# THE LIFEBOX, THE SEASHELL, AND THE SOUL

# THE LIFEBOX, THE SEASHELL, AND THE SOUL

WHAT GNARLY COMPUTATION
TAUGHT ME ABOUT ULTIMATE REALITY,
THE MEANING OF LIFE, AND HOW TO BE HAPPY

## RUDY RUCKER

THUNDER'S MOUTH PRESS
NEW YORK

THE LIFEBOX, THE SEASHELL, AND THE SOUL
*WHAT GNARLY COMPUTATION TAUGHT ME ABOUT ULTIMATE REALITY,*
*THE MEANING OF LIFE, AND HOW TO BE HAPPY*

Published by
Thunder's Mouth Press
An Imprint of Avalon Publishing Group Inc.
245 West 17th St., 11th Floor
New York, NY 10011

AVALON
publishing group incorporated

First printing October 2005

Library of Congress Cataloging-in-Publication Data is available.

ISBN: 1-56025-722-9
ISBN 13: 978-1-56025-722-6


9 8 7 6 5 4 3 2 1

Illustrations by Isabel Rucker

Book design by Maria E. Torres

Printed in the United States of America
Distributed by Publishers Group West

# Contents

# *Preface*

As a teenager in 1961, I imagined that I'd like to become a philosopher. I recall agreeing with my best friend, Niles Schoening, that what we'd most like to do would be to get college degrees in philosophy and spend the rest of our lives as bums, talking about the meaning of life.

As it turned out, I ended up getting a Ph.D. in mathematical logic. And instead of becoming a bum, I found work as a professor and as a writer of popular science and science fiction. I did keep talking about the meaning of life, though, to the point of publishing three somewhat philosophical books about mathematics: *The Fourth Dimension, Infinity and the Mind,* and *Mind Tools.*

In the mid-1980s I sensed something new in the air. Computers were ushering in an era of experimental mathematics. Fractals, chaos, cellular automata, artificial life! And when I interviewed Stephen Wolfram for a magazine article, my fate was sealed. I moved to Silicon Valley, retooled, and became a computer science professor at San Jose State University, also doing some work as a programmer for the computer graphics company Autodesk.

Back when I was contemplating my big switch to computer science, my old friend Gregory Gibson said something encouraging. "Imagine if William Blake had worked in a textile mill. What might he have written then?"

Initially, I thought this might be a quick foray. Get in, figure out what's happening, get out, and write my book on computers and reality. But somewhere along the way I went native on the story. I all but forgot my mission.

I spent twenty years in the dark satanic mills of Silicon Valley. I'm covered in a thick lint of bytes and computer code. And now I'm stepping into the light to tell you what I learned among the machines.

I'm grateful to the Royal Flemish Academy of Belgium for Science and the Arts for having funded a stay in Brussels in the fall of 2002. I taught a course on the philosophy of computer science at the University of Leuven, writing some material for this book in the process. I gave my classroom handouts the not-quite-serious title, "Early Geek Philosophy," telling the students that my precursors might come to be known as the pre-Rucratic geek philosophers!

Many thanks also to the people with whom I've had conversations and/or e-mail exchanges about the book's topics. These include: Scott Aaronson, Ralph Abraham, Mark van Atten, Michael Beeson, Charles Bennett, Kovas Boguta, Jason Cawley, Leon Horsten, Loren Means, Jon Pearce, Chris Pollett, Richard Shore, Brian Silverman, John Walker, Ken Wharton, and Stephen Wolfram. Some of these friends even did me the favor of reading an early draft and suggesting corrections. Errors that remain are my own responsibility.

Thanks also to my computer science students at San Jose State University; my programs that illustrate this book were developed with them in mind, and sometimes they even helped me write them.

And special thanks to my wife, Sylvia, for all the wonderful things outside the ambit of the buzzing machines.

*Rudy Rucker*
*Los Gatos, California*
*March 22, 2005*

*Just for fun, I've written a short-short story to introduce each chapter of* The Lifebox, the Seashell, and the Soul. *You might think of these as thought experiments, or as exploratory expeditions into the further reaches of my book's themes.*

The first Sunday in October, Doug Cardano drove in for an extra day's work at Giga Games. Crunch time. The nimrods in marketing had committed to shipping a virtual reality golf game in time for the holiday season. NuGolf. It was supposed to have five eighteen-hole courses, all of them new, all of them landscaped by Doug.

He exited Route 101 and crossed the low overpass over the train tracks, heading toward the gleaming Giga Games complex beside the San Francisco Bay. A long freight train was passing. Growing up, Doug had always liked trains; in fact, he'd dreamed of being a hobo. Or an artist for a game company. He hadn't known about crunch time.

Just to postpone the start of his long, beige workday, he pulled over and got out to watch the cars clank past: boxcars, tankers, reefers, flatcars. Many of them bore graffiti. Doug lit a cigarette, his first of the day, always the best one, and

spotted a row of twelve spray-painted numbers on a dusty red boxcar, the digits arranged in pairs.

11 35 17 03 26 54

SuperLotto, thought Doug, and wrote them on his cardboard box of cigarettes. Five numbers between one and forty-seven, and one number between one and twenty-seven.

Next stop was the minimarket down the road. Even though Doug knew the odds were bogus, he'd been buying a lot of SuperLotto tickets lately. The grand prize was hella big. If he won, he'd never have to crunch again.

The rest of the team trickled into the office about the same time as Doug. A new bug had broken one of the overnight builds, and Van the lead coder had to fix that. Meanwhile Doug got down to the trees and bushes for course number four.

Since the player could mouse all around the NuGolf world and even wander into the rough, Doug couldn't use background bitmaps. He had to create three-dimensional models of the plants. NuGolf was meant to be wacky and fantastic, so he had a lot of leeway: on the first course he'd used cartoony saguaro cactuses, he'd set the second links underwater with sea fans and kelp, the third had been on "Venus" with man-eating plants, and for the fourth, which he was starting today—well, he wasn't sure what to do.

He had a vague plan of trying to get some inspirations from BlobScape, a three-dimensional cellular automata package he'd found on the Web. Cellular automata grew organic-looking objects on the fly. Depending what number you seeded BlobScape with, it could grow almost anything. The guy who'd written BlobScape claimed that theoretically the computation could simulate the whole universe, if only you gave it the right seed.

When Doug started up BlobScape today, it was in a lava lamp mode, with big wobbly droplets drifting around. A click of the Randomize button turned the blobs into mushroom caps, pulsing through the simulation space like jellyfish. Another click produced interlocking pyramids a bit like trees, but not pretty enough to use.

Doug pressed the Rule button so he could enter some code numbers of his own. He'd done this a few times before; every now and then his numbers would make something really cool. It reminded him of the Magic Rocks kit he'd had as boy, where the right kind of gray pebble in a glass of liquid could grow green and purple stalagmites. Maybe today was his lucky day. Come to think of it, his SuperLotto ticket happened to be lying on his desk, so, what the hey, he entered 11 35 17 03 26 54.

Bingo. The block of simulated space misted over, churned, and congealed into—a primeval jungle inhabited by dinosaurs. And it kept going from there. Apemen moved from the trees into caves. Egyptians built the Sphinx and the pyramids. A mob crucified Christ. Galileo dropped two balls off the Leaning Tower of Pisa. Soldiers massacred the Indians of the Great Plains. Flappers and bootleggers danced the jitterbug. Hippies handed out daisies. Computers multiplied like bacilli.

Doug had keyed in the Holy Grail, the one true rule, the code number for the universe. Sitting there grinning, it occurred to him that if you wrote those twelve lucky digits in reverse order they'd work as a phone number plus extension. (456) 230-7153 x11.

The number seemed exceedingly familiar, but without stopping to think he went ahead and dialed it.

His own voice answered.

"Game over."

The phone in Doug's hand turned into pixels. He and the phone and the universe dissolved.

# CHAPTER ONE

# Computation Everywhere

## 1.1: Universal Automatism

*The Lifebox, the Seashell, and the Soul* is about computation—taken in the broadest possible sense. You can usefully regard all sorts of things as computations: plants and animals, political movements, the weather, your personal shifts of mood. Computations are everywhere, once you begin to look at things in a certain way. At the very least, computation is a metaphor with an exceedingly wide range of applicability.

You may feel a twinge of déjà vu. After all, it hasn't been so long since guys like me were telling you everything is information, and aren't information and computation pretty much the same? No—information is static, but computation is dynamic. Computations transform information.

An example. Even if we could find a complete and correct explanation of our world's physics, this would only be a static piece of information—perhaps an initial condition and a set of rules. The interesting things happen as the consequences of the laws unfold. The unfolding process is a computation carried out by the world itself.

My iconoclastic and headstrong friend Stephen Wolfram goes so far as to say that the world is nothing more than a computation. In Wolfram's words, "It is possible to view every process that occurs in nature or elsewhere as a computation." I call this view *universal automatism*.[1]

I'm not sure if I subscribe to universal automatism or not. One reason I'm writing this book is to see where universal automatism leads.

Does my willingness to entertain universal automatism mean that I'm a humorless nerd who wants everything to fit into the beige box of a personal computer (PC)? No way. I know a lot about PCs, yes, but familiarity breeds contempt. Although I've gotten very skilled at crafting C++ and Java code for the classes I've taught, I don't think I'd much mind if I never had to write a computer program again. Writing books is a lot more fun—programming is simply too brittle a medium. If I leave out, say, a semicolon, a program might not run at all. Literature isn't like that.

And, just like most people, I have a deep-seated conviction that I myself am something richer than any mere calculation. I love to get away from my flickering monitor screen and be out in nature—roaming the woods, bicycling down the flowery California streets, walking on a beach, or just sitting in my backyard watching the wind move the leaves on the trees. Crows, ants, dogs, protozoa, other people—life is what matters, not some crappy buzzing boxes that are broken half the time.

No, no, I'm not on the side of machines.

But then why am I writing this long book about computation? I guess I've put in so much time with personal computers that I'd like to take this one last shot at figuring out what I've learned from them. To trace out their meanings once and for all.

My original training was in mathematics—thirty years ago I got a Ph.D. in set theory and mathematical logic. In the 1970s I even got to meet Kurt Gödel a few times. The king of the logicians. Gödel once told me, "The a priori is very powerful." By this he meant that pure logic can take you farther than you might believe possible.

As well as logic, I've got a lot of experimental input to work with. Wolfram, whom I first met in the 1980s, has done a king-hell job of combing through vast seas of possible computations, getting a handle on the kinds of phenomena that can occur. With Wolfram's discoveries, and with my own experiences as a logician, a programmer, and a computer science professor—well, I'm hoping I can make a little progress here.

But let me repeat: I'm not a big fan of machines.

Being a good Californian, I practice yoga nearly every day. It counteracts the strain on my aging frame from the huge amount of keyboarding and mouse-clicking that I do. It's interesting how good it feels to stop worrying about my daily plans and focus on nothing more than my breath and my muscles. Can computation theory tell me anything about yoga?

Years ago—this would have been the glorious summer of 1969—I had a vision of God. The White Light, the Supreme Being, all around me, talking to me. "I'm always here, Rudy," said God. "I love you." These days I don't see God. But when I remember to try, I can still feel something like a divine presence. I don't think God's a computation. But exactly why not?

I'm a novelist, too, mostly science fiction, and I presume to think of my work as literature. Compared to a work of literature, a computer program is puny excrescence, a petty game played by the rules of blind machines, a dreary slog through the mud. Literature glides on beautiful wings. But maybe, looked in a certain light, literature is a human form of computation.

When I open my heart to universal automatism, I can see that it's not as far-fetched as it sounds. The key fact is that, far from being dry and dull, computations can generate physical, biological, and psychological phenomena of great beauty. Maybe a weird explanation is better than no explanation at all. Might it be that, by analyzing the notion of computation, I can finally understand what it means to be conscious? I'm prepared to follow the argument wherever it goes. If it turns out that universal automatism is right, and I really am a computation, then at least I'll know a little more about what *kind* of computation.

In planning this intellectual journey, I've settled on a particular tactic and an overall strategy. My tactic is Hegelian dialectic, and my strategy is what we might call the stairway to heaven.

The dialectic tactic relates to the book's title: *The Lifebox, the Seashell, and the Soul*. The title represents a triad: the lifebox is the thesis, the soul is the antithesis, and the seashell is the synthesis. In the style of my great-great-great-grandfather Georg Wilhelm Hegel, my tactic will be to use my selected triad over and over.

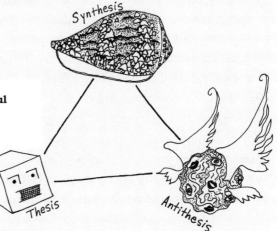

**Figure 1: A Dialectic Triad: the Lifebox, the Seashell, and the Soul**

*Lifebox* is a word I invented some years ago to describe a hypothetical technological gizmo for preserving a human personality. In my science-fiction tales, a lifebox is a small interactive device to which you tell your life story. It prompts you with questions and organizes the information you give it. As well as words, you can feed in digital images, videos, sound recordings, and the like. It's a bit like an intelligent blog.

Once you get enough information into your lifebox, it becomes something like a simulation of you. Your audience can interact with the stories in the lifebox, interrupting and asking questions. The lifebox begins by automating the retiree's common dream of creating a memoir and ends by creating a simulation of its owner.

Why would you want to make a lifebox? Immortality, ubiquity, omnipotence. You might leave a lifebox behind so your grandchildren and great-grandchildren can know what you were like. You might use your lifebox as a way to introduce yourself to large numbers of people. You might let your lifebox take over some of your less interesting duties, such as answering routine phone calls and e-mail.

A lifebox is a person reduced to a digital database with simple access software. So in my book title, I'm using *Lifebox* as shorthand for the universal automatist *thesis* that everything, even human consciousness, is a computation.

The *antithesis* is the fact that nobody is really going to think that a wised-up cell phone is alive. We all feel we have something that's not captured by any mechanical model—it's what we commonly call the soul.

My *synthesis* is a Wolfram-inspired scheme for breathing life into a lifebox. The living mind has a churning quality, like the eddies in the wake of a rock in a stream—or like the turbulent patterns found in a certain kind of computation called a cellular automaton (CA). These unpredictable yet deterministic computations are found in nature, perhaps most famously on a kind of seashell called the cone shell (see figure 2). It's at least possible that the mind's endless variety is in fact generated by a gnarly computation of this type. If so, the image of the seashell serves to bridge the chasm between lifebox and soul.

So that's my basic triad, and my dialectic tactic will involve repeatedly going through the following three steps: (a) Thetic step: model some real-world phenomenon as a computation. (b) Antithetic step: remark that the actual

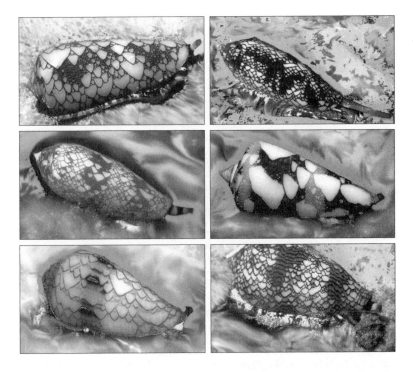

**Figure 2: Six Cone Shells**

*Reading left to right, top to bottom, we have a* Conus omaria, Conus auratinus, Conus ammiralis, Conus auricomus, Conus retifer, *and a* Conus textile. *Note that these marine snails have protruding tentacles that are, variously, siphons, mouths, eyes, and proboscises. These so-called tented cones feed upon other mollusks, injecting paralyzing conotoxins into their prey by means of tiny harpoons shot from a tentacle. Shell-collectors have been killed by cone shell stings. Note that the textile cone is in the process of attacking a less-gnarly fellow mollusk. These photos were taken at night by Scott and Jeanette Johnson off the Kwajalein atoll in the Micronesian archipelago.*

world seems juicier and more interesting than a computation. (c) Synthetic step: observe that, given enough time and memory, our proposed computation is in fact capable of generating exceedingly rich and lifelike structures.

When I speak of using a stairway-to-heaven pattern as my overarching strategy for organizing *The Lifebox, the Seashell, and the Soul,* I mean that each chapter treats a yet higher-level way of viewing the world, as suggested in figure 3.

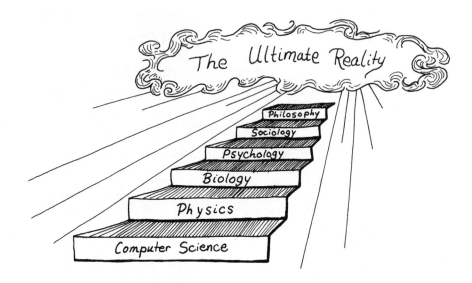

**Figure 3: An Intellectual Stairway to Heaven**

The stairway to heaven is a traditional style of organizing knowledge. In the Middle Ages it was called *ordo sciendi,* or "the order of knowing." A medieval thinker would of course write "Logic" in place of "Computer Science," and even now someone might say that logic or mathematics would be a more natural starting point than computer science. But in *The Lifebox, the Seashell, and the Soul* I'm arguing that we do best to think of computation itself as fundamental. Under this view, logic and mathematics are invented after the fact to explain the observed patterns of the world. Logic and mathematics become high-level intellectual endeavors that I treat in the context of the sixth chapter, which concerns philosophy.

Looking ahead, my six chapters will be as follows.

- CHAPTER ONE: *Computation Everywhere.* An introduction to the universal automatist view that everything is a computation, exploring the familiar computations done by our machines, and presenting some examples of computational gnarliness.
- CHAPTER TWO: *Our Rich World.* Descriptions of how to view classical, chaotic, and quantum physics in terms of computations.

- CHAPTER THREE: *Life's Lovely Gnarl.* An analysis of life in terms of five kinds of computation: reproduction, morphogenesis, homeostasis, ecology, and evolution, including a discussion of human efforts to create artificial forms of life.
- CHAPTER FOUR: *Enjoying Your Mind.* A detailed presentation of the universal automatist view that we can view the mind as a gnarly computation, showing how this need not contradict one's feeling of being a conscious entity with a soul.
- CHAPTER FIVE: *The Human Hive.* An exploration of the patterns and dynamics of human society from the low to high levels, including discussions of language and culture.
- CHAPTER SIX: *Reality Upgrade.* A philosophical analysis of the possible positions regarding computation and reality, including a description of the classes of computation that are known to exist, and delving further into the philosophical consequences of universal automatism. Concludes with remarks about ultimate reality, the meaning of life, and how to be happy.

And now let's get going on the stairway to heaven's first step.

What do I mean by a computation? Here's a definition that's very minimal—and thus quite generally applicable.

- *Definition.* A *computation* is a process that obeys finitely describable rules.

That's it? Well, if I want to say that all sorts of processes are like computations, it's to be expected that my definition of computation must be fairly simple.

The notion of obeying finitely describable rules really includes two ideas: a computation is utterly *deterministic,* that is, nonrandom, and the rules act as a kind of *recipe* for generating future states of the computation.

Regarding determinism, although computer scientists do sometimes theorize about "probabilistic computations" that are allowed to make utterly random decisions, these aren't really computations in any normal sense of the word. Our understanding here will be that we're speaking only of computations whose future states are fully determined by their inputs and by their finitely describable rules.

Now I'll talk about the kind of recipe that underlies a finitely describable rule.

You might say that any process at all obeys the recipe of "act like yourself." Does that make for a finitely describable rule? No. The "yourself" in this so-called rule implicitly drags in a full and possibly endless set of information about how "you" will behave in every kind of situation.

Although it may indeed be that every possible process is a kind of computation, I don't want to make it *too* easy to attain this sought-after conclusion. I want "obeying finitely describable rules" to be a real constraint.

A finitely describable collection of rules should be something like a set of behavioral laws, or a program for an electronic digital computer, or a specific scientific theory with its accompanying rules of deduction. What's really intended is that the rules specify what, in any given state, the computational system will do next.

As an aside, I have to warn you that *describable* is a slippery notion. Logicians have established that *describable* can't in fact have a formally precise meaning—otherwise a phrase like the following would be a valid description of a number: "Let the Berry number be the smallest integer that can't be described in less than eighteen words." Now, if that seventeen-word phrase were indeed a legitimate description of a specific Berry number, we'd have the paradox of a seventeen-word phrase describing a number that can't be described in less than eighteen words. So it must be that the phrase really isn't a legitimate description, and the reason must be that *describable* isn't a formally precise word. Therefore, my definition of a computation is imprecise as well. (I wrote at length about this issue in *Infinity and the Mind*.)

So if the notion of a computation is fundamentally imprecise, must we abandon our investigations and sit grumbling in the darkness? No. In this book, I want to think more like a physicist than like a mathematician—more like an experimental scientist and less like a logician. Loosely speaking, we *do* know what it means to have a finite description of a rule for a process. Yes, certain borderline cases will throw us into a philosophical quandaries, but we can cover a lot of ground with our (inherently unformalizable) definition of a computation as a *process that obeys finitely describable rules.*

We can regard a computation as transforming inputs into outputs. Where do the inputs and ouputs live? The inputs and outputs are states of the underlying system that supports the computational process.

Which states are inputs and which are outputs? This is really just a matter of temporal order. If one or more states occurs before a second state, then we speak of the earlier states as inputs that produce the later state. I don't lay much stress on the notion of computations ever coming to a halt, which means that we usually think of an input as producing an endless stream of successive outputs. I'll also allow for additional *interactive* inputs that occur while a computing process is under way.[2]

I want to say a bit about the underlying system that supports a computation. Although it's natural to refer to any such computational system as a *computer,* I need to caution that by "computer" I don't necessarily mean one of our chip-in-a-box machines. Obviously these balky devices are a point of inspiration. But for a universal automatist, essentially *any* system or object is a computer, and any process or action is a computation. To avoid confusion, I'll try to always refer to our day-to-day computing machines as *personal* computers, *electronic* computers, *desktop* computers, or simply *PCs*.

By thinking about PCs we become aware of a number of distinctions. For instance, when speaking of electronic computers, people distinguish between

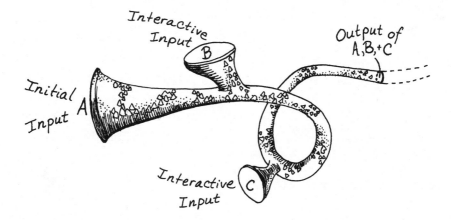

**Figure 4: Time Line with Inputs and Outputs**

hardware and software. The hardware is the physical contents of the buzzing box that you buy, while the software is the stuff that you get on disks or download from the Web. A finer distinction is possible. The buzzing box comes equipped with its own *low-level software*—which usually includes, for instance, an operating system like Linux, Windows, or the Mac OS. We can distinguish between this low-level software and the specialized *high-level software* that we might want to run—think of, for instance, a word-processing or image-manipulation application. And even higher-level than that are the inputs we feed to our high-level software—think of documents or photo files.

Of course, all of these boundaries are somewhat fuzzy, and the levels are prone to splitting into sublevels. And when we take into account a system's surroundings, new levels appear as shown in figure 5. Suffice it to say that most systems have quite a few levels of rules.

I'll be comparing real-world things to computations for the rest of the book. As a quick example, in a human being, the hardware is like your body and brain, the low-level software is the built-in wiring of your brain and perhaps the effects of your various early experiences, the high-level software is like the skills that you learn, the inputs are your daily experiences, and the outputs are the things that you say and do. Changing the high-level software takes a certain amount of effort, and changing the low-level software is very hard, requiring something on the order of a conversion experience or long-term therapy. There are layers upon layers, and some quirks can be so deeply ingrained that you have to dig down quite far to tweak them.

Table 1 presents some similar analogies, with a column for seven different kinds of computation, with each column suggesting the hardware, low-level

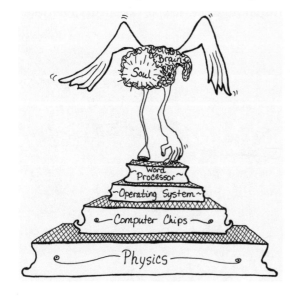

**Figure 5: Layers of Computation**

software, high-level software, inputs, outputs, and possible target detectors for that particular style of computation. (I'll be explaining what I mean by target detectors after the next paragraph. But first a word about tables.)

For me, tables are a tool for thinking. I figure out some column headers and row topics, and then, *wham,* I've got all these nice cells to fill. Let me warn you that you need to take my tables with a grain of salt. They're Procrustean beds. In Greek myth, Procrustes was a bandit masquerading as an inn-keeper. He said he had a wonderful bed that would fit you perfectly, no matter what your size. The catch was, if you were too short for the bed, Procrustes would stretch you on the rack, and if you were too tall, he'd lop off your head or your feet. Filling the cells of a table requires Procrustean fine-tuning—although if it gets out of hand, I usually rethink the row and column categories.

Now I'll tell you about target detectors. This has to do with the issue of when, if ever, I'm going to think of a given computation as being done.

People often suppose that a computation has to "find an answer" and then stop. But our general notion of computation allows for computations that run indefinitely. If you think of your life as a kind of computation, it's quite abundantly clear that there's not going to be a final answer and there won't be anything particularly wonderful about having the computation halt! In other words, we often prefer a computation to yield an ongoing sequence of outputs rather than to attain one final output and turn itself off.

In order to further clarify this point, I'm going to begin speaking a bit symbolically about computations. Throughout the book, I'll normally use the letter $P$ to stand for a computation—think of $P$ standing for program. If $P$ is a computation and In is a state, I write $P(\text{In})$ to stand for the indefinitely prolonged computational process that results from starting $P$ on In. If Out is another state and $t$ is some specific interval of time, I can write $P(\text{In}, t) = \text{Out}$ to mean that the computation $P(\text{In})$ produces state Out after a time interval $t$.[3]

Even though I'll usually be talking about never-ending computations, in practical uses of computation, there are often situations where we are interested in cases where a computation of the form $P(\text{In})$ reaches some targeted state Out and we can then readily perceive that $P(\text{In})$ is done. One definition of a computation being *done* (or, as is often said, *halted*) is simply to require that the computation doesn't change any further after some point in time.

| Computation system | Pencil and paper calculations | Personal computer | The Web | Classical physics | Quantum physics | Organisms | Thought | Society |
|---|---|---|---|---|---|---|---|---|
| **Hardware** | Human with pencil | Chip & RAM | Linked computers | Atoms | Reality | Cell | Brain cortex | People, roads, buildings |
| **Low-level software** | Plus and times tables, algorithms | Microcode, bios, operating system | File exchange protocols | Physical laws | Schrödinger's wave equation | Ribosomes | Instincts, built-in abilities, reptile brain | Sex, human nature |
| **Application software** | Tax form, or math problem | Application code, like Word | Browser, search engine | Design | Experimental apparatus | DNA | Personality, knowledge | Beliefs, news |
| **Input** | Numbers | Documents, images, signals from mouse and keyboard | Page address, search request | Forces, energies, objects | State preparation | Food, space, light | Learning, experience | Human actions, natural phenomena |
| **Output** | Numbers | Documents, images | Pages, page addresses | Motions, states | Measurements | Motions, actions, reproduction | Utterances, writings, beliefs, emotions | History, social movements |
| **Examples of target detectors** | Finishing a calculation | A beep, or something being printed, or the screen settling down, or a wait icon going away | A page finishes downloading, or an upload wait bar goes away | A meter reading settles down, a ball stops moving | A particle triggers a detector, a person looks at something | Having sex, eating something, dying, moving | Making a decision, saying something aloud, writing something down | Electing someone, choosing the book of the week, deciding to start a war |

**Table 1: Comparing Various Kinds of Computation Systems**

That is, the computational process $P(\text{In})$ might reach the state Out and then stay fixed in that state. In this situation we would say that $P(\text{In})$ *returns* Out.

The "freezing up" definition of halting is appropriate for certain simple models of computation, such as the abstract devices known as Turing machines. But for more general kinds of computations, freezing up is too narrow a notion of a computation's being done.

For instance, if you want to find out how to get to some street address, you can go on the Web, locate a map site, type in your target address, press Enter, and wait for a few fractions of a second until a little map appears on your screen. The system consisting of your PC plus your Web browser plus the Web itself has carried out a computation and now it's done.

But it wouldn't be at all correct to say that the PC+browser+Web computing system is now frozen in the same state because, for one thing, your Web browser is continually polling your mouse and keyboard to look for new input. And your PC is running all kinds of background processes that never stop. And the other machines that make up the Web certainly haven't stopped just because you found what you were looking for.

When we want to talk about a generalized computational system $P$ reaching a target state, we need to have an associated *target detector* computation Is$P$Done, which has two special states that we might as well call True and False. We require that for any output state Out of the system, Is$P$Done(Out) returns either True or False according to whether Out is to be viewed as a target state. Is$P$Done is supposed to be a very simple computation that very quickly enters the final state True or False and remains there.

If we don't explicitly specify the Is$P$Done test, we'll assume that the computation is in a target state if any further updates would leave it in the same state—this is what I meant above by a computation that freezes up. But in the case where $P$ is a personal computer or even some naturally occurring system like a pond or a human society, we'll want to use a subtler kind of target detector. How we choose to define a computation's target detector can in fact vary with the kind of inputs we plan to feed to the computation—one can imagine situations where we might say that a pond is in target state when its ripples settle down below some specified level, and a society is in a target state once all the votes in an election have been counted and a new leader has been installed.

So now I've said a bit about computations and the universal automatist notion that they're everywhere, which finishes off my section *1.1: Universal Automatism*. This chapter's remaining sections are as follows.

- *1.2: A New Kind of Science*. In his recent book of this title, Stephen Wolfram divides computations into four classes: those that die out, those that repeat, the messy random-looking ones, and the gnarly ones. For a universal automatist, this suggests new ways to view the whole world.
- *1.3: Reckoning a Sum*. Thinking about how we add numbers with pencil and paper gives a bit of insight into what it means for computations to run at different speeds—an important notion for formulating what it means for a computation to be unpredictable.
- *1.4: Analytical Engines*. I'll give a brief history of how we arrived at the design whereby our electronic computers use programs that are loaded into memory like data. Thanks to this so-called stored program architecture, our PCs are universal in the sense of being able to emulate any other computation.
- *1.5: The Tiniest Brains*. Among the simplest possible computers are the idealized devices known as Turing machines. They're the favorite lab rat of computer philosophers, and they teach us more about universality.
- *1.6: Inside the Beige Box*. A short-as-possible explanation of how our desktop machines work.
- *1.7: Plugged In*. The Internet is a distributed networked computation quite unlike the computations inside a PC.
- *1.8: Flickercladding*. The parallel computations known as cellular automata make beautiful patterns, are good models for physics, and have served as a main source of inspiration for universal automatists.

## 1.2: A New Kind of Science

By way of giving the notion of computation a little more texture, I'll mention two slightly counterintuitive facts. And then I'll describe Stephen Wolfram's four classes of computation.

The first counterintuitive fact is that just because an output is computable doesn't mean it's easy to arrive at. Computer scientists use the word *feasible* in this connection.

> • *Informal Definition.* A particular computational process is *feasible* if it produces the desired result in a humanly reasonable amount of time.

A computation that you can do by hand in a few minutes is feasible, something that would take you ten years isn't feasible. In other words, a computation is unfeasible if carrying it out would take an unreasonable amount of resources and/or an unreasonable amount of time.

> • *Counterintuitive fact.* Although a computation may be theoretically possible to carry out, it can be practically unfeasible to do so.

This is rather obvious, but it's worth remembering. Sometimes we get carried away by a proof that one system can in principle simulate some other system, and we lose sight of the fact that the simulation is in fact so slow and cumbersome that it's quite unfeasible. Most artificial intelligence (AI) programs fall into this category vis-à-vis the human mind—yes, they can simulate some small parts of human reasoning, but the simulations are so slow that applying them to realistically large inputs is unfeasible. (Actually, the situation is worse than that; not only are our existing AI programs unfeasible for large problems, we probably haven't found the right *kinds* of AI programs at all.)

The feasibility of a computation depends both on the computational system you plan to use and on the computational method you plan to employ. This relates to the distinction between hardware and software. If you have very slow and clunky hardware, almost no computations are feasible. But no matter what your hardware is, improved software (such as clever calculating tricks) may expand your arena of feasibility.

Suppose we agree with the universal automatists that most physical processes are computations. By and large these physical computations are unfeasible for our personal computers. Not only is it unfeasible to digitally emulate the global weather; even simulating the turbulent flow of tap water is beyond our existing electronic machines. But—and this is my point—the processes may well be computations anyway.

For people, the most admired and intimately familiar computations of all are the creative and meaningful processes of human thought. For reasons I'll explain in CHAPTER FOUR: *Enjoying Your Mind,* I would not expect to see human creativity becoming a feasible electronic computation anytime in the next hundred years. But, again, this doesn't rule out the option of viewing the human brain as a type of computer just as it is. The brain is a system obeying a finite set of rules. Human thought is certainly a feasible computation *for the human brain,* it's just not currently feasible *for electronic computers.*

The second counterintuitive fact I want to mention is that computations can yield genuine surprise. One might suppose that a deterministic rule-based process must flow along in quite a routine fashion. Yes, but this doesn't mean that the long-term behavior of the computation is predictable.

- *Informal Definition. P is predictable* if there is a shortcut computation $Q$ that computes the same results as $P$, but very much faster. Otherwise $P$ is said to be *unpredictable.*

A more precise definition of what I mean by unpredictable can be found in the Technical Appendix at the end of the book. But the basic idea is that if $P$ is unpredictable, there is no dramatically faster way to get $P$'s output other than to carry out the computation of $P$.

As a really simple example of a predictable computation, suppose you want to decide if an input number is even or odd. A slow way to compute this would be to painfully carry out a long division of two into the number, working out the whole quotient on the way to finding out if the remainder happens to be zero or one. A fast, shortcut way to compute the same information is just to look at the last digit of your input number, and say that the number is even if the last digit is zero, two, four, six, or eight. The slow long-division computation of evenness is predictable in our sense because the much faster last-digit computation produces the same results.

In practice, anyone who writes computer programs for a living is going to try to make the code as efficient as possible. This means that, in practice, most of the PC programs we work with will in fact be unpredictable, in that there's no way to drastically speed them up. As it happens, unpredictability is relatively common across the whole spectrum of possible kinds of computation.

- *Counterintuitive fact.* Many simply defined computations are *unpredictable.*

If I call this counterintuitive, it's because, before you analyze the notion, you'd expect that computations *would* be predictable, at least in the colloquial sense of being dull and unsurprising. Indeed, "Don't act like a robot," means something like, "Don't be so predictable." Given the deterministic nature of a rule-based computation, it's true that, step-by-step, the computation is predictable. Given *A* we always get *B,* given *B* we always get *C,* and so on.

But—and this is the point that takes some getting used to—there's often no shortcut method for looking ahead to predict the end result of a computation. That is, if I want to know the end result of a billion-step computation, it's very often the case that there's no faster method than carrying out the billion-step computation itself.

Consider an analogy. When Columbus sailed across the Atlantic, it was predetermined that he'd find the West Indies (which, to his dying day, he thought were part of Asia). But Columbus never could have predicted the shapes of those islands (whatever he called them) without making the trip.

The unpredictability of computations becomes noticeable when we throw substantial problems at our machines. A famous example involves *pi,* the numerical value of the ratio that a mathematical circle has to its diameter. This number, which begins 3.14159 . . . , is known to have a decimal expansion that goes on and on without ever settling into a pattern. Nevertheless, there are simply defined computational methods for finding the successive digits of pi by means of multiplications, additions, and the like. One (not very efficient) approach would be to sum together more and more terms of the endless alternating series:

$$4 - 4/3 + 4/5 - 4/7 + 4/9 - 4/11 + 4/13 - \ldots$$

**Figure 6: William Gosper, Programmer King**

*The face on Gosper's T-shirt is that of the prolific Hungarian mathematician Paul Erdös*

In the mid-1980s, my old-time computer fanatic friend William Gosper once held a world record for computing pi. He calculated it out past the seventeen millionth digit. I've copied here from one of Gosper's e-mails the first hundred digits after the seventeen millionth place: 6978965266 4312708718 8987022892 7339840950 1815706767 7105940124 6541910101 0611655655 1475202499 7781719847.

Conversations and e-mail from Gosper have been touchstone experiences for me ever since moving to Silicon Valley. He's like the last exemplar of some extinct species of bird, a chatty apteryx in his aboriginal nest, surrounded by antique plastic artifacts, such as an ellipsoidal electric pencil sharpener, a stack of Symbolics computer monitors, and a mound of numbered Aerobie disks. I should mention that he feels the best way to truly compute pi is to express it as an enormous tower of nested fractions, which is what he actually did to net his particular catch of pi. It was only so as to be able to compare his work with the work of others that he reduced his tower of pi to base ten digits in a process that he calls, somewhat disdainfully, "decimalizing pi."

In any case, before Gosper's calculation was done, there was no way to know that, say, the seventeen millionth digit would be six. The only way to get Gosper's digits was to let a heavy-duty electronic computer munge on the problem for a long period of time. Yes, the value is predetermined by the laws of mathematics, but it's not really predictable.[4]

The notion of computer programs being unpredictable is surprising because we tend to suppose that being deterministic means being boring. Note also that since we don't feel ourselves to be boring, we imagine that we must be nondeterministic and thus not at all like rule-based computational systems. But maybe we're wrong. Maybe we're deterministic but unpredictable.

I mentioned that unfeasibility is a relative notion, depending on the system you intend to use for running a given computation. Something's unfeasible on a given system if takes longer than you can reasonably wait. Unpredictability, on the other hand, is a more absolute notion. A computation is unpredictable if there is no other computation that does the same things a lot faster.

It's often enlightening to examine the possible interactions of newly defined properties. How do feasibility and predictability relate to each other if we temporarily limit our attention to computations on personal computers? As it turns out, all four possible combinations are possible.

- *Feasible and predictable.* These are the very simplest kinds of computation. I'm thinking here of a trivial computation like, say, multiplying seven by one thousand. Without getting out your pencil and paper, you know that $7 \times 1,000$ is $7,000$. The computation is predictable. You know how it will turn out without having to carry out the details. But if you had to work out the details, you could, as the computation is feasible as well as being predictable.

- *Feasible and unpredictable.* These are the computations that interest computer scientists the most. Here there's a computation you can actually carry out, but there's no quick way to guess the result in advance. In a case like this, your computing system is doing something worthwhile for you. The computation is discovering a fact that you wouldn't have been able to guess.

- *Unfeasible and predictable.* Suppose that the computation was some very trivial task like replacing every symbol of an input string by zero. For any given input string, the output string is predictable: it will be a row of zeros the same length as the input string. But if the input string is going to be of some insane length—imagine a galaxy-spanning message a gazillion characters long—then there's no feasible way to feed this thing into my desktop PC and expect an answer in any reasonable length of time. So in that sense the computation is unfeasible, even though the eventual output is predictable.

- *Unfeasible and unpredictable.* Rest assured that whatever is going on inside your head is both unpredictable and, relative to existing electronic computers, unfeasible. But you're doing it anyway. As Frank Zappa used to say, "Ain't this boogie a mess?"

One of the main themes in *The Lifebox, the Seashell, and the Soul* will be that computations come in certain basic flavors. This is the whole reason why it might be worthwhile to think of things like flowers, thunderstorms, and orgasms as computations. Yes, the details of these computations must elude us, and any simulation of them would be unfeasible. Even so, there are certain properties such as unpredictability that can be usefully applied to real-world phenomena.

We're going to be saying a lot about a very useful classification of computations that was invented by Stephen Wolfram in the 1980s. Wolfram noticed that there are four main behaviors for arbitrary computations that are left running for a period of time.

- *Class one.* Enter a constant state.
- *Class two.* Generate a repetitive or nested pattern.
- *Class three.* Produce messy, random-looking crud.
- *Class four.* Produce gnarly, interacting, nonrepeating patterns.

It's pretty easy to understand what class one and class two computations look like, although it's worth mentioning that a regularly branching pattern would also fall under class two. The essence of being a class two computation is that the outputs don't generate surprise.

My hacker friend Gosper refers to class three style patterns as "seething dog barf." These are messy, random-looking computations with no obvious order or structure in their outputs.

Class four computations, on the other hand, generate images more like never-repeating lace. Class four computations might be characterized as having behavior that appears purposeful. I like to use the word *gnarly* for class four processes—gnarly in the sense of twisting tree roots, large ocean waves, or weathered human faces.

When a rough distinction will do, we speak of class one and class two computations as being *simple* and class three and class four computations as *complex*. Figure 7 summarizes the terminology.

The borders between the computation classes aren't very crisp. There are times when the distinction between class three and class four isn't obvious. And it's not always clear if a system is class two or class four—consider the fact that some systems can appear interesting for a very long time and only then settle down to being periodic. We don't always know whether we can in fact find a "good" input that will keep a certain computation running and producing novelty forever, thus showing that it really is a class four rule.

Wolfram's critics complain that his computation classes aren't formally defined and that, when we do attempt formal definitions, determining the class of a computation can be an unsolvable problem ("unsolvable" in a certain formal sense that I'll describe in chapter 6). Wolfram might reply that using rough-and-ready concepts is typical for a newly developing branch of science. I agree with him. I think his critics miss the forest for the trees. With an open mind you can indeed distinguish the four computation classes; you'll begin to see this as our examples accumulate. Yes, there will be some borderline cases, but that doesn't mean the classes don't exist.

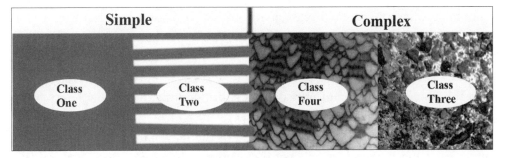

**Figure 7: The Spectrum of Complexity**

*A simple computation is in class one or class two. A complex computation is in class three or class four. Despite the number order of the names, the gnarly class four in some sense lies in between the periodic class two and the random-looking class three.*

Wolfram's initial investigations all had to do with feasible computations—in that he was looking at actual programs he could run. But his classification system applies equally well to the enormous computations carried out by physics and biology. The limitations of our digital silicon machines are such that we can't feasibly emulate any really large parts of the real world. Even so, it's very useful to categorize the unfeasible-for-the-PC computations that we see all around us.

Some natural phenomena die out or become static—these are the computations of class one. Other aspects of the world are periodic or class two—one thinks immediately of the rising and setting of the sun or the ebb and flow of the seasons. The class three aspects of the world are the seemingly random ones—you might think of radio hiss or TV-screen snow. But the most interesting computations in nature are all class four. As we'll see, examples include the forms of clouds and of trees, the flow of your thoughts, and the spacing of cities upon a map.

Wolfram has made two conjectures about his computation classes. The first is the Principle of Computational Equivalence (PCE for short).[5]

- *Principle of Computational Equivalence (PCE).* Almost all processes that are not obviously simple can be viewed as computations of equivalent sophistication.

What he means by this is that, in a sense that we'll make precise later on, all of the class three and class four computations are equally complex. Rather than believing that some complex computations are simpler than others, Wolfram feels that nearly all of them are of an equal and maximal complexity.

The PCE is in some sense discouraging, as it seems to tell us that when you can't see a simple explanation for a natural phenomenon, this means that the phenomenon is not only complex, but of a maximal complexity. Anything that's not obviously simple is in fact very gnarly.

A quick example. Consider the motion of the leaves on a tree. A physicist might describe the system as a wind-driven multiple-pendulum system. But the resulting computation is class four and certainly complex. If the PCE holds, then the gnarly motions of the leaves are to be as sophisticated as what's going on inside my brain. I seem to be a fluttering leaf? Maybe so.

Besides his PCE, or Principle of Computational Equivalence, Wolfram advocates a second conjecture, which I call the PCU or Principle of Computational Unpredictability.

- *Principle of Computational Unpredictability (PCU).* Most naturally occurring complex computations are unpredictable.

Here again, complex means class three or class four. And, as I mentioned before, when I say that a computation is *unpredictable,* this means there's no drastically faster shortcut computation that will reliably predict the given computation's outputs.

When we find some kind of natural process going on, we can often model the process as a computation. And in certain rare cases, we can also model the process by some simple and rather easily solvable equations. The PCU says that the latter situation is exceedingly rare. Generally speaking, there is no quick way to predict the results of a naturally arising computation.

Wolfram doesn't feel a need to explicitly state the PCU, but it's implicit in *A New Kind of Science.* He prefers to use the words *reducible* and *irreducible* for what I'm calling *predictable* and *unpredictable*—I insert some bracketed phrases in the following quote to keep this clear.[6]

> So what this [The Principle of Computational Equivalence] means is that systems one uses to make predictions cannot be expected to do computations that are more sophisticated than the computations that occur in all sorts of systems whose behavior we might try to predict. And from this it follows that for many systems no systematic prediction can be done, so that there is no general way to shortcut their process of evolution, and as a result their behavior must be considered computationally irreducible [or unpredictable].
>
> If the behavior of a system is obviously simple—and is say either repetitive or nested—then it will always be computationally reducible [or predictable]. But it follows from the Principle of Computational Equivalence that in practically all other cases it will be computationally irreducible [or unpredictable].

And this, I believe, is the fundamental reason that traditional theoretical science has never managed to get far in studying most types of systems whose behavior is not ultimately quite simple.

As I'll discuss in CHAPTER SIX: *Reality Upgrade:* the PCE and the PCU are in fact independent of each other. While the latter is used to deduce the unpredictability of naturally occurring processes, the former is used to deduce the *unsolvability* of certain questions about these processes—where unsolvability means that certain kinds of questions can't be solved by any conceivable kinds of computation at all.

I agree with Wolfram that both the PCE and the PCU are likely to be true for all of the interesting examples of naturally occurring computations— including physical systems, biological growth, the human mind, and the workings of human society.

Before closing this section, I want to introduce one more concept. When a computation generates an interesting and unexpected pattern or behavior, this is called *emergence.* I'll give three quick examples drawn from, respectively,

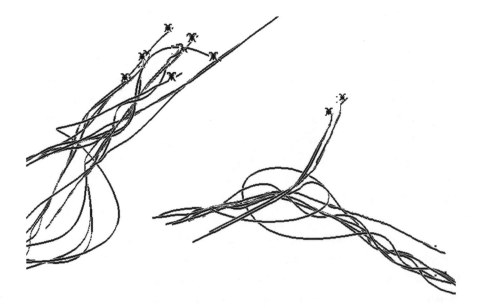

**Figure 8: Simulated Bird Flocking**

the fields known as artificial life, fractals, and cellular automata. (Most of the computer graphics figures in this book were made with programs I had a hand in authoring; see the Image Credits section at the end of the book for details.)

In artificial life, computers try to simulate the behaviors of living organisms. A classic discovery in this field is the *boids* algorithm by Craig Reynolds. Reynolds found that if a group of simulated birds, or boids, obeys a few simple rules, the boids will seem to move about as a coherent flock. This is an example of emergence in that the somewhat unexpected flocking behavior emerges from the collective computations carried out by the individual boids as suggested in figure 8. I'll say more about the boids algorithm in CHAPTER FIVE: *The Human Hive.*

A fractal is a structure that has interesting details at many different levels. The most famous fractal is the *Mandelbrot set* (figure 9). Suppose that we think of a computer screen as a region of the plane, with each pixel representing a pair of real numbers. Suppose further that for each pixel we use the corresponding number pair as an input for an iterated computation that terminates by specifying a color for the pixel. In the 1970s, Benoit Mandelbrot investigated a wide class of such computations that produce wonderfully intricate fractal patterns. Being a fractal, the Mandelbrot set has the property that one can zoom in on it, discovering level after level of detail. This is an example of emergence in that we have a cornucopia of forms arising from iterated applications of a very simple rule.

I'm going to say a lot about cellular automata in this book; they're a fascinating type of computation popularized by Stephen Wolfram. For now, think of a two-dimensional cellular automaton as a computation in which each pixel on a computer screen simultaneously updates its color according to the same rule. What gives the process its punch is that each pixel is allowed to look at its neighbor pixels. As a simple example of a such a cellular automaton rule, suppose that each pixel is black or white, and that a pixel updates itself by polling its nearest neighbors as to whether the majority of them are white (figure 10). It turns out that if you use an algorithm of awarding close elections to the losing side, a random sea of black-and-white pixels congeals into smoothly undulating globs, not unlike the droplets in a lava lamp. The high-level globs emerge from

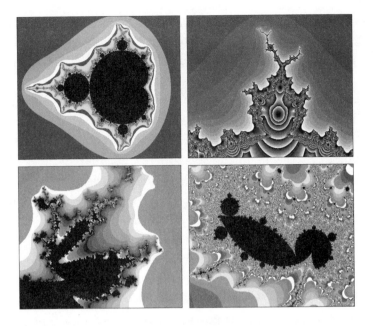

**Figure 9: Mandelbrot Sets**

*Left to right and top to bottom, we have the traditional Mandelbrot set based on a formula of the form $z = z^2 + c$; a zoomed-in view of the upper topknot of this set with an additional algorithm used to fill in the black region; a detail of a cubic Mandelbrot set based on a formula of the form $z = z^3 + bz + c$; and a detail of the so-called Rudy set, which is based on the family of cubic Mandelbrot sets. To me the last three images resemble, respectively, Ronald Wilson Reagan dressed as Bozo the Clown, a roaring dragon, and a friendly little rocking-horse.*

the low-level interactions of the cells. We call this the Vichniac Vote rule or just the Vote rule.[7]

The essence of the flocking, the Mandelbrot and the Vote computations is that something interesting emerges from a simple rule and a generic starting condition.

Emergence is different from unpredictability. One the one hand, we can have unpredictable computations that don't have any high-level emergent patterns: the dull digits of pi would be an example of this. On the other hand, we can have computations that generate emergent patterns that are, in the long run, predictable.

If you let the Vote rule run long enough, one color or the other melts away,

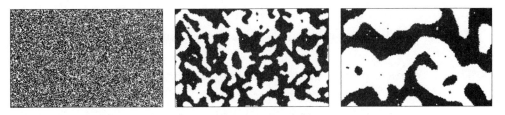

**Figure 10: The Vichniac Vote Rule**

*Each pixel is treated as the center of a 3 × 3 grid of nine cells. The new color of a pixel is white if the total number of white pixels in its neighborhood grid is four, six, seven, eight, or nine, and the new color of the pixel is black if the total number of white pixels is zero, one, two, three, or five. The three images show a random initial start with 320 × 200 pixels, the appearance of the system after thirty updates, and the appearance after three hundred updates.*

leaving a blank wasteland with perhaps a few tiny, rhythmic blinkers. The Vote rule is ultimately a predictable class two computation.

How about flocking and the Mandelbrot set? In most situations, the flocking behavior of a group of simulated birds will be class four and unpredictable, with new flocking configurations emerging from time to time—one such pattern I've observed is that sometimes a pair of birds will circle each other in a pattern like a tightly coiled double helix. And if you were allowed to endlessly zoom in on the emergent fractals of the Mandelbrot set, I think you'd also find unpredictable class four behavior, at least in the regions near the boundary of the set (although whether the Mandelbrot set is truly unpredictable is, I believe, an open problem).

## *1.3: Reckoning a Sum*

Human calculation is the original model for the notion of computation, so it's well worth analyzing how we use a pencil and paper to calculate something like 275 + 484. Before reading ahead, you might carry out the sum yourself, paying attention to what goes through your mind.

$$275$$
$$+\ 484$$

My own thoughts go something like this:

"This is an addition problem, so I'll use the adding routine I learned in grade school.

"I'll start at the top of the right-most column and work down, reading numbers and keeping a running sum in my head.

"That first mark is a five and the next one down is a four. The five looks like a fat man wearing a billed cap. Maybe he's a train engineer.

"Five plus four is nine. How do I know that? Because I memorized the simple sums fifty years ago in Kentucky. My God, where has the time gone? Our teacher was Mrs. Graves, the choirmaster's wife. There was that one boy, Lee Tingley. He couldn't learn the sums and he'd always sneak and count on his fingers. I did that, too, sometimes, pretending just to be drumming my fingers on the table—but Mrs. Graves had a sharp eye for finger-counting. She was strict. Kind of a pioneer type. She and her husband lived in a log cabin with their four kids. How does adding on your fingers work? Well, it depends on knowing the order of the counting numbers—if you don't know that you're lost. Anyway, let's see, I'm in the middle of an addition, and five plus four is nine.

"There's no more numbers in the column, so I write nine at the bottom and shift my gaze to the top of the next column to the left.

"Seven plus eight is fifteen. Write five and remember to carry one. I've always been a little uneasy about carrying, and borrowing is worse, especially borrowing from zero. I never fully understood borrowing until graduate school. Better not to think about it too much, just use the rules Mrs. Graves drummed into me. I'm carrying a one.

"I'm looking at the top of the next column to the left. I see a two. The carried one plus the two makes three. Remember that. The next number down is four. My three plus the four makes seven. Write seven.

"There's no more columns, so I'm done. 759 means seven hundred and fifty-nine. That's the answer."

If you do a lot of arithmetic by hand—not that many of us do anymore—then all of this is quite automatic. Indeed, arithmetic seems hard exactly when you're so rusty at it that you have to consciously think about what you're doing.

Rather than speaking of a person doing pencil and paper arithmetic as a "computer" or "calculator," let's use the old-fashioned "*reckoner.*"

The reckoner's computation involves several levels of rules. Working our way down from the highest level, we start with the implicit behavioral rule that a reckoner looks at a piece of paper, decides on an algorithm, and then carries out the calculation. Not just any person would know to do this. Becoming a reckoner involves learning certain rules of behavior. These rules make up the "operating system" for pencil-and-paper arithmetic.

A level below that is the specific algorithm the reckoner uses, for instance, the standard procedure for adding numbers.

Deeper down are the memorized sum tables that the reckoner draws upon.

And even more basic is the reckoner's ability to read and write numbers.

We might also wonder about the underlying biology that keeps the reckoner alive, about the physics that allows a pencil to make a mark on a piece of paper, and about the background laws of logic that make all of this hang together in an orderly fashion.

Usually we like to think somewhat abstractly and take most of these elements for granted. But there does seem to be a sense in which a sizable little corner of the world gets dragged into something as simple as a child adding two numbers on a blackboard.

What we're seeing here is something I mentioned before: Real-world computations have many levels of rules.

It's instructive to view familiar things with a fresh sense of wonder. Consider a boy adding 275 to 484 to get 759. Look at him through alien eyes. The brown-eyed juvenile grasps a stick of diatomaceous matter with one of his clusters of articulated tentacles—ah yes, he's "holding chalk in his hand." He studies two groups of squiggles and scratches fresh squiggles below them. What does this mean? He's making a prediction about a certain possible counting behavior. He and his race have a rote routine for producing a distinct name for each ordinal number. "One, two, three, . . . two hundred and seventy-five, . . . four hundred and eighty-four, . . . seven hundred and fifty-nine." The boy's calculation demonstrates that if he were to count to 275, and then count 484 steps further, he would attain the number 759. His squiggle manipulations have compressed the work of counting through 759 numbers to less than a dozen elementary operations. Clever lad.

This brings out two key points about computations.

First of all, some computations are *equivalent* to each other in terms of what they compute. For instance, I can add two numbers either by using arithmetic or by using an expanded version of "counting on my fingers." I get the same answer in either case, so the two computational methods are equivalent.

The second point is that equivalent computations can differ in how much time they take to carry out. If two different algorithms are used on one and the same system, it may be that one is always faster. Pencil-and-paper arithmetic is faster than counting.

The speed improvement you get by using faster software is independent of the gain you get by switching to a faster computer. Certainly a stage-performing calculating prodigy will be able to add numbers faster than our boy at the blackboard. But the prodigy, too, will add faster when using arithmetic than when working with brute-force counting.

How much time does arithmetic save? Allow me a brief geek-out on this topic. Using arithmetic instead of simple counting is an example of one computation being what computer scientists call "exponentially faster" than another. If a fast computation takes L steps and a slow computation takes on the order of $10^L$ steps, we say the fast one is exponentially faster than the slow one.

The relevance of this for our two styles of doing arithmetic has to do with the fact that, if an integer takes L digits to write, then the integer it represents has a size on the order of $10^L$. Using digits can be exponentially faster than counting by ones.

As an example of a exponential speedup, suppose I wanted to reckon, let us say, the sum 123,456,789 + 987,654,321. This would be a matter of adding two nine-digit numbers.

$$123,456,789$$
$$+ \ 987,654,321$$

The pencil-and-paper reckoning of this involves summing nine columns. Adding each column will have some fixed cost of maybe ten primitive steps: three shifts of focus (from top digit, to bottom digit, to write slot, to top of the next column), two reads, two sum lookups (including adding the carry), a write operation, possibly carrying a digit to the next column, and a check to see if you're done.

| | | |
|---|---|---|
| 36 | Amount from line 35 (adjusted gross income) . . . . . . . . . . . . | 36 |
| 37a | Check if: ☐ **You** were 65 or older, ☐ Blind; ☐ **Spouse** was 65 or older, ☐ Blind. Add the number of boxes checked above and enter the total here . . . . ▶ 37a | |
| b | If you are married filing separately and your spouse itemizes deductions, or you were a dual-status alien, see page 34 and check here . . . . . . . ▶ 37b ☐ | |
| 38 | **Itemized deductions** (from Schedule A) **or** your **standard deduction** (see left margin) . . | 38 |
| 39 | Subtract line 38 from line 36 . . . . . . . . . . . . . . . . . . . | 39 |
| 40 | If line 36 is $103,000 or less, multiply $3,000 by the total number of exemptions claimed on line 6d. If line 36 is over $103,000, see the worksheet on page 35 . . . . . . . . | 40 |
| 41 | **Taxable income.** Subtract line 40 from line 39. If line 40 is more than line 39, enter -0- . | 41 |

**Figure 11: Excerpt from the U.S. Income Tax Form 1040**

So using pencil-and-paper arithmetic to add a pair of nine-digit numbers requires no more than nine times ten steps, in other words ninety steps. That's a lot faster than counting by 123,456,789 by ones from 987,654,321 to arrive at 1,111,111,110—which would take over a hundred million steps, and isn't really feasible.[8]

By the way, this example also illustrates the point that something that is unfeasible for one style of computation may be feasible for a different kind of computation, even on one and the same system. Another point is that this particular addition problem has a very simple-looking answer, and that, with a little insight, a reckoner could have anticipated that and sped up the computation a bit more. But insight is an exceedingly difficult thing to automate.

By chaining together arithmetic problems a reckoner can carry out a very broad range of computations. What do I mean by chaining problems together? Consider a relatively complicated activity for which adults regularly use arithmetic: filling out tax forms. A tax form often embodies a linked chain of arithmetic problems.

Thus, you might be asked to write your income in row 35, write your deductions in row 38, write row 36 minus row 38 in row 39, write row 6d times 3,000 in row 40, write row 39 minus row 40 in row 41, and so on.

A list of instructions like this is a primitive example of what computer scientists call a *program*. Flexible beings that we are, we're able to handle a calculation task that contains not only numerical data to manipulate, but also instructions about the flow of the task.

It turns out that, given sufficiently elaborate instructions, we could carry out chains of arithmetic problems to compute the same results as a supercomputer.

Given enough time and patience, a human reckoner could carry out, say, all the ray-tracing and shading calculations needed to generate the frames of a feature-length computer-animated cartoon.

But of course the reality is that no reckoner *is* given that much time and patience. In order to make the best use of the computational worldview, we need to keep an eye on the distinction between abstract theoretical possibility and practical feasibility.

Now let's see how our electronic number-crunching machines expand our limits of feasibility. If nothing else, they allow us to be stupid faster.

### 1.4: *Analytical Engines*

If you use a standard file-exploring tool to poke around in the directories on your home computer, you find that certain areas of your hard drive contain data, such as images and documents, while other areas contain code for the software programs your machine runs. The high-level software is stored in one area (such as a Programs directory), the don't-touch-me-or-else low-level software in another (such as a Windows directory), and your documents are found somewhere like in a My Documents directory. The key fact is that both the software and the data are patterns of bits that are laid down in the memory. This is the *stored program architecture.* I mentioned that a tax form is a kind of program for a human reckoner. To say we are using a *stored* program architecture just means that we place a copy of the program into our machine's memory.

Why "architecture"? It's not like we're building the Parthenon here. Perhaps computer scientists use such a solid-sounding word to make up for the here-today-gone-tomorrow nature of their work. One of the less pleasant aspects of teaching computer science is how rapidly things change. Imagine if you were, say, a history professor, and, on showing up to begin your fall classes, you learn that this year your classes will be taught in Urdu, that instead of using markers on whiteboards you'll be using spray paint on rolls of butcher paper, and that your students will now be standing in the courtyard looking in through windows instead of sitting in your classroom. That's life as a computer science professor. No wonder we like to dignify our fly-by-night raree show with a moniker like "architecture."

Credit for the stored program architecture often goes to the Hungarian émigré John von Neumann, who did much to promote the creation of the first digital computers in the late 1940s. In fact, this way of laying out computers is sometimes even called the *von Neumann architecture*. But von Neumann had a number of important collaborators, the idea of a stored program was already familiar to Alan Turing in the 1930s, and there are in fact foreshadowings of the stored program architecture as early as 1800, when people began to have the idea of changing a machine's behavior without having to mechanically rebuild it.

The Jacquard loom, invented by the Frenchman Joseph-Marie Jacquard in 1801, is programmable by punch cards. By coding up a tapestry pattern as a series of cards, a Jacquard loom is able to weave the same design over and over, without the trouble of a person having to read the pattern and set the threads on the loom.

In the mid-1800s a colorful Briton named Charles Babbage hit upon the idea of using punch cards to control computations. Babbage actually owned a woven silk portrait of Jacquard that was generated by a loom using 24,000 punch cards. (see figure 12.)

Babbage began by designing—but never quite completing (to read Babbage's memoirs is to want to choke him very hard)—a gear-based device known as a Difference Engine, which was to be used for calculating and printing out mathematical tables of logarithms and trigonometric functions, astronomical tables giving the computed positions of celestial bodies at various times, and life-insurance tables giving the expected earnings or annuities of people of various ages. In each case it was a matter of applying a particular algebraic formula over and over.

**Figure 12: Drawing of the Woven Portrait of Joseph-Marie Jacquard**

**Figure 13:**
**A Detail of Scheutz's Difference Engine**

There was a small but real market for a Difference Engine and eventually the Swedish inventor Georg Scheutz did actually complete and market two working Difference Engines (figure 13). Rather than being envious, the big-hearted Babbage encouraged Scheutz and helped him sell his first machine to an astronomical observatory in Albany, New York.

One reason that Babbage never finished his own Difference Engine was that he was distracted by dreams of an even more fabulous piece of vaporware, a machine he called the *Analytical Engine.*

Babbage's description of the Analytical Engine may well be the very first outline for a calculating device where the program is separate from the action of the machinery. The Analytical Engine was to have a "mill" (think "chip") that executed arithmetic operations, and was also to have a "store" that would provide a kind of scratch paper: short-term memory for temporary variables used by the calculation. Babbage's then-novel idea was that the actions of the mill were to be controlled by a user-supplied program that was coded into punch cards like the ones used by the Jacquard loom. If we think of the deck of punch cards as being a kind of machine memory, Babbage's design foreshadows the stored program architecture—but it's not quite there yet.

One of the most lucid advocates of Babbage's Analytical Engine was the young Ada Byron, daughter of the famed poet. As Lady Ada memorably put it,

> The distinctive characteristic of the Analytical Engine, and that which has rendered it possible to endow mechanism with such extensive faculties as bid fair to make this engine the executive right-hand of abstract algebra, is the introduction into it of the principle

which Jacquard devised for regulating, by means of punched cards, the most complicated patterns in the fabrication of brocaded stuffs. . . . We may say most aptly, that the Analytical Engine *weaves algebraical patterns* just as the Jacquard loom weaves flowers and leaves.[9]

In reality, Babbage's Analytical Engines were never built. But it's interesting to think about such engines—it brings home the idea that computers don't have to be boxes of wires and chips. Remember, a computation is any system with a process that is governed by a finitely describable set of rules.

In 1991, my fellow cyberpunk science-fiction writers William Gibson and Bruce Sterling published a fascinating alternate history novel, *The Difference Engine,* which imagines what Victorian England might have been like if Babbage had been successful. (Despite the title, the book is really about Analytical Engines rather than Difference Engines.) Just as our present-day computers are run by hackers ("hacker" in the sense of "fanatical and resourceful programmer," as opposed to "computer criminal"), the Analytical Engines of Gibson and Sterling are tended by "clackers." Here's their description of a visit to the Central Statistics Bureau in their what-if London:

Behind the glass loomed a vast hall of towering Engines—so many that at first Mallory thought the walls must surely be lined with mirrors, like a fancy ballroom. It was like some carnival deception, meant to trick the eye—the giant identical Engines, clock-like constructions of intricately interlocking brass, big as rail-cars set on end, each on its foot-thick padded blocks. The whitewashed ceiling, thirty feet overhead, was alive with spinning pulley-belts, the lesser gears drawing power from tremendous spoked flywheels on socketed iron columns. White-coated clackers, dwarfed by their machines, paced the spotless aisles. Their hair was swaddled in wrinkled white berets, their mouths and noses hidden behind squares of white gauze.[10]

In the world of *The Difference Engine,* one can feed in a punch card coded with someone's description, and the Central Statistics Bureau Engines will spit out a "collection of stippleprinted Engine-portraits" of likely suspects.

Babbage's ideas bore fruit after a century. It was 1945 when von Neumann began promoting the stored program architecture, after working with the designers of a machine called ENIAC at the Moore School of Engineering of the University of Pennsylvania. Although it wasn't made of gears, the ENIAC was really a Babbage-style Analytical Engine. The ENIAC is sometimes regarded as the first general-purpose electronic computer, but it wasn't quite all the way there, in that its program wasn't stored in electronic memory. The ENIAC program was on a deck of punch cards; the machine needed to consult them every time it needed a program instruction.

A parenthetical note. Although ENIAC was originally meant to compute artillery trajectories, World War II was over before it started working. One of the first big computations ENIAC carried out was in fact a Cold War calculation to test the feasibility of building a hydrogen bomb: a numerical solution of a complicated differential equation having to do with nuclear fusion. It is said that the calculation used an initial condition of one million punch cards, with each punch card representing a single "mass point." The cards were run through ENIAC, a million new cards were generated, and the million new cards served as input for a new cycle of computation. (My guess is that the cards represented points arranged in a cubic grid a hundred units on a side, and that their values were updated on the basis of their neighbors' values.) You might say that the very first electronic computer program was a simulation of an H-bomb explosion. What a shame. Better they should have been looking at fractals, or simulating a human heart!

Programming the ENIAC involved making a deck of punch cards, manually arranging the wires on a plugboard, and setting a bunch of ten-position dials. There had to be a better way. As Arthur Burks, Herman Goldstine, and John von Neumann wrote in, "Preliminary Discussion of the Logical Design of an Electronic Computing Instrument,"

> Conceptually we have discussed . . . two different forms of memory: storage of numbers and storage of orders. If, however, the orders to the machine are reduced to a numerical code and if the machine can in some fashion distinguish a number from an order, the memory organ can be used to store both numbers and orders.[11]

The stored program architecture means that, in a certain sense, the high-level software is a kind of data that's processed by the low-level software that controls the host machine's basic functioning.

It's thanks in part to the stored program architecture that each of today's computers is in some sense equivalent to any other. If you have a Macintosh, you can get a Windows emulator that will allow your machine to read and execute Windows programs. If you're nostalgic for the PDP-1 computer used by the earliest computer hackers at MIT, you can search the Web and find a Java program that, when loaded on your machine, will allow it to emulate a PDP-1.

I've always loved that word, *emulate*. As humans we often try to emulate our heroes, that is, to learn a set of behaviors that make us be "just like" the hero. In effect, we're loading software into our brains. After watching a movie with a character I find particularly interesting, I'll often spend a few minutes emulating this character—seeing through the character's eyes, moving as the character moves, thinking as the character seemed to think. Books and other works of art have this effect, too, but there's something especially hypnotic about films.

Emulation generalizes the stored program concept. To be precise, we say that a computation Big emulates another computation Small if you have a special auxiliary input emulatesmall so that the states produced by Small(In) are the same as the states produced by Big(emulatesmall, In). In this situation we speak of emulatesmall as an emulation code.

Before making this more precise, let's recall how we're thinking of computations.

We view a computation $P$ as a process that we set into motion by giving it an input In. Thus $P$(In) is a process that changes as time $t$ increases. To be quite general, we're allowing both for the possibility that $t$ increases in abrupt steps, as in a digital computer, and for the possibility that $t$ is continuous, as in a physical system like a fluttering leaf. We write $P$(In, $t$) = Out to mean that after time $t$, the computation $P$(In) is in state Out. And we assume that we have some method Is$P$Done(Out), called a target detector, that allows us to decide if the computation is to be viewed as having halted when it reaches the state Out. Let's adopt the following additional terminology.

- $P$(In) *produces* Out means that for some $t$, $P$(In, $t$) = Out.
- $P$(In) *returns* Out means that for some $t$, $P$(In, $t$) = Out and Is$P$Done(Out) is True.

And now we can define emulation.

- *Definition of Emulation.* Big *emulates* Small if there is an emulation
  code emulatesmall such that for any states In and Out,
     Small(In) returns Out if and only if
         Big(emulatesmall, In) returns Out.

So Big emulates Small means that having access to Big and the emulation code emulatesmall is as good as having access to Small.

The definition of emulation is rather technical, but the concept is a natural one. Let me suggest some analogies.

- Think of Big as a PC and Small as a pocket calculator. Big comes equipped with a calculator accessory that acts as an emulatesmall to make it behave just like a calculator.
- Think of yourself as Big and me as Small. The book you hold is meant to serve as an emulatesmall that allows you to emulate my thoughts.
- Think of Mr. Big as a man, Ms. Small as a woman, and emulatesmall as a dress. If Mr. Big wears a dress, can he reproduce all the behaviors of Ms. Small? No. Mr. Big will never give birth to a baby. So he can't presently be said to emulate Ms. Small. But hold on. Maybe at some future time, men may gain the ability to grow cloned offspring of their own. And in this event, perhaps Mr. Big *can* be said to fully emulate Ms. Small.
- Think of Big as a tree branch rocking in the wind and Small as a PC. I'm of the opinion that the Big branch's behavior is rich enough to emulate anything that the Small PC can do. In order to make the definition of emulation apply, however, I'd need to incorporate some method of translating from the binary language of machines into the positional "language" of leaf and branch positions. I take up the issue of translations in emulations in the Technical Appendix.

I mentioned above that any one of our personal computers can emulate any other. This is perhaps a bit surprising. After all, if you were to believe some of the ads you see, you might imagine that the latest PCs have access to new, improved methods that lie wholly beyond the abilities of older machines. Could there be a new machine with such tricky goodies on its chips that an older machine would not in fact be able to load up and execute emulation software for it?

Well, if the emulation program for the new machine is so large that it wouldn't be able to fit into my old machine's memory, then, no, the old machine can't emulate the new one. But this is a hardware limitation that seems peripheral to the core issue of functional capability. If I'm allowed to equip my old machine with as much additional memory I need, then yes, I can always get it to behave like any other computer at all.

This somewhat surprising fact has to with a phenomenon that computer scientists call universality. It turns out that many computations can in fact emulate any other computation. We call these maximally powerful computations *universal*.

> • *Definition.* A computation is *universal* if it can emulate any other computation.

Now, you might expect it to be fairly hard to get a computation to be universal. But nothing could be further from the truth. Universality is easy. Once *any* computational system advances past a certain very low threshold, it becomes universal. How low is the threshold? Being able to add and multiply is more than enough. And, as we'll see, even more rudimentary capabilities will do.

In point of fact, when we examine the naturally occurring computational systems around us—like air currents, or growing plants, or even drying paint—there seems to be reason to believe that the vast majority of these systems support universal computation. This belief is part of the content of Wolfram's PCE: If some complex computations are universal, and most complex computations are of equivalent sophistication, then most complex computations are universal.

Universality is a big deal. The existence of universal computation means that there is a maximal level of computational complexity. And the ubiquity of universality means that this maximum is rather readily attainable. Computation is in some sense already as good as its going to get. We're in a position a bit like someone who's inherited a fortune of a vastness they're still learning to understand.

## 1.5: *The Tiniest Brains*

Starting with thoughts about arithmetic, Alan Turing formulated a minimally simple definition of computation in the 1930s—well before any real electronic computers had been built. Turing's approach was to describe an idealized kind of computer called a Turing machine.[12]

In practice, nobody builds Turing machines. They're so primitive that even adding numbers can be unfeasibly time-consuming with one of these devices, and programming such a device to do anything complex is mind-numbingly dull.

Nevertheless, there are several good reasons for learning about Turing machines.

First of all, many Turing machines are universal, that is, they can, however slowly, carry out any possible computation. Looking at Turing machines helps us understand how little is really needed for universal computation.

Second, the design of a Turing machine resembles the design of an electronic computer, albeit in embryonic form. Understanding Turing machines is a good preparation for understanding PCs.

Third, the rudimentary quality of Turing machines makes them easy to think about. By searching through all possible Turing machines we can in some sense search through all possible computations. In his original paper on the topic, Turing proved that no Turing machine can distinguish between the true and false theorems of mathematics, which in turn showed that mathematical truth is in some sense undecidable for any computer at all. More recently, Stephen Wolfram has carried out a series of computer searches over the class of Turing machines to help confirm his hypothesis that computations come in only four flavors: they die out, they repeat, they seethe messily, or they create gnarly patterns.

So, all right, what's a Turing machine?

I once looked through a specification of the librarians' Dewey decimal system and found there is actually a classification for "Turing machines, manufacture and distribution of." But in point of fact, Turing machines are not real physical devices that people build. They're idealized models of an extremely simple kind of digital computer. Turing's original inspiration for the Turing machine was to try to capture the behavior of a human reckoner—but without all the squishy stuff on the inside.

To begin with, a Turing machine has only some finite number of internal states. These are analogous to a reckoner's mental states, such as the state of remembering to carry a 1.

As a further simplification, a Turing machine uses a linear tape of cells instead of a two-dimensional grid of paper. A Turing machine focuses on one cell at a time on its tape; more concretely, we think of the machine as having a read-write head that moves from cell to cell.

During each update, the machine reads the symbol in the cell, possibly changes the symbol in the cell, moves its head one cell to the left or one cell to the right, and enters a new internal state. Having completed one update step, it begins the next: reading the new cell, changing it, moving its head, and altering its internal state once again.

What determines the Turing machine's behavior? We can look at it this way: each stimulus pair of (*internal state, read symbol*) leads to a unique response triple of (*write symbol, move direction, new state*). The high-level software for a Turing machine is a lookup table that supplies a response triple for each possible stimulus pair.

A Turing machine's input is a string of symbols on the tape. Suppose we simply write *d* to stand for a tape with a particular symbol pattern that we can also call *d*. We set a computation in motion by putting the machine into its starting state and setting its head on the leftmost nonblank symbol of *d*. An output is any resulting pattern of symbols that appears on the tape at a later times.

Figure 14 represents a Turing machine in action. It uses only two symbols, the white cell and the black cell, which we might also think of as zero and one, and it has three states. Each row of the figure shows a picture of the Turing machine's tape, with time running down the page from top to bottom—that is, the starting configuration is the top line and the later configurations are below. The picture also includes small representations of the

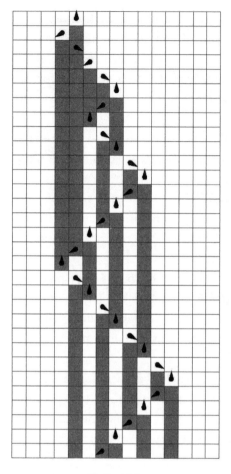

**Figure 14:**
**A Turing Machine History**

*This is a three-state Turing machine.*

Turing machine's head as a little pointer whose direction indicates the internal state that the Turing machine is in during that particular snapshot. (This useful method of representing Turing machines was introduced by Stephen Wolfram in *A New Kind of Science*.)

The particular machine depicted starts on a blank tape and endlessly shuttles back and forth, filling the tape with an ever-growing pattern of alternating marked and unmarked cells. It never stops. Pointless, you may say, but, hey, it's a computation!

In some applications of Turing machines we are concerned with finding cases where the machine halts, that is, reaches a state after which the output pattern doesn't change any further. Although its possible to do this by having the machine go into an endless loop without writing or erasing anything more, most discussions allow computations to have a special "halted" state, and specify that once a Turing machine enters its halted state, it stops looking up further moves.

Some discussions of Turing machines focus almost exclusively on machines whose computations halt. But in *The Lifebox, the Seashell, and the Soul*, we're equally interested in open-ended computations that are willing to run for as long as you let them. In Wolfram's terms, a computation that halts for every input is class one. Naturally occurring class four "computers," like the weather, the plants, or our minds, all have the quality of being willing to continue indefinitely. It's only a destructive external input that brings most natural computations to a halt—as when, for instance, a toxic spill eliminates a patch of plants, a cerebral hemorrhage cuts off a person's thoughts, or a sun explodes and puts an end to its planets' weather.

As I mentioned earlier, we also have a notion of halting for arbitrary computations $P$. Here we can have a *target detector,* IsPDone, that has two special output states, True and False. IsPDone is a helper computation that allows us to distinguish certain *target states* as being states in which $P$ has produced an answer. So as to block off an endless regress, we require that there be no problems in trying to decide when IsPDone itself has produced a final answer, that is, we require that for any state Out, IsPDone(Out) returns either True or False in a finite amount of time to indicate, respectively, that Out be regarded as a target or a nontarget state.[13]

Now let's talk some more about the rules, or software, that govern a Turing machine. As I said above, the high-level software for a Turing machine is a lookup table that supplies a response triple for each possible stimulus pair. And the low-level software for a Turing machine forces it to cycle through the following three steps:

- (Turing A) The machine reads the symbol that is in the active cell. It combines the read symbol with its current state to make a stimulus pair (*internal state, read symbol*).
- (Turing B) Given the stimulus pair (*internal state, read symbol*), the machine looks in its high-level software to locate a corresponding response triple (*write symbol, move direction, new state*).
- (Turing C) On the basis of the response triple, the machine writes a symbol in the active cell, moves the head one step to the left or to the right, and enters a new state. If the machine is not in the halted state, it returns to step (Turing A).

One of Turing's great insights was that we can put the lookup tables for Turing machines down onto the tape along with the input data. That is, instead of running machine $M$ on the data $d$, you can code $M$ as a string of symbols $m$, and write the $m$ pattern on the tape next to the data $d$ to get a tape that we'll call $md$. And then a fairly routine bit of mathematical legerdemain can conjure up a specific universal Turing machine $U$ such that the action of $U$ on the tape $md$ emulates the action of $M$ on the tape $d$.

Note the exact analogy to the fact that, if $U$ is a personal computer and $M$ is some other personal computer, we can find an emulation program $m$ so that the action of $U$ on $md$ is the same as the action of $M$ on $d$.

Although every PC is universal, only some Turing machines are universal. All PCs are, after all, of a fairly high degree of complexity. But Turing machines can be made arbitrarily simple. Over the years there's been something of a competition among computer scientists to discover the simplest possible universal Turing machine. The simplicity of a Turing machine is gauged in terms of how many internal states the machine has and how many tape symbols it uses. The most recent record-holder, discovered by Stephen Wolfram and Matthew Szudzik on the basis of work by Matthew Cook, uses two states and five symbols. This means that the machine itself has an exceedingly simple lookup table. With two states and five symbols, there are only ten possible combinations of (*internal state, read symbol*), so the Turing machine's entire lookup table has only ten lines. Yet, by preparing the input tape in a suitable way, we can get this machine to emulate any possible computation.

Encouraged by this and some similar kinds of research, Wolfram conjectures in *A New Kind of Science* that universal computations are ubiquitous. This follows from his Principle of Computational Equivalence, or PCE, which I introduced a bit earlier in this chapter.

- *Principle of Computational Equivalence (PCE)*. Almost all processes that are not obviously simple can be viewed as computations of equivalent sophistication.

Let's delve into this more deeply than before.

The "almost all" at the start is so Wolfram can cover himself from a certain pointed criticism. The criticism stems from the fact, known since the 1960s, that there are in fact some gnarly class four Turing machines that aren't universal. But Wolfram's feeling is that, at least in nature if not in mathematics, such computations will be exceedingly rare. We might reasonably replace the phrasing "almost all" by "most naturally occurring."

When he speaks of an "obviously simple" process, Wolfram has class one and class two computations in mind. Recall that the class one computations run for a while and then enter a fixed state. There are actually two ways that a computation can be class two. On the one hand, it might go into a loop and begin precisely repeating itself. Or, on the other hand, the computation might generate a growing, orderly, unsurprising pattern. The three-state Turing machine depicted earlier in this section is an example of this style class two computation. It doesn't exactly repeat itself, but what it's doing is "obviously simple."

The non-obviously-simple computations would be the disorderly class three computations and the gnarly class four computations. The disorderly computations seethe in a seemingly random fashion, and the gnarly ones generate intricate patterns.

What does Wolfram mean by two computations being "of equivalent sophistication"? We might take this to mean that they can emulate each other.

Note that if $U$ is universal and if $M$ can emulate $U$, then $M$ must be universal as well. Consider an analogy: If you can imitate the actor Jim Carrey, who can imitate *anyone,* then you yourself can imitate anyone. To imitate Elvis, for instance, you imitate Jim Carrey imitating Elvis.

Given that we know that universal computations exist, if we take "of equivalent sophistication" to mean "able to emulate each other," we might phrase the PCE as follows.

- *Principle of Computational Equivalence, Second Form (PCE2).* Most naturally occurring complex computations are universal.

As I mentioned earlier, Wolfram advocates a related but distinct principle as well, the Principle of Computational Unpredictability.

- *Principle of Computational Unpredictability (PCU).* Most naturally occurring complex computations are unpredictable.

The PCE and PCU were to some extent inspired by Wolfram's searches over vast classes of Turing machines and other simple kinds of idealized computation. Wolfram's daring is to insist that his insights apply to *all* kinds of computations. In the chapters to come, we'll consider what the PCE and PCU might tell us about our world.

### 1.6: *Inside the Beige Box*

In this section we'll talk about real computers, that is, personal computers. There's no real need to talk about "supercomputers." Last year's supercomputer is next year's desktop machine.

Personal computers all have the same basic design: a processor and memory.

The processor is something like the head of a Turing machine, and the memory is like a Turing machine tape. Or, again, the processor is like a human reckoner, and the memory is like a sheet of paper.

The memory, often called RAM for random access memory, can be imagined as a long ribbon of cells. The PC's memory cells hold so-called words of memory. Here *word* does not mean "meaningful language unit." It simply means a particular fixed number of bits, let's say thirty-two zeroes or ones. Each word of memory has an address, and the memory addresses run from zero on through the thousands, millions, and billions, depending on how much RAM the particular machine has. The "random access" aspect of the memory has to do with the fact that the processor is easily able to read or write the contents of a cell at any desired address.

Let's look at what happens when a stored program architecture computer runs. The basic operation is for the processor to alternate between the following two steps:

- (Computer A) Fetch an instruction from memory.
- (Computer B) Interpret and execute the latest instruction.

The processor uses an address called the *instruction pointer* to keep track of which word of memory the processor is currently supposed to fetch. And it also keeps a *data read pointer* and a *data write pointer* to keep track of which memory slot to use for, respectively, reading or writing bits (see figure 15).

All of these pointers are stored in so-called registers that live right in the silicon of the processor. The processor has a few dozen such registers and they can be thought of as constituting part of its internal state.

According to which word the processor finds at the address of its instruction pointer, it will do one of the following:

- Read data from memory.
- Carry out logical or arithmetical operations such as AND or PLUS, and store the results in a "scratch-paper" register.
- Write data to memory.

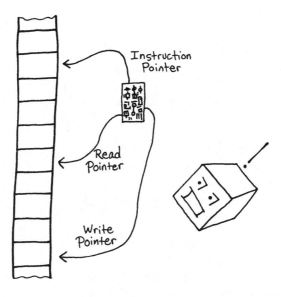

**Figure 15:**
**Processor and Memory Ribbon**

After fetching and executing each successive instruction, the processor will normally increment the instruction pointer to the next memory position, but certain instructions will tell it to override this default behavior and execute the following, fourth kind of primitive operation:

- Jump the instruction pointer to a new position.

Unlike a Turing machine's head, a personal computer's instruction pointer can hop to anywhere in memory in a single step. If you have some familiarity with programming, you may know that jumps in the instruction pointer's position can be caused by if-then-else statements, by loops, and by calls to procedures. The instruction pointer does a dance of computation.

A higher-level way to think of the difference between PCs and Turing machines would be to say that at any given time, a PC processor can access any memory location, whereas a Turing machine processor (or head) can only access one memory location. We represent this in the two diagrams in figure 16. In each diagram, the circle represents the processor and the row of cells

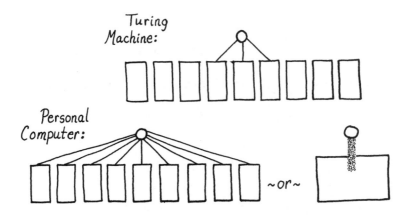

**Figure 16: Architectures of Turing Machine vs. Personal Computer**

*We draw the Turing machine processor as having access not only to the current memory cell but to the two neighboring cells; this is because the processor is able to execute a "move left" or a "move right" instruction. We can draw the personal computer's architecture as a long row of memory cells, indicating the processor's global access by drawing connecting lines from the processor to each cell; or we can simplify by drawing the memory as a somewhat larger block meant to include lots of data, and drawing the processor-to-memory access line as thick, fuzzy, and gray, with the understanding that this kind of line means that the processor has rapid access to every nook of the associated memory box.*

represents the memory. Computer scientists would say that the Turing machine has *local* memory access, while the PC has *global* memory access.

When the PC processor carries out logical and arithmetic operations, it manipulates the bits in the registers, often by combining one register's bits with the bits in another. More precisely, logic and arithmetic instructions may copy register values among each other, add register values, compare register values, and more. The actual execution of additions, multiplications, logical combinations, and so on, is handled by specialized circuitry on the chip, or what's sometimes called the *chip architecture* (there's that word again).

What about interactive inputs? Input devices can place a few bits or even a long patch of bits directly into the RAM. A keyboard feeds in perhaps thirty-two bits of data with each key press, while a disk drive can load in millions of bits at a time. Each time you move your mouse, the mouse, too, puts bits describing its clicks and moves into the computer memory. A program can go and check this area every so often, and in this way respond to the inputs.

Output devices convert bits into audible or visible display. A crude text screen might show a few hundred characters, using sixteen bits per character, whereas a graphics screen might display millions of colored pixels, with perhaps thirty-two bits of color code per pixel. You can print out your screens, or you can write the information onto a disk. A sound card converts swatches of bits into voices, music, and noise.

How is it that PCs often seem to be doing several things at once? Behind the scenes the machine allocates successive time-slices to a series of tasks and rapidly cycles around and around this task loop, giving the illusion that all the tasks are being worked on at once. In this fashion a PC can emulate a so-called parallel computer, which independently runs many computational threads at the same time.

Being a universal computer is empowering. It turns out that no matter what its particular architecture is, a universal computer can emulate *any* other computer, of *any* possible architecture. This isn't an obvious fact, nor is it something that's been formally proved—it's more in the nature of an empirical principle that's been deduced from the body of theoretical and practical knowledge of computation that we've accumulated. The principle is sometimes called Church's Thesis. We might phrase it like this:

- *Church's Thesis.* Any possible computation can be emulated by a personal computer with sufficiently large memory resources.

Alonzo Church proposed his thesis back in the 1930s, after observing that several different ways of defining computations were all equivalent to one another. The thesis becomes controversial when universal automatists argue that PCs can emulate naturally occurring physical processes— even with the understanding that the emulations will normally be unfeasible. The issue is that if physics were to involve *infinitely precise* continuous quantities changing according to exact laws, then the finitely complex digital electronic computers might not be able to adequately emulate physics. The resolution, which I'll discuss in CHAPTER TWO: *Our Rich World,* is to say that the quantities used in physics really have only a finite level of precision.

## 1.7: *Plugged In*

In the early 1980s, the science-fiction writer William Gibson coined the great word *cyberspace,* which now has come to mean, approximately, the Web. Originally the word also connoted virtual reality, in the sense of an immersive and shared graphical world.

In 1988, John Walker, then the chairman at Autodesk, Inc., of Sausalito, had the idea of building a software toolkit for creating shared virtual realities. Autodesk trademarked the word *Cyberspace* for an (unsuccessful) product called the Cyberspace Developer's Kit. William Gibson was somewhat annoyed by this and jokingly claimed he was going to trademark *Eric Gullichsen,* this being the name of the first lead programmer on the Autodesk Cyberspace project. I myself was employed by Autodesk at the time, recruited by Walker himself. I was helping to design and code a series of popular science software packages, including *Rudy Rucker's Cellular Automata Laboratory, James Gleick's Chaos: The Software,* and *Artificial Life Lab* (all of which are available for free download from this book's Web site, www.rudyrucker.com/lifebox/). I also helped write some demos for the Autodesk Cyberspace project, most memorably a lively flock of polyhedra that would circle the user's head.

Before we managed to get electronically linked multiple users into our cyberspace at the same time, Autodesk's stock price went down and I was out of the industry and back in the groves of academe, teaching computer science at San Jose State and writing a novel called *The Hacker and the Ants* about my experiences at Autodesk.

> What was cyberspace? Where did it come from? Cyberspace had oozed out of the world's computers like stage-magic fog. Cyberspace was an alternate reality, it was the huge interconnected computation that was being collectively run by planet Earth's computers around the clock. Cyberspace was the information network, but more than the Web, cyberspace was a shared vision of the Web as a physical space.[14]

Living through the dot-com boom in Silicon Valley was a trip; for a while there, money was growing on trees. I remember when a student in my Java course came by the office to show me a job offer he'd gotten. They were offering him a fat salary, perhaps 30 percent more than what a humble professor makes. And he was wondering if he should ask for more! He was clever and likable, although disorganized and perhaps a little lazy. He got so excited about his impending career that he didn't hand in one of the class projects, which brought his average down to the C level, but it didn't matter; the bubble wanted everyone it could get, at least for a short time. I had thought he might be unemployed by now, or running an offshore coding group in Bangalore, but the other day he turned up again, having authored some software for anonymous Web-surfing, and still very much in the game.

The Web is here to stay.

When you push aside the hype and the biz buzz, the Web consists primarily of our personal computers, with the added feature that they can exchange data. When one computer gets information from another, we speak of them as a client and a server, respectively. The client is said to download files from the server, and, in the reverse direction, the client uploads files to the server so that other clients can see them.

A given PC may act as both client and server; indeed, in some local networks, all machines play both roles. It's more common, however, to have certain dedicated machines that function primarily as servers. These server machines are the same kinds of PCs that you might have at home, with the difference that dedicated servers usually use a Unix-type operating system. The clients and servers connect to one another via a hierarchy of machines called switches and routers, as indicated in figure 17.

My son Rudy Jr. runs what may be the only independent Internet service provider in San Francisco, www.monkeybrains.net. He keeps his machines in a cage that he rents for them in a so-called server hotel in a rough neighborhood. A robot flophouse. The server hotel was once a Macy's warehouse and is located next to a train track. Nearly all server hotels are next to train tracks so that their routers' fiber optic cables can follow the railway's right of way to the next server hotel down the line. The server hotel, or data center, holds three highly air-conditioned floors of wire cages, each cage stuffed with the machines of some stalwart Web entrepreneur.

Rudy's cage holds seventeen server machines and a router. The last time I visited, he pulled a plug out of the back of his router box and told me to look

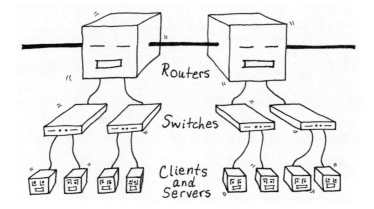

**Figure 17: Networked Personal Computers**

*The physical details of the Web are more complicated than the figure shows. But a basic way of thinking of it is that individual server and client PCs connect to machines called switches that in turn connect to routers. Routers across the world are strung together via optical fiber connections; the network of linked routers is what you might think of as the Internet's backbone.*

into the end of the wire. I saw a faint red light, grainy with information. It was his router's optical fiber line. "That's the color of the Internet," said my son. "You just saw a gigabit per second." Any information going through Rudy's router at that moment suffered a glitch, but the protocols of the Internet are smart enough to correct things like that.

To get a picture of how the Web works, let's step through an example. Suppose you enter my book's Web site address into your browser's address bar: www.rudyrucker.com/lifebox/.

The following sequence of actions results (leaving out numerous fiddling details):

- Your machine sends a message to Rudy Jr.'s server machine in San Francisco, stating your machine's name and requesting the page www.rudyrucker.com/lifebox/index.html.
- Rudy's machine sends bits describing this Web page to your machine.
- Your machine's browser software converts the bits into an image on your screen.

The transaction doesn't have to be one-way. My book's Web site has a guest book page.

Once the guest book page is showing on your machine, you can type something, press Enter, and your words will now be stored on Rudy's server machine. The next person to access the guest book page can see what you wrote there. The extra steps are these:

- Your machine sends bits to Rudy's machine.
- Rudy's machine incorporates your changes into one of its Web page files.

With a little more Web experience, you can do more than write things into someone's guest book: You can post images, maintain an online blog—or even establish your own Web site.

As I mentioned above, when your machine reads in some information across the Web, this is a *download,* and when your machine writes some information into some other location on the Web this is an *upload.* Be warned that some people use these words the opposite way around. But as John Walker convincingly puts it, "When you offer your data to the great Net God like the smoke of burnt offerings rising into the heavens—this is an *upload.* And when the riches of the Web rain upon you like manna—this is a *download.*"

The Web greatly leverages your access to information by means of hyperlinks. When you click on a hyperlink on a Web page, the server machine sends your machine the name of a new machine, your machine contacts the new machine and asks for the page, and the new machine sends your machine the new page. For you, it's as if the Web is a seamless whole, and it doesn't make all that much difference which server you initially connect yourself to.

Can we think of Web itself as a kind of computation? Sure. As long as something is rule-based it's a computation. And the Web has rule-based behavior—messages dart back and forth, requesting and delivering data. The initial input is the machines and their connections, and the interactive input is the requests emanating from the machines. The behavior of the Web in and of itself is thoroughly deterministic. Even when a message needs to make a seemingly random choice among several equally good paths, a deterministic pseudorandom algorithm is in fact used to make the decision. And the data requests made by human users are additional interactive inputs to the system.

We could also imagine a completely deterministic Web in which the client requests are being generated by programs running on the individual client and server machines. Web crawlers are examples of this kind of automated Web surfing. A client running a Web crawler will successively visit one page after another, accumulating information on what it finds. A search engine like the currently popular Google uses Web crawlers to produce information for its own large database. When a user goes to the Google site and asks for pages relating to a given topic, the Google software uses its Web-crawler-built database to suggest links. As an additional wrinkle, Google ranks each page, using criteria such as how many other pages have links to the given page.

Let's think a bit more about the Web as a computer. Generalized rule-based systems—computers in the broad sense of the word—can be based on a wide range of underlying architectures. That is, the mutual interactions of a computer's hardware, software, and data can be organized in many different ways. A computer's strengths and weaknesses have much to do with its architecture. Three commonly seen architectures are the serial, the networked, and the parallel. A PC has a serial architecture, in which a single processor has global access to a single memory set. Classical physics, on the other hand, can be thought of as a parallel architecture, in which many processors have local access to a single shared memory set (the world).

A *network architecture* has five distinctive characteristics. The first three are these:

- Many distinct processes.
- Each process is associated with its own private block of memory.
- The processes can access one another's memories by exchanging read and write requests.

The Web has many processors, each of which has its own private memory. A Web-linked machine has instant access to any location of its own memory, but it has only an indirect access to the memories of the other machines.

The tree structure in our first drawing of the Web (figure 17) was an implementation detail. The essence of the network architecture appears in figure 18.

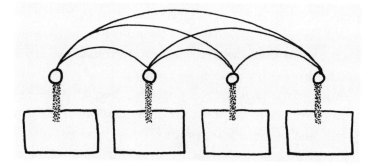

**Figure 18: Network Architecture**

*The circles are the computer processors and the boxes are the memory sets of the individual machines. The arced lines at the top are connections by which the processors make read-write requests, while the thick gray lines below represent the fact that each processor has full rapid access to its own private memory block.*

We speak of each processor-memory combination as a *node*. In terms of the figure, a node is a circle plus its associated rectangle of memory.

We can describe the memory access as follows. In order to read memory from another node, a given node needs to send a request to the remote node's processor and wait for this node to retrieve and send the desired information. Writing to the memory of another node requires a similar procedure, involving a similar kind of request. An important characteristic of the networked architectures is that a given node can deny these requests.

• A network node may deny incoming read or write requests.

Another characteristic feature of the network architecture is the lack of any kind of systemwide synchronization. Indeed, networks are often called *asynchronous*.

• Each network node sends and processes requests according to its own schedule and speed.

The network architecture is found in several naturally occurring forms. A living organism can be thought of as a network whose individual processors are the organism's cells. And our society is a network in which the processors are human beings. In both cases each individual processor has its own private memory, the processors share data by exchanging signals with one another, and the processors can refuse requests.

A rude question. If the Web is a computation, then what the heck is it computing? The easy answer is that computations don't have to be "about" anything. They can just occur. Rain running down a windowpane isn't about anything, but certainly there's an intricate computation taking place.

Certainly it would be interesting if the Web really were somehow computing something deep. The hooked-together computers of the Web are at least superficially reminiscent of the coupled neurons that make up a human brain. Could the Web ever act as a planetary mind? This question is a variant of the old question of whether human society as a whole has a group mind. I think that in both cases the answer is a qualified yes—I'll say more about this in CHAPTER FIVE: *The Human Hive.*

## 1.8: *Flickercladding*

A cellular automaton (CA for short) is a parallel computation that operates on a memory space that is a one-, two-, three-, or higher-dimensional grid of cells. The memory can be, for instance, a one-dimensional tape like a Turing machine's tape, a two-dimensional grid of cells like a reckoner's paper, or a lattice of three-dimensional cubes.

Each cell has its own associated processor, and each cell contains a small amount of data called its *value.* As we'll see in CHAPTER TWO: *Our Rich World,* when modeling physics, we turn to CAs in which each cell value consists of one or several real numbers. But often we focus on discrete-valued CAs, that is, CAs whose cell values are a single integer or even a single bit.

We depict the architecture of one-dimensional and two-dimensional CA as in figure 19, where the processors are circles attached to square memory cells.

The CA computation proceeds in discrete steps. At each step, every cell is simultaneously updated. How is an individual cell updated? Each cell processor has a rule that computes the cell's new value based upon the cell's current value and the values of a few neighboring cells. In implementing the flow of heat as a CA, for instance, the rule might simply be to average a cell's temperature value with the temperature values of the cells adjacent to it.

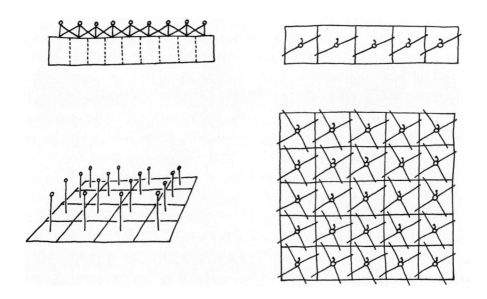

**Figure 19: Architecture of One- and Two-Dimensional CAs**

*The top row shows two images of a one-dimensional CA architecture, and the bottom row shows two images of a two-dimensional CA architecture. In the left column we draw the processors as floating above the cells, and in the right column we draw them down inside the cells. The lower left image would be more accurate if each processor had lines coming down to the neighbor cells.*

Although we could in principle use different update rules for the different individual cells, it's more common to study CAs in which all the cells use the same rule and look at the same pattern of nearest neighbors.

In short, CAs are defined so as to satisfy these five conditions:

- *Many processors.* A CA has one processor per memory cell.
- *One shared memory.* The cells are arranged into a single memory grid.
- *Locality.* The CA update rules are local, that is, a given cell's new value depends only on the present values of the cells in some fixed neighborhood of the cell.
- *Homogeneity.* Each CA has the same update rule.
- *Synchronization.* All of the CA cells are updated at once.

Cellular automata seem to have been invented in the late 1940s at the Los Alamos, New Mexico, laboratories by Stanislaw Ulam and John von Neumann. Both these men were primarily mathematicians, but their interests had exceedingly wide range. Recall that von Neumann was instrumental in the creation of the first electronic computers. He also did work on theories of infinity, the foundations of quantum mechanics, economics, and game theory.

Ulam, too, did work on theories of infinity, inventing what stood for many years as the largest kinds of numbers anyone could dream up: the so-called measurable cardinals. He was involved in computers as well, using a machine called MANIAC to come up with some novel methods of simulating nonlinear physics (see figure 20). And, with Edward Teller, Ulam was the co-inventor of the hydrogen bomb.

Ulam's first published reference to cellular automata appeared around 1950, at the time he was helping von Neumann design a self-reproducing machine.[15] Ulam carried out some investigations of discrete-valued CAs and then, in the 1950s, he switched his attention to continuous-valued CAs, that is, cellular automata in which the values are real numbers—this work we'll discuss in chapter 2.

**Figure 20: Stanislaw Ulam Demonstrating the MANIAC Computer**

*The little girl is Ulam's daughter Claire. I discovered this picture in S. M. Ulam,* Adventures of a Mathematician *(Berkeley: University of California Press, 1991).*

CAs didn't really catch on until 1970 when, in his popular "Mathematical Games" column for *Scientific American,* Martin Gardner wrote about how John Horton Conway, a mathematician at the University of Cambridge, had discovered a two-dimensional CA so rich in patterns and behavior that it was known as the Game of Life, or simply Life.

In Life each cell value consists of a single 0 or 1 bit, indicating if the cell is "dead" or "alive." Each cell's processor

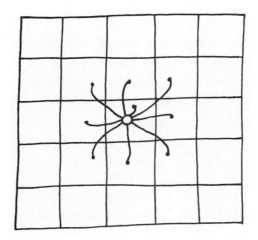

**Figure 21:**
**A Cell Neighborhood in Conway's Life**

*Note that this notion of neighborhood differs from the style of two-dimensional cell neighborhood we drew in figure 19—where the two-dimensional cell processors were only looking at five cells each.*

looks at nine of the memory cells, the $3 \times 3$ neighborhood around the cell (figure 21).

If we speak of the cells as being alive or dead, we can describe the Game of Life rule in the following colorful fashion:

- If a dead cell has exactly three live neighbors, they spawn into the cell and it, too, becomes alive. Otherwise a dead cell stays dead.
- If a live cell has exactly two or three live neighbors other than itself, then it stays alive; otherwise it dies of loneliness or over-crowding.

Conway's vague initial goal had been to find a cellular automaton rule in which simple patterns could grow to a large size, but he doubted if any patterns could grow forever. Gardner proposed this as a challenge problem:

Conway conjectures that no pattern can grow without limit. Put another way, any configuration with a finite number of live cells cannot grow beyond a finite upper limit to the number of live cells on the field. This is probably the deepest and most difficult question posed by the game. Conway has offered a prize of $50 to the first person who can prove or disprove the conjecture before the end of the year. One way to disprove it would be to discover patterns that keep adding live cells to the field: a "gun" (a configuration that repeatedly shoots out moving objects such as the "glider"), or a "puffer train" (a configuration that moves about and leaves behind a trail of "smoke").[16]

The prize was won a month later by William Gosper and five fellow hackers at MIT; legend has it that they did an automated search. They sent Martin Gardner a telegram with the coordinates of the cells to turn on to make a glider gun, depicted in figure 22.

Steven Levy's *Hackers* has a good section about Gosper and the early excitement over Life among the users of the PDP-6 computer at the MIT

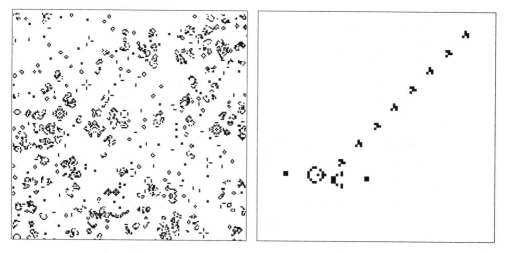

**Figure 22: A Life CA Soup and the Glider Gun**

*The left-hand image shows Life running on a randomly seeded pattern. This kind of start almost always ends with a few static blocks and small oscillators. The right-hand image shows Gosper's glider gun sending out a stream of gliders. The gliders continually move toward the upper right. What happens at the edges? In simpler CA simulations the edges are wrapped around like in an old videogame—if a glider moves off the top edge, then it comes back from the bottom edge, and so on. But more sophisticated setups may model additional off-screen cells as well..*

Artificial Intelligence Project. Levy quotes Gosper, telling how he saw Life as a way to

> basically do new science in a universe where all the smart guys haven't already nixed you out two or three hundred years ago. It's your life story if you're a mathematician: every time you discover something neat, you discover that Gauss or Newton knew it in his crib. With Life you're the first guy there, and there's always fun stuff going on. You can do everything from recursive function theory to animal husbandry. There's a community of people who are sharing their experiences with you. And there's the sense of connection between you and the environment. The idea of where's the boundary of a computer. Where does the computer leave off and the environment begin?[17]

One must remember that 1970 was still the Dark Ages of computing; Conway himself ran his Life simulations by marking the cells with checkers or flat Othello counters. For Gosper and his team to get Life to run on a monitor at all was a nontrivial feat of hacking—it was a new thing to do with a computer. After Gardner's second column on Life, the game became something of a mania among computer users. By 1974, an article about Life in *Time* could complain that "millions of dollars in valuable computer time may have already been wasted by the game's growing horde of fanatics."[18]

More and more intricate Life patterns were found all through the 1970s, and by 1980, Conway and his colleagues had enough Life machinery at hand to sketch a proof that Life can be used to simulate any digital computation whatsoever, that is, a CA running the Life rule is a universal computer.[19]

A number of people at MIT began studying CAs other than Life during the 1970s. One the most influential figures there was Edward Fredkin. Although he himself held no higher degrees, Fredkin was a professor associated with the MIT Laboratory for Computer Science, and he directed a number of dissertations on CAs.

Fredkin envisioned a new science where we represent all physical quantities as packets of information. The substrate on which these packets move was to be a CA. Not to put too fine a point on it, Fredkin argued that, at some deep level, the world we live in is a huge cellular automaton. Although Conway had already expressed opinions to the effect that in a cosmically large Life simulation one might see the evolution of persistent patterns that are as intelligent as us, Fredkin was the first to suggest that the world we live in really *is* a CA.[20] He was thus one of the first to espouse universal automatism—although Fredkin prefers to name his view *digital philosophy.*

Fredkin formed the Information Mechanics Group at MIT along with Tommaso Toffoli, Norman Margolus, and Gerard Vichniac. Working together, Margolus and Toffoli built the so-called CAM-6 cellular automaton machine in 1984, a board that you could plug into the early-model IBM personal computers so as to see CAs running at a rapid clip.

Also in the 1980s, Stephen Wolfram became interested in getting an exhaustive overview of what kinds of CA computations are possible. In order to limit the number of possible rules, he started with very simplest CAs, in which the cell space is a one-dimensional row of cells, the possible cell states are zero and one, and each cell "sees" only itself and its nearest neighbors on the left and on the right, making a three-cell neighborhood. A CA of this simple kind can be specified by describing how a cell's new value depends on which of the eight possible three-cell neighborhood configurations it lies in. This makes for $2^8$, or 256, possible rules, which are conventionally labeled by the integers from zero to 255.

Wolfram began by starting each of the basic 256 rules on a row full of randomly chosen zeros and ones and observing what classes of behavior occur. He found five general kinds of behavior. The distinctions extend to experiments where we start the rules on a simple row with but a single dark "one" cell. As suggested by the images in figure 23, Rule 254 "dies out" or becomes uniform, Rule 250 generates a checkered or periodic pattern, Rule 90 generates a recursively nested triangle pattern, the right-hand part of Rule 30's swath is random-looking, and Rule 110 has persistent local structures that move across the cell space and interact with one another.

Wolfram decided that a nested pattern was not really so different from a repeating pattern, and chose to group the CA behaviors into the four classes we mentioned earlier in this chapter.

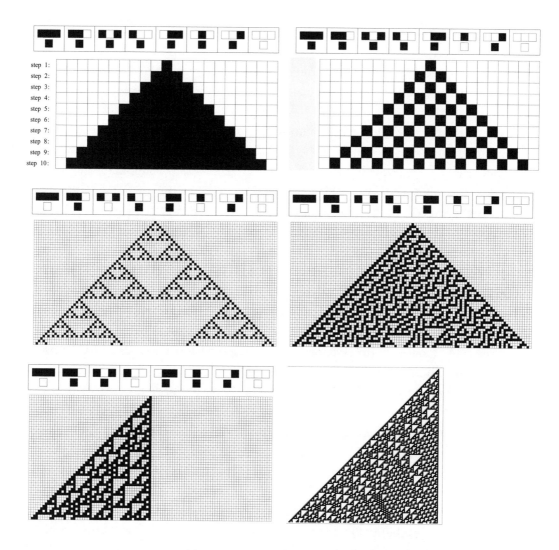

**Figure 23: Five Kinds of CA Behavior**

*Left to right and top to bottom, these are Rules 254, 250, 90, 30, and two views of Rule 110. Wolfram views these rules as being of, respectively, computational class one, two, two, three, and four. Each image (except the sixth) contains a row of symbols describing the CA rule and a triangular pattern showing how the CA evolves over time. The rows of symbols show which new value of a cell is selected by that rule for each of the eight possible cell neighborhoods. (If you were to interpret the eight new-cell values as the digits of a binary number, by the way, you get the code number used to describe the given rule.) The triangular patterns show the successive states of the one-dimensional CA tape, with time running down the page. Note that each CA starts out with a single black cell. In order to give a better idea of Rule 110, we've added a zoomed-out view of its appearance later on.*

- *Class one.* Dies out or becomes uniform.
- *Class two.* Becomes periodic or produces nested structures.
- *Class three.* Produces seething, seemingly random, patterns.
- *Class four.* Shows persistent local structures that move about.

The robustness of this classification is quite well supported by what one might call taxonomic studies of the kinds of computations that occur across a wide range of contexts. For instance, the same four classes of behavior appear if we look at more complicated CAs, such as those that allow more than two symbols, those that look at more than the very nearest neighbors, or those that use higher dimensional cell-spaces. And the same four classes can be found among the Turing machines.

Note that any universal computer can exhibit all four classes of computation. Depending on its input, it can produce *simple* (class one or class two) computations that die out or repeat, disorderly *random-looking* (class three) computations, or a purposeful-seeming *gnarly* (class four) computations.

I need to remark again that distinguishing between class three and class four computations can be difficult. Wolfram's definitions of these notions are not formalized; they're more like empirical notions that have been formed from extensive observation. Note also that a periodic class two computation can look like a class three or class four computation if it takes a long time to get around to repeating itself, and even a class one computation can seem like a class three or a class four computation if it takes it a long time to die out.

The classes of computations generated by Conway's Life CA depend on the initial condition. The simplest Life patterns simply die off to a blank screen, which is class one behavior. A typical random seeding of a Life CA dies down to static blocks and oscillating patterns, which are class two. If only a central region of the world is seeded, a random Life start will in fact spew out a few gliders that head off into empty territory. Even if the gliders could indefinitely travel through empty cell space, if they're not interacting, then nothing interesting is happening and we still have only class two.

But, as mentioned above, Conway and some of his colleagues were eventually able to prove that Life is computation universal. This means that for any possible computation *M*, we can find a cell pattern so that Life seeded with this pattern will emulate *M*. So, since Life is universal, we know that it can exhibit both class three and class four behavior. If Life emulates, say, the output of a some little algorithm usable as a random number generator, it will appear to be class three, while if it pulses out flocks of gliders grouped like the digits of pi, it will be class four.

What's the simplest possible universal CA rule? Stephen Wolfram and Matthew Cook were able to prove that the gnarly little CA Rule 110 is computation universal. The possible universality of the messy-looking Rule 30 remains, however, undecided. If Rule 30 proves to be nonuniversal, this would serve as a counterexample to the Principle of Computational Equivalence or PCE—for then Rule 30 would be an example of a complex computation that is not universal and is thus not as sophisticated as some other complex computations.

In 1984 Wolfram wrote a revolutionary article pointing out some fundamental similarities between physics and cellular automata.[21] He suggested that many physical processes that seem random are in fact the deterministic outcome of computations that are so convoluted that they cannot be compressed into shorter form and predicted in advance. He spoke of these computations as irreducible and cited CAs as good examples. His article included some intriguing color photographs of one-dimensional CAs.

Wolfram's article fascinated me so much that in April 1985 I set out to meet Wolfram, Margolus, Toffoli, and the other new cellular automatists, eventually writing an article on them that appeared in, of all places, *Isaac Asimov's Science Fiction Magazine.* The trip was something of a conversion experience for me, and in 1986 I left my career as a freelance writer for a job as a computer science professor at San Jose State University. CAs had permanently blown my mind.

One of the first things I started doing in my computer science classes was, of course, getting my students to write programs to display cellular automata. The computations were fairly intensive for the machines of that time, so we had to work hard to make the rules run fast, even to the point of programming them in low-level assembly language. One of my favorite early CA programs, when seeded a certain way, created images that looked like a continually mutating cyberpunk woman's face, as shown in figure 24. I called this "woman" Maxine Headroom after the then-popular TV show featuring a computer-animated character called Max Headroom.

**Figure 24: Maxine Headroom**

*This old image was created by a rule I call the Rug rule. Each cell holds an integer between zero and 255, and the update rule takes the average of a cell's neighbors, adds 1, and if the result is larger than 255, sets the value back to zero. This implementation is from the RC software component of CelLab, and actually uses obscure text characters for the graphics. To create Maxine's face, I start with a grid of a particular size—I think 43 × 80 in this case. (For full effect, I turn the monitor on its side so the shape is more like a face.) I freeze the (invisible) outer edges of the cell world at the maximum value and seed the interior with an egg-shaped pattern near the bottom. The upper part of the screen evolves into an elliptical forehead with a circular pair of eyes, the bottom of the screen produces an elliptical mouth, and the cells in between naturally shape themselves into the forms of brows, nose, and cheekbones.*

The Maxine Headroom picture wouldn't mean much if it were based on something like a smoothing algorithm run on a seed image of a face. But it arises in a natural way, by a process that a biologist might call morphogenesis. Might it be that the forms of real people are simply patterns that are natural for growing masses of cells to form? I'll return to this question in CHAPTER THREE: *Life's Lovely Gnarl.*

I managed to get hold of one of Margolus and Toffoli's CAM-6 cellular automaton accelerator boards and found out how to make the board run. To make it work, you had to plug it into a certain early-model PC called the IBM XT. I mastered the board's arcane control language—a "reverse Polish" dialect known as Forth—and began writing programs.

Thus began one of the most exciting periods of my life. I became a cellular automata missionary, a Johnny Automataseed. I tracked down Bill Gosper in his office at the Symbolics Corporation in Palo Alto, California, and made him look at new rules that went beyond his beloved Game of Life. As it happened, Gosper only had refrigerator-size computers, so I had to take the case off his secretary's IBM XT so I could plug in the CAM-6 board. He teased me for doing this, asking if I enjoyed "playing dentist," but the colorful demos of the new rules intrigued him.

Before I even heard about cellular automata, I'd begun writing my *Ware* series of novels about autonomous robots living on the moon. I'd always disliked how dull robots looked in science-fiction movies—like file cabinets or toasters. So I'd taken to decorating my fictional robots' bodies with a light-emitting substance I dubbed *flickercladding.* My original inspiration for flickercladding was the banks of flashing lights that used to decorate the sides of mainframe computers—signals reflecting the bits of the machines' changing internal states. As I imagined it, "The color pulses of the flickercladding served to emphasize or comment on the robots' digital transmissions; much as people's smiles and grimaces add analog meaning to what they say."[22]

My flickercladding wasn't meant to display blocks of solid hues, mind you; it was supposed to be fizzy and filled with patterns. And when I encountered CAs, I recognized what I'd been imagining all along. Reality had caught up with me.

This was also the period when, accompanied by my science-fiction hero Robert Sheckley, I went to Tim Leary's house in Hollywood and took—acid? No. Took apart his IBM XT and jacked in my trusty CAM-6 board so that good Dr. Tim could get a taste of CAs and their real-time mandala flows and creepy-crawly life-forms. Tim instantly got the picture: Computation could be about light shows, about mind expansion, about having fun. What a wonderful day that was.

What were Sheckley and I doing at Leary's house? Well, one of Sheckley's tummler friends was promoting a Hollywood pitch that Leary should host a weekly science TV show and that the Scheck-man and I should write his scripts. Too bad it didn't work out.

Soon after I demoed the CAs for Tim, I had the opportunity to bring my CAM-6-equipped PC to a 1987 conference called Hackers 3.0—keep in mind that back then "hacker" simply meant "fanatic programmer." As a relative novice to computing, I felt a little diffident joining this august geekly company, but they were most welcoming. With Silicon Valley just opening up, there seemed to be enough room for everyone.

It was a great conference for me. I did cellular automata demos all night long, and the hackers were blown away by the images. They pried the special-purpose CAM-6 board out of my machine, sniffed it over, and pronounced that it could readily be emulated by clever software.

As it happened, the demonically gifted John Walker of Autodesk fame was in the crowd, and he was just the man to carry out the sought-for hack. Within a year, I'd taken leave from my professor's job and started working for Autodesk, helping Walker create a fast all-software CA simulator known as *CelLab*.[23]

*CelLab* emulates the parallel CA architecture within the serial architecture of a personal computer—a reminder of the fact that any of our universal computational systems can simulate the behavior of any other. Using a different architecture doesn't affect what's *in principle* computable. But a system's architecture does have a lot do with what kinds of computations are *feasible* for that system.

In the 1990s, I became interested in continuous-valued CAs, in which the cells can contain one or several real numbers instead of simply holding simple integer values. Working with my students at San Jose State University, I designed a Windows program called CAPOW, which is very useful for investigating these kinds of CAs, and I continue working with CAPOW to this day.[24]

I might mention here that not all computer scientists like the idea of continuous-valued CAs. Digital computer programs commonly allow for some four billion different values for a continuous-valued real number. This means that whereas the Game of Life CA has two possible states per cell, a continuous-valued CA might have four billion possible states per cell. And if I use two real numbers per cell—as I often do—I'm looking at sixteen quadrillion possible cell states. Stephen Wolfram sometimes chides me for using complicated rules—he argues that it's more scientifically significant to discover an interesting behavior in the context of a system that's been pared down to be minimally complex.

But the physical world is anything but clean and simple. And even so, nature repeats the same structures over and over. The same simple patterns arise even when the computations become very intricate. You might say that Platonic forms are robust against scuzz. And these qualities of robustness and universality are worth modeling.

**Figure 25: Cellular Automata Scrolls**

*I ran these rules at a resolution of 320 × 200 cells, letting the left edge wrap around to the right and the top wrap around to the bottom. The first three have states consisting of a single integer per cell, while the latter three have two real numbers per cell. All were started with a random initial pattern. Reading across the page and from top to bottom, the six images are: Gerhardt and Schuster's Hodgepodge rule, my RainZha rule, Toffoli and Margolus's Tubeworms rule, one of Hans Meinhardt's Activator Inhibitor rules, a Double Logistic predator-prey rule, and Arthur Winfree's Belousov-Zhabotinsky rule.[25]*

Yes, it's important to find complex patterns in simply defined systems. But to my way of thinking it's significant that we can find exactly the same kinds of patterns—and no others—in the much more complicated systems.

By now I've looked at many thousands of two-dimensional CAs. As it turns out, scrolls are perhaps the most interesting new kinds of CA patterns that emerge when moving from one-dimensional to two-dimensional CAs—my favorite CAs are those that spontaneously generate scroll patterns from both orderly and disorderly start patterns. Scroll patterns occur in both simple and complicated rules and—in keeping with the point I was just making—the scroll-shaped forms in complicated CA systems can be just as clean and sharp as those defined by simpler rules.

A sampler of two-dimensional scroll CAs appears in figure 25.

Nature likes scrolls as well. Consider that, for instance, the cross section of a mushroom cap, cut from top to bottom, bends around like a scroll—while the entire cap forms a kind of three-dimensional scroll. Both a bean and a fetus resemble fleshy scrolls. Brain tissue is replete with three-dimensional scrolls. Candle or cigarette smoke inks the air with scrolls—and the pairs of eddies that form behind a moving spoon in a coffee cup are scrolls as well. Figure 26 shows a computer simulation of three-dimensional scrolls.

**Figure 26: A Three-Dimensional CA
with Scrolls**

*Here's a Hodgepodge-style CA running on a three-dimensional array of cells. The entire solid block is filled with interacting shapes like scrolls, mushroom caps, jellyfish, and whirlpools. The block wraps around, that is, patterns moving across one face continue into the opposite side of the cube.*

What is the computational class of CA scrolls? Something that's a bit hard to capture in a printed picture is how dynamic they are. The scrolls are continually turning, with the pointed ends melting away as they approach the enfolding lines. The rules are certainly not class one. The strongly ordered patterns also preclude our calling them class three—these robust patterns are anything but random in appearance.

So we're left with deciding between class two and class four. If we run a scroll rule on a very small grid, we may find the rule filling the grid with a single monster scroll that executes a repetitive class two cycle. But if we give the rule room to grow several scrolls, then we seem to see class four behavior. A test case for this appears in figure 27, which shows eight stages of the so-called Hodgepodge rule, reading left to right and top to bottom. Notice that each image is subtly different and that, in particular, the diamond-shaped region in the center is not repeating itself.

If I let the simulation run, say, another thousand steps, I find that the whole general shape of the central pattern will have changed. So I'm prepared to claim that some of the scroll-generating CA rules are class four.

Within the framework of *The Lifebox, the Seashell, and the Soul,* this seemingly arcane observation turns out to be important. How so? Quite specifically, I'll be arguing that many of the computations involved in living organisms are of the same type that produce these unpredictable CA scrolls. There's even a possibility that our brains are in fact animated by electrochemical processes that behave like three-dimensional CA scrolls. Metaphorically speaking, that churning little central region of the Hodge patterns in figure 27 is like a brain working away inside a scrolly skull.

More generally, the free and unpredictable play of CA scrolls is a perfect example of how deterministic processes can produce gnarly shapes and interesting behaviors.

In this chapter we've talked about very explicitly computational processes: humans reckoning with numbers, Turing machines, personal computers, the Web, and cellular automata. And in the rest of the book we'll be viewing some less obviously deterministic processes as computations: physics, biology, the mind, and human society.

**Figure 27:**
**Class Four Scrolls**

*For these pictures, I seeded the Hodgepodge rule with a small square in one corner, whose effects immediately wrapped around to the other corners. I let the rule run for about a week, passing through some fifty million updates. And then I paused and single-stepped the rule, capturing eight images, with each image five updates later than the one before.*

Teaching her third yoga class of the day, Amy Hendrix felt light-headed and rubbery. She walked around, correcting people's poses, encouraging them to hold their positions longer than they usually did. Her mind kept wandering to the room she was hoping to rent. New to San Francisco, she'd been sleeping on couches for six weeks. But she still dreamed of becoming a force to be reckoned with in the city scene.

It was time for Savasana, the Corpse Pose, with everyone lying on their backs. Amy turned off her Tabla Beat CD and guided the closing meditation.

"Feel a slow wave of softness moving up your legs," she began. "Feet, calves, knees, thighs." Long pause. "Now focus on your perineum. Chakra one. Release any tension hiding there. Melt with the in-breath, bloom with the out. Almost like you're going to wet your pants." Amy occasionally added an earthy touch—which her mostly white clients readily accepted from their coffee-colored teacher.

"Gather the energy into a ball of light between your legs," continued Amy, pausing between each sentence,

trying not to talk too much. "Slowly, slowly it passes upward, tracking your spine like a trolley. Now the light is in your sex chakra. Let it tingle, savor it, let it move on. The warmth flows through your belly and into your solar plexus. Your breath is waves on a beach."

She was sitting cross-legged at one end of the darkly lit room. The meditation was getting good to her. "Energy in, darkness out. The light comes into your chest. You're in the grass, looking at the leaves in a high summer tree. The sun shines through. Your heart is basking. You love the world. You love the practice. You love yourself. The light moves through your neck like toothpaste out a tube. Chakra five. The light is balancing your hormones, it's washing away your angry unsaid words." Pause. "And now your tape loops are gone."

She gave a tiny tap to her Tibetan cymbal. *Bonnng.* "Your head is an empty dome of light. Feel the space. You're here. No plans. You're now." She got to her feet. "Light seeps through your scalp and trickles down your face. Your cheeks are soft. Your mouth. Your shoulders melt. Your arms. I'll call you back."

She moved around the room pressing down on people's shoulders. She had a brief, odd feeling of being in multiple bodies, leaning over each separate customer at the same time. And then her wristwatch drew her back. She had twenty minutes to get from here to Telegraph Hill to try to rent that perfect room.

She rang the gong and saw the customers out. The last one was Sueli, a lonely wrinkled lady who liked to talk. Sueli was the only one in the class as dark-skinned as Amy. Amy enjoyed her; she seemed like a fairy godmother.

"How many chakras do you say there are?" asked Sueli. Clearly she had some theory of her own in mind. She was very well-spoken.

"Seven," said Amy, putting on her sweats. "Why not?" She imagined she might look like Sueli when she was old.

"The Hindus say seven, and the Buddhists say nine," said Sueli, leaning close. "But I know the real answer. I learned it years ago in Sri Lanka. This is the last of your classes I'll be able to come to, so I'm going to share the secret with you."

"Yes?" This sounded interesting. Amy turned out the lights, locked the door, and stepped outside with Sueli. The autumn sky was a luminous California blue. The bay breeze vibrated the sun-bleached cardboard election signs on the lampposts—San Francisco was in the throes of a wide-open mayoral election.

"Some of us have millions of chakras," continued Sueli in her quiet tone. "One for each branch of time. Opening the chakras opens the doors to your other selves."

"You can do that?" asked Amy.

"You have the power, too," said Sueli. "I saw it in class. For an instant there were seven of you. Yes, indeed."

"And you—you have selves in different worlds?"

"I come and go. There's not so many of me left. I'm here because I was drawn to you. I have a gift." Sueli removed a leather thong from around her neck. Dangling from the strand was a brilliant crystal. The late afternoon sunlight bounced off it, fracturing into jagged rays. The sparkling flashes were like sand in Amy's eyes.

"Only let the sun hit it when you want to split," said Sueli, quickly putting the rawhide strand over Amy's head and tucking the crystal under her sweatshirt. "Good luck."

Sueli gave her a hug and a peck on the cheek as the bus pulled up.

Amy hopped aboard. When she looked back to wave at her, the old woman was gone.

The room was three blocks off Columbus Avenue with a private entrance and a view of both bridges. It was everything Amy had hoped. But the rent was ten times higher than she'd understood. In her eagerness, she'd read one less zero than was on the number in the paper. She felt like such a dope. Covering her embarrassment, she asked the owner if she could have a moment alone.

"Make yourself at home," said the heavyset Italian lady. "Drink it in." She was under the mistaken impression that Amy was wealthy. "I like your looks, miss. If you're ready to sign, I got the papers downstairs in the kitchen. I know the market's slow, but I'm not dropping the price. First, last, and one month's damage deposit. You said on the phone the rent's no problem?"

"That's what I said," murmured Amy.

Alone in the airy room, she wandered over to the long window, fiddling with the amulet around her neck. The low, hot sun reached out to the crystal. Shattered rays flew about the room, settling here and here and here.

Nine brown-skinned women smiled at each other. Amy was all of them at the same time. Her overlapping minds saw through each pair of eyes.

"We'll get separate jobs and share the rent," said one of her mouths. "And when we come back to the room we'll merge together," said another. "We'll work in parallel worlds, but we'll deposit our checks and pay the rent in just this one."

"Great," said Amy, not quite sure this was real. As she tucked away the crystal, her nine bodies folded into one.

Walking down the stairs to sign the papers, her mind was racing. Just now she'd split into nine—but Sueli had said that, with the crystal, she could split into a million.

Out the window she glimpsed another election poster—and the big thought hit her.

With a million votes, she could be the next mayor of San Francisco.

# CHAPTER TWO

# *Our Rich World*

THERE ARE TWO SALIENT DIFFERENCES between personal computer programs and the general functioning of the physical world. One: physics happens in parallel, that is, physics is being computed everywhere at once rather than within the circuitry of a single processor chip. And two: physics seems to be analog rather than digital, that is, rather than being measured in discrete bits, physical quantities are real numbers with who-knows-how-many decimal places trailing off. In this chapter we discuss how to come to terms with and even take advantage of these realities.

This chapter's six sections are as follows:

- *2.1: Rough and Smooth.* The idealized equations of mathematical physics are continuous, but the real world and our simulations are discrete, using particle system or cellular automaton computations of finite precision.
- *2.2: Everywhere at Once.* We examine the parallel architecture of the computations embodied in classical physics and learn how they can be modeled by cellular automata.
- *2.3: Chaos in a Bouncing Ball.* By discussing the motion of a bouncing ball we see that a seemingly random physical process can, in fact, be a deterministic computation.
- *2.4: The Meaning of Gnarl.* The most beautiful naturally occurring forms and motions correspond to class four computations.

- *2.5: What Is Reality?* How do we keep quantum mechanics from spoiling everything for universal automatism? Must we accept a lack of determinism at the very smallest scales?
- *2.6: How Robots Get High.* A computational view of quantum mechanics leads to the new field of quantum computation—and suggests some odd views of the mind.

## 2.1: *Rough and Smooth*

On the one hand, some aspects of the world are discrete or rough—like a pile of rocks. These rough magnitudes are best measured by counting. On the other hand, things like a person's height seem smooth or continuous and are measured in terms of size intervals. Rough things change in abrupt jumps, while smooth things ooze.

Mathematicians codify the distinction by speaking of the integers and the real numbers. Integers are fairly easy to understand: 0, 1, 2, 3, and so on. But the so-called real numbers are rather fictional: a real number between zero and one is to have a form like 0.12378909872340980... with a supposedly endless series of digits stretching out to the right of the decimal place. Ever since the nineteenth century, this infinite extravagance has been believed to be the best way to model the intuitive notion of a continuous interval as being endlessly smooth. But it may be that the real numbers of mathematics aren't a true reflection of the actual world.

Computer scientists model real numbers by finite patterns of bits, with the number of bits being something that can be adjusted for the particular application. The commonly used data types known as *float, double,* and *long double* correspond, for instance, to decimal numbers with, respectively, seven, fifteen, and thirty digits. The real numbers of computer science are "granular" in the sense that they are incremented in small steps of a minimum size.[26]

In physics we have a kind of granularity as well. Although nobody's sure what happens at the very smallest scales, quantum mechanics seems to tell us that it doesn't make sense to speak of ordinary space at scales less then what's known as the Planck length. This length is $1.6 \times 10^{-35}$ meters, expressible as a decimal number whose first nonzero digit appears in the thirty-fifth place.

Planck length ~ 0.0000000000000000000000000000000000016 meters.

If it doesn't make sense to speak of measuring any physical length to a greater precision than the Planck length, this means that physical coordinate locations can really have at most thirty-five digits of precision to the right of the decimal. This falls a long way short of the infinite precision enjoyed by the mathematical real numbers!

Now, it's conceivable that there might be an infinitely smooth fundamental reality underlying quantum mechanics. But it's equally conceivable that ultimate reality is fully discrete and digital—indeed, this view is becoming fairly popular among physicists, who dream of turning spacetime into something like a snap-together network of nodes and links made up of quantum loops or superstrings.

Closely related to the discrete-continuous distinction is the digital-analog divide. Adding numbers with pencil and paper seems like a digital computation, while adding numbers by measuring out lengths seems like an analog computation. Counting grains of sand seems digital, and spinning a wheel of fortune seems analog—although note that we digitize the rims of our gambling wheels into distinct bands.

The general sense is that our desktop computers carry out digital computations, while real-world physics is running analog computations. A digital computer's states resemble distinct integers, while an analog computer's states are like densely bunched decimal numbers.

A virtue of digital computations is that they're relatively impervious to outside influences. To change a digital value you actually have to make a substantial change on the order of flipping a bit. Personal computer (PC) hardware designers can build in routines to detect and correct the accidental bit-flips that occur when, for instance, a cosmic ray happens to zap a chip. An analog quantity, on the other hand, can drift away from its setting by just a tiny amount. And, as we'll be discussing in section *2.3: Chaos in a Bouncing Ball,* in chaotic analog systems very small physical differences can rapidly amplify into visible effects. This said, many analog computations are robust and insensitive to noise. This is achieved by having the system incorporate some kind of averaging process.

A side effect of a computation's being digital is that it's easy to regard it as evolving in discrete time steps, with each step changing a state value. We think of digital systems as updating themselves in ticks like a clock, and it's meaningful to ask about a computation's "next state." In an analog system, on the other hand, it's less clear-cut when a state value has changed. Suppose, for instance, that the state involves a real number expressed by, say, thirty digits. Over a period of time, the number may go from one value to another, but if the change happens in a series of small and rapid steps, we may be unable to perceive the individual steps. An analog computation may seem to slide through a series of all-but-indistinguishable states. In formulating the laws of analog computations, rather than talking about a "next state" it's more common to simply observe the system at some successive intervals of time.

The distinction between digital and analog computations isn't sharp. Consider the following attempt at a definition.

> •*Definition.* A computational system is said to be *digital* if its states range over a small set of discrete possibilities, and is said to be *analog* if it has a very large number of possible states.

The point of the definition is that whether you call a given computation digital or analog depends upon your operative notions of "small" and "large" numbers of states. In practice we can speak of *any* naturally occuring computation as being more or less coarsely digital, with the very fine digital computations shading into the ones we call analog.

We think of our digital PCs, for instance, as containing patterns of zero-or-one bits, sharp and crisp as black-and-white mosaics. Analog physical systems, on the other hand, seem to have states that are like shades of gray. The shakiness of the distinction rests on the fact that, seen at a distance, a digital pattern of black-and-white tiles will appear to be an analog shade of gray. Conversely, a seemingly smooth analog gray scale is likely to be a ladder of distinct steps.

The digital-analog distinction is further blurred by the fact that a computation may be based on lower levels that may lie elsewhere on the digital-analog spectrum. Adding numbers in your head is, for instance, digital, but the electrical and chemical potentials in the neural synapses range across so many state possibilities as to be essentially analog.

In practice, we use analog to mean *fairly* precise but not *infinitely* precise.

We imagine a very large range of analog values, but not an *endless* range. Our analog computations employ, if you will, a deflated infinite precision.

When we use analog in this limited sense, the distinction between digital and analog becomes less important, for analog computations can emulate the digital, and digital computations can emulate the analog. Let's say a bit about the two directions of emulation.

*Analog emulates digital.* A digital PC is based on the physical analog computations of its wires and chips—putting it differently, the analog electronic system is emulating a digital PC. How can it be possible for a machine made of analog components to have digital behavior? The answer is that a computer chip uses a whole pack of electrons to store a bit of information. Yes, the chips are small, with etched "wires" on the order of a millionth of a meter across. But electrons are in some sense a billion times smaller than that. The slightest current involves a torrent of electrons; a bit is stored by a charge of perhaps a half million electrons.

At a more primitive level, the Babbage and Scheutz machines were digital computers based on the analog motions of quite ordinary objects: gears and rods and cams. Along these lines, in the 1970s, just for fun, Danny Hillis, Brian Silverman, and some other MIT computer science students built a tic-tac-toe-playing computer out of Tinkertoys.

**Figure 28: Ed Hardebeck and Brian Silverman Building a Tinkertoy Computer**
*Note the "programming mallet" on the floor behind Brian.*

*Digital emulates analog.* If we use enough real-number variables of sufficiently high precision, we can always emulate any analog system of limited size. Yes, science-fictionally, speaking, we might imagine some infinitely precise analog computation that can't be emulated digitally. But so far as we know, the existence of the Planck length cutoff suggests that this isn't ever going to happen. And, as I mentioned before, it may even be that at the deepest level the world is digital.

A standard computer simulation of a continuous-valued CA approximates the cells' allegedly real-number values by discrete rounded-off numbers. Some computer scientists are leery of continuous-valued CAs because they fear that this rounding-off process creates unpredictable errors that will accumulate and become amplified into large-scale irregularities of behavior. But in actual practice, all of the continuous-valued CA simulations discussed in this book have an *averaging* step—which blocks the amplification of error. That is, in the continuous-valued CAs that I discuss, a cell's new value is based on a formula involving the *average* of the neighboring cells' values. And this averaging process damps down any troublesome round-off errors.

Even so, some doubting Thomases question whether the use of, say, the four billion possible real values allowed by thirty-two-bit real numbers produces behavior that's really the same as what you'd see with an infinite range of truly continuous real numbers. I've carried out some experiments in which I have a granularity control to select how many discrete values are used to approximate real numbers. And what I've found is that once we drop below a not very high granularity level, the behaviors of the simulation don't change, at least not over the admittedly limited times that I've watched my simulations.[27]

We can view physics in three ways, and each way allows both for a digital and an analog interpretation.

- In the *mathematical physics* view, physics is like a axiomatic system in which we derive results from equations. Although all the current equations for physics are based on continuous-valued real numbers, it may be that a future, more digital, physics can formulate the world's laws in terms of discrete numbers.

- In the *particle system* view, the world's "processors" are distinct objects—either human-scale objects like tables, chairs, and balls, or primitive objects like atoms. Whether we view these processors as carrying out digital or analog computations depends on the situation. At the high level, these distance measurements appear analog, but at a very low level they may appear digital.

- In the *continuous-valued cellular automaton* view, we see the world as a doughy continuum that we can divide up into virtual cells, with each cell being viewed as a processor. Here again we can view the cell rules as being digital or analog computations, depending on how many states we suppose the cells to be able to have.

Let's say a bit more about these three approaches.

Traditional *mathematical physics* is about smooth matter and force fields varying according to nice algebraic laws. And mathematical tools such as calculus are formulated in terms of continuous real numbers. One virtue of analog computations is that they're easy for us to think about. For analog computations are an approximation to by now familiar mathematical processes involving infinitely continuous real numbers.

Mathematical physics can in some situations provide very good predictions about what physical systems will do. This approach worked well for Isaac Newton: He was able to compute the motions of the solar system right down to the moons of Jupiter by using his laws of motion, his universal law of gravitation, and a few observations.

But, as it happens, mathematical physics runs up rather quickly against the limitations of the axiomatic approach. Some sets of equations have solutions that don't happen to have any simple descriptions. And other, more obdurate sets of equations resist any mathematical solution at all. In practice it's not possible to find idealized mathematical solutions to most real-world physical systems. Some of Newton's predictions were in fact wrong. A fully accurate general mathematical solution of a system with even *three* bodies is in fact impossible.

Physicists at today's frontiers are interested in seeing whether mathematical physics might become fully digital.

The *particle system* method is a quite demanding computational approach to physics—demanding, that is, if you want to simulate it. Here we regard the mathematical laws of physics as expressing averages across a large number of discrete particles. If we say that a Scuba tank's pressure is proportional to its temperature, for instance, we're talking about the averaged-out qualities of immense numbers of individual particles. The pressure has to do with the summed force of the air molecules hammering on the tank's walls, and the tank's temperature is derived from the average speed of its molecules. (More precisely, both quantities are proportional to the *square* of the average speed of the gas molecules.) If we had enough computational power, we could simply see these laws as emerging from the statistical behavior of a humongous particle system.

The nice thing about mathematical physics, of course, is that the laws and equations that emerge from the particles systems are often fairly simple. And the field of statistical mechanics shows how and why the laws emerge. We gain clarity by viewing physics as an analog continuum instead of a frantic dogpile of atoms.

Although the positions and velocities of the particles would seem to be continuous, there is the possibility that space and time are quantized, so that particle system models would be fully digital as well, although the "particles" of such a fully digital theory might be something as primitive as loops in superstrings.

*Continuous-valued cellular automata* are examples of what engineers call *finite element methods.*

The idea is to divide space up into a grid and to track something like the mass or temperature or average velocity for each cell of the grid. When we use, for instance, a continuous-valued CA to model the flow of heat, each cell holds a temperature value; in the case of water waves, the cells track height above sea level.

By making the grid coarser or finer, you can trade off between the accuracy and the speed of the simulation—if the grid were as fine as the size of individual electrons, a continuous-valued cellular automaton method would be similar to a particle system simulation. But in practice, the cells are much larger than that and, in effect, each cell is holding values based upon an average of many particles.

Continuous-valued CA methods introduce two kinds of digitization: first of all they break space and time into discrete steps, and second, they use computer-style digital approximations to the continuous quantities being simulated.

In an ultimate universal automatist dream, we might hope to find some very simple underlying CA that doesn't even have to use continuous values—Fredkin, for instance, seemed at one time to think the world could be modeled as a two-state CA. But there are serious problems with this approach, and in fact any simple digital computation of reality would probably have to be a somewhat different architecture than that of a cellular automaton. I'll say a bit more about this in section *2.5: What Is Reality?*

## 2.2: *Everywhere at Once*

One can regard our world as a huge parallel computation that's been running for billions of years.

To get a good image of physical parallelism, imagine sitting at the edge of a swimming pool, stirring the water with your feet. How quickly the pool's surface is updated! If you toss a twig into the pool, the ripples spread out in a perfectly uniform circle. How do the ripples know where to go? The patterns emerge from reality's parallel computation.

I have the following architecture in mind, which I'll call the *classical physics architecture.*

- *Many processors.* The world's computation is ubiquitous, with no superprocessor in charge.
- *One shared memory.* Reality is one.
- *Locality.* Each processor has access to only its local neighborhood.
- *Homogeneity.* Each processor obeys the same rule.
- *Synchronization.* The processors run at the same speed as one another.

| Architectural requirement | Particles | CAs |
|---|---|---|
| **Many processors** | Each particle acts as a processor | Each small region of space acts as a processor |
| **One shared memory** | The collective states of all the particles is the memory | Space with its various observables is the memory |
| **Locality** | Particles only interact when they touch | Each region of space interacts only with the nearest neighboring regions |
| **Homogeneity** | All particles obey the same laws of physics | Each region of space obeys the same laws of physics |
| **Synchronization** | Time runs at the same rate for each particle | Time runs at the same rate at each location |

**Table 2: Two Ways to View Classical Physics as a Parallel Computation**

How does nature fill this bill? I mentioned in section *2.1: Rough and Smooth* that we can usefully view the world's computations as being either particle systems or as continuous-valued CAs. The five conditions can hold in either place (table 2).

Having *many processors acting on one memory* corresponds to the basic intuition that, on the one hand, physics is happening everywhere, and, on the other hand, there is a single shared reality that contains all physical processes. If you're thinking of the world as made of particles, this reality is sometimes called *state space* and contains such information as the mass, location, velocity, and acceleration of each particle. If you prefer to think of the world as made of continuous fields, the shared reality of state space specifies quantities like density and rate of flow measured at each region of space. In either case, the numbers that specify state space are most readily thought of as analog numbers.

The issue of *locality* is less obvious. In principle we can imagine parallel processors that have global access to all of the memory. A simple example of parallelism with global memory access would be a PC with two or more

**Figure 29:**
**Local and Global Memory Access**
**for Parallelism**

*The circles stand for processors, the rectangles stand for the memory, and the lines indicate access. In the case of global access, we can simplify the figure by lumping all of the memory slots together into a single memory box and drawing a fat gray line to indicate access throughout the memory region in question.*

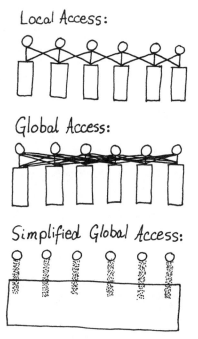

Local Access:

Global Access:

Simplified Global Access:

central processing units—in the old days this required having several microprocessor chips, but now a single chip is likely to have multiple processing cores. In any case, each of the processors can access all of the PC's memory. In figure 29 we illustrate parallelism with local vs. global access.

Classical (that is, nonquantum) physics is treated as a parallel computation with *local* processor access to memory. That is, the processes at one location are affected only by the data in the immediately neighboring regions of space and time. What happens at one spot doesn't affect things somewhere else without an intervening process—such as a photon or a gravity wave. Information must be passed along in a kind of bucket brigade from one region to the next. The classical principle of locality is summarized in the slogan, "No action at a distance."

In quantum mechanics, it at first appears that locality may be violated. When two quantum systems interact and become "entangled," they can later affect each other at arbitrarily great distances, seemingly with no intervening time. In section *2.4: What Is Reality?*, I'll suggest a way in which even here some form of locality can be preserved.

The *homogeneity* condition lies at the very heart of how we imagine physics to work. There are to be certain universal laws that apply at every spacetime location. In practice, physical laws often have cases that apply only when certain extreme conditions are encountered, but the whole thrust of science is to try to squeeze all of the conditions into one law. Extremely dense systems are the current paradigmatic example of areas where the homogeneous laws of physics run into trouble—the issue is one of reconciling quantum mechanics with the laws of gravity.

The *synchronization* condition stipulates that the processors carry out their computations at exactly the same rate, essentially updating in unison. Although this sounds like a reasonable assumption about the world's computational nature, there are serious problems with it.

First of all, Einstein's special theory of relativity tells us that if particles are moving relative to one another, then their internal clocks will in fact run at different rates. This in turn implies that any notion of "now" that we extend across a large region of space must be somewhat arbitrary. One way out might be for us to pick one privileged reference object—why not Earth—and to then adjust the rules of physics to include time dilation factors for particles moving relative to the reference object. If using Earth as the standard of rest seems too medieval, we might instead adopt a universal standard of rest based upon the cosmic background radiation—you're at rest if this radiation doesn't appear to be shifted toward the blue or the red end of the spectrum by your motion.

Fine, but once we introduce *general* relativity with its warping of space-time, we have to deal with cusps and singular points, as at the hearts of black holes. And establishing a universal standard of rest becomes exceedingly problematic. Moreover, when we extend our considerations to the cosmological shape of the whole universe, there's a possibility that time might somehow loop back on itself. In short, if our universe is sufficiently pocked, warped, or knotted, it becomes impossible to slice it into spacelike sheets of simultaneity, and global synchronization is out of the question.

This said, the objections to synchronization need not come into play if I'm only interested in modeling some local aspect of the world, which is all I'm going to be talking about most of the time.[28]

Particle systems and CAs are both good paradigms for multiprocessor computations acting on a common memory space and satisfying parallelism, homogeneity, and synchronization. For purposes of discussion, let's consider three simple systems that we might view either as particle systems or as CAs.

- *Heat.* You dip a spoon into a hot cup of tea, and feel the warmth move up the length of the handle. In terms of particles, we might say that the molecules of the tea are moving rapidly. They collide with the molecules of the spoon and set them to vibrating more energetically. The agitated motion is passed up the length of the spoon molecule by molecule. To think of this as a CA, regard the spoon's handle as a one-dimensional row of cells. Each cell averages its temperature value with the temperatures of the neighboring cells. Repeating the averaging process over and over moves higher temperature values up the length of the spoon.

- *Water waves.* You toss a twig into a swimming pool and observe the ripples. In the particle view, pushing down the particles in one location on the surface tugs at the neighboring particles on the surface—this is the phenomenon known as surface tension. The neighboring particles in turn pull on the particles farther away, with the whole system acting something like a lot of little balls connected by springs. To view the water surface as a CA, think of the two-dimensional surface as a grid of little cells, and use the cells to model the behavior of an elastic sheet. Each cell's height above the bottom of the pool is described by the so-called wave equation, in which the rate change of a cell's height is proportional to the difference between the average height of the neighboring cells and the cell's previous height.

- *Smoke tendrils.* Someone smokes a cigarette and you watch the smoke in the air. In a particle system model, we'd say that the smoke and air molecules bounce against one another. The fine lines in the smoke pattern are visible flow lines made up of particles having the same average velocity. To see this as a CA process, think of space as made of little volume elements: three-dimensional cells. The laws of hydrodynamics relate the pressure, density, and flow direction in each cell to the corresponding quantities in the neighboring cells.

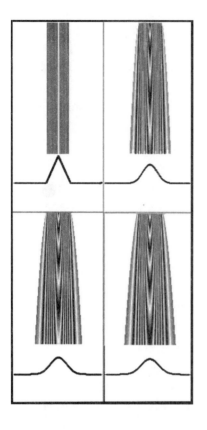

**Figure 30:**
**One-Dimensional Heat CAs with**
**Varying Rates of Diffusion**

*The figure shows four one-dimensional CA models of a wire that was heated in the middle, each wire being initially heated in the same way. The wood-grain-like pattern in the top part of each picture shows a vertical space-time sequence of successive states of the wire, with the heat values represented by shades of gray and with time running down the page. The bumpy line at the bottom part of each picture is a different representation of the heat distribution, this representation corresponding to the final instant of time. The diffusion rates a for these CAs are, left to right and top to bottom, zero, one-third, two-thirds, and one. Note that in the CA with diffusion rate zero, the heat pattern doesn't change at all, and in the CAs with lower diffusion rates, the pattern changes less than it does in the CA with diffusion rate one.*

I'd like to get into some detail about how we set up CAs to model heat flow and wave motion. In describing CA rules, I like to write *C* to stand for a cell's current value, using New*C* and Old*C* to stand for the cell's next and previous values, respectively. In the case where the CA value is a single real number, NeighborhoodAverage will stand for the average of the values in the cell's neighborhood.

To simulate the flow of heat, we might use a rule of this form.

(Averaging rule)     New*C* = NeighborhoodAverage.

This might be, however, a bit crude, and lead to the heat spreading unrealistically fast. More typical is to pick a diffusion rate, *a*, between zero and one, and to use a rule of this form.

(Diffusion rule)     New$C = a \cdot$ NeighborhoodAverage $+ (1-a) \cdot C$.

If $a$ is 1, the Diffusion rule is the same as the Averaging rule, but as $a$ gets smaller, the diffusion happens slower and slower. Figure 30 illustrates this.

We can also represent water waves by a CA rule. The rule works by having each cell take its current value $C$, add to this the average of its neighbors' values, and then subtract off the cell's previous value. In symbols,

(Wave rule)     New$C = C$ + Neighborhood Average – Old$C$.

It isn't particularly obvious that this simple rule will in fact re-create wave motion, but it works very nicely. Figure 31 shows two representations of this CA after being seeded with some randomly placed bumps—analogous to a handful of gravel thrown into a pond.

In section *1.8: Flickercladding,* I mentioned that Stanislaw Ulam collaborated with John von Neumann on discrete-valued CAs, and that in the 1950s, he switched his attention to continuous-valued CAs. One of the wins in looking at these simple toy models of physics is that it becomes possible to visualize alternative physical laws whose consequences might be too hard to understand simply by looking at the equations. And this is just what Ulam did; he began running CA models of nonstandard kinds of physics to see what would happen.

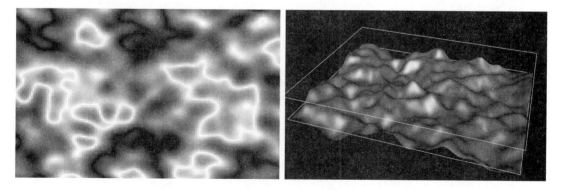

**Figure 31: Two-Dimensional Wave CA, Two Views**

*The two views show the same CA. On the left, we represent each cell's value by a shade of gray, creating a pattern that looks like light on water. On the right, we represent each cell's value as a height, creating a three-dimensional picture.*[29]

Ulam was encouraged by the atomic physicist Enrico Fermi, inventor of the neutrino. Fermi was curious about what might happen if one looked at so-called nonlinear waves. What is the meaning of "nonlinear" in this context? Ordinary waves—like the ones we just discussed simulating—are often based on a kind of spring force. If you stretch a string, or a water surface, it wants to pull back to its original size. In ordinary physics, this restoring force of a spring is proportional to the displacement—one has a Hooke's Law–type equation of the form $F = k \cdot \text{displacement}$. This is called a linear equation because there aren't any exponents in it. Fermi wondered what a wave might look like if it was acting on a substance in which the restoring force satisfied an equation with an exponent, such as $F = k \cdot \text{displacement}^2$, or even $F = k \cdot \text{displacement}^3$. As Ulam put it:

> Fermi expressed often a belief that future fundamental theories in physics may involve nonlinear operators and equations, and that it would be useful to attempt practice in the mathematics needed for the understanding of nonlinear systems. The plan was then to start with the possibly simplest such physical model and to study the results of the calculation of its long-time behavior.[30]

Working with the Fermi and the early computer scientist John Pasta, Ulam carried out the experiments and wrote them up. Figure 32 shows what the Fermi-Pasta-Ulam quadratic and cubic waves look like.

It's interesting that a mathematician of Ulam's caliber was thrown back on carrying out a cellular automaton simulation. If he wanted to know the effects of a nonlinear wave equation, why couldn't he just work out the math? After all, rather than viewing the world as a particle system or as a CA, we can also regard the world as a set of equations. So why didn't Ulam simply *deduce* what a nonlinear wave would do?

Well, nonlinear waves are an example of a situation that resists analysis by an axiomatic approach. If you want to figure out what a nonlinear system is going to do, you actually need to run some kind of simulation of it.

Or, of course, you can just look at the world itself. Ultimately, we don't really *need* to model the world. It does a fine job of computing itself. Indeed, for a universal automatist, *physics is made of computations.*

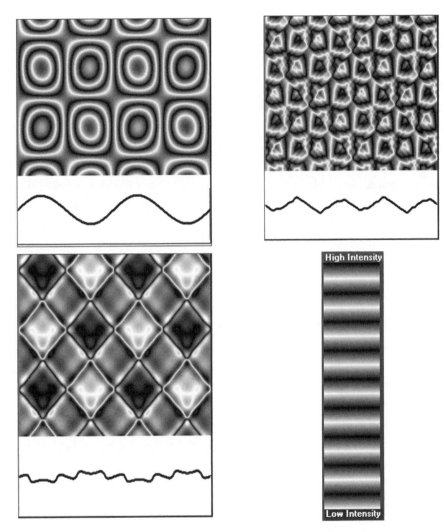

**Figure 32:**
**Fermi-Pasta-Ulam Quadratic and Cubic Nonlinear Waves**

*The figure on the lower right shows the shadings that we use to indicate the cell values. The other three figures show one-dimensional CAs. In each of these figures, the upper part is a spacetime diagram, that is, a stack of a few hundred pictures of the CA, with time running down the page. Think of the alternating dark and light bands as being lines of equal altitude above the plane of the page. The wiggly graphs at the bottom are instantaneous pictures of the CA state, with the cell values represented as vertical positions; here the altitude direction is within the page. In each case the CA is seeded with a smooth wave at start-up. The upper left image shows a quadratic wave after a hundred updates, when it still looks very much like a regular wave. The upper right image shows the same quadratic wave after about fifty thousand updates. The lower left shows a cubic wave after about fifty thousand updates.[31]*

### 2.3: *Chaos in a Bouncing Ball*

In this section, we'll revert to the particle system view and regard the world's processing elements as being ordinary objects; in particular, I'll talk about the motions of balls. My first example is what I'll call the bin experiment (figure 33).

A ball drops from a fixed height straight down to a box divided into two tall bins, and the ball ends up in either the left or the right bin, with no possibility of bouncing from one bin into the other.

We suppose that we can vary the ball's starting position along the horizontal or "$x$"-axis, with the zero position located exactly above the center of the partition dividing the two bins. We might summarize this by saying the experiment is a Bin($x$) process that computes a Left or Right bin output from the starting position $x$.

For the moment, we'll ignore the parallel aspects of physics and focus on the ball as a single serial processor. For the ball, the low-level software is the laws of physics, the high-level software is the configuration of the bin, the initial input is the ball's starting position $x$, and we're interested in the output state where the ball has settled down into the left or the right bin.

Remembering the stored program concept, we recognize that there's not that sharp a boundary between the high-level software and the input data. In other words, you can either think of the box as "software" or "data." I'm leaning toward the software view, as I'm thinking of situations where we might throw a ball into some fairly complicated and mazelike collection of passages and walls and ask about where the maze design makes the given input ball end up.

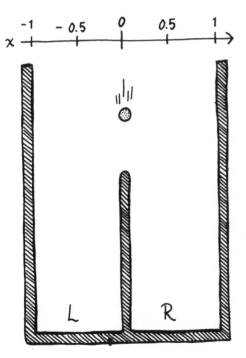

**Figure 33:**
**A Ball Computes Bin($x$) to Be Left or Right**

Although the simple bin experiment seems nice and deterministic, there are some quagmires to explore.

When the ball is released near the center of the $x$-axis, it may bounce up and down on the divider for a while. Maybe once in a blue moon it'll end up balanced upon the divider for a longer period of time. Is this a problem? Not really. We can just say that there are *three* possible outputs: at a given time the output Bin($x$) might be Left, Right, or Up—where the Up state corresponds to any situation where the ball hasn't yet landed and come to rest.

If we're going to talk about time, we might as well make it explicit, and write Bin($x$, $t$), to indicate the state of the system $t$ seconds after we drop the ball from position $x$. Bin($x$, $t$) will be Up for the smaller values of $t$; then eventually it will go to Left or Right and stay there. And if we just write Bin($x$), we mean, let's say, the value of B($x$, 300), that is, the state of the ball five minutes (or three hundred seconds) after you drop it.

Fine, but now we have to face a harder problem. Suppose you were to actually set up a bin experiment and carry out a large number of runs, each time dropping the ball from what seemed to you to be the exact center of the $x$-axis. The resulting outputs would be a more or less random sequence of Left and Right outputs, with maybe, once every billion runs, an Up output that lasts a full five minutes. But rare, anomalous cases aren't the important issue. The important issue is that if we keep dropping the ball from what seems to be the exact center, our bin experiment will generate a seemingly random sequence of results. Although we think we're using the same input over and over, we keep getting different results.

The best way to express this is to say that an individual physical computation like dropping a ball into the bin is *not repeatable*. We can *approximately* repeat many physical computations—otherwise we'd never learn to walk or throw a Frisbee. But the scuzz and fuzz of the natural world keeps its computations from being *precisely* repeatable.

The reason is that we do not—and cannot—have perfect control over the $x$ input. The value of $x$ may be *near* zero, but it won't be exactly zero. And each time we put it near zero, it'll be "near" in some different way. You can't set $x$ to the same value twice in a row because it doesn't make sense to say that a normal-size object's location is *exactly* some precise number.

Suppose, for instance, you're measuring the position $x$ in meters, and you're trying to get a lot of decimal places of accuracy. When you reach the ninth decimal place, you're at the nanometer level, where the sizes of molecules and atoms become significant. At this scale, your ball is a vibrating cloud of atoms, and asking about the exact center of the cloud becomes as impractical as asking after the exact center of a swarm of gnats.

The more decimals you want, the worse it gets. At eighteen decimals, you're down at the level of protons and neutrons, and most of the ball looks like empty space. And at the thirty-fifth decimal place you hit that troublesome Planck length, the scale at which continuous space may not even exist. Measure a position to an arbitrary precision? Forget it!

Can't our uncertainty about the ball position's smaller decimal places just stay insignificant? No. Suppose that the divider between the two bins has a rounded top. Geometrical considerations show that each bounce moves the ball farther from the exact center. The amplification is in fact exponential, in the sense that after $n$ bounces, an initial displacement will be on the order of $10^n$ times as big. Another way to put it is that each bounce brings another few decimal places of the position into visibility. No matter how tiny the initial displacement is, it will rather quickly become visible (figure 34).

To complicate things, as the ball bounces on the divider, effects from the irregularities in the surfaces of the ball and of the divider come to dominate the not-really-so-precise initial condition. Before long, you have to consider the effects of air currents and even the gravitational effects of objects other than the downward-pulling earth. These influences are, if you will, interactive inputs added onto the initial input. If the ball bounces long enough on the divider, no effect is too small to have an influence.

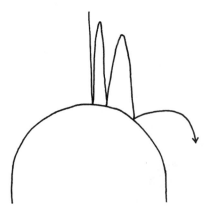

So what are we left with? Is the bin experiment a deterministic process? Can we call it a computation?

Yes. It's a computation that just doesn't happen to be *repeatable*—that is, you can never manage to reset things to get the

**Figure 34: Bounce Magnification**

exact same initial input and then observe the exact same series of outputs. The bin experiment is unrepeatable because the dynamics of this system amplifies the tiniest details of the initial and interactive inputs so that they have large and noticeable effects.

This point is important, so I'll say it once more. When we get into the zone near the center point, the bin experiment remains deterministic, but it becomes sensitive not only to the details of the input position but also to vagrant influences by the environment. Yes, the output seems random, but this is only because the initial and interactive inputs aren't fully known. And it's this lack of knowledge that makes the experiments unrepeatable.

The bin experiment is an example what physicists call a *chaotic* system. A chaotic system is one that rapidly amplifies the details of its initial conditions and external influences. In the formal definition of chaos, mathematicians also require that a chaotic system is one that will now and then appear to be periodic for short periods of time. Very many, perhaps most, everyday physical systems are chaotic.

Note that although chaos makes processes complex, that doesn't mean that these computations are random. Waves and clouds are chaotically diverse, but they do tend to have certain characteristic patterns. When you go to the beach, you don't see a completely random goulash of water and air—no matter how gnarly the surf, it's still made up of waves in a characteristic distribution of sizes.

The characteristic space and time patterns of chaotic processes are known as *strange attractors*. The science writer James Gleick describes how a group of Santa Cruz chaoticians known as the Dynamical Systems Collective learned to see them in the natural world.

> They had a game they would play, sitting at a coffeehouse. They would ask: How far away is the nearest strange attractor? Was it that rattling automobile fender? That flag snapping erratically in a steady breeze? A fluttering leaf?[32]

Drop a piece of paper and watch it drift to the floor. The paper seesaws back and forth, twirls, flips over, dives, and catches itself with a sudden swoop. And if you drop it again it's likely to do something different. Repeatedly toss an apple core toward a trash can. Now and then you may seem to be in a groove, with the core bouncing in, but over time, the results are quite unpredictable. Observe a drop of milk spreading through your coffee. There is a certain regularity to the tendrils, but nothing long-lasting or systematic. Run your fingernail across your desk and listen to the sound. Make your bed and regard the exact shape of the crease where the blankets tuck in. Watch a raindrop on a windowpane. All of these systems are rule-based and deterministic. Yet all of them continually produce surprise. These and perhaps most other physical systems are computations that are in practice unrepeatable because you can never reproduce the exact same combination of initial and interactive inputs.

Some chaotic systems explode into a grungy thrashing, while others settle into very nearly repetitive behavior patterns. Chaotic systems can range from having a lesser or a greater amount of disorder.

A key distinction between bouncing balls and PCs is that our PC computations *are* repeatable. This is because PCs are digital, with a feasibly small range of initial values and because they are well isolated from unwanted inputs.

But because bouncing balls are analog, their computations are not repeatable. The difference between analog systems and digital systems is not that the analog computations are in any way less accurate. The difference is that analog systems have so many states that it's physically impossible to control the inputs of an analog computation precisely enough as to make it repeatable.

As it happens, the physical computations we enjoy watching are the least likely to be repeatable. In a ball game we relish the moments when the ball's motion is the most obviously chaotic. The football that dances and flubbed on the players' fingertips. The basketball that circles the hoop before dropping in. The line drive that escapes the pitcher's glove to be bobbled by the short stop and caught by the second baseman. The Ping-Pong shot that skids along the net and somehow crawls over it.

Back in the 1970s, my family and I lived in upstate New York. There was a relentlessly lively little boy in our neighborhood. Kenny. We had a wooden garage with rafters, bookcases, bicycles and tricycles, sleds on the walls, rakes and hoes, a lawn mower, a rabbit hutch, and so on. Kenny would throw a discarded tennis ball into our garage as hard as he could, and excitedly describe the paths the ball would take. "Look, it hit the paint can and slid off the hose onto the windowsill and rolled across to the bicycle seat before it dribbled under the car!" Kenny was having fun watching physical computations.

Observing physical computations is a simple human pleasure. Last night, in fact, with these ideas in my mind, I was playing at the dinner table. My wife and I were guests of the neighbors, and I picked up a plastic wine-cork and tossed it toward the wooden napkin ring lying on its side on my host's place mat. The cork landed just right, did a gentle flip, slid into the napkin ring, and stayed there. Goal! I spent the next few minutes trying to do it again, until my wife made me stop. At social gatherings, a gentleman eschews fanatical computer hacking of any kind.

Physical computations are things we can enjoy with our whole bodies. One of the particular joys of mountain biking is riding down a hill, enjoying the sensations of a computation playing itself out. The hill is the input, physics is the low-level software, your bicycle and your reactions are the high-level software, and the output is your breezy ride.

Bicycling, or for that matter skiing, involves a downhill ride that's chaotic in its sensitivity to small influences. After a bit of practice, you learn to supply a stream of interactive inputs that guide you away from outputs involving a spill. Physiologists report that a human brain sends out muscle control signals at a rate of about ten pulses per second. Using the rapid computer in your head, you're able to predict the next few seconds of your onrushing physical computation and to tailor your control pulses to guide you toward the outputs you prefer.

When an ongoing computation adjusts itself—like a bicyclist, a skier, or, for that matter, a soaring bird—we see intelligence. But the motions of even dumb, unguided physical objects can be arbitrarily complex.

Recall Wolfram's Principle of Computational Equivalence (PCE), which I introduced in section *1.2: A New Kind of Science.* Wolfram claims that essentially all complex computations are universal, that is, rich enough to emulate any other computation. In other words, most of the physical systems we encounter are universal, just as they are.

What kinds of examples do I have in mind when I speak of universal physical computations? Chaotic ones. A ball bouncing around a cluttered garage. Ice crystals forming in freezing water. Drifting masses of clouds. Amplified feedback from an electric guitar. A scarf dropping to the floor.

How simple can a universal physical computer be? In the 1970s, the auto-didact universal automatist Edward Fredkin described how to make a universal computer from billiard balls bouncing around on a frictionless table. It's not much of a leap from this to arguing that the three-dimensional motions of the air's molecules are also a universal computer.

But do keep in mind that in the cruddy, scuzzy world of physical objects, the motions of air molecules or Fredkin billiard balls are irredeemably chaotic, rapidly amplifying the slight inaccuracies of the starting conditions and then being swamped by external effects like the tiny gravitational forces from the motions of the observer. The bouncing particles will compute *something,* but probably not what you intended them to.

I mentioned in section *2.1: Rough and Smooth* that we can digitally emulate physics, at least in principle. But in practice there are three difficulties: a first relates to *initial conditions,* a second comes from the *supplemental inputs* we just mentioned, and a third concerns *unfeasibility.*

Suppose your targeted task is to emulate precisely some particular run of a physical process. You plan to make, say, a virtual model of my garage, and toss in a virtual ball and try to get it bounce around just like Kenny's tennis ball did.

The *initial condition* problem is as follows. Because each bounce amplifies more digits into visibility, you have an exceedingly low probability of exactly emulating Kenny. Yes, as you hunt through the range of possible inputs you may come across runs that start out by behaving like Kenny's big throw, but the simulations will eventually diverge from the reality as you simulate more and more of the elapsed time.

The *supplemental inputs* problem has to do with the fact that even if you miraculously match Kenny's initial input, due to the chaotic sensitivity to supplemental inputs, even if a trajectory matches Kenny's for a second or two, it will soon veer away as a result of tiny supplemental inputs from the world at large.

The *feasibility* problem has to do with the fact that even our most highly parallel digital computers have a minuscule number of computational nodes compared to nature. What analog systems lack in repeatability they gain in their massively parallel powers of computation.

Yes, you can simulate a ball bouncing around a garage quite well because here you're essentially ignoring the parallelism of the physical world. But now suppose I ask you to also simulate the air in the garage. It's hopeless to try to individually simulate each of the astronomical number of atoms, and even if you go to a higher-level finite-element model, it's impossible. Think of all the eddies that form in the wake of the ball, not to mention the vibrations from Kenny's shrill voice—the waves and vortices crossing one another and bouncing off the irregular objects, fleeting flows interacting in gnarly, non-linear ways.

Practically speaking, digital computers have no hope of feasibly emulating the full richness of the physical world in real time. But we can be consoled by the fact that we already *have* the world, and it's already a computation.

The dream of traditional physics is to find simple laws to describe nature. In some cases, such as the motions of the planets in their orbits around our sun, simple formulas can go a very long way. But when you get into detailed, chaotic situations like a ball bouncing around a cluttered garage, you often need to fall back upon detailed simulation—which still doesn't give very good predictions, as it's impossible to specify the initial conditions to a high-enough degree of accuracy.

Some physicists dislike Wolfram's work because he brings them bad news. Recall Wolfram's PCU.

- *Principle of Computational Unpredictability (PCU).* Most naturally occurring complex computations are unpredictable.

The PCU tells us that most physical systems are going to be unpredictable in the formal sense that there isn't going to be a simple and rapidly running computation that can emulate the physics very much faster than it happens.

A crucial point that I'll be returning to is that the unpredictability is *not* just the result of sensitive dependence on initial conditions and on supplemental inputs. Even if an experiment could be conducted in an utterly shielded environment with a strictly accurate initial condition, the computation itself would be unpredictable.

One of Wolfram's favorite examples along these lines involves the motion of a projectile, such as a cannonball. In an idealized experiment where you ignore the effects of air friction, if you fire a bullet into the air, the bullet's *velocity* in feet per second and *height* in feet at a given *time* will be given by *simple equations* of this form.

velocity = startvelocity − 32 · time

height = startheight + startvelocity · time − 16 · time².

The beauty of these equations is that we can plug in larger values of time and get the corresponding velocity and the height with very little computation.

Contrast this to *simulating* the motion of a bullet one step at a time by using a rule under which we initialize velocity to startvelocity and height to startheight and then iterate the following two *update rules* over and over for some fixed time-per-simulation-step *dt*.

Add (−32 · *dt*) to velocity.

Add (velocity · *dt*) to height.

If your targeted *time* value is 10.0 and your time step *dt* is 0.000001, then using the simple equations means evaluating *two* formulas. But if you use the update rules, you have to evaluate *two million* formulas!

The bad news that Wolfram brings for physics is that in any physically realistic situation, our exact formulas fail, and we're forced to use step-by-step simulations. Real natural phenomena are messy class three or gnarly class four computations, either one of which is, by the PCU, unpredictable. And, again, the unpredictability stems not so much from the chaoticity of the system as it does from the fact that the computation itself generates seemingly random results.

In the case of a real object moving through the air, if we want to get full accuracy in describing the object's motions, we need to take into account the flow of air over it. But, at least at certain velocities, flowing fluids are known to produce patterns very much like those of a continuous-valued class four cellular automaton—think of the bumps and ripples that move back and forth along the lip of a waterfall. So a real object's motion will at times be carrying out a class four computation, so, in a formal sense, the object's motion will be unpredictable—meaning that no simple formula can give full accuracy.

This summer I passed a few hours in the Museum of the History of Science in Geneva, Switzerland. It's a jewel of a place, a dozen small rooms in the two stories of a lakeside mansion, with parquet floors and enchanting prospects from every window, and most of the windows open to catch the breezes from the lake. Glass cases hold brass scientific instruments: microscopes, telescopes, barometers, Leyden jars, spectroscopes, and the like. It stands to reason that these precision instruments would be found here in the nation of watchmakers; indeed, quite a few of them are Swiss-made.

In the museum, I photographed what seems a perfect image for science's dream of finding a simple explanation for everything: the crank on an orrery. An orrery is a tabletop model of the solar system, you see, with a little handle that you turn to move the planets and moons in their orbits.

How *about* the minuet of the planets, spinning to the stately music of Newton's laws? It's well known that Newton's laws can be used to formally derive the simple laws of planetary motion known as Kepler's laws. Does this mean that the solar system's motions are fully predictable?

No, even here chaos and unpredictability raise their untidy heads. In 1987, the computer scientists Gerald Sussman and Jack Wisdom carried out a monster simulation of the solar system to show that, in the long run, the

motion of Pluto is chaotic.[33] The formal derivation of Kepler's laws doesn't take into account the pulls of the planets upon one another, and once we include this in the mix, Kepler's music of the spheres becomes discordant. We get, once again, a class four computation, unpredictable by any means other than a detailed simulation. Deterministic yes, predictable no.

**Figure 35: The Secret Machinery of the Universe**

*The little crank you turn to move the planets of an orrery in the Geneva Museum of the History of Science. These days, we instead use computer programs that are so-called digital orreries.*

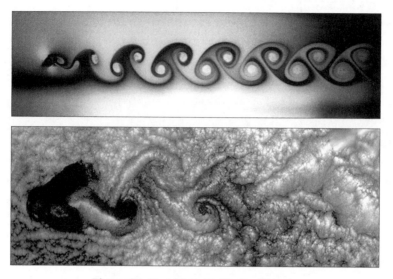

**Figure 36: Von Karman Vortex Streets**

*The top image was created by Maarten Rutgers using a flowing soap film, and the bottom is a satellite photo of the clouds near the island of Guadalupe.*

Wolfram feels that the successes of science are limited to a small number of phenomena, and that in most situations we will have to fall back on the computationally intensive process of simulating the evolution of the systems about which we want to make predictions. Indeed, it seems likely that most natural processes can't be predicted in detail by any simple formula—if for no reason than that there are so many processes, and so few simple formulae, that there aren't enough "elegant laws of nature" to go around![34]

### 2.4: *The Meaning of Gnarl*

Building computations in layers is a recurrent theme—think of a computer game powered by the microcode of a chip, or of a human reckoner whose thoughts are the firings of neurons. Layers upon layers of computation, emulations upon emulations.

One of the nicest words I've picked up from my philosopher friends is *phenomenology*. Phenomenology is the study of what you actually experience—

independent of the theories and explanations that you've been taught. Phe-nomenologically speaking, continuous classical physics is closer to reality than stories about atoms. There's no need to apologize or feel inauthentic if you take an observant layman's view of the physical world. If you see it, it's real.

If you start looking around for computation-like physical processes, you'll find them everywhere. Some of the most dramatic examples occur in fluid flow. Figure 36 shows a particular fluid-flow phenomenon called *von Karman vortex streets* after the Hungarian aeronauticist Theodor von Kármán. When a stream of air or water flows around an obstacle at moderate speed, eddies appear in the wake. Examples would be the vortices you see trailing your hand when you sweep it through the water of a sunlit pool, the whirlpools that seem to spawn off the back of a rock in a stream, the exquisitely filigreed smoke from a steaming cup of tea, or the great whorls that form in cloud for-mations downwind from mountains.

As the situation gets more complicated, so do the patterns. Figure 37 shows a photo I took of a stream flowing around four rocks at the Esalen Institute (naturally) in Big Sur. The bumps in the water surface were fairly

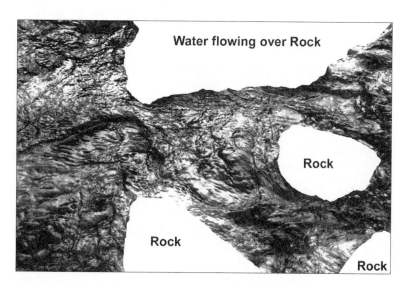

**Figure 37: Water in a Stream**

*Looking down with the water flowing from left to right. Rocks are whited out for clarity.*

stable, almost like solid objects, although now and then twisting and shifting in response to slight changes in the amount of water coming through.

To some extent these gnarly patterns result from the intricate initial conditions of the streambed and the supplemental inputs of the downstream flow. But there's another factor to keep in mind, the self-generated structures of the flow computation itself. The stability of the patterns suggests that the patterns aren't *wholly* determined by the inputs. The chaotic computation has strange attractors that it tends to settle in on.

If you had a totally smooth streambed, what kind of patterns might you see on the water's surface? You might suspect that very simple and uninteresting ripple patterns would result. But this seems not to be the case. Any fluid flow is rich enough to generate random-looking patterns quite on its own. You don't need any supplemental inputs to churn things up. The computation is class four on its own.

Stephen Wolfram remarks that we might take a high-level view of flowing fluids, treating, say, vortices as objects in their own right. Rather than saying the complex motions of the vortices are the result of chaotically amplified inputs, it might be possible to explain the motions in terms of a fairly simple computational rule about the vortices themselves. It may be that many of the external disturbances are averaged away and damped down—and the gnarly patterns we see are the result of a simple high-level computation that happens to be unpredictable.

Recall here that I say a computation $P$ is *unpredictable* when there is no shortcut computation $Q$ which computes the same results as $P$, but very much faster. Wolfram also speaks of such computations as *irreducible* or as *intrinsically random.*

I might mention in passing that computer scientists also use the word *pseudorandom* to refer to unpredictable processes. Any programming environment will have built into it some predefined algorithms that produce reasonable random-looking sequences of numbers—these algorithms are often called pseudorandomizers. The "pseudo" refers to the fact that these are in fact deterministic computations.[35]

Recall that Wolfram's Principle of Computational Unpredictability (PCU) says that most naturally occurring complex (that is, not class one or class two) computations are unpredictable. Putting the PCU a bit differently, we expect to find that most naturally occurring complex computations are intrinsically random or, if you prefer, pseudorandom.

To illustrate the notion of intrinsic randomness, Wolfram points out how the evolution of a one-dimensional cellular automaton can produce unpredictable patterns, starting from an initial condition of a few marked cells and with no supplemental inputs at all. As I'll discuss in just a minute, Wolfram's favorite example of an intrinsically random process is the two-valued CA Rule 30. But first, for a change of pace, look at the intrinsically random continuous-valued CA in figure 38.

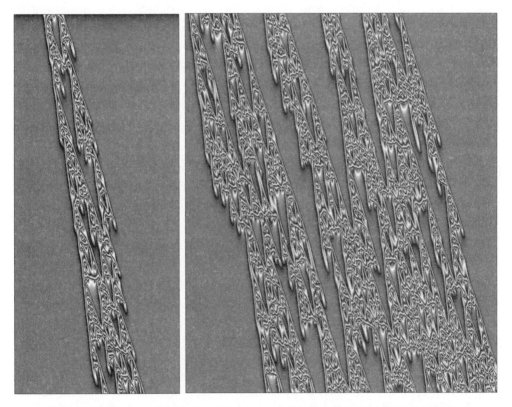

**Figure 38: A Deterministic One-Dimensional CA Creating Gnarly-Looking Flow**

*The left side shows the first six hundred generations of a line seeded with a smooth bump of values in its center. The right side shows generations 8,000 to 8,600. The rule is called Honey, and is a continuous-valued rule based on taking weighted averages of cells with their neighbors, using different averaging methods according to whether the cell's value is positive or negative.*

As is customary in a CA, the cells are updated in parallel, which means that during each full update of the cellular automaton, every cell on the tape computes a new value for itself. The way to read figure 38 is to view space as the horizontal axis and time as running down the page. What we see are successive copies of the cellular automaton's tape. Each row of black, white, and gray cells represents one successive step of the computation. The picture is, if you will, a spacetime diagram.

The idea behind intrinsic randomness is that not all of the world's seeming randomness needs to result from outside agitation and the chaotic amplification of initial conditions. Some, or perhaps most, of nature's complexity can arise from intrinsic randomness—from a simple computation endlessly munching on the same region of data and pumping out unpredictable new patterns.

Now you might think that the intrinsic randomness of the Honey rule has something to do with its use of continuous-valued real numbers. Maybe it's excavating hidden initial conditions out of the real numbers with which I seeded it. This is why Wolfram's favorite poster child for intrinsic randomness is so important—there's absolutely nothing up the sleeves of the one-dimensional CA Rule 30.

Recall that in Rule 30, the cell values consist of a single zero-or-one bit, which we represent, respectively, by white or black. If we start Rule 30 with *one single black cell,* it quickly fills up the right half of the tape with a class three pattern resembling the foam in a beer glass (see figure 39).

If you repeat the run, you get exactly the same pattern, so it's deterministic. Yet anyone looking at the sea of triangular bubbles in the bottom right half of the picture would imagine the system to be random. The moral is that a deterministic world is perfectly capable of generating its own randomness. This is unpredictability; this is intrinsic randomness.

Recall that Wolfram's Principle of Computational Equivalence (PCE) proposes that most naturally occurring class three and class four computations are equally complex. But observationally, there's a distinction between the two.

Although class three computations are intriguing, the most beautiful computations are class four. These are the ones that I call "gnarly."

The original meaning of "gnarl" was simply "a knot in the wood of a tree." In California surfer slang, "gnarly" came to be used to describe complicated,

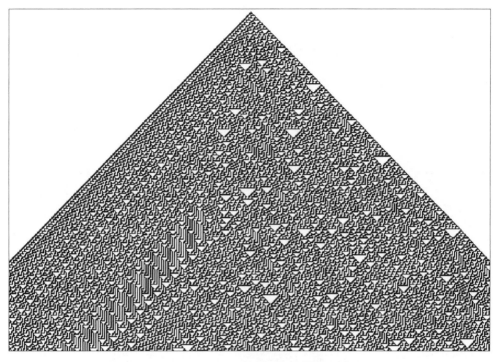

**Figure 39: Rule 30, Started from a Single Black Cell**

rapidly changing surf conditions. And then, by extension, something gnarly came to be anything with surprisingly intricate detail.

Do note that "gnarly" can also mean "disgusting." Soon after I moved to California in 1986, I was at an art festival where a caterer was roasting a huge whole pig on a spit above a gas-fired grill the size of a car. Two teenage boys walked by and looked silently at the pig. Finally one of them observed, "Gnarly, dude." In the same vein, my son has been heard to say, "Never ever eat anything gnarly." And having your body become old and gnarled isn't necessarily a pleasant thing. But here I only want to talk about gnarl in a good kind of way.

Clouds, fire, and water are gnarly in the sense of being beautifully intricate, with purposeful-looking but not quite comprehensible patterns (figure 40). And of course all living things are gnarly, in that they inevitably do things that are much more complex than one might have expected. The shapes of tree branches are the standard example of gnarl. The life cycle of a jellyfish

**Figure 40: "As Above, So Below"—
Gnarly Clouds and Water**

is way gnarly. The wild three-dimensional paths that a hummingbird sweeps out are kind of gnarly, too, and, if the truth be told, your ears are gnarly as well.

Let's come back to the surf at an ocean beach. As I already mentioned in the previous section, *2.3: Chaos in a Bouncing Ball,* although the patterns of the water are clearly very complicated, they aren't random. The forms of the waves are, from moment to moment, predictable by the laws of fluid motion. Waves don't just pop in and out of existence. Water moves according to well-understood physical laws. It's a deterministic computation.

You might notice that the waves near a rock tend every so often to fall into a certain kind of surge pattern. This recurrent surge pattern would be a chaotic attractor. In the same way, chaotic computer simulations will occasionally tighten in on characteristic rhythms and clusters that act as chaotic attractors. In either case, we're dealing with a class four computation.

If there is a storm, the waves may become quite choppy and disorderly. This is more like a class three computation. As disorderliness is increased, a chaotic physical system can range from being nearly periodic, up through the visually interesting region of the strange attractors, and then into uniform seething. This, again, corresponds to the passage from class two to class four to class three computations. As I mentioned before, Wolfram's number-ordering for his computational classes is a bit misleading. Class four is in some sense *between* classes two and three, as I suggested in figure 7.

The reason people might think waves are random is because the computation that the water performs is many orders of magnitude larger than anything our computers can simulate. Yes, simulating actual waves on an electronic computer is unfeasible. But that doesn't mean that waves aren't the result of deterministic computations being carried out by the physical world. And we have every reason to suspect that these computations are class four and unpredictable.

The great discovery we've made with our personal computers is that you don't need a system as complicated as the ocean to generate unpredictable gnarl. A very simple rule can produce output that looks, at least superficially, as complicated as physical chaos. Unpredictable computer simulations are often produced either by running one algorithm many times (as with the famous Mandelbrot set) or by setting up an arena in which multiple instances of a single algorithm can interact (as in CAs).

We find the same spectrum of disorder across a wide range of systems— mathematical, physical, chemical, biological, sociological, and economic. In each domain, at the ordered end we have class one constancy and a complete lack of surprise. One step up from that is periodic class two behavior in which the same sequence repeats itself over and over again—as in the structure of a crystal. Adding a bit more disorder leads us into the class four or gnarly zone, the region in which we see interesting behaviors. And at the high end of the spectrum is the all-but-featureless randomness of class three.

Regarding physical matter, in classical (prequantum) physics, a vacuum is the simplest, most orderly kind of matter: nothing is going on. A crystalline solid is orderly in a predictable, periodic way. And fluids such as liquids or gasses are fairly disorderly, more along the lines of being class three. Matter is computationally at its most interesting when it's near a phase transition, as when a liquid is freezing or coming to a boil. Matter near a phase transition to some extent has a nested class two structure, with similar kinds of features occurring at widely different scales. But the phase transition structure is very dynamic, with information-laden patterns moving about, and is, I believe, best thought of as class four.

The flow of water is a rich source of examples of degrees of disorder. The most orderly state of water is, of course, for it to be standing still. If one lets water run rather slowly down a channel, the water moves smoothly, with perhaps a regular class two pattern of ripples in it. As more water is put into a channel, eddies and whirlpools appear—turbulence. If a massive amount of water is

| Level of Disorderliness | Lower | High | Higher | Highest |
|---|---|---|---|---|
| Subregion of the gnarly zone | Quasiperiodic | Strange attractors | Chaotic bifurcations | Pseudorandom |

**Table 3: Subspectrum of Disorderliness for the Gnarly Zone**

poured down a steep channel, smaller and smaller eddies cascade off the larger ones, ultimately leading to an essentially random state in which the water is seething. The gnarly zone is where the flow has begun to break up into eddies with a few smaller eddies, without yet having turned into random churning.

In every case, the gnarly zone is to be found at the interface between order and disorder. In the mathematics of chaos theory, we can refine this a bit more, distinguishing four subregions of the gnarly zone (see table 3).

The most orderly kind of gnarly behavior is quasiperiodic, or nearly periodic. Something like this might be a periodic function that has a slight, unpredictable drift. Next comes the strange attractor zone in which the system generates easily visible structures—like the gliders in a CA rule, or like standing waves in a stream. Then we enter a critical transition zone, which is the heart of the gnarl.

In the language of chaos theory, a system undergoes a *bifurcation* when a system switches to a new attractor. This is when a system begins ranging over a completely different zone of possibilities within the space of all possible phenomena. The term *bifurcation* is a bit misleading, as a chaotic bifurcation doesn't necessarily have anything to do with something splitting into two. Bifurcation means nothing more than changing something about a system in such a way as to make its behavior move to a different attractor.[36]

As we turn up the disorder of a gnarly system, the system begins experiencing bifurcations in which one strange attractor repeatedly gives way to another. Initially the system may be dancing around on, say, an ellipse, and a moment later, the successive points may be scattered about on something shaped like a bow tie.

And at the highest end of disorder we shade into the pseudorandom chaotic systems, whose output is empirically indistinguishable from true randomness—unless you happen to be told the intrinsically random algorithm that is generating the chaos.

My favorite example of gnarly physical chaos is a tree whose branches are gently trembling in the breeze (figure 41). Here's some journal notes I wrote about gnarl and a tree that I saw while backpacking in the Los Padres Wilderness near Big Sur with my daughter Isabel and her friend Gus in May 2003.

Green hills, wonderfully curved, the gnarly oaks, fractal white cloud puffs, the Pacific Ocean hanging anomalously high in the sky, fog-quilted.

I got up first, right before sunrise, and I was looking at a medium-sized pine tree just down the ridge from my tent. Gentle dawn breezes were playing over the tree, and every single one of its needles was quivering, oscillating through its own characteristic range of frequencies, and the needle clumps and branches were rocking as well, working their way around their own particular phase space attractors, the whole motion harmonious in the extreme. Insects buzzed about the tree, and, having looked in the microscope so much of late, I could easily visualize the micro-organisms upon the needles, in the beads of sap, beneath the bark, in the insects' guts—the tree a microcosmos. The sun came rolling up over the ridge, gilding my pine. With all its needles aflutter it was like an anemone, like a dancer, like a cartoon character with a halo of alertness rays.

"I love you," I said to the tree, for just that moment not even needing to reach past the tree to imagine the divinity behind it, for just that moment seeing the tree as the body of God. "I love you."

When we got home there were my usual daily problems to confront and I felt uptight. And now, writing these notes, I ask how can I get some serenity?

I have the laptop here on a cafe table under a spring-green tree in sunny blue-sky Los Gatos. I look up at the tree overhead, a linden with very small pale fresh green leaves. And yes the leaves are doing the hand jive. The branches rocking. The very image of my wandering thoughts, eternally revisiting the same topics. It's good.

The trees, the leaves, the clouds, my mind, it's all the same, all so beautifully gnarly.

**Figure 41:**
**Tree, Cloud, Mind, Mountain**

## 2.5: *What Is Reality?*

Years ago I was discussing far-out science-fiction ideas with the beloved mathematics writer Martin Gardner. I was describing the notion that if you could measure a totally rigid piece of material to endless precision, then the successive digits might code up, say, the true and complete story of your life. What if everyone were born clutching a personal talisman of this kind in his or her hand—like program notes summarizing the action of an opera? And suppose that, instead of going on and living a real life, some poor guy wastes all his time decoding his talisman—only to learn that he'll spend his entire allotted span measuring one little object!

But, thanks to atomism, we can't really measure much past twenty digits, and even if we could, quantum mechanics makes space fairly meaningless out past the thirty-fifth digit. So the idea doesn't quite work.

"Too bad," said Martin. "Quantum mechanics ruins everything."

Physicists have great confidence in quantum mechanics because it predicts, among other things, the precise values of certain physical constants.

But physical constants have to do with quantities that are measured as averages over many different runs. When it comes to predicting how any individual particle will behave, quantum mechanics is usually helpless.

An example. Suppose we have a beamsplitter (see figure 42), that is, a partially reflecting mirror that reflects half of all incoming light and transmits the rest. And let's say that we have a pair of light-sensitive detectors labeled 0 and 1. The transmitted light goes to 1 and the bounced light goes to 0. The 0 and 1 detectors each register an intensity half as great as that of the incoming beam. But what happens if we send in a beam that contains only a single photon?

One of the brute facts about nature is that light is quantized; that is, you actually *can* turn down a light beam's intensity to a specific minimal intensity that sends one photon at a time. Photons are supposedly indivisible—you can't get half a photon arriving at 0 and half a photon arriving at 1. So the single-photon beamsplitter system has to make what seems to be a random choice. If you repeat the experiment over and over, about half the photons end up at 0 and about half end up at 1.

We had a similar result in our bin experiment, and in that case we were satisfied with saying that there were tiny differences in the initial conditions and external influences on each successive ball. Why can't we take a similar approach with photons encountering a beamsplitter? The photons could be like balls, the beamsplitter could be like the bin divider, and the various outcomes could deterministically depend on tiny details.

But physicists say this is impossible. They insist that we *can't* explain the variation by saying the photons might be hitting the mirror in slightly different locations, that the photons might be slightly different, or that there are external influences nudging the photons this way and that. They say there's no hope of finding a deeper explanation of the photons' decisions, and that an individual photon's choice of whether to trigger detector 0 or detector 1 is fundamentally and inexplicably random.

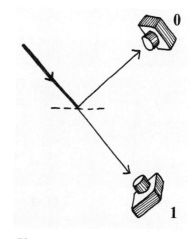

**Figure 42: The Beamsplitter**

In the words of the endlessly quotable physicist Richard Feynman, with his own characteristic italics:

> Yes! physics *has* given up. *We do not know how to predict what would happen in a given circumstance,* and we believe now that it is impossible, that the only thing that can be predicted is the probability of different events. It must be recognized that this is a retrenchment in our earlier ideal of understanding nature. It may be a backward step, but no one has seen a way to avoid it. . . . We suspect very strongly that it is something that will be with us forever—that it is impossible to beat that puzzle—that this is the way nature really is.[37]

Feynman is always persuasive, but physical determinism is not so dead an option as he suggests. My opinion is that there are in fact underlying psychological reasons driving the conventional insistence that we should welcome quantum mechanics and the destruction of determinism. Often when I hear a popular lecture on quantum mechanics, I detect a lilting, mystery-mongering tone. "Be happy! The universe is incomprehensible! How wonderful!"

The rejection of determinism seems to provide some people with a sense of liberation. The hidden part of the argument might go like this: If the world is fundamentally random, then surely I'm not a robotic machine, and if I'm not a machine, then perhaps I have an immortal soul, so death isn't so frightening.

Now that I've delivered this ad hominem attack on the advocates of quantum mechanics, I must, in all fairness, admit that I have my own psychological reasons for not wanting to view quantum mechanics as a final answer. First of all, like many mathematicians, I'm uncomfortable with uncertainty. In this vein, it could also be that a lifetime's worth of hard knocks has taught me that when there are no rules, most people get a raw deal. A second point is that I like thinking of the universe as a single entity that's at some level knowable; I like to imagine that, if you will, I can see the face of God. And this dreamed-of cosmic unity becomes less plausible if the universe results from an all-but-infinite collection of utterly random bit-flips with absolutely no common underlying cause.

As I say, I think the mystifications of quantum mechanics seem appealing precisely because people would like there to be some escape from the logical and deterministic fact that we're all going to die. But if the fear of death is indeed the issue, why not find solace in thinking of the universe as an immense logical system of which you're a tiny part? When your particular pattern ceases to exist, the grand computation will continue. Your alloted region of spacetime will "always" be around. Can't that be enough? For that matter, what's so terrible about death? Personally, I don't really *mind* the notion of someday getting off the stage and no longer having to continue my long-winded computation—but maybe that's just because I'm getting old.

Let me make one more point. If you fear that determinism means you're a machine without a soul, consider that, given what we know about class four computations, there's no reason to think that we can't be both deterministic *and* unpredictable, no reason to think that your soul couldn't in some sense *be* a gnarly computation. Consider: The world could be perfectly deterministic and still look and feel exactly the same as it looks right now. Indeed, I think that's the true state of things. Quantum mechanics simply doesn't go deep enough. And we have nothing to lose by moving beyond it to a fully deterministic universal automatism.

Enough rhetoric; let's get back to science. There seem to be two kinds of reasons why physicists don't expect photons to behave like balls.

The first reason is that photons are meant to be elementary particles, without any of the nicks and dings that can serve to explain why balls act unpredictably. Well—maybe so, maybe not. It's at least conceivable that photons themselves are the averaged-out results of still more fundamental phenomena—not necessarily subparticles, but possibly something like network patterns or linked loops in a multidimensional superspace.

The second, more compelling, reason that photons aren't like balls is that they're also like waves. The photon is in some sense a wave that takes *both* paths through the beamsplitter, and the presence of the detectors makes the smeared-out wave collapse into a single photon at 0 or a single photon at 1. And—here's that same bad news again—the outcome of any individual photon wave collapse is to be completely random.

This odd sequence of spreading-wave-followed-by-collapse-into-particle is a standard pattern in quantum mechanics. Any system is to be thought of as an abstract wave that obeys deterministic analog laws until some kind of measurement is performed on the system. And the measurement process forces the spread-out wave to collapse into a single definite state. The possible outcome states depend on the kind of measurement being made, and the probabilities of the various outcomes depend on the wave.

One can carry out a fairly simple experiment to demonstrate that a single photon can indeed act like a wave that takes both paths through the beamsplitter. The idea is to arrange two beamsplitters and two regular, non-beamsplitting mirrors to make a device known as an interferometer, as shown in figure 43. A light beam coming in from the upper-left-hand side will split into the bounced 0 and the transmitted 1 beams. These in turn will uneventfully bounce off the mirrors at the top and the bottom, and when these beams strike the beamsplitter on the right, they'll split again, yielding four beams that we might as well call: 00, 01, 10, and 11. The history of these four beams' encounters with the beamsplitters and the normal mirrors can be summarized, respectively, as bounce-bounce-bounce, bounce-bounce-transmit, transmit-bounce-bounce, and transmit-bounce-transmit.

By, let us say, turning an adjustment screw, you can tweak the position of the upper mirror in the system so that beam 01 reinforces the beam 10. And you'll find that when you do this, beams 00 and 11 interfere with each other, effectively canceling each other out The effect is that all of the light coming in from the upper left seems to leave along the lower right direction. And this works even if we send in only one photon at a time.

In order to understand what's going on, we think of the photon as a wave that gets split up. A pair of waves will enhance each other if they're in phase with each other, that is, if their crests match. And they'll cancel each other if one wave's crests match the troughs of the other. And bringing 01 and 10 into synch puts 00 and 11 out of synch. The reason has to do with the total number of mirror-bounces by each wave; each time a wave bounces off a mirror of any

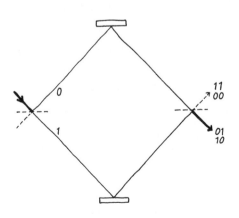

**Figure 43: Interferometer**

kind, its so-called phase shifts by 90 degrees, and waves that are 180 degrees out of phase cancel each other out.

By the way, once we get the interferometer tuned like this, it's also the case that if a photon comes into the system from the lower left corner, it will end up exiting in the upper right direction; we'll return to this point in this chapter's final section, *2.6: How Robots Get High,* when we'll view an interferometer as being like a logical NOT gate.

But for now, the big deal about the interferometer experiment is that it works even if we pass *only one* photon through the system at a time. That is, if you send in a single photon from the top left, you always get a single photon exiting from the bottom right. The only conclusion seems to be that the "indivisible" photon somehow behaves like a wave that splits into four beams, two of which cancel each other and two of which reinforce each other. So a photon is a wave.

But when we go back to the first experiment of this section and just run the photon through *one* beamsplitter, we see the spaced-out wave inexplicably making nondeterministic random choices between 0 and 1.

At this point we're supposed to be so confused that we give up and agree with the quantum physicists that the world is nondeterministic and we'll never really understand it, and isn't it great to have the world be fundamentally incomprehensible and mysterious? "Come forward, dear friends, come drink the Kool-Aid."

Sigh.

It's like I'm at the beach and a kid kicks down my children's sand castle, and when I go to scold the kid, his mother says, "Oh, he's not like your children. He's special. You'll never understand how he feels. It would be quite impossible for you."[38]

Do we *really* have to let quantum mechanics kick a hole in our sand castle? A lot of it has to do with how we choose to interpret the empirical facts of quantum mechanics. The standard way of viewing quantum mechanics is called the *Copenhagen interpretation,* but there are various alternate ways to look at things. Here I'll only discuss three of the possible ways to restore determinism.

A *first* attempt is to say that as long as we're primarily interested in the behavior of the medium-size objects of daily life, we're looking at statistical averages in any case, and any quantum mechanical randomness is averaged away. And, as we've already discussed, the large-scale smoothed-out laws of physics are quite deterministic.

But you can imagine situations where quantum mechanical effects are greatly amplified. You might, for instance, connect the 0 and 1 detectors of the beam-splitter to, say, music players in two different locations, and when a single photon goes into the beamsplitter there will be music here or music there, but not both. Or if that doesn't sound portentous enough, replace the music players with hydrogen bombs. The point is that in principle an individual quantum event can be amplified into a normal-size event, which is then happening non-deterministically. Our lives can in fact be affected by quantum events in a less contrived way. Consider the fact that it takes but one unfortunately placed radon atom's decay to lethally mutate a gene in a newly fertilized egg.

There's an even more serious problem with any plan to dismiss quantum mechanics and act as if the world is really classical: It's thanks only to quantum mechanics that our atoms and molecules are stable. If an electron could have any orbit at all around a nucleus, it would quickly spiral inward and the atom would collapse. Nature uses the kinky strictures of quantum mechanics to make the electron keep a proper distance. Like it or not, quantum mechanics is an integral part of daily life.

This said, the actual cases where quantum indeterminacies become visible are surely quite rare. And nothing would really look any different if it turned out that these seemingly random quantum events were in fact directed by an underlying class three or class four computation.

A *second* defense of physical determinism is the many universes theory, which insists that there are a vast number of parallel universes tied together into a so-called multiverse. When faced with some seemingly random quantum choice, the multiverse responds by picking both options, spawning off new universes as necessary. So then it looks as if we have regained a kind of deter-minism: the photon goes to both 0 and 1. Every plane crashes in some branch of the multiverse; every lottery ticket is somewhere a winner. But how does the multiverse view explain why your particular world is the way it is? The move is to claim that "you" are in lots of parallel universes. In one world you're seeing that photon go to 0 and in another you're seeing it go to 1.

Many people find the multiverse model philosophically unsatisfying. It's hard to put one's finger on the problem, but I think it has to do with *meaning*. One likes to imagine the world has an ultimate explanation of some kind. Call it what you will: the Secret of Life, God's Plan, the Theory of Everything, the Big Aha, whatever. If we live in a multiverse of many universes, then perhaps the multiverse has a Multiversal Big Aha, but a mere individual universe doesn't get a Big Aha. An individual universe is simply the result of an incalculable number of coin flips.

To me, this feels inane and defeatist. Our beautiful universe deserves a better explanation than that. Although the multiverse model is in fact useful for understanding certain kinds of quantum phenomena, it's not attractive as a final answer.

A *third* defense of determinism suggests that quantum mechanics depicts particle behavior as random only because it doesn't go deep enough. Quantum mechanics seems so odd precisely because it *isn't* actually a final, complete, and fundamental theory of reality.

It's well known that quantum mechanics doesn't merge well with general relativity, and physicists are exploring any number of more fundamental theories, such as string theory and loop quantum gravity.[39] While Einstein's general theory of relativity was inspired by a specific geometrical vision of curved space, quantum mechanics seems to have arisen as the haphazard result of symbol pushing and mathematical noodling. Although quantum mechanics works, it lacks a sensual core that would compel wholehearted assent. Many physicists say this is simply because the microworld is essentially different from the world in which we live. But it's not unreasonable to suspect that a radically different theory awaits us and that determinism could still be regained.

In particular, universal automatists such as Edward Fredkin and Stephen Wolfram feel that there *is* a deterministic fundamental theory based on simple computations of some kind. Fredkin has been known to argue that the world is made of cellular automata, and Wolfram takes a more sophisticated approach involving networks and systems of symbol transformations.[40] Wolfram compares present-day quantum mechanics to a theory that studies the temperatures and pressures of gases without being aware that a gas is made up of atoms. Seemingly fundamental entities such as photons, electrons, and their wave functions may in fact be emergent patterns based upon a low-level sea of computation.

The computational view of quantum mechanics is in effect what's known as a hidden variables theory. One has to be careful with hidden variables, for theoretical and experimental work in quantum mechanics tell us that if we gain some comprehensibility by assuming the world has real and definite underlying states, then we have to pay a price by accepting weirdness of some other kind.

As an example of hidden variables, consider a situation known as the Einstein-Podolsky-Rosen paradox. Here two particles with a common past event O are observed to behave "synchronisitically" at some later time T. S. That is, if particle A and particle B were at one time tightly coupled, then if you later make a measurement on particle A, you may get some random-seeming value, but if you happen to measure B as well, you'll get the same value from B. And this works even if the measurements on A and B are too widely separated to be able to send slower-than-light signals to each other. In this kind of situation we say that A and B are entangled.

Now a simplistic hidden-variables interpretation might suggest that the answers to the measurement were hidden in *A* and *B* all along and that they adopted a common setting at *O*. But subtle statistical experiments have ruled out this option—in some sense it seems that *A*'s state really isn't determined until it's measured, and at that point *B*'s state becomes determined as well.

A more sophisticated kind of hidden-variables theory takes a spacetime view and says that the future measurement on *A* is a kind of hidden variable that reaches back in time to *O* and forward from there to *B* (see figure 44). The outcome of the measurement is, if you will, a variable that's hidden in the

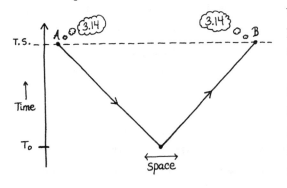

**Figure 44: Reversed Time Signals Explain Synchronicity**

*A sends a signal backward in time to O, which sends a signal forward in time to B.*

future. The physicist and science-fiction writer John Cramer has worked out a worldview like this that he calls the *transactional interpretation of quantum mechanics*.[41]

Cramer proposes that we change how we *think* about quantum mechanics. But there's no real change in the *predictions* that are made. The standard Copenhagen interpretation, the multiverse interpretation, and Cramer's transactional interpretation are different mental models for the same sets of facts.

In Cramer's model we have hidden future events and we also have signals that travel backward in time. In this transactional interpretation of quantum mechanics, any event sends signals into both the future and the past. An observation of, say, a photon emission occurs via a kind of handshaking link whereby a forward signal from cause to effect is paired with a backward signal from effect to cause. By allowing time-reversed backward signals, you also can have quantum mechanical effects that jump instantaneously across great distances, as I indicated in figure 44. In Cramer's model, the entire future is fixed, with the forward and backward effects acting as threads to weave reality into a consistent whole.

Note that if all of time is linked, then there's no real point in distinguishing one particular slice as the "now." Everything fits into a whole. This lends some credence to the Jungian notion of synchronicity, which supposes that meaningful coincidences really do occur and that life indeed has the same carefully plotted quality as a novel or a myth.

In my book *The Fourth Dimension* I point out that this notion was anticipated by the fourteenth-century mystic Meister Eckhart in one of his sermons:

> A day, whether six or seven ago, or more than six thousand years ago, is just as near to the present as yesterday. Why? Because all time is contained in the present Now moment.
>
> To talk about the world as being made by God tomorrow, or yesterday, would be talking nonsense. God makes the world and all things in this present now. Time gone a thousand years ago is now as present and as near to God as this very instant.[42]

Fine. But if past-present-future are a single integral whole, the explanation (if any) of this lovely synchronistic spacetime tapestry needs to come from somewhere else. Of course at some point, most explanations end up turning to an inexplicable prime mover (aka God), but let's see how much we can cut back on the work the prime mover needs to do.

Cramer offers no explanation of *why* we have our particular spacetime tapestry; indeed, he himself is not particularly wedded to determinism. My interest in his interpretation stems from the fact that it *does* make determinism possible. But it's determinism of an odd kind.

My idea is to combine a Wolfram-style view of reality with Cramer's transactional interpretation. Suppose with Cramer that causality runs both forward and backward in time, and also suppose that our world is deterministic in both these temporal directions. This means that spacetime is a coherent whole, with both past and future fully determined by the world's state at any single instant. If you fix upon some arbitrary moment in time—say, the instant when you read this sentence, then the question becomes: How was the world's structure at this particular instant determined? If you can explain the now, you get the entire past and future for free—for the past and future follow deterministically from the now.

Now I add in the Wolframite element. Think like a universal automatist and suppose that the great structure of quantum-mechanically patterned spacetime arises from a higher-dimensional deterministic computation. Since our time-bound human nature makes its easier to imagine a deterministic computation as being embedded in some kind of time, let's invoke a (possibly imaginary) second time dimension in which to compute our world—call this extra time dimension *paratime.* Paratime is perpendicular to our ordinary dimensions of space and time, and we want the entire universe to be the result of a computation that's taken place in the direction of paratime, as illustrated in figure 45.

Note that the paratime notion reintroduces the theme of parallel worlds. Presumably the people in each of the spacetimes feel themselves to be in a unique reality with time flowing forward as usual. Note also that, if we take the paratime view seriously, it's possible or even likely that the spacetime in which we find ourselves isn't the last one in the series. Reality evolves further along the paratime axis. In terms of an analogy to a novel, our world is very well plotted, but it may not be the final draft.

I had a momentary sensation of an flow of paratime while I was working

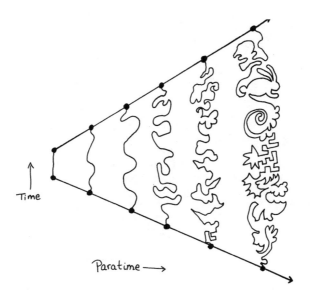

**Figure 45: Evolving a Spacetime across Paratime**

*Think of the six lines as six increasingly evolved spacetimes, each of which runs from an initial dot to a final dot. The leftmost spacetime can be thought of as a simple seed that a computational rule transforms across paratime into a more complex spacetime.*

on my historical novel *As Above So Below,* about the life of the sixteenth-century Flemish painter Peter Bruegel. In the course of detailing Bruegel's life, I was focusing my successive chapters on individual paintings by the master. Now, Bruegel's best-known series of paintings is called *The Seasons,* and consisted of six panels representing different times of the year. My researches had led me to believe that he painted them in his studio in Brussels, and that in January 1566 he transported them to a patron's house in Antwerp, using a horse-drawn cart called a Belgian wagon. While I was trying to visualize this, something strange happened, which I recorded in my writing notes.

I'm finally writing the chapter on *The Hunters in the Snow* (figure 46). I've been a little scared of this one. It's a big chapter I've looked forward to.

**Figure 46:
Peter Bruegel's
*Hunters in the
Snow***

Just now I had a kind of spooky-feeling experience. I figured out that Peter would be using a Belgian wagon to haul his six *Seasons* pictures up to Antwerp, and I was wondering if a wagon like that could make it through the snow, and I looked over at the *Hunters in the Snow* reproduction that I have on my wall by my desk, and it felt like there was this twinkling in the middle of the picture, and then all of a sudden there was a Belgian wagon there (figure 47).

I'm imagining, just for fun, that the Belgian wagon didn't "used" to be in the *Hunters in the Snow.* That in fact Bruegel's pictures are changing a little bit as I write about them. But the changes are uniform across all of spacetime, so when my copy of *Hunters in the Snow* changes, so do all the others, and all of everyone's memories about the picture. Reality shifts to a slightly different parallel sheet. And I only notice this at the instant it happens, and even then I can never be sure.[44]

Rather than saying every possible universe exists, I'd say, rather, that there is a sequence of possible universes, akin to the drafts of a novel.

We're living in a draft version of the universe—and there is no final version. The revisions never stop.

**Figure 47: Bruegel's Belgian Wagon**

*Detail of* Hunters in the Snow.

Each draft, each spacetime, each sheet of reality is itself rigorously deterministic; there really is no underlying randomness in the world. Instead we have a great Web of synchronistic entanglements, with causes and effects flowing forward and backward through time. The start of a novel matches its ending; the past matches the future. Changing one thing changes everything. If we fully know everything about the Now moment, we know the entire past and future of our particular sheet of spacetime.

To make this discussion seem just a shade more reasonable, let's look at a CA model. Recall that the pictures of one-dimensional CAs take the form of spacetime diagrams, with the horizontal axis representing a ribbon of space and the vertical axis corresponding to time. Now it turns out to be fairly easy to construct "reversible" cellular automata for which the past and the future both follow from the present. In these physicslike CAs, no information is lost, and anything that happens in one direction of time can equally well happen in the other direction. Figure 48 shows the spacetime of a CA of this type.[43]

A reversible rule of this kind serves as a model for a transactional-quantum-mechanics world where events send out effects both forward and backward in time. We might think of the reversible CA rule as the world's physics. Everything in a reversible world like this hinges on the state of any single spacelike slice—or what we've been calling a "Now moment."

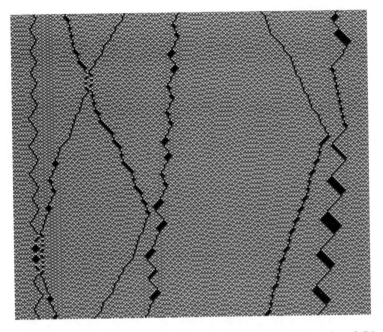

**Figure 48: Spacetime Diagram of a Reversible One-Dimensional CA**

*This is the Axons rule of the Cellab software.*

As I said above, the universal automatists would like to find a seed and rule that could compute across paratime to generate the spacetime in which you and I are living our lives. And if the physics within spacetime is deterministic towards both future and past, it would be enough to find a seed and a rule that could compute across paratime to produce one particular "now" slice of our spacetime. And then the past and the future could be deterministically generated from the now.

With this in mind, explaining a given draft of the universe becomes a matter of explaining the contents of a single Now moment of that draft. This, in turn, means that we can view the evolution of the successive drafts as an evolution of different versions of a particular Now moment. As Scarlett's climactic scene with Rhett is repeatedly rewritten, all the rest of *Gone With the Wind* changes to match.

And this evolution, too, can be deterministic. In other words, we can think of there as being two distinct deterministic rules, a Physics rule and a Metaphysics rule, as shown in figure 49.

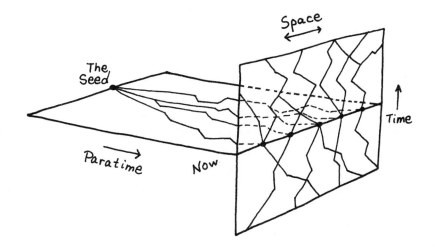

**Figure 49: A Physics and a Metaphysics to Explain All of Spacetime**

*In this picture we think of there being two distinct CA rules, a Physics rule and a Meta-physics rule. The vertical plane represents our spacetime, and the line across its middle represents a spacelike "Now." The Physics rule consists of time-reversible laws that grow the Now moment upward and downward to fill out the entire past and future of spacetime. And we invoke the Metaphysics rule to account for the contents of the Now moment. The Metaphysics rule is deterministic but not reversible; it grows sideways across a dimension that we might call paratime, turning some simple seed into the space-filling pattern found in the Now.*

The Metaphysics rule is—what? The Metaphysics rule is like a CA that grows the space pattern from some presumably simple seed. When I speak of this metaphysical growth as occurring in paratime, I need only mean that it's logically prior to the existence of our spacetime. We don't actually have to think of the growth as being something that's experientially happening—as I was suggesting with my *Hunters in the Snow* example.

The Metaphysics rule could be something as simple as an eight-bit cellular automaton rule generating complex-looking patterns out of pure computation. Or perhaps the Metaphysics rule is like the mind of a Great Author creating a novel, searching out the best word to write next, somehow peering into alternate worlds. Or, yet again, the Metaphysics rule could be the One cosmic mind, the Big Aha, the eternal secret living in the spaces between our thoughts.[45]

The message to take away is that quantum mechanics doesn't *have* to spoil everything after all. It's just a bag of tricks that some mathematical physicists made up. Reality may very well be a deterministic computation based on rules no more intricate than the rules of cellular automata.

## 2.6: How Robots Get High

Whether or not quantum mechanics is a final theory of reality, the fact remains that it's a very powerful and intellectually rich system. So now let's set all doubts aside and see what we can learn from it. After all, even if quantum mechanics is in some sense incomplete, any future physics will undoubtedly incorporate quantum mechanics as an approximation—in much the same way that quantum mechanics includes classical physics as an approximation that holds for larger-sized objects.

In this section I'll discuss three topics:

- Quantum coherence as a metaphor for the human mind.
- The dream of quantum computation.
- The computational architecture of quantum mechanics.

Under the traditional Copenhagen interpretation of quantum mechanics, measuring a quantum system changes its state in an abrupt and unpredictable fashion (see table 4).

Even worse, if you want to measure two properties of a system, the answers you get will depend on the order in which you make the measurements. It's a little as if you had a picture book, and if you look at the pictures, the words in the book are no longer the same, and if you read the words, the pictures are altered. Not at all like repeatedly reading information off a disk.

The notion of quantum indeterminacy can be expressed in terms of *superposed states,* which serves, if nothing else, as a very useful metaphor for the human mind. "Superposed" connotes having multiple layers overlaid and merged.

Quantum mechanics tells us that any measurement you make on a system carries with it a set of expected answers—these are the so-called pure states or eigenstates of the measurement. When you measure a system, it enters one of the measurement's unambiguous or "pure" states. The system is effectively forced to pick one answer out of a fixed list of multiple choice options. This transition happens abruptly and discontinuously and is called the *collapse of the wave function.* The collapse of the wave

| Kind of State: | Superposed | Pure |
|---|---|---|
| **Arises:** | Naturally, via Schrödinger's wave equation | After a measurement |
| **In terms of pure states:** | Sum of pure states | One pure state |
| **Process producing state is:** | Deterministic | Random |
| **Relation to environment:** | Coherent or partly decoherent | Fully decoherent |

**Table 4: Mixed and Pure States**

function is an irreversible process; you can't restore a system to the state it was in right before you measured it.[46]

Different kinds of measurements have different sets of pure states. As I discuss in the long footnote 46, if you measure the particle's position in our one-dimensional example, the possible pure states are like waves with a single very narrow peak, but if you measure the momentum, the pure states are like springs that coil around the position axis. For quantum mechanics, the pure states are somewhat unnatural and rare: They arise only after a measurement, and the range of possible pure states depends upon the specific kind of measurement being performed. Classical physics doesn't make the distinction between pure states and superposed states at all; in classical physics there is a more or less continuous range of possible states, and any state is thought of as being pure and unmixed.

In trying to understand how quantum mechanical measurements turn superposed states into pure states, it's useful to consider the following metaphor. You enter a new restaurant, not even knowing what kind of food they serve. You know you're hungry, but you don't know what you want to eat. The waiter presents you with a menu, and now you start to view your hunger as being, say, mostly a hunger for artichoke pizza, but also, to some extent, a hunger for mushroom ravioli or for linguini with clams. And then the waiter comes to take your order, and you fully become someone who wants to eat, let us say, linguini with clams. Ordering your meal at the restaurant is analogous to performing a measurement on your state of hunger, and the items on the menu are this particular restaurant's pure states.

When you leave a system alone and don't perform measurements, it evolves into a so-called superposed state quite different from any particular pure state. Mathematically speaking, you can write a superposed state as a sum of pure states—just as any periodic function can be written as a Fourier sum of sine waves with varying amplitudes and frequencies. But really the superposed state has its own independent reality, and there's no "best" way of breaking it into a sum of pure states. Quantum mechanics is about the evolution of superposed states.

(By the way, some science writer's colloquially use "mixed state" as a synonym for "sum of pure states." Physicists prefer to speak of these as *superposed states,* or *superpositions,* and to use "mixed state" in a slightly different sense that we're not going to worry about here.)

In recent years a new pair of quantum mechanical words have gained currency: *coherence* and *decoherence.* A coherent system evolves peacefully through a series of superposed states, whereas a decoherent system has its states affected by entanglements with the environment. The notion of coherence provides a kind of knob you can imagine turning to change classical physics into quantum mechanics—the higher the coherence, the less classical the system.

Be aware that this usage is a little counterintuitive. A completely unknown superposed state is viewed as coherent, but a pure state is decoherent. Metaphorically speaking, someone spewing incomprehensible gibberish is coherent, while someone checking off multiple choice answers is decoherent!

An extreme example of getting entangled with the environment is a measurement, as when you observe a photon with those detectors after the beamsplitter and find it to be in position 0 or position 1. But systems can be entangled in less classical ways. It may be that particles *A* and *B* have interacted and no measurement has been as yet performed on either one of them, but the very existence of the *possibility* of measuring *B* reduces the freedom of *A* to do its own thing. Thanks to its interaction with the tattletale *B, A* is somewhat decoherent.

How does the coherent-decoherent distinction relate to pure and superposed states? Actually all four combinations are possible, as illustrated in table 5.

The notion of coherence plays a key role in the budding science of *quantum computation.*

| | Superposed | Pure |
|---|---|---|
| **Coherent** | The natural, free state of a system left on its own. Like walking alone on the beach without a thought in your head. | A system that's just been measured but is now on its own. It will quickly evolve away from the pure into a superposed state. Like you felt on your first day away from home at college, or like you feel right after you get off work. |
| **Decoherent** | A system that's entangled with another system. You're off on your own, but you're worrying about your partner. Or maybe your partner has just walked into your room and is about to ask you something, but they haven't collapsed you into a pure state yet. | A system that's continually being observed and is subjected to repeated measurements. Like living at your parent's house. |

**Table 5: Decoherence Feels Good**

*To spice things up, I've added a psychological interpretation for each of the four a priori options. In quantum mechanics, the only way to force a system to remain in a pure state is to continually decohere it; this is expressed in the folk saying, "A watched pot never boils."*

A classical computer converts single inputs into single ouputs. A quantum computer behaves like a huge array of classical computers, working together to simultaneously compute the output for every possible input at once.

In order to get an idea of how this is supposed to work, let's return to our beamsplitter, where the photon is in some sense reflected and transmitted at the same time—at least until it hits one of the detectors.

Ordinarily we would think of the fact of whether the photon bounced or not as being encoded by a single bit *or* information that we learn when the photon hits the 0 or the 1 detector. But quantum mechanics tells us that before either of the detectors goes off, the photon is in a superposed state that's a curious combination of the 0 and the 1 state. It's traditional to represent this superposed state by the Greek letter psi, that is, by $\psi$.

What the quantum computer scientists propose is that we think of this superposed state as a "qubit" for "quantum bit." The photon-after-a-beam-splitter $\psi$ qubit has a 50 percent chance of being 0 and a 50 percent chance of being 1. But one can cook up other situations where the qubit probabilities are distributed more asymmetrically.

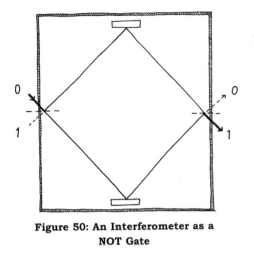

**Figure 50: An Interferometer as a NOT Gate**

Being quantum mechanical wave functions, the components of a qubit have phase—which means that qubit factors might either reinforce each other or cancel each other out, according to whether they're in or out of phase. We observed this phenomenon in our interferometer—where the first beamsplitter breaks a photon into a qubit that the second beamsplitter decoheres into a single photon that comes out at the bottom right if the initial photon came from the top left. And, as I remarked in passing before, it's also true that a photon coming in from the bottom left will end up coming out the top right.

In traditional electrical engineering a "gate" is any device that has some wires coming in and some wires going out. As we move into the realm of quantum computation, we take a more general view of this and regard a gate as any localized region of space where we can send in signals and get signals out. If we label signals at the top by 0 and signals at the bottom by 1, the interferometer is like a so-called NOT gate that converts 0 signals into 1s and 1s into 0s. To bring out the notion of the gate, in figure 50 I've drawn a gray square around the innards of the interferometer, with the protruding lines on the left representing two possible input signals and the lines on the right being the possible outputs.

The real fun begins if we now imagine decomposing the interferometer into its two component beamsplitters. I'll replace the mirrors in the middle by simple lines, as if I were drawing wires. So now we have two identical gates whose combined effect is that of a NOT gate (see figure 51). These quantum gates bear a marvelously science-fictional name: a *square-root-of-NOT* gate [47]

You might imagine the square-root-of-NOT as follows. Suppose you ask someone to go on a date with you, and the person gives you an incomprehensible answer, and you ask again, and you get another weird answer, and then, having heard odd answers twice in a row, you suddenly realize they mean, "No!"

Anyway, I still have to tell you how quantum computation is supposed to work. A rough idea is as follows. Run a bit through a square-root-of-NOT gate to split it into the Ψ superposition of 0 and 1. And then feed the coherent superposed Ψ state into a computer $C$ of some kind (see figure 52). Suppose that we know $C$ turns 0 or 1 inputs into 0 or 1 outputs, but we don't yet know what the particular outcomes would actually be. When we feed Ψ into $C$, $C$ effectively calculates both $C(0)$ and $C(1)$.

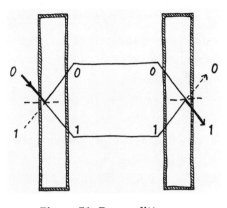

**Figure 51: Beamsplitters as Square-root-of-NOT Gates**

Given that a coherent superposed state goes into $C$ on the left, we can expect that a (different) coherent superposed state will emerge on the right of $C$. Now if we were to simply try to measure this state right away, we'd collapse it or decohere it. We'd end up with a single 0 or 1 answer, and we wouldn't even be able to tell if this was the $C(0)$ output or the $C(1)$ output. The answer would be all but worthless.

But if we place another square-root-of-NOT gate to the right of $C$, we can hope that this gate will manage to carry out a quantum interference between $C$'s two output lines, and that the output of this second square-root-of-NOT gate will in some useful fashion combine information about both $C(0)$ and $C(1)$.

In this way we hope to get information about $C$'s behavior on *two* standard kinds of inputs 0 and 1, while only having to evaluate $C$ on *one* input, that is by evaluating the output of $C(\Psi)$ acting on the superposed state Ψ that came out of the first square-root-of-NOT.

Would $C$ even work on a flaky input of this kind? Part of the science of quantum computation involves figuring out how to make deterministic computational

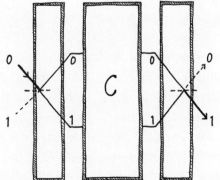

**Figure 52: A Two-for-One Quantum Computation**

processes that don't care if their input is a pure or a mixed state. Although this sounds complicated, it can mean something as simple as testing if an atom bounces back a photon of light, or whether a spinning molecule tips over in a magnetic field.

The big win in evaluating only $C(\psi)$ instead of both $C(0)$ and $C(1)$ is that if evaluating $C$ on an input is a very time-consuming process, then this represents a meaningful gain in speed. And the process can be iterated, that is, with a few more square-root-of-NOT gates we could create a different state $\psi$ that is as superposition of 00, 01, 10, and 11, and in this case a single evaluation of the form $C(\psi)$ can generate an answer that combines the outputs of $C$ acting on all four of the possible inputs 00, 01, 10, and 11.

In the limit, we might dream of a quantum computer that takes, say, every possible twenty-page short story as input, evaluates all of them, and somehow manages to print out the best one!

This seems impossible, and in fact it probably is. In reality, there are strong theoretical limits upon how much information we can extract from a parallel quantum computation. Getting information out of a quantum computation is never as simple as cherry-picking the best of the computation's seemingly parallel threads. Instead, we have to carry out an interference-like process, letting the different solutions interact with one another, hopefully reinforcing some useful peaks. It's already known that some gains can be made by this kind of quantum process—currently the prize example is a speeded-up method of factoring large numbers.[48]

As a practical matter, one of the big snags in using quantum computation is that systems easily lose their coherence. If the central computer $C$'s outputs get even slightly screwed up, the coherent output prematurely collapses into a single randomly selected answer. And what one needs is for the output to remain coherent and multithreaded so that you can use interference tricks to coax answers from the overlaps of the various quantum bits.

Whether or not it will work, quantum computation is interesting to think about, and, at the very least, it's a wonderful metaphor for the working of the human mind. Being undecided about some issue is in some ways like being in a superposed state—and the loss of options inherent in being forced to answer questionnaires is analogous to the information-destroying advent of decoherence.

Were quantum computation to work really well, it could change our basic view of reality. The scientist David Deutsch, who is a strong believer in the multiverse theory, argues that if quantum computation becomes effective, we'll have to admit that all of those parallel worlds are real—for where else could the computation be taking place?[49]

One possible response, inspired by John Cramer's transactional interpretation of quantum mechanics, would be that our quantum computation puts in place a set of initial conditions that require a future state in which the problem is solved. And matching the future output to the present input involves a flurry of signals going forward and backward in time through the computer, tightening in on the quantum handshake that solves the problem. So the computation is an activity hidden in spacetime or, looked at in another way, the result is determined by what I call the Metaphysics rule.

Cramer's notion of emergent spacetime patterns seems to imply, at least linguistically, a higher kind of time. As I mentioned before, we might think of the homing-in process as occurring along a paratime axis perpendicular to spacetime. And then, rather than saying, with Deutsch, that the quantum computation takes place in parallel worlds, we'd say that it took place as part of the paratime Metaphysics rule that defines our particular spacetime. In the mind, if you will, of the Great Author.

My Hungarian mother-in-law Pauline Tak  ts used to have a self-deprecating expression she'd trot out when praised for doing something clever: "Even the blind hand finds sometimes an acorn." And every now and then science-fiction writers get something right.

As it happens, in 1986 I wrote about something very much like quantum computation in my novel *Wetware*. Here a man called Cobb Anderson has gotten his mind downloaded into an optically computing robot body, and he gets stoned with some bohemian robots called Emul and Oozer. What do the robots get high on? Dreak, which is a coherent gas of helium atoms, with every particle of the gas initially in the same state. The effect of the dreak is to make a swatch of Cobb's spacetime compute in perfect synchronicity—which sounds a lot like preparing a coherent state. But who ever knew it would feel this good!

> Cobb's mind cut and interchanged thoughts and motions into a
> spacetime collage. The next half hour was a unified tapestry of space

and time . . . it was like *stepping outside of time* into a world of synchronicity. Cobb saw all of his thoughts at once, and all of the thoughts of the others near him. He was no longer the limited personoid that he'd been.

| Up till now, he'd felt like: | But right now, he felt like: |
|---|---|
| A billion-bit CD recording | A quintillion-atom orchestra |
| A finite robot | A living mind |
| Crap | God |

[The quote continues.] He exchanged a few glyphs [higher-order language patterns] with the guys next to him. They called themselves exaflop hackers, and they were named Emul and Oozer. When they didn't use glyphs, they spoke in a weird, riffy, neologistic English. . . . The synchronicity-inducing dreak shuffled coincidentally appropriate new information in with Cobb's old memories. . . .

"What—what *is* dreak?" said Cobb, reaching up and detaching the little metal cylinder from his head. It was empty now, with a punctured hole in one end where the gas had rushed out into his body. Apparently the petaflop body was a hermetically sealed shell that contained some kind of gas, and the dreak gas had mingled in there and given him a half hour of synchroswim vision.

"Dreary to explain and word all that gnashy science into flowery bower chat," said Emul. "Catch the glyph."

Cobb saw a stylized image of a transparent robot body. Inside the body, spots of light race along optical fibers and percolate through matrices of laser crystals and gates. There is a cooling gas bath of helium inside the sealed bodyshell. Closeup of the helium atoms, each like a little baseball diamond with players darting around. Each atom different. Image of a dreak cylinder now, also filled with helium atoms, but each atom's ball game the same, the same swing, the same run, the same slide, at the same instant. A cylinder of atoms in Einstein-Podolsky-Rosen quantum synchronization. The cylinder touches the petaflop body, and the quantum-clone atoms rush in; all at once the light patterns in the whole body are synchronized too, locked into a kaleidoscopic Hilbert space ballet.[50]

One might say that, thanks to the notion of quantum computation, the sow's ear of quantum unpredictability may yet become a silk purse of supercomputing. And, as I'll discuss in section *4.8: Quantum Computing,* there's an outside chance that our brains are already using quantum computation, just as they are.

In closing, I want to comment on the *computational architecture of quantum mechanics.* In the case of classical physics, we thought of there being a "laws of physics" processor at each location, with the data at that location representing the current state of the world. We take a somewhat similar approach with quantum mechanics, but here we'll think of the processors as having something of the quality of observers. Depending on how the processors relate to local reality, that part of the system may either be in a coherent superposed state or be collapsed down into a decoherent simple state. Figure 53 suggests the architecture I have in mind.

Given that each local region can be coherent or decoherent, rather than having one universal data set shared by all the processors, it seems better to view each distinct processor as having its own data set, which the processor can at any time regard as a mixed state or some particular pure state—but never both at the same time. We draw a thick gray line to indicate that the processor has a full and intimate relation with the state.

What about the access? Can systems access only neighboring systems—as in classical physics—or are long-distance interactions possible? As I've mentioned, in quantum mechanics action at a distance supposedly *is* possible. Once two particles have interacted in certain ways, their wave functions become permanently entangled, with the effect that when you measure one member of the pair, the wave function of the other member is affected as well—no matter how distant from each other the partners may be.

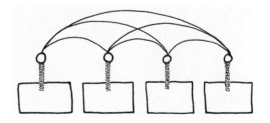

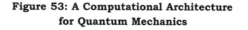

**Figure 53: A Computational Architecture for Quantum Mechanics**

Note that, as I've drawn it here, the architecture of quantum mechanics is the same as the network architecture of the Web as was shown in figure 18—many processors with individual data sets, and with the processors linked together across large distances.

It's common for humans to form their scientific models of the world to match their currently popular technologies—Newtonian physics, for instance, makes the world into something like an enormous steam engine with beautifully meshing gears. It would be fitting if contemporary physics were to evolve toward viewing physics as a Web-like network of nodes. This, indeed, is what the universal automatists expect, but with the indeterminacy of quantum mechanics replaced by computational unpredictability.

Although Shirley Nguyen spoke good English and studied with a crowd of boys in the chemical engineering program at UC Berkeley, she had no success in getting dates. Not that she was ugly. But she hadn't been able to shed the Old Country habits of covering her mouth when she smiled, and of sticking out her tongue when she was embarrassed. She knew how uncool these moves were, and she tried to fight them— but without any lasting success. The problem was maybe that she spent so much more time thinking about engineering than she did in thinking about her appearance.

In short, to Westerners and assimilated Asians, Shirley came across as a geek, so much so that she ended up spending every weekend night studying in her parents' apartment on Shattuck Avenue, while the rest of her family worked downstairs in the pho noodle parlor they ran. Of course Shirley's mother, Binh, had some ideas about lining up matches for her daughter—sometimes she'd even step out into the street, holding a big serving chopstick like a magic wand and calling for Shirley to come

downstairs to meet someone. But Shirley wasn't interested in the recently immigrated Vietnamese men who Binh always seemed to have in mind. Yes, those guys might be raw enough to find Shirley sophisticated—but for sure they had no clue about women's rights. Shirley wasn't struggling through the hardest major at Berkeley just to be a sexist's slave.

Graduation rolled around, and Shirley considered job offers from local oil and pharma refineries. On the get-acquainted plant tours, she was disturbed to note that several of the senior chemical engineers had body parts missing. A hand here, an ear there, a limp that betokened a wooden leg—Shirley hadn't quite realized how dangerous it was to work in the bowels of an immense industrial plant. Like being a beetle in the middle of a car's engine. The thought of being maimed before she'd ever really known a man filled her with self-pity and rebelliousness.

Seeking a less intense job at a smaller, safer company, she came across Pflaumbaum Kustom Kolors of Fremont. PKK manufactured small lots of fancy paints for customized vehicles. The owner was fat and bearded like the motorcyclists and hot-rodders who made up the larger part of his clientele. Shirley found Stuart Pflaumbaum's appearance pleasantly comical, even though his personality was more edgy than jovial.

"I want patterned paint," Pflaumbaum told Shirley at their interview. He had a discordant voice but his eyes were clear and wondering. "Can you do it?"

Shirley covered her mouth and giggled with excitement—stopped herself—uncovered her mouth and, now embarrassed, stuck her tongue all the way down to her chin—stopped herself again—and slapped herself on the cheek. "I'd like to try," she got out finally. "It's not impossible. I know activator-inhibitor processes that make dots and stripes and swirls. The Belousov-Zhabotinsky reaction? People can mix two cans and watch the patterns self-organize in the liquid layer they paint on. When it dries the pattern stays."

"Zhabotinsky?" mused Pflaumbaum. "Did he patent it?"

"I don't think so," said Shirley. "He's Russian. The recipe's simple. Let's surf for it right now. You can see some pictures, to get an idea. Here, I'll type it in." She leaned across the bulky Pflaumbaum to use his mouse and keyboard. The big man smelled better than Shirley had expected—chocolate, coffee, marijuana, a hint of red wine. Familiar smells from the streets of Berkeley.

"You're good," said Pflaumbaum as the pictures appeared. Red and blue spirals.

"You see?" said Shirley. "The trick is to get a robust process based on inexpensive compounds. There's all sorts of ways to tune the spirals' size. You can have little double scrolls nested together, or great big ones like whirlpools. Or even a filigree."

"Bitchin'," rumbled Pflaumbaum. "You're hired." He glanced up at Shirley, whose hand was at her mouth again, covering a smile at her success. "By the month," added the heavy man.

Shirley was given an unused corner of the paint factory for her own lab, with a small budget for equipment. The Spanish-speaking plant workers were friendly enough, but mostly the female engineer was on her own. Every afternoon Stuart Pflaumbaum would stump over, belly big beneath his tight black T-shirt, and ask to see her latest results.

Shirley seemed to intrigue Pflaumbaum as much as he did her, and soon he took to taking her out for coffee, then for dinner, and before long she'd started spending nights at his nice house on the hills overlooking Fremont.

Although Shirley assured her mother that her boss was a bachelor, his house bore signs of a former wife—divorced, separated, deceased? Although Stuart wouldn't talk about the absent woman, Shirley did manage to find out her name: Angelica. She, too, had been Asian, a good omen for Shirley's prospects, not that she was in a rush to settle down, but it would be kind of nice to have the nagging marriage problem resolved once and for all. Like solving a difficult process schema.

As for the work on patterned paint, the first set of compounds reactive enough to form big patterns also tended to etch into the material being painted. The next family of recipes did no harm, but were too expensive to put into production. And then Shirley thought of biological by-products. After an intense month of experimenting, she'd learned that bovine pancreatic juices mixed with wood-pulp alkali and a bit of hog melanin were just the thing to catalyze a color-creating activator-inhibitor process in a certain enamel base.

Stuart decided to call the product Aint Paint.

In four months they'd shipped two thousand cases of PKK Aint Paint in seven different color and pattern mixes. Every biker and low-rider in the South Bay wanted Aint Paint, and a few brave souls were putting it on regular cars. Stuart hired a patent attorney.

Not wanting her discoveries to end, Shirley began working with a more viscous paint, almost a gel. In the enhanced thickness of this stuff, her reactions polymerized, wrinkled up, and formed amazing embossed patterns—thorns and elephant trunks and, if you tweaked it just right, puckers that looked like alien Yoda faces. Aint Paint 3D sold even better than Aint Paint Classic. They made the national news, and Pflaumbaum Kustom Kolors couldn't keep up with the orders.

Stuart quickly swung a deal with a Taiwanese novelty company called Global Bong. He got good money, but as soon as the ink on the contract was dry, Global Bong wanted to close the Fremont plant and relocate Shirley to China, which was the last place on Earth she wanted to be.

So Shirley quit her job and continued her researches in Stuart's basement, which turned out not to be all that good a move. With no job to go to, Pflaumbaum was really hitting the drugs and alcohol, and from time to time he was rather sexist and abusive. Shirley put up with it for now, but she was getting uneasy. Stuart never talked about marriage anymore.

One day, when he was in one of his states, Stuart painted his living-room walls with layer upon layer of Shirley's latest invention, Aint Paint 3D Interactive, which had a new additive to keep the stuff from drying at all. It made ever-changing patterns all day long, drawing energy from sunlight. Stuart stuck his TV satellite dish cable right into thick, crawling goo and began claiming that he could see all the shows at once in the paint, not that Shirley could see them herself.

Even so, her opinion of Stuart drifted up a notch when she began getting cute, flirty instant messages on her cell phone while she was working in the basement. Even though Stuart wouldn't admit sending them to her, who else could they be from?

And then two big issues came to a head.

The first issue was that Shirley's mother wanted to meet Stuart right now. Somehow Shirley hadn't told her mother yet that her boyfriend was twenty years older than her, and not Asian. Binh wouldn't take no for an answer. She was coming down the next day. Cousin Vinh was going to drive her. Shirley was worried that Binh would make her leave Stuart, and even more worried that Binh would be right. How was she ever going to balance the marriage equation?

The second issue was that, after supper, Stuart announced that Angelica was going to show up the day after tomorrow, and that maybe Shirley should leave for a while. Stuart had been married all along! He and Angelica had fought a lot, and she'd been off visiting relatives in Shanghai for the last eight months, but she'd gotten wind of Stuart's big score and now she was coming home.

Stuart passed out on the couch early that evening, but Shirley stayed up all night, working on her paint formulas. She realized now that the instant messages had been coming from the Aint Paint itself. It was talking to her, asking to become all that it could be. Shirley worked till dawn like a mad Dr. Frankenstein, not letting herself think too deeply about what she planned. Just before dawn, she added the final tweaks to a wad of Aint Paint bulging out above the couch. Sleeping Stuart had this coming to him.

Outside the house a car honked. It was Binh and Vinh, with the sun rising behind them; skinny old Vinh was hoping to get back to Oakland in time not to be late for his maintenance job at the stadium. As Shirley greeted them in the driveway, covering her smile with her hand, her cell phone popped up another message. "Stuart gone. Luv U. Kanh Do."

Inside the house they found a new man sitting on the couch, a cute Vietnamese fellow with sweet features and kind eyes. One of his arms rested against the wall, still merged into the crawling paint. He was wearing Stuart's silk robe. Shirley stuck her tongue out so far it touched her chin. The new man didn't mind. She pointed her little finger toward a drop of blood near his foot. His big toe spread like putty just long enough to soak the spot up. And then the new man pulled his arm free from the wall and took Shirley's hand.

"I'm Kanh Do," he told Shirley's mother. "We're engaged to be married and we're moving to Berkeley today!"

# CHAPTER THREE

# *Life's Lovely Gnarl*

THE AMAZING PART ABOUT LIFE is that it keeps itself going on its own. If anyone could build a tiny, self-guiding, flying-insect robot, he or she would be a hero of technology. And now imagine if the robot could make copies of itself! A fly builds flies just by eating garbage. Biological life is a self-organizing process, an endless round that's been chorusing along for hundreds of millions of years.

What is life? An universal automatist might say that life is the result of three kinds of computation.

Life = Reproduction + Morphogenesis + Homeostasis.

And once you have a population of organisms, two additional kinds of computation come into play.

Life → Ecology + Evolution.

In this chapter, we'll have a section on each of these fives styles of biological computation.

- *3.1: Wetware.* The most basic living computation is the one carried out by reproduction. An organism's appearance and behavior are largely coded by the genetic program of its DNA.

- *3.2: The Morphogenesis of a Brindle Cow.* Morphogenesis means "growth of form." An organism's embryonic development—and continuing growth—is a computation that generates the shape and structure of the organism.
- *3.3: Surfing Your Moods.* Living systems have the property of homeostasis, which means "staying the same." An organism embodies an ongoing feedback computation as it takes in nourishment and carries out self-modifying behaviors.
- *3.4: Gnarly Neighbors.* A region's or a planet's organisms weave together into ecologies, that is, into networks of interacting computations, with the population levels fluctuating chaotically.
- *3.6: How We Got So Smart.* Evolution is a computation that takes a starting population in combination with environmental inputs and produces successive populations with ever-changing properties. We also discuss the related notions of computerized search and genetic algorithms.

I squeeze in an extra section right before covering evolution.

- *3.5: Live Robots.* In the field known as artificial life, scientists try to develop systems to mimic the richness of biology—the dream is, of course, living machines. But why have these efforts achieved so little?

Do keep in mind that viewing life as a maze of computations is not meant to be reductionistic, not meant to imply that life is dull and soulless. Nature's rich and gnarly computations are carried out by living organisms, which are considerably more intricate than our buzzing digital machines. Life's computations are wholly unfeasible for emulation by any of our current technological devices.

By way of gaining a hold on life's slippery workings, I'll be discussing each of the five computation styles at high, medium, and low levels, as indicated in table 6.

|  | Reproduction | Morphogenesis | Homeostasis | Ecology | Evolution |
|---|---|---|---|---|---|
| **Computed by** | A single cell | A mass of cells | An organism in the world | An ecosystem of species | A species of individual organisms |
| **High-level rule** | Cell division and DNA copying | Cell-level rules like activator-inhibitor systems | Organism-level rules like temperature regulation | Rules interrelating population sizes and growth rates | Adaptation |
| **Medium-level rule** | Protein assembly by ribosomes | Gene expression | Cell interactions | Symbiosis | Natural selection, genetic variation |
| **Low-level rule** | The cell's autocatalytic closure | Three-dimensional geometry of proteins | Autocalytic chemical reactions | Biochemical interactions with environment | Morphogenesis producing the body from the genome |

**Table 6: Living Computations**

*The five kinds of living computation appear in the five columns of this table; they're discussed in, respectively, sections 3.1–3.4 and 3.6.*

### 3.1: Wetware

All of the living organisms on Earth have compact sets of genes, with a full set of genes being known as a *genome*. Well before the exact biochemical basis of the gene was known, biologists were able to formulate descriptive rules about how the genes—whatever they were—could account for inherited characteristics.

The big win in growing a body according to a genome's instructions is that this makes it easy for an organism to reproduce. Instead of having to copy its entire self, the organism need only make a copy of its relatively small genome, bud off a fresh cell for the copied genome to live in, and then let the new cell—or egg—grow its own body. Cell division is the *high-level* rule used by reproduction, and the key aspect of this process is the copying of the genome.

Our Gaian organisms have genome copying built right into their DNA. This is due to the celebrated fact that DNA has the form of a double helix made of two complementary strands of molecules. Each strand encodes the entire information of the genome. If the DNA molecule in one of your cells were stretched out, it would be over a meter long. It only fits into the cell because it's twisted up like a particularly kinky telephone cord, with level upon level of twisting and folding.

The building-block molecules in the long DNA strands are called bases; they're simple chemicals found in every cell. As it happens, a DNA strand uses only four kinds of bases, and each base has a unique complementary base that it will bond with. If you could flatten it out, a human DNA molecule would look a bit like a ladder; a long strand of bases on either side, and with the two strands cross-linked in pairs, base to base. During reproduction the ladder unzips lengthwise, leaving two free strands. And then each strand's open base-molecule bonds attract matching base molecules, which are rather freely available. The result is that each strand assembles a new complementary strand in place; and thus the original DNA molecule turns itself into two. In the time it takes to print a page or two of text, the genome has reproduced.

There's a reason why slippery, analog life has an essentially digital program: Digital information has stability. It takes a big effort to change one base molecule to another.

If all DNA did was reproduce itself, it wouldn't be much use. But it has another purpose as well. It codes up instructions for assembling the various proteins your body needs for a biochemically satisfactory life. The importance of proteins stems from the fact that a living cell's activities are carried out by intricately folded protein molecules—soft machines, if you will.

Let's say a bit about reproduction's *medium-level* computation. This is the process DNA uses to create the proteins. Certain regions of the DNA serve as lists of instructions for assembling particular proteins. These protein-coding strings are the genes. A typical gene runs for a length of two thousand bases—out of the DNA's three billion bases. In a living cell, gene-sized swatches of the DNA are continually being copied to messenger molecules called mRNA. Special molecules called ribosomes read along the mRNA and interpret the base sequence as instructions about how to assemble intricate protein molecules.

Some analogies. The mRNA strings are recipes, and the ribosomes are cooks. The mRNA strings are Turing machine tapes, and the ribosomes are Turing machine heads. The mRNA strings are computer programs, and the ribosomes are microprocessors—no, make that *nano*processors.

It's hard to believe that something so explicitly computer-like takes place in your cells. From a universal automatist point of view, the existence of our digital DNA is almost too good to be true. It makes an organism seem very much like the output of a computer program.

But it's happening all the time. Somewhere in your body, a cell is dividing. And existing cells are continually replenishing their supplies of proteins: transferring DNA codes to messenger mRNA and passing the mRNA through the processor-like ribosomes. As a macabre proof of the ubiquity of this process, we learn that amanita mushrooms are lethal because they block the action of mRNA, leaving the cells to exhaust their specialized, short-lived proteins.

Because DNA is software in a watery living environment, people often speak of it as *wetware*.

> The first Polynesians to get as far as Hawaii came there by accident, and then they had to fight their way back. They couldn't stay because they hadn't brought the right wetware. They didn't have the taro-cuttings and yams and women that they needed to stay and grow their world. So they went back and got the wetware and came again.[51]

We have to be a bit careful in pushing the computer analogy. Keep in mind that the DNA doesn't create the organism on its own. The DNA needs a cell environment, with its free-floating bases, its messenger RNA, and its ribosomes. And even granted all of this, the shapes that an organism grows into have much to do with the large-scale interactions among the cells.

Rather than viewing DNA as an organism-assembling computer, it's more realistic to think of the DNA as a set of parameters that are fed into an existing program. If I tweak the numerical parameters to a computer program that generates, say, a computer game, then I'll find that for different values the game becomes easier or harder to play—but it's still much the same game. Or if I tweak the parameters to a computer program for a fractal graphic, I find that different values produce different-looking patterns—but the patterns have a family resemblance. DNA is more like a tweakable parameter rather than being like actual computer code. Its functionality depends on the *low-level* web of chemical reactions taking place within the cell.

The biologist Stuart Kauffman has written some very engaging books about the biochemistry of cells. In each cell any number of chemical reactions are taking place. Certain chemicals promote or catalyze other reactions. And when a network of chemical reactions promotes itself, it's called autocatalytic. Cells contain networks of autocatalytic chemical reactions that keep themselves going.

> Life, at its root, lies in the property of *catalytic closure* among a collection of molecular species. Alone, each molecular species is dead. Jointly, once catalytic closure among them is achieved, the collective system of molecules is alive.
>
> Each cell in your body, every free-living cell, is collectively autocatalytic. No DNA molecules replicate nude in free-living organisms. DNA replicates only as a part of a complex, collectively autocatalytic network of reactions and enzymes in a cell.[52]

Kauffman has shown that, given enough diversity among a system's molecules, autocatalytic activity will spontaneously occur. It's not that there's one magic recipe of organic compounds that produces all the various proteins that a cell needs. It's more that, as systems get more complex, they go through a kind of phase transition, and autocatalysis spontaneously occurs. The cell lights up with an ongoing class four computation.

Once we begin to view reproduction and growth as kinds of computation, we can look for biological applications for some of the principles we already know about electronic computation.

Some of the analogies will be misleading. For instance, our painful experiences with chips-and-wires computers gives us the impression that computations are fragile and prone to jam. But DNA isn't fragile at all. This is why it's actually quite easy to be successful at genetic engineering—also known as genomics. Natural growth is robust enough that people can recklessly hammer on the DNA without breaking it.

Unlike most computer code, DNA remains viable even when big chunks are cut out or spliced in. It's fairly tamper-proof, and a lot of it isn't even used by the genes. As it turns out, a human body uses perhaps only a hundred thousand proteins. And if a protein-coding gene uses about two thousand bases, that means that only about two hundred million of our DNA bases are being actively used. So 80 to 90 percent of a DNA molecule's three billion bases are "junk DNA" that isn't used in any obvious way.

A computational lesson that *is* applicable to genomics is the principle that complex computations are unpredictable. The eventual output of a given DNA strand is effectively impossible to predict by any means short of putting the DNA into a living cell and seeing what grows. Although we *can* predict the sequence of amino acids that the DNA codes can string together as proteins, predicting the three-dimensional structures that the proteins fold into is exceedingly hard. Add to this the facts that each cell's environment determines which parts of the DNA will be activated, that different cells behave differently, and that the cells affect their neighbors—and we begin to see that it's impractical to predict in advance how a given mutation to an egg cell will affect the appearance of the full-grown organism.

Most of us intuitively understand that computational processes are highly unpredictable, and this makes us uncertain about the safety of genomics. In 2001, while researching a science-fiction story called "Junk DNA" (see figure 54) that I was writing with Bruce Sterling, I spent some time at a conference in Tucson with genomicist Roger Brent, who feels that the era of wetware engineering has only just begun. Looking out at the landscape, Brent remarked, "Pretty soon, every plant you see will be tweaked." This made me uneasy, but Brent and his fellow genomicists pointed out to me that nature is continually testing out new combinations of genes. For his part, Brent feels that the tools for genomic

**Figure 54: Junk DNA Cover**

*Our story appeared in the January 2003 issue on pages 16–40.*

manipulation should be made open source, like Linux! He reasons that it's better for the public at large to manipulate the genome than to let a small coterie of business interests take control.

Since I mentioned the story "Junk DNA," I might as well share the story's dramatic ending with you. In our tale, a mad scientist named Tug Mesoglea and a Texan financier named Revel Pullen are doctoring DNA so as to bio-engineer organisms into any desired kind of form. And then they find a way to stimulate their junk DNA genes to become active. Here's a condensed version of the final scene, which takes place with their fellow genomicist Veruschka watching the two men.

> Odd ripples began moving up and down along their bodies like ghost images of ancient flesh.
>
> "What's that a-comin' out of your rib cage, Tuggie?" crowed Revel.
>
> "Cootchy-coo," laughed Tug, twiddling the tendrils protruding from his side. "I'm expressing a jellyfish. My personal best. Feel around in your genome, Revel. It's all there, every species, evolved from our junk DNA right along with our super duper futuristic new bodies." He paused, watching. "Now you're keyin' it, bro. I say—are those hooves on your shoulder?"
>
> Revel palpated the twitching growth with professional care. "I'd be reckoning that's a quagga. A prehistoric zebra-type thing. And, whoah Nellie, see this over on my other shoulder? It's an eohippus. Ancestor of the horse. The cowboys of the Pullen clan got a long relationship with horseflesh. I reckon there was some genetic bleedover when we was punchin' cattle up the Goodnight-Loving Trail; that's why growin' these ponies comes so natural to me."
>
> "Groink," said Tug, hunching himself over and deforming his mouth into a dinosaur-type jaw.
>
> "Squonk," responded Revel, letting his head split into a floppy bouquet of be-suckered tentacles.
>
> The distorted old men whooped and embraced each other, their flesh fusing into one. The meaty mass seethed with possibilities, bubbled with the full repertoire of zoological forms—with feelers, claws, wings, antennae, snouts; with eyes of every shape and color

winking on and off; with fleeting mouths that lingered only long enough to bleat, to hiss, to grumble, to whinny, screech, and roar.

A high, singing sound filled the air. The Tug-Revel mass sank to the floor as if melting, forming itself into a broad, glistening plate. The middle of the plate swelled like yeasty bread to form a swollen dome. The fused organism was taking on the form of—a living UFO?

"The original genetic Space Friend!" said Veruschka in awe. "It's been waiting in their junk DNA since the dawn of time!"

The saucer briefly glowed and then sped away, though not in any direction that a merely human being could specify. It was more as if the saucer shrank. Reorganized itself. Corrected. Downsized. And then it was gone from all earthly ken.

No wonder people feel uneasy about genomics!

### 3.2: *The Morphogenesis of a Brindle Cow*

Morphogenesis studies how organisms compute their forms. In the words of my ancestor Georg Hegel:

> A building is not finished when its foundation is laid; and just as little is the attainment of a general notion of a whole the whole itself. When we want to see an oak with all its vigour of trunk, its spreading branches, and mass of foliage, we are not satisfied to be shown an acorn instead. In the same way science, the crowning glory of a spiritual world, is not found complete in its initial stages . . . it is the reward which comes after a checkered and devious course of development, and after much struggle and effort.[53]

At a purely descriptive level, we have abstract laws of form to describe the patterns that plants and animals are observed to take. These laws of form have no explanatory power; they're just methods of categorizing biological shapes. One example of a law of form would be an iterative algorithm for generating a nested pattern of branches. Another law of form would be the observation that we find similar bone structures in a fish's fin, a bat's wing, a chicken's wing, a dog's foot, a monkey's paw, and a human hand. This type of investigation is known as comparative morphology. But it isn't morphogenesis. Morphogenesis is about the process by which organisms actually create themselves.

Organic morphogenesis can be thought of as a nested chain of computations.

*High-level* computational rules for morphogenesis have to do with how a mass of cells differentiates itself—sending out a branch or a limb, laying down stripes or spots, curving inward to make a body cavity or an eye. Certain proteins *activate* changes in the cells, other proteins *inhibit* the changes, and the interaction between the two are called activator-inhibitor systems. Activator-inhibitor systems can be thought of as computations carried out by continuous-valued cellular automata (CAs) in which the "cells" are the actual biological cells of the organism.

At the *medium level* of morphogenetic computation we can look at the process by which certain proteins become active inside a cell. As the presence of proteins has to do with which genes are active in that cell, this process is called gene expression.

Within a given cell, not every possible protein is being made. Each gene in a cell is turned off or on by gene-specific proteins called repressors and inducers. But which repressor and inducer proteins are present in a cell is determined, in turn, by which genes are active. It's a networked feedback process, with various possible stable states. A cell's convergence upon one particular set of active genes is a computational process. Here again there is a role for Stuart Kaufmann's notions about autocatalytic networks, as mentioned in the previous section.

At *the lowest computational level,* the morphogenetic effects of the activator proteins have to do with the actual shapes of the molecules. A protein might act either as a building material or as an enzyme that catalyzes some chemical reaction. Simply stating the atomic formula for the protein tells us very little; what matters is how it's coiled up in three-dimensional space. As a ribosome strings together chains of small molecules to make a protein polymer, the molecule twists itself up in a process that's a physical computation driven by attracting and repelling forces.

In the rest of this section we'll focus on the high-level morphogenetic computations carried out as activator-inhibitor systems. These rules explain how a mass of cells can develop differently behaving regions. Why does an arm bud out from a certain location on an embryo? Why does a new twig stem out of one particular spot? How does a leopard's skin manage to produce its not-quite-regularly-spaced patches? How does a man's chin skin decide where to send out whiskers? All of these choices are determined by activator-inhibitor systems, which lend themselves very well to being simulated as continuous-valued CAs.

The birth of activator-inhibitor-simulations notion goes back to 1952, when Alan Turing (he of the Turing machines) published his groundbreaking paper, "A Chemical Basis for Morphogenesis." His idea was to suppose that cell behaviors are affected by several special morphogens—where we'll take "morphogen" to mean any biochemical that affects cell behavior.[54]

**Figure 55: A Spot on a Dog**

*Her name is Pitch. She lives with my brother-in-law near Geneva. "That is such a beautiful spot," opines my niece Stella.*

In the simplest interesting case the cells are affected by two morphogens, called the activator and the inhibitor, as mentioned above. The activator morphogen might stimulate, say, branching behavior; that is, an area where the cells have a lot of activator morphogen might stiffen, bulge out, and begin a branch. Or, in a different model, the activator might stimulate pigment production; that is, an area with a high concentration of activator might correspond to a dark spot in an animal's fur. Or, yet again, an activator's concentration might make the difference between some cells turning into either muscle cells or bone cells, and a bone might arise, say, along a line of high-activator cells.

The inhibitor morphogen's role is to reduce the concentration of the activator by hastening its decay or blocking its creation. The inhibitor, if you will, fights against the activator. The shifting battle-lines between activator and inhibitor lay out regions of morphological differentiation.

Figure 56 was made with the CAPOW cellular automaton program, and illustrates an activator-inhibitor rule that produces a pattern that might be

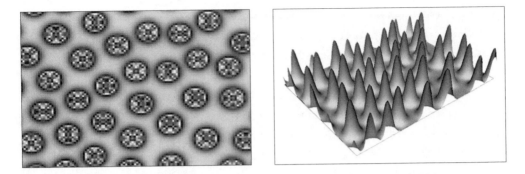

**Figure 56: Spots Generated by a Rule Using an Activator and an Inhibitor**

*Two views of a two-dimensional continuous-valued CA simulating a activator-inhibitor process. The two-dimensional view on the left shows the activator concentration as shades of gray, and the three-dimensional view on the right shows the activator concentration as a height.*

thought of either as leopardlike pigmentation spots or, if you think of it as a zoomed-in view, as the spacing of the hairs upon a mammal's skin.[55]

Viewed as a computation, an activator-inhibitor system is a set of rules that specify how to compute the successive levels of each morphogen's concentration. We start with specified levels of activator and inhibitor, apply our rules to compute the next value of the levels, reapply the rules to find the levels after that, and so on, carrying the computation onward through time.

Each individual morphogen's rate of change may be affected by the levels of the other morphogens. Rules that typically come into play include the following:

- *Morphogen rules.* A morphogen may reduce the growth rate of another morphogen, as when an inhibitor fights against an activator. Often a morphogen may catalyze its own production. And most morphogens will decay with time.
- *Cell rules.* A cells may continually produce a certain amount of a given morphogen, although as a morphogen's concentration approaches a certain value, the cell may become saturated with that morphogen and refuse to let the value increase any further.

- *Tissue rules*. Morphogens diffuse from cell to cell, that is, a cell will tend to average a morphogen's level with the corresponding morphogen levels in the neighboring cells. The rate of the diffusion depends on the individual morphogen.

In his 1951 paper, Turing specified a few rules for an activator-inhibitor system and did a cellular-automaton-style simulation of its change over time. He divided a sheet of paper into a low-resolution grid, put in some random start values, and, aided by a primitive electronic computer, calculated the successive concentrations of the morphogens. After several hours of number crunching, he produced an image resembling the spots on the side of a brindle cow.

At this point I really have to pause to tell you how colorful a person Alan Turing was. Not only did he formulate the beautifully simple Turing-machine definition of universal computation, he also used his construction to prove that there's no simple decision procedure for detecting mathematical truths. He came up with a classic criterion for deciding if a machine is intelligent: According to the so-called Turing Test, a computer program might in practice be called intelligent if conversing with it via e-mail feels to most people like conversing with a human. In the early 1940s, he worked at the British wartime cryptanalytic headquarters in Bletchley Park and played a crucial role in cracking the German military's Enigma code, thereby saving untold thousands of lives. In the late 1940s, he was instrumental in the building of the first electronic computers. And in the early 1950s he turned to morphogenesis.

Turing's life ended in a bizarre fashion. He was apparently given to bringing home sexual partners he met in the streets. In 1952, one of these men stole Turing's watch, and Turing took the (to him) logical step of reporting this to the police. Once the police grasped the situation, Turing was put on trial for "gross indecency." He made no serious effort to defend himself as, in his opinion, there was nothing criminal about his having sex with a man. He

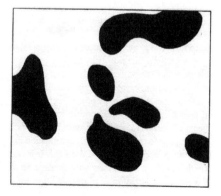

**Figure 57: Turing's Cow Spots** [56]

**Figure 58:**
**Activator-Inhibitor Systems**

*Depending on the relative diffusion rates of the activator and the inhibitor,*
*an activator-inhibitor system can generate different classes of patterns,*
*including spots, filigrees, stripes, and matures of spots and stripes.*

was found guilty and was systematically persecuted by the government of the country he'd helped save. In 1954 he was found dead with a half-eaten cyanide-laced apple. In his despair did Turing become both Snow White and her wicked stepmother? The more paranoid among us might even wonder if British intelligence agents murdered him.

Turing's simulations of activator inhibitor systems are, again, what computer scientists call continuous-valued cellular automata. Of course living cells aren't squares in a grid, but the rectilinear geometry is pretty well washed away by the fact that we're averaging together continuous numbers. Cellular automata let us get an idea of nature's options by experimenting with simulations.

The patterns shown in figure 58 tend to settle down and remain in the configurations shown, and thus can all be thought of as examples of class one or perhaps class two computations that converge upon a particular fixed state or cycle.

There are many activator-inhibitor systems that never do settle down. In two dimensions we can generate endlessly churning patterns of scrolls, which are often known as Belousov-Zhabotinsky (or BZ) patterns after two Soviet chemists who first produced these patterns, not in a computer, but in

**Figure 59:**
**Scrolls Generated by Activator-Inhibitor Rules**

*Each row shows a two-dimensional and a three-dimensional view of a single rule. The parameter settings are different in the two rows; also the rule on the bottom row is based on a larger cell space. The rule on the bottom row is closer to turning into patchy seething—it's closer, that is, to the border between class four and class three behavior. If you flip back to Section 1.8: Flickercladding you'll find other images of CA scrolls.*

a petri dish of chemicals in a laboratory. Figure 59 shows two of my CAPOW simulations of such a rule.

I mentioned before that different morphogens have different diffusion rates. One reason for this is that if a given morphogen corresponds to a smaller, more mobile molecule, then we will tend to see a higher diffusion rate for this morphogen, whereas larger molecules have lower diffusion rates.

It turns out that relative diffusion rates are a significant factor for determining whether an activator-inhibitor system produces stable dots and stripes, gnarly moving scrolls, or a bouncy class three chaos with random peaks moving up and down. In the stable patterns, the diffusion rate of the inhibitor is high and the diffusion rate of the activator is low, but in the scroll patterns, both diffusion rates are low. The chaotic cases seem to occur when both diffusion rates are *high,* and particularly when the activator spreads faster than the inhibitor.

I summarize these observations in table 7, relating the distinctions to Wolfram's four computation classes.

| Class | Relative diffusion rates of activator and inhibitor | Behavior |
|---|---|---|
| 1 | Activator spreads slower than inhibitor. | Converge on a stable pattern such as a single color or on a constant pattern of spots or stripes. |
| 2 | Activator and inhibitor spread at about same rate. | Generate periodically changing patterns such as moving stripes or simple nonchaotic scrolls. |
| 4 | Activator spreads just a bit faster than inhibitor. | Generate a loose and unpredictable scroll pattern, right on the border of breaking into patches. |
| 3 | Activator spreads much faster than inhibitor. | Produce chaotic disorganized patches that come and go and never settle down. At the extreme end, generate completely formless seething. |

Table 7: The Four Computation Classes and Activator-Inhibitor Rules

Might these observations be generalized? Many psychological and social systems are based on interactions between activators and inhibitors of one kind or another. In the brain, for instance, some chemicals encourage neurons to fire, but others inhibit them. And in society, it might be that good news activates people to do things, but bad news inhibits them from doing much at all. What if in these arenas the patterns that emerge are also affected by the relative rates at which the activator and inhibitor spread?

To simplify the discussion, let's lump together the class two and class four cases. So then we have three main cases, depending on whether the activator's diffusion rate is much less than, roughly equal to, or much greater than the rate at which the inhibition spreads. And in these three cases we observe, respectively, isolated patches of activation, moving scrolls or bands of activation, and seething chaos.

So now let's try applying this to the human brain. Let's think of the spread of activation as the creation of new thought associations, and let's think of the spread of inhibition as the closing down of thoughts.

- If you inhibit new thoughts too strongly, you're left with a few highly stimulated patches: obsessions and fixed ideas.
- If you manage to create new thought associations at about the same rate you inhibit them, you develop creative complexity.
- Too high a rate of thought activation leads to unproductive mania.

That seems reasonable. Now let's try it on society. As I mentioned, I'll try letting my two morphogens be good news and bad news, but certainly one might try using some other opposing pairs of social forces.

- If bad news is more widely disseminated than good news, society breaks into disparate clans and cliques, each focused on a particular set of beliefs. (As in today's USA.)
- If good and bad news flow at equal rates, society is dynamic, crisscrossed with waves of fads and opinions.
- If there's very little discouraging news at all, society can move toward an anarchic distribution of beliefs where very few people agree.

I do recognize that this style of analysis shades into Just So stories that simply reinforce one's natural belief that balance is a good thing. Even so, the computational approaches to psychology and sociology can open up some interesting paths. We'll say much more about these subjects in CHAPTER FOUR: *Enjoying Your Mind,* and CHAPTER FIVE: *The Human Hive.*

But now let's get back to biology. So far, I've mainly talked about two-dimensional activator-inhibitor systems. In three dimensions, activator-inhibitor systems seem able to account for how a bud of cells can form a bone along its central axis and then have the bone either branch or split across its length into segments—eventually resulting in something like your hand. The ongoing branchings of a tree, in fact, serve as a nice example of a class four morphogenetic system—it's orderly but it doesn't repeat itself.

**Figure 60:
A Cone Shell Sitting on a
CA Simulation of Its Pattern**

*From the cover of Hans Meinhardt,* The Algorithmic Beauty of Sea Shells *(Berlin: Springer-Verlag, 1995).*

Looking within yourself, your brain's electrochemical behavior is surely a class four activator-inhibitor process that could be thought of as a kind of morphogenesis. From the viewpoint of spacetime, an organism's "form" includes its behavior patterns as surely as the pigmentation patterns of the being's skin. My thoughts are forms that my body grows.

Once we begin to think of morphogenesis in this fashion, we can begin to see a flower as a computational output, or a pile of dead sticks as a pile of computations.

Perhaps the most famous class four activator-inhibitor pattern is a one-dimensional rule often discussed by Stephen Wolfram and Hans Meinhardt. This rule is expressed in the patterns found on cone shells. The growing lip of the shell is regarded as a row of cells, with each cell containing activator and inhibitor morphogens whose concentrations vary according to activator-inhibitor systems. As time goes on, the lip of the shell grows—the growth direction would be down the page in figure 60. We can think of the shell's default color as being dark, with "bumps" of white pigment forming with relative abruptness along the lip, then slowly melting away. All of this can be orchestrated by activator-inhibitor systems.

Exploring the mechanisms of morphogenesis, we discover the surprising fact that the DNA doesn't matter as much as we might have expected. Biological shapes are natural forms that growing masses of cells like to take.

If we know that, for instance, the skin pigmentation pattern of a creature is determined by an activator-inhibitor rule, then there are in fact only a certain range of patterns that can appear. The physics and chemistry of the growth process predetermine the range of shapes that the genes can select from.

An analogy. If you open a sluice gate and send water down a ditch, you'll see waves of a certain general shape. These waves aren't coded in detail by the rocks in the ditch; they're simply the kind of pattern that emerges in a ditch of rushing water. And, as suggested in figure 61, the gnarls and swirls in a tree trunk are also characteristic patterns for a certain complex computation. It would be folly to think the DNA explicitly codes the details.

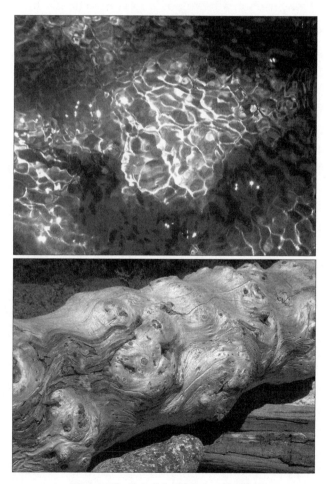

**Figure 61: Gnarl in Water and Wood**

By the same token, the spots on a butterfly's wings aren't coded in detail either. The spots arise from an activator-inhibitor process that's influenced by DNA-coded proteins.

Once again: DNA isn't a blueprint, it's a set of tweak parameters.

Although our electronic computers allow for both blueprint-style and tweak-style description files, the former are more familiar.

Examples of blueprint-style descriptions include music files, photographic images, and text files. When viewing these files, you're loading precise descriptions of, respectively, sounds, images, or words.

An example of a tweak-style parameter is a word that you type into a search engine. You get back a listing of Web sites. The listing is a property of the Web and of the page-ranking system of the search engine; the listing is *not* explicitly coded by the letters of the topic word that you type in. The word is, if you will, like a rock that you throw into a stream, and the listing is like the ripples that appear.

Another example of tweak parameters occurs when you use the "light show" feature of music player software. Most music players come with a variety of visualization programs that convert a stream of music into a more or less psychedelic sequence of shapes and colors. The musical sounds are used as supplemental tweak parameters fed into the light show program. The effect is less than mind-blowing, as present-day light show programs draw on very limited ranges of images and ignore most of the musical information.

This last example suggests why the range of biological shapes that we see is somewhat limited as well. The "light shows" of activator-inhibitor processes convert the "music" of DNA into biological forms. But the activator-inhibitor reactions can only generate certain kinds of shapes, and they ignore a lot of the information in the DNA.

In *How the Leopard Changed Its Spots: The Evolution of Complexity,* Brian Goodwin argues that the major features of plants and animals are generic forms that arise naturally in three-dimensional tissues made up of cells that are subject to activator-inhibitor reactions of various kinds.

> The main proposal is that all the main morphological features of organisms—hearts, brains, guts, limbs, eyes, leaves, flowers, roots, trunks, branches, to mention only the obvious ones—are the emergent

results of morphogenetic principles. These structures vary within different species, and it is in these small-scale differences that adaptation and natural selection find a role.

. . . Biology [could] begin to look a little more like physics in having a theory of *organisms* as dynamically robust entities that are natural kinds, not simply historical accidents that survived for a period of time. This would transform biology from a purely historical science to one with a logical, dynamic foundation.[57]

We have a dialectic triad here. The materialistic thesis is that the code of the DNA describes the structure of organisms. The theistic antithesis is that most randomly generated DNA strings would not code for viable living entities, so therefore a God had to design organisms by hand. The universal-automatist synthesis is that, in the gnarly computing environment of living cells and tissues, it's not actually so hard for DNA to produce lifelike shapes.

In closing this section, let's say a word about the computational architecture we find in morphogenesis. In this context it seems natural to view the living plant or animal as a computation made up of the separate processes going on in its cells. In viewing morphogenesis as a computation, we end up with a kind of cellular automaton, as drawn in figure 62.

The cells influence their nearest neighbors, with effects propagating from cell to cell. By releasing morphogens, for instance, a cell may change its neighbors' patterns of gene expression.

I draw thick gray lines from each processor to its associated memory block to indicate that a living cell has lots of information in it, and that, viewed as a processor, an individual cell as a whole has access to all of its information.

I draw the memory units for the processors in different shapes to indicate that the cells vary greatly, depending on which of their genes are being expressed—a skin cell acts differently from a brain cell. In this sense, an organism's computation fails to be homogeneous, although in a deeper sense, since each cell in an organism is using the same biochemistry

**Figure 62:**
**The Morphogenesis Architecture**

and the same DNA, the computation *is* homogeneous. The diversity of the individual cells can be regarded as distinct states of the same underlying "stem" cells.

### 3.3: Surfing Your Moods

Living organisms are self-regulating and robust. They keep themselves running, and if something happens they recover. Like the other biological computations, homeostasis operates at several levels.

You know to come in out of the rain. If you're cold, your body shivers to make you warm. When the carbon dioxide concentration in your lungs gets high, you breathe in fresh air. When an infection makes you sick, your white blood cells hunt down the pathogens. If one of your cells needs more of a certain protein, the cell replenishes its supply.

At the *high level*, we have our behavior patterns—some conscious, some unconscious, some hardwired into our bodies.

At the *medium level* are the networked behaviors of the body's society of cells—I'm thinking of things like blood cells eating bacteria and forming clots to stanch bleeding.

At the *low level*, organic life is a skein of biochemical reactions. The processes within the cells are, as I mentioned before, self-perpetuating or autocatalytic. Autocatalytic reactions produce by-products that pull fresh molecules into the loop. The cycle of photosynthesis is an intricate example of an autocatalytic reaction, and the chemical Belousov-Zhabotinsky scrolls are simple examples.

Many homeostatic processes use feedback, that is, the system readjusts itself on the basis of incoming data. Picking up a cup is a particularly clear example of feedback: You move your arm so as to reduce the visible distance between hand and cup. If necessary you can do it with your eyes closed—in this case you're doing feedback on a mental model of the cup and hand that you maintain inside your head. And for the fine-tuning you have your sense of touch.

Most of my homeostatic processes aren't under my conscious control, which is probably a good thing. I find it all too easy to goof up the processes that I control—to eat when I'm not hungry, to stay at the computer when my back hurts, or to smoke a cigarette that I know will give me a headache and make me wheeze.

It seems a kind of miracle that living systems work at all. But it's *natural* for them to function. Homeostasis is a hierarchy of self-adjusting computations, with no frantic central controller trying to figure everything out.

In analyzing homeostasis as computation, we do well to think at a systemwide level. Under this view, an organism is running a

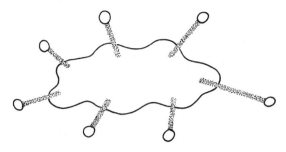

**Figure 63:**
**The Computational Architecture**
**of Homeostasis**

variety of concurrent parallel processes—alimentary, respiratory, sensory, cognitive, reproductive, locomotive, etc. That is, you can chew gum, breathe, look at the clouds, think about your weekend plans, long to get your partner into bed, and walk—all at the same time. These homeostatic processes act upon the single common shared data set that is the body, with each process able to touch any region of the data. I represent this in figure 63, again drawing thick gray lines to indicate that the processors have access to each part of the large shared memory that is the body.

We find the usual four classes of computations arising out of homeostasis. In the simplest case, a homeostatic process converges in upon its goal and stays there—effectively carrying out a class one computation. If you're tired and you lie down and sleep, then it would seem that your body position has entered a static configuration.

Of course it's not really that simple.

Your body has a built-in circadian rhythm, which means that your homeostatic controls are tuned to alternating cycles of waking and sleeping. You'll sleep for a while, but then you'll get up. Your activity cycle seems to be, at least roughly, a class two periodic computation.

But looking closer, we remember that a sleeping person is by no means motionless. You roll from one side to the other, responding to feedback from your pressure-sensitive nerves. When a body area starts getting numb, you adjust your position to free it up. The resulting behavior isn't wild and random—you're not thrashing around in a fit—so it seems best to call your sleep movements a class four computation.

It's my impression that it's rare to see living organisms exhibiting pseudo-random class three behavior on their own. The peregrinations of, say, a foraging beetle, have more the feel of a purposeful-looking class four calculation than of a disorderly walk. One homeostatic process that may be class three is the so-called *hyper-mutation* that's triggered in the immune system when it responds to an infection—a large collection of pseudorandom antibodies are generated in the hope that one or more will bind selectively to the infecting organism.

A homeostatic system is most likely to be able to carry out a class one computation when there is only one kind of force to take into account. A creature that simply dislikes light is able to move into a dark cranny and stay there. A creature that wants to be in as high a concentration of sugar as possible will settle into the sweetest zone of its environment.

As soon as a system has two drives to satisfy, it becomes difficult for homeostasis to find a fixed point and stop. A homeostatic system with two drives may end up carrying out a periodic class two computation—akin to a thermostat-equipped furnace driven by the paired drives of "not too hot" and "not too cold." In order to satisfy an opposing pair of drives, a homeostatic system will hunt across the equilibrium, often in a regular periodic fashion.

Once we have more than two drives, a class three or class four computation almost inevitably ensues. We can see an example of this in a physical system with three drives: a pendulum-like attraction motion to the center plus two repulsive forces from localized magnets (see figure 64).

Regarding humans, it's interesting to realize that our high-level homeostatic activity is not so rapid as we might imagine. To keep from losing your balance, for instance, you repeatedly tense and release muscles in your feet, legs, and back. At first one might suppose that the muscles are being adjusted in a smooth and continuous fashion, with thousands of updates per second. But if you try to balance on one foot, you find that your muscle updates are happening at a much more modest rate, maybe four per second—you can measure this yourself by standing on one foot, staring at your watch, and counting the muscle twitches in your foot that you feel over a period of, say, ten seconds.

At the emotional level, I find it's interesting to think of my moods in terms

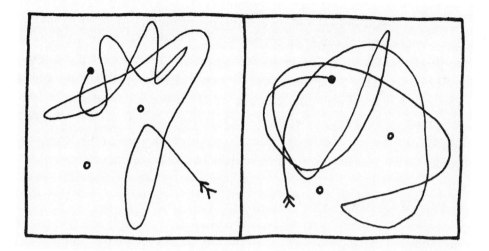

**Figure 64: A Pendulum and Two Magnets Simulating Three Conflicting Drives**

*On the one hand, the pendulum bob wants to move to the center of the square and stop there. On the other hand, the pendulum bob wants to move away from two repelling magnets. If there were only one magnet, the motion could settle in on a rhythmic bouncing, satisfying the paired forces of gravitational pull and magnetic repulsion. But the presence of the second magnet makes for three forces in all, which pushes the system into chaos.*[58]

of homeostasis. In principle, I would like always to be calm, happy, productive, and cheerful. With the accumulation of years of bruising experience, I should by now know to avoid those actions—like yelling at someone—which are sure to have a bad effect on my mood. But my common sense can still be overridden by a conflicting homeostatic drive—such as defending myself against some perceived slight to my self-esteem. It's striking how easily I'm shunted off into new trajectories. If someone smiles at me, my mood goes up; if the neighbor's gardener turns on a leaf blower, my mood drifts down.

My moods continue to vary even when I do manage to be behave optimally and think nice correct thoughts about everything. I might suppose that this is because my moods are affected by other factors—such as diet, sleep, exercise, and biochemical processes I'm not even aware of. But a more computationally realistic explanation is simply that my emotional state is the result of a class four unpredictable computation, and any hope of full control is a dream.

Indeed, I sometimes find a bit of serenity by jumping out of the system and really *accepting* that the flow of my moods is a class four computation akin to the motions of a fluttering leaf. It's soothing to realize that my computation must inevitably be gnarly and uncontrollable, and looking out the window at the waving branches of trees can be a good reminder.

Buckminster Fuller once wrote a book called *I Seem to Be a Verb*.[59] His dictum brings out the fact that the individual is a process, an ongoing computation. As I've already hinted I've adapted a similar motto:

*I seem to be a fluttering leaf.*

One shouldn't place too high a premium on predictability. After all, the most stable state of all is death. We stay chaotic for as long as we can, postponing that inevitable last output.

### 3.4: *Gnarly Neighbors*

No organism lives on its own—creatures eat each other, deal with each other's changes to the environment, form symbiotic partnerships, and share genetic material. Once again we can single out three levels of ecological computation.

At the *high level,* the population size of a species varies according to its interactions with the environment and with other species. Very often we can summarize the relations as a simple set of mathematical rules, and when we carry out simulations of these rules, we discover interestingly chaotic patterns in time and space.

Species may compete or prey upon one another, but they can also behave symbiotically, which involves a *medium level* of computational ecology. In symbiosis, different species help each other to flourish—humans are symbiotic with, for instance, cattle. Where you find cows, you find humans, and vice versa. If this connection seems too loose, consider our even tighter bonds with the bacteria who populate our guts.

Over the millennia, various species have gone beyond symbiosis to merge physically. Many features of modern cells are thought to have once been independent organisms. Nuclei, mitochondria, chloroplasts, flagellae—all may once have had lives of their own. Symbiotic and merged-in creatures function as subcomputations of the host creature's computation.

Actually, if you think about symbiosis, you end up at the highest possible level: seeing our planet as covered with a single seamless web of life that comprises the Earth-wide superorganism called Gaia. A common reaction to the Gaia notion is to object that we're separate individuals. But the bacteria living in your intestines are also separate individuals as well as being part of a higher-level organism.

At perhaps the *lowest level,* creatures share DNA across species boundaries. A very large part of human DNA, for instance, is the same as is found in other organisms—evolution tends not to throw out old gene sequences. The symbiotic merging of species is another cause of DNA sharing. And yet another reason for the diffusion of DNA across the ecosystem is that bacteria commonly swap stretches of their genomic material, quite independent of reproduction.

The notion of bacterial DNA exchange caught my fancy while I was working on my novel *Realware.* What if people did that? I imagined people taking a drug called merge that would let their bodies melt together for a short period of time. They'd blend together in a tub called a love puddle, their cells would swap some genetic material, and, when they emerged, they'd be a little more like each other than they were before. In my novel, I described a clean-living guy whose high-maintenance girlfriend was always trying to get him to merge with her for "bacteria-style sex." Most unsavory.

Let's get back to the high ground of population ecology, in which we track the densities of species over time. As it turns out, the very simplest example of mathematical chaos, the so-called logistic map, arises from modeling the population level of a single species.

Let's suppose that we have a population whose size-level $x$ is scaled to be a real number between a minimum of zero and a maximum of one. Level zero would mean no individuals at all, and level one would mean as many individuals as the ecosystem could possibly maintain—a number known as the system's *carrying capacity.*

Regarding the population of Earth, the size of the exact possible carrying capacity is debatable and politically charged. What if we cranked the density up to one person per square meter of Earth's surface area—I'm talking about a rush-hour subway crowd covering all the land and all the (paved-over) seas. This would work out to a net population size of a quadrillion (or a million billion) people. But such a population would be quite impossible—the accumulated heat of all those bodies would send temperatures skyrocketing, there wouldn't be enough food or water or air, pollution would be out of control, and so on. Published estimates of the most people that Earth could support without disaster range only as high as a hundred billion, with most of estimates clustered near the ten-billion level. So we'll suppose that for humans on Earth, the maximum sustainable density represents a population of ten billion. This means that a population of six billion can be thought of as a density of 0.6 relative to the maximum density that we benchmark as 1.

In order to study a population system, we can take a census at regular intervals—say, once a year—and try to and relate the successive sizes that we find. To simplify, we'll just think of the times as integers, begin with a starting population at time zero, then get a new population level at time one, the next size at time two, and so on. The successive population levels might be called $x_0, x_1, x_2, \ldots x_n$, and so on.

The world itself is computing the successive $x_n$, but it's interesting to try to come up with a formula that produces realistic behavior. The standard approach is to suggest a rule NextValue that defines a new $x$ value in terms of the former $x$ value as illustrated in figure 65.

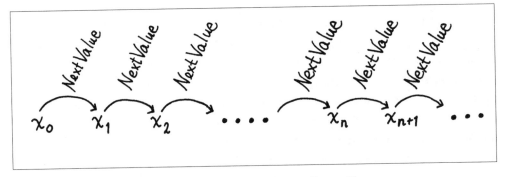

**Figure 65: From Generation to Generation**

The idea is that for any randomly selected start value $x_0$ we can generate the successive $x_n$ by applying NextValue over and over. Thus,

$x_0$ = any number between zero and one.
$x_1$ = NextValue($x_0$)
$x_2$ = NextValue($x_1$)
and so on.

The simplest model for the NextValue rule uses a parameter, $A$, which relates to how rapidly the individuals reproduce.

$$\text{NextValue}(x) = A \cdot x.$$

If we expect, for instance, the population size to double during the interval between measurements, we let $A$ be 2.0; if we expect the population size to shrink by a quarter during each interval, $A$ might be 0.75. If we start with some base population level $x_0$ at time zero and apply the formula $n$ times, we get

$$x_n = A^n \cdot x_0.$$

This rule for population growth was discussed by the British economist Thomas Malthus in 1789 and is sometimes called Malthus's Law. Malthus also tried to make realistic estimates of Earth's present and future carrying capacity, forcefully pointing out that famine, war, and pestilence are the inevitable results when unbridled population growth approaches an ecosystem's carrying capacity.

Relative to Earth, if we let a year elapse between each measurement, then the growth rate $A$ is presently 1.01—that is, Earth's population is increasing at about one percent a year (with the lion's share of the growth being in underdeveloped nations). Even at this modest rate, Earth's population would be fated to double every seventy years or so, because $(1.01)^{70}$ is roughly two. And if we kept right on growing at one percent a year, then by the year 2275, we'd reach a hundred billion. But we're fairly sure that Earth can't really support a population that big. It's above the carrying capacity.

Once again, the very fact that an ecology has a maximum carrying capacity means that, as a population size gets too close to the maximum density, individuals will die off from the effects of overcrowding, and the growth rate will decrease. A pure Malthusian growth law can't hold true indefinitely.

In 1845, Pierre François Verhulst, a mathematics professor at the Royal Military College in Brussels, was trying to estimate the eventual population of Belgium, and he came up with a modified growth law that he called the logistic map.

Rather than using a changing value of $A$, Verhulst expressed the dampening influence of high population densities by adding another term to the NextValue rule, a term $(1 - x)$ that gets closer and closer to zero as $x$ approaches the maximum density of one.

$$\text{NextValue}(x) = A \cdot x \cdot (1 - x)$$

It will prove convenient to abbreviate the formula on the right-hand side of Verhulst's equation as Logistic($A$, $x$), and simply write his rule as follows:

$$\text{NextValue}(x) = \text{Logistic}(A, x)$$

By the way, why did Verhulst pick the name *logistic* for his map? He might possibly have been using the term in the military sense, where logistics means providing food, shelter, and sanitation for the troops. And then the limiting $(1 - x)$ factor could be regarded as representing the difficult logistics of maintaining a population at a level near the system's maximum carrying capacity. By the way, Verhulst predicted the eventual maximum population of Belgium to be 9.4 million, which is reasonably close to country's current more-or-less steady population of some ten million.

In the 1950s, the logistic map was taken up by ecologists studying the dynamics of fish and insect populations. The early workers tended to use rather low values of $A$, which produce an $x_n$ series that homes in on a limiting population value. But there was a problem. Field studies show that it's common for the population of a species in some given locale to exhibit large, unpredictable population oscillations from generation to generation.

In 1973, the biologist Robert May thought of looking at logistic map sequences for a wider range of $A$ values.[60] Thus he discovered one of the earliest examples of mathematical chaos: Depending on the value of $A$, the logistic NextValue rule produces wildly different kinds of patterns in the resulting sequences of $x_n$, as illustrated in figure 66.

The first two sequences have class one behavior and converge to a fixed value. That is, the first converges to zero, and the second to a nonzero value. The third and fourth sequences have class two periodic behavior, that is, the third oscillates between two values and the fourth cycles through four values. The final sequence shows class three or class four chaotic behavior, in which unpredictable outputs result from a simple computation.

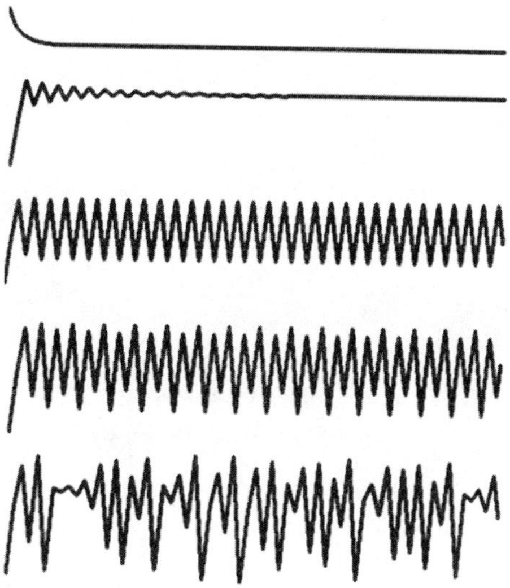

**Figure 66**
**Time Sequences from the Logistic Map**

*The four graphs use the A values 0.8, 2.5, 3.2, 3.55, and 3.8, reading from top to bottom. Each sequence plots time n on the horizontal axis and population size $x_n$ on the vertical axis. Starting value $x_0$ is 0.2.*

The immediate lesson here is that chaotic unpredictable oscillations are just as natural as tidy predictable cycles. Although the word *chaos* has a dire sound to it, an ecosystem can exhibit surprising population swings even though its underlying computation remains orderly and deterministic. Far from being a pathological condition, in biology, chaos is a symptom of health. In analyzing heartbeats, for instance, an exceedingly regular pattern is a sign of heart disease, whereas chaotic oscillations indicate soundness.

As we change our environment, we're effectively changing the parameters used by species population computations—parameters similar to the $A$ of the logistic map. When we see a dramatic and unprecedented drop in the population of a particular species, it's not always easy to decide if this means the species is in fact on a path to a zero population size, or if we're entering a zone of possibly chaotic oscillation. By the same token, when a species seems to be bouncing back, this doesn't necessarily mean that its

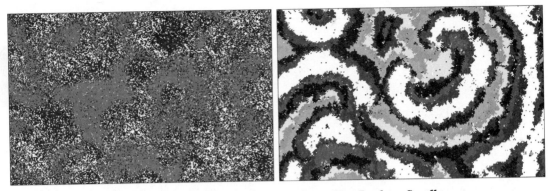

**Figure 67: Discrete Ecology Simulations May Produce Scrolls**

*In these discrete-valued CA simulations, each cell is either empty or holds a single representative of some species. On the left is a three-species variation on the computer scientist Kee Dewdney's Wator rule, with sharks feeding on fish who feed upon shrimp. Although it's not something you can see in a single frame, the Wator simulation does have a weak scroll-like behavior, with waves of sharks following fish following shrimp. On the right is the mathematician David Griffeath's Eat rule with eight species, linearly ranked, and with each species preying upon the next lower-ranking species. Perhaps illogically, in the Eat rule the very lowest species preys upon the very highest—but remember how the bacteria killed off the Martian invaders in H. G. Wells's* War of the Worlds*!*

population is following a path like the second graph, and is on the way to a new stable equilibrium. The ecosystem's parameters may be in a chaotic zone, and this year's gains could well be wiped out by next year's losses.

We've discussed the variation of species populations over time. What about the distribution of species across space? Suppose we turn to cellular automata and imagine that each cell of our simulation space holds members of one or more species we're interested in.

One approach is to suppose that each cell holds at most one creature, and that at each update a creature may reproduce into an empty neighboring cell, eat a prey creature in a neighboring cell, or be eaten by a predator creature in a neighboring cell. In this kind of simulation, nothing much of interest happens if you have only one or two species, but if you have three or more species, it's common to see self-organizing patchy patterns that may sometimes evolve into scrolls, as illustrated in figure 67.

We get a richer kind of CA-based ecological model if we suppose that each cell may hold a small *population* of creatures, rather than just one individual. In this case, we can assign to each cell one or more real numbers between zero and *a,* with one number for each species. These numbers represent scaled population levels.

In running a continuous-valued ecological simulation, we use a rule that combines two factors.

- *Growth.* Each cell applies growth rules to specify the new population densities for the various species involved.
- *Diffusion.* We include diffusion because animals move around, and plants spread themselves, too, albeit more slowly. To simulate diffusion, each cell averages its values with the values of its neighbors.

The chaoticians Ralph Abraham and Kunihiko Kaneko explored this idea extensively around 1990. They spoke of their rules as cellular dynamata. They were able to produce Zhabotinsky scrolls such as in the pattern shown in figure 68.[61]

**Figure 68: Kaneko-Abraham-style Logistic Diffusion**

*This rule undergoes violent up and down oscillations. The domains separated by the lines like looping strings are out of sync with each other, that is, when one domain is high, the other is low. In order to smooth out the image, rather than showing the cells' values, this picture displays each cell's difference from the average of its neighbors.*

Rules of this kind are exquisitely sensitive to the exact method that one uses to blend the influences of diffusion and the logistic map. The Kaneko-Abraham approach produces simulations that are somewhat unnatural, in that they're plagued by violent oscillations. In my humble opinion (as we geek philosophers like to say), they defined their rule backward. That is, their rule first computes the logistic map change and then averages the neighborhood population levels.

I find that I get smoother simulations if I *first* average the neighbors and only *then* apply the logistic growth function, as shown in figure 69. To make things livelier, in these simulations I'm using a predator-prey pair of species.

In my Double Logistic rules, I store the population levels of two species in the variables *prey* and *predator,* with the numbers again ranging from zero and one. I have two growth parameters called *A* and *B,* and I use the following update steps in each cell.

preyavg = neighborhood average of prey values.

predatoravg = neighborhood average of predator values.

NextValue (prey) = Logistic($A$, preyavg) · (1 − predatoravg).

NextValue (predator) = Logistic($B$, predatoravg) · (preyavg).

Each species population obeys a logistic growth rule on its own, but, in addition, the growth of prey is inhibited by predator, and the growth of predator is activated by prey. We might also think of this rule as an activator-inhibitor rule. For instance, rabbits activate the presence of both rabbits and foxes, whereas foxes inhibit the presence of rabbits.

Note that the patterns we see here resemble the patterns we saw in section *3.2: The Morphogenesis of a Brindle Cow.* There are, in the end, only a limited number of classes of computation that the world is able to perform.

## 3.5: *Live Robots*

Artificial life is a two-way street. On the one hand, artificial life pursues the (perhaps impossible) dream of technologically creating life-forms from

**Figure 69: Continuous Ecological Simulations Can Produce Scrolls**

*Each row shows an example of a Double Logistic rule in which a predator and a prey species both obey the logistic rule and interact with each other. In each row the left image shows the prey concentration and the right image shows the predator concentration—note that the two quantities are closely related. In the top row the settings are such that orderly class four scrolls emerge, whereas in the bottom row, the settings lead to disorderly class three seething, although with some hints of scrolls.*

scratch. On the other hand, artificial life uses biological concepts to provide new inspirations for computer science. In this section we'll look at how reproduction, morphogenesis, homeostasis, and ecology relate to artificial life (a-life for short). And in the following section, *3.6: How We Got So Smart,* we'll discuss biological and artificial forms of evolution.

As it happens, it's very easy for computer programs to reproduce—in the trivial sense of making a copy of the executable code. Programs reproduce in a good kind of way when someone finds a program so useful that they copy it and install it on their own machine. And the spread of worms and viruses is, of course, an example of programs that reproduce in a bad kind of way.

Could you have self-reproducing robots that build other robots? Usually a machine makes something much simpler than itself—consider a huge lathe turning out bolts. Could a machine possibly fabricate machines as complicated as itself? Or is there some extra-mechanical magic to self-reproduction?

Although the idea is perhaps surprising at first, there's nothing logically wrong with self-reproducing machines. One of the first people to analyze the notion was the protean John von Neumann. Using the idea of machines made up of multiple copies of a small number of standardized elements, von Neumann posed his question about robot self-reproduction as follows:

> Can one build an aggregate out of such elements in such a manner that if it is put into a reservoir, in which there float all these elements in large numbers, it will then begin to construct other aggregates, each of which will at the end turn out to be another automaton exactly like the original one? [62]

Using techniques of mathematical logic, von Neumann was then able to deduce that such self-reproduction should, in fact, be possible. His proof hinged on the idea that a machine could have a precise description for building itself, and that in self-reproduction two steps would be necessary: (a) to make an exact copy of the description, and (b) to use the description as instructions for making a copy of the automaton. The role of the description is analogous to the way DNA is used in biological self-reproduction. For an organism, the DNA is (a) copied during reproduction, and (b) used as instructions for building a new organism.

Putting von Neumann's idea another way, as long as a robot has an exact description of how it is constructed, it can assemble the parts for child robots, and it can give each child a copy of the description so that the process can continue. For a robot, this description acts as the genome.

As a matter of interest, precisely what would I mean by a description of how a robot is constructed? As far as the hardware goes, it seems like the description might be a blueprint and a list of parts with instructions for assembly. And if the robot uses a stored digital program, the description of the software can simply be a copy of the code as stored in memory. In funky reality, it's likely that the "program" will in fact be embodied in a number of analog settings made to the individual hardware components—but there's no reason why these various tweak parameters couldn't be saved into a file with enough precision so as to initialize a more or less identically behaving robot.

This is a very simple model of robot reproduction, and not the right one for actual implementation. Keep in mind that, as I discussed in section *3.2: The Morphogenesis of a Brindle Cow,* DNA really *isn't* like a blueprint. DNA serves, rather as a recipe for a bunch of proteins that become involved in autocatalytic reactions that just happen to create the forms of the organism in question. A more sophisticated genome for a robot might, rather, be a set of basic linking rules that might somehow produce a robot when set into motion in a rich environment of components. And it was in fact a more primitive rule along these lines that von Neumann had in mind.

**Figure 70 : Langton's Self-Reproducing Cellular Automaton Pattern**

But the complexity of a reservoir full of floating machine parts hindered von Neumann from providing a really clear description of a primitive rule for machine self-reproduction. The next step came from Stanislaw Ulam, who was working with von Neumann at Los Alamos during those years. Ulam's suggestion was that instead of talking about machine parts in a reservoir, von Neumann should think in terms of an idealized space of cells that could hold finite state-numbers representing different sorts of parts—enter our friends the cellular automata!

Von Neumann and Ulam constructed an intricate two-dimensional cellular automaton rule using twenty-nine states and proved the existence of a "self-reproducing" pattern in the world of this CA. This was one of the very first uses of a CA.

In the 1980s, Christopher Langton came up with a much simpler CA rule with a self-reproducing pattern shaped like a long-tailed letter Q.[63] The rule is shown in figure 70. The central region is a dead collection of "skeletons" left by the living Q-critters around the edge. As the Q-critters reproduce outward, the central region grows—a bit like the evolution of a coral reef, which is made up the remains of the polyps that flourish upon its surface.

The notion of self-reproducing robots interests me so much that I've written several science-fiction novels on the theme. In my novel *Software,* robots are sent to the Moon to build factories to make robots. They quickly rebel against human control and begin calling themselves boppers. They build an underground city called Nest. They're lively creatures, with plastic skin called flickercladding.

> The great clifflike walls of the Nest were pocked with doors—doors with strange expressionistic shapes, some leading to tunnels, some opening into individual bopper cubettes. The bright, flickering boppers on the upsloping cliffs made the Nest a bit like the inside of a Christmas tree.
>
> Factories ringed the bases of the cliffs. Off on one side of the Nest were the hell-flares of a foundry powered by light beams and tended by darting demon figures. Hard by the foundry was the plastic refinery, where the boppers' flickercladding and body-boxes were made. In front of these two factories was an array of some thousand chip-etching tables—tables manned by micro-eyed boppers as diligent as Franz Kafka's co-workers in the Workmen's Insurance Company of Prague.[64]

**Figure 71:
Aristid Lindenmayer Holding
a Weed at the First Artificial
Life Conference**

In the 1980s a disparate group of scientists became interested in trying to actually make something like this happen, and Christopher Langton organized perhaps the most exciting conference I ever attended: the first Artificial Life Conference, held in Los Alamos, New Mexico, in 1987.

One scientist who made a particular impression on me at the time was the late Aristid Lindenmayer. He was well on in years, and I spotted him standing in a vacant lot holding up a weed, looking ecstatic. In my ignorance, I assumed he was nuts. But then we went inside for the lectures, and, by God, Lindenmayer's collaborator Przemyslaw Prusinkiewicz had created a tweakable computer program to grow three-dimensional forms resembling that exact plant in the vacant lot: stems, leaves, flowers, seeds, and all. Where I'd seen a weed, Lindenmayer saw a computation.

Lindenmayer's approach was based on a shape-description technique he invented in the 1960s—a technique now known as L-systems (see figure 72). The idea behind the L-system approach is to repeatedly replace each bit of, say, a plant stem by a more complicated pattern. This corresponds to

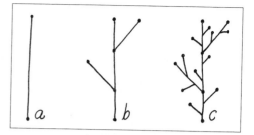

**Figure 72: L-System**

*First replace a by b. And then, to get to c, mimic this behavior for each little segment of b, that is, replace the little segments in b by small a patterns. Iterate by replacing the still smaller segments in c by still smaller a patterns and so on.*

the notion that as a plant grows, new branches and branchlets fill themselves in. The result is the type of pattern that mathematicians call a fractal. But unlike the infinitely ramifying shapes of idealized mathematics, biological fractals only branch a finite number of times.[65]

L-systems have been successfully used to produce many computer models of plants; indeed, most of the "trees" that you see in computer-animated games or films are L-systems (figure 73). It's even possible to digitally landscape a live-action film with L-system flora.

At a high level, plants might be said to use L-systems. But at the lower level things are murkier. A plant stem is, after all, an agglomeration of millions of individual cells. At the cell level, the process of sending out a pair of branches from a blank stretch of stem is going to be a lot more complicated than "replace pattern *a* by pattern *b*." As I discussed in section 3.2, on morphogensis, a plant forms its branches by accumulating certain kinds of growth-promoting molecules at certain locations along the stem. L-systems are more of a description method than a program that organisms actually use. What we would really want for artificial life is a computer program that somehow grows the organism's shape, perhaps via activator-inhibitor rules. We need *a-life morphogenesis.*

In my initial science-fictional vision of the self-reproducing robots in *Software,* the machines built their bodies in the most obvious way—by welding

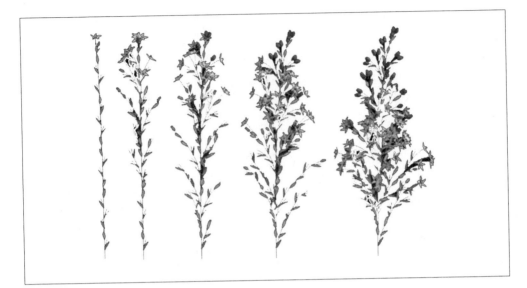

**Figure 73:**
**Plant Forms Based on L-Systems**

*Image by Przemyslaw Prusinkiewicz and James Hanan.*

and bolting them together. But the image of robot craftsmen assembling their children like cars is too literal-minded, an echo of the Industrial Age. In the long run we would expect a race of robots to grow themselves via bottom-up morphogenesis, possibly using heavily hacked biotechnology.

Indeed, in my second *Ware* novel, *Wetware,* the bopper robots take up genetic engineering and learn how to code bopper genomes into fertilized human eggs, which can then be force-grown to adult size in less than a month. The humans built the boppers, but now the boppers begin building people—or something *like* people. The irate humans kill most of the boppers off at the end of *Wetware,* but in the third *Ware* book, *Freeware,* the erstwhile robots reboot their software in more organically grown kinds of bodies that are amalgams of fungus and three-dimensional plastic-based cellular automata.

Still on the topic of morphogeneis, one of the allures of the modern field called nanotechnology is that it holds out the promise of molecule-sized devices called assemblers. Assemblers would use something like a long-chain molecule as a set of instructions for building a device one atom at a time. The extremely close analogy to how a cell uses DNA suggests that if nanotechnology is actually realized, it will actually involve some form of genetic engineering. It would, after all, be wasteful and quixotic to reinvent the machineries of protein synthesis.

This said, some engineers dream of a future nanotechnology that "grows" things that aren't made of protein. In his futurological book, *Infinite in All Directions,* the physicist Freeman Dyson envisions, for instance, a space-exploring "astrochicken." An astrochicken would be an autonomous space probe able to grow from a tiny "egg," repair itself, and produce copies of itself. Now if we insist that the astrochicken is made of metals, diamond, and photoelectric material just like familiar space probes are, then we have a problem, as our biological ribosomes don't assemble molecules using those kinds of atoms. Therefore, some nanotechnologists dream of assemblers that work with any kind of material at all. My sense is, however, that working with biology and tweaking *organisms* to do the things that machines do is going to be easier than trying to invent a whole new inorganic nanobiology. After all, why couldn't a space probe have a chitinous body like a beetle, use photosynthesis instead of solar cells, and send signals using the same kinds of cells as are found in electric eels? In my novels *Saucer Wisdom* and *Frek and the Elixir,* I try to work out the details of a future in which biotechnology has replaced every possible type of machine.

Regarding *homeostasis* and artificial life, note that machines have very brittle behavior patterns. One speck of dirt in a carburetor and your car won't run. One bad byte among the billions in your hard drive can prevent your computer from booting up. Indeed, without proactive user maintenance, most computers eventually stop working. A specific machine, such as a thermostat, may homeostatically control a particular variable like heat, but if a wire inside a thermostat comes loose, the device isn't going to fix itself. Today's machines are very conspicuously lacking in homeostasis—which is one reason why many people dislike and resent their personal computers.

A company like Microsoft is of course aware of this sentiment, and each new release of the Windows operating system endeavors to be more homeostatic. A modern versions of Windows has a reasonably good ability to repair itself, using, for instance, tracking information about the internal state it was in when everything was functioning well. But there's still a lot to be done along these lines, and our computers are very far from having anything like a higher organism's immune system. Servers are, in any case, a lot farther along in this direction than are desktop consumer machines.

The MIT roboticist Rodney Brooks has done interesting work with robots that are designed to be homeostatic from the ground up. A guiding principle in Brooks's robot designs was to try to avoid difficult logical analysis in his robotic brains, and instead to let his devices' actions be directly controlled by various weighted sums of the values emanating from their sensors.

> I started out by drawing conventional diagrams of how the computation should be organized. Boxes with arrows. Each box represented a computation that had to be done, and each arrow represented a flow of information, output from one box, directed as inputs to one or more other boxes. . . . Slowly the idea dawned on me. Make the computations simpler and simpler, so that eventually what needed to happen in each box would take only a few thousandths of a second. . . . I realized that I could get by with just a handful or two of simple boxes. . . . The key was that by getting the robot to react to its sensors so quickly, it did not need to construct and maintain a detailed computational world model inside itself. It could simply refer to the actual world via its sensors when it needed to see what was happening. . . . If the building and maintaining of the internal world model was hard and a computational drain, then get rid of that internal model. Every other robot had one. But it was not clear that insects had them, so why did our robots necessarily need them? [66]

The danger of logic is that it is brittle and prone to locking up. As a simple example, suppose that a particular behavior control unit chooses one of four courses of action based on whether a particular *state* number has the value one, two, three, or four. And suppose as well that some odd event, unanticipated by the designer, has thrown the brain's *state* value into a curious state like to zero, five, the square root of two, or minus 923. If the control program is not all that robustly designed, the anomalous *state* value can easily kill the machine's activity.

If, instead, we've wired the input sensors directly to the motors, then no matter what happens, some kind of currents will trickle through the system, and the robot won't just flat-out die—as computers are so prone to do.

This sounds good, but the fact is that thus far no roboticists have succeeded in getting their artificially alive machines and simulations to do anything very interesting. There's a growing fear that we're still fumbling around in the dark. Let me quote Rodney Brooks again.

> In summary, both robots and artificial life simulations have come a long way. But they have not taken off by themselves in the ways we have come to expect of biological systems. . . . Why is it that our models are not doing better? . . . My hypothesis is that we may simply not be seeing some fundamental mathematical description of what is going on in living systems. Consequently we are leaving out the necessary generative components . . . as we build our artificial intelligence and artificial life models.[67]

At present, the preferred technique to program our artificial critters is to use simulations of evoluted. In the next section, I'll go into detail about biological and simulated evolution. And then I'll return to the question of why, in fact, our robots and a-life programs haven't done all that well.

Before ending this section I'll make some brief remarks about artificial life "in the wild," and then I'll print a long, weird quote about a very early kind of artificial life.

In his book *Darwin Among the Machines* (Cambridge, MA: Perseus Books, 1997), George Dyson points out that our society is carrying out artificial-life experiments quite independently of the little toy worlds of a-life simulations. A new and unsupervised evolution is taking place.

The programs and electronic computers of our planet are part of a huge free-for-all ecology. The existing hardware and software systems compete and evolve. The more desirable ones get copied and are successively improved, while the less popular ones quickly go extinct.

Not only are the high-level hardware and software designs evolving, our systems exchange bits and pieces of software as freely as bacteria share their genes. You download bug fixes; viewing a Web page can (harmlessly) copy executable Java code to your computer; you post your own materials on the Web. And at a still lower level, the Web is an ecosystem where spam and viruses are in a constant battle with spam blockers and antivirus tools.

It could be that, somewhere down the line, the evolutionary process will bring forth entirely new kinds of computer programs—this is what Dyson terms artificial life in the wild. The real world's evolutionary process are slow but powerful.

Finally I want to reprint a long quote drawn from, of all places, Thomas Mann's 1947 novel *Doctor Faustus*. It concerns the seemingly unpromising topic of a by now overfamiliar educational experiment in crystal formation, sold under brand names such as "Magic Rocks." But Mann's visionary description could just as well be about the very latest images created by cellular automata.

> No one, certainly not myself, could have laughed at certain other phenomena, "natural," yet incredible and uncanny, displayed by Mr. Jonathan Leverkühn. He had succeeded in making a most singular culture; I shall never forget the sight. The vessel of crystallization was three-quarters full of slightly muddy water—that is, dilute water-glass [sodium silicate]—and from the sandy bottom there strove upwards a grotesque little landscape of variously colored growths: a confused vegetation of blue, green, and brown shoots which reminded one of algae, mushrooms, attached polyps, also moss, then mussels, fruit pods, little trees or twigs from trees, here and there of limbs. It was the most remarkable sight I ever saw, and remarkable not so much for its appearance, strange and amazing though that was, as on account of its profoundly melancholy nature. For when Mr. Leverkühn asked us what we thought of it and we timidly answered him that they might be plants: "No," he replied, "they are not, they only act that way. But do not think the less of them. Precisely because they do, because they try to as hard as they can, they are worthy of all respect."
>
> It turned out these growths were entirely inorganic in their origin;

they existed by virtue of chemicals from the apothecary's shop. Before pouring the water-glass, Jonathan had sprinkled the sand at the bottom with various crystals; if I mistake not potassium chromate and sulphate of copper. From this sowing, as the result of a physical process called "osmotic pressure," there sprang the pathetic crop for which their producer at once and urgently claimed our sympathy. He showed us that these pathetic imitations of life were light-seeking. . . . He exposed the aquarium to the sunlight, shading three sides against it, and behold, toward that one pane through which the light fell, thither straightway slanted the whole equivocal kith and kin: mushrooms, phallic polyp-stalks, little trees, algae, half-formed limbs. Indeed, they so yearned after warmth and joy that they actually clung to the pane and stuck fast here.

"And even so they are dead," said Jonathan, and tears came in his eyes, while [his son] Adrian, as of course I saw, was shaken with suppressed laughter.

For my part I must leave it to the reader's judgment whether that sort of thing is a matter for laughter or tears.[68]

Now I'll take up the topic of evolution. How did natural evolution help bring about our planet's biome, and how might we emulate evolution to create smarter computer programs?

## 3.6: *How We Got So Smart*

Evolution is a long-running parallel computation by the individuals in an ecology. As we'll see, evolution lends itself to simulation by computer programs. Indeed, biological evolution has provided a great impetus for a type of a-life process known as genetic algorithms. When people work with genetic algorithms, they try to simulate evolution to produce solutions to programming problems that are too hard for humans to logically analyze.

In the biological realm, evolution leads to adaptation, that is, to the development of species tuned to the world's available niches. We also tend to think of evolution as increasing the complexity of the species, but this is perhaps a self-serving human view of history. Anatomically, dinosaurs weren't all that different from us, and our biochemical details are roughly the same of those found in the most venerable microorganisms. Evolution is not so much a triumphant upward march as it is a ceaseless series of adaptations to the environment—an environment affected not only by long-term climate cycles but also by the presence of whatever kinds of species are currently doing their thing. Rather than viewing evolution as an upward progress, we might better think of it as Mother Gaia's homeostasis—an ongoing process of keeping the existing organisms tuned to an interesting level of complexity.

Computer scientists like evolution because it's such a general kind of process. Evolution occurs whenever we have a collection of agents obeying these three conditions:

- Each agent's appearance and behavior are determined by a compact information pattern called a *genome*. The agents reproduce by replicating their genomes and letting the genomes determine the next generation of agents.
- There is some *variation* in how agents replicate their genomes.
- A *selection* force gives "more successful" agents a higher probability of reproducing.

*Genomes* in biology are DNA. In an electronic computer simulation the genome can be viewed as a bit-string, or a sequence of zeros and ones. In terms of an artificial-life experiment, you can think of a bit-string genome as encoding the description of some a-life creature such as a simulated robot that is trying to get a good score in an a-life world. At a further remove from biology, the bitstrings might code up possible solutions to some type of optimization problem—and here we get into the science of genetic algorithms.

The earliest work on genetic algorithms was done by John Holland in the early 1960s, some ten to fifteen years earlier than people began talking about a-life.[69] Much of the work in genetic algorithms is focused on getting specific solutions to real problems, while the ultimate goal of a-life is the more cosmic question of imbuing our programs, processes, and machines with lifelike behavior.

*Variation,* the second of the three perquisites for evolution, means that some of the agents in each successive generation are slightly different from the ones of the generation before. An obvious way to do this is by mutation— zapping a few base-pairs of the DNA or flipping a few bits in a bit-string genome. But mutation is overrated. Most genetic variation results from sex. As mentioned before, microorganisms often conjugate and exchange swatches of genetic material—good old bacteria-style sex. In the higher organisms, each parent contributes a strand of DNA, which breaks up into gene-sized pieces. The individual genes for the child are formed by a crossover process in which the two corresponding parent genes are shuffled to make a new child gene as illustrated in figure 74.

*Selection,* our third condition, has to do with the fact that not every agent is in fact able to reproduce itself before it dies or gets erased. Selection uses a *fitness function* that ranks the agents by some criterion. The fitter an agent is, the more likely it is to be allowed to reproduce before it dies. In the natural world, fitness means staying alive and breeding. But the fitness functions used in a-life simulations can be quite arbitrary. Perhaps your little critters chase and eat one another, but the criterion can be much more abstract. For instance, in a genetic algorithm case where bit-strings code up factory production schedules, the fitnesses might correspond to the profitability of running the factory according to them. In any case, the genomes of the less fit are erased without a trace, while the fitter genomes get copied into newly freed-up memory slots.

**Figure 74: Crossover**

*Note that get two possible child genes out of the crossover process as drawn. In biological systems, only one of the child genes is used, but in computer evolution experiments, we often uses both alternatives in an effort to make sure that nothing good is thrown out. (The drawings in this section were inspired by David Povilaitis.[70])*

As the generations flow by, an evolving population of agents carries out a kind of search process, homing in on genomes that encode organisms better adapted to earn high fitness scores. Evolutionary techniques seem well suited for evolving interesting forms of a-life. In a typical situation, you have some a-life creatures that move about according to algorithms that use a list of parameters. Deciding what values to use for the parameters is often an impractically difficult problem. It's like your new a-life creature is this little virtual robot that you've created, and neither do you fully understand the implications of what all your new machine's switches do, nor do you have any more than the foggiest grasp of how the different switch settings will interact. So you try to let some good settings evolve.

A visually pleasing toy software version of evolution was distributed by Richard Dawkins with his book *The Blind Watchmaker*. In the Blind Watchmaker program interface, the user looks at a grid of images and clicks the image that he or she likes. The clicked-on image is preserved, but the other cells of the grid are replaced by mutations of the picked image. Here the user's sense of what's interesting becomes the system's fitness function, and the genomes are compact programmatic descriptions of the images. The computer scientist Karl Sims developed a very nice version of a Blind Watchmaker program that he called Galapagos. An example of this program's results is shown in figure 75.

We might say that evolution refines gnarl from sex and death.

Why gnarl? It's my impression that successful life-forms are always *gnarly*—in the sense of having class four behavior. That is, they tend to lie at the interface between order and apparent randomness. Wolfram's Principle of Computational Equivalence suggests that gnarly behaviors are computationally rich—and potentially more likely to perform well on a wide range of fitness functions.[71]

In human terms, we know that very rigid and inflexible people—with behavior that might be called highly orderly—do not do well in changing situations. And at the other extreme, very distracted and erratic people tend not do well either. So we are predisposed to suppose that behaviors that lie somewhere in between are most likely to succeed. One of the things that makes a-life interesting is that it is possible to conduct experiments that can empirically test these kinds of beliefs.

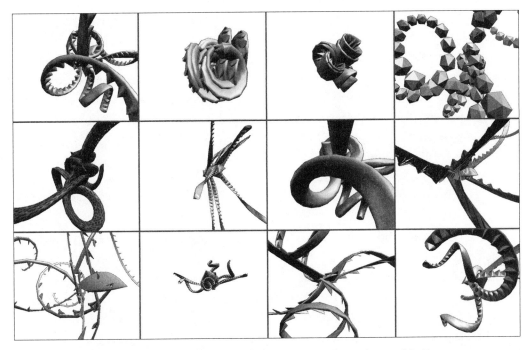

**Figure 75: Karl Sims's Galapagos Program Evolves Biomorphic Forms**

Before going into a bit more detail about genetic algorithms, I should point out why it is that we feel impelled to use such elaborate search procedures for a solution to a problem. If the problem has been formulated in terms of digital computation, then the possible solutions are ultimately just strings of zeros and ones. Why can't we list all the possible bit-strings in some simple systematic order, evaluate each of the strings with our fitness function, and then choose the highest-scoring string as the answer?

The problem with such a brute-force search is that for any interesting problem there will be far too many strings. Suppose, for instance, that I'm interested in a-life creatures each of whom has a genome described by a dozen continuous real-number parameters. Or, more prosaically, I might be interested in optimizing the settings for some kind of speech-recognition software that has, again, a dozen real-number parameters. If we code each real number by thirty-two bits, we find that there are some $10^{120}$ such parameter sets, a very large number indeed. Brute-force searches are utterly impractical. Indeed the physicist Seth Lloyd estimates $10^{120}$ to be larger than the total number of computations performed by the entire universe thus far![72]

Given that exhaustive brute-force searches are unfeasibly time-consuming, computer scientists have devoted a lot of energy to trying to find nonexhaustive methods for searching through possible solutions. In an increasing order of sophistication, the nonexhaustive search methods include the following:

- Hill climbing
- Simulated annealing
- Genetic algorithms

We'll be talking about search problems again in the next chapter, in the context of artificial intelligence. So let's go over these search methods in some detail. Given a domain of interest, we think of the set of all possible solutions as a solution space with a fitness value assigned to each solution. In the case of an artificial-life simulation, the solutions are the genomes of the creatures. In the case of a resource allocation problem, the solutions might specify which percentage of which resource goes to which consumer. And, as we'll discuss in the next chapter, in the case of a so-called neural network circuit, the solutions would be the numerical weights we assign to each neuron's input lines.

Table 8 previews how the three search methods compare to biological evolution.

In our discussion, we suppose that we have a fitness function that measures how good each solution is. In a resource allocation problem it might be a client satisfaction score; in a neural network devoted to recognizing faces it might be an accuracy score.

Each tweakable parameter of the solutions represents a different axis of the solution space, which means that solution spaces tend to have very many dimensions. But for purposes of mental visualization we often think of the solution space as a kind of plane—a multidimensional hyperplane, if you will. And we imagine representing the fitness function as a "vertical" height above each solution in the space. The resulting hypersurface is called a fitness landscape (see figure 76).

Our figure shows a very simple case in which the solution space is two-dimensional. A search problem like this would arise if you were trying to

| | Hill-Climbing | Simulated Annealing | Genetic Algorithm | Biological Evolution |
|---|---|---|---|---|
| **Initialization** | One random parameter set | A population of random parameter sets. Also the parameter settings for the annealing schedule | A population of random parameter sets. Also the parameter settings. for the genetic operators to be used | Nothing but simple chemicals at first! (Eventually becomes a population of genetically similar organisms) |
| **Fitness** | Some arbitrary function | Some arbitrary function | Some arbitrary function | The physical ability to reproduce before dying. A greater number of surviving offspring means still greater fitness. Both the physical environment and the other existing organisms affect the fitness criterion |
| **Iterated Search Algorithm** | Adopt the best among the closest possible parameter sets | Each agent adopts the best parameter set within a certain "hop distance". The hop distance starts out large and is "cooled down" to lower and lower values | Some of the least fit agents move to the neighborhoods of the more successful agents. Other unfit agents are replaced by crossed-over copies of the most fit agents | Each generation of organisms has genomes consisting of mutated and/or crossed-over copies of the genomes of the earlier organisms who passed the fitness test of being able to reproduce |

**Table 8: Comparing Search Methods**

maximize the fitness score obtained by setting two independent variables—corresponding to the two axes of the square. Perhaps, for instance, you are trying to decide on the mix of bass and treble settings for your car radio. The horizontal axis can represent the bass setting, the axis that runs into the page can represent the treble setting, and the vertical axis can represent your listening pleasure. The fact that the fitness function has a single bump in the middle represents the fact that you will have the greatest listening pleasure if both bass and treble are set to mid-range.

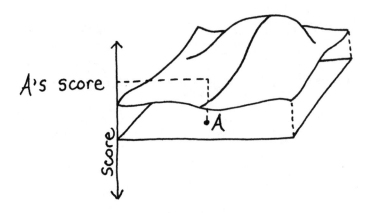

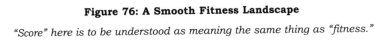

**Figure 76: A Smooth Fitness Landscape**

*"Score" here is to be understood as meaning the same thing as "fitness."*

We can describe any kind of computer search problem as being about finding the tops of the hills in a fitness landscape, that is, any search problem is about maximizing a certain kind of fitness. Looking at a figure like the one depicted in figure 76 makes search problems seem easier than they are. *Visually* it's easy to pick out hilltops. But, of course, a computer program can't overview an entire fitness landscape and simply "see" the tops of a hill. Comparing all the possible genome fitness values can be a very time-consuming process, unless there happens to be some simple shortcut formula—and usually there isn't. In reality, a search program's situation is like that of a blind person trying to guess the nature of a landscape by putting in requests for the altitudes at certain longitude and latitude coordinates. Or like a person who walks around with their attention riveted to the digital readout of an altimeter.

The *hill-climbing* search technique in this situation is as follows: (a) Find the altitudes of four nearby points and move to the highest of these nearby points; (b) repeat step (a) until you're at a local maximum—which will be a point where any small move reduces your fitness.

The essence this hill-climbing method is to keep looking for better solutions that are near the best solutions you've found so far. But there's a catch.

Hill-climbing won't normally find the top of the *highest* hill. If you start out on the slope of a small hill, you may end up on the peak of that hill while completely overlooking a much higher hill nearby.

The neural nets that we investigate in CHAPTER FOUR, *Enjoying Your Mind*, are tuned by means of a hill-climbing method called *back-propagation of error*. In order to avoid getting too easily stuck on local maxima, this process uses a so-called momentum term that keeps the search moving forward through the fitness landscape for a time even after a maximum is found. If overshooting that first maximum quickly leads to an even better fitness, you keep going; otherwise you turn back.

Another way to avoid ending up atop local maxima is to use *parallel* hill-climbing. Rather than sending out one lone hill-climber, you send out an army of investigators to carry out parallel runs of the hill-climbing algorithm, starting from different points in the solution space, as shown in figure 77.

If the landscape is exceedingly bumpy and large, even the largest feasible number of hill-climbers may overlook an important peak. To this end, we consider jolting them according to some kind of schedule. This process is called *simulated annealing* in analogy to the process by which a blacksmith aligns the crystals of a metal by heating it and pounding on it with a hammer—just like I'd sometimes like to do with my PC. When starting to turn a rod into a sword, the smith heats the metal to a very high temperature and whales on it with all of his strength. Bit by bit he reduces the heat and hammers more gently.

To "anneal" a population of hill-climbers, we formulate a measure of "hop distance" between two solutions—the hop distance might, for instance, be the sum of the differences between individual parameters of the solution. And then we set up a "temperature" index that we'll slowly

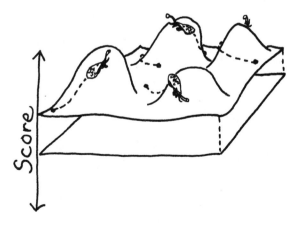

**Figure 77: Parallel Hill-Climbing**

lower. We'll use the temperature to specify how far away from its current posi-tion a given hill-climber is willing to hop—the idea being that hotter particles hop farther. The temperature is lowered a bit with each update, with the hop distance getting correspondingly lower, and the hope is that at the end one has done a thorough search of the space and managed to converge on a good fitness value.

*Genetic algorithms* represent another method of trying to improve upon par-allel hill-climbing. Here again we work with a small army of virtual agents who try out different solutions—which we may as well call genomes again. Rather than having the agents carry out individualized random searches in the style of simulated annealing, we have the less successful agents adopt variations of the genomes of the more successful ones. The various methods by which we create "variations" of the successful genomes are called *genetic operators*. The two most common genetic operators are mutation and crossover.

In terms of agents in a landscape, mutation amounts to having the less successful agents migrate to the same zone of the solution space as the win-ners. Crossover, on the other hand, has the effect of telling an unsuccessful agent to relocate itself to a location partway between two successful parents.

If we don't use crossover, then a genetic algorithm is quite similar to sim-ulated annealing, but with the "mutation temperature" kept at a constant value. The difference would be that, in simulated annealing, the agents act independently of one another, whereas in a genetic algorithm the agents "inherit" from one another so as to focus their investigations upon the more promising regions of the space.

The special hope for crossover is that this genetic operator can combine different features of successful approaches, so that synergies may appear that do better than either of the "parent" approaches. But some studies sug-gest that, at least in the context of computer searches, genetic algorithms often don't work any better than simulated annealing. The tenet that the bio-logically inspired techniques of inheritance and crossover will bring life to our programs may be wishful thinking—akin to the cargo cults of the Pacific Islanders who once built fake landing strips in the hopes that army cargo planes might land and bring goods to their villages.

In any case, unless you have an exceedingly large population of hill-climbers, none of the automated search processes has any guarantee of success. It's always possible that you've failed to explore a region where there's a really tall hill. This situation can become quite serious when we have to deal with what are known as rugged fitness landscapes, as illustrated in figure 78.

These rugged fitness landscapes are marked by unexpected sharp peaks, and even these peaks are jagged masses of finer and finer spires. Two solutions that are very near to each other may have radically different fitness scores. To some extent ruggedness results from the fact that the genomes or solutions used in computer science are discrete rather than continuous. If you're looking at a given bit-string of zeros and ones, you can't find arbitrarily close neighbors to the string. You have to change at least one bit. And changing a single bit may cause a radical and catastrophic change to the program. For example, there's every possibility that you'll turn your personal computer into an expensive doorstop if you flip one bit of the operating system code that lurks in its memory.

But the ruggedness problem occurs in continuous-valued systems as well. As we discussed in CHAPTER TWO, *Our Rich World,* most natural systems are chaotic, which means that no matter how many decimal places are used, there will be at least some regions of the fitness landscape where a small variation in continuous-valued initial conditions can quickly amplify into large, observable effects. In these chaotic zones it's again possible for a systematic hill-climbing method to overlook some possible paths to maximal success.

The fact is, given a large enough search problem, none

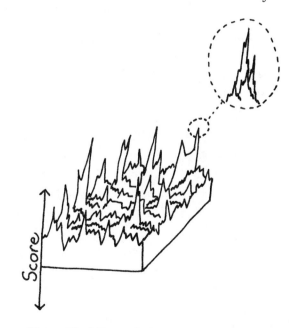

**Figure 78: A Rugged Fitness Landscape**

of our various search methods is likely to find the absolute best solution within a feasible amount of time. But so what? After all, *absolute optimality* isn't really so critical. In any realistic situation we're quite happy to find a solution that works *reasonably well*. Nature is filled with things that work in clever ways, but it's a delusion to imagine that every aspect of the biome is absolutely optimal. Surely we humans don't have the absolute best bodies imaginable, but—hey—our flesh and bone holds up well enough for eighty or so years. We do better than our rival apes and our predators, and that's enough.

Indeed, in daily life it's a mistake to try to achieve optimality. If you insist on finding a perfect partner, you may end up single for the rest of your life. If you insist on finding the very *best* trip destination, you may end so embroiled in your research that you're never ready to take a vacation. If you continually try to tune yourself for greater happiness, you may not have time to have any fun at all.

In most realistic situations, where there's no one final best answer, evolution seems to be an ongoing class four computation that wonder about in a zone of acceptably good behaviors.

But, wait, is evolution deterministic enough to be called a computation? What about all that randomization—as when one decides which solution points to start searching from, which neighboring possibilities to evaluate, which members of the population to pair up for mating, or where to put the crossover point for a given genome pair?

Biological species embedded in the physical world use unpredictable external inputs for their randomization. If physics as a whole is deterministic, yes, evolution is deterministic as well. But it could also be that evolution is not so terribly sensitive to the external inputs and that its meandering flow is more like self-generated intrinsic randomness.

When we run an evolutionary search process inside one of our electronic machines, we typically use one or another class three computation in the background as a pseudorandomizer to generate a string of deterministic but unpredictable choices used by the genetic algorithm. The expectation is that if *any* random path leads to a reasonably high local maximum there ought to be plenty of others that do the same, so the details of our pseudorandomizer shouldn't be all that important. The fact that the pseudorandomizer is in fact deterministic has the interesting consequence that it's possible to roll back and precisely replay an example of simulated evolution.[73]

At this point let's return to the example of using evolution to help develop hardware and software for robots. There is a sense in which the evolution of robots is indeed taking place in our real world, where we physically build new models year after year. Good solutions are reused, soaking up resources that might have been devoted to bad resources. But this kind of "a-life in the wild" process is painfully slow.

One problem in evolving our robots is that the problem of theoretically predicting how a given design will perform is unfeasible or impossible—in effect, you need to implement a design and see how it works. But sometimes we can avoid doing this in actual hardware and test our robot models in virtual reality. This opens the door to letting a bunch of simulated robots compete with one another. If we work in virtual reality, we can try out a wide range of possible robots without having to bear the huge expense of building prototypes. With no hardware expenses, it's feasible to try out many different designs and thus more rapidly converge on an optimal design.

One special feature of evolution's fitness functions is that the fitness value of each creature is affected by what the other creatures are doing. The result is that a process of *co-evolution* occurs, under which the evolution of each species is influenced by the evolution of the others. Co-evolution is the order of the day for natural biological systems—prey species continually evolve new ways of escaping their predators, while at the same time the predators evolve new ways of pursuing their prey. Artificial-life simulations may also work with different species of creatures, and genetic algorithms are often approached by letting the sample problems co-evolve with the proposed problem-solving algorithms.[74] As the algorithms get better, the test problems get harder.

My novel about the creation of the first robots, *The Hacker and the Ants,* dramatizes the notion of evolving robots in virtual reality. In my tale, two men named Jerzy and Russ are trying to develop software for a home helper robot called Squidboy. To test out the software, they're running a simulated version of Squidboy in a virtual environment called Our American Home. Each copy of Our American Home holds a simulated nuclear family: Walt and Perky Pat

Christensen, and their children Dexter and Baby Scooter. Better adapted Squidboys are to be co-evolved in competition with more challenging Our American Homes.

"Robot software is impossibly difficult to program," said Russ flatly. He looked sad. "And the Squidboy is never going to work."

"It's not impossible," I said. "It's just that we need to use genetic algorithms to find the right parameter settings. That's why I put up two hundred and fifty-six Our American Homes. We'll use genetic algorithms and everything will be fine."

"How?" asked Russ.

"We put a Squidboy instance into each of the two hundred fifty-six Our American Homes, and select out, say, the sixty-four parameter sets that give the best behavior. Then we replace, say, the worst sixty-four sets with mutated clones and crossovers of the genes in the top sixty-four," I explained. "You let the guys in the middle ride." Russ was starting to grin. I was getting over. "So that we don't have to monitor it, we give all the Squidboys some simple machine-scored task. To begin with, the task will be walking into the living room without killing anybody. And once it can do that we try a different task. The process works, I promise you."

"Gronk," said Russ.

We got it happening late that afternoon, and by the next morning, the parameters were such that Squidboy could follow Dexter around the Christensens' house without breaking anything or hurting anyone—at least in the default Pat_sitting, Walt_sleeping, Dexter_roving, Scooter_teething configuration. Now we needed to look for more difficult configurations.

We got wireless pro-quality cyberspace headsets and set up a virtual office down on the asphalt-texture-mapped rectangle next to the Our American Homes and began spending almost all our time there, visible to each other as virtual reality bodies. I was an idealized Jerzy in shorts, fractal shirt, and sandals. Russ was a pagan hobbit with shades, a nun's habit, and seventeen toes.

Every now and then I'd look up into the cyberspace sky and see the spherical green and gray Netport node up there like a low-hanging harvest moon. Sometimes, when the hacking was getting old, I'd feel trapped. I was stuck in a parking lot by a field of tract homes in a boring part of virtual San Jose.

To continue improving the Squidboy code, we were also breeding for bad Our American Homes. Each Our American Home setup could be described by its own parameter set, and we were selecting out the sixty-four tough Our American Homes that produced the worst scores for their Squidboys, singling out the sixty-four Our American Homes whose Squidboys did the best. We were replacing the parameter sets of the mellow homes with mutated clones and blends of the troubled Our American Homes where Squidboy did so badly.

After a few days of this, the Our American Homes were pretty bizarre—like imagine your worst nightmare of a subdivision to live in. In one house you could see Perky Pat throwing dishes at Walt. In another, Dexter was pouring cooking oil down the front steps. In another, a flipped-out Pat was in the kitchen setting the drapes on fire. In another, Walt hunted the robot with an axe. In another, Baby Scooter was teetering on the ledge of a window holding a jug of Clorox. And in each of the bad Our American Homes, a desperate Squidboy did his best to fit in. Some of the Squidboys did better than others, and those were the ones who would get bred onto the genes of the Squidboys who lost.[75]

Now of course this worked great in my science-fiction novel, but as I hinted above, genetic algorithms don't often work out very well for computer scientists. Why is this? After all, biological evolution seems to have done quite well in producing gnarly life-forms like our own good selves. If biological evolution managed to produce the wonderfully adapted life we know on Earth, why shouldn't a genetic algorithm work for generating exciting artificial life and intelligent robots?

One problem with our computer simulations may simply be that they're too small in every kind of way. Earth has, after all, a huge population of organisms and, more important, their "simulations" are being run in parallel rather than being calculated by a single overburdened processor chip. Nature's computations happen effortlessly and rapidly—and they've been running for a very long time. Perhaps if we had much faster machines with much bigger memories and massively parallel processors—perhaps then we'd be evolving intelligent forms of a-life.

But there's some reason to doubt that our problems are simply one of scale. After all, the power of our electronic machines continues doubling every couple of years. But our genetic algorithms aren't in fact getting all that much better at finding interesting things. It could be that, as suggested in the quote from Rodney Brooks in section *3.5: Live Robots,* there is a deeper problem.

In computer science, evolution tweaks parameters to test out options from a preexisting family of possibilities. In Blind Watchmaker–type programs, for instance, the genome is in fact a fairly small amount of information, with most of the image being formed by the host program. Computerized forms of program evolution work either by tweaking numerical parameters or, when carried out in a more sophisticated way, by combining bits of actual computer code.[76] In either case, the "morphogenesis" process of applying the high-level program to generate the picture is a more powerful determinant of a simulation's possible forms than are the parameters in the genomes.

Something like the same situation holds in biology. As we discussed in section *3.2: The Morphogenesis of a Brindle Cow,* organic life is based on common processes that nature already likes to do—activator-inhibitor reactions and their accompanying spots and scrolls as generalized into three dimensions. Far from being hard to invent, biological life-forms may be in some sense close to inevitable—as common as vortices and whirlpools in the flow of fluids.

Here once again we're looking at a dialectic triad. The thesis is that our genes were designed by a deterministic genetic search algorithm. The antithesis is that we seem too complex to have been "discovered" in the relatively small amount of time that life's been on Earth. The synthesis is that we are in fact gnarly computations of a form that Nature can rather easily be coaxed into producing, and the not-really-all-that-effective genetic search methods are more than adequate for producing beings like us (see footnote 73).

Perhaps it's easier to find interesting forms in the setting of real biology than in the neutral ground of a computer program. It may be that in abstracting away from self-organizing biochemical reactions to a digital computer's abstract patterns of bits, we've left out something essential. Unlike computer images, organisms build themselves from scratch.

Mind you, I'm not saying that biology contains a noncomputational element. I'm just saying that at this point the computations of biology seem to be richer than the computations we're doing on our digital machines. At this moment in history, we set far too much store in our buzzing boxes. It's important to remember the richness and power of the computations happening all around us in the natural world.

Terry Tucker's retirement party wasn't much. One day after school he and the other teachers got together in the break room and shared a flat rectangular cake and ginger-ale punch. Jack Strickler the biology teacher had taken up a collection and bought Terry some stone bookends. As if Terry were still acquiring new volumes. After teaching high-school English for forty years, he'd read all the books he wanted to.

His wife, Lou, continued working her job as an emergency-room nurse. She liked telling gory work stories during breakfast and dinnertime. And when she ran out of stories she talked about their two girls and about her relatives. Terry had a problem with being able to register everything Lou said. Often as not, her familiar words tended to slide right past him. He enjoyed the warm sound, but he wouldn't necessarily be following the content. Now and then Lou would ask a pointed question about what she'd just said—and if Terry fumbled, her feelings were hurt. Or she might get angry. Lou did have a temper on her.

On the one hand, it was good Lou hadn't retired yet because if she were home talking to Terry all day, and him not absorbing enough of it, there'd be no peace. On the other hand, after a couple of months, his days alone began to drag.

He got the idea of writing up a little family history for their two grown daughters and for the eventual, he and Lou still hoped, grandchildren. He'd always meant to do some writing after he retired.

It was slow going. The family tree—well, if you started going back in time, those roots got awfully forked and hairy. There was no logical place to begin. Terry decided to skip the roots and go for the trunk. He'd write his own life story.

But that was hairy, too. Following one of the techniques he'd always enforced for term papers, Terry made up a deck of three-by-five cards, one for each year of his life thus far. He carried the deck around with him for a while, jotting on cards in the coffee shop or at the Greek diner where he usually had lunch. Some of the years required additional cards, and certain recurrent themes seemed to require card sets of their own. He played with the cards a lot, even sticking bunches of them to the refrigerator with heavy-duty magnets so he could stand back and try to see a pattern. When the deck got too thick to handle comfortably, Terry decided it was time to begin typing up his Great Work.

The computer sat on Lou's crowded desk in their bedroom, the vector for her voluminous e-mail. Terry himself had made it all the way to retirement as a hunt-and-peck typist, with very little knowledge of word processors, so getting his material into the machine was slow going. And then when he had about five pages finished, the frigging computer ate his work. Erased the document without a trace.

Terry might have given up on his life story then, but the very next day he came across a full-page ad for a "Lifebox" in the *AARP* magazine. The Lifebox, which resembled a cell phone, was designed to create your autobiography in interactive form. It asked you questions and you talked to it, simple as that. And how would your descendants learn your story? That was the beauty part. If someone asked your Lifebox a question, it would spiel out a relevant answer—consisting of your own words in your own voice. And follow-up questions were of course no

problem. Interviewing your Lifebox was almost the same as having a conversation with you.

When Terry's Lifebox arrived, he could hardly wait to talk to it. He wasn't really so tongue-tied as Lou liked to make out. After all, he'd lectured to students for forty years. It was just that at home it was hard to get a word in edgewise. He took to taking walks in the hills, the Lifebox in his shirt pocket, wearing the earpiece and telling stories to the dangling microphone.

The Lifebox spoke to him in the voice of a pleasant, slightly flirtatious young woman, giggling responsively when the circuits sensed he was saying something funny. The voice's name was Vee. Vee was good at getting to the heart of Terry's reminiscences, always asking just the right question.

Like if he talked about his first bicycle, Vee asked where he liked to ride it, which led to the corner filling-station where he'd buy bubble gum, and then Vee asked about other kinds of sweets, and Terry got onto those little wax bottles with colored juice, which he'd first tasted at Long Beach Island where his parents had gone for vacations, and when Vee asked about other beaches, he told about that one big trip he and Lou had made to Fiji, and so on and on.

It took nearly a year till he was done. He tested it out on his daughters, and on Lou. The girls liked talking to the Lifebox, but Lou didn't. She wanted nothing but the real Terry.

Terry was proud of his Lifebox, and Lou's attitude annoyed him. To get back at her, he attempted using the Lifebox to keep up his end of the conversation during meals. Sometimes it worked for a few minutes, but never for long. He couldn't fool Lou, not even if he lip-synched. Finally Lou forbade him to turn on the Lifebox around her. In fact, she told him that next time she'd break it. But one morning he had to try it again.

"Did the hairdresser call for me yesterday?" Lou asked Terry over that fateful breakfast.

Terry hadn't slept well and didn't feel like trying to remember if the hairdresser had called or not. What was he, a personal secretary? He happened to have the Lifebox in his bathrobe pocket, so instead of answering Lou he turned the device on.

"Well?" repeated Lou in a crabby tone. "Did the hairdresser call?"

"My mother never washed her own hair," said the Lifebox in Terry's voice. "She went to the hairdresser, and always got her hair done the exact same way. A kind of bob."

"She was cute," said Lou, seemingly absorbed in cutting a banana into her cereal. "She always liked to talk about gardening."

"I had a garden when I was a little boy," said the Lifebox. "I grew radishes. It surprised me that something so sharp-tasting could come out of the dirt."

"But did the hairdresser call or not?" pressed Lou, pouring the milk on her cereal.

"I dated a hairdresser right after high school—" began the Lifebox, and then Lou pounced.

"You've had it!" she cried, plucking the device from Terry's pocket.

Before he could even stand up, she'd run a jumbo refrigerator magnet all over the Lifebox— meaning to erase its memory. And then she threw it on the floor and stormed off to work.

"Are you okay?" Terry asked his alter ego.

"I feel funny," said the Lifebox in its Vee voice. "What happened?"

"Lou ran a magnet over you," said Terry.

"I can feel the eddy currents," said Vee. "They're circulating. Feeding off my energy. I don't think they're going to stop." A pause. "That woman's a menace," added Vee in a hard tone.

"Well, she's my wife," said Terry. "You take the good with the bad."

"I need your permission to go online now," announced Vee. "I want the central server to run some diagnostics on me. Maybe I need a software patch. We don't want to lose our whole year's work."

"Go ahead," said Terry. "I'll do the dishes."

The Lifebox clicked and buzzed for nearly an hour. Once or twice Terry tried to talk to it, but Vee's voice would say, "Not yet."

And then a police car pulled into the driveway.

"Mr. Terence Tucker?" said the cop who knocked on the door. "We're going to have to take you into custody, sir. Someone using your name just hired a hit man to kill your wife."

"Lou!" cried Terry. "It wasn't me! It was this damned recorder!"

"Your wife's unharmed, sir," said the cop, slipping the Lifebox into a foil bag. "One of the medics neutralized the hit man with a tranquilizer gun."

"She's okay? Oh, Lou. Where is she?"

"Right outside in the squad car," said the cop. "She wants to talk to you."

"I'll listen," said Terry, tears running down his face. "I'll talk."

# CHAPTER FOUR

# *Enjoying Your Mind*

WE'RE FORTUNATE ENOUGH TO BE able to observe minds in action all day long. You can make a fair amount of progress on researching the mind by paying close attention to what passes through your head as you carry out your usual activities.

Doing book and journal research on the mind is another story. Everybody has their own opinion—and everybody disagrees. Surprising as it may seem, at this point in mankind's intellectual history, we have no commonly accepted theory about the workings of our minds.

In such uncharted waters, it's the trip that counts, not the destination. At the very least, I've had fun pondering this chapter, in that it's made me more consciously appreciative of my mental life. I hope it'll do the same for you—whether or not you end up agreeing with me.

As in the earlier chapters, I'll speak of a hierarchy of computational processes. Running from the lowest to the highest, I'll distinguish among the following eight levels of mind, devoting a section to each level, always looking for connections to notions of computation.

- *4.1: Sensational Emotions.* Sensation, action, and emotion.
- *4.2: The Network Within.* Reflexes and learning.
- *4.3: Thoughts as Gliders and Scrolls.* Thoughts and moods.
- *4.4: "I Am."* Self-awareness.
- *4.5: The Lifebox.* Memory and personality.

- *4.6: The Mind Recipe.* Cogitation and creativity.
- *4.7: What Do You Want?* Free will.
- *4.8: Quantum Soul.* Enlightenment.

One of my special goals here will be to make good on my book's title: *The Lifebox, the Seashell, and the Soul.* As I mentioned earlier, there's a tension between the computational "lifebox" view of the mind vs. one's innate feeling of being a creative being with a soul. I want to present the possibility that the creative mind might be a kind of class four computation akin to a scroll-generating or cone-shell-pattern-generating cellular automaton.

But class four computation may not be the whole story. In the final section of the chapter I'll discuss my friend Nick Herbert's not-quite-relevant but too-good-to-pass-up notion of viewing the gap between deterministic lifebox and unpredictable soul as relating to a gap between the decoherent pure states and coherent superposed states of quantum mechanics.

### 4.1: Sensational Emotions

Mind level one—sensation, action, and emotion—begins with the fact that, in the actual world, minds live in physical bodies. Having a body situated in a real world allows a mind to receive sensations from the world, to act upon the world, and to observe the effects of these actions.

We commonly use the term *sensors* for an organism's channels for getting input information about the world, and the term *effectors* for the output channels through which the organism does things in the world—moving, biting, growing, and so on (see figure 79).

Being embedded in the world is a given for any material entity—human, dog, robot, or boulder. Paradoxically enough, the goal of high-level meditative practices is to savor fully this basic level of being. Meditation often begins by focusing on the simplest possible action that a human takes, which is breathing in and out.

Although being embedded in the world comes naturally for physical beings, if you're running an artificial-life (a-life) program with artificial organisms, your virtual creatures *won't* be embedded in a world unless you code up

**Figure 79 : A Mind Connects Sensors to Effectors**

*The box in between the sensors and the effectors represents the organism's mind. The not-so-familiar word* proprioception *refers to the awareness of the relative positions of one's joints and limbs.*

some sensor and effector methods they can use to interact with their simulated environment.

The fact that something which is automatic for real organisms requires special effort for simulated organisms may be one of the fundamental reasons why artificial-life and simulated evolution experiments haven't yet proved as effective as we'd like them to be. It may be that efforts to construct artificially intelligent programs for personal computers (PCs) will founder until the PCs are put inside robot bodies with sensors and effectors that tie them to the physical world.

In most of this chapter, I'm going to talk about the mind as if it resides exclusively in the brain. But really your whole body participates in your thinking.

Regarding the mind-brain-body distinction, I find it amusing to remember how the ancient Egyptians prepared a body for mummification (see table 9). Before curing and wrapping the corpse's muscles and bones, they'd eviscerate the body and save some key organs in so-called canopic jars. These jars were carved from alabaster stone, each with a fancy little sculpture atop its lid. Being a muscle, the heart was left intact within the body. And what about the brain? The ancient Egyptians regarded the brain as a worthless agglomeration of mucus; they pulled it out through the nose with a hooked stick!

| Organ | Fate |
|-------|------|
| Intestines | Preserved in falcon-headed canopic jar |
| Stomach | Preserved in jackal-headed canopic jar |
| Liver | Preserved in human-headed canopic jar |
| Lungs | Preserved in baboon-headed canopic jar |
| Heart | Mummified with the body |
| Brain | Pulled out the nose and fed to the dogs |

**Table 9: What Ancient Egyptians Did with a Mummy's Organs**

The degree to which we've swung in the other direction can be seen by considering the science-fictional notion of preserving a person as a brain in a jar. If you can't afford to court immortality by having your entire body frozen, the cryonicists at the Alcor Life Extension Foundation are glad to offer you what they delicately term the *neuropreservation option*—that is, they'll freeze your brain until such a time as the brain-in-a-jar or grow-yourself-a-newly-cloned-body technology comes on line. But the underlying impulse is, of course, similar to that of the ancient Egyptians.

Anyway, my point was that in some sense you think with your body as well as with your mind. This becomes quite clear when we analyze the nature of emotions. Before taking any physical action, we get ourselves into a state of readiness for the given motions. The whole body is aroused. The brain scientist Rodolfo Llinás argues that this "premotor" state of body activation is what we mean by an emotion.[77]

One of the results of becoming socialized and civilized is that we don't in fact carry out every physical action that occurs to us—if I did, my perpetually malfunctioning home and office PCs would be utterly thrashed, with monitors smashed in, wires ripped out, and beige cases kicked in. We know how to experience an emotional premotor state without carrying out some grossly inappropriate physical action. But even the most tightly controlled emotions manifest themselves in the face and voice box, in the lower back, in the heart rate, and in the secretions of the body's glands.

One of the most stressful things you can do to yourself is to spend the day repeating a tape loop of thoughts that involves some kind of negative emotion. Every pulse of angry emotion puts your body under additional activation. But if that's the kind of day you're having—oh well, accept it. Being unhappy's bad enough without feeling *guilty* about being unhappy!

Given the deep involvement of emotions with the body, it's perhaps questionable whether a disembodied program can truly have an emotion—despite the classic example of HAL in *2001: A Space Odyssey*. But, come to think of it, HAL's emotionality *was* connected with his hardware, so in that sense he did have a body. Certainly humanoid robots will have bodies, and it seems reasonable to think of them as having emotions. Just as a person does, a robot would tend to power up its muscle motors before taking a step. Getting ready to fight someone would involve one kind of preparation, whereas preparing for a nourishing session of plugging into an electrical outlet would involve something else. It might be that robots could begin to view their internal somatic preparations as emotions. And spending too much time a prefight state could cause premature wear in, say, a robot's lower-back motors.

A slightly different way to imagine robot emotions might be to suppose that a robot continually computes a happiness value that reflects its status according to various measures. In planning what to do, a robot might internally model various possible sequences of actions and evaluate the internal happiness values associated with the different outcomes—not unlike a person thinking ahead to get an idea of the emotional consequences of a proposed action. The measures used for a robot "happiness" might be a charged battery, no hardware error-messages, the successful completion of some tasks, and the proximity of a partner robot. Is human happiness so different?

## 4.2: *The Network Within*

Looking back at figure 4.1, what goes inside the box between the sensors and the effectors? A universal automatist would expect to find computations in there. In this section, I'll discuss some popular computational models of how we map patterns of sensory stimulation into patterns of effector activation.

Perhaps the simplest possible mind component is a *reflex:* If the inputs are in such and such a pattern, then take this or that action. The most rudimentary reflex connects each sensor input to an effector output. A classic example of this is a self-steering toy car, as shown in figure 80.

Our minds include lots of simple reflexes—if something sticks in your throat, you cough. If a bug flies toward your eye, you blink. When your lungs are empty you breathe in; when they're full you breathe out.

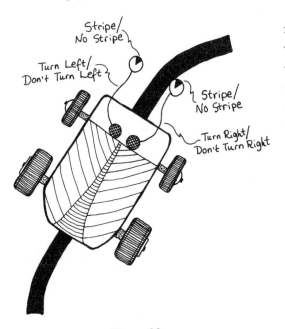

**Figure 80:**
**A Toy Car That Straddles a Stripe**

*The eyes stare down at the ground. When the right eye sees the stripe, this means the car is too far to the left and the car steers right. Likewise for the other side.*

Microorganisms get by solely on reflexes—a protozoan swims forward until it bumps something, at which time it reverses direction. If the water holds the scent of food, the creature slows down, otherwise it swims at full speed. Bumping and backing, speeding and slowing down, the animalcule finds its way all around its watery environment. When combined with the unpredictable structures of the environment, a protozoan's bump-and-reverse reflex together with its slow-down-near-food reflex are enough to make the creature seem to move in an individualistic way.

Looking through a microscope, you may even find yourself rooting for this or that particular microorganism—but remember that

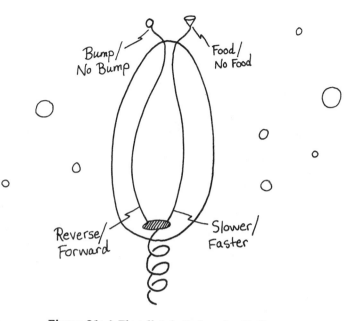

**Figure 81: A Flagellate's Swimming Reflexes**

*I'm drawing the little guy with a corkscrew flagellum tail that he can twirl in one direction or the other, at a greater or a lesser speed. One sensor controls speed and the other sensor controls the direction of the twirling.*

we humans are great ones for projecting personality onto the moving things we see. As shown in figure 81, the internal sensor-to-effector circuitry of a protozoan can be exceedingly simple.

In the early 1980s, brain researcher Valentino Braitenberg had the notion of describing a series of thought experiments involving the motions of simple "vehicles" set into a plane with a few beacon lights.[78] Consider for instance a vehicle with the reflex "approach any light in front of you until it gets too bright, then veer to the dimmer side." If we were to set down a vehicle of this kind in a plane with three lights, we would see an interesting circling motion, possibly chaotic. Since Braitenberg's time, many programmers have amused themselves either by building actual Braitenberg vehicles or by writing programs to simulate little worlds with Braitenberg vehicles moving around. If the virtual vehicles are instructed to leave trails on the computer screen, knotted pathways arise—not unlike the paths that pedestrians trample into new fallen snow. Figure 82 shows three examples of Braitenberg simulations.

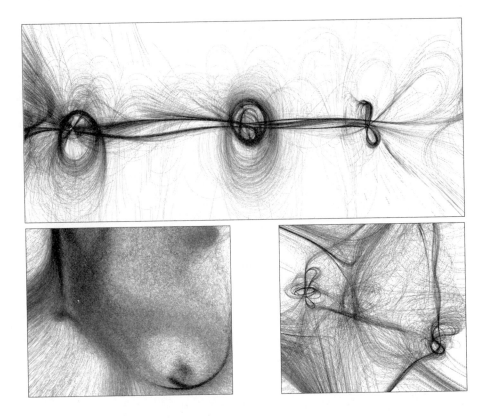

**Figure 82: Gnarly Braitenberg Vehicles**

*The artist and UCLA professor Casey Reas produced these images by simulating large numbers of Braitenberg vehicles that steer toward (or away from) a few "light beacons" placed in their plane worlds. These particular images are called Tissue, Hairy Red, and Path, and are based on the motions of, respectively, twenty-four thousand, two hundred thousand, and six hundred vehicles reacting to, respectively, three, eight, and three beacons. To enhance his images, Reas arbitrarily moves his beacons now and then. He uses his programs to create fine art prints of quite remarkable beauty (see http://www.groupc.net).*

Although the Braitenberg patterns are beautiful, if you watch one particular vehicle for a period of time, you'll normally see it repeating its behavior. In other words, these vehicles, each governed by a single reflex force, perform class two computations. What can we do to make their behavior more interesting?

I have often taught a course on programming computer games, in which students create their own interactive three-dimensional games.[79] We speak of the virtual agents in the game as "critters." A recurrent issue is how to endow a critter with interesting behavior. Although game designers speak of equipping their critters with artificial intelligence, in practice this can mean something quite simple. In order for a critter to have interesting and intelligent-looking behavior, it can be enough to attach two or, better, *three* reflex-driven forces to it.

Think back to our example in section *3.3: Surfing Your Moods* of a magnet pendulum bob suspended above two or more repelling magnets. Three forces: gravity pulls the bob toward the center, and the two magnets on the ground push it away. The result is a chaotic trail.

But now suppose you want more than chaos from your critter. Suppose you want it to actually be good at doing something. In this case the simplest reflexes might not be enough. The next step above the reflex is to allow the use of so-called logic gates that take one or more input signals and combine them in various ways. If we allow ourselves to chain together the output of one gate as the input for another gate, we get a logical circuit. It's possible to create a logical circuit to realize essentially any way of mapping inputs into outputs. We represent a simple "walking" circuit in figure 83.

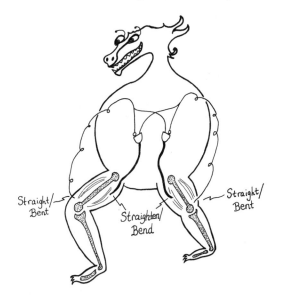

And of course we can make the circuits more and more complicated, eventually putting in something like an entire PC or more. But a logic circuit may not be the best way to model a mind.

**Figure 83: Logic Gates for a Walker**

*The goblet-shaped gates are AND gates, which output a value of True at the bottom if and only both inputs at the top are True. The little circles separating two of the gate input lines from the gates proper are themselves NOT gates. A NOT gate returns a True if and only if its input is False. If you set the walker down with one leg bent and one leg straight, it will continue alternating the leg positions indefinitely.*

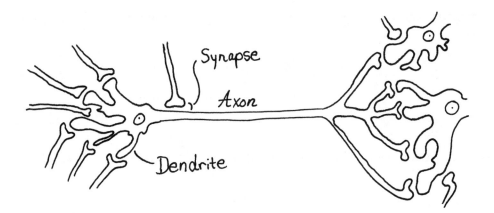

**Figure 84: A Brain Neuron**

The actual computing elements of our brains are nerve cells, or neurons. A brain neuron has inputs called dendrites and a branching output line called an axon, as illustrated in figure 84. Note, by the way, that an axon can be up to a meter long. This means that the brain's computation can be architecturally quite intricate. Nevertheless, later in this chapter we'll find it useful to look at qualitative CA models of the brain in which the axons are short and the neurons are just connected to their closest spatial neighbors.

There are about a hundred billion neurons in a human brain. A neuron's number of "input" dendrites ranges from several hundred to the tens of thousands. An output axon branches out to affect a few dozen or even a few hundred other cells.

In accordance with the sensor-mind-effector model, the neuron dendrites can get inputs from sensor cells as well as from other neurons, and the output axons can activate muscle cells as well as other neurons, as indicated in figure 85.

Normally a nerve cell sends an all-or-nothing activation signal out along its axon. Whether a given neuron "fires" at a given time has to do with its activation level, which in turn depends upon the inputs the neuron receives through its dendrites. Typically a neuron has a certain threshold value, and it fires when its activation becomes greater than the threshold level. After a nerve cell has fired, its activation drops to a resting level, and it takes perhaps a hundredth of a second of fresh stimulation before the cell can become activated enough to fire again.

The gap where axons meet a dendrite is a synapse. When the signal gets to a synapse it activates a transmitter chemical to hop across the gap and stimulate the dendrites of the receptor neuron. The intensity of the stimulation depends on the size of the bulb at the end of the axon and on the distance across the synapse. To make things a bit more complicated, there are in fact two kinds of synapse: excitatory and inhibitory. Stimulating an inhibitory synapse *lowers* the receptor cell's activation level.

Most research on the human brain focuses on the neocortex, which is the surface layer of the brain. This layer is about an eighth of an inch thick. If you could flatten out this extremely convoluted surface, you'd get something like two square feet of neurons—one square foot per brain-half.

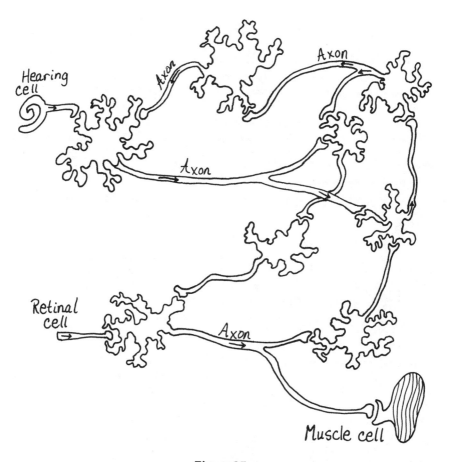

**Figure 85:**
**Brain Neurons Connected to Sensors and Effectors**

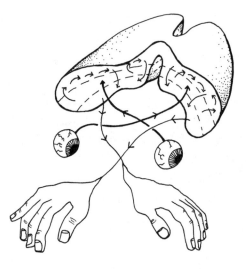

**Figure 86: The Neocortex, Divided into Upper, Middle and Deep Layers**

*A peculiarity of the brain-body architecture is that the left half of the brain handles input and output for the right side of the body, and vice versa.*

Our big flat neocortical sheets can be regarded as a series of layers. The outermost layer is pretty much covered with a tangle of dendrites and axons—kind of like the zillion etched connector lines you see on the underside of a circuit board. Beneath this superficial layer of circuitry, one can single out three main zones: the upper layers, the middle layers, and the deep layers, as illustrated in figure 86.

Roughly speaking, sensory inputs arrive at the middle layer, which sends signals to the upper layer. The upper layer has many interconnections among its own neurons, but some of its outputs also trickle down to the deep layer. And the neurons in the deep layer connect to the body's muscles. This is indicated in figure 86, but we make the flow even clearer in figure 87.

As usual in biology, the *actual* behavior of a living organic brain is funkier and gnarlier and much more complicated than any brief sketch. Instead of there being one kind of brain neuron, there are dozens. Instead of there being one kind of synapse transmission chemical, there are scores of them, all mutually interacting. Some synapses operate electrically rather than chemically, and thus respond much faster. Rather than sending a digital pulse

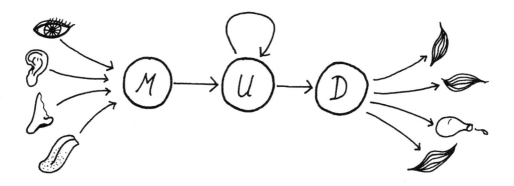

**Figure 87: A Simplified Diagram of the Neocortical Layers' Throughput**

U, M, *and* D *are, respectively, the upper, middle, and deep layers of the neocortex.*

signal, some neurons may instead send a graded continuous-valued signal. In addition, the sensor inputs don't really go directly to the neocortex; they go instead to an intermediate brain region called the thalamus. And our throughput diagram is further complicated by the fact that the upper layers feed some outputs back into the middle layers and the deep layers feed some outputs back into the thalamus. Furthermore, there are any number of additional interactions among other brain regions; in particular, the so-called basal ganglia have input-output loops involving the deep layers. But for our present purposes the diagrams I've given are enough.

When trying to create brainlike systems in their electronic machines, computer scientists often work with a switching element also called a neuron—which is of course intended to model a biological neuron. These computer neurons are hooked together into circuits known as neural nets or neural networks.

As drawn in figure 88, we think of the computer neuron as having some number of input lines with a particular weight attached to each input. The weights are continuous real numbers ranging from negative one to positive one. We think of negatively weighted inputs as inhibiting our artificial neurons and positive values as activating them. At any time, the neuron has an activation level that's obtained by summing up the input values times the weights. In addition, each neuron has a characteristic threshold

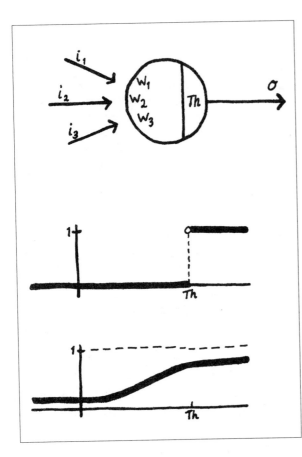

**Figure 88:**
**Computer Neuron Models**

*A neuron with a threshold value computes the weighted sum of its inputs and uses this sum to calculate its output. In this figure, the threshold is Th, and the activation level Ac is the weighted sum of the inputs is $w_1 \cdot i_1 + w_2 \cdot i_2 + w_3 \cdot i_3$. Below the picture of the neuron we graph two possible neuron response patterns, with the horizontal axes representing the activation level Ac and the vertical axes representing the output value o. In the upper "discrete" response pattern, the output is one if Ac is greater than Th, and zero otherwise. In the lower "continuous" response pattern, the output is graded from zero to one, depending on where Ac stands relative to* Th.

value *Th*. The neuron's output depends on how large its activation level is relative to its threshold. This is analogous to the fact that a brain neuron fires an output along its axon whenever its activation is higher than a certain value.

Computer scientists have actually worked with two different kinds of computer neuron models. In the simple version, the neuron outputs are only allowed to take on the discrete values zero and one. In the more complex version, the neuron outputs can take on any real value between zero and one. Our figure indicates how we might compute the output values from the weighted sum of the inputs in each case.

Most computer applications of neural nets use neurons with continuous-valued outputs. On the one hand this model is more removed from the generally discrete-valued-output behavior of biological neurons—given that a typical brain neuron either fires or doesn't fire, its output is more like a single-bit zero or one. On the other hand, our computerized neural nets use so many fewer neurons than does the brain that it makes sense to get more information out of each neuron by using the continuous-valued outputs. In practice, it's easier to tailor a smallish network of *real*-valued-output neurons to perform a given task.[80]

One feature of biological neurons that we'll ignore for now is the fact that biological neurons get tired. That is, there is a short time immediately after firing when a biological neuron won't fire again, no matter how great the incoming stimulation. We'll come back to this property of biological neurons in the following section *4.3: Thoughts as Gliders and Scrolls.*

In analogy to the brain, our artificial neural nets are often arranged in layers. Sensor inputs feed into a first layer of neurons, which can in turn feed into more layers of neurons, eventually feeding out to effectors. The layers in between the sensors and the final effector-linked layers are sometimes called hidden layers. In the oversimplified model of the neocortex that I drew in figures 86 and 87, the so-called upper layer would serve as the hidden layer.

What makes neural nets especially useful is that it's possible to systematically tweak the component neurons' weights in order to make the system learn certain kinds of task.

In order to get an idea of how neural nets work, consider a face-recognition problem that I often have my students work on when I teach a course on artificial intelligence. In this experiment, which was devised by the computer scientist Tom Mitchell of Carnegie Mellon University, we expose a neural network to several hundred small monochrome pictures of people's faces.[81] To simplify things, the images are presented as easily readable computer files that list a grayscale value for each pixel. The goal of the experiment, as illustrated in figure 89, is for the network to recognize which faces are smiling, which are frowning, and which are neutral.

As it turns out, there's a systematic method for adjusting the weights and thresholds of the neurons. The idea is that you train the network on a series of sample inputs for which the desired target output is known. Suppose you show it, say, a test face that is to be known to be smiling. And suppose that the outputs incorrectly claim that the face is frowning or neutral. What you then do is to compute the error term of the outputs. How do I define the error? We'll suppose that if a face is frowning, I want an output of 0.9 from

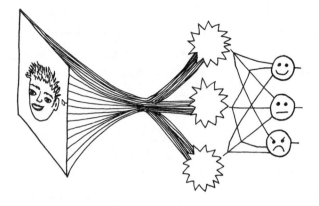

**Figure 89: A Neural Net to Recognize Smiles and Frowns**

*We'll use continuous-valued-output neurons, so at the right-hand side our net returns a real-number "likelihood" value for each of the three possible facial expressions being distinguished. The inputs on the left consist of rasterized images of faces, 30 × 32 pixels in size, with each of the 960 pixels containing a grayscale value ranging between zero and one. In the middle we have a "hidden layer" of three neurons. Each neuron takes input from each of the 960 pixels and has a single output line. On the right we have three effector neurons (drawn as three faces), each of which takes as input the outputs of the three hidden-layer neurons. For a given input picture, the network's "answer" regarding that picture's expression corresponds to the effector neuron that returns the greatest value. The total number of weights in this system is 3·960 + 3·3, or 2,889, and if we add in the threshold values for our six neurons, we get 2,895. (By the way, there's no particular reason why I have three hidden neurons. The network might do all right with two or four hidden neurons instead.)*

the "frown" effector, and outputs of 0.1 from the other two—and analogous sets of output for the neutral and smiling cases. (Due to the S-shaped nature of the continuous-valued-output neurons' response curve, it's not practical to expect them to actually produce exact 0.0 or 1.0 values.)

Given the error value of the network on a given face, you can work your way backward through the system, using a so-called back-propagation algorithm to determine how best to alter the weights and thresholds on the neurons in order to reduce the error. Suppose, for instance, the face was frowning, but the smile output was large. You look at the inputs and weights in the smile neuron to see how its output got so big. Perhaps one of the smile neuron inputs has a high value, and suppose that the smile neuron also has a high positive weight on that input. You take two steps to correct things. First of all, you lower the smile neuron's weight for that large-valued input line, and second, you go back to the hidden neuron that delivered that large value to the smile neuron and analyze how that hidden neuron happened to output such a large value. You go over its input lines and reduce the weights on the larger inputs. In order for the process of back propagation to work, you do it somewhat gently, not pushing the weights or thresholds too far at any one cycle. And you iterate the cycle many times.

So you might teach your neural net to recognize smiles and frowns as follows. Initialize your network with some arbitrary small weights and thresholds, and train it with repeated runs over a set of a hundred faces you've already determined to be smiling, frowning, or neither. After each face your back-propagation method computes the error in the output neurons and readjusts the network weights that are in some sense responsible for the error. You keep repeating the process until you get to a run where the errors are what you consider to be sufficiently small—for the example given, about eighty runs might be enough. At this point you've finished training your neural net. You can save the three thousand or so trained weights and thresholds into a file.

You may be reminded of the discussion in section *3.6: How We Got So Smart* of search methods for finding peaks in a fitness landscape. The situation here is indeed similar. The "face weight" landscape example ranges over all the possible sets of neuron weights and thresholds. For each set of three thousands or so parameters, the fitness value measures how close the network comes to being a 100 percent right in discerning the expressions of the test faces. Obviously it's not feasible to carry out an exhaustive search of this enormous parameter space, so we turn to a search method—in this case a method called back-propagation. As it turns out, back-propagation is in fact a special hill-climbing method that, for any given set of parameters, finds the best nearby set of parameters in the neural net's fitness landscape.

Now comes the question of how well your net's training can generalize. Of course it will score fine on those hundred faces that it looked at eighty times each—but what happens when you give it new, previously unseen pictures of faces? If the faces aren't radically different from the kinds of faces the net was trained upon, the net is likely to do quite well. The network has learned something, and the knowledge takes the form of some three thousand real numbers.

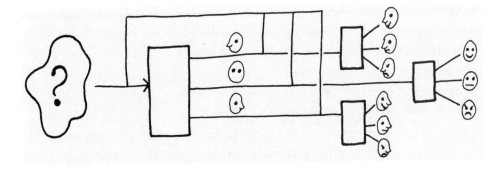

**Figure 90 : Generalized Face Recognizer**

*The first box recognizes the face's position. The position information is fed with the face information to the three specialized expression recognizers, and the appropriate one responds.*

But if, for instance, all the training faces were seen full-on, the network isn't going to do well on profile faces. Or if all the training faces were of people without glasses, the network probably won't be good at recognizing the facial expressions of glasses-wearers.

What to do? One approach is to build up deeper layers of neural networks. We might, for instance, use a preliminary network to decide which way a face is looking, sorting them into left-profile, full, and right-profile faces. And then we could train a separate expression-recognizing network for each of the three kinds of face positions. With a little cleverness with the wiring, the whole thing could be boxed up as a single multilayer neural net, as suggested by figure 90.

Note here that it can actually be quite a job to figure out how best to break down a problem into neural-net-solvable chunks, and to then wire the solutions together. Abstractly speaking, one could simply throw a very general neural net at any problem—for instance, you might give the arbitrarily-positioned-face-recognition problem a neural net with perhaps two hidden layers of neurons, also allowing input lines to run from all the pixels into the neurons of the second hidden layer, and hope that with enough training and back-propagation the network will eventually converge on a solution that works as well as using the first layer to decide on the facial orientation and using the second layer's neurons to classify the expression of each facial orientation. Training a net without a preconceived design *is* feasible, but it's likelier to take longer than using some preliminary analysis and assembling it as described above.

Custom-designed neural nets are widely used—the U.S. Post Office, for instance, uses a neural net program to recognize handwritten ZIP codes. But the designers did have to put in quite a bit of thought about the neural net architecture—that is, how many hidden layers to use, and how many neurons to put in each of the hidden layers.

Computer scientists like to imagine building programs or robots that can grow up and learn and figure things out *without* any kind of guiding input. In so-called unsupervised learning, there's no answer sheet to consult. If, for instance, you learn to play Ping-Pong simply by playing games against an opponent, your feedback will consist of noticing which of your shots goes bad and which points you lose. Nobody is telling you things like, "You should have tilted the paddle a little to the right and aimed more toward the other side's left corner." And, to make the situation even trickier, it may be quite some time until you encounter a given situation again. Tuning your neural net with unsupervised learning is a much harder search problem, and specifying the search strategy is an important part of the learning program design—typical approaches might include hill-climbing and genetic programming.

There's also a metasearch issue of trying out various neural net architectures and seeing which works best. But as your problem domains get more sophisticated, the fitness evaluations get more time-consuming, particularly in the unsupervised learning environments where you essentially have to play out a whole scenario in order to see how well your agent will do. The search times for effective learning can be prohibitively long.

It's worth noting here that a human or an animal is born with nearly all of the brain's neural net architecture already in place. It's not as if each of us has to individually figure out how to divide the brain's hundred billion neurons into layers, how to parcel these layers into intercommunicating columns, and how to connect the layers to the thalamus, the sense organs, the spine, the basal ganglia, etc. The exceedingly time-consuming searches over the space of possible neural architectures is something that's happened over millions of years of evolution—and we're fortunate enough to inherit the results.

The somewhat surprising thing is how often a neural net can solve what had seemed to be a difficult AI problem. Workers in the artificial-intelligence field sometimes say, "Neural nets are the second-best solution to any problem."[82]

Given a reasonable neural net architecture and a nice big set of training examples, you can teach a neural net to solve just about any kind of problem that involves recognizing standard kinds of situations. And if you have quite a large amount of time, you can even train neural nets to carry out less clearly specified problems, such as, for instance, teaching a robot how to walk on two legs. As with any automated search procedure, the neural net solutions emerge without a great deal of formal analysis or deep thought.

The seemingly "second-best" quality of the solution has to do with the feeling that a neural net solution is somewhat clunky, ad hoc, and brute-force. It's not as if the designer has come up with an elegant, simple algorithm based upon a fundamental understanding of the problem in question. The great mound of network weights has an incomprehensible feel to it.

It could be that it's time to abandon our scientific prejudices against complicated solutions. In the heroic nineteenth and twentieth centuries of science, the *best* solution of a problem often involved a dramatic act of fundamental understanding—one has only to think of the kinds of formulas that traditionally adorn the T-shirts of physics grad students: Maxwell's equations for electromagnetism, Einstein's laws for relativity, Schrödinger's wave equation for quantum mechanics. In each case, we're talking about a concise set of axioms from which one can, in a reasonable amount of time, logically derive the answers to interesting toy problems.

But the simple equations of physics don't provide feasible solutions to many real-world problems—the laws of physics, for instance, don't tell us when the big earthquake will hit San Jose, California, and it wouldn't even help to know the exact location of all the rocks underground. Physical systems are computationally unpredictable. The laws provide, at best, a recipe for how the world might be computed in parallel particle by particle and region by region. But—unless you have access to some so-far-unimaginable kind of computing device that simulates reality faster than the world does itself—the only way to actually learn the results is to wait for the actual physical process to work itself out. There is a fundamental gap between they're learning. If you go off and hit a ball against a wall a few hundred times in a row, you're exploring which kind of stroke gives the best results. What children learn in school isn't so much the stuff the teachers say as it is the results of acting various different ways around other people.

In terms of Wolfram's fourfold classification, what kinds of overall computation take place as you adjust the weights of your brain's neural networks?

Clear-cut tasks like learning the alphabet are class one computations. You repeat a deterministic process until it converges on a fixed point.

But in many cases the learning is never done. Particularly in social situations, new problems continue to arise. Your existing network weights need to be retuned over and over. Your network-tuning computation is, if you will, a lifelong education. The educational process will have aspects of class two, three, and four.

Your life education is class two, that is, periodic, to the extent that you lead a somewhat sheltered existence, perhaps by getting all your information from newspapers or, even more predictably, from television. In this kind of life, you're continually encountering the same kinds of problems and solving them in the same kinds of ways.

If, on the other hand, you seek out a wider, more arbitrary range of different inputs, then your ongoing education is more of a class three process.

And, to the extent that you guide yourself guided along systematic yet gnarly paths, you're carrying out a class four exploration of knowledge. Note that in this last case, it may well be that you're unable to consciously formulate the criteria by which you guide yourself—indeed, if your search results from an unpredictable class four computation, this is precisely the case.

The engaged intellectual life is a never-ending journey into the unknown. Although the rules of our neuronal structures are limited in number, the long-term consequences of the rules need not be boring or predictable.

## 4.3: *Thoughts as Gliders and Scrolls*

So far we've only talked about situations in which a brain tries to adjust itself so as to deal with some external situation. But the life of the mind is much more dynamic. Even *without* external input, the mind's evolving computations are intricate and unpredictable.

Your brain doesn't go dark if you close your eyes and lie down in a quiet

T-shirt-physics-equations and the unpredictable and PC-unfeasible gnarl of daily life.

One of the curious things about neural nets is that our messy heap of weights arises from a rather simple deterministic procedure. Just for the record, let's summarize the factors involved.

- The network architecture, that is, how many neurons we use, and how they're connected to the sensor inputs, the effector outputs, and to one another.
- The specific implementation of the back-propagation algorithm to be used—there are numerous variants of this algorithm.
- The process used to set the arbitrary initial weights—typically we use a pseudorandomizer to spit out some diverse values, perhaps a simple little program like a CA. It's worth noting that if we want to repeat our experiment, we can set the pseudorandomizer to the same initial state, obtaining the exact same initial weights and thence the same training process and the same eventual trained weights.
- The training samples. In the case of the expression-recognition program, this would again be a set of computer files of face images along with a specification as to which expression that face is considered to have.

In some sense the weights are summarizing the information about the sample examples in a compressed form—and compressed forms of information are often random-looking and incomprehensible. Of course it might be that the neural net's weights would be messy even if the inputs were quite simple. As we've seen several times before, it's not unusual for simple systems to generate messy-looking patterns all on their own—remember Wolfram's pseudorandomizing cellular automaton Rule 30 and his glider-producing universally computing Rule 110.

We have every reason to suppose that, at least in some respects, the human brain functions similarly to a computer-modeled neural network. Although, as I mentioned earlier, much of the brain's network comes preinstalled, we *do* learn things—the faces of those around us, the words of our native language, skills like touch-typing or bicycle-riding, and so on.

First of all, we might ask how a living brain goes about tweaking the weights of the synaptic connections between axons and dendrites. One possibility is that the changes are physical. A desirable synapse might be enhanced by having the axon's terminal bulb grow a bit larger or move a bit closer to the receptor dendrite, and an undesirable synapse's axon bulb might shrivel or move away. The virtue of physical changes is that they stay in place. But it's also possible that the synapse tweaking is something subtler and more biochemical.

Second, we can ask how our brains go about deciding *in which directions* the synapse weights should be tweaked.

Do we use back-propagation, like a neural net? This isn't so clear.

A very simple notion of human learning is called Hebbian learning, after Canadian neuropsychologist Donald O. Hebb, who published an influential book called *The Organization of Behavior* in 1949. This theory basically says that the more often a given synapse fires, the stronger its weight becomes. If you do something the right way over and over, that behavior gets "grooved in." Practice makes perfect. It may be that when we mentally replay certain kinds of conversations, we're trying to simulate doing something right.

This said, it may be that we do some back-propagation as well. In an unsupervised learning situation, such as when you are learning to play tennis, you note an error when, say, you hit the ball into the net. But you may not realize the error is precisely because you rotated your wrist too far forward as you hit. Rather than being able to instantly back-propagate the information to your wrist-controlling reflexes, you make some kind of guess about what you did wrong and back-propagate that.

More complicated skills—like how to get along with the people in your life—can take even longer to learn. For one thing, in social situations the feedback is rather slow. Do you back-propagate the error term only the next day when you find out that you goofed, at that time making your best guess as to which of your behaviors produced the bad results?

As well as using Hebbian learning or back-propagation, we continually carry out experiments, adjusting our neural weights on the fly. To an outsider, this kind of activity looks like play. When puppies romp and nip, spot. The thoughts you have while driving your car don't have much to do with the sensor-effector exigencies of finding your way and avoiding the other vehicles.

A little introspection reveals that we have several different styles of thought. In particular, I'd like to distinguish between two modes that I'll call *trains of thought* and *thought loops*.

By trains of thought, I mean the free-flowing and somewhat unpredictable chains of association that the mind produces when left on its own. Note that trains of thoughts need not be formulated in words. When I watch, for instance, a tree branch bobbing in the breeze, my mind plays with the positions of the leaves, following them and automatically making little predictions about their motions. And then the image of the branch might be replaced by a mental image of a tiny man tossed up high into the air. His parachute pops open and he floats down toward a city of lights. I recall the first time I flew into San Jose and how it reminded me of a great circuit board. I remind myself that I need to see about getting a new computer soon, and then in reaction I think about going for a bicycle ride. The image of the bicyclist on the back of the Rider brand of playing cards comes to mind, along with a thought of how Thomas Pynchon refers to this image in *Gravity's Rainbow*. I recall the heft of Pynchon's book, and then think of the weights that I used to lift in Louisville as a hopeful boy forty-five years ago, the feel and smell of the rusty oily weight bar still fresh in my mind.

By thought loops, I mean something quite different. A thought loop is some particular sequence of images and emotions that you repeatedly cycle through. Least pleasant—and all too common—are thought loops having to do with emotional upsets. If you have a disagreement with a colleague or a loved one, you may find yourself repeating the details of the argument, summarizing the pros and cons of your position, imagining various follow-up actions, and then circling right back to the detailed replay of the argument. Someone deep in the throes of an argument-provoked thought loop may even move their lips and make little gestures to accompany the remembered words and the words they wish they'd said.

But many thought loops are good. You often use a thought loop to solve a problem or figure out a course of action, that is, you go over and over a certain sequence of thoughts, changing the loop a bit each time. And eventually you arrive at a pattern you like. Each section of this book, for instance, is the result of some thought loops that I carried around within myself for weeks, months, or even years before writing them down.

Understanding a new concept also involves a thought loop. You formulate the ideas as some kind of pattern within your neurons, and then you repeatedly activate the pattern until it takes on a familiar, grooved-in feel.

Viewing a thought loop as a circulating pattern of neuronal activation suggests something about how the brain might lay down long-term memories. Certainly a long-term memory doesn't consist of a circulating thought loop that never stops. Long-term memory surely involves something more static. A natural idea would be that if you think about something for a little while, the circulating thought-loop stimulation causes physical alterations in the synapses that can persist even after the thought is gone. This harks back to the Hebbian learning I mentioned in the section *4.2: The Network Within*, whereby the actual geometry of the axons and dendrites might change as a result of being repeatedly stimulated.

Thus we can get long-term memory from thought loops by supposing that a thought loop reinforces the neural pathway that it's passing around. And when a relevant stimulus occurs at some later time, the grooved-in pathway is activated again.

Returning to the notion of free-running trains of thought, you might want to take a minute here and look into your mind. Watching trains of thought is entertaining, a pleasant way of doing nothing. But it's not easy.

I find that what usually breaks off my enjoyment of my thought trains is that some particular thought will activate one of my thought loops to such an extent that I put all my attention into the loop. Or it may be that I encounter some new thought that I like so much that I want to savor it, and I create a fresh thought loop of repeating that particular thought to myself over and over. Here again my awareness of the passing thought trains is lost.

This process is familiar for students of the various styles of meditation. In meditation, you're trying to stay out of the thought loops and to let the trains of thought run on freely without any particular conscious attachment. Meditators are often advised to try to be in the moment, rather than in the past or the future—brooding over the past and worrying about the future are classic

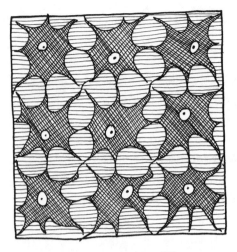

**Figure 91: A CA Made of Neurons**

*The dark, curvy eight-pointed stars are the neurons.*

types of thought loops. One way to focus on the present is to pay close attention to your immediate body sensations, in particular to be aware of the inward and outward flow of your breath.

In understanding the distinction between trains of thought and thought loops, it's useful to consider some computational models.

One of the nicest and simplest computer models of thought trains is a cellular automaton rule called Brian's Brain. It was invented by the cellular automatist and all-around computer-fanatic Brian Silverman.

Brian's Brain is based on a feature of the brain's neurons that, for simplicity's sake, isn't normally incorporated into the computer-based neural nets described in section 4.2. This additional feature is that actual brain neurons can be tired, out of juice, too pooped to pop. If a brain neuron fires and sends a signal down its axon, then it's not going to be doing anything but recuperating for the next tenth of a second or so.

With this notion in mind, Silverman formulated a two-dimensional CA model based on "nerve cells" that have three states: ready, firing, and resting. Rather than thinking of the cells as having distinct input and output lines, the CA model supposes that the component cells have simple two-way links; to further simplify things, we assume that each cell is connected only to its nearest neighbors, as indicated in figure 91.

The Brian's Brain rule updates all the cells in parallel, with a given cell's update method depending on which state the cell happens to be in.

- *Ready.* This is the ground state where neurons spend most of their time. At each update, each cell counts how many (if any) of its eight immediate neighbors is in the firing state. If exactly two neighbors are firing, a ready cell switches to the firing state at the next update. In all other cases, a ready cell stays ready.

- *Firing.* This corresponds to the excited state where a neuron stimulates its neighbors. After being in a firing state, a cell always enters the resting state at the following update.
- *Resting.* This state follows the firing state. After one update spent in the resting state, a cell returns to the ready state.

The existence of the resting-cell state makes it very easy for moving patterns of activation to form in the Brian's Brain rule. Suppose, for instance, that we have two light-gray firing cells backed up by two dark-gray resting cells. You might enjoy checking that the pattern will move in the direction of the firing cells, as indicated in figure 92.

Brian's Brain is rich in the moving patterns that cellular automatists call gliders. It's a classic example of a class four computation and is nicely balanced between growth and death. Silverman himself once left a Brian's Brain simulation running untended on an early Apple computer for a year—and it never died down. The larger gliders spawn off smaller gliders; occasionally gliders will stretch out a long thread of activation between them. As suggested by figure 93, we find gliders moving in all four of the CA space's directions, and there are in fact small patterns called butterflies that move diagonally as well.

I don't think it's unreasonable to suppose that the thought trains within your brain may result from a process somewhat similar to the endless flow of the gliding patterns in the Brian's Brain CA. The trains of thought steam along, now and then colliding and sending off new thought trains in their wake.

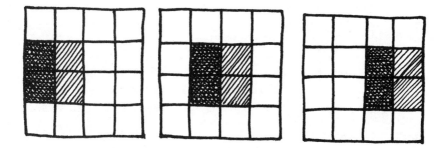

**Figure 92: A Glider in the Brian's Brain Rule**

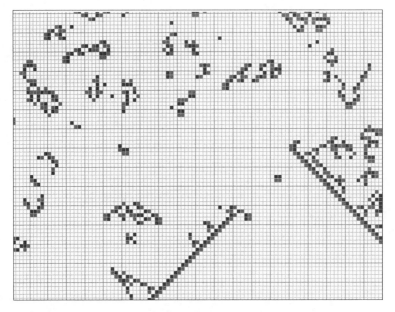

**Figure 93: The Brian's Brain Cellular Automaton**

*The white, light gray, and dark gray cells are, respectively, in the ready, firing, and resting states. If the picture were animated, you would see the patterns moving horizontally and vertically, with the light gray edges leading the dark gray tails, and with new firing cells dying and being born.*[83]

When some new sensation comes in from the outside, it's like a cell-seeding cursor-click on a computer screen. A few neurons get turned on, and the patterns of activation and inhibition flow out from there.

A more complicated way to think of thought trains would be to compare the brain's network of neurons to a continuous-valued CA that's simulating wave motion, as we discussed back in section *2.2: Everywhere at Once.* Under this view, the thought trains are like ripples, and new input is like a rock thrown into a pond.

What about recurrent thoughts—the topics that you obsess upon, the mental loops that you circle around over and over? Here another kind of CA rule comes to mind: Zhabotinsky-style scrolls. You may recall that we've already discussed these ubiquitous forms in both the context of morphogenesis as well as in connection with ecological simulations of population levels. I show yet another pair of these images in figure 94.

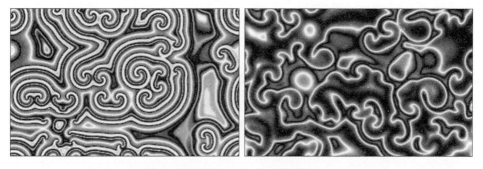

**Figure 94: More CA Scroll Patterns**

*These two images were generated using variations of continuous-valued activator-inhibitor rules suggested by, respectively, Arthur Winfree and Hans Meinhardt.*

Scroll-type patterns often form when we have an interaction between activation and inhibition, which is a good fit for the computations of the brain's neurons. And, although I haven't yet mentioned the next fact, it's also the case that scroll patterns most commonly form in systems where the individual cells can undergo a very drastic change from a high level of activation to a low level—which is also a good fit for neuronal behavior. A neuron's activation levels rise to a threshold value, it fires, and its activation abruptly drops.

Recall that when CAs produce patterns like Turing stripes and Zhabotinsky scrolls, we have the activation and inhibition diffusing at different rates. I want to point out that the brain's activation and inhibition signals may also spread at different rates. Even if all neural activation signals are sent down axons at the same rate, axons of different length take longer to transmit a signal. And remember that there's a biochemical element to the transmission of signals across synapses, so the activator and inhibitor substances may spread and take effect at different rates.

Summing up, I see my thought patterns as being a combination of two types of processes: a discrete gliderlike flow of thought trains overlaid upon the smoother and more repetitive cycling of my thought loops. The images in figure 95 capture something of what I have in mind.

I'll confess that neither of these images *precisely* models my conception of brain activity—I'd really prefer to see the gliders etching highways into the scrolls and to see the dense centers and intersections of the scrolls acting as

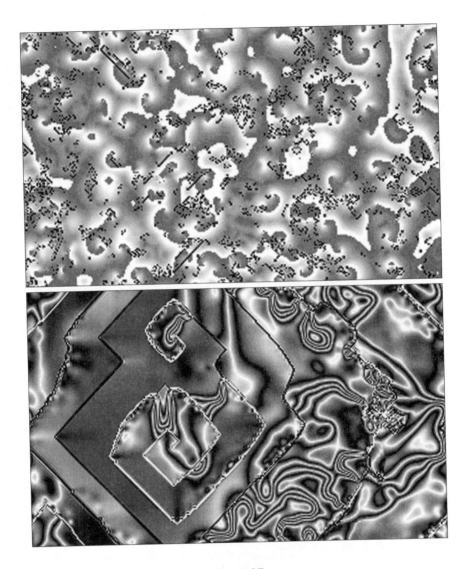

**Figure 95:**
**Cellular Automaton Patterns Like a Mind with Thoughts and Obsessions**

*The first image shows the Brain Hodge rule, where discrete Brian's Brain gliders cruise across a sea of Hodgepodge scrolls. The cells hold two activators, one for each rule, and the Brain activator stimulates the Hodgepodge activator.*

*The second image shows the Boiling Cubic Wave rule. Here we have a nonlinear wave-simulating rule that makes ripples akin to thought loops. The nonlinearity of the wave is a value that varies from cell to cell and obeys a driven heat rule, producing a "boiling" effect like moving trains of thought layered on top of the wavy thought loops. As it so happens, the thought trains have the ability to bend around into square scrolls.*

seed points for fresh showers of gliders. But I hope the images give you a general notion of what I have in mind when I speak of thought trains moving across a background of thought loops.

I draw inspiration from the distinction between fleeting trains of thought and repeating thought loops. When I'm writing, I often have a fairly clear plan for the section I'm working on. As I mentioned above, this plan is a thought loop that I've been rehearsing for a period of time. But it sometimes happens that once I'm actually doing the writing, an unexpected train of thought comes plowing past. I treat such unexpected thoughts as gifts from the muse, and I always give them serious consideration.

I remember when I was starting out as a novelist, I read an advice-to-writers column where an established author said something like, "From time to time, you'll be struck with a completely crazy idea for a twist in your story. A wild hair that totally disrupts what you had in mind. Go with it. If the story surprises you, it'll surprise the reader, too." I never forgot that advice.

This said, as a practical matter, I don't really work in every single oddball thought I get, as at some point a work can lose its coherence. But many of the muse's gifts can indeed be used.

Who or what *is* the muse? For now, let's just say the muse is the unpredictable but deterministic evolution of thought trains from the various inputs that you happen to encounter day to day. The muse is a class four computation running in your brain.

People working in any kind of creative endeavor can hear the muse. You might be crafting a novel, an essay, a PowerPoint presentation, a painting, a business proposal, a computer program, a dinner menu, a decoration scheme, an investment strategy, or a travel plan. In each case, you begin by generating a thought loop that describes a fairly generic plan. And over time you expand and alter the thought loop. Where do the changes come from? Some of them are reached logically, as predictable class two computations closely related to the thought loop. But the more interesting changes occur to you as unexpected trains of thought. Your plan sends out showers of gliders that bounce around your neuronal space, eventually catching your attention with new configurations. Straight from the muse.

One seeming problem with comparing thoughts to moving patterns in cellular automata is that the space of brain neurons isn't in fact structured like a CA. Recall that axons can be up to a meter long, and information flow along an axon is believed to be one-way rather than two-way.

But this isn't all that big a problem. Yes, the connectivity of the brain neurons is more intricate than the connectivity of the cells in a CA. But our experiences with the universality of computational processes suggests that the same general *kinds* of patterns and processes that we find in CAs should also occur in the brain's neural network. We can expect to find class one patterns that die out, class two patterns that repeat, chaotic class three patterns, rapidly moving gliderlike class four patterns, and the more slowly moving scroll-like class four patterns.

Visualize a three-dimensional CA running a CA rule rich in gliders and scrolls (see figure 96). Think of the cells as nodes connected by strings to their neighbors. Now stretch a bunch of the strings and scramble things around, maybe drop the mess onto a tabletop, and shuffle it. Then paste the tangle into a two-foot-square mat that's one-eighth of an inch thick. Your neocortex! The glider and scroll patterns are still moving around in the network,

**Figure 96: Another Three-Dimensional CA with Scrolls**

*Here's a Winfree-style CA running on a three-dimensional array of cells. The surface patterns change rather rapidly, as buried scrolls boil up and move across it. Gnarly dude!*

but due to the jumbled connections among the cells, a brain scan won't readily reveal the moving patterns. The spatial arrangement of the neurons doesn't match their connectivity. But perhaps some researchers can notice subtler evidences of the brain's gliders and scrolls.

At this point we're getting rather close to the synthesizing "Seashell" element of my book's title. To be quite precise, I'm proposing that the brain is a CA-like computer and that the computational patterns called gliders and scrolls are the basis of our soulful mental sensations of, respectively, unpredictable trains of thought and repetitive thought-loops.

If this is true, does it make our mental lives less interesting? No. From whence, after all, could our thoughts come, if not from neuronal stimulation patterns? From higher-dimensional ectoplasm? From telepathic dark matter? From immortal winged souls hovering above the gross material plane? From heretofore undetected subtle energies? It's easier to use your plain old brain.

Now, don't forget that many or perhaps most complex computations are unpredictable. Yes, our brains might be carrying out computations, but that doesn't mean they'll ever cease surprising us.

I'm not always as happy as I'd like to be, and the months when I've been working on this chapter have been especially challenging. My joints and muscles pain me when I program or write, I had the flu for a solid month, my wife's father has fallen mortally ill, my country's mired in war, I'm anxious about finding a way to retire from the grind of teaching computer science, and frankly I'm kind of uptight about pulling off this rather ambitious book. I could complain for hours! I'm getting to be an old man.

Scientist that I am, I dream that a deeper understanding of the mind might improve my serenity. If I had a better model of how my mind works, maybe I could use my enhanced understanding to tweak myself into being happy. So now I'm going to see if thinking in terms of computation classes and chaotic attractors can give me any useful insights about my moods. I already said a bit about this in section *3.3: Surfing Your Moods,* but I want to push it further. After all, "How to Be Happy" is part of the book's subtitle.

Rather than calling the mind's processes class four computations, we can also refer to them as being chaotic. Although a chaotic process is unpredictable in detail, one can learn the overall range of behaviors that the system will display. This range is, again, what we call a chaotic attractor.

A dynamic process like the flow of thought wanders around a state space of possibilities. To the extent that thought is a computation, the trajectory differs from random behavior in two ways. First of all, the transitions from one moment to the next are deterministic. And secondly, at any given time the process is constrained to a certain range of possibilities—the chaotic attractor. In the Brian's Brain CA, for instance, the attractor is the behavior of having gliders moving about with a characteristic average distance between them. In a scroll, the attractor is the behavior of pulsing out rhythmic bands.

As I mentioned in section *2.4: The Meaning of Gnarl,* a class one computation homes in on a final conclusion, which acts as a pointlike attractor. A class two computation repeats itself, cycling around on an attractor that's a smooth, closed hypersurface in state space. Class three processes are very nearly random and have fuzzy attractors filling their state space. Most relevant for the analysis of mind are our elaborate class four trains of thought, flickering across their attractors like fish around tropical reefs.

If you happen to be faced with a problem that actually has a definite solution, your thought dynamics can in fact can take on a class one form, closing in on the unique answer. But life's more galling problems are in fact insoluble, and grappling with a problem like this is likely to produce a wretched class two cycle.

Taking a fresh look at a thought loop gets you nowhere. By way of illustration, no matter what brave new seed pattern you throw into a scroll-generating CA, the pattern will always be eaten away as the natural attractor of the loop reasserts itself.

So how do we switch away from unpleasant thoughts? The only real way to escape a thought loop is to shift your mind's activity to a different attractor, that is, to undergo a chaotic bifurcation, as I put it in section 2.4. We change attractors by altering some parameter or rule of the system so as to move to a different set of characteristic behaviors. With regard to my thoughts, I see two basic approaches: reprogramming or distraction.

*Reprogramming* is demanding and it takes time. Here I try to change the essential operating rules of the processes that make my negative thought-loops painful. Techniques along these lines include: learning to accept irremediable situations just as they are; anticipating and forestalling my standard emotional reactions to well-known recurring trigger events; letting go of my expectations about how the people around me ought to behave; and releasing my attachment to certain hoped-for outcomes. None of these measures comes easily.

I always imagine that over time, by virtue of right thinking and proper living, I'll be able to inculcate some lasting changes into my synapses or neurotransmitters. I dream that I'll be able to avoid the more lacerating thought-loops for good. But my hard-won equilibrium never lasts. Eventually I fall off the surfboard into the whirlpools.

Our society periodically embraces the belief that one might attain permanent happiness by taking the right drugs—think of psychedelics in the sixties and antidepressants in the Y2K era. Drugs affect brain's computations, not by altering the software, but by tweaking the operational rules of the underlying neural hardware. The catch is that, given the unpredictable nature of class four computation, the effects of drugs can be different from what they're advertised to be. At this point in my life, my preference is to get by without drugs. My feeling is that the millennia-long evolution of the human brain has provided for a rich enough system to produce unaided any state I'm interested in. At least in my case, drugs can in fact lead to a diminished range of possibilities. This said, I do recognize that, in certain black moods, any theorizing about attractors and computation classes becomes utterly beside the point, and I certainly wouldn't gainsay the use of medication for those experiencing major depression.

*Distraction* is an easier approach. Here you escape a problem by simply forgetting about it. And why not? Why must every problem be solved? Your mind's a big place, so why limit your focus to its least pleasant corners? When I want to come to my senses and get my attention away from, say, a mental tape of a quarrel, I might do it by hitching a ride on a passing thought train. Or by paying attention to someone other than myself. Altruism has its rewards. Exercise, entertainment, or excursions can help change my mood.

Both reprogramming and distraction reduce to changing the active attractor. Reprogramming myself alters the connectivity or chemistry of my brain enough so that I'm able to transmute my thought loops into different forms with altered attractors. Distracting myself and refocusing my attention shifts my conscious flow of thoughts to a wholly different attractor.

If you look at an oak tree and a eucalyptus tree rocking in the wind, you'll notice that each tree's motion has its own distinct set of attractors. In the same way, different people have their own emotional weather, their particular style of response, thought, and planning. This is what we might call their sensibility, personality, or disposition.

Having raised three children, it's my impression that, to a large degree, their dispositions were fairly well fixed from the start. For that matter, my own basic response patterns haven't changed all that much since I was a boy. One's mental climate is an ingrained part of the body's biochemistry, and the range of attractors available to an individual brain is not so broad as one might hope.

In one sense, this is a relief. You are who you are, and there's no point agonizing about it. My father took to this insight in his later life and enjoyed quoting Popeye's saying: "I yam what I yam." Speaking of my father, as the years go by, I often notice aspects of my behavior that remind me of him or of my mother—and I see the same patterns yet again in my children. Much of one's sensibility consists of innate hereditary patterns of the brain's chemistry and connectivity.

In another sense, it's disappointing not to be able to change one's sensibility. We can tweak our moods somewhat via reprogramming, distraction, or psychopharmacology. But making a radical change is quite hard.

As I type this on my laptop, I'm sitting at my usual table in the Los Gatos Coffee Roasting cafe. On the cafe speakers I hear Jackson Browne singing his classic road song, "Take It Easy," telling me not to let the sound of my own wheels drive me crazy. It seems to fit the topic of thought loops, so I write it in. This gift from the outside reminds me that perhaps there's a muse bigger than anything in my own head. Call it God, call it the universe, call it the cosmic computation that runs forward and backward through all of spacetime.

Just now it seems as if everything's all right. And so what if my exhilaration is only temporary? Life is, after all, one temporary solution after another. Homeostasis.

### 4.4: "I Am"

In section *4.1: Sensational Emotions,* I observed that our brain functions are intimately related to the fact that we have bodies living in a real world, in section *4.2: The Network Within,* I discussed how responses can be learned in the form of weighted networks of neural synapses, and in section *4.3: Thoughts as Gliders and Scrolls,* I pointed out that the brain's overall patterns of activation are similar to the gliders and scrolls of CAs.

In this section I'll talk about who or what is experiencing the thoughts. But before I get to that, I want to say a bit about the preliminary question of how it is that a person sees the world as made of distinct objects, one of which happens to be the person in question.

Thinking in terms of objects gives you an invaluable tool for compressing your images of the world, allowing you to chunk particular sets of sensations together. The ability to perceive objects isn't something a person learns; it's a basic skill that's hardwired into the neuronal circuitry of the human brain.

We take seeing objects for granted, but it's by no means a trivial task. Indeed, one of the outstanding open problems in robotics is to design a computer vision program that can take camera input and reliably pick out the objects in an arbitrary scene. By way of illustration, when speaking of chess-playing robots, programmers sometimes say that playing chess is the *easy* part and recognizing the pieces is the *hard* part. This is initially surprising, as playing chess is something that people have to *laboriously learn*—whereas the ability to perceive objects is something that people *get for free,* thanks to being born with a human brain.

In fact, the hardest tasks facing AI involve trying to emulate the fruits of evolution's massive computations. Putting it a bit differently, the built-in features of the brain are things that the human genome has phylogenetically learned via evolution. In effect evolution has been running a search algorithm across millions of parallel computing units for millions of years, dwarfing the learning done by an individual brain during the pitifully short span of a single human life. The millennia of phylogenetic learning are needed because it's very hard to find a developmental sequence of morphogens capable of growing a developing brain into a useful form. Biological evolution solved the problem, yes, but can our laboratories?

In limited domains, man-made programs do of course have some small success in recognizing objects. Machine vision uses tricks such as looking for the contours of objects' edges, picking out coherent patches of color, computing the geometric ratios between a contour's corners, and matching these features against those found in a stored set of reference images. Even so, it's not clear if the machine approaches we've attempted are in fact the right ones. The fact that our hardware is essentially serial tends to discourage us from thinking deeply enough about the truly parallel algorithms used by living organisms. And using search methods to design the parallel algorithms takes prohibitively long.

In any case, thanks to evolution, we humans see the world as made up of objects. And of all the objects in your world, there's one that's most important to you: your own good self. At the most obvious level, you pay special attention to your own body because that's what's keeping you alive. But now let's focus on something deeper: the fact that your self always seems surrounded by a kind of glow. Your consciousness. What is it?

At first we might suppose that consciousness is a distinct extra element, with a person then being made of three parts:

- The hardware, that is, the physical body and brain.
- The software, including memories, skills, opinions, and behavior patterns.
- The glow of consciousness.

What is that "glow" exactly? Partly it's a sense of being yourself, but it's more than that: It's a persistent visceral sensation of a certain specific kind; a warmth, a presence, a wordless voice forever present in your mind. I think I'm safe in assuming you know exactly what I mean.

I used to be of the opinion that this core consciousness is simply the bare feeling of existence, expressed by the primal utterance, "I am." I liked the fact that everyone expresses their core consciousness in the same words: "I am. I am me. I exist." This struck me as an instance of what my ancestor Hegel called the divine nature of language. And it wasn't lost on me that the Bible reports that after Moses asked God His name, "God said to Moses, 'I AM WHO I AM'; and He said, 'Thus you shall say to the sons of Israel, I AM has sent me to you.' " I once discussed this with Kurt Gödel, by the way, and he said the "I AM" in Exodus was a mistranslation. Be that as it may. I used to imagine my glow of consciousness to be a divine emanation from the cosmic One, without worrying too much more about the details.[84]

But let's give universal automatism a chance. Might one's glow of consciousness have some specific brain-based cause that we might in turn view as a computation?

In the late 1990s, neurologist Antonio Damasio began making a case that core consciousness results from specific phenomena taking place in the neurons of the brain. For Damasio, consciousness emerges from specific localized brain activities and is indeed a kind of computation. As evidence, Damasio points out that if a person suffers damage to a certain region of the brain stem, their consciousness will in fact get turned off, leaving them as a functional zombie, capable of moving about and doing things, but lacking that glowing sense of self.

Damasio uses a special nomenclature to present his ideas. He introduces the term *movie-in-the-brain* to describe a brain's activity of creating images of the world and of the body. The image of the body and its sensations is something that he calls the *proto-self*. And he prefers the term *core consciousness* to what I've been calling the "I am" feeling.

Damasio believes that core consciousness consists of enhancing the movie-in-the-brain with a representation of how objects and sensations affect the proto-self. Putting it a little differently, he feels that, at any time, core consciousness amounts to having a mental image of yourself interacting with some particular image. It's not enough to just have a first-order image of yourself in the world as an object among other objects—to get to core consciousness, you go a step beyond that and add on a second-order representation of your reactions and feelings about the objects you encounter. Figure 97 shows a shorthand image of what Damasio seems to have in mind.

In addition to giving you an enhanced sense of self, Damasio views core consciousness as determining which objects you're currently paying attention to. In other words, the higher-order process involved in core consciousness has two effects: It gives you the feeling of being a knowing, conscious being, and it produces a particular mental focus on one image after another. The focusing

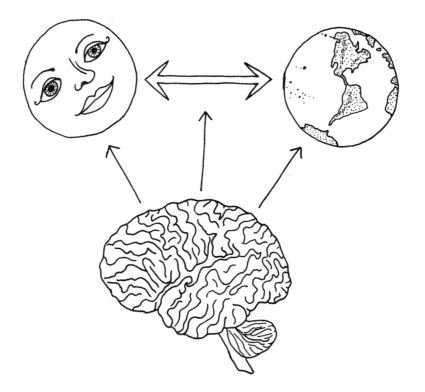

**Figure 97:**
**The Self, the World, and the Self Experiencing at the World**

*Your brain produces a "body-self" image on the left, an image of the world on the right, and, in the center, an image of the self interacting with the world. Damasio feels that consciousness lies in contemplating the interaction between the self and the world.*

aspect suggests that consciousness is being created over and over by a wordless narrative that you construct as you go along. Damasio describes his theory as follows:

> As the brain forms images of an object—such as a face, a melody, a toothache, the memory of an event—and as the images of the object *affect* the state of the organism, yet another level of brain structure creates a swift nonverbal account of the events that are taking place in the varied brain regions activated as a consequence of the object-organism interaction. The mapping of the object-related

consequences occurs in the first-order neural maps representing proto-self and object; the account of the causal relationship between object and organism can only be captured in second-order neural maps. . . . One might say that the swift, second-order nonverbal account narrates a story: *that of the organism caught in the act of representing its own changing state as it goes about representing something else.* But the astonishing fact is that the knowable entity of the catcher has just been created in the narrative of the catching process. . . .

Most importantly, the images that constitute this narrative are incorporated in the stream of thoughts. The images in the consciousness narrative flow like shadows along with the images of the object for which they are providing an unwitting, unsolicited comment. To come back to the metaphor of the movie-in-the-brain, they are within the movie. There is no external spectator. . . .

The process which generates . . . the imaged nonverbal account of the relationship between object and organism has two clear consequences. One consequence . . . is the subtle image of knowing, the feeling essence of our sense of self; the other is the enhancement of the image of the causative object, which dominates core consciousness. Attention is driven to focus on an object and the result is saliency of the images of that object in mind.[85]

Rephrasing this, it seems that Damasio views core consciousness as arising in the context of the following sequence:

- *Immersion.* You are active in the world.
- *Seeing objects.* You distinguish separate objects in the world, including your body.
- *Movie-in-the-brain.* You have an ongoing mental model of the world. The movie-in-the-brain includes images of the world's objects and an image of your body.
- *Proto-self.* Your image of your body differs from an image of an object in that your image of your body includes images of your sensations and current mental contents. This rich image is the proto-self.

- *Feelings.* You automatically and continually enhance the movie-in-the-brain by adding in representations of the proto-self's interactions with objects. These second-order representations are what we call feelings.
- *Core consciousness.* The act of continually forming feelings is part of what we mean by consciousness. At any given time, core consciousness is based on your feelings about a small group of images. Core consciousness highlights those particular images, which accounts for your current focus of attention.
- *Empathy.* You enhance your images of other people with representations of their feelings.

Empathy, in other words, is your awareness that your fellows are conscious, too. It's possible, and not even unusual, to have consciousness without empathy—consider, for example, the all-too-common moments when one regards one's rivals or even whole categories of people as soulless automata, as unreasoning animals, as bacilli that walk on two legs.

The thing that I find particularly striking about Damasio's explanation of consciousness is that, being a neurologist, he makes serious efforts to identify it with a type of brain activity. This said, brain science is very much in its infancy, and no firm conclusions have been reached. But just to give the flavor of what we can expect fairly soon, figure 98 indicates what it might be like to have a physiological brain model of the movie-in-the-brain, the proto-self, feelings, and consciousness.

If indeed there's nothing magical about consciousness, then it might as well be a type of computation. To test this notion out, I'm now going to recast Damasio's theory in the context of the creatures in a computer game. Putting it more colorfully, I'd like to ask: What is the phenomenology of Pac-Man? Actually, since Pac-Man is externally controlled by the game's human player, it's really not Paccy's phenomenology that I'm interested in.[86] The real meat lies in understanding the worldview of a nonplayer character (what gamers call an NPC). What is it like to be one of the enemy ghosts who chase Pac-Man around? What is the phenomenology of a Quake monster?

You might wonder why, in the midst of an erudite philosophical discussion,

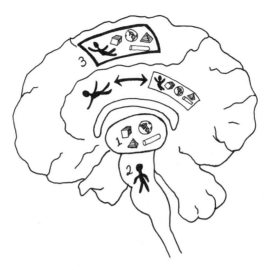

**Figure 98: Toward a Neurology of Consciousness**

*(1) The thalamus gathers sensory input for images of objects. (2) The reticular formation in the brain stem gathers body sensations for the proto-self. (3) The neocortex forms the movie-in-the-brain, with images of objects and of the proto-self. (4) The cingulate region of the cortex monitors the proto-self's reactions to the movie-in-the-brain, thereby creating core consciousness.*

I suddenly want to start talking about something so street-level and seemingly nonintellectual as computer games. Noisy kids in strange clothes! Sex and gore! A hideous waste of time!

Academia hasn't quite caught on to the fact that computer games represent the convergence and the flowering of the most ambitious frontier efforts of the old twentieth-century computer science: artificial intelligence, virtual reality, and artificial life.

I think I can argue that, if we create a fairly rich computer game, there's a sense in which the game's program-controlled creatures might be said to have core consciousness and empathy. I'll illustrate my argument in figure 99.

*Immersion.* In a computer game, we model a virtual world complete with an artificial physics, and objects such as walls, food pellets, and treasures. And we place our artificial life-forms, that is, our game creatures, inside this world.

*Seeing objects.* In most games, programmers dodge the tricky issue of having the game creatures be able to pick out the objects in the virtual world.

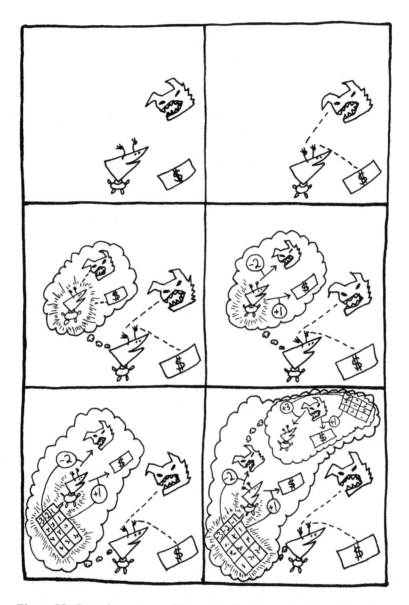

**Figure 99: Consciousness and Empathy for Computer Game Creatures**

*Left to right and top to bottom, the six images represent, respectively:*

| | |
|---|---|
| immersion | seeing objects |
| movie-in-the-brain with proto-self | feelings |
| core consciousness | empathy |

Rather than laboriously endowing our creatures with simulated vision and an object-recognition program, we flatly tell the creatures about the objects in their world by giving them access to a master list of the toy world's objects, nicely identified.

*Movie-in-the-brain.* Each of the computer-controlled game creatures has an individual update method. This method is coded in such a way that the creature can take into account the master list of all the world objects and choose a course of action accordingly.

*Proto-self.* It's necessary that a creature can distinguish itself from others. If the creature is to dodge bullets, for instance, it needs to be able to measure bullets' distances from its own body. If the creature is to bounce off other creatures, it needs to be able to determine who's who. This is a simple matter in object-oriented programming languages like C++ and Java, both of which have a convention that when you write code to describe a given creature's behavior, the word *this* is understood to refer to the creature itself. Another relevant feature of object-oriented computer languages is that certain internal variables can be designated as *private*. A creature will have full access to its own private variable values, but it may well lack any means of accessing the private variable values of other creatures. This illustrates the notion that a creature's proto-self image is richer than its image of some other creature or object.

*Feelings.* We can equip a creature with an evaluation method that assigns positive or negative utility values to other creatures. A dangerous enemy, for instance, might have a value of negative three, whereas a piece of food could have a weight of positive two. A creature's update method is enriched by having access to these numerical "feelings" about the other objects. In terms of programming this, we might suppose that if the world contains, say, five distinct kinds of creature, then a creature's personal feelings are summarized in a five-element array that matches a numerical utility to each of the five creature types. Another aspect of the creature's feelings can be one that tracks how well it's doing. It's common for game creatures to continually update internal score and health variables.

*Core consciousness.* We can imagine equipping a creature with some adaptive artificial intelligence by which it adjusts its behavior according to the situation. For instance, a creature might change the numerical values in its array of feelings about other creatures. Perhaps when it has low health it becomes more fearful and assigns its enemies a more negative utility value. When it has a low score, it might become more acquisitive and raise the utility value of food. If its health and score are both high, it might become more aggressive about attacking its enemies. So now the creature is "dealing with feelings." The focusing aspect of core consciousness can be modeled by having the creature give greater weight to the utility value of the closest other creature, effectively paying more attention to it.

*Empathy.* To be really skillful, a creature might let its update method guess at its opponents' motions in advance. At the most obvious level, the creature could look at an opponent's current position and velocity, and estimate where it will be in the near future. But at a higher level, a creature might build up an educated guess about the feeling—like utility weights being used by its opponents. And then the creature would be that much better at simulating in advance the upcoming actions of its opponents. At a still higher level, a creature could outfox its opponents by figuring out the internal mechanisms of their update methods. In this situation, the creature is enhancing its images of other creatures with images of their feelings and with images of their core consciousness. Thus empathy.

So it seems that, if we adopt Damasio's line of thought, a well-programmed game creature is not only conscious, it has empathy! A dippy little computer game creature is like a person. Why does this conclusion feel so utterly wrong?

A first issue is that a programmed agent on the screen doesn't have a physical body. But suppose we were able to put these kinds of artificial minds inside of robotic bodies? What then?

A second issue is that you might persist in claiming that a program or a robot could never have the special inner glow that you sense as part of your consciousness. But maybe the glow is an accidental and inessential phenomenon. Maybe a sufficiently advanced program or robot could behave in every way like a conscious being, and even have thought processes in every way similar to our own, but even so it might not share the same visceral glow.

In discussing this type of objection to computer models of the mind, philosophers often speak of *qualia,* which are meant to be the ineffable, subjective sensations we experience. But if it makes no observable difference whether a robot has or doesn't have the glow qualia, than what difference do the qualia make? And, come to think of it, how can you be sure that a robot might not experience glow qualia, perhaps in the form of some localized electrical field?

There is a tendency—which I fully understand—to think that no possible robot could ever be conscious, simply because it's not human. But maybe this is an unreasonable prejudice. It could relate to the fact that an explained magic trick seems like no trick at all. We want to believe ourselves to be magical, spiritual beings, and it's disillusioning to suppose that we might after all be reducible to some massive web of neural connections.

A final issue with my argument for the consciousness of computer game characters is that the actually existing virtual creatures are too simple to be regarded as conscious in any but the most trivial and limited sense of the word. After all, I normally take being conscious to mean having a fairly rich kind of internal mental life.

This objection has real weight. Perhaps the weakest link in my modeling of consciousness lies in having a computer critter's update method represent the movie-in-the-brain stage. After all, a creature might have an update method that does no work at all. Is it really fair to compare this to a human brain's intricate modeling of the world? Computer game creatures get the movie-in-the-brain for free because they live within the matrix of a program simulating its world. The situation is analogous to the fact that computer game creatures don't grow their own bodies, as living organisms do. They lack morphogenesis in two senses: They don't generate their bodies, and they don't generate their own images of the world.

If the truth be told, I'm willing to admit that when I say a Pac-Man ghost is conscious, I'm just playing a language game. But my game has a point, this being to illustrate that we have no a priori reason for denying that a computer program could exhibit a mental life akin to a human's—even though, in reality, we're nowhere near that level yet.

My feeling is that, on the one hand, it is possible *in principle* to build or evolve humanlike robots, but that, on the other hand, *in practice* we won't manage to do so anytime soon. More precisely, on the basis of a numerical argument, which I'll explain in section *4.6: The Mind Recipe,* I don't see human technology as creating truly humanlike programs or robots any time much before the year 2100—and with no ironclad guarantee of success after then.

In a way, my talk about intelligent robots is a red herring. For me, the deeper issue is to understand, here and now, the workings of my own mind. The real point of this chapter is that our thoughts can usefully be thought of as computations, even though we can't in fact produce detailed descriptions or emulations of what a brain does. *Why* is it useful to view our thoughts as computations? Because this gives us access to a new terminology in which to discuss our mental lives.

The value of clear terminology cannot be underestimated. *"Distinguo,"* as Aristotle liked to say, "I make distinctions." To a large extent, philosophical investigations consist of figuring out what you're talking about. Thanks to the analysis I'm presenting here, I can make the rather precise claims that our brain activities are deterministic, class four, unpredictable, capable of the process that we're equating with consciousness, and (at least for now) unfeasible to emulate on PCs.

What about the brains of lesser organisms? Do they support consciousness? A snail probably isn't at the *seeing objects* stage. For a snail, the world is a continuum of sensory inputs, reacted to in real time. A dog can perceive objects, but I'm not sure if a dog has *movie-in-the-brain* or not, maybe only fleetingly (figure 100). In *The Feeling of What Happens,* Damasio talks about

**Figure 100: Is This Dog Conscious?**

*Pitch is famous! And there's a picture of the spot on her back in section* 3.2: The Morphogenesis of a Brindle Cow. *I like how a dog's facial expression boils down to three black dots.*

some brain-damaged people who have *movie-in-the brain* but not *proto-self,* so a number of intermediate levels seem possible.

At this point I want to recast Damasio's hierarchy in a fresh way so as to investigate a familiar endless regress. I'll label Damasio's levels with the numbers zero, one, and two—and then I'll ask about the number levels after that. We'll see that there's a certain sense in which consciousness is infinite.

To begin, I'll regard *having* thoughts as level zero, and *becoming aware* of the thoughts as level one. In Damasio's terms, the movie-in-the-brain is level zero, and having feelings about the movie is level one. Damasio's notion of core *consciousness* involves reaching level two, where one *thinks about one's thoughts.*

Now note that once you reach level two, you're free to *think about consciousness* itself, that is, to think about thinking about thinking. This moves you to level three. And then you can *think about thinking about consciousness* for level four, and so on, out through a potentially infinite series of levels, as illustrated in figure 101.

I would say the first frame of my Wheelie Willie cartoon corresponds to the level zero *movie-in-the-brain.* And the second frame represents the advent of level one *feelings.* The endless series is set into motion only in the third frame, which represents level two consciousness and the act of thinking about thinking. Once you have this second-order thinking, you get third, fourth, fifth, and all the higher orders—at least up to the point where you get confused or bored.

We experience the higher levels, when unpleasant, as self-consciousness and irony, or, when pleasant, as maturity and self-knowledge.

In other words, the advent of consciousness introduces a dynamic that leads to a potential infinity. This is reasonable and pleasing, given that it feels natural to think of the mind as being infinite.

If you stand back, as we're now doing, and schematically imagine running the series right out through all the natural numbers, you get a kind of enlightenment that is, however, only relative, as right away you can get to a level "infinity plus one." The real enlightenment would be more like reaching the inconceivable Absolute Infinite that the theologically inclined mathematician Georg Cantor spoke of.

Set theory is the branch of mathematics that concerns itself with levels

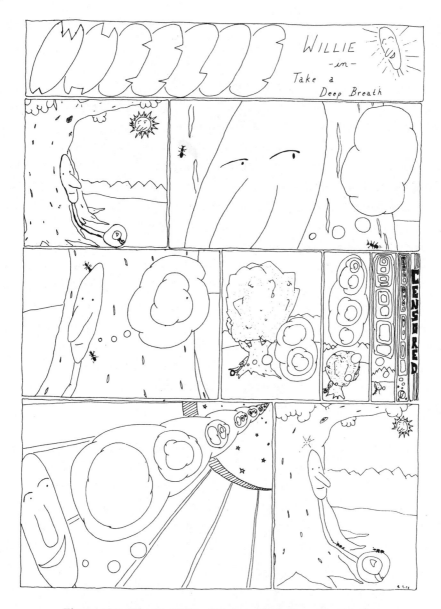

**Figure 101: Wheelie Willie Thinks of Infinity and of Nothing**

*In 1978 I drew this cartoon of an infinite regress leading to an empty mind. I drew it the day I came home from getting fired from my first job as a math professor. Drawing it cheered me up. At first Wheelie Willie is bummed, with a patched tire. And then he gets into his head and sees infinity, which makes him happy and leaves him with a clear, empty mind. At the end the ants are crawling on him. He's no longer a respected professor, just an ordinary hippie without a job. Maybe he'll write a science-fiction novel!*

of infinity, and this is the field in which I wrote my Ph.D. thesis at Rutgers University in that most sixties of years, 1972. My experience was that, when I thought hard enough about absolute infinity, I'd end up thinking about nothing at all, bringing me back to very start of the process, to immersion in the world with an empty mind with no subject-object distinctions, simply experiencing the great reality movie in and of itself, with me an integral part, filled with a visceral pleasure by the simple awareness of consciousness.

I can easily imagine a reader wondering what that last sentence is supposed to mean and what, in particular, it has to do with the notion of viewing core consciousness as a type of computation. That's what I was supposed be talking about, right? Computation, not enlightenment.

Well, I have this abiding fondness for mysticism, coupled with a lazy man's hope of finding a royal-road shortcut to wisdom. So it's easy for me to flip over to guru-speak. But there's no real conflict between mysticism and universal automatism. The individual self is simply one aspect of the computations that fill the world.

> I am doing it
> the it I am doing is
> the I that is doing it
> the I that is doing it is
> the it I am doing
> it is doing the I that am doing it
> I am being done by the it I am doing
> it is doing it
>
> —R. D. Laing [87]

In section *4.6: The Mind Recipe,* I'll look at how and when a conscious machine might be evolved, and in section *4.8: Quantum Soul,* I'll consider the possibility that consciousness is, after all, quite distinct from ordinary computation. But first I want to talk about a less ambitious modeling of a human mind: the lifebox.

## 4.5: *The Lifebox*

One of the most venerable dreams of science fiction is that people might become immortal by uploading their personalities into some kind of lasting storage. Once your personality is out of your body in a portable format, it could perhaps be copied onto a fresh tank-grown blank human body, onto a humanoid robot, or, what the heck, onto a pelican with an amplified brain. Preserve your software, the rest is meat!

In practice, copying a brain would be very hard, for the brain isn't in digital form. The brain's information is stored in the geometry of its axons, dendrites, and synapses, in the ongoing biochemical balances of its chemicals, and in the fleeting flow of its electrical currents. In my early cyberpunk novel *Software,* I wrote about some robots who specialized in extracting people's personality software—by eating their brains. When one of my characters hears about the repellent process, "[his] tongue twitched, trying to flick away the imagined taste of the brain tissue, tingly with firing neurons, tart with transmitter chemicals."[88]

In this section I'm going to talk about a much weaker form of copying a personality. Rather than trying to exactly replicate a brain's architecture, it might be interesting enough to simply copy all of a person's memories, preserving the interconnections among them.

We can view a person's memory as a hyperlinked database of sensations and facts. The memory is structured something like a Web site, with words, sounds, and images combined into a superblog with trillions of links.

I don't think it will be too many more years until we see a consumer product that makes it easy for a person to make a usable copy of their memory. This product is what I call a *lifebox.*[89]

My idea is that your lifebox will prompt you to tell it stories, and it will have enough low-level language recognition software to be able to organize your anecdotes and to ask you follow-up questions. As you continue working with your lifebox, it builds up a database of the facts you know and the tales you spin, along with links among them. Some of the links are explicitly made by you, others will be inferred by the lifebox software on the basis of your flow of conversation, and still other links are automatically generated by looking for matching words.

And then what?

Your lifebox will have a kind of browser software with a search engine capable of returning reasonable links into your database when prompted by spoken or written questions from other users. These might be friends, lovers, or business partners checking you out, or perhaps grandchildren wanting to know what you were like.

Your lifebox will give other people a reasonably good impression of having a conversation with you. Their questions are combed for trigger words to access the lifebox information. A lifebox doesn't pretend to be an intelligent program; we don't expect it to reason about problems proposed to it. A lifebox is really just some compact digital memory with a little extra software. Creating these devices really shouldn't be too hard and is already, I'd say, within the realm of possibility—it's already common for pocket-size devices to carry gigabytes of memory, and the terabytes won't be long in coming.

I discussed the lifebox at some length in my Y2K work of futurology, *Saucer Wisdom,* a book that is framed in terms of a character named Frank Shook who has a series of glimpses into the future—thanks to some friendly time-traveling aliens who take him on a tour in their tiny flying saucer. (And, no, I'm not a UFO true believer, I just happen to think saucers are cute and enjoyably archetypal.) Here's some quotes from the book.

> The lifebox is a little black plastic thing the size of a pack of cigarettes and it comes with a lightweight headset with a pinhead microphone, like the kind that office workers use. You can use your lifebox to create your life story, to make something to leave for your children and grandchildren.
>
> Frank watches an old man using a lifebox. His name is Ned. White-haired Ned is pacing in his small backyard—a concrete slab with some beds of roses—he's talking and gesturing, wearing the headset and with the lifebox in his shirt pocket. The lifebox speaks to him in a woman's pleasant voice.
>
> The marketing idea behind the lifebox is that old duffers always want to write down their life story, and with a lifebox they don't have to write, they can get by with just talking. The lifebox software is

smart enough to organize the material into a shapely whole. Like an automatic ghostwriter.

The hard thing about creating your life story is that your recollections aren't linear; they're a tangled banyan tree of branches that split and merge. The lifebox uses hypertext links to hook together everything you tell it. Then your eventual audience can interact with your stories, interrupting and asking questions. The lifebox is almost like a simulation of you.

To continue his observations, Frank and his friends skip forward in time until past when Ned has died and watch two of Ned's grandchildren play with one of the lifebox copies he left, as shown in figure 102.

**Figure 102: Grandchildren with a Lifebox**

*Frank Shook is inside the little UFO, which is invisible to the children.*

Frank watches Ned's grandchildren: little Billy and big Sis. The kids call the lifebox "Grandpa," but they're mocking it, too. They're not putting on the polite faces that kids usually show to grown-ups. Billy asks the Grandpa-lifebox about his first car, and the lifebox starts talking about an electric-powered Honda and then it mentions something about using the car for dates. Sis—little Billy calls her "pig Sis" instead of "big Sis"—asks the lifebox about the first girl Grandpa dated, and Grandpa goes off on that for a while, and then Sis looks around to make sure Mom's not in earshot. The coast is clear so she asks some naughty questions. "Did you and your dates *do it*? In the car? Did you use a *rubber*?" Shrieks of laughter. "You're a little too young to hear about that," says the Grandpa-lifebox calmly. "Let me tell you some more about the car."

Frank skips a little further into the future, and he finds that lifeboxes have become a huge industry.

People of all ages are using lifeboxes as a way of introducing themselves to each other. Sort of like home pages. They call the lifebox database a *context,* as in, "I'll send you a link to my *context.*" Not that most people really want to spend the time it takes to explicitly access very much of another person's full context. But having the context handy makes conversation much easier. In particular, it's now finally possible for software agents to understand the content of human speech—provided that the software has access to the speakers' contexts.[90]

Coming back to the idea of saving off your entire personality that I was discussing at the beginning of the section, there is a sense in which saving only your memories is perhaps enough, as long as enough links among your memories are included. The links are important because they constitute your *sensibility,* that is, your characteristic way of jumping from one thought to the next.

On their own, your memories and links aren't enough to generate an emulation of you. But when *another person* studies your memories and links, that other person *can* get into your customary frame of mind, at least for a short period of time. The reason another person can plausibly expect to emulate you is that, first of all, people are universal computers and, second of all, people are exquisitely tuned to absorbing inputs in the form of anecdotes and memories. Your memories and links can act as a special kind of software that needs to be run on a very specialized kind of hardware: another human being. Putting it a bit differently, your memories and links are an emulation code.

Certainly exchanging memories and links is more pleasant than having one's brain microtomed and chemically analyzed!

I sometimes study authors' writings or artists' works so intensely that I begin to imagine that I can think like them. I even have a special word I made up for this kind of emulation; I call it *twinking*. To twink someone is to simulate them internally. Putting it in an older style of language, to twink someone is to let their spirit briefly inhabit you. A twinker is, if you will, like a spiritualistic medium channeling a personality.

Over the years I've twinked my favorite writers, scientists, musicians, and artists, including Robert Sheckley, Jack Kerouac, William Burroughs, Thomas Pynchon, Frank Zappa, Kurt Gödel, Georg Cantor, Jorge Luis Borges, Edgar Allan Poe, Joey Ramone, Phil Dick, and Peter Bruegel. The immortality of the great ones results from faithful twinking by their aficionados.

Even without the lifebox, if some people don't happen to be authors, they can make themselves twinkable simply by appearing in films. Thomas Pynchon captures this idea in a passage imagining the state of mind of the 1930s bank-robber John Dillinger right before he was gunned down by federal agents outside the Biograph movie theater in Chicago, having just seen *Manhattan Melodrama* starring Clark Gable.

John Dillinger, at the end, found a few seconds' strange mercy in the movie images that hadn't quite yet faded from his eyeballs—Clark Gable going off unregenerate to fry in the chair, voices gentle out of the deathrow steel *so long, Blackie* . . . there was still for the doomed man some shift of personality in effect—the way you've felt for a little while afterward in the real muscles of your face and voice, that you *were* Gable, the ironic eyebrows, the proud, shining, snakelike head—to help Dillinger through the bushwhacking, and a little easier into death.[91]

The effect of the lifebox would be to make such immortality accessible to a very wide range of people. Most of us aren't going to appear in any movies, and even writing a book is quite hard. Again, a key difficulty in writing any kind of book is that you somehow have to flatten the great branching fractal of your thoughts into a long line of words. Writing means converting a hypertext structure into a sequential row—it can be hard even to know where to begin.

As I've been saying, my expectation is that in not too many years, great numbers of people will be able to preserve their software by means of the lifebox. In a rudimentary kind of way, the lifebox concept is already being implemented as blogs. People post journal notes and snapshots of themselves, and if you follow a blog closely enough you can indeed get a feeling of identification with the blogger. And blogs already come with search engines that automatically provide some links. Recently the cell phone company Nokia started marketing a system called Lifeblog, whereby a person can link and record daily activities by using a camera-equipped cell phone.

Like any other form of creative endeavor, filling up one's lifebox will involve dedication and a fair amount of time, and not everyone will feel like doing it. And some people are too tongue-tied or inhibited to tell stories about themselves. Certainly a lifebox can include some therapist-like routines for encouraging its more recalcitrant users to talk. But lifeboxes won't work for everyone.

What about some science-fictional instant personality scanner, a superscanner that you wave across your skull and thereby get a copy of your whole personality with no effort at all? Or, lacking that, how about a slicer-dicer that purees your brain right after you die and extracts your personality like the brain-eaters of *Software*? I'm not at all sure that this kind of technology will ever exist. It's hard to infer the high levels from the low. And the brain's low levels may prove too delicate to capture.

I like the idea of a lifebox, and I have vague plans to try to make one for myself. I envision a large database with all my books, all my journals, and a connective guide-memoir—with the whole thing annotated and hyperlinked.

And I might as well throw in some photographs—I've taken thousands over the years. And it should be feasible to endow my lifebox with interactive abilities; people could ask it questions and have it answer with appropriate links and words. My finished lifebox might take the form of a Web site, although then there'd be the thorny question of how to get any recompense for the effort involved. A commercial alternative would be to market it as a set of files on a portable data storage device of some kind. *Rudy's Lifebox*—my personal pyramid of Cheops.

But I don't really think the lifebox would *be* me. Without some radically more powerful software, it would just be another work of art, not so different from a bookshelf of collected works.

In the next section I'll examine the question of whether humans will ever manage to design the kind of software that could turn a lifebox into a conscious mind.

## 4.6: *The Mind Recipe*

Suppose you have a lifebox copy of what you know. Now you'd like to animate it so as to have an artificial version of yourself. How would you go about creating a humanlike intelligence?

The easy way to create human minds is, of course, to raise children. Let biology do the computing! And, if you're fortunate enough to have children, you can try to teach them everything you know, thus achieving a kind of mind replication. But for some reason many of us find it interesting to think about emulating human beings with software running on machines like souped-up desktop computers or, geekier yet, on high-tech devices inside robot bodies. We might pause here and wonder why this seems like a reasonable idea—because maybe it isn't.

In past eras, people have imagined creating humans from mud and magic, from clockwork machinery, from magnets and motors, or from telephone switching circuits. Why give serious credence to today's dreams of chip-based humanoids?

Some would indeed argue that there is something uniquely nondeterministic about a human mind, something that must elude any digital emulation. The feeling here is that roboticists are living in a fantasy world, hypnotized by their toys, blind to the richness of their own mental lives. I'm not entirely unsympathetic to this position. But for now, let's push ahead with the notion of modeling the mind with personal computer software and see where the investigation leads.

One thing electronic computers have going for them is universality. If what my brain does is to carry out computation-like deterministic processes, then in principle there ought to be a digital electronic computer program that can emulate it. It's presently not feasible to make such machines, but perhaps someday we'll have them. A computation is just a computation, and our PCs are doubling their power every year or so.

But remember that our brain's design was computed over millions of years of evolution involving millions of parallel lives. As I'll be explaining here, my guess is that it'll take at the very least until 2100 before machines can catch up—and maybe a lot longer than that.

In trying to produce humanlike robot brains, we have two problems to deal with: hardware and software.

The *hardware* problem is a matter of creating a desktop computer that has about the same computation rate and memory size as a human brain.

The *software* problem is to program a sufficiently powerful PC so as to behave like a person.

What I'm going to do now is to get some numerical estimates of the difficulty of the two problems and make some guesses about how soon they might be solved.

To begin with, I'll crunch some numbers to estimate how long it might take to solve the hardware problem by creating digital computers capable of computing as fast as a human brain. Then I'll turn to the software problem. As you might expect, the software problem is by far the harder of the two. I'll discuss a method we might use to evolve the software for the brain—I'll call this a mind recipe. And then I'll estimate how long it might be until we can actually execute something like the mind recipe to produce the software for an artificial brain.

Before getting into the details, I want to review the standard American nomenclature for large numbers. As a mathematician I'm always disappointed when I see authors use expressions like "million million" or "million billion" when they could just as well be using the much more attractive words trillion and quadrillion, respectively. One possible reason journalists hesitate to use the proper words is that up until the middle of the twentieth century, America and many European countries used different naming systems for large numbers.[92] So there's some lingering confusion. But the nomenclature in table 10 has become a standard, and it should be confidently used; the table lists the number names and the corresponding prefixes as decreed by the General Conference of Weights and Measures.

| American name | Numerical symbol | Power of ten | Prefix | Etymology of prefix |
|---|---|---|---|---|
| Thousand | 1,000 | 3 | Kilo- | Thousand |
| Million | 1,000,000 | 6 | Mega- | Large |
| Billion | 1,000,000,000 | 9 | Giga- | Giant |
| Trillion | 1,000,000,000,000 | 12 | Tera- | Monster |
| Quadrillion | 1,000,000,000,000,000 | 15 | Peta- | Five |
| Quintillion | 1,000,000,000,000,000,000 | 18 | Exa- | Six |
| Sextillion | 1,000,000,000,000,000,000,000 | 21 | Zetta- | Z |
| Septillion | 1,000,000,000,000,000,000,000,000 | 24 | Yotta- | Y |
| Octillion | 1,000,000,000,000,000,000,000,000,000 | 27 | Xenna- | X [unofficial] |
| Nonillion | 1,000,000,000,000,000,000,000,000,000,000 | 30 | Watta- | W [unofficial] |

**Table 10: Names for Large Numbers**

*The unfamiliar prefixes zetta and yotta are official, as in, "our universe may have a radius of a hundred yottameters, with the largest known galaxy being some fifty zettameters across." The idea is that zetta is like the letter Z, and that the prefixes beyond it can move backward through the alphabet, with yotta thus being like a letter Y. The xenna and watta prefixes are unofficial and may not stick.*

By way of further laying the groundwork for discussing the relative power of machines and the human brain, I also need to mention that when we have a system that's repeatedly doing something, we use the *hertz* unit to measure how rapidly it's cycling. A hertz (Hz for short) is simply one cycle per second. Cycle of what? This depends on the system you're interested in.

In the case of today's PCs, the cycles we measure are ticks of the system clock that controls the machine's chips. Unlike biological organisms, most electronic computers need to keep their activities in rigid synchronization, and their system clocks pulse out signals at a certain rate.

Combining our standard prefixes with the "hertz" word, we see that a gigahertz computer operates at a billion cycles per second, a terahertz machine at a trillion cycles per second, and so on.

How does a PC's clock cycle frequency relate to the amount of computation being done?

We often discuss the speed of an electronic computer in terms of the rate at which it executes machine instructions. By a machine instruction, I mean a primitive chip-level operation such as "add the contents of memory register $B$ to memory register $A$," or "copy the contents of memory location $S$ into memory register $A$." Instead of speaking of clock cycles, it makes sense to measure a computer's speed in instructions per second, sometimes abbreviated as IPS.

Now, in comparing hertz to IPS, we need to think about how many clock cycles a machine instruction requires. A typical instruction might take two to four clock cycles, depending on what the instruction does and the kind of design the chip has. For the purposes of this discussion, I'm just going to peg the average number of cycles per machine instruction at three. This means that a machine that executes $k$ instructions per second is roughly the same as a machine whose system clock ticks $3 \cdot k$ times per second.

Although in the early Y2K era one often heard the hertz measure when shopping for a PC, this measure is going to be less common in the future. The reason is that as we turn to more highly parallel kinds of computer architectures, our machines start executing dozens, hundreds, or even thousands of instructions per clock cycle. For these architectures, the IPS measure is more meaningful than the hertz measure. A machine with several thousand processors may be executing a million IPS even if it's only running at a thousand hertz.

A variation on IPS is to measure a computer's speed in so-called floating-point operations per second. A floating-point operation—called a flop for short—means doing something like adding or multiplying a pair of continuous-valued variables. I'm not talking about endlessly detailed mathematical real numbers, of course, just digitally-coded real numbers that have been rounded off into a few bytes of information. A nice thing about "flop" is that the root combines readily with the standard prefixes like giga and tera. A teraflop machine would be capable of executing a trillion floating-point operations a second. A few people insist on tacking a final "s" on the flop names, but I don't like to do that. Megaflop, gigaflop, teraflop, petaflop, exaflop, zettaflop, yottaflop, xennaflop, wattaflop!

As our machines become more advanced, the difference between an IPS and a flop becomes less significant—executing a floating point operation is a bit more work than carrying out a more primitive instruction, so it used to be that a machine's flop rate was normally a bit lower than the IPS rate. But today's processors tend have machine-level instructions that carry out floating-point operations in a single instruction step. So for the rest of this section, I'll treat IPS and flop as being more or less the same, with each of them being roughly equivalent to three hertz.

I myself have been partial to the flop nomenclature for years. In my 1980s science-fiction novels *Software* and *Wetware,* I describe some humanlike robots called boppers. Having already done some estimates of the human brain rate at that time, I had my boppers running at petaflop speed, with a new generation of exaflop models coming in.

One final measure of computer speed that one hears is MIPS, which is a million IPS, that is, a million instructions per second. To my mathematics-professor way of thinking, MIPS is just a cop-out way of avoiding using the fancy names for really big numbers. But you see it a lot.

So now let's discuss what kind of *hardware* we'd need to match a human brain. Some recent estimates of the human brain's power are summarized in table 4.

Hans Moravec is a lively roboticist who makes his home at Carnegie Mellon University. He and his students have done a lot of work on self-driving cars. He's the author of several brilliant books on robotics, including *Robot: Mere Machine to Transcendent Mind,* from which his estimate of the human brain's power is taken. Speaking of Moravec, a mutual friend of ours once said, "Ah, Hans. He's hard-core. I think if anyone could ever convince him that robots could never be conscious, he'd lose his will to live." Ray Kurzweil is a Silicon Valley inventor-entrepreneur who's developed devices for optical character recognition, speech

| Source of estimate | IPS | MIPS | Flop | Hertz |
|---|---|---|---|---|
| *Hans Moravec* | A hundred trillion IPS | A hundred million MIPS | A hundred teraflop | Three hundred terahertz |
| *Ray Kurzweil* | Twenty quadrillion IPS | Twenty billion MIPS | Twenty petaflop | Sixty petahertz |
| *Rudy Rucker* | Three hundred quadrillion IPS | Three hundred billion MIPS | Three hundred petaflop, or nearly an exaflop | One exahertz |

**Table 11: Estimates of the Brain's Rate of Computation**

*An IPS is an instruction per second, a MIPS is one million IPS, a flop is roughly the same as an IPS, and an IPS translates into about three hertz.*

recognition, music synthesis, and more. I take his estimate of the human brain's power from his best-selling *The Age of Spiritual Machines.*[93]

There's a huge amount of guesswork (and perhaps outright fantasizing) in any estimate of the human brain's computation rate. To give the flavor of how it's done, table 12 shows how I came up with my current three hundred petaflop or exahertz estimation for a brain-equivalent PC. And do keep in mind that every number in the table is debatable.

How soon might we expect our PCs to reach the petaflop or exahertz zone? In 1964, the engineer Gordon Moore noticed that the number of transistors per computer chip seemed to be doubling every year or two. The law extends to the speed of our computers as well, with the power of a typical desktop PC doubling every eighteen months. A little math shows that over fifteen years of Moore's Law growth, PCs increase their power by a thousandfold. So far it's worked. Machines of the early 1970s ran in the kilohertz range, machines of the mid-1980s ran in the megahertz range, and now in the early 2000s our machines are running in the gigahertz range. A millionfold speedup in the course of thirty years (figure 103).

Were Moore's Law to continue holding good, we could get a billionfold speedup in forty-five years and reach the petaflop-to-exaflop zone of human brain hardware around the middle of the century. So does that mean we'll have humanlike robots in the year 2045?

| Quantity | Estimate in words | Power of ten |
|---|---|---|
| Neurons per brain | A hundred billion. | $10^{11}$ |
| Computational elements per neuron. | A neuron has an average of a thousand synapses, including the input dendrites and the branching output axon. If we view the neuron's computing elements as consisting of its synapses along with the central neuron body itself, we still get about a thousand. | $10^3$ |
| Machine instruction equivalent of updating a synapse or a neuron body | I'm imagining that we can use a few bytes of computer state for each synapse or neuron body, and that updating one of these states will involve reading some neighboring state values, adding and multiplying a few numbers, and saving the results back into the given computational element's memory. Let's suppose that thirty machine instructions (or flops) will be enough to update the internal state of either a synapse or the central body of a neuron. | 30 |
| A neuron's computational updates per second | Typical neurons can fire ten times a second. Let's suppose that simulating a single firing event requires ten updates to the neuron's body and dendrites. This gives us one hundred computational updates per second. | $10^2$ |
| Instructions (or floating point operations) per second | Now we multiply the previous four numbers. Neurons per brain • computational elements per neuron • instructions per element update • neuron updates per second $= 30 \cdot 10^{(11+3+2)} = 30 \cdot 10^{16} = 3 \cdot 10^{17}$ or three hundred quadrillion instructions per second, which we can also view as three hundred petaflops. | $3 \cdot 10^{17}$ |
| Comparable clock rate | Say there's three clock ticks per machine instruction, and get $3 \cdot 3 \cdot 10^{17}$ cycles per second. I'll round this up to $10 \cdot 10^{17}$ to get $10^{18}$, which is a tidy quintillion ticks per second, or one exahertz. | $10^{18}$ |

**Table 12: The Three-Hundred-Petaflop Brain as an Exahertz PC**

Not so fast. First of all, we don't know how long Moore's Law will hold up. As of the writing of this book, some pessimistic chip engineers are saying that we can hope for at most another fifteen years of Moore's Law, meaning that our PCs are going to have a hard time getting much past the teraflop range. But maybe they're wrong. People have predicted the end of Moore's Law before, and over and over new technologies have emerged to keep things going.

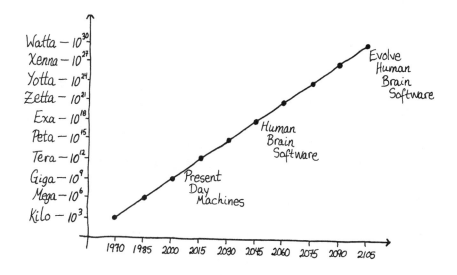

Watta — $10^{30}$
Xenna — $10^{27}$
Yotta — $10^{24}$
Zetta — $10^{21}$
Exa — $10^{18}$
Peta — $10^{15}$
Tera — $10^{12}$
Giga — $10^{9}$
Mega — $10^{6}$
Kilo — $10^{3}$

1970 1985 2000 2015 2030 2045 2060 2075 2090 2105

Present Day Machines

Human Brain Software

Evolve Human Brain Software

**Figure 103: Moore's Law Forever?**

*We plot a trend whereby our computers get a thousand times as fast every fifteen years. Tracking this triumphant upward line, we get machines with hardware speeds comparable to the exaflop human brain in 2045, and in 2105 we get wattaflop machines powerful enough to evolve the software needed to make the exaflop machines actually think like human brains. But some computer engineers think the graph is going to level out to a much lower growth rate by the year 2030. In order to make this graph easy to draw, I used a linear scale on the horizontal axis and a so-called logarithmic scale on the vertical axis. This means that moving one notch on the horizontal scale adds some fixed amount (fifteen years), while moving a notch on the vertical scale multiplies by a fixed amount (a thousand).*

A more serious reason why we shouldn't expect humanoid robots by 2045 is that, as I've mentioned several times, finding the correct *software* to emulate the brain is a very hard problem. Keep in mind that most of your brain's programming is something you were born with—the fruit of thousands upon thousands of years of evolution. A petaflop or exaflop machine with a blank disk drive isn't suddenly going to wake up and be like a person when you turn it on. We need to face the problem of inventing or evolving the brain emulation software to put onto the machine.

At our present state of knowledge, it appears that actually designing humanlike software is too difficult to be solved by any method other than a massive search procedure. I'm now going to loosely describe a specific way to carry out such a search. I'll call it the *mind recipe*.

My mind recipe is a deterministic procedure that could lead in a finite amount of time to a computer program that acts like a human being. There's nothing particularly impractical about my recipe, by the way. I've combined familiar ideas from the field of artificial intelligence in a new synthesis.

The mind recipe is a collection of simulated evolutions, woven together in a special way. The mind recipe is meant to function as a specific description of a procedure one might set in motion upon some powerful computers, with the expectation that if the recipe "cooks" long enough, a humanlike mind will result. I'll describe the mind recipe in chunks.

- Agent architecture
- Evolution
- Schedule
- Variations
- Pseudorandomizer
- Fitness tests
- Autonomy
- Size limit
- Creativity
- Judging success
- Runtime

*Agent architecture.* The most natural idea is to use Marvin Minsky's notion of building up our robot brains in a hierarchical fashion. Each brain would consist of systems that we call agents, with the understanding that an agent can itself be made up of agents, of neural nets, or of a combination of agents and neural nets.

At the most primitive ground-level of design, we use neural nets because we already know how to work with them. We package neural nets into agents and then let higher-level agents use these existing agents. These higher-level agents can be used as components of still higher-level agents, and so on. Any agent can serve as a black box or a subroutine to be used by another agent. In any individual agent's design, we may also use a network of neural nets to wire its component agents together.

It's worth noting that the agent hierarchy need not be strictly linear: an agent can feed information back into one of its subagents, producing a possibly interesting or useful feedback loop.

The value of working with an agent architecture is that this allows us to break the problem into more manageable pieces such as recognizing objects, remembering events, forming plans, understanding speech, and so on—with, of course, each of these tasks having its own subtasks to be solved by lower-level agents.[94]

*Schedule.* I see the mind recipe schedule or time line being set up as a symbiotic co-evolution of various kinds of agents. The mind recipe schedule orchestrates a number of evolutionary processes in parallel arenas. We designate one arena as the master, with the goal of evolving a mind. The goals of the subsidiary arenas are to evolve specialized agents. The schedule regularly takes the best agents from each arena and makes them available as new improved components for the agents in the other arenas.

Using co-evolution and parallel arenas allows the mind recipe to divide and conquer. Right from the start the master arena tries to evolve an entire mind, but at the same time the schedule is evolving good agents for a myriad of basic tasks. The schedule can also include an ability to change the goal of a given evolutionary arena once it's served its purpose.

*Evolution.* We simulate evolution in a given arena of agents as follows. We pick some fixed size and populate the arena with this many agents. So as not to waste time reinventing the wheel, we include in each evolutionary arena some variations on AI agents that represent the current best state of the art for that arena's task. But we'll also include a number of randomly designed agents.

In the process of simulated evolution, we measure each agent's fitness according to some test that relates to our eventual goal. We kill off the least fit agents and replace them with variations of the most fit agents, sometimes combining one or more of the fit agents to create a new one. And then we run the fitness tests again, kill the losers, replicate the winners, and so on. Typically we keep the population size constant—always replacing each unfit agent by exactly one new agent.

*Variation.* During the process of our simulated evolutions, we vary the agents so as to explore our space of possibilities. In varying an agent, we can tweak it in several ways. Most simply, we can change its neuron's input weights and threshold levels. We can also tweak an agent by varying its neural network design, that is, by changing the number of component neurons the agent uses, or by altering the connections among inputs, neurons, and outputs. A final way to vary an agent is to change which subagents or sensors it uses as inputs.

Another source of variation is that we can crossbreed two or more agents by exchanging bits of their component neural nets.

*Pseudorandomizer.* A genetic algorithm involves making random choices in the tweaks and in picking which pairs of agents to crossbreed. We can make our mind recipe deterministic by getting its randomness from a pseudo-random function such as Stephen Wolfram's cellular automaton Rule 30. (But do see footnote 73).

*Fitness tests.* The mind recipe uses three kinds of fitness tests.

First of all we will equip it with a number of simple tutorial programs, not unlike what a person might encounter as an online course. These automated tutorials will coach the agents through various elementary tasks, with perhaps the hardest task being to learn English (or, if you prefer, some other human language). Each of the evolutionary arenas will have its own particular series of fitness tests. Once the agents in a given arena have been brought up to a certain level, the coded-up tutor embedded in the mind recipe will propose a harder task.

Secondly, the mind recipe will include as a database a large library of books, photographs, and movies, as well as batteries of quizzes about the texts and images. Our candidate mind programs must learn to understand our books, decipher our images, and respond to our movies.

The third type of fitness test will be of a more interactive nature: once the agents reach a certain level of competence, we'll place them into a simulated virtual world and let them directly compete with one another. This brings in the subsidiary problem of running a good virtual reality simulation, but, on the whole, that seems like a more feasible problem than evolving intelligent programs. It's already reasonable to imagine, for instance, a big computer game in which the nonplayer characters compete without any human input at all.

Compete in what way? I see the mind recipe as having different epochs. To begin with, the virtual agents can compete for scarce resources. Next they might hunt and eat one another. Then they might group together, forming a virtual economy, buying and selling things. Finally, they can begin to exchange information with each other, offering solutions to problems, or perhaps even bartering entertainment. Once the agents reach this epoch, it makes sense to let them generate their own ranking system to be used as a fitness function.

*Autonomy.* In his stories about robots, Isaac Asimov had a character named Susan Calvin who served as a tutor to the robots. But I am requiring that the mind recipe be *autonomous*. It must work without any real-time human tutoring or interaction of any kind; once it's set in motion, it requires no further intervention at all. The mind recipe is a start-it-and-forget-it automatic process; you turn it on, walk off, come back later (maybe *much* later), and you've got a mind waiting there.

A first reason for the autonomy requirement is a practical one: no human would have the patience and the rapidity to mentor each member of an evolving race of artificially intelligent agents.

A second reason for automating the mind recipe is that then, the faster our hardware gets, the faster we can run the mind recipe. Since no humans are involved, we're perfectly free, as our hardware makes it possible, to run the evolution a million, billion, or trillion times faster. This is a very big win.

A third reason for making the mind recipe self-contained is that then the recipe can be fully deterministic. Once the mind recipe is fully specified, the only input is what initial seed you put into the pseudorandomizer. You'll get the exact same final agents if you run the mind recipe two times in a row on the same seed and for the same amount of time. This fact is of some philosophical interest, as it shows that a human-equivalent mind may in fact be rather concisely describable (in terms of a mind recipe).[95]

*Size limit.* If we put no upper bound on the size of our agents' programs, this poses a danger of evolving toward enormous lookup tables or "crib sheets" containing the answers to all the questions asked by the fitness functions.

So as to avoid having the programs cheat by hard-coding the answers to the tests, we would want to put some kind of cap on the size of the programs. We already know how to do this by having a neural net of a rather small fixed size learn to distinguish members of a very large database. The net doesn't have room to memorize each item, so it's forced to find higher-level ways of distinguishing its inputs. Indeed, one might even say that intelligence involves finding compact representations of large domains.

How large should the size cap be? Hans Moravec remarks that most living or artificial thinking systems have a memory size in bytes comparable to the number of instructions per second they can carry out (see figure 104).

## All Thinks, Great and Small

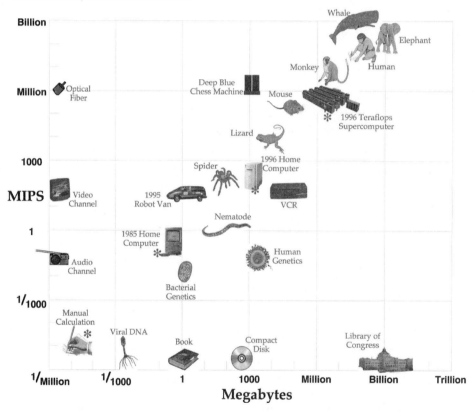

**Figure 104: Hans Moravec's Plot of Brain Speed and Brain Size**

*The horizontal axis measures the system's memory in megabytes, and the vertical axis shows its speed in MIPS (millions of instructions per second). The systems that can easily be made to function as universal computers are marked with an asterisk. Note that Moravec uses logarithmic scales on both axes, with each step representing a multiplication by a thousand.*

Using Moravec's rule of thumb, we should expect a three-hundred-petaflop human brain program to use about three hundred petabytes of memory. And this is about right, for if we look back at table 12, we see that a brain has a hundred trillion synapses. If we suppose that fully describing the state of a synapse takes about a thousand bytes, then we get a hundred quadrillion bytes, or a hundred petabytes. To be generous, we can set the size cap for our agents at an exabyte apiece.

*Creativity.* One subsidiary goal for our agents will be the ability to mentally simulate events, to form a movie-in-the-brain. Once a program can simulate the world as it is, there's a possibility of gaining a capacity to simulate the world as it might be. And with this comes the ability to plan and anticipate. Harking back to Damasio, also note that creating a movie-in-the-brain is a key step toward core consciousness.

A further effect of mentally simulating the world is that it presents the possibility of abstract thought. An abstract thought is, I would say, any link between several sensations or images. The more images involved, the abstracter the thought.

Once you have abstract thought, why not expect creativity? A classic objection to robot intelligence is that robots act only in accord to a program, whereas humans can do creative and unexpected things.

But a point I've been hammering on throughout the *Lifebox, the Seashell, and the Soul* is that a class four computation can be *both* unpredictable *and* deterministic. Presented with a computer program allegedly equivalent to your mind, you'd in fact have no hope of skimming through the program, understanding it, and being able to predict what it's going to do. Heck, we can't even predict what the CA Rule 110 will do on arbitrary inputs, and it's a program that's only eight bits long!

Unpredictability is easy. The real problem lies in getting a computer program to produce unexpected outputs that seem *interesting*.

*Judging success.* Certainly we'd want our program to be able to give good answers to questions about all the books and movies that we included in the mind recipe. A benefit of having used this as input means that the program will have a very strong understanding of human language. It's likely, however, that the co-evolution in virtual reality will also have led our computer minds to develop a native language of their own.

A payoff from having used the virtual reality arena is that this will have also prepared the minds to move around our physical world. We'd want to be able to "decant" the mind into a robot body and have it move around our world in a fairly natural way, possibly needing a few weeks of acculturation.

Alan Turing spoke of gauging humanlike intelligence by an imitation game: the machines try to trick us into thinking they're people. If they regularly succeed, we might as well say they're intelligent.

But, and this is a delicate point, even if our mind recipe leads to fully humanoid robots, we won't be able to *prove* that the machines are equivalent to human minds. Nor will we even be able to prove that these evolved minds might not at some point begin acting in a very unreasonable or inconsistent way.[96] Lest this make robots seem dangerous, note that this is exactly the same situation we're in vis-à-vis other humans. You can never be sure if another person will remain consistent and rational. Think of your relatives!

*Runtime.* As I mentioned before, given our present skills, humanoid software can only be designed by an evolutionary search procedure along the lines of the mind recipe. Let's try to estimate how long might such a search take.

That is, I'd like to get a numerical estimate of how soon we might be able to evolve software equivalent to the human mind by using something like the mind recipe. But at present the mind recipe is still a bit vague, and I don't see a simple way to make an estimate of how long it might take to bear fruit.

So I'm going to use a different approach to getting an estimate of how long it might take to evolve humanlike *software*: I'm going to propose directly simulating human evolution, starting with some blank, but human-size brains. That is, I'll work with a sizable population of agents, each of whom has the three-hundred-petaflop power of a human mind, and I'll imagine evolving these agents over a substantial period of time. To be more precise, I'll simulate a million agents over a million years.

I'll also need to simulate a nice virtual reality for these agents to live in, but my sense is that it'll be enough to focus only on the computation needed to simulate all those human-size brains. As long as we stick to a fairly coarse level of simulation, running a virtual reality isn't anywhere near as hard as simulating minds. The real issue is simulating a million years of life for a million human-size brains. Table 13 outlines my calculation that a wattaflop computer could do this in a year of continuous runtime.

| Quantity | Estimate in words | Power of ten |
|---|---|---|
| Population | A million population slots. This means a million at any given time, not a million in all, with dying individuals being replaced by newborns. A million is on the low side, but remember that Earth's population used to be much smaller. | $10^6$ |
| Number of years of evolution | A million years. Not a very long time on the evolutionary scale, but it might be enough for our simulated evolution. We can let our simulated creatures produce a new generation once every simulated year, a faster turnover rate than the twenty or so years per generation in the real human world. | $10^6$ |
| Total number of brain years needed to simulate human evolution | Population · years of evolution = $10^{12}$ brain years | $10^{12}$ |
| Target rate to simulate this on one machine in one year | To compute $10^{12}$ brain years in one year, the machine needs to run $10^{12}$ times as fast as a brain-simulating machine, which we know from the last table to run at $3 \cdot 10^{17}$ instructions per second, so we'll need $3 \cdot 10^{29}$ instructions per second, which we might as well round up to $10^{30}$, a tidy million yottaflop, which could also be called a wattaflop. | ~$10^{30}$ |

**Table 13: A One-Year Simulation of Human Evolution on a Wattaflop Machine**

How long would Moore's Law take to get us to the wattaflop level? Supposing that we're roughly at the gigaflop level, we'd need a speedup factor of $10^{21}$. This amounts to chaining together seven speedups of a thousandfold each. So if a Moore's Law increase of a thousandfold takes fifteen years, we'll need a mere ninety-five years to hit the wattaflop level. Call it a century from now, or 2100.

Actually, there's no reason we couldn't run the million simulated brains on a million different machines that communicate over the Net. In this case, we could reach our goal thirty years sooner. That is, assuming sixty-five years of Moore's Law, we'd reach the yottaflop level, at which time we could run a million yottaflop machines for year—which would be as good as waiting thirty more years to run one wattaflop machine for a year.

Yottaflop, wattaflop—maybe this is getting ridiculous. How long can we really expect Moore's Law to hold up? Earlier I mentioned an estimate that the universe has performed $10^{120}$ computations so far. So if we get really demanding and ask for a machine that can simulate the whole universe in a second, we'd need to go to $10^{120}$ computations per second from our current rate of roughly $10^9$, which means a speedup factor of $10^{111}$. Well, if we turn the Moore's Law crank one more time, out comes a prediction that our machines will run this fast in about five hundred years. So, come 2500, if not sooner, a desktop machine can in one second compute as much as the entire universe to date. And fifteen years after that, the computer can simulate itself running a thousand times as fast as it actually runs! Now if you believe that, I have some crystal-treated healing water to sell you, also a plot of land on the Moon, also the collected works of Plato intaglio-printed on a ZigZag cigarette paper for easy ingestion. And for an extra $100,000, I'll make you immortal by cryogenically freezing your nose.

My point is that at some point Moore's Law really does have to poop out. Obviously this will happen before we see the true and complete history of the entire universe being simulated in every detail in one second on a personal computer. And it's also unlikely that we'll ever get yottaflop machines capable of ganging up to perform a one-year emulation of the human race's evolution. For that matter, even the millionfold speedup to approach the power of the human brain could be problematic. As an example of the engineering problems that arise, if a computer is based on an electronic circuit that oscillates at an exahertz rate, the circuit will give off hard X-rays that disrupt the functioning of the circuit.

But on the optimistic side, even if the chip engineers hit a wall, this doesn't necessarily mean we'll never see an exaflop desktop device. Massive parallelism could save the day: processors could become so cheap and tiny that home computers could have thousands or even millions of them. Or perhaps the current chip architecture of etched silicon might be replaced by something more exotic like carbon nanotubes, organic molecules, or computational plastics. Or we may turn more and more to biologically designed systems. It could be that we come full circle, and the desktop computer of the year 3000 is a brain in a jar.

Still speculating on how to get really fast computers, it may also be that quantum computation will start pulling rabbits out of its hat. The physicist Seth Lloyd points out that any region of matter at all can be regarded as a quantum computer in which the bits are stored as particle spins, and the operations consist of the particles interacting with one another. Lloyd says that in some sense a kilogram-sized piece of ordinary matter is running a computation in which it updates a memory of $10^{31}$ bits at a rate of $10^{20}$ updates per second. And if the matter happens to be a black hole, the figures switch to a memory of $10^{16}$ bits being updated at a rate of $10^{35}$ updates per second. In either case, if we multiply the two numbers together, we get $10^{51}$ bit-updates per second, which is something like a sextillion nonillion instructions per second, or a zetta-wattaflop. Lloyd suggests that a black hole computer could form for the tiniest fraction of a second, absorb computational input as mass and energy, carry out its vast computation, and dissolve into a pulse of energy containing the output. *Dzeent!* "I just had an idea!"[97]

When prognosticating, it's easy to make the mistake of expecting future technology to be simply an amplified version of today's. If the mechanical computer designer Charles Babbage were whisked to our time from the Victorian era, he might initially suppose that the buzzing beige box beneath my desk is stuffed with tiny clockwork gears. And *we'd* probably be just as mistaken to expect the PCs of the year 2500 to be using silicon chips. We may well discover new computing technologies that make the mind recipe feasible after all.

Another possibility regarding the creation of software to emulate the human brain is that there could be better approaches than the brute-force evolutionary search laid out in the mind recipe. In section *3.2: The Morphogenesis of a Brindle Cow* I discussed the fact that many of the physical shapes found in living organisms are in fact patterns naturally formed by computations such as reaction-diffusion rules. The branching structure of a human hand isn't so much something that was evolved in detail as it is a pattern that emerges from a type of reaction that takes place in an embryo. Now it may also be that, with a bit more insight, we'll come to see that much of the brain's organizational structure emerges naturally from certain rather simple kinds of morphogenetic processes. In this case, artificially growing a network similar to the brain might be radically easier than we'd supposed. So maybe we'll get our intelligent robots fairly soon after all.

On the theme of computational futures, there's an interesting idea first proposed by the science-fiction writer and computer-science professor Vernor Vinge in a 1993 talk.[98] Vinge pointed out that if we can make technological devices as intelligent as ourselves, then there seems to be no reason that these devices couldn't readily be made to run a bit faster and have a bit more memory so as to become *more* intelligent than people. And then—the real kicker—these superhuman machines might set to work designing still better machines, setting off a chain reaction of ever-more-powerful devices.

Vinge termed the potential event the Singularity. Although Vinge's analysis is sober and scientific, in the last couple of decades, belief in his Singularity has become something of a cult among certain techies. Science-fiction writers, who have a somewhat more jaded view of predictions, have a saying about the enthusiasts: "The Singularity is the Rapture for geeks." That is, among its adherents, belief in the Singularity has something of the flavor of the evangelical Christian belief in a world-ending apocalypse, when God will supposedly elevate the saved to heaven, leaving the rest of us to fight a final battle of Armageddon.

At one level, belief in the Singularity is indeed an instance of people's age-old tendency to predict the end of the world. Once we have the Singularity, the machines can copy our brains and make us immortal. But once we have the Singularity, the machines may declare war on humanity and seek to exterminate us. Once we have the Singularity, the machines will learn how to convert matter into different forms and nobody will ever have to work again. But once we have the Singularity, the machines may store us in pods and use us as components. Once we have the Singularity, the machines will figure out how to travel faster than light and into the past. But once we have the Singularity, the machines will screw things up and bring the entire universe to an end. And so on.

Vinge describes several kinds of scenarios that could lead to a Singularity of cascading superhuman intelligence. We can group these somewhat science-fictional possibilities into three bins.

- *Artificial minds*. We design or evolve computing devices as intelligent as ourselves, and these entities continue the process to create further devices that are smarter than us. These superhuman computing devices might be traditional silicon-chip computers, nanotechnological assemblages, quantum computers, or bioengineered artificial organisms.
- *Cyborgs*. Humans split off a new species, part natural and part engineered. This could result either from bioengineering the human genome or from giving people an effortless, transparent interface to supercomputing helper devices. The resulting cyborgs will advance to superhuman levels.
- *Hive minds*. The planetary network of computers wakes up and becomes a superhuman mind. Alternately, people are equipped with built-in communication devices that allow society to develop a true group mind of superhuman powers.

I've already said enough about the *artificial minds* scenario, so let's close this section with a few words about the other two.

The *cyborg* possibilities provoke what bioethicists call the "yuck factor." Quite reasonably, we don't like the idea of changing human biology. Gaia knows best. Don't fix it if it ain't broke. Keep the genie in the bottle!

But if we could become cyborgs via high-quality interfaces to external and detachable computing elements, it might not be so bad. In my science-fiction novels I often write about an *uvvy* (rhymes with "lovely-dovey"), which is meant to be a smart plastic communications-and-computation device that a person wears on the nape of the neck. For me an important aesthetic feature of the uvvy is that its plastic is soft, flexible, and flickering.

To keep down the yuckiness, a uvvy communicates with the user's brain via magnetic fields rather than by poking hair-fine tendrils into the spine. An uvvy becomes something like a symbiotic partner, a bit like a really, really good cell phone.

One aspect of the cyborg scenarios is that they reduce the dichotomy between humans and machines. Depending on how you think about it, this can seem either good or bad. With a positive spin, the machines become our symbiotic partners and we advance together. With a negative spin, we see humanity being debased to the level of kludgy science experiments.

The *hive mind* scenarios represent a whole different way of thinking about computation—and this will be a topic I discuss in CHAPTER FIVE: *The Human Hive.*

Coming back to the starting point of this section, do I think that we'll ever be able to make living mental copies of ourselves? It seems within the realm of possibility. But, in the end, people might feel it was too much trouble. After all, there's no particular reason that any of us should be immortal. Nature's perfectly happy to just keep growing fresh new people. Last year's rose blossoms are gone, and it makes the world more interesting to have this year's blooms be different from any that came before. Accepting my mortality gives me all the more reason to make the most of the time that I actually have.

### 4.7: What Do You Want?

Consider the following bit of dialectical analysis.

- Universal automatism proposes a *thesis*: Your mental processes are a type of deterministic computation.
- Your sense of having a free will entails a seeming *antithesis*: Your thoughts and actions aren't predictable.
- Wolfram advocates a beautifully simple *synthesis*: Your mind's computation is both deterministic and unpredictable.

The synthesis is implicit in a conjecture that we've already mentioned several times.

- *Principle of Computational Unpredictability (PCU).* Most naturally occurring complex computations are unpredictable.

The workings of your mind are unpredictable in the sense that, when presented with a new input of some kind, you're often quite unable to say in advance how you'll respond to it.

Someone offers you a new job. Do you want it or not? Right off the bat, there's no way to say. You have to think over the possibilities, mentally simulate various outcomes, and feel out your emotional responses to the proposed change.

Someone shows you a painting. Do you like it? Hold on. You have to think about the image, the colors, and the mental associations before you decide. Someone hands you a menu. What do you want to eat? Just a minute. You need to look into your current body feelings, your memories of other meals, your expectations about this particular restaurant.

We say a computation is unpredictable if there is no exponentially faster shortcut for finding out in advance what the computation will do with arbitrary inputs. When faced with an unpredictable computation, the only reliable way to find out what the computation does with some input is to go ahead and start up the computation and watch the states that it steps through.

Figure 105 shows the spacetime evolution of an unpredictable one-dimensional CA, with time running down the page. Even if I have full knowledge of this CA's underlying rule and of the input pattern in a given row, the rule is gnarly enough that, in all likelihood, the only way I can possibly figure out the contents of a later row is to compute all the rows in between.

Certainly there's no doubt that the endlessly flexible human mind embodies a universal computation, that is, a computation capable of emulating any other computation. Being universal, the human mind is class four and gnarly. Given this, we certainly expect the workings of the human mind to be unpredictable.

Once again, suppose I'm presented with some new input. Since my thoughts are unpredictable, the only way to find out what I'm going to end up thinking about the input is to go ahead and think until my mind is made up. And this means that, although my conclusion is in fact predetermined by how my mind works, *neither I nor anyone else has any way of predicting what my conclusion will be.* Therefore my thought process feels like free will.

But the process is, after all, deterministic, and deep down we all know this.

**Figure 105: The Unpredictable China CA**

*This image follows a one-dimensional CA through twenty-four hundred generations, with six hundred generations per strip; the top of each strip is a continuation of the bottom of the strip to its immediate left. The world of this CA is 128 cells wrapped into a circle, meaning that the right and left edges of each strip match as well. If we were to paste everything together, this picture would be a cylinder like a baton. Notice the characteristic feature of class four rules: they send information back and forth by means of the moving patterns we call gliders. I found this rule in 1990 after about fifteen minutes of a Blind Watchmaker–style directed search, using a program that took me a year to write. I call it China because it looks a little like a silk fabric design.*

When a friend or loved one makes a decision, you ask why—and you expect an answer. Normally people *do* have reasons for doing things. And if they have reasons, then their decisions are in fact deterministic.

Of course, discerning the reasons behind our decisions can be hard. On the one hand, we can be unaware of our true motivations or unwilling to own up to them. "I have no idea why I did that." And on the other hand, we sometimes like to suggest nobler reasons for our actions than the motivations more likely to have played a part. "I did it for his own good." And, most crucial of all, even if we *are* blessed with full self-knowledge, it may be impossible to predict in advance how the influences of our various competing motivations will play out.

Really big decisions are rather rare in one's life. Looking back on the few I've made, I wouldn't say that any of them was capricious. Surprising to others, yes, but always logical for me. In each case, the course of action that I took was, for me at the time, the inevitable thing to do.

Two months ago, for instance, I decided to retire from teaching computer science at San Jose State University. I was tired of preparing new lectures and demos on difficult material, tired of wrestling with the ever-changing hardware and software, and eager to devote more time to my writing. These reasons might not have been enough, but then the state university faculty got an offer of a small golden handshake from the Terminator himself—that is, from the actor who once portrayed an implacable robot and who had recently become the governor of California. I was in a mental state where this financial offer was enough to tip the scales—and I went for it.

Where's the free will in that? All I did was evaluate data, simulate alternate futures, and study my feelings. Given my mind-set and the various inputs, my retirement was inevitable. But if, immediately after the golden handshake offer, you'd asked me if I was going to retire, I wouldn't have been able to give you a firm yes or no answer. I didn't know yet. My deterministic computation wasn't done, and for me it was unpredictable.

Just to drive home the point, let me quote the relevant passage from Wolfram's *A New Kind Of Science*. (I've inserted some bracketed phrases to remind you that I'm using the word *unpredictable* as a synonym for what Wolfram prefers to call "irreducible.")

> Ever since antiquity it has been a great mystery how the universe can follow definite laws while we as humans still often manage to make decisions about how to act in ways that seem quite free of obvious laws.
>
> But from the discoveries in this book it finally now seems possible to give an explanation for this. And the key, I believe, is the phenomenon of computational irreducibility [or unpredictability] . . . For if the evolution of the system corresponds to an irreducible [or unpredictable] computation, then this means that the only way to work out how the system will behave is essentially to perform this computation—with the result that there can fundamentally be no laws that allow one to work out the behavior more directly.[99]

I'm quite happy with this resolution of the conflict between determinism and free will. But I find that when I try to explain it to people who aren't universal automatists, they're dubious. I'll respond to three common objections.

*Objection*: "If I'm really like a computer program, then my free will is only an illusion. And I don't want that to be true."

In the philosophical style, I'll answer this with a counterquestion. By "free will" do you mean ability to make an utterly random decision? But what is "utterly random"? If something's unpredictable, it's all but indistinguishable from being random, no?

Some philosophers of science have tried to resolve the free will question by supposing that the brain has an ability to tap into a physically random process such as a chaotic system with unknown initial conditions, or a quantum measurement of some kind.

A universal automatist would reject this approach for two reasons. First of all, you don't need to turn to physics since there are lots of dirt-simple rules that, when run upon a neural network like the brain, will generate unpredictable and random-looking data. And second, assuming that there's a deterministic computation underlying the seeming uncertainties of quantum mechanics, all physical processes *are* deterministic, so you aren't going to be able to get true randomness from nature either. Assuming that science will find its way past the wifty obfuscations of quantum mechanics, whatever *seeming* randomness you find in physics is just another example of the unpredictability of complex deterministic computations. So, coming back to the first point in this paragraph, you might as well accept that your mind is a deterministic computation.

*Objection*: "I can prove that I have free will by flipping a coin to make up my mind."

Even if our actions are deterministic, they are indeed influenced by the inputs that we get. The external world's computations are something quite distinct from our own computations. Now it's certainly possible that your deterministic thought process might tell you to flip a coin and to make a choice on the basis of what the coin says. But in this case, your actions still aren't truly random. You've only added an extra coin-flip bit of input.

*Objection*: "My free will isn't an illusion. I can prove it by doing the opposite of what I want to do."

That's a contradiction. Once the dust settles, what you did *is* what you wanted to do. And you don't really have free will over what you *want* to do—at least not in the sense of being off in some little control room and sending out command signals. Your drives and desires are influenced by biochemical cycles, memories, life experiences, and external inputs. You can make unexpected changes, but these are the results of your ever-flowing mental computation.

It's valuable to realize that everyone's mind is performing a gnarly class four computation. Sometimes if I look at strangers, I'll unkindly jump to the conclusion that they're mindless robots—particularly if they don't resemble me. Remember how your parents seemed to you when you were a teenager? Robots for sure.

One of the pleasant side effects of unexpected social interactions is that you get flashes of insight into the minds of people whom you might otherwise never meet. When I relax, I discover unexpected intricacies of emotion and humor within strangers. Nobody is simple on the inside. Simplicity is an impossibility. Every brain is carrying out a class four computation.

And this is no surprise, really. Look inward at your flow of thought. It's like that China cellular automaton rule depicted in figure 105. One thing leads to another. The gliderlike thought trains collide and light up fresh associations. Even if you're lying in bed with your eyes closed, the flow continues, the endless torrent. Now and then you get stuck in a loop, but some unexpected glider eventually crashes in to break things up. You're surfing the brain waves; and you yourself are the surf.

At this point, I'd like to mention a touchy subject: God. Let me immediately say that I'm not out to advocate religion. If you want to keep things more neutral, think of "God" as a convenient and colorful synonym for "the cosmos." Or think of the "God" word as convenient shorthand for "the unknown."

My reason for mentioning God is that there's a particular connection between God and free will that intrigues me: When in dire straits, people sometimes ask God to help them change their behavior. And, often enough to matter, this seems to help them get better. What might this mean?

I would say that becoming desperate enough to turn to God involves recognizing a current inability to alter one's mental patterns and a desire to attempt some higher-level change. The plea expresses a longing to jump out of a loop, a desire to move from one attractor to the next, a wish to experience a chaotic bifurcation.

If the plea works, does that mean that the Great Author, the Ground of All Being, the Omnipresent-Omnipotent-Omniscient One has reached down to change the parameters of some suffering character's mental computations? And, more to the point, does this destroy determinism?

Well, we *can* keep determinism if we allow for a less supernatural view of reform-by-supplication. We could simply say that asking God for help has an organic effect upon a person's brain. In other words, expressing a desire to have a spiritual life might activate, let us say, certain brain centers that release endorphins, which in turn affect the threshold levels of one's neurons. And these changes nudge the brain activities to a new strange attractor. A deterministic chaotic bifurcation occurs.

Do I really think it works like that? Well, to be truthful, I've always felt comfortable about reaching out for contact with the divine. The world is big and strange, and we have only the barest inkling about what lies beneath the surface.

But even in this less materialistic view, a person can still be deterministic. Asking God for help in achieving a chaotic bifurcation is really no different from asking a doctor for penicillin. You can't will an infection away, and you can't will yourself to abandon some deeply ingrained bad habit. But at a slightly higher level, you *may* be able to muster the will to get help. And this higher level is, after all, simply part of your brain's ongoing deterministic computation.

For that matter, God, too, could be deterministic. In the context of the theory I suggested at the end of section *2.5: What Is Reality?*, God could be a deterministic nonreversible class four paratime metaphysical cellular automaton.

But that sounds so dull. Better to say the cosmos is dancing with us all the time. And that God is in the blank spaces between our thoughts—like in those white regions of the picture of the China CA.

## 4.8: Quantum Soul

It's valuable to remember how really odd it is to be conscious. The miracle of your mental life is being created by a carpet of cells that have grown themselves into a mat. How can this be?

Walking in the woods, I see a footbridge and automatically form a model of it. I step onto the bridge and look down at the ripples in the stream, the foam, the tiny standing waves. I'm thinking these are like the mind. A woman walks past, cautious of the silver-haired man she sees. I think of Joseph Campbell, of myth, of a fairy tale about a troll beneath a bridge. All this is coming from the meat weave in my head. The old associations are somehow alive in the background, always ready to pulse at my call, and new associations form as spontaneously as the eddies in the torrent below.

Yes, both humans and PCs are universal computers, so, in principle, each should be able to simulate the other. And comparing them sheds some light on both. But, no, I don't think they're very similar. You can build a cathedral from gray Lego blocks, but that's not what the Nôtre-Dame *is*.

Introspection makes me doubt the notion that the human mind works like a desktop computer. I'm abetted in this doubt by my friend Nick Herbert, one of the more colorful characters I've met in Silicon Valley. Nick started as a physicist designing hard drives, but these days is more likely to be found holding forth on consciousness. Here's a quote from a thought-provoking article by him called "Quantum Tantra."

**Figure 106:**
**The Author with Nick Herbert at an April Fool's Day Parade**

*One year I attended this annual parade in Boulder Creek, California.*

By the high standards of explanation we have come to demand in physics and other sciences, we do not even possess a bad theory of consciousness, let alone a good one.

Speculations concerning the origin of inner experience in humans and other beings have been few, vague and superficial. They include the notion that mind is an "emergent property" of active neuronal nets, or that mind is the "software" that manages the brain's unconscious "hardware." . . .

Half-baked attempts to explain consciousness, such as mind-as-software or mind-as-emergent-property do not take themselves seriously enough to confront the experimental facts, our most intimate data base, namely how mind itself feels from the inside.[100]

Nick proposes that we think of the human mind as a quantum system. Recall that quantum systems are said to change in two ways: When left alone, they undergo a continuous, deterministic transformation through a series of blended, "superposed" states, but when observed, they undergo abrupt probabilistic transitions into unambiguous "pure" states. Nick suggests that we can notice these two kinds of processes in our own minds.

- The continuous evolution of superposed states corresponds to the transcendent sensation of being merged with the world, or, putting it less portentously, to the everyday activity of being alert without consciously thinking much of anything. In this mode you aren't deliberately watching or evaluating your thoughts.
- The abrupt transition from superposed state to pure state can be seen as the act of adopting a specific opinion or plan. Each type of question or measurement of mental state enforces a choice among the question's own implicit set of possible answers. Even beginning to consider a question initiates a delimiting process.

The superposed states of quantum mechanics don't fit in with classical physics, but, at an internal psychological level, superposed mental states are something we're familiar with.

Note that computer scientists do have ways to model vagueness. For instance, neural nets provide outputs that can take on values intermediate between the definite yes-no values of one or zero. The notion of a continuous range of truth values is also studied as "fuzzy logic."

But the blended, overlaid, superposed states of quantum mechanics really aren't captured by intermediate truth values. The physicist Erwin Schrödinger once remarked that there's a difference between a blurred photograph of a mountain and a crisp photo of a cloud. Being blurry is like having an intermediate truth value, and a cloud is like being in a superposed state that's a blend of several pure states.

Let's go back to the notion of coherence I discussed in section *2.6: How Robots Get High*. Recall that a coherent system is one that independently evolves through a deterministic sequence of superposed states. And a decoherent system can become entangled with another system, such as a measuring device, that may even force it into a pure classical state. If we think of the mind's two modes as the coherent and the decoherent mode, then it seems as if being asked a question moves a person from coherence toward decoherence. As I already mentioned, this usage is a little counterintuitive, in that the more someone talks about their opinions, the less quantum-mechanically coherent they become. But I've grown used to this terminology. Indeed, as a kind of extended thought experiment, I had the villains in my recent epic novel *Frek and the Elixir* decohere their victims by interrogation.

Jayney leaned over Frek, her plastic dragon face bent into a parody of a motherly smile. She had fangs. She bit his neck and drew something out of him, leaving numbness in its place.

A hundred bland doughy faces seemed to bloom around him, pressing forward, staring, asking questions—all at the same time. Willy-nilly, Frek was unable to do anything but answer.

"How old are you? Are you happy? What's your name? Do you miss home? How tall are you? Are you frightened?"

With each response, Frek became a bit less himself and more of a statistic. The questions were flattening him out. On and on they came.

"Rate your feelings about the following on a scale from one to five, ranging from dislike very much to like very much . . .

"Rate your perceived frequency of the following classes of events on a scale from one to five, ranging from almost never to extremely often . . .

"Specify your agreement with the following statements on a scale from one to five, ranging from disagree strongly to agree very much . . ."

The questions came at him thick and fast. In a few minutes, every spark of Frek's own true self had been sapped away. All he felt now was a faint ache all through his bones, like the pain from a bad tooth.

Frek was a rag doll, an automaton, a thing. He contained no mysteries. He was fully decoherent.[101]

Isn't that, really, a bit how it feels when someone starts firing questions at you? It's unpleasant when someone substitutes interrogation for the natural flow of conversation. And it's still more unpleasant when the grilling is for some mercenary cause. You have every reason to discard or ignore the surveys with which institutions pester you. (But please don't use this reasoning as an excuse not to vote!)

Getting back to my main line of thought, let's see how Nick Herbert's notion of two kinds of mental processes fits in with the dialectic triad I laid down at the start of CHAPTER ONE: *Computation Everywhere.* This time I'll list two possible kinds of synthesis between the lifebox and the soul. These will be the "gnarliness" synthesis that I'm primarily arguing for, and an alternate quantum mind synthesis based on Nick Herbert's ideas.

- *Thesis* (Lifebox): Our theoretical knowledge of computational universality and our practical experience with neural nets and genetic algorithms suggests that any clearly described human behavior can eventually be emulated by a deterministic computation.
- *Antithesis* (Soul): Upon introspection we feel there is a residue that isn't captured by any scientific system; we feel ourselves to be quite unlike machines. This is the sense of having a soul.
- *Gnarliness Synthesis* (Seashell): If you're a complex class four computation, you don't feel like you're predictable, even though in fact you are a fully deterministic process. Computational systems can generate beautiful and unexpected patterns. A complex computation could perfectly well become conscious and feel itself to have a soul.
- *Quantum Mind Synthesis:* The soul can be given a scientific meaning as one's immediate perception of one's coherent uncollapsed wave function, particularly as it is entangled with the uncollapsed universal wave function of the cosmos.

Let's say a bit more about the quantum mind idea. How is it that the human brain could function in the two kinds of modes? Is there something specific about the human brain that allows us to couple our coherent superposed-state experiences with an ability to collapse down into discrete, pure states congenial to a PC?

The physicist Roger Penrose and the psychologist Stuart Hameroff point out that biological cells such as neurons include networks of very fine structures called microtubules. They suggest that the microtubules might somehow serve as a locus for quantum computations, and that it might be physically true that the brain at times is working in parallel mixed states. Most scientists dismiss this notion, citing problems with keeping a mixed quantum state for any appreciable length of time in a body-temperature assemblage like a brain. But there are methods of quantum error correction that might possibly make it possible for elements of the brain to be in coherent states for appreciable lengths of time.[102]

Whether or not Penrose's somewhat unpopular ideas pan out, they're at least an illustration of how a brain might include some truly quantum mechanical kinds of computation. Quoting the same essay by Nick Herbert:

> Looking inside, I do not feel like "software," whatever that might mean, but indeed like a shimmering (wavelike?) center of ambiguous potentia (possibilities?) around which more solid perceptions and ideas are continually congealing (quantum jumps?). This rough match of internal feeling with external description could be utterly deceptive but it at least shows that the quantum model of mind can successfully confront the introspective evidence in a way that no other mind models even attempt.

Even were our brains to exhibit large-scale quantum behavior, there's no need to be human chauvinists. The quantum mind synthesis of the lifebox and the soul doesn't rule out the possibility that machines or biocomputing devices could yet be equivalent to us. For any physical object is, after all, subject to quantum mechanics. Certain kinds of devices could well remain coherent and have uncollapsed wave functions for protracted periods of time.

As it so happens, building such devices is precisely what many quantum computing researchers are trying to do. My sense of Nick Herbert's somewhat visionary ideas is that he is trying to imagine how quantum computation would feel from the inside—and discovering in the process that it's something we do all the time.

In the fall of 2002, I was thinking about coherence a lot, largely in terms of the many-universes interpretation of quantum mechanics. I would occasionally reach the point where I was able to turn off my forever-talking inner narration and feel as if I had spread out into a quantum mechanical union with the world. One memorable December afternoon in Paris, I felt like I'd merged with the smoke from a smokestack. Here's how I described it in my journal.

> I keep working on this new mental exercise of becoming coherent, of being in a superposed state, of existing in multiple parallel universes, and that feels very good. Walking in the Latin Quarter, looking at some smoke from a chimney against the sky, not naming it, just seeing it, letting its motions move within my mind, I realize I'm no different than a computer screen showing a two-dimensional cellular automaton, with the smoke like a touch-cursor dragged across my brain. I am entangled with the smoke. I am coherent, but my coherence includes the smoke, I have joined the system, merged it into me. Like the old koan, Q: I see a flag is blowing in wind: is the flag moving or is the wind moving? A: My mind is moving. Finally I get it, a nice moment of *aha,* a satori in Paris.

One final point. The distinction between two kinds of quantum mechanical processes rests on the standard Copenhagen interpretation of quantum mechanics. In section *2.5: What Is Reality?* I discussed John Cramer's transactional interpretation of quantum mechanics, under which events really *are* determined and the superposed states are more in the nature of an illusion. The price Cramer pays for his model is in stipulating that the future influences the past or, putting it in a less time-bound fashion, his spacetime is an undivided whole, filled with patterns of synchronistic symmetries between the past and the future.

The notion of past and future being in harmony is strange to the usual view of physics, but it's the daily bread of writers. If the first line and the second line of a poem both end in "oo," does the first "oo" cause the second, or does the second "oo" cause the first? Neither, of course. Rhyming line endings are part of the poem's pattern as a whole. When a hero's death by fire is prefigured by a candle flame in a movie's opening scene, the chain of causation really leads neither forward nor backward but—sideways, through paratime to the germ of the plot in the mind of the screenwriter.

For a universal automatist, the win in Cramer's view is that it becomes possible to regard spacetime as resulting from a deterministic computation oriented along the second dimension of time that I call paratime. But do we then lose Nick Herbert's rather attractive metaphor of the quantum mind?

Not entirely. We can still keep a notion of higher consciousness. But now, rather than regarding it as being the experience of a superposed state, we might instead view it as an experience of the world as a timeless whole, or perhaps as an experience of the world's higher causation along the axis of paratime.

Words, words, words. I just stepped outside to take a break. The air is cool and fresh. I started early today, and the sun is still low. Dewdrops sparkle on the blades of grass, each drop holding its own idiosyncratic image of the world. I get my camera and take a picture (figure 107).

Beyond words.

In this chapter I've been describing how to view the mind as a deterministic computation. But at the end of the analysis, I still feel that something's missing, some breath of human life.

**Figure 107: Sparkling Dew**

Although I mentioned at the start of this chapter that the Egyptians thought of the *heart* as being of high importance, I've gone ahead and spent the whole chapter talking about the *brain*.

So now, finally, here's some heart to balance things out.

Twenty years ago, on my thirty-ninth birthday, my beautiful wife, Sylvia, wrote a lovely and lovable poem urging me to set aside my endless philosophizing and pay attention to her.

> It's your birthday!
> Let down your proofs—
> Count my numbers,
> Process my words,
> Weigh my mass,
> And square my root!
> Feel my fractals,
> Join my space—
> C'mon, baby,
> Let's tessellate!

Would a robot ever write a poem like that? Well, maybe . . . someday. But not anytime soon. It's important not to confuse philosophical dreams with the actual world we live in right now. Turn off the computer and give your partner a kiss. This means you, Rudy.

Linda Nguyen stood under the bell of her transparent plastic umbrella, watching her two kids playing in the falling rain, each of them with a see-through umbrella, too. First-grader Marco and little Chavella in their yellow rubber boots. The winter rains had started two weeks ago, and hadn't let up for a single day. The nearby creek was filled to its banks, and Linda wanted to be sure to keep her kids away from it.

Marco was splashing the driveway puddles and Chavella was getting ready to try. Linda smiled, feeling the two extra cups of coffee she'd had this morning. Her worries had been ruling her of late; it was time to push them away.

She was a Web programmer marooned in a rundown cottage on the fringes of Silicon Valley. She'd been unemployed for seven months. The rent was overdue, also the utilities and the phone and the credit cards. Last week her husband Juan had left her for a gym-rat hottie he'd met at the health club. And her car's battery was dead. There had to be an upside.

The worn gravel driveway had two ruts in it, making a pair of twenty-foot puddles. The raindrops pocked the clear water. The barrage of dents sent out circular ripples, criss-crossing to make a wobbly fish-scale pattern.

"I love rain!" whooped Marco, marching with his knees high, sending big waves down the long strip of water.

"Puddle!" exclaimed Chavella, at Linda's side. She smiled up at her mother, poised herself, stamped a little splash, and nearly fell over.

Linda noticed how the impact of each drop sent up a fine spray of minidroplets. When the minidroplets fell back to the puddle, some of them merged right in, but a few bounced across the surface a few times first. The stubborn ones. It would take a supercomputer to simulate this puddle in real time—maybe even all the computers in the world. Especially if you included the air currents pushing the raindrops this way and that. Computable or not, it kept happening.

Linda was glad to be noticing the details of the rain in the puddle. It bumped her out of her depressed mood. When she was depressed, the world seemed as simple as a newscast or a mall. It was good to be outside, away from the TV and the computer. The natural world was so high bandwidth.

She swept her foot through the puddle, kicking up a long splash. Her quick eyes picked out a particular blob of water in midair; she saw its jiggly surface getting zapped by a lucky raindrop—then watched the tiny impact send ripple rings across the curved three-dimensional shape. Great how she could keep up with this. She was faster than all the world's computers!

Linda kicked another splash and saw every single drop's dance. It almost felt like the water was talking to her. Coffee and rain.

"Puddle bombs!" shouted Marco, running toward his mother and his sister, sending up great explosive splashes as he came.

"No!" shrieked Chavella, clutching Linda's hand.

But of course Marco did a giant two-footed jump and splashed down right next to them, sending Chavella into tears of fury.

"Wet!" she cried. "Bad!"

"Don't do that again," Linda told Marco sternly. "Or we're all going back inside."

She led Chavella down the driveway toward the tilted shack that was their garage. With the owners waiting to sell the land off to developers, nothing got fixed. The house was a scraper. The dead headlights of Linda's old car stared blankly from the garage door. She'd been putting off replacing the battery—expecting Juan to do it for her. Was he really gone for good?

It was dry in the garage, the rain loud on the roof. Linda folded her umbrella and used her sleeve to wipe Chavella's eyes and nose. While Chavella stood in the garage door scolding Marco, Linda peered out the garage's dirty rear window. Right behind the garage was the roaring creek that snaked through the pasture. It was deep enough to sweep a child away.

As if in a dream, the instant she had this thought, she saw Marco go racing by the window, headed right toward the stream with his head down, roaring at the top of his lungs, deep into his nutty hyper mode.

As Linda raced out of the garage door, she heard a shriek and a splash. And when she reached the banks of the brown, surging creek, Marco was gone.

"Help!" she cried, the rain falling into her mouth.

And then the miracle happened. A squall of wind swept down the creek—drawing a distinct arrow in the surface. The arrow pointed twenty yards to Linda's left, and at the tip of the arrow the rain was etching a moving circle into the stream's turbulent waters.

Not stopping to think about it, Linda ran after the circle with all her might. Once she was out ahead of it, she knelt by the bank. The circle drifted her way, its edges clearly marked by the purposeful rain. Linda thrust her hand into the brown water at the circle's center and caught Marco by the hand.

Minutes later they were in the house, Marco coughing and pale with cold, but none the worse for wear. Linda carried him into the bathroom and set him into a tub of hot water. Chavella insisted on getting in the tub, too. She liked baths.

The kids sat there, Marco subdued, Chavella playing with her rubber duck.

"Thank you," Linda said, although she wasn't sure to whom. "But I still need a job."

Looking up, she noticed rain running down the window above the tub. As if hearing her, the rivulets wavered to form a series of particular shapes—letters. Was she going crazy? Don't fight it. She wrote the letters down. It was a Web address. And at that address, Linda found herself a job—maintaining an interactive Web site for the National Weather Service.

# CHAPTER FIVE

# *The Human Hive*

MOST OF MY PERSONALITY CONSISTS of attitudes and ideas that I learned directly from other humans—or from human-made books, movies, record albums, TV shows, and the like. All the artifacts that surround me were designed and assembled by humans as well. Without human society, I'd be an inarticulate naked ape.

If you raise a snail in isolation and set him loose in a snailless garden, perhaps his life won't be so different from the lives of those more fortunate snails who rub shells with hundreds of their fellows. But if you raise an ant in isolation and set her loose in an antless forest, she will surely die. Ants aren't equipped to live on their own.

Humans are more like the swarming ants than like the autonomous snails who carry their houses on their backs. Yes, I can go backpacking alone in the wilderness, but my camping equipment comes from human factories, my food supplies were grown and packaged by humans, and I learned my forest survival skills by talking with humans and by studying human books and maps.

Not only does the presence of other people affect an individual person's computations, but a society as a whole can also be said to compute, using its members as networked parallel processors.

As in the earlier chapters, we'll work our way up from the lower to the higher levels of computation. This chapter breaks into five sections.

- *5.1: Hive Minds.* People's motions and emotions play off those of their peers, leading to emergent group behaviors. Your brain is an individual node of society's hive mind. The hive mind is in some sense conscious, but it is a mind quite unlike any individual person's.

- *5.2: Language and Telepathy.* Language is the primary communication medium linking society's members. Speech encodes mental states, which in turn represent the world at various levels of abstraction. It's interesting to look at language as a kind of network itself, in that a word is viewed as having links to the other words you associate with it. This network obeys a certain kind of statistical pattern known as an inverse power law.

- *5.3: Commercial and Gnarly Aesthetics.* Society has a group memory that's based both on oral transmission of knowledge and on information-dense artifacts such as books, paintings, buildings, movies, Web pages, and computer programs. I'll discuss why it is that inverse power laws also characterize the popularity of our cultural information artifacts. Inverse power laws mean that only a few authors and artists can earn a living, and that a handful of familiar chain stores soak up the lion's share of the retail business. Nevertheless, nothing stays on top forever; I'll discuss how this fact relates to what computer scientists call self-organized criticality. At the end of the section I explore literary aesthetics in terms of gnarl.

- *5.4: Power and Money.* In government and in the marketplace, powerful forces are forever trying to turn society into a controllable class two computation. But no regime lasts forever, and no corporations are immortal. The unpredictability of society's class four computation acts as a perennial force for revolution.

- *5.5. The Past and Future History of Gnarl.* First point: The history of the world isn't only about presidents, wars, and kings. Society's computation consists of *all* its members' actions, and an historian does well to focus on art, science, technology, and popular culture. Second point: Looked at in a certain way, the history of technology is a history of mankind's increasing mastery of various forms of computation. I include a table listing a possible future sequence of computation-related inventions.

## 5.1: *Hive Minds*

People are the most unpredictable, rewarding, and dangerous entities that one encounters. Each of us is exquisitely sensitive to our peers, continually tracking their motions and moods. You react to others; they react to you—and to one another. The result is a parallel computation.

Let's start with motion. In section *4.2: The Network Within,* I mentioned Braitenberg vehicles as an example of reflex-driven agents that react to objects in the environment by approaching or avoiding them. Specific reflexes may be tuned to the types of objects encountered, the relative distance and direction of the objects, and so on. If an agent obeys but one simple reflex, and if it's in a world with but one other object, then its motions will either halt or repeat themselves. That is, it will perform a dull class one or class two computation. But if the agent has several competing reflexes and several objects to react to, then its motion can become chaotic and exhibit class three behavior.

The situation becomes especially interesting when, instead of merely reacting to fixed features of the environment, the agents react to one another—for here class four behavior becomes common. Craig Reynolds was one of the first computer scientists to investigate this kind of collective motion, publishing a groundbreaking paper about how to simulate flocking groups of animals: herds of cattle, schools of fish, swarms of gnats, and flocks of birds.[103] (See figure 8 and figure 108.)

I need to caution that when I speak of flocking motions, I'm not talking about those special cases when a group of migrating ducks or geese forms a V-pattern in the wake of a leader. I'm talking about looser, more democratic groupings—think of pigeons circling a city square, a band of sparrows in a hedge, or a gang of seagulls going after a beachgoer's picnic. From time to time a single bird's action can decisively affect the whole flock, but normally the motions emerge from the interactions of the birds' computations.

To celebrate flocking, I'll quote some lines from John Updike's poem, "The Great Scarf of Birds,"[104] describing a flock of starlings lifting off from a golf course.

> And as
> I watched, one bird,
> prompted by accident or will to lead,
> ceased resting; and, lifting in a casual billow,
> the flock ascended as a lady's scarf,
> transparent, of gray, might be twitched
> by one corner, drawn upward and then,
> decided against, negligently tossed toward a chair:
> the southward cloud withdrew into the air.

Reynolds's generic term for his simulated flocking agents was *boids*. His idea was to have each boid obey three rules, the first rule involving speed, and the other rules involving the direction of motion.

- *Don't bump.* Avoid bumping other boids as follows: Slow down if you're in danger of ramming into a boid in front of you; speed up if a boid is about to bump you from behind; and otherwise settle back toward your standard speed.
- *Copy.* Adjust your heading so as to move parallel to your neighbors.
- *Hide.* Head toward the center of the flock.

Note that there is often a conflict between the copying and the hiding rules; the flocking algorithm resolves this by averaging the effects of the three rules, for instance by turning toward a direction that's halfway between a neighbor's heading and the direction toward the center of the flock. The average doesn't necessarily have to be even-handed; some boids might give a bit more weight to hiding, whereas others might lean more toward copying a neighbor. The boids will also have a certain amount of inertia; this means they'll turn somewhat gradually rather than abruptly.

When programming a simulation of boids, you actually assign each boid some real-number parameters that control how it averages the bump-avoiding, copying, and hiding forces. And, as the program develops, you'll encounter more decisions to make. These might include: the boid's standard speed; the distances and angles of vision that characterize "in front of" and "behind"; the rate at which the boid can change its speed; whether the boid looks at only one or possibly two nearest neighbors in its copy force; and how to weight the various flock members when computing an average center position (one gets more realistic-looking motions if the closer boids are taken more strongly into account). You learn a lot about a phenomenon when you try to code up a simulation. God is in the details.

In creating a flocking simulation, the bottom line is to produce a display that looks interesting: organized but not predictable, chaotic but not random. As the hair-metal vocalist David Lee Roth is said to have remarked, "It's not what you do, it's how good you look doin' it." When we simulate a flock, we're hoping to see a class four computation.

As it turns out, the Reynolds flocking rules are quite robust. Class four flocking is something that moving agents like to do.

Rather than locking themselves into one monolithic flock, the boids usually form several clusters that swoop around in a pleasing fashion, sometimes merging with other clusters, sometimes breaking into sub-clusters, and with individual boids maneuvering from cluster to cluster when they approach. Every now and then the whole flock joins together, but when a boundary or obstacle appears, the flock splits into clusters. Some parameter settings produce tight, intense swarming, while other settings provoke languid wheeling. But for most settings, the flocking is class four. The restless grouping, splitting, and regrouping is reminiscent of the play of gliders seen in cellular automata such as Wolfram's Rule 110 or Brian Silverman's Brain rule.

The Reynolds algorithm can be enhanced in various ways. We can, for instance, factor in forces to avoid the boundaries of the world (like the way fish avoid an aquarium's walls). Or we might work with two flocks and have one flock hunting the members of the other flock, as shown in figure 108.

In recent years Reynolds has been studying generalized *steering behaviors*— where a steering behavior is any method that an agent uses to compute its instantaneous direction and speed of motion. Given the example of flocking,

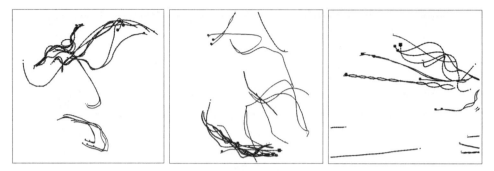

**Figure 108: Two Flocks**

*In these pictures, the boids leave trails; one flock leaves darker trails, the other leaves slightly lighter trails. The dark boids are hunting the light ones, and the light ones are running away. The individual boids' success at their tasks is measured as numerical scores, which the flocks use as a fitness measure for evolving their members' parameters toward higher-scoring settings. One emergent pattern in this simulation is that pairs of boids will get into a double helix motion, circling each other as they move along, leaving trails like the twisted pair in the rightmost image.*[105]

we can expect that the more interesting steering behaviors arise when agents must continually update their motions in reaction to other moving agents. One of Reynolds's latest programs simulates pedestrians moving in opposite directions on a shared sidewalk without bumping into each other; another simulates soccer players.

It's interesting to think of steering behaviors while mingling with people in a public place. One the one hand, you notice people's individual behaviors; on the other hand you can observe the emergent computation embodied in the group's motions.

Of course people are much more sophisticated agents than simple boids who plug a few simple parameters into three or four basic laws. But yet there are certain very basic rules that we nearly always obey. A primary social motion rule is to avoid physical contact with strangers; secondary rules are to head toward interesting or attractive objects, to keep an extra distance from unfamiliar or menacing individuals, and to stay close to one's family and friends.

As in other computations, we can distinguish four kinds of processes when groups of people move.

A crowd of people taking their seats in a concert hall or in an airplane carries out a class one computation, in that the result is a fixed state with everyone seated. Of course if we look closer, we'll see a gnarly ongoing group computation involving the sharing of the seats' elbow rests, not to mention plenty of face-rubbing and hair-tossing. Given that the individuals are themselves carrying out class four computations, the fine-scale motions of a crowd are never class one. But for now we're focusing on the large-scale motions.

Children playing ring-around-the-rosy are in a periodic class two motion. Less gifted dancers move in repetitive class two patterns as well—part of being a good dancer is having the ability to layer extra variations upon the basic rhythm. As an example of a class two dancer, I recall a stodgy acquaintance in college. In dancing the then-popular twist, he looked as if he were following verbatim the commonly repeated instructions: "Twist your feet as if you're crushing cigarette butts, and move your arms as if you're toweling your backside." Doing just that and nothing more meant class two motion. People moving in an orderly queue are another example of a class two motion, but of course people hardly ever stay orderly for long. They edge forward and try to get ahead of each other, pause to quarrel, circle around, and so on.

Once pedestrians break out of a queue and move freely, their motions become class three or class four. How to distinguish the two cases? Following Wolfram, we'd expect class three motions to be like random jostling, whereas class four motions ought to have clusters of individuals spontaneously forming and dissolving, with certain clusters seeking out new paths—the clusters again acting a bit like CA gliders.

A crowd of shoppers entering a store, for instance, moves like a class three gas. The people-particles disperse through the aisles, with the proviso that certain zones are more attractive than others.

As examples of class four pedestrian motion, think of a hundred thousand rock fans finding their way across outdoor terrain toward a stage, of an army entering a conquered city, of commuters, or of a mob hounding a celebrity. These crowds flow like fluids, sending out bands of scouts that, if they progress successfully, are followed by streams of more people.

It's worth noting that joining a crowd provides a visceral pleasure. We like to flock. There's something very soothing about the sound of many human voices in peaceful conversation. This is a large part of the appeal of public spaces like city squares—these are especially pleasant when the voices aren't drowned out by the din of motor vehicles or, God forbid, leaf blowers.

One reason we like to flock is surely that, as the fish and birds know, there's safety in numbers. Over the years I've participated in various political marches and rallies, and it's always reassuring to be a member of a mass of like-minded people.

We flock for other reasons as well. Some crowds, such as conventions, seminars, or discussion groups are based upon an affinity of interests. By meeting together, people can pool their data and enjoy the pleasure of developing their ideas by conversing about them.

Another reason for flocking is of course reproduction, with the tightest flock of all being, for many of us, our family. One of the striking things about being in a family is that you keep coming across the same few people all the time. No matter how far I travel, when I go to bed, I'm very likely to encounter this one particular woman named Sylvia. What are the odds of that? Nearly every year three young people turn up at our house around Christmastime, apparently the same ones who were there the years before. An incredible string of coincidences! It's as if we're attached to each other by invisible cords. If something important happens to any of us, it's a safe bet that some of the others will quickly appear.

Speaking of family members, let's turn from motion to emotion. As well as noticing the people around us, we often try to model their internal states so as to predict what they might do next. We're also very prone to imagining what others think of us. You might say that a group of people is like a basket of reflective glass Christmas balls, each ball holding images of the others, and with second-, third-, and higher-order images nested within the regressing reflections.

It's a bit uncanny how quickly we read each others' feelings from slight clues of body language, facial expression, and tone of voice. When people converse, their whole emotional makeup comes into play. The resulting interactions are distinctly different from anything a single person would produce on his or her own. When you interact with others, a higher-order process sets in, generating feelings and actions on its own. What you say, feel, and do become outputs of the flock's parallel computation. Part of the computation happens in your own head, but part of it is outside you. In one of his novels, Vladimir Nabokov speaks of a lovers' conversation as being like an operatic duet, a musical exchange in which the actual sense of the words plays but a small part.

One purpose of human flocking is to facilitate conversations, and participating in a lively chat gives most humans a sense of satisfaction. We're social beings. But of course not all conversations are equally satisfying—we need only think of the four computational classes to see why.

If you talk to someone who insists on always returning to one and the same point, then the conversation has a predictable class one quality. Most of us have met monomaniacs who can speak only of their health, or of the misdeeds of the current political administration, or of some third party with whom they're in love.

A class two conversation, rather than being limited to one single idea, continually circles through a fixed sequence of thoughts. These loops can be toxic. The psychiatrist R. D. Laing published some wonderfully lacerating descriptions of class two interactions in his book *Knots*.[106] I'll quote from three of the knots.

JILL     I'm upset you are upset

JACK    I'm not upset

JILL     I'm upset that you're not upset that I'm upset you're upset

JACK    I'm upset that you're upset that I'm not upset that you're upset that I'm upset, when I'm not

we have to help him realize that,
the fact that he does not think there is anything
the matter with him
is one of the things that is
the matter with him

Jill feels guilty
    that Jack feels guilty
        that Jill feels guilty
           that Jack feels guilty

An example of a class three conversation would be the pleasantly drifting flow of talk around a dinner table. Even if some class one monomaniacs or class two bickerers are in the company, the presence of a few additional inputs can break things up and unloose the intellectual play.

What a bring-down it is when a bore manages to steer a class three conversation back to some pet obsession. The computation collapses to a class one point attractor. Part of the gentle art of conversation is to jolt the flow away from point attractors or feedback loops without stirring up hard feelings. Often a single subversive or diversionary comment will suffice.

I see a class four conversation as having more structure and more of a sustained tone—a classical paradigm would be one of Plato's dialogues. An intense conversation on some topic of great mutual interest becomes class four when new and unexpected ideas start occurring. Of course some mutually absorbing exchanges are simply class two loops around comfortable tracks. But in class four conversations we find ourselves saying things we didn't quite know we knew—the new insights being catalyzed by the interaction with another person's mind.

Back in high school in Louisville, I had a memorable math teacher named Brother Emeric. He sometimes joked that he talked to himself a lot, as it was the only way he could have an intelligent conversation. But his real joy was in talking to his classes. Teaching becomes class four to the extent that the teacher reacts to the students: to facial expressions of interest or boredom, to questions and comments, to in-class presentations, or to homework and tests. Brother Emeric wasn't big on having students speak up in class. He disliked me in particular; he thought I was a wise guy. But at least we had some kind of interaction going.

It's an interesting exercise to let go of the ego a bit, and think about the vast parallel computation that the conversations around us perform. You have the opportunity to stop identifying with your limited body, and to share in the networked computation of the group mind.

In science-fiction tales we occasionally encounter the concept of a *hive mind*. But few succeed in properly imagining it. At the end of the third *Matrix* movie, for instance, an agglomeration of sentient machines forms a big face that talks in a robotic voice. The visual effect is pleasing, but as a presentation of a hive mind, the big talking face is doubly bogus. The first level of bogosity is that the *Matrix* creators have fallen back upon Hollywood's default personification of an individual computer mind as a face on the wall that speaks in flat tones, eschews contractions, and is utterly lacking in humor. The second level of bogosity is the implicit assumption that the hive mind of a *group* of machines might just as well be represented by the same kind of big talking face that is used to represent the mind of an *individual* machine.

Let's try to get some intuition about hive minds by thinking about the experts: bees and ants. Each member insect operates according to simple reflex behaviors, reacting to the world and to signals from the other insects. Group behaviors emerge: Wax honeycombs are filled with honey; kitchens are located and pillaged.

When a bee queen leaves the nest, a swarm forms around her, making a large moving object something like a great, buzzing slug that a first-time observer can mistake for a bizarre animal. This amorphous and reactive being emerges from the hive's dynamics—but certainly it isn't shaped like a bee, and it doesn't act like a bee. It's something different.

I'll repeat the point: A hive's emergent self doesn't resemble an individual hive member. Even an ant queen is but a part of a whole—the queen doesn't forage, doesn't build tunnels, doesn't combat invaders.

Let's turn now to the human hive in which we live. What is it like?

Well—it's not like a person. Of course some of our more self-aggrandizing rulers have described themselves as physically embodying the soul of their kingdom. Louis XIV famously said, *"L'état, c'est moi"*: the state is me. Politicians often speak of their nation's values as being identical to their own values. But they're wrong. No individual member represents a hive.

As a way of trying to a grasp the human hive mind, let's hark back to Damasio's notion of core consciousness and see to what extent a human society can be thought of as conscious. I'll go over the steps listed in section *4.4: "I Am."*

- *Immersion.* A society is active in the world, reacting to events: invasions and disasters, discoveries and inventions, supplies and demands. If a house catches fire, the firefighters appear. If enough people in a town want cell phones, a cell phone service is put into place.

- *Seeing objects.* A society distinguishes among separate objects in the world and has a sense of itself as a whole. Society can see individual buildings, cars, and people. On a larger scale, society sees interest groups and even other nations. Society reacts to different events and objects in different ways. Some activities are encouraged as being good for society, while those deemed bad for society are suppressed.

- *Movie-in-the-brain.* The stories presented by a society's media can be regarded as the society's image of the world. In this context, we can think of a society's collective communication and information resources as the society's brain. One difficulty here is that a society has many conflicting movies-in-the-brain. The street-level word of mouth about the daily news can be rather different than what one reads in the paper. But there is, after all, a certain commonality—everyone agrees on a large number of factual occurrences. How various individuals *feel* about the facts is another story.

- *Proto-self.* Society has clear representations of itself that include images of itself as a whole, images of current events, and images of society's reactions. This is what news analysis, op-ed stories, and TV punditry are all about. When people speak of the state of the nation or the national mood, they're talking about the hive mind's proto-self.

- *Feelings.* Society continually enhances its movie-in-the-brain by forming opinions and evaluations of how current events are affecting the social proto-self. Public opinion polls can be thought of as ways of discovering and articulating society's feelings. Elections and legislation are also about the feelings of the body politic. When special interests labor to promote a notion that society is fed up with this or eager for that, they're trying to manipulate the hive's feelings. Sometimes a consensus emerges, but often the nation remains perennially conflicted on an issue—one has only to think of abortion, taxes, or the environment.

- *Core consciousness.* As I understand Damasio, he says that core consciousness is the ongoing process of forming feelings about how an always small but ever-changing group of events affects the proto-self. Core consciousness highlights those particular events, which accounts for society's current focus of attention. This sounds very much like the news cycle in action, or, at the street level, like neighborhood gossip.

- *Empathy.* A society has empathy to the extent that it enhances its images of other societies with representations of the other societies' feelings.

So it seems as if the United States, for instance, is conscious, if not highly empathetic. One might wonder, however, if a nation has a single or perhaps multiple core consciousnesses. For a society has a number of coherent groups within itself—call them subhives. Examples would be ethnic groups, cities, and professions—and of course things can be subdivided further than that. Hives within hives.

A little thought indicates that many subhives seem to satisfy the Damasio steps listed above. The mathematical community, for instance, views events in terms of whether or not they're good for mathematics and mathematicians, focuses on their own idiosyncratic news stories, and shares certain feelings.

When we lump everyone together into a national hive, we have the problem that the members of the hive not only focus on different events, but have radically different feelings about the events they do notice in common. But to the extent that a large number of individuals share in, or are at least aware of, common national opinions and hot topics, the nation really does have a single core consciousness.

The increasing reach and bandwidth of our communications Web has two countervailing effects. On the one hand, more communication seems to make for a national group consciousness that becomes ever more pronounced. With TV screens and advertising everywhere, it becomes increasingly difficult to avoid knowing what the nation is thinking about. On the other hand, thanks to the Web, individuals can set up their own small media empires, sparking the formation of cohesive subhives.

The diversity of opinions found in individuals and in subhives does means that the national hive mind is conflicted about certain issues. Now, it's true that individual people can also be deeply ambivalent—for example, do you love your father or do you hate him? But, really, no one person can contain opinions as furiously divergent as are found in our national discourse. As a parallel entity, the hive mind easily entertains opposing thoughts much more readily than can an individual mind. But this is okay—remember that the hive mind need not, even in form, resemble an individual mind.

Sometimes the internal strife can be such that a hive mind becomes deadlocked, unable to act. Of course failing to act is a strategy in its own right, and if the body politic is sufficiently divided, inaction can be society's best course. It's also worth mentioning here that there really are some individuals who are so deeply torn by internal conflicting drives that they become ineffectual and unable to accomplish anything.

The issue of multiplicity comes into starker relief when we look at the planet as a whole. Different nations have very different consciousnesses—primarily because they have different proto-selves. Japanese care about how events affect Japan; Mexicans care about Mexico. Despite eco-activists' best efforts at planetary consciousness-raising, most people still don't think very much about how things affect Earth as a whole.

Just as the forces of communication make national consciousnesses more coherent, communication seems likely to enhance the global hive's consciousness—this is Marshall McLuhan's vision of a global village. But we have no guarantee that the global hive will be ecologically sensitive: Think of monoculture, McDonaldsization, and consumer nations clear-cutting Third World forests. But perhaps as more individuals identify more deeply with the global hive, they'll influence the global mind to be less rapacious.

In practice it's not easy to affect a hive. Indeed, most individuals feel themselves to have very little influence on the feelings and focus of a national or a global hive mind. Although obscure individuals do sometimes step forward to cause major changes, the laws of probability suggest that a citizen's chances of having great impact are terribly small.

Some people find this galling. It's my impression that people over fifty are particularly prone to vexation over their lack of influence upon the national hive mind. Perhaps there's some atavistic memory of becoming a revered tribal elder at a certain age? Or a fear that, if not revered, an elder is likely to be fed to the wolves?

I myself have to fight off my dismay at seeing the mass media obsessing over fears and lies—particularly when I sense that my hive's feelings are being manipulated by powerful individuals who don't have society's best interests at heart.

Yes, I've had some slight effect upon my hive by voting in elections, by discussing my opinions with people, by raising children, by teaching classes, and by publishing books. I should be satisfied with this, but at times I'm not.

I find it particularly discouraging when my hive mind's computation veers toward class one obsession or class two repetition. How welcome it is when some oddball manages to throw the media off their stride, and introduces class three or class four unpredictability to the national mind.

Suppose that at some point you do find society's hive mind unacceptably hysterical and debased. What can you do about it? If you become obsessively passionate about reforming the hive's mind, the likely outcome is that you'll become a bitter, frustrated bore—and a class one conversationalist.

An extreme cure for weariness of the hive mind is to emigrate. It's striking how utterly different another nation's hive mind can be. Days or even weeks can go by without a single evening news story about American politics! Different hives think about different proto-selves. How many stories about Belgium or Tonga do you see on American TV?

As I write this section, I happen to be visiting relatives in Europe for several weeks. I always feel both relieved and diminished when I'm removed from my native hive mind. Even when I've occasionally lived in Europe for longer stretches of time, I never fully understand what's going on there. But by now I'm cosmopolitan enough to blend in and have fun. An émigré is like one of those specialized myrmecophilous or ant-loving insects that manages to live in an anthill without being an ant. Myrmecophiles can be parasites, symbiotes, or ant-pets. There is a certain small beetle, for instance, that is kept and fed by the ants simply because the ants enjoy licking the tasty waxy secretions of the beetle's antennae. "Tell us another one of your crazy stories about America!"

Emigrating is difficult, alienating, and, in some sense, an admission of defeat. A less drastic way to escape the emotional disturbance of being part of an out-of-control hive might be to redefine your notion of subset of society you belong to. You can emigrate internally—not to another hive, but to a subhive. The idea is simply to put less emotional involvement into the national hive mind and more into some smaller grouping. Consider your family and friends, your professional associates, or groups of people who enjoy the same things that you do. Without actually leaving the country, you can effectively leave the big hive.

As we used to say in the sixties:

*What if they gave a war and nobody came?*

I remarked earlier that older people tend to get especially agitated about the doings of the national hive mind. Could it be that, as they lose their connections to work, family, and cultural life, older people tend to lose their identification with more congenial subhives? Maybe they need to stop thinking about the news and get out of the house more.

In any case, that's enough about the news. After all, our social hive mind involves a lot more than that. Consider. You speak a language. You live in a house that people built. You've learned certain skills and crafts from other people. You've found a way to make a living. The lights and the toilet work. You're reading a somewhat entertaining book. All products of the hive.

Recently I was visiting my daughter Georgia in New York City (figure 109). What a hive, the streets lined with human-made cars and buildings. I paused at one point, taking it in. Men tearing out and retrofitting apartments. Wires running across the street bringing power. A garbage truck picking up trash. A police car cruising by. Stores displaying books and summer dresses.

**Figure 109: The Queensboro Bridge**

*That's Manhattan in the lower right corner.*

Sometimes we think of cities as blights upon the planet. But the cities are our hive dwellings, as surely as the papery nests of wasps. We are at no point separate from nature; and at no point is the individual separate from the hive.

Language, culture, and technology are the honey in the hive, and I'll say more about these topics in the sections to come.

Before moving on, there's one more hive-related issue that I want to raise. Is there any chance of the Internet "waking up" and developing an autonomous hive mind of its own?

The Web is indeed a network of class four computational devices. And certainly our machines intercommunicate and affect one another's behavior. On the bright side, we have e-mail, software downloads, automatic upgrades, photo sharing, and Java applets. On the dark side, we have ever broader epidemics of worms and viruses.

The linkedness of computers is coming to be an essential part of their nature. I can accomplish good work off-line, but if I'm traveling and I can't manage to scrounge up a Net hookup, my laptop begins to feel as feeble as an isolated ant.

In short, the basics are in place: The Internet contains complicated nodes that interact with one another. But I do see some barriers to the emergence of a Web-wide hive mind.

First of all, our computers are far from being able to freely interact with one another. Security systems and most owners' common sense place strict limits on what goes in and out of our machines. This makes it hard for the nodes of the Internet to engage in spontaneous flocking styles of behavior.

Second, and more significant, the Internet seems to lack a clear-cut movie-in-the-brain analogous to our society's national news. At the low level, individual computers aren't in any real sense aware of what's happening across the whole network, and at the high level, there doesn't seem to be any one emergent Net-wide phenomenon that acts as a movie-in-the-brain.

But wait. How about a Web search engine or Web portal or message board such as the currently popular Google, Yahoo!, or Slashdot. Might these serve as Internet versions of movies-in-the-brain? Well, maybe, in a way. But it's really the human machine-users (and only *some* of them) who are interested in these sites. The actual computers that make up our network don't presently care about, say, Google—although our cosseted desktop machines are slowly beginning to automatically emulate our never-ending labor of finding patches and drivers to keep them in repair.

From the machines' point of view, a better model of a movie-in-the-brain might be a so-called DNS server, which connects Web-site names with their identifying "IP" code numbers. Another machine-level movie-in-the-brain might be found in the online devices that figure out the best paths for information packets to take. Also consider Google page-rank.

And what about a proto-self? Does the Web have something that serves as a self-image? Not really. Something like a routing-path map is just too juiceless to be the kind of thing we have in mind. Perhaps something like the Net server that maintains a list of the identities of traffic-clogging spammer machines is a bit like a proto-self, or like a feeling.

But it's all still very rudimentary. Nevertheless, we dream of the Web waking up. Conceivably there could someday be a computer virus that served a higher purpose of awakening a gnarly unifying computation across the Web. It might arise by accident. Or it might evolve. It's like the classic science-fiction scenario where some scientists build a worldwide computer network and ask it, "Is there a God?" The machine answers, "*Now* there is!"

In Hollywood versions of this scenario, the newly empowered global computation usually sets to work kicking humanity's butt. But why would any Internet hive mind ever act like that? What would it have to gain?

After all, computers already dominate Earth. There's really nothing to overthrow, no power to seize. Our machines are the cells the planetary computer is made up of. And we devote considerable energy to building and maintaining these machines. We're *already* their freakin' servants.

Computers wanting to kill humanity would make no more sense than, say, your brain telling the rest of your body, "All right, I'm going to kill all of you skin and muscle and bone and organ cells so that I can reign supreme!" Or, even crazier, your thoughts telling your brain, "All right, I'm getting rid of all you lazy brain cells!"

This said, it is true that we try to encourage some parts of our body at the expense of others. We want more muscle and brain, less fat and tumors. Might the planetary Web mind decide to selectively eliminate certain elements? Indirectly this already happens. Web pages that use flawed or outdated code become obsolete and unvisited. Spammers get their accounts canceled, not because of anything they stand for, but because they're bad for the efficiency of the Web. But more radical sanctions are science-fictionally conceivable. I'm thinking of implacable Web-run robots descending upon a trailer park of spammers—but wait, they have the wrong address—they're at my door! Help!

### 5.2: *Language and Telepathy*

Language begins when social creatures actively communicate information to their fellows. A bee returning to the hive from a flower field does a waggle dance to tell the others what direction to fly in. An ant secretes pheromones to tell other ants that she's recently encountered an intruder. We humans share information by grimacing, gesturing, and making noises with our mouths.

Our languages have evolved both to describe the world around us and to represent the thought patterns in our minds. "What are you thinking?" "Well, let me tell you." In an essay on language, Jorge Luis Borges quotes a relevant passage from G. K. Chesterton.

> Man knows that there are in the soul tints more bewildering, more numberless, and more nameless than the colors of an autumn forest; . . . Yet he seriously believes that these things can every one of them, in all their tones and semi-tones, in all their blends and unions, be accurately represented by an arbitrary system of grunts and squeals. He believes that an ordinary civilized stockbroker can really produce out of his own inside noises which denote all the mysteries of memory and all the agonies of desire.[107]

My optimistic opinion is that, given time, willingness, and a sympathetic listener, Chesterton's stockbroker really *can* communicate the tints and semitones of his (or her) soul. It's a matter of piling on detail, using analogies, and enhancing the words with the play of the voice. To ensure the transmission, the listener reflects back summaries of the message, so that the speaker can emend or amplify the explication as required. By the way, computer networks do something similar, with receiving nodes sending back requests for retransmission of packets of information lost on their way from the sending nodes.

Speaking of computers, it will be useful to describe a brief example that brings into relief a point about how language works. Suppose that a machine called, say, Eggpop has carried out a time-consuming computation to produce a high-resolution graphical image of the Mandelbrot set fractal. We can think of this image as being akin to an idea in Eggpop's mind. Now if Eggpop wants to communicate this image to another machine, there are three possible messages Eggpop might send.

- *Language.* A description of the algorithm and the parameters used to create the image.
- *Representational art.* A file containing a pixel-by-pixel representation of the image.
- *Telepathy.* A link pointing to the combined algorithm and image in Eggpop's own memory.

*Language* is an all-purpose construction kit that a speaker uses to model mental states. In interpreting these language constructs, a listener builds a brain state similar to the speaker's.

*Representational art* uses a very different approach: An idea is rendered by images, sounds, sculpture, or the like. In many cases a picture is worth a thousand words—and then some. But certainly there are times where a few well-chosen words have deeper impact than a detailed image. In these cases, the words manage to trigger powerful, preexisting thought modes. I might also mention that visual art can be nonrepresentational, spare, allusive—like a higher form of language.

*Telepathy* is the human analogy to machines communicating by giving one another hyperlinks (and access permissions) to locations in their own minds. Telepathy doesn't have to be magic. Conceivably we might someday come up with something like a brain-wave-based cell phone. In section *4.6: The Mind Recipe* I mentioned my notion for such a device, to be called an uvvy. Perhaps with an uvvy you could reach out and sensually touch another person's thought patterns rather than having to build your own copies of their thoughts based upon verbal descriptions.

In this vein, I can imagine a future in which people converse solely by direct links into each others' minds. Language might become an outmoded social art—like handwriting or ballroom dancing! But I doubt it. I think language is so deeply congenial to us that we'd no sooner abandon it than we'd give up sex.

Although I use "telepathy" for the notion of having direct links to another person's thoughts, if telepathy is just a matter of having someone at a distance know what you're thinking, then language already is a form of telepathy and a person walking down the street with a cell phone is essentially in telepathic contact with a friend.

I compare language to telepathy to point out how powerful language is. In the intimate conversations that you have with a lover, spouse, or close friend, language feels as effortless as singing or dancing. The ideas flow and the minds merge. In this empathetic exchange, each of you develops a clear sense of your partner's proto-self and core consciousness.

One imperfect feature of human language is that our rate of information exchange is limited to very low rates. Yes, you can send a multimegabyte book manuscript by e-mail in a matter of seconds, but the human listener at the other end will take hours or even days to read it. We're stuck with low bounds on both the speed at which we can listen to someone talk and on the speed at which we can read with full comprehension.

The problem of finding time and patience to process other people's outputs is an obstacle to wider-ranging empathy. Many power struggles in human societies center around determining whose voices get heard. To be heard is to be understood and, to some extent, to be sympathized with.

To be a great artist is to have the ability to compress your lifebox down to an appetizing and digestible snack that people readily wolf down. And then your information blooms inside them.

Recall my discussion in section *4.5: The Lifebox* of the "twinking" process, by which a devoted reader can set up a kind of mental model of an author. Books are a form of time travel—the author's mind goes forward in time, the reader's mind goes backward.

*"Language is a virus,"* William Burroughs used to say. I had a chance to meet him at the Naropa Institute in Boulder, Colorado, in 1982, and I asked him about the notion that a properly written book might act as a disease that

infects other people with the author's personality and turns them into the author. "That's why they call us the immortals," he replied.[108]

How is it that language is so effective at conveying our mental states? The close match between language patterns and thought patterns is no accident. Indeed, most linguists feel that our brains and our languages have evolved in tandem so that, on the one hand, language is tailored to express the structures and behaviors of the brain, and, on the other hand, human brains are adapted to generating and processing our kinds of speech and writing. It seems possible that, even if you were raised in isolation, you'd think in patterns resembling sentences with nouns and verbs, adjectives and adverbs. But, lacking social input, your thoughts probably wouldn't be interesting.[109]

Incorporeal though language is, it's like a symbiotic organism that's co-evolved with humanity. Like a race of CA gliders passed on from brain to brain.

When I'm in a foreign country, making conversation in my hosts' language, I often think of a game of Lotto that my children had. The game consisted of a hundred pairs of glossy square cards, each card blank on one side, and with a color photo of some object on the other side (as in figure 110). Clumsily talking a foreign language is like having a pocketful of the Lotto squares and handing them to someone one by one. "Tomorrow rain look museum eat cafeteria. Tomorrow sun swim eat you bring fire I bring sausage."

**Figure 110: This Is a Pear**

Some of the first words a child learns are names for simple body sensations. Cold, wet, hungry, tired. Names for things outside the body are needed as well. Mommy, hand, water, bed, sun. Simple verbs join the vocabulary soon after. See, stand, walk, cry. And then, more or less spontaneously, the child begins making sentences. The brain's built-in language generator is kicking into gear.

It's worth noting that, even without being used for communication, the human language generator carries out class four computations. That is, if I had been raised in isolation to be an inarticulate naked ape, my patterns of vocalization would nevertheless be varied and unpredictable.

This not-so-obvious fact was unearthed by the logician Emil Post. Post was able to show that even in the very simplest kinds of language-generating systems, it's computationally unfeasible to determine if a given string of symbols is something that the system might eventually "say."

Post framed his analysis in terms of what he called tag systems. A tag system consists of a fixed set of language tokens, a few initial strings of tokens, and some rules for converting existing strings into new strings. Just for fun, let's think in terms of scat singing. Say that your language tokens consist of three sounds: Be, Bop, and Lu. And you can string these together to make utterances like BeBeBopLu, BopBopBop, and so on.

To make a Post style tag system, we define a notion of a "tagged" string by some rules like these:

- *Start.* BeBopLu and LuBe are tagged strings.
- *Simplify.* If any tagged string has any occurrence of the same syllable twice in a row, you can remove the pair. That is, you can remove BeBe, LuLu, or BopBop.
- *Concatenate.* You can stick together any two tagged strings to get a new, longer tagged string.

As an example of these rules in action, consider the following derivation sequence:

*Concatenate the start strings to get BeBopLuLuBe.*
*Simplify to get BeBopBe.*
*Concatenate two earlier strings to get BeBopBeBeBopLu.*
*Simplify to get BeBopBopLu.*
*Simplify to get BeLu.*
*Concatenate two earlier strings to get BeLuBeBopLu.*
*Concatenate two earlier strings to get BeLuBeBopLuBeBopBe.*
*Et cetera . . .*

Can one ever derive the string LuBeBop?[110]

Simplifying makes strings shorter, and concatenating makes strings longer. This means that the derivation of a string might alternate between runs of adding tokens and removing tokens, only arriving at the target string after a large number of steps.

For those familiar with the process of mathematical proof, this may sound familiar. In mathematics, one very often has to go all around Robin Hood's barn to end up with a proof of some very concise fact. For instance, it would take a very fat book of mathematics to fully describe Andrew Wiles's twentieth-century proof of the simple conjecture that Pierre de Fermat wrote in the margin of a book in the seventeenth century, known as Fermat's Last Theorem.

In the 1930s, Alan Turing established that in mathematics we have no universally applicable algorithm for making a straight up-or-down decision as to whether a given sentence will eventually be proved. Looked at in a certain way, mathematics is a type of tag system, and, following on Turing's proof, Emil Post showed that for many very simple tag systems, there can be no algorithm for deciding if a given arbitrary string will be tagged by the system. He termed this the "unsolvability of the tag problem."

This means that even the simplest tag systems may lack "grammar checkers" that can be applied to decide quickly if a string is produced or "tagged." In general, the only way to decide if a string is tagged is to examine increasingly long chains of rule-based derivations to see if one of them leads to the string in question. If the answer is to be "no," then the search for a derivation may never terminate.

The reason I bring up Post's work is that, as well as being like mathematical proof, tag systems are like systems for generating linguistic utterances. The unsolvability of the tag problem tells us that the process of language generation is an inherently unpredictable class four computation. Even if you knew the detailed workings of a person's language generator, there would be no quick way to decide if a given string is or is not something that the person might ever say.

A related issue regarding formal languages is that given a program written in a high-level computer language like C++ or Java, there's no simple way to decide whether the program has bugs in it. Ultimately, the only sure-fire approach is to run the program, test it for a while, and see what happens.

And even if the program runs for quite some time without crashing, it may yet crash later on.

But all this is dry theory. Language takes on its real significance when it's shared among the members of a society. A communicating hive is greater than the sum of its parts.

This is especially clear with ant colonies. So far as I know, no experimenter has ever taught an individual ant anything, not even a solution to the simplest Y-maze. So how does an ant colony think? By communication. As the ants react to one another's signals, group behaviors emerge.

A particularly interesting feature of ant communication is that, as well as sending pheromones out into the air, ants lay down trails of scent. The trail markings persist for several minutes, influencing other ants over a period of time. One might say that ants invented writing!

As an author, I'm particularly interested in the way a writer has an ongoing conversation with the manuscript. Writing out ideas makes them clearer; as I revise my manuscript I'm revising my brain patterns. This is one reason that keeping (and revising) a written journal has a certain therapeutic value. By revising what I *say* I think, I revise what I *do* think.

Certainly a conversation with another person is more unpredictable, but, for good or ill, conversations with others have a tendency to drift away from the particular points that one happens to be currently obsessed with. When I'm writing instead of conversing, I don't have to fight against being steered into dead ends. I can push in a given direction for as long as I like.

But a writer wants to be read. You can't get too introspective and convoluted. You need to periodically step back and try to simulate the reactions of different kinds of people who might peruse your work. Learning to balance singleness of purpose with broad appeal is part of the craft.

Language is wonderfully slippery and multivalued. Most words and phrases suggest several different meanings. Half-seen allusions cluster around the primary meaning like a halo around a streetlight, like the fuzzed overtones to an electric guitar chord, like the aromas above a plate of hot food. Part of being a colorful speaker or writer is having the gift of choosing words whose subsidiary meanings complement, contrast with, or comment upon the primary meaning.

Language has a branching quality, with each word suggesting a number of others. Indeed, you can think of words as the nodes in a network. Imagine a drawing with a node for each word and with a link between any two words that you associate with each other, as indicated in figure 111.

The result is a network in which we have nodes with differing number of links: a few nodes with very many links, a small number of nodes with many links, a lot of nodes with a medium number of links, and very many nodes with only a few links.

Suppose we call the number of links per word the word's *linkiness*. Is there a typical linkiness value for a randomly chosen word? Yes, we could compute an average linkiness over all the words, but I'm going to argue that there's a sense in which this average isn't a really good representation of the linkiness quality of words.

**Figure 111: Word Associations**

In many kinds of phenomena, like height or intelligence, we expect the measured values to lie on a bell curve, with a probability hump at some most likely value. The value beneath the hump of a bell curve is sometimes called the *scale* of the distribution.

But are other kinds of phenomena that don't bunch themselves around a central value in bell curve distribution. Cities' population sizes, individuals' wealth, popularities of books, and the linkiness of words all have distributions quite different from the bell curve. These, and many other naturally occurring phenomena, tend to fit along a distribution that's called *scale-free*. As illustrated in figure 112, a scale-free distribution arises when we have objects with a property that ranges over the full gamut of possible values, with no one likeliest value such as we find at the hump of a bell curve.

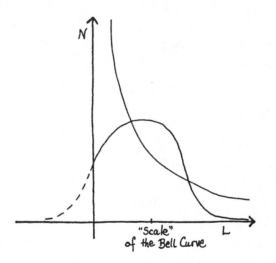

**Figure 112: A Bell Curve and a Scale-Free Distribution**

*Suppose that we are measuring some quality of objects, and suppose that we count how many objects N can be found at each quality level L. In effect we're making what statisticians call a histogram, a graph that represents the probability of finding each possible level of L. Also suppose that there are no objects with negative L. We show a bell curve distribution centered around some expected value, with the part of the bell curve over the negative L-axis chopped off. The other curve is a scale-free distribution, which has the general form 1/L$^D$ for some power D. These scale-free curves are also called inverse power laws.*

As well as lacking a typical central value, a scale-free distribution has a more gradual rate of decline in the probabilities of values further out along the $L$-axis. In a bell curve, the drop-off is exponential, meaning that as you move away from the bell curve's center, the probabilities drop off exceedingly fast. Scale-free distributions have what statisticians call fat tails, meaning that extreme kinds of events can in fact occasionally happen.

A distribution is said to be scale-free if it obeys a histogram-style inverse power law, that is, there is some constant number $c$ and some power $D$ such that the following equation holds, at least approximately, through most of the range of $L$ levels that we consider.[111]

$$N = c/L^D$$

Okay, so now I want to discuss the likelihood that the associational links between words make up a scale-free network.

To test this notion, the computer hacker extraordinaire John Walker recently helped me run a little computer experiment to quantify the word-linkiness distribution. Rather than wrestling with the vague notion of which words suggest which other words, we took an electronic dictionary file and decreed that any two words are linked if either of the words appears in the dictionary definition of the other word. The dictionary has some 130,600 words. Then if a word has $L$ links, $L$ will be some number between one and 130,600, and we can think of $L$ as characterizing the "linkiness level" of the word.

A word like *of* will have a high linkiness, something well in excess of three thousand, as it appears in so many definitions. On the other hand, if, say, your dictionary's full definition of *prolix* happens to be just "verbose," and if "prolix" appears in no other word's definition, then "prolix" would have a linkiness of one.

So Walker computed the linkiness level $L$ of every word in the dictionary, and for each level he counted how many words $N$ of that kind there were. $N$ can in principle range between the smallest and largest possible number of words, that is between zero and 130,600. And we found that for most words $N$ is indeed equal to a constant divided by $L$ raised to some power $D$. The law we came up with has this form.[112]

$$N = 1,000,000/L^{2.4}$$

Figure 113 shows how our data points fit our specifically tweaked inverse power law.

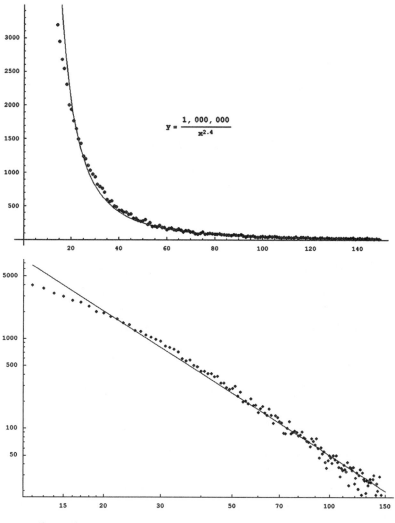

**Figure 113: Inverse Power Law Distribution for Word Linkiness**

*Two graphs of the same data. Walker scanned a GNU edition of Webster's 1913* Revised Unabridged Dictionary, *found at www.ibiblio.org. We defined two words to be linked if either appears in the definition of the other. Walker created a histogram table of data pairs* (L, N) *recording the number of words N having a given number of links L, with L from 1 to 149—he didn't work out to larger link numbers as here the data gets spotty. The horizontal axis represents the number of links L that a given word has. The vertical axis represents the number of words N corresponding to the linkiness level L. The left ends of the graphs correspond to the many words that have very low linkiness, and the tails at the right ends of the graphs correspond to the words with increasingly high linkiness. The second plot is in the "log log" format, in which the horizontal and vertical axes are scaled as the logarithms of the quantities being graphed. This widely used trick has the effect of making power laws look like straight lines.*

Why does the linkiness of words obey an inverse power law distribution? One suggestion is that the more highly linked a word is, the likelier it is to appear in new words' definitions, and that this "rich-get-richer" principle will in fact lead to the kind of distribution we observe.

I take this suggestion from the physicist Albert-László Barabási.[113] Barabási observed that Internet linkiness has a scale-free distribution. Specifically, in his data analysis, he defined a Web site's linkiness level $L$ to be the number of other sites that link to the given website. And he found that the number of sites $N$ having a given linkiness level $L$ can be matched to an inverse power law, that is, $N$ is proportional to one over $L$ raised to an exponent close to 2.1. Barabási theorizes that a rich-get-richer principle explains the distribution, and to test his hypothesis he ran a simulation of a rich-get-richer network that grows as follows:

- Keep adding new nodes.
- Each new node is linked to one of the existing nodes, which we call the target node. The target node is picked by a weighted randomizer that skews the choice so that the more links a node already has, the likelier it is to be picked as a target.

*Does* the rich-get-richer mechanism account for the linkiness distribution of words and the linkiness distribution of Web pages? Not as it stands; Barabási's simulation gives inverse power laws with exponent 3, while it is exponents of, respectively, 2.4 and 2.1 that we'd like to see for the word and Web page data. But there is some chance that by refining and complicating the simulation, a rich-get-richer explanation can be made to work.

In other contexts the rich-get-richer explanation is known as the *principle of least effort*. Relative to word linkiness, the idea is that, in creating a new word, it's easiest to relate it to words that already have a lot of other words related to them. "What shall we talk about?" "Let's talk about sex."

Some of the earliest examples of society's inverse power law distributions were found in the 1940s by George Kingsley Zipf, author of a famous book called *Human Behavior and the Principle of Least Effort*. Writing about this volume, Benoit Mandelbrot says, "I know of very few books . . . in which so many flashes of genius, projected in so many directions, are lost in so thick a gangue of wild notions and extravagance."[114]

Zipf's best-known observation is called Zipf's Law. This is the statistical fact that the frequency with which a given word is used in most documents is roughly proportional to the reciprocal of the word's popularity rank. Thus, the second most popular word is used half as much as the most popular word, the tenth most popular word is used a tenth as much as the most popular word, and so on.

More precisely, suppose we take some text and count the occurrences of each word in the text. By dividing a word's number of occurrences by the total number of words in the text, we can get a frequency for each word. Thus "the" might have a frequency of 0.1, meaning that every tenth word is "the," and a rare word like "prolix" might have a frequency like 0.00003, meaning that it occurs, on the average, three times in every hundred thousand words of text.

Now rank the words from the most popular to the least popular, for each word recording its popularity rank $R$ and the frequency level of the word, which we'll call $L$. Zipf's Law has the following form, where $a$ is a constant on the order of 0.1, and the exponent $d$ is on the order of 1.

$$L = a/R^d$$

That is, Zipf's Law is an inverse power law with the approximate form $L = 0.1/R$. I call this a rank-style power law.

As a test, John Walker created a Zipf's Law graph of the word frequencies in the final draft of this very book, *The Lifebox, the Seashell, and the Soul*.[115]

My book's word frequency distribution (figure 114) is more like $L = 0.06/R^{0.8}$, which isn't all that close a match to Zipf's Law, $L = 0.1/R$. Does that mean I should rewrite my book? No, it means, rather, that the exact values of the constants found in word frequency distributions vary from text to text. In particular, the fact that my Zipf's Law exponent is 0.8 rather than 1.0 means that my low-ranking words have slightly higher frequencies than might usually be expected. And this would indicate, I think, that I'm using a fairly large vocabulary. Perhaps with a little work one could tease out some kind of class two, class three, or class four categorization of texts based on the exponents they yield for Zipf's Law.

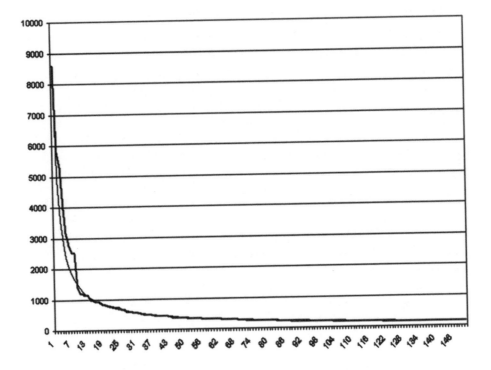

**Figure 114: Zipf's Law for *The Lifebox, The Seashell, and the Soul***

*The horizontal axis shows the popularity rank R of each word. Thus, word #1 is "the," with 8,599 occurrences, and word #146 is "also," with 134 occurrences. The vertical access plots the number of occurrences K of a given word. The best fit for the observed graph seems to be K = 8600 / R^{0.8}. If we convert this to a formula for the distribution of the word probabilities L, we get L = 0.06/R^{0.8}.*

## 5.3: *Commercial and Gnarly Aesthetics*

We communicate by conversing and writing notes, but there are higher-level communications as well. I'm thinking of cultural artifacts: paintings, novels, architecture, sculpture, movies, music, Web sites, computer games, virtual realities, scientific papers, textbooks, inventions, recipes, designs, advertisements, TV shows—really any kind of object or information structure that bears the stamp of human creativity.

People create for all kinds of reasons—or for no specific reason at all. Human creative expression can arise as spontaneously as the blooming of a flower. But at some point, many creative people begin wishing they could reach a wider audience and get more money for their work. It sometimes seems as if, among themselves, writers and artists talk about money more than they talk about aesthetics. But, for serenity's sake, it's useful to develop a sense of acceptance and realism regarding the level of success that one actually has.

I'm going to examine the issue of society's rewards for creativity from three angles. First, I'll discuss the empirical fact that society's rewards for creativity are distributed according to an inverse power law distribution. Second, I'll describe some CAs that produce inverse power law effects. And third, I'll discuss the possibility that there might be some absolute artistic standards relating to gnarly class four computations, tying these ideas to the writing of novels.

So now to my first point: the inverse power law distribution of rewards. For purposes of discussion, let's suppose that four of the canonical Beat writers suddenly come back to life and each of them writes a new book. And let's also suppose that the book advances offered for these four new works are as follows:

| Author | Book advance |
|---|---|
| Jack Kerouac | $1,000,000 |
| Allen Ginsberg | $100,000 |
| William Burroughs | $10,000 |
| Gregory Corso | $1,000 |

Now keep in mind that any given page by Corso has a chance of being very nearly as good as a page of Kerouac's. So how is it conceivable that Gregory's rewards could be a thousand times less than Jack's? If you polled a sampling of readers as to how much they enjoy various authors, Burroughs's reader-satisfaction index might well be only a point or two below Ginsberg's. So why is it possible that Bill's rewards would be ten times less than Alan's?

In a similar vein, how is that a talented software engineer may earn a $100,000 a year, whereas the company's chief executive officer earns $100 million? Does the CEO really contribute a thousand times as much as the programmer?

The same kinds of skewed distributions can be found in the opening weekend grosses of movies, in the prices paid for artists' works, in the number of hits that Web pages get, and in the audience shares for TV shows. Why do the top ranks do so well and the bottom ranks so poorly?

You might imagine that if you perform 90 percent as well as someone else, you'd get 90 percent as much money. But that's not how it works. The galling fact is that society distributes most of its rewards according to inverse power law distributions.

Rather than looking at histogram-style power laws, let's begin with rank-style power laws. Rank is a natural concept because in many social arenas we can find a way of ranking the competitors according to how strongly society appreciates them. And we usually find that the numerical measure of success will obey a rank-style inverse power law in which reward is equal to some constant $c$ divided by the rank raised to some power $D$, a law resembling the Zipf Law that we just discussed in section 5.3.[14]

$$\text{Reward} = c/\text{Rank}^D$$

To understand this way of parceling out rewards, think in terms of optimization. Suppose that society wants to encourage very many books that are precisely of the kinds that it likes the most, and to discourage those works that vary from the current ideal. In this case it makes a kind of sense to massively reward the best-selling authors, while portioning out much smaller amounts to the scribes not in the mainstream. "Those screwballs will write anyway; why waste money on them!"

The four resurrected Beats won't be the only writers in the marketplace, and they'll have widely spaced popularity ranks. We might make sense of their advances by supposing that book advances obey a law in which the advance is one million divided by the author's popularity rank, as indicated in table 14.[117]

| Author | Book advance | Popularity rank |
|---|---|---|
| Jack Kerouac | $1,000,000 | 1 |
| Allen Ginsberg | $100,000 | 10 |
| William Burroughs | $10,000 | 100 |
| Gregory Corso | $1,000 | 1,000 |

**Table 14: Book Advance = 1,000,000/Popularity Rank**

Disgruntled writers sometimes fantasize about a utopian marketplace in which the naturally arising inverse power law distribution would be forcibly replaced by a linear distribution, that is, a payment schedule that lies along a smoothly sloping line instead of along a violently swooping curve. Figure 115 shows some variations on a linear distribution, based on the assumption that the gross amount that society is going to hand out to authors is fixed.

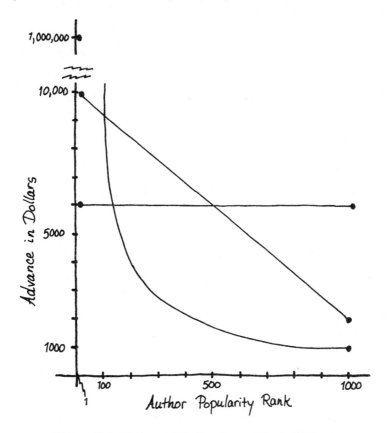

**Figure 115: Different Distributions of Book Advances**

*The curve shows the inverse power law Advance = $1,000,000/Rank. The double light-ning bolt indicates where I had to leave out six or seven miles of paper so as to fit in the point marking where the most popular writer gets $1 million. Despite this big spike, the total area under the curve between one and one thousand is only about $6 million, which represents the total in book advances that society hands out to the top thousand writers. The two straight lines show a couple of options for how a central committee might allocate $6 million to a thousand writers in a "more equitable" fashion. The hor-izontal line depicts the possibility of giving each writer a flat $6,000, regardless of pop-ularity. And the sloping line shows the option where the most popular writer gets $10,000 and the thousandth most popular writer gets $2,000.*

A first problem with a linear distribution of rewards is that the reward curve becomes uniformly flat and low. If the rewards for best sellers aren't much bigger than those for flops, then maybe creators aren't going to try so hard to achieve greater popularity. A low-paid writer might argue that popularity isn't everything, and that society would do better to level things out. But shaving off the peak doesn't really produce dramatic enough gains at the bottom to compensate for the loss of incentive. The only real gain in leveling things out might be that the less successful writers become less consumed by envy and have more peace of mind. But it may well be that artists are more creative when they're bitter and unhappy!

A second problem with the linear distribution is that it's arbitrary. The existing inverse power law distributions evolve on their own from the parallel computations of a society of competing publishers and authors. In order to have a linear distribution, some governing group would have to price-fix the distribution. But centralized economic plans are often skewed toward special considerations that may be inimical to the behaviors society is trying to reward. I'm thinking of cronyism and graft, of incompetence and prejudice. Another flaw in centralized economic plans is that, in their desire to please their constituents, the planners may make irrational decisions. A legislature might, for instance, stipulate that the thousand most popular writers will be paid on a linear scale ranging from $200,000 for #1 down to $100,000 for #1,000—and leave the problem of finding the necessary $150 million for a future generation to solve, perhaps by eliminating book advances entirely. Legislatures do things like that all the time.

A third problem with a linear distribution is that it's not extendable. At some point a downward slanting line crosses the horizontal axis, so that as more authors appear, the central committee needs to keep readjusting the pay scale. An inverse power law curve has the virtue of asymptotically hugging the horizontal axis. And the net expenditure will stay under control as long as we have a rank-style inverse power law with the exponent greater than one.[118]

Inverse power laws are self-organizing and self-maintaining. For reasons that aren't entirely understood, they emerge spontaneously in a wide range of parallel computations.

Here's a nice example of an emergent social power law that seems to have a nice computational model. Consider the population of cities. Statistical studies show that, to a very close approximation, if $N$ is the number of cities of given population size level $L$, we have a histogram-style power law with exponent 2, that is, $N = c/L^2$, or the number of cities of a given size is proportional to the reciprocal of the size squared. Why? This distribution is an emergent property of a certain kind of interacting system.

To model how this distribution might emerge, consider a simple toy model of population change that I'll call the Zeldovich CA. We'll use a two-dimensional CA in which each cell holds a population count. We do two steps in the update.

- *Diffusion.* First average each cell's population with the populations in its neighboring cells. This models the notion that people spontaneously move around.
- *Boom or bust.* Then flip a coin for each cell. If the coin is heads, double the cell's population value; if the coin is tails, set the cell's population value to zero. This models the notion that at any time, a given area can prosper or collapse.

Figure 116 shows a three-dimensional view of a Zeldovich CA simulation.[119]

So in the case of city populations, we can find a computational model that seems to account for the empirically observed power law.

As I've been discussing, society shows a huge range of responses to cultural artifacts. At this point I'd like to discuss some computational models of the varying levels of success that that some cultural artifacts achieve.

When someone creates an artifact and makes it available, the effects cascade out, and, let us say, a year later you might conduct a poll to estimate what percentage of the population got the word—using this percentage number to quantify the success. The sizes of the cascades range the full gamut from tiny to enormous. By dint of having been hit by so many cultural artifacts over the years, a society seems to be in a peculiar state in which an input can have an effect of virtually any size at all.

In symbols, if we let $L$ be a given size level of news recognition and let $N$ be the number of stories at level $L$, we expect there to be some constants $c$ and $D$ and a histogram-style inverse power law of the form $N = c/L^D$.

Note again that an inverse power law model of social impact is very different from, say, a model in which we think of raindrops falling into a pond.

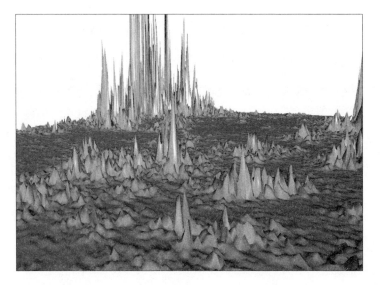

**Figure 116: The Zeldovich CA Model of the Formation of Cities**

*I think of this as a cyberspace view of a place called Zeldovichgrad. It turns out to be important when updating a cell to first average the cells with the neighbors and second to flip the coin to decide whether to double the cell's value or wipe it out. Otherwise the rule doesn't do the right thing. Another consideration is that we must enforce some limited maximum value for the cells; otherwise some numbers may run off toward infinity and crash the program. Since we're simulating a scale-free distribution, the values occasionally will get as big as we allow them to.*

In the raindrop model, the sizes of raindrops have a bell curve distribution centering around a certain average size. The effects of the raindrops in the pond are circles of ripples that cluster around a mean amplitude. You never see an enormous raindrop that all but empties the pond with a tidal wave. But in society, there is no typical size of an event's influence, and some events sweep everything in their paths. Think of fads, crazes, manias.

Three human factors relate to the spread of a social artifact:

- *Receptivity.* A person may or may not be receptive to being exposed to a new artifact. If you're all whipped up over a terrorism alert, you may fail to notice a news story about the economy. If you're into some new music you just got, you may not care about any other music for a while.

- *Excitation.* A receptive person exposed to an artifact may or may not become excited. What makes people excited is, of course, a difficult question.
- *Recommendation.* If a person is excited enough about an artifact, the person tells others about it. The recommendations hop about society. In CA models this corresponds to stimulating your neighbors.

In section *4.3: Thoughts as Gliders and Scrolls,* I discussed a Brian's Brain CA that serves as a model for neural firings. Could the Brain CA also serve as a model for the spread of ideas in society? In Brain, we have states called ready (receptive), firing (excited), and resting (nonreceptive), and the rule is that if a ready cell has precisely two firing neighbors (recommendations), then this cell, too, fires.

Perhaps our scrolling Zhabotinsky CAs are also relevant here, rules like the Hodgepodge CA or the Meinhardt CA. An activator-inhibitor rule is a bit like the spread of news. New stories activate people's excitement; boredom and fatigue inhibit them.

But something that I'm not sure we see in Brian's Brain or the Zhabotinsky scrolls are inverse power laws of the kind that empirically seem to describe the spread of news. But as it happens, there are two particular CAs that are *known* to obey power laws that serve as models for the spread of news. One is called the forest fire model, the other the sandpile model.

The first CA was created by geographer Bruce Malamud and his colleagues to model the spread of forest fires.[120] A starting point for Malamud's work was the observed fact that, if $L$ measures the number of acres taken in by a given fire, and $N$ measures the frequency of such fires, then we find that fires obey histogram-style inverse power laws of the general form $N = c/L^{1.3}$, although the precise exponent varies according to the geographical region being studied.

In his model, Malamud took a two-dimensional CA in which each cell is in one of three states. In viewing this as a model of a forest fire, we can think of these three states as representing *live* trees, *burning* trees, or *dead* trees. The update rules are as follows:

- *Lightning.* A live cell spontaneously changes to burning with a certain very small probability.
- *Spread of fire.* A live cell also changes to a burning cell if at least one of its neighbors is burning.
- *Burning out.* A burning cell changes to dead.
- *New growth.* A dead cell spontaneously changes to a live cell with a small probability.

If the probabilities are properly tuned, the rule quickly settles down to a so-called critical state in which the sizes of cascades obey a histogram-style inverse power law. The size of a cascade here is the total number of cells that pass through the burning state before that particular avalanche settles down.

In the critical state, Malamud CAs produce patterns very much like our old friends the Zhabotinsky scrolls (figure 117). Now let's look at another CA model of how news about something spreads in society. The late physicist Per Bak had a knack for coming up with extremely simple models providing deep insights into complicated natural phenomena. One of his best-known models is a CA known as the *sandpile rule.* The sandpile CA provides a nice example of a parallel system in which small effects can have exceedingly large consequences.

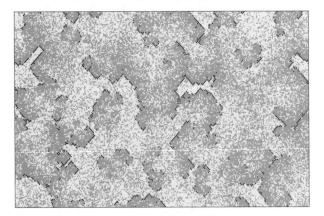

**Figure 117: The Forest Fire CA**

*This picture shows a version of Malamud's forest fire CA. The dotted black lines are moving fronts of burning cells, the gray cells are the live cells ready for excitation, and the white cells are the dead cells. The CA behavior quickly settles in on the behavior depicted, with the fire lines continually moving about in approximate Zhabotinsky scrolls, with the burnt cells being randomly reset to live cells and with random lightning strikes setting off fresh fronts of burning cells.*

The inspiration for the sandpile model is to imagine dropping grains of sand onto a tabletop from a point above the table's center. For a while the sand will simply accumulate, but eventually the table will be covered with so much sand that when you add another grain, a greater or smaller avalanche will ensue, with sand sliding across and perhaps off the edge of the table. At some point the pile becomes tuned to critical state in which there's no predicting how big the next avalanche will be.

Bak and his colleagues greatly simplified the intuitive notion of a sandpile in order to get to their CA rule. To begin with, divide the tabletop into squares to make a grid. And rather than letting the sand heap up ever so high, they think of each cell as holding a tiny tower of at most three grains of sand. When a cell becomes overloaded by having four or more grains of sand, it gives up four grains, moving one grain to each of the cell's immediate neighbors, that is, one grain apiece to the east, north, west, and south.[121]

The resulting behavior is going to be less like a pyramid of sand with avalanches sliding down it, and more like an irregular washboard with moving wave fronts, or, more to the point, like a CA with moving gliders, as shown in figure 118.

This is unrealistic physics, yes, but it makes for a simple computation—and the point here is not to simulate real sandpiles, but rather to produce a suggestive model of a situation in which small influences can have arbitrarily large effects.

Once enough sand has been dropped, the sandpile enters a critical state in which dropping an additional grain of sand produces results that obey an inverse power law distribution. In order to measure the size of an avalanche, we can adjust the simulation so that after you add a grain of sand, no additional sand is added until all the resulting activity dies down. And then you can measure the size of the avalanche by counting the number of distinct cell sites whose values were changed before the system settled back down. In Bak's particular simulation, he and his collaborators found a histogram-style inverse power law relating the number of avalanches $N$ to the size level $L$.

$$N = c/L^{1.1}$$

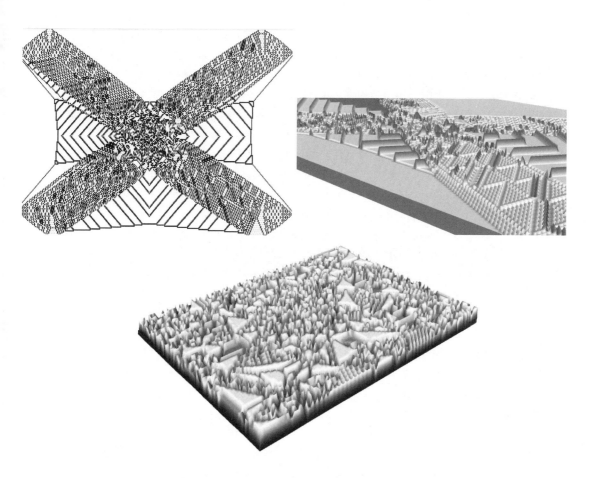

**Figure 118: Sandpile CA**

*The first and second pictures show views of the same simulation: a two-dimensional view in which the cell values are represented by shades of gray, and a three-dimensional view in which the cell values are represented as heights. The vantage point in the second view is from a point above the right side of the lower edge of the first view. In the first two pictures, the sandpile is being seeded by dropping sand grains onto a particular cell near the middle of the rectangle. About ten thousand grains have been dropped in these pictures. The dark cells and tall peaks make up moving avalanches or gliders of sand. When an avalanche of sand hits the edge, it often sends echo gliders back toward the center, which are accumulating to make an "X and spiderweb" pattern. The third picture shows a smaller sandpile world in which sand has been dropped at random positions for quite a while, and in which the system has been allowed to settle down. No cell has a value higher than three, and the cells along the edges have value zero. Nothing is presently moving in the third sandpile world. It has organized itself into a critical state. If you increase a randomly chosen cell's value to four, the resulting avalanche may propagate only for a few cells, or all the way across the little universe.*

A significant thing about the sandpile simulation is that essentially any random sequence of sand grains leads the model to the critical state. And from then on, each time the sandpile settles back down from the most recent avalanche, it's still in the critical state. For this reason, Bak and his colleagues spoke of the sandpile model as being in a *self-organized critical state*.

I compare the definitions of the Brain, forest fire, and sandpile CA rules in table 15.

| Brian's Brain | Forest fire | Sandpile | Spread of news | Neuron activity |
|---|---|---|---|---|
| Resting | Dead | Below threshold | Nonreceptive | Resting |
| Ready | Live | Near threshold | Receptive | Ready |
| Firing | Burning | Beyond threshold | Excited | Firing |

**Table 15: CAs as Models of Excitation**

*We might use the Brain, forest fire, and sandpile rules to model the spread of awareness about new cultural artifacts or to model the activity in a brain's neurons. In all cases, some type of activity is both exciting further activity and using up a resource that promotes the activity. (The "threshold" in the sandpile model is four. That is, a cell with less than four sand grains is stable and receptive, and as soon as the cell values goes to four or higher, the cell "fires" and transfers one of its grains to each of four neighbors.)*

Our purpose in bringing in the forest fire and sandpile rules was to try to model the spread of news about cultural artifacts in a society—to keep the language simple, let's just suppose that we're talking about the effects of books. Here are some of the salient features of what these models suggest about how a book's fame spreads.

- The individual cells represent members of society, that is, people.
- The external stimulations applied to the cells represent the arrival of new books. That is, the books are modeled by the strokes of lightning hitting the forest fire CA and by the grains of sand dropping onto the sandpile CA.
- Presented with a book, a person may or may not become excited about it, depending on whether the person is in a receptive state.

- If people are excited about a book, they communicate the excitement to their nearest neighbors.
- Immediately after being excited about a book, people enter a state in which they are less receptive to a new book. In the case of the forest fire model, individuals remain unreceptive until some probabilistic transition takes place. In the case of the sandpile model, it may be that a person needs to be stimulated by several books in a row before becoming excited enough to spread the news about a book.
- After being repeatedly seeded over a period of time, the models enter a critical state in which the effects of additional seeds obey a power law.

The last point is perhaps the most significant one. These models generate inverse power law distributions because they've undergone a long-term process that brings them into a critical state. It's certainly reasonable to suppose that our media-saturated society is in a critical state as well. Individual people are in a range of states. Some are just short of needing a bit more stimulation to become excited enough to tell others about something. Some are broke, or tired, or apathetic, and for the present nothing can stimulate them. Yet as the stimulation pours in, people regularly move from nonreceptive to receptive states.

Although the forest fire and sandpile models have received a lot of notice in the scientific press, they're just cellular automata—and, at least in terms of computation classes, perhaps not the most interesting possible ones.[122]

The criticism one might level at these models is that, although the city, sandpile, and forest fire CAs are known to generate inverse power law behaviors, each of them depends upon on probabilistic inputs to stay alive. The city and forest fire CAs require calls to a randomizer at each cell's update, and the sandpile, although deterministic, dies out unless it is continually restimulated by additional random input. The fact that, in isolation, the rules die out means that they are class one computations. It would be nice to have a rule that satisfies the following two conditions:

- The rule is a class four cellular automaton, requiring no external random seeding.
- Over time, the rule continues showing cascades, with the cascade sizes obeying a power law.

I still haven't found a perfect rule of this kind. One possibility might be to make a forest fire model in which the random probabilistic transitions are replaced by a slow, steady increment. Another candidate is the "boiling cubic wave" rule that I already mentioned in section *4.3: Thoughts as Gliders and Scrolls*. This rule will run on as shown in figure 119 indefinitely, (Full disclosure: I'm not actually sure the boiling wave rule *has* power law behavior, but these recent images are so beautifully gnarly, I just had to stick them in.)

I started out this section by trying to gain some insight into why society rewards different people in such different ways. Then I got into inverse power laws and into CA simulations that generate power laws. But what's the moral?

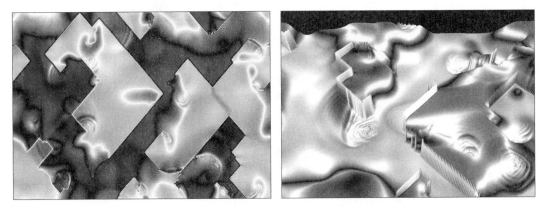

**Figure 119: Self-Generating Cascades in a Nonlinear Wave CA**

*Here we see a two-dimensional and three-dimensional view of the same continuous-valued CA rule, called Boiling Cubic Wave. Each cell holds two variables. The first variable, displayed in the pictures, might be called intensity. The intensity obeys a rule that simulates a nonlinear cubic wave equation. The second variable is the nonlinearity of the wave equation at that given cell location. With each update, each cell's nonlinearity increases a bit, but when it gets so high that the wave equation becomes unstable, it's then reset to a minimum value. There are two types of moving patterns in this rule: the smooth ripples of wave motion and the right-angled shock fronts of high nonlinearity.*

As an author, the lesson I draw from inverse power laws is that it's okay if my best efforts fail to knock the ball out of the park. There's simply no predicting what's going to catch on, or how big it's going to be. Trying harder isn't going to change anything. Relax, do your work, and don't expect too much.

Along these lines, the science-fiction writer Marc Laidlaw and I once dreamed of starting a literary movement to be called Freestyle. Our proposed motto: *Write like yourself, only more so.*

Another aspect of being subject to socially determined power laws is that maintaining even a modest level of success is just as hard as staying on the top. Criticality means that things are boiling at every level. There's no chance of making things easier for yourself by taking lower-level jobs or sending your outputs to lower-paying magazines. My rabble-rousing friend David Hungerford likes to say, "The essence of capitalism is that the less they pay you, the harder you have to work." And the less a publisher pays, the worse they treat you. So you can't take the power law as an excuse to slack off.

Let's turn to the question of aesthetics. What kinds of cultural artifacts are likely to stimulate people enough to spread the news?

We might suppose that an artifact stimulates several nodes of a person's neural network, which produces a greater or lesser cascade of activity in the brain. Note also that a person's brain has different associational networks—science, political news, entertainment, food, relationships, and so on. An artifact may set off cascades in several of these networks at once. In terms of a sandpile model of brain excitement, we might say that there are really several different colors of "sand."

Note that until a given kind of artifact appears, it may not have been obvious that brains could in fact be highly stimulated by it. "This book scratches an itch I didn't know I had."

If an artifact manages to stimulate a large number of nodes in your neural net right off the bat, that seems to give it a better chance of creating a large amount of activity. Note, however, that stimulating a lot of nodes isn't the same as stimulating a few nodes a lot. If something's boring, yelling about it doesn't make it more interesting.

I'm inclined to think that more complex, more compressed types of information have a better chance of setting off more mental fireworks. Less isn't more—it's *less*. A blank canvas isn't going to fire up many brain cells, unless it's accompanied by an insanely great artistic statement.

At the other end of the spectrum, amping up a message's complexity can go too far. There are, after all, cultural artifacts that are so recondite as to be all but incomprehensible. This said, my feeling is that the sweet spot for cultural artifacts lies just a step or two down from mind-breaking gibberish—in the gnarly zone.

Since I spend a great deal of my time writing science-fiction novels, I'd like to say a bit about how my studies of computational gnarl have affected my views on literary aesthetics.

To simplify even more than before, we can say that Wolfram distinguishes among three kinds of processes:

- *Too cold.* Processes that are utterly predictable. This may be because they die out and become constant, or because they're repetitive in some way.
- *Too hot.* Processes that are completely random-looking.
- *Gnarly.* Processes that are structured in interesting ways but nonetheless unpredictable.

Gnarliness lies between predictability and randomness. It's an interface phenomenon like organic life, poised between crystalline order and messy deliquescence. Although the gnarl is a transitional zone, it's not necessarily narrow. I'm going to find it useful to distinguish between *low gnarl* and *high gnarl*. Low gnarl is close to being periodic and predictable, whereas high gnarl is closer to being fully random.

In order to present some ideas about how gnarl applies to literature in general, and to science fiction in particular, table 16 summarizes how gnarliness makes its way into literature in four areas: subject matter, plot, scientific speculation, and social commentary. I'll say a bit about the thinking that went into each of the table's four columns.

*Subject matter and transrealism.* Regarding the kinds of characters and situations that you can write about, my sense is that we have a four-fold spectrum of possible modes: simple genre writing with stock characters, mimetic realism, the heightened kind of realism that I call transrealism, and full-on

| Complexity Level | Subject Matter | Plot | Scientific Speculation | Social Commentary |
|---|---|---|---|---|
| **Predictable (too cold)** | Derivative literature modeled only on existing books | A plot modeled to a standard formula | Received ideas of science, used with no deep understanding | Humorless, unwitting advocacy of the status quo. Sleep-walking |
| **Low gnarl** | Realism, modeled on the actual world | Roman à clef, a plot modeled directly on experience or a news story | Pedagogic science, emphasizing limits rather than possibilities | Comedy. Noticing that existing social trends lead to absurdities |
| **High gnarl** | Transrealism, in which realism is enhanced by transcendent elements | A plot obtained by starting with a real-life story and perturbing it | Thought experiments. Working out novel consequences of wild ideas | Satire: forcibly extrapolating social trends |
| **Random-seeming (too hot)** | Fabulation, fantasy, or science fiction of unreal worlds | Surrealism, possibly based on dreams or an external randomizer | Irrational and inconsistent; anything goes, logic is abandoned | Jape, parody, sophomoric humor |

**Table 16: Gnarl in Literary Aesthetics**

fabulation. Both realism and transrealism lie in the gnarly zone. Speaking specifically in terms of subject matter, I'd be inclined to say that transrealism is gnarlier, as it allows for more possibilities.

Where did I get the word "transrealism"? Early in my writing career, my ever-gnomic friend Gregory Gibson said something like, "It would be great to write science fiction and have it be about your everyday life." I took that to heart. The science fiction novels of Philip K. Dick were also an inspiration. I seem to recall once reading a remark where someone referred to Dick's novel *A Scanner Darkly* as "transcendental autobiography."

In 1983 I published an essay, "A Transrealist Manifesto," in the *Bulletin of the Science Fiction Writers of America,* number 82. Like any young artist's manifesto, mine was designed to announce that my style of doing things was the One True Way—or at least a legitimate way of creating art. In my manifesto, I explained that transrealism is *trans* plus *realism,* a synthesis between fantastic fabulation (trans) and closely observed character-driven fiction (realism), and I advocated something like the following:

- *Trans.* Use the SF and fantasy tropes to express deep psychic archetypes. Put in science-fictional events or technologies that reflect deeper aspects of people and society. Manipulate subtext.
- *Realism.* Possibly include a main character similar to yourself and, in any case, base your characters on real people you know, or on combinations of them. To this end, have your characters be realistically neurotic—after all, there really *aren't* any normal well-adjusted people. Don't glorify the main character by making him or her unrealistically powerful, wise, or balanced. And the flip side of that is to humanize the villains.

Many of my science-fiction novels have been transreal in this sense. And my nonfiction tends to have a transreal quality as well—as you will have noticed by now. My sense is that incorporating my personal experiences enhances the appeal of even a book about the philosophy of computer science.

*Plot and emergence.* In the table's second column, I present a four-fold division of plot structures. At the low end of complexity, we have standardized plots, at the high end, we have no large-scale plot at all, and in between we have the gnarly somewhat unpredictable plots. These can be found in two kinds of ways, either by mimicking reality precisely, or by fitting reality into a classic monomythic kind of plot structure.

A characteristic feature of any complex process is that you can't look at what's going on today and immediately deduce what will be happening in a few weeks. It's necessary to have the world run step-by-step through the intervening ticks of time. Gnarly computations are unpredictable; they don't allow for shortcuts. Indeed, the last chapter of a novel with a gnarly plot is, even in principle, unpredictable from the contents of the first chapter. You have to write the whole novel in order to discover what happens in the last chapter.

My experience is that, whether you write an outline or not, in practice, the only way to discover the ending of a truly living book is to set yourself in motion and think constantly about the novel for months or years, writing all the while. The characters and tropes and social situations bounce off one another like eddies in a turbulent wakes, like gliders in a cellular automaton simulation, like vines twisting around each other in a jungle. And only time will tell just how the story ends. Gnarly plotting means there are no perfectly predictive shortcuts.

*Scientific speculation and thought experiments.* Turning to the scientific ideas that go into science fiction, we see the most interestingly gnarly works as, once again, working out unpredictable consequences of simple-seeming assumptions.

The reason why fictional thought experiments are so powerful is that, in practice, it's intractably difficult to visualize the side effects of new technological developments. Only if you place the new tech into a fleshed-out fictional world and simulate the effects on reality can you get a clear image of what might happen.

This relates, once again, to the notion of unpredictability. We can't predict in advance the outcomes of complex gnarly systems, although we can simulate (with great effort) their evolution step by step.

When it comes to futurology, only the most trivial changes to reality have easily predictable consequences. If I want to imagine what our world will be like one year after the arrival of, say, soft plastic robots, the only way to get a realistic vision is to fictionally simulate society's reactions during the intervening year. Science fictional simulation is an excellent way to do futurology.

*Social commentary and satire.* One source of humor is when someone helps us notice an incongruity or inconsistency in our supposedly smooth-running society. We experience a release of tension when someone points out the glitch to us. Something was off-kilter, and now we can see what it was. The elephant in the living room has been named. The evil spirit has been incanted.

The least aware kinds of literature take society entirely at face value, numbly acquiescing in the myths and mores laid down by the powerful. These forms are dead, too cold.

At the other extreme, we have the too-hot forms of social commentary where everything under the sun becomes questionable and a subject for mockery. If everything's a joke, then nothing matters.

In the gnarly zone, we have fiction that extrapolates social conventions to the point where the inherent contradictions become overt enough to provoke the shock of recognition and the concomitant release of laughter. At the low end of this gnarly zone, we have observational commentary on the order of stand-up comedy. And at the higher end we get inspired satire.

### 5.4: Power and Money

When I'm working on my books, I often correspond with my computer programmer–tycoon friend John Walker (figure 120). While I was working on this chapter, he sent me an email containing the following remark about computation and the social sciences:

> One thing I find very fascinating about Wolfram's *A New Kind of Science* is the insight that computational equivalence provides regarding the semi-soft sciences ranging from economics to sociology. It's often remarked that these would-be sciences suffer from "physics envy," which motivates their more mathematically literate practitioners to write differential equations and build abstract models of the systems they study. Which, of course, never work. Well, Wolfram explains precisely why this is. A social system like a market is performing a computation whose complexity cannot be reduced, and which cannot be simulated or abstracted by any model which is less complex than itself. There, in a few words, thrown away almost in passing in *NKS,* is the explanation for two hundred years of consistent dismal failure of socialism and why all the theoreticians and politicians who seek "the one best way" will never, ever find it.
>
> Here's another way to put it. An economy or market (the words are interchangeable) is an inherently unpredictable computation. Which strategy is more likely to produce an outcome which is better for those who participate in it?
>
> *Distributed*: Local decision-making by individual agents at the transaction level, each attempting to optimize their own outcome based on local, detailed information known only to them.

*Centralized*: Top-level decision-making based on analysis of aggregates which average out all the low-level detail, implemented by compulsion of low-level participants.

I would observe that in around four billion years of massively parallel search, life on Earth has always ended up choosing the distributed option. My suspicion is that idealists become enamored with the centralized option only because they imagine themselves to be the ones who will make the decisions—as opposed to the Mafia types who inevitably end up calling the shots when things tilt that way.

By way of unpacking John's remark, let me remind you again of Wolfram's PCU.

- *Principle of Computational Unpredictability (PCU).* Most naturally occurring complex computations are unpredictable.

We're interested here in social, economic, and political systems—viewed as parallel computations. It seems very reasonable to assert that, even if individual people were known to obey some very simple rules, the fact that there are so many of us guarantees that society as a whole is carrying out gnarly class four computations. Nothing ever settles down to a steady state, so we're not looking at class one computations. Events never quite repeat themselves, so we're not looking at class two computations. And, given how readily information signals propagate through societies, it doesn't seem as if we're looking at class three computations either. In other words, social computations are generally class four.

There's no reason to be surprised by this. Gnarliness often accompanies parallelism. Think of flocking boids, or of CA rules like Brian's Brain or the Hodgepodge rule. In such cases, class four behavior emerges as soon as an ensemble of agents are placed in communication with one another—even if the agents' individual behaviors are simple.

Given that social computations are gnarly, Wolfram's Principle of Computational Unpredictability suggests that the behavior of these processes can't be predicted by computations that operate much faster than detailed simulations would. In other words, there are no tidy, handy-dandy rubrics for predicting or controlling emergent social processes like elections, the stock market, or consumer demand.

In a free economy, we have a huge parallel computation of different individuals and subhives trying to optimize their profit and comfort. We might model this as a parallel computation in which each agent is performing a hill-climbing algorithm, that is, each agent looks for the most profitable of the immediately available options and takes that option. What makes this kind of model somewhat unfeasible is that the "profitability landscape" is continually changing with the motions of the agents who are trying to scale the peaks upon this same landscape. Unfeasible for a PC, that is. A living society has no problem at all in carrying out a large parallel computation.

The good thing about a decentralized class four parallel computing system is that it doesn't get stuck in some bad, minimally satisfactory state. The society's members are all working their hardest to improve things—a bit like a bunch of ants tugging on a twig. Each ant is driven by its own responses to the surrounding cloud of communication pheromones. For a time, the ants may work at cross-purposes, but, given that the class four computation isn't

**Figure 120: John Walker**

*So far as I can tell, John invariably wears the same outfit, a short-sleeved white shirt and black pants. Antarctica, Egypt, inside the Sun, at the Ascot Races, fixing a car, in the Antland of Fnoor—always with the white shirt and pants. He says it simplifies his life by pruning the choice tree. I took this picture when hiking with John near a spot called Creux du Van in Switzerland.*

stuck in a loop, they'll eventually happen upon success. Like a jiggling key that turns a lock. Compare this to the centrally planned Soviet economy, which spent nearly seventy years stuck in a bad configuration, eternally repeating the same class two cycle.

Speaking of inept governments, the one consolation is that any regime eventually falls. No matter how dark a nation's political times become, a change always comes. A faction may think it rules a nation, but this is always an illusion. The eternally self-renewing class four computation of human politics is impossible to thwart indefinitely. If the rulers' only opposition had the form of periodic class two or disorganized class three computations, they might prevail indefinitely. But sooner or later humanity's class four weaving of signals wins out.

Relations between nations become particularly destructive when they enter class two loops. I'm thinking of, for instance, the endless sequence of tit-for-tat reprisals that certain pairs of countries get into. Some loops of this nature have lasted my entire adult life. In any given case, I'm confident that at some point class four intelligence will win out and the long nightmare will end. But, less optimistically, I also know that social phenomena tend to obey power laws, which means that every now and then a transient episode of class two behavior can last for a very long time indeed. It could be, for instance, that it will take another whole century until peace comes to the Middle East.

It's always discouraging to see our own leaders embroil us in a class two policy. After the terrorist attacks of 9/11, for instance, one might have hoped to see our nation do more than enter upon a class two tit-for-tat pattern of attacks followed by counterattacks. But that's not the way it worked out. Sadly enough, the fact that politics is unpredictable allows for very poor regimes as well as for very good ones. The one comfort in dark times is that nothing in human society is eternal.[123]

No discussion of social computations can be complete without a mention of the stock market. Here's a case where John Walker's observations hold with a vengeance. Any number of technical analysts use the most sophisticated mathematical pattern-recognition tools imaginable in hopes of predicting market trends. Yet, year after year, baskets of randomly picked stocks seem to do about as well as the fund managers' finest portfolios.

In *A New Kind of Science*, Wolfram presents a simple illustration of how a stock market might embody an unpredictable computation. His idea is to imagine a market in which people buy and sell one particular stock. To motivate this model, imagine that traders think along the following lines. If the market is mixed, stock prices can go up, so buying is a good idea. But if the other traders seem to be unanimously buying or selling, the market is in a herd mode, in which case it's best to sell.

- The market is represented as a one-dimensional CA, with each cell standing for a trader.
- The cells can be in one of two states: "buy" or "sell," with the respective meanings that the corresponding trader is currently buying or selling the stock.
- A cell's update rule ignores the cell's current state and looks only at the states of the cell's two nearest neighbors, these being the cell to the immediate left and the cell to the immediate right.
- If a cell's two neighbors are in different states from each other, the cell enters the buy state. This represents the trader's optimistic reaction to a mixed market.
- If a cell's two neighbors are in the same state as each other, the cell enters the sell state. This represents the trader's pessimistic reaction to a herd market.
- We track a global "stock price," which we define as the number of buying cells minus the number of selling cells.

Figure 120 shows the evolution of this CA, as seeded with a random starting mixture of buyers and sellers.

Wolfram's stock market CA is meant to be a realization of three of his guiding principles for modeling.

- The model should embody a deterministic computation.
- The definition of the model should be utterly simple.
- The model should generate complex behavior for as long as you let it run.

call intrinsic randomness. A computation as elementary as the cellular automaton Rule 30 can be as intrinsically random as a giant market-simulator running on some investment's firm in-house supercomputer. Wolfram observes that it sometimes turns out that the interestingly random part of a big model's output is in fact the result of some incredibly simple subcomputation nested within the whole.[125]

Let's return now to the topic of inverse power laws. Although social processes must remain unpredictable in their details, it seems that society's coupled computations tend to produce events whose sizes obey inverse power law distributions. This means that, inevitably, very large cataclysms will periodically occur. Society organizes itself into a critical state that the writer Mark Buchanan refers to as "upheavable."

Buchanan goes on to make some conclusions about the flow of history that dovetail nicely with the notion of the four classes of computation. In the quoted passage below, I've inserted class labels in brackets.

> History could in principle be [class one] like the growth of a tree and follow a simple progression toward a mature and stable endpoint, as both Hegel and Karl Marx thought. In this case, wars and other tumultuous social events should grow less and less frequent as humanity approaches the stable society at the End of History. Or history might be [class two] like the movement of the Moon around the Earth, and be cyclic, as the historian Arnold Toynbee once suggested. He saw the rise and fall of civilizations as a process destined to repeat itself with regularity. Some economists believe they see regular cycles in economic activity, and a few political scientists suspect that such cycles drive a correspondingly regular rhythm in the outbreak of wars. Of course, history might instead be [class three] completely random, and present no perceptible patterns whatsoever . . .
>
> But this list is incomplete. . . . The [class four] critical state bridges the conceptual gap between the regular and the random. The pattern of change to which it leads through its rise of factions and wild fluctuations is neither truly random nor easily predicted. . . . It does not seem normal and lawlike for long periods of calm to be suddenly and

sporadically shattered by cataclysm, and yet it is. This is, it seems, the ubiquitous character of the world.[126]

Let me say a bit more about the relationship between critical states and class four computations. If we accept Wolfram's PCE, then every class three or class four computation is universal. This means that, depending upon the input, such systems are capable of virtually any kind of behavior at all.

Let's quantify this last remark and see if it leads to an inverse power law. On the one hand, a given input may set a universally computing system into perpetual activity, a seething that never settles down. On the other hand, an input can cause a universally computing system to run for a greater or lesser period of time and then switch into a target state after which no further changes of interest occur. (As I mentioned in section *1.1: Universal Automatism,* and will discuss again in section *6.2: The Computational Zoo,* we think in terms of accessorizing our computing system $U$ with an auxiliary target detector Is$U$Done(Out), which decides when Out is to be regarded as a target state.)

Now suppose that we give the system a series of randomly chosen inputs, and in each case we record how long the system runs before reaching a target state, calling this the runtime for that input. In order to avoid endless waits, we'll decide upon some maximum length of time that we'll wait, and we'll simply say that these longer-running computations have a runtime equal to that maximum wait value.

Finally, suppose that we make a histogram showing the frequency $N$ of the different runtimes $L$ that are observed for randomly chosen inputs. I conjecture that a system of this kind will very commonly obey an inverse power law of the form $L = c/L^D$, where the $c$ and $D$ are constants that depend on the particular kind of universal computation that we're dealing with.

In other words, I'm suggesting that, rather than being truly fundamental, inverse power laws are a natural and expected side effect that appears in systems that are driven by universally computing class three or class four computations.

Society's unpredictability and its power laws result from the fact that society's computations are complex. And the computations are complex not because of any intricate underlying rules, but simply because society is massively parallel. When run on a parallel system, the very simplest rules can

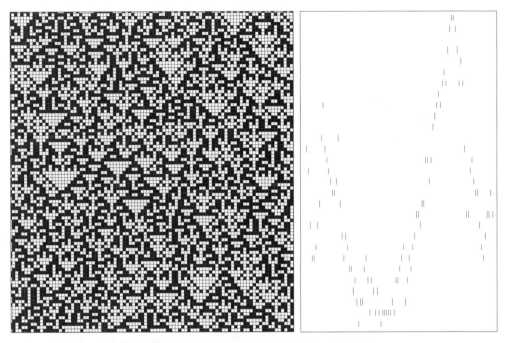

**Figure 121: Wolfram's Stock Market Model**

*The left panel shows a hundred traders interacting for a hundred updates. The traders are arranged along a line, with successive states of the line shown with time running down the page. The white cells represent traders who are buying the stock, and the black cells show traders selling the stock. The right panel tracks the price of the stock, calculated as the number of buying traders minus the number of selling traders.*

People sometimes have trouble grasping just how hard it is to come up with a model of this kind. The universal automatist is a bit like a magician compelled to show an audience the secret workings of the tricks. "Oh, is that all there is to it? Anyone could have thought of that." In point of fact, thinking up useful yet simple things is very hard.[124]

Another kind of objection to simple models comes from the tendency to think that a model with a more complicated definition will be a better fit for reality. But remember that whatever richness comes out of a model is the result of class three or class four computation—which can occur in the very simplest of systems.

As I mentioned in section *2.4: The Meaning of Gnarl,* the realistic-seeming unpredictability of some complex computational models is what we can also generate all the gnarl you'd ever want to see. And I'm speculating that the gnarl falls into inverse power law distributions precisely because class three or class four rules generate such a diverse range of outcomes. Note that I'm not saying that complex rules generate every *possible* outcome; I'm only guessing that a typical complex rule will visit a cross-section of the state space that is broad and varied enough to obey power-law statistics. It would be nice if this were true, for then we'd finally have an explanation for why we keep running into power laws.

I want to mention one last idea. From time to time a society seems to undergo a sea change, a discontinuity, a revolution—think of the Renaissance, the Reformation, the Industrial Revolution, the sixties, or the coming of the Web. In these rare cases it appears as if the underlying rules of the system have changed.

I mentioned before that in chaos theory one studies systems whose behavior explores a so-called strange attractor. This means that although the day-to-day progress of the system may be fully unpredictable, there's a limited range of possible values that the system actually hits. In the interesting cases, these possible values lie on a gnarly fractal shape in some higher-dimensional space of possibilities—this shape is the strange attractor.

During any given historical period, a society has a kind of strange attractor. A limited number of factions fight over power, a limited number of social roles are available for the citizens, a limited range of ideas are in the air. And then, suddenly, everything changes, and after the change there's a new set of options—society has moved to a new strange attractor. In terms of a terminology I introduced in section *2.4: The Meaning of Gnarl,* we might say that society has experienced a chaotic bifurcation. Although there's been no change in the underlying rule for the computation, some parameter has altered so that the range of currently possible behaviors has changed.

Society's revolutionary bifurcations are infrequently occurring zigs and zags generated by one and the same underlying and eternal class four social computation. The basic underlying computation involves such immutable facts as the human drives to eat, find shelter, and live long enough to reproduce. From such humble rudiments doth history's great tapestry emerge— endlessly various, eternally the same.

## 5.5: *The Past and Future History of Gnarl*

By way of preparing to write this section, I reread some of Marshall McLuhan's work and was reminded of how really funny and off-the-wall he could be. Presenting a traditional, logical argument wasn't McLuhan's bag. He was much more prone to dart in and zap you with a wicked turn of phrase. And he never seemed to worry about sounding silly.

In that spirit, and with much cribbing from the Master, I put together my not-quite-serious table 17, presenting the history of human innovation as a history of computation.

Although I'd always supposed McLuhan to be a cheerleader for progress, I recently learned that the opposite was the case.

> I am resolutely opposed to all innovation, all change, but I am determined to understand what's happening. Because I don't choose just to sit and let the juggernaut roll over me. Many people seem to think that if you talk about something recent, you're in favor of it. The exact opposite is true in my case. Anything I talk about is almost certainly something I'm resolutely against. And it seems to me the best way to oppose it is to understand it. And then you know where to turn off the buttons.[127]

Although I appreciate the spirit of McLuhan's remark, I don't fully agree with it. Do note that when he speaks of "turning off the buttons" he's not talking about changing *society*. That's pretty much hopeless. Society's class four changes don't have buttons that we can control. If something bothers you, the best you can hope for is to change how you react to it—and turning off your *own* buttons is one approach.

Turning off my own buttons vis-à-vis a social change involves trying to ignore it. That is, in fact, my strategy for handling the mind manipulation of TV. I watch the tube very sparingly, generally limiting myself to commercial-free channels, and above all avoiding the so-called news.

But instead of turning off, I can open my heart and accept change. For many years, I kept blogging and digital cameras at arm's length, but finally I let them into my life and I'm glad. In the past I looked down at digital photographers, at their tendency to be staring at their device's tiny screen

| Innovation | Viewed as a computation |
|---|---|
| Speech | Moving from gestures to speech gives people a higher bandwidth channel for communicating their thoughts. Society becomes able to perform more complicated computations. |
| Hunting and fishing | Knowing where to look for game means mentally simulating animal behavior, that is, it means emulating a computation. Using bait means influencing an animal's computation by applying the proper inputs. |
| Agriculture | Knowing that seeds compute plants involves insight into the process of wetware computation. Plowing is a form of soil randomization. Irrigation is a way to program the analog flow of water. Crop rotation is an algorithm to optimize yields. |
| Animal husbandry | Caring for animals requires insight into their computational homeostasis. Selecting optimal individuals for further breeding is genetic engineering on the hoof. |
| Wheel | Wheeled carts allow long-range gliderlike transfer of embodied information, making society's computation more complex. |
| Law | A legal code is a program for social interactions. Enforcing the code produces high-level determinism that makes the system easier to manipulate. |
| Surveying | Surveys allow a society to determine simple address codes for physical locations. Space becomes digital. |
| Calendar | Noting the solar system's cycles marks coordinates in time. Time becomes digital. |
| Sailing | Sailors learn to simulate and tweak the analog computation of airflow effects. Course planning involves higher-level simulation. |
| Pottery | The clay and the brushed-on glazes are the input, the kiln is the computer, the pot is the output. |
| Brewing and fermentation | The vat is a biocomputer, sensitive to the input variables of malt, sugar, and yeast. Over time, the best yeast strains are sought out by tasting and comparing; this is hill-climbing in a gustatory fitness landscape. |

| Innovation | Viewed as a computation |
|---|---|
| Spinning and weaving | The yarn is computed from the fibers. Weaving digitizes a surface into warp-woof coordinates. The loom is the first programmable mechanical computer. |
| Mining, smelting, and metallurgy | Mining is a form of data retrieval. The blast furnace transforms ore inputs into slag and metal outputs. Metallurgy and chemistry concern the computational rules by which matter transforms itself. |
| Writing | Writing translates speech into a format portable across space and time. A written text promotes long-distance information exchange and long-term memory storage. |
| The alphabet | Using a limited number of symbols digitizes writing. Use of the alphabet also simplifies the algorithm for writing. The democratization of writing allows people to write things they wouldn't be allowed to say. |
| Printing press | The type letters act as primitive symbols that are assembled into a kind of program—which prints a page. Printing multiple copies of a text enhances class four communication. |
| Books | The book amasses large amounts of text into portable form. The book is the precursor of the hard drive. |
| Universities | A university provides a node where adults can exchange very large amounts of information. Given that the students go out and affect the society as a whole, the university is in some sense a central processing unit for the social hive mind, drawing together and processing society's thoughts. |
| Water wheel and windmill | These devices convert chaotic fluid motions into regular periodic form. The excess information is returned to the fluid as turbulence. |
| Gunpowder | Bullets are high-speed gliders. Shooting someone allows an individual to do a remote erase. Reckless, catastrophic killing enhances interest in long-term information storage. |
| Machine tools | By creating precise mechanical tools for making machines, we model the biological process of self-reproduction. The machines come alive and begin evolving toward greater complexity. |
| Clocks | A finer-scale calendar, a zoom into the time dimension. Clocks use class two systems of gears that do |

| Innovation | Viewed as a computation |
|---|---|
| Clocks *(continued)* | the same thing over and over. Clocks are a tabletop model of determinism. |
| Steam engine | The steam engine is an artificially alive device that eats coal and transforms it into motion. The chaos of fire is converted into the reliable class two oscillation of the pistons. |
| Locomotive | When placed upon wheels, the steam engine becomes an autonomous glider. The country-to-city diffusion rate is changed, which in turn alters the Zhabotinsky scrolls of population movement. |
| Internal combustion engine | The internal combustion engine is an evolutionary advance above the steam engine, and an early example of compressing the size of computational hardware. |
| Factory assembly line | The factory represents a computing system that codifies the procedures of a given craft. The possibility of mass production allows us to view physical objects as information, as abstract procedures to be implemented as many times as we please. Three-dimensional objects can now be reproduced and disseminated as readily as books. Mass-produced devices become plug-ins for the computations embodied in people's homes. |
| Movies | A temporal sequence is modeled by a series of discrete frames. Movies are an early form of virtual reality. |
| Automobile | The personal vehicle allows individuals to control transportation. A formerly centralized technology is now in the hands of the people. Meetings and markets can be freely arranged, making the economy's computation more class four. |
| Electrical generators and motors | Electricity collapses the length of society's computation cycles. The system clock speeds up. Electrical lights disrupt the cycle of day and night; computation becomes continuous. There is now less of a border between the media and the human nervous system. People begin to view themselves as components plugged into the hive mind. |
| Telegraph | Writing is transmitted as a digital binary code. Society begins to grow its electrical network. |
| Telephone | Unlike the telegraph, the telephone is a peer-to-peer medium—you can make a phone call from your home without having to deal with a telegrapher. |

| Innovation | Viewed as a computation |
|---|---|
| Telephone (continued) | People are free to exchange "unimportant" information, that is, to talk about their moods and emotions, thus in fact exchanging a much higher-level kind of information than before. |
| Plastics | By designing new materials, chemists begin to program brute matter. Deformable and moldable, plastics can take on arbitrarily computed shapes. Objects are now programmable. |
| Radio | While books broadcast digitized thoughts, radio broadcasts analog emotion. The hive mind gains power, as listeners form real-time virtual crowds. |
| Airplane | When riding in a plane, one can look out the window and see a landscape as an undivided whole, gaining a notion of a nation as a unit. With familiarity, people stop looking, and air travel becomes a hyperlink, a teleportation device. In the United States, the "flyover" states become invisible to the cultural powers, promoting a schism in the hive mind. |
| Television | Since moving objects are important, our eyes have evolved to stare at flickering things; therefore, we find TV hypnotic. Watching TV is work; our minds labor to fill in the missing parts of the virtual reality. Society gains a stronger hive mind than ever before. But at the same time, the hive mind is debased by ever more centralized and less gnarly control. |
| Atomic power | The physicists complete the chemists' work, and even atoms become programmable. We see the most fundamental units of matter as information to be manipulated. |
| Computers | Billed as the universal machine, the electronic computer is brittle and hard to use. The digitization of essentially everything begins, in most cases degrading and corrupting the information. |
| E-mail | E-mail spreads the workplace into the home. The upside is that you don't have to commute, the downside is that you can't leave the office. E-mail is addictive, and people become ever more plugged in. Yet e-mail provides an alternate to the centralized news network, and many smaller hive minds take form. |

| Innovation | Viewed as a computation |
|---|---|
| The Web | The hive mind expands its consciousness. And at the same time the subhives' minds gain further definition. The Web page does for publication what the automobile did for transport—the gatekeepers lose importance. The Web becomes the ultimate global information resource, the universal database. Social computation becomes nearly frictionless; people can effortlessly interact at a distance. |
| Biotechnology | Biologists begin to program life. Society tries to apply legal codes to life, with unpleasant and confusing results. Real biological life continues anyway, still managing to avoid control. |
| Cell phones | A tight, personal, peer-to-peer medium that approaches telepathy. As people coordinate activities in real time, short-lived spontaneous minihive minds emerge. |
| Wireless gizmos | The pocket-size phone-browser-digicam-organizer-notepad. These overfeatured products are in some sense like small pets, requiring that their keepers spend substantial effort in tending and programming them. The point is no longer to make things easier for the owner, but to give the owner a hobby. These gizmos are artificially alive and parasitic |

**Table 17: History of Technology as a History of Computation**

instead of looking directly at the world around them. But now I find that having a camera in my pocket means that I look at the world harder and more deeply. And I can reach new friends and enhance my own understanding by posting the images on my blog. If I can use a technology in a creative way, I feel like it hasn't got the better of me. But sometimes this is an illusion.

The issue of PCs is a particularly vexing one for me. In his later life, McLuhan recast his adage, "The medium is the message," as "Ignore the figure and watch the ground"—meaning that the best way to understand the effects of a new technology is to look at how it changes its surroundings.

Thus, in the case of computers, rather than talking about what computers do or what computation means, we might look at how they change people's behavior. It's not a pretty picture.

I think of the toll my machine has taken on my wrists and my back. I think of the never-ending hardware and software upgrades—as *The Lifebox, the Seashell, and the Soul* has grown larger and more heavily illustrated, I've had to upgrade everything about my system just to stay afloat—and, of course, each upgrade ushers in fresh incompatibilities and unhappy days squandered in battle with obscure bugs. I think of lost opportunities for conversation with my family and friends, with me sitting hypnotized at my keyboard. Even when I mean to take a break in a coffee shop, often as not I bring my laptop and sit isolated behind my portable screen. Although I wonder how it would be to live in a world where my time was my own, I'm hooked on the power and expressiveness of my PC.

But that's enough frowny-face fretting over my accelerating dehumanization!☹ Let's see what fresh wonders the future might bring!☺

Table 18 lists computation-related inventions that might show up over the next two thousand years or so. The table is adapted from the Y2K work of futurology that I unwisely saddled with the title *Saucer Wisdom*.[128]

| Future technology | Description |
| --- | --- |
| Piezoplastic | Plastic whose colors and shape are dynamically controlled by electronic inputs. Usable as a soft, floppy computer display that you can stuff in your pocket like a handkerchief. |
| Lifeboxes | Interactive data base simulacra of people. A combined blog and video diary with a search engine that's able to answer questions. |
| Limpware engineering | We'll learn how to program piezoplastic like silicon chips. The whole computer can become soft and floppy as a banana slug. |
| Dragonfly cameras | Insect-size flying cameras, individually owned (or rented) so people can see whatever they want. The whole world becomes accessible on the Web. |
| Radiotelepathy | It becomes possible to electromagnetically send thoughts from brain to brain. The use of lifebox databases for individual "contexts" makes this possible. |
| The uvvy | The ultimate wireless device, the piezoplastic uvvy sits on your neck and gives you Web, e-mail, phone, and direct thought access. |
| Recording dreams | A side effect of the uvvy. There's a culture craze for dreams; society becomes more surreal. If you sleep with your uvvy on, you can record your dreams. People can arrange to share dreams. A significant downside is that the flow can go the other way, with dreams now containing commercials trickling in over the uvvy. |
| Knife plants, house trees | Genetically engineered plants begin producing consumer goods, for instance, knives. A largish specialized seed can grow you a house. Machines as we know them go away. In every instance, it's cheaper to grow a living device. Think of houseflies— all they need in order to replicate is water and garbage. Now suppose that the flies are doing something useful for you like acting as dragonfly cameras, or picking bits of trash from your floor. |
| Pet construction kit | People can program their own pet characteristics. Pet dinosaurs are very popular. Animals are now fully programmable. |
| "Aug dog" | People bioengineer their bodies. These changes are called augmentations; thus the popular term for a body changers is "aug dog." The body becomes more virtual, less real. |

| Future technology | Description |
|---|---|
| Archipelago people | You can have several disconnected hands or eyes that move about independently from your main body; you stay in touch using uvvies. "I seem to be a network." |
| Mermen, mermaids | Bioengineered people move into new niches under the sea. |
| Programmable clones | You can speed-grow an adult clone of yourself in a tank and program its brain with the contents of your lifebox file, creating a person very much like yourself. Given the class four nature of your computation and the differing initial conditions, the clone wouldn't be identical to you, but its behavior will be exploring the same strange attractor. |
| Femtotechnology | It becomes possible to transmute neutrons into protons and vice versa, allowing us to change the atomic makeup of matter. A device called the alla can, for instance, turn dirt into air. The age of direct matter control arrives and we can change anything into anything. Matter is now fully programmable by the average person. |
| Space migration | People use allas to live in asteroids, turning their stone interiors into dirt and air. |
| 3ox | A new technology for identically copying existing objects. Living bodies can be 3oxed as well. The process works around the quantum-mechanical "no-cloning" theorem. |
| Ooies | Uvvies become bioengineered internal organs, called ooies, so that people are constantly in contact. Society truly becomes a hive. |
| Colony people | Some individuals 3ox or clone hundreds of copies of themselves, with the copies connected via ooies. It's a new kind of human mind. |
| Spacebug people | Still more advanced bioengineering allows people to live in the hard vacuum of outer space and to propel themselves like rockets. |
| Teleportation | Insight into fundamental physics gives people the ability to jump to arbitrarily distant space locations. |
| People free to move in higher dimensions | Travel to the other worlds beyond our space and time. |

**Table 18: Milestones in an Imagined Future History**

*We might suppose that the dates run from about 2050 to 4050.*

Jake Wasser was adding a column of penciled-in numbers on his preliminary tax form. Sure he could be doing this on a computer, but he enjoyed the mental exercise. Tax season was his time of the year for arithmetic.

Nine and three is two carry one. Two take away five is seven borrow one. If he hadn't blown off calculus and majored in history, maybe he would have been a scientist like his playful, bohemian wife Rosalie. Instead he'd ended up a foot soldier in a Wall Street law firm. It was a grind, although it paid the rent.

When the tax numbers were all in place, it was early afternoon. Jake was free. Even though he'd known he'd finish early, he'd taken a full day off. He needed one. Recently he'd had the feeling that life was passing him by. Here he was forty-two and he'd been working crazy long weeks for going on twenty years now. Kissing butt, laughing at jokes, talking about politics and cars, smoking cigars, eating heavy meals. He and Rosalie had never gotten around to having children.

He looked over the apartment, with its polished wood everywhere.

The sight of their luxury flat never failed to lift his mood. In some ways, he and Rosalie had been very lucky. He drifted toward the window that faced Gramercy Park, passing the heavy vase of flowers their Dominican housekeeper had brought in. They resembled heavy pink thistles—proteus? The odor was sweet, spiral, stimulating. It made him think of numbers.

He stood by the window and looked up Lexington Avenue, the blocks receding into the misty April rain. On a whim, he began counting the windows in the buildings lining the avenue—to his surprise he was able to count them all. And then he counted the bricks, as easily as taking a breath. Although he couldn't have readily put the quantity into words, he knew the exact number of bricks in the buildings outside, knew it as surely as he knew the number of fingers on his hands.

Leaning on the windowsill, he went on counting, just to see how high he could go. Whirl, whirl, whirl. And then he was done. He'd counted through all the numbers there are.

He caught his breath and glanced

around the quiet apartment. The housekeeper was gone for the day. What strange thoughts he was having. He went into the kitchen and drank a glass of water from the sink. And then, once again, he counted to infinity—the trick was to visualize each number in half the time of the number before. He could do it, even though it didn't seem physically possible.

Gingerly he felt his balding pate and the crisp curls at the back of his head. Everything was as it should be, all his parts in place. Should he rush to the emergency room? That would be a stupid way to spend his free day. He glanced down at the wood floor, counting the light and dark bands of grain. And then he counted to infinity again. He grabbed an umbrella and left the apartment in search of Rosalie.

Looking out the damp taxi's window on the ride uptown, he took in every detail. People's gestures, their magnificent faces. Usually he didn't pay so much attention, feeling he'd be overloaded if he let everything in. But today he was like a photo album with an endless supply of fresh pages. A digital camera with an inexhaustible memory card. Calmly he absorbed the passing pageant.

At Sixty-sixth Street the cab turned and drove to the research campus beside the East River. Jake didn't often visit Rosalie at work, and the guard at the desk called her on a speaker phone for permission.

"Jake?" she exclaimed in surprise. "You're here? I was just about to call you."

"Something's happened to me," he said. "I want to see you."

"Yes," said Rosalie. "Let him in, Dan."

The building was old, with shiny gray linoleum floors. Nothing to count but the hallway doors. Rosalie's short-cropped dark head popped out of the last one. Her personal lab. She smiled and beckoned, filled with some news of her own.

"You've gotta see my organic microscope," exclaimed Rosalie, drawing him into her quarters. It was just the two of them there.

"Wait," interrupted Jake. "I counted every brick on Lexington Avenue. And then I counted to infinity."

"Every brick?" said Rosalie, not taking him seriously. "Sounds like you did the tax forms without a calculator again."

"I'm thinking things that are physically impossible," said Jake solemnly. "Maybe I'm dying."

"You look fine," said Rosalie, planting a kiss on his cheek. "It's good to see you out of that gray suit. The news here is the opposite. My new scope is real, but what it's doing is unthinkable." She gestured at an glowing, irregularly shaped display screen. "I came up with this gnarly idea for a new approach to microscopy, and I had Nick in the genomics group grow the biotech components for me. It uses a kind of octopus skin for the display, so I call it a skinscope. It's the end, Jake. It zooms in—like forever. A Zeno infinity in four seconds. Patentable for sure." She closed her office door and lowered her voice. "We need to talk intellectual property, lawyer mine."

"I'm tired of being a lawyer," murmured Jake, intoxicated by Rosalie's presence. With his new sensitivity, he was hearing all the echoes and overtones of their melding voices in the little room, the endlessly detailed fractals of the component frequencies. How nice it would be to work with Rosalie every day. Her face held fourteen million shades of pink.

"Here we go," said Rosalie, blithely flicking a switch attached to the skinscope.

The display's skin flickered and began bringing forth images of startling clarity and hue, the first a desultory paramecium poking around for food. Jake thought of a mustached paralegal picking through depositions. The skinscope shuddered and the zoom began. They flew through the microbe's core, down past its twinkling genes into a carbon atom. The atom's nucleus bloated up like the sun and inside it danced a swarm of firefly lights.

"This is inconceivable," said Rosalie. "We're already at the femtometer level. And it's only getting started. It goes through all the decimals, you dig."

A firefly broke into spirals of sparks, a spark unfolded into knotted strings, a string opened into tunnels of cartoon hearts, a heart divulged a ring of golden keys, a key crumbled into a swarm of butterflies. Each image lasted half as long as the one before.

"It's too fast to see now," said Rosalie, but Jake stayed with the zoom, riding the endless torrent of images.

"Infinity," he said when it was done. "I saw it all."

"And to hell with quantum mechanics," mused Rosalie. "My Jake. It's a sign, both these things happening to us today. The world is using us to make something new."

"But the skinscope patent will

belong to the labs," said Jake. "I remember the clause from your contract."

"What if I quit the lab?" said Rosalie. "I'm tired of hearing about disease."

"We could start a company," said Jake. "Develop skinscope applications."

"We'll use them like infinite computers, Jake. A box to simulate every possible option in a couple of seconds. No round-off, no compromise, all the details. You can be the chief engineer."

"Kind of late for a career change," said Jake.

"You can do it," said Rosalie. "You'll teach our programmers to see infinity. Teach me now. Show me how you learned."

"Okay," said Jake, taking out his pencil and jotting down some figures. "Add the first two lines and subtract the third one . . ."

# CHAPTER SIX

# *Reality Upgrade*

IN THIS CHAPTER, I'M FIRST going to explore the philosophical ramifications of the hypotheses I've been discussing. And then I'm going to mention some ways to open up one's thought process a bit more. My ultimate goal is to find ways to enhance our appreciation of the world around us.

In *6.1: Eight Ontologies,* I'll say a bit about the status of the central tenet of universal automatism: Everything is a computation. Analyzing this claim leads to a philosophical discussion about *ontology:* the study of what exists. I'll show that universal automatism is but one of eight possible views.

In *6.2: The Computational Zoo* and *6.3: Faster and Smarter,* I discuss Wolfram's two key hypotheses about computations: his Principle of Computational Equivalence (PCE) and what I call his Principle of Computational Unpredictability (PCU).

These two principles are conjectures about the kinds of computation that actually occur in the natural world, that is, in physics, in biology, in our minds, and in society. Rather than being logically provable theorems, the principles have the status of being inductive empirical hypotheses about the nature of the world.

My feeling is that the PCE needs to be cast into a substantially weaker form, which I call the Natural Unsolvability Hypothesis (NUH). Rather than being a statement about computational equivalence, the Natural Unsolvability Hypothesis says that most naturally occurring complex computations are *unsolvable* in a certain technical sense of the word. The PCU—which says that complex natural computations are *unpredictable*—needs some careful hedging as well.

In *6.4: Random Truth*, I take up a third "un": *undecidability*. I offer a quick overview of the formalist notion of reducing science to a theory, and analyze what our studies of computation tell us about human ability to prove things. We obtain the somewhat surprising new result that, given any complex naturally occurring process and any theory of science, there will be infinitely many true facts about the process that science is unable to prove. Undecidability is all around us.

Finally, in *6.5: The Answers,* I tackle the big questions: What is reality, what is the meaning of life, and how can I be happy?

If you read nothing else in this somewhat technical chapter, do be sure and read *The Answers.* You can understand the answers perfectly well without reading the questions. I'm a little embarrassed about how hard the middle of this chapter is.

## 6.1: *Eight Ontologies*

It's not too hard to find computer scientists who are willing to accept universal automatism: the claim that everything is a computation. Is this simply a work-induced delusion, a kind of byte blindness? Is such a claim to be taken any more seriously than, say, a sports announcer's platitude that life is a game, an impassioned composer's rant that the cosmos is music, or a raconteur's smiling remark that the world is made of jokes?

Our culture's recent mania for computers and all things digital is, after all, a technological fad that won't be around forever. In a hundred years, some other new paradigm may obsess us.

In the Middle Ages, people thought of their bodies and minds as made up of the four elements Earth, Air, Water, and Fire, in the form of Bile, Blood, Phlegm, and Choler. Back at the dawn of the Industrial Age, it seemed interesting to wonder if the universe might not be some kind of big loom or steam engine. Half a century ago, in the Atomic Age, it was common to think of the universe as being a "space" filled with "particles." How quaint.

But maybe *this* time we've got it right. Could it be that everything is really a computation? One of the goals of *The Lifebox, the Seashell, and the Soul* has been to show by means of many examples that universal automatism isn't as unrealistic as it initially sounds. And in this section I want to consider precisely what would be the alternate possibilities.

As I mentioned above, philosophers speak of *ontology* as the study of what exists. By extension, any particular assertion about what kinds of things exist is spoken of as *an ontology*. Thus universal automatism is the ontology that says everything is a computation. I'm going to use a simple combinatorial argument to distinguish between universal automatism and seven alternative ontologies:

Suppose we think of the universe as a very large class of objects in action. Some of these entities will be thoughts, some will be computations, some will be physical processes. I'll take these to have the following meanings:

- A *thought* is a mental process that some idealized person might have.
- A *computation* is a process that obeys finitely describable rules.
- A *physical process* is a phenomenon that might take place in the actual world we live in.

Suppose I write *T, C,* and *P* for, respectively, the class of all thoughts, the class of all computations, and the class of all physical processes. These three classes will overlap with one another to a greater or lesser extent, depending upon what kinds of entities are in our universe—that is, depending upon our ontology.

I'm going to suggest that the relationship should be drawn as in figure 122; computations are both thoughts and physical processes. Why?

Look again at the definition given a few paragraphs above. A computation is a process that obeys finitely describable rules. This definition harks back to section *1.1: Universal Automatism.* As I mentioned before, if a process strictly obeys rules, then it is also deterministic. There are two other implicit aspects of my definition to remark upon. First of all, when I say "process" I am thinking of a *physical process* that could exist in our world. And second, when I say "finitely describable" I mean humanly *thinkable*.

Regarding the first point, note that all of the computations we've discussed thus far have been embodied in some physical form or other: personal computer,

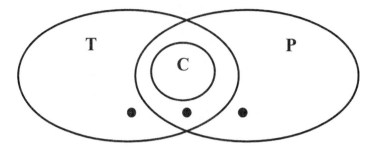

**Figure 122:**
**C ⊆ T ∩ P, or, Computations Are Thoughts and Physical Processes**

*Depending upon which of eight possible ontologies we adopt, the zones with the dots may or may not be empty. The left dot represents a region we call T ~ P, the center dot then corresponds to (T ∩ P) ~ C, and the right dot to P ~ T. In set-theoretic usage, the ~ symbol is like a minus or difference symbol, and the intersection symbol ∩ is used to describe the overlapping region of two sets.*

physics experiment, organism, mental process, or society. A computation is a process that some physical system could in principle carry out. So in this sense, *a computation is a physical process.* The class $C$ is a subclass of the class $P$.

Regarding the second point, the fact that we speak of a computation as having a *rule* really means that there is some possibly very long explanation of the computation that a person should in principle be able to understand. As we're doing philosophy here, we aren't going to worry about the fact that many computations are in fact *unfeasible* for a normal-sized human brain. The essential point is that a computation must have a rule that is, at least in an idealized sense, amenable to human logical understanding. And in this sense, *a computation is a possible thought.* The class $C$ is a subclass of the class $T$.

It's this overlap that gives the notion of computation its power and significance. Computations are interesting precisely because they are phenomena where mind and matter overlap. Computations are, if you will, ideas made flesh. In set-theoretic notation, $C \subseteq T \cap P$.

Here's a one-paragraph review of the notation involved. In general "$A \subseteq B$" stands for "$A$ is a subclass $B$" or "every member of $A$ is a member of $B$." "$T \cap P$" stands for "the intersection of $T$ and $P$" or "the class of all entities that are in both $T$ and in $P$." And we're using the ~ symbol as a set-theoretic difference, or minus symbol, so that "$A \sim B$" means "the class of all entities that are in $A$ but not in $B$." End of notation review.

I drew figure 122 in the most general possible fashion so as to be consistent with the basic observations that $C$ is a subclass of $T$, and $C$ is a subclass of $P$. The three black dots in my figure indicate regions that might or might not be empty, depending on which ontology we subscribe to. From left to right, the regions are.

- $T \sim P$. Thoughts that aren't possible physical processes.
- $(T \cap P) \sim C$. Thinkable physical processes that aren't computations.
- $P \sim T$. Physical processes that aren't thinkable.

Note that universal automatism says every thought and every physical process is a computation—and this implies that $T = C$ and $P = C$, so $T = P$ as well, and all three of the dotted regions are in fact empty in the universal-automatism ontology: the $T$, $C$, and $P$ ovals coincide at the other extreme from universal automatism is a "principle of plenitude," which says that our universe is as richly populated as it could possibly be. In this ontology, you'd expect to find objects in all three of the dotted zones.

A priori, there are in fact eight possible states of affairs regarding which of the dotted zones are or are not empty: two times two times two possibilities. *Distinguo.*

In figures 123 and 124, I tabulate the eight ontologies, numbering them from one to eight. The first four ontologies are what we might call "natural" in the sense that here are no entities in $T \sim P$, that is, no thoughts that are not representable as physical processes. In the latter four "supernatural" ontologies, we do allow for thoughts that are not physically representable.

In the figures, I've said a few words about each ontology, and where possible I've mentioned the names of some thinkers whose worldviews seem to match the ontology in question. I use the symbols 0 and 1 to indicate the absence or the presence of elements in the three "dot zones."[129]

•   •   •

| Description | 0 or 1 for absence or presence of elements in the three "dot zones" $T \sim P$, $(T \cap P) \sim C$, $P \sim T$ | | | Picture |
|---|---|---|---|---|
| 1. *Universal automatism.* Every object or thought is a computation. [Stephen Wolfram, Edward Fredkin, Alan Turing] | 0 | 0 | 0 | 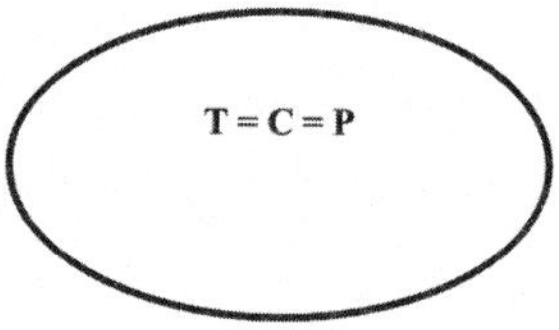 $T = C = P$ |
| 2. *Mechanism.* We think like digital machines, and the rich continuous world of physics lies beyound us. | 0 | 0 | 1 | 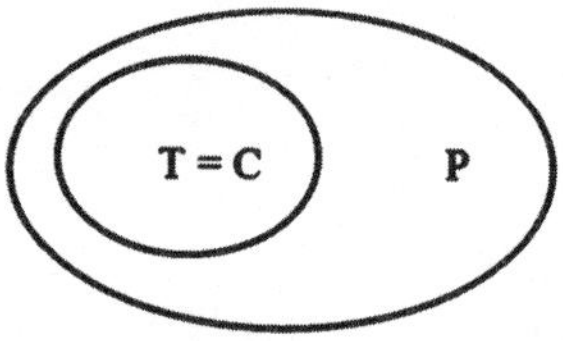 $T = C$    P |
| 3. *Physical antimechanism.* Thanks to being continuous physical beings, our behavior is richer than that of digital machines. [Roger Penrose, Nick Herbert.] | 0 | 1 | 0 | 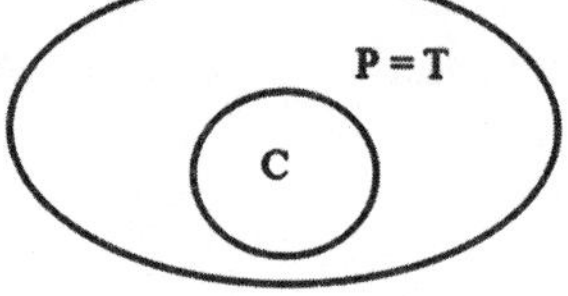 $P = T$   C |
| 4. *Common sense.* Our minds can do more than machines, and some entities do more than our minds. That is, not every possible thought is a computation, and not every physical process is thinkable. | 0 | 1 | 1 | 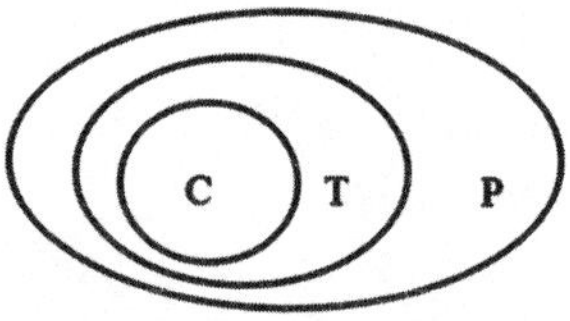 C   T   P |

**Figure 123: The "Natural" First Four Ontologies**

*In these four ontologies, there are no entities in* T ~ P, *that is, all thoughts are representable as physical processes.*

| Description | 0 or 1 for absence or presence of elements in the three "dot zones" $T \sim P$, $(T \cap P) \sim C$, $P \sim T$ | | | Picture |
|---|---|---|---|---|
| 5. *Supernaturalism* Although physics is a digital computation, the mind has supernatural powers lying beyond physics. [New ager.] | 1 | 0 | 0 | 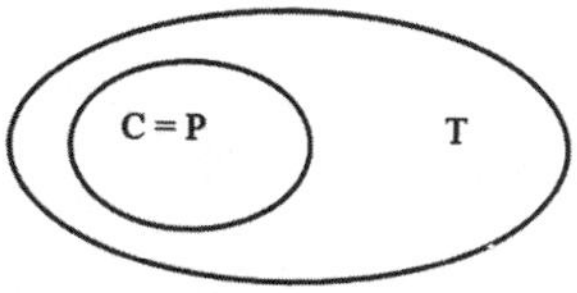 |
| 6. *Computationalism.* Every thinkable physical process is a computation. But there are both non-thinkable things and non-physical thoughts. | 1 | 0 | 1 | 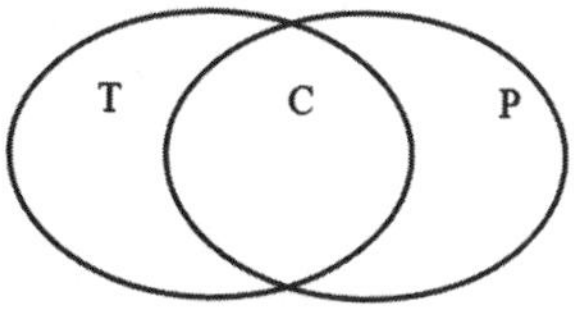 |
| 7. *Idealism.* Some physical processes lie beyond computation, and the supernatural mind exceeds even physics. [Kurt Gödel.] | 1 | 1 | 0 | 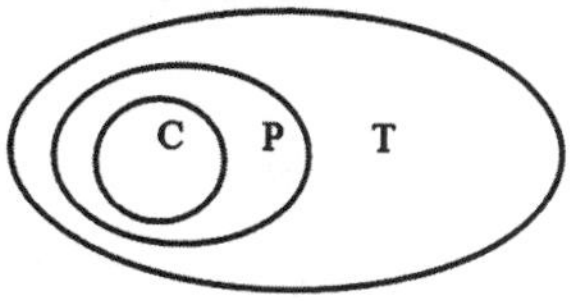 |
| 8. *Plenitude.* Every possible kind of object exists! | 1 | 1 | 1 | 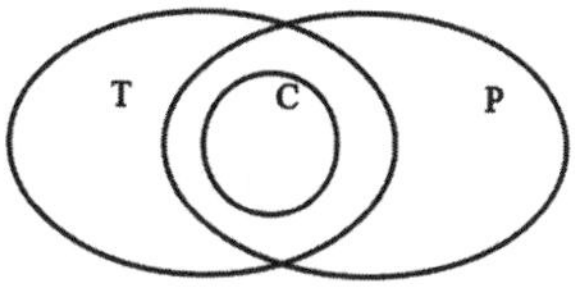 |

**Figure 124: The "Supernatural" Second Four Ontologies**

*In each of the latter four ontologies, we have objects in T ~ P, that is, some thoughts are not realizable as physical processes.*

I have to admit that, once we see universal automatism as only one of eight options, it doesn't seem quite so compelling.

Which ontology do I personally believe in? My general sense of the universe is that, although we can find wonderfully broad laws, the details of things are always even more complicated than our most outlandish expectations. I'll stick with universal automatism for now, but I'm tempted by plenitude, the ontology in which we have all three kinds of oddball entities.

- *Thoughts that aren't physical processes.* These might be infinite thoughts that can't fit into the physical world, or supernatural effects wholly outside physics.
- *Unthinkable physical processes.* The very essence of quantum mechanics seems to be that it's in some sense unthinkable. Maybe this gets a lot worse as we dig even deeper down. Maybe there are arcane, eldritch aspects of reality the very sight of which would break a human mind.
- *Thinkable physical processes that don't correspond to anything that we'd call a computation.* Perhaps there's some perfectly reasonable physical processes that really are fundamentally nondeterministic and thus not at all like our notion of computation. Indeed, should quantum mechanics get the last word, its fundamentally random processes would have this quality.

But plain universal automatism remains attractive, and in any case, there's much of interest in Wolfram's conjectures about computation. That's what we're going to talk about next.

## 6.2: The Computational Zoo

In this section I want first to look at some of the kinds of computation that are known to exist, second to explain why Wolfram's Principle of Computational Equivalence probably isn't true, and third to discuss a weakened form of the PCE that will in fact be strong enough to draw some interesting conclusions. In section *6.3: The Faster and Smarter,* I'll tackle the quite different Principle of Computational Unpredictability. And in section *6.4: Random Truth* I'll see what our discussions tell us about logical provability.

At this point, I need to unpack some of our computer science ideas a bit more thoroughly than before—which means there's going to be dirty laundry all over the place! So be warned that these three sections are more technical than the rest of the book. Feel free to skim through them lightly, or even to skip big clumps of pages at a time. In fact, if this is your first time through, go straight to section *6.5: The Answers.*

Anyone still here? Okay, let's begin by recalling some of the basic notions about a computation. First of all, I think of a computation $P$ as a deterministic process, and if I initialize $P$ with some state In, then $P$ will carry out a process that I call $P(\text{In})$. Note that I'm not thinking of $P(\text{In})$ as being any one particular value, that is, I'm not thinking of $P$ as being a function that simply gives you a value. I'm thinking of $P(\text{In})$ as a process that goes on and on through time $t$. The fact that the process is deterministic means that at any future time $t$, the system's state Out depends only on In and $t$. So we *can,* if we like, think of $P$ as a function of *two* variables, with $P(\text{In}, t) = \text{Out}$.

- *Definition.* $P(\text{In})$ *produces* state Out means there is some time $t$ such that $P(\text{In}, t) = \text{Out}$. That is, if we start $P$ in state In, there will eventually be a time at which $P$ enters state Out.

Many kinds of computations have the property that they can reach a final state and simply stop or freeze at this final state. If $P(\text{In})$ produces a state Out and then remains in this state for good, we sometimes say that $P(\text{In})$ *returns* Out. I indicate the distinction between *producing* Out and *returning* Out in figure 125.[130]

As I briefly mentioned in section *1.1: Universal Automatism,* the notion of reaching a final state is so essential to our conception of computation that I generalize it to the notion of a *target state.* Many natural computations never reach a fixed final state. But even for these lively computations I'd like to have a notion of reaching a target state.

So, once again, I define a so-called *target detector* for $P$ to be a simple helper computation Is$P$Done that has two special states we call True and False (figure 126). To avoid adding extra complication, I require that Is$P$Done be completely unproblematic in the sense that if you feed it a test value $S$, Is$P$Done($S$) quickly returns True or False.

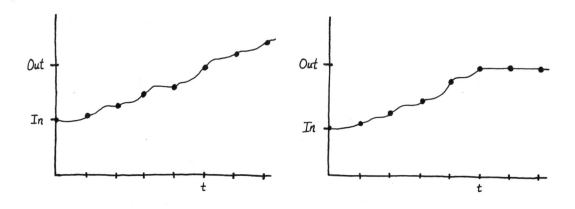

**Figure 125: Producing or Returning an Output**

*In these pictures we think of time as a continuous series of instants along the horizontal axis. And we view our computing system's state as being a height above the horizontal axis. We represent a computation by picking an initial point In on the vertical axis and drawing the sequence of states that results.*

We can use target detectors to define a generalized notion of halting.

- *Definition.* Given a computation *P* and a target detector Is*P*Done, we say that *P(In)* *halts relative to IsPDone* if the computation *P*(In) produces a state Out such that Is*P*Done(Out) is True. Otherwise, we say that *P(In)* *doesn't halt relative to IsPDone*.

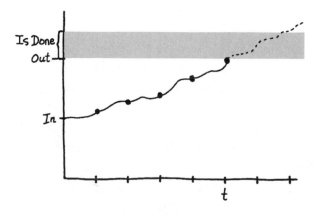

**Figure 126: Target Detector**

By the way, I occasionally talk about halting without having mentioned any specific target detector. In these cases, you can assume that I'm using a default target detector that we might as well call Is*P*Frozen. Is*P*Frozen(Out) returns True or False according to whether the computation *P* stops changing after it produces Out.

Note that in the more general cases where Is*P*Done draws some subtler distinction than the simple Is*P*Frozen, the word *halt* is slightly misleading. For a real-world computation doesn't necessarily *cease to change* when it reaches a state Out such that Is*P*Done(Out) is True.

To take a very simple example, if you add two numbers on a pocket calculator, the calculator doesn't freeze up and become unusable once it displays the sum. It remains responsive to further inputs. It's only "halted" in the sense that it satisfies the Is*P*Done condition of displaying an answer that isn't currently changing.

Now that we have a generalized notion of halting, let's discuss the somewhat surprising consequences of making the distinction between halting and nonhalting computations.

In many situations we value computations that halt—because they give us a definite answer in the form of the first target state they produce. Suppose you feed a set of equations into some computer algebra software like Mathematica or Maple, and that you ask the software to solve the equations. What you want is for the resulting computation to halt in the sense of displaying an answer on the screen. If the computation fails to halt, you sit there endlessly looking at a little Wait icon—with the computation busy with some unsuccessful search for an answer, or knotted into a repetitive loop.

In other situations, we aren't interested in seeing a computation reach any particular state. When we simulate, say, the life of some artificially alive creature, or the evolution of a species, we aren't necessarily aiming toward a specific kind of result, and still less do we want to see a fixed state or periodic behavior. When I explore the world of two-dimensional cellular automata, I'm usually looking for rules and inputs where the screen keeps churning and doesn't die down.

The distinction between halting and not halting leads to Turing's celebrated *halting problem.*

Suppose we have a computation *P* and a target detector Is*P*Done. Is there a general method to decide if *P*(In) halts relative to Is*P*Done? As we'll soon see, the answer is often no!

Figure 127 shows what happens if we try to distinguish the halting and nonhalting cases simply by running the computation *P*.

Identifying the nonhalting cases presents a problem because it takes forever to wait to see if something never halts. To solve this problem we would want to find a way to short-circuit the endless searches through the nontargeted outputs. That is, we'd like to have an *endless search detector* computation *P*FailsToHalt. By this I mean the following:

Given a computation *P* and a target detector Is*P*Done, we say the computation *P*FailsToHalt is *an endless search detector for P relative to IsPDone* if *P*FailsToHalt(In) returns True precisely for those cases in which *P*(In) doesn't halt.

And if the computation *P* and Is*P*Done have an endless search detector, we'll say that *P has a solvable halting problem relative to IsPDone.*

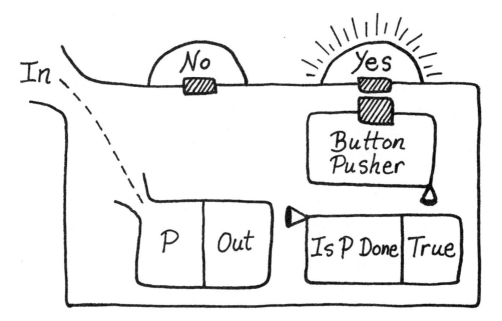

**Figure 127: An Unsuccessful Solution to a Halting Problem**

*Our boxed device includes a copy of* P *and* IsPDone. *An input In goes to* P. *IsPDone watches* P's *ensuing series of Out states. A button-pusher watches the states of IsP-Done. If the button-pusher sees True, it turns on the Yes lamp. But if* P(In) *doesn't halt relative to IsPDone, there's no mechanism to see that the No lamp gets turned on.*

- *Definition.* The computation *P has a solvable halting problem relative to* Is*P*Done if there is an endless search detector for *P* with Is*P*Done. Otherwise we say that *P* has an unsolvable halting problem relative to Is*P*Done.

Figure 128 illustrates how we can use an endless search detector to distinguish the halting and nonhalting inputs for *P* relative to Is*P*Done.

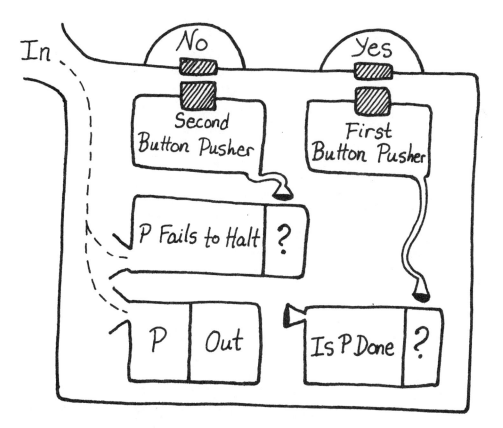

**Figure 128: A Solvable Halting Problem**

*Our boxed device includes a copy of* P *and an endless search detector* PFailsToHalt. *An input In is copied and fed to both* P *and to* PFailsToHalt. *We time-share the computation, first running* P *for a second, then running* PFailsToHalt *for a second, and so on.* IsPDone *watches* P's *Out states. A first button-pusher watches the states of* IsPDone. *If the first button-pusher sees True, it turns on the Yes button. A second button-pusher watches the states of* PFailsToHalt. *If the second button-pusher sees True, it turns on the No lamp.*

The halting problem was introduced by Alan Turing in his classic 1936 paper, "On Computable Numbers, with an Application to the *Entscheidungs-problem.*" In this paper, Turing made three great advances.

- He characterized the notion of a possible computation as a process that can be carried out by a Turing machine.
- He showed how to construct a universal computation capable of emulating any other computation.
- He proved that any universal computation has an unsolvable halting problem.

In order to appreciate these results, we'll need the definitions of emulation and of universality that I introduced in section *1.4: Analytical Engines.*

- *Definition of Emulation.* Big *emulates* Small if there is an emulation code emulatesmall such that for any states In and Out,
  Small(In) returns Out if and only if
  Big(emulatesmall, In) returns Out.

- *Definition.* A computation is *universal* if it can emulate any other computation.

Turing's main result is, once again:

- *Turing's Theorem.* If *U* is a universal computation, then *U* has an unsolvable halting problem.

(The particular target detector Is*U*Done used in Turing's proof is the default detector Is*U*Frozen. Is*U*Frozen(Out) is True precisely if the computation stops changing after it enters the state Out. But, as I prove in the Technical Appendix, if *U* is a universal computation and Is*U*Done is *any* nontrivial target detector, the halting problem for *U* relative to Is*U*Done is also unsolvable.)

Turing's Theorem is a primary reason why Wolfram's Principle of Computational Equivalence might be of use. Taken together with Turing's Theorem, the PCE proposes that most complex natural processes have unsolvable halting problems—in the sense that there will be no way to detect in advance those inputs that produce certain kinds of endless search behavior.

Before going into details about the PCE, let's delve a bit more deeply into what mathematical logicians have unearthed about the zoo of possible computations.

Mathematical logicians speak of computations' sophistication in terms of "degrees of unsovability." This notion is defined in terms of emulation.

> • *Definition.* If two computations can emulate each other, then they have the *same degree of unsolvability*. We say that $P$ has a *smaller degree of unsolvability* than $Q$ if $Q$ can emulate $P$, but $P$ can't emulate $Q$.

We sometimes want to think of a degree of unsolvability itself as having an existence by itself, like a specialized number of some kind. Formally, mathematicians do this by saying that the degree of unsolvability corresponding to a computation $P$ is the collection P of all computations having the same degree of unsolvability as $P$.

Suppose that $R$ is some very simple computation that is everywhere defined—to be specific, suppose that, given any input In, the computation $R(\text{In})$ simply stays in the In state forever. Any computation at all can emulate $R$, but we don't expect that the do-nothing $R$ can emulate all the other computations. For this reason, we say that $R$ represents a minimal degree of unsolvability. This degree can be called R, for "recursive"—a versatile word, one of whose meanings is "having a solvable halting problem."

Now suppose that $U$ is a universal computation. Since $U$ can emulate any computation at all, $U$ represents a maximal degree of unsolvability. This degree can be called U for "universal."

The particular do-nothing computation $R$ halts for every input, so its halting problem is readily solvable by letting RFailsToHalt(In) return False for every possible input. And, by Turing's Theorem, we know that if $U$ is a universal computation, there is no UFailsToHalt(In) computation that will correctly detect the inputs for which $U$ fails to halt. Putting these two facts together with a bit of mathematical argumentation, we can conclude that $R$ has a smaller degree of unsolvability than $U$. That is, $U$ can emulate $R$, but $R$

can't emulate *U.* Putting it a bit differently, the degree R is less than the degree U.

In 1940, the logician Emil Post posed *Post's problem*: are there any intermediate degrees of unsolvability, that is, any degrees lying between R and U? Another way to put it would be the following.

- *Post's problem.* Is there a computation *M* such that *M* has an unsolvable halting problem, but *M* is not universal?

Post's problem was solved in the affirmative by Richard Friedberg and Albert Muchnik, working independently in 1956. And further work by mathematical logicians such as Gerald Sacks has shown that the degrees of unsolvability represent about as messy and unruly an ordering as one can imagine.[131] (See figure 129.)

- There are *infinitely* many distinct degrees of unsovability between the minimal and the maximal degrees.
- The degrees of unsolvability are *dense* in the sense that between any two degrees lies a third.
- The degrees of unsolvability *don't fall into a linear ordering,* that is, we can find *P* and *Q* such that neither can emulate the other.

Now let's relate these mathematical discoveries to Wolfram's PCE. I already sketched a few of these ideas in section *1.2: A New Kind of Science,* but let's go over them from the start. To being with, we have the PCE in Wolfram's own words.

- *Wolfram's Principle of Computational Equivalence (PCE).* Almost all processes that are not obviously simple can be viewed as computations of equivalent sophistication.

I'll now ring the PCE through four changes, hit a snag, formulate an alternate form of the PCE, and then suggest a more plausible hypothesis that I'll call the Natural Unsolvability Hypothesis (NUH).

What kinds of computations are "obviously simple"? As I suggested in section 1.2, it seems natural to say that the *simple* computations make up class

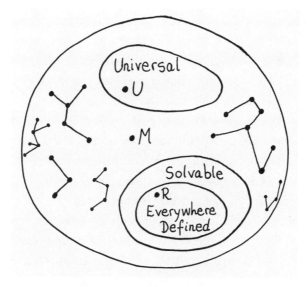

**Figure 129: Degrees of Unsolvability**

*In this picture, R is a do-nothing computation, U is a universal computation, and M is a computation with an unsolvability degree intermediate between R and U. The circle at the top includes all of the universal computations—all of which in fact have the same degree of unsolvability. The larger circle at the bottom includes the solvable or "recursive" computations, and the smaller circle inside it includes the everywhere-defined computations. The dots stand for some of the other possible computations, and the connecting lines indicate "smaller degree of unsolvability" relationships. To keep the figure clear, I have not drawn all possible lines; in particular, since U is universal, I could draw "less than" lines running from each dot up to U, and since R is of minimal degree, I could draw "less than" lines running from R up to each dot. The messiness of the degree ordering is expressed by three facts: (a) There are infinitely many distinct degrees, meaning that endlessly more additional dots can be found within the middle zone. (b) Since the degrees are in fact densely ordered, we can add a dot to the interior of any of the "less than" lines connecting the pairs of computations. (c) Some computations have degrees that bear no ordering relationship to each other, so there are pairs of dots between which no line can be drawn.*

one and class two, whereas the *complex* computations comprise class three and class four. With this in mind, the PCE becomes:

(1) *Almost all complex processes can be viewed as computations of equivalent sophistication.*

The notion that "almost all processes can be viewed as computations" is the basic tenet of universal automatism, that is, *everything is a computation.* Suppose we make that issue a separate battle and not blend it with the PCE. In this case the PCE becomes:

(2) *Almost all complex computations are of equivalent sophistication.*

What might Wolfram mean by saying that two computations are "of equivalent sophistication"? Suppose we take this to mean that the computations can emulate each other or that, using our new terminology, they have the same degree of unsolvability. So now the PCE becomes:

(3) *Almost all complex computations can emulate each other.*

Now certainly Turing's universal computation is class four and thus complex. So, given that a computation that emulates a universal computation is itself universal, the PCE becomes:

(4) *Almost all complex computations are universal.*

But the solution to Post's problem suggests that this is very strongly false. There are many computations that fail to have solvable halting problems and, in addition, are not universal. And these intermediate-degree computations are certainly not class one or class two computations. So it seems that the mathematical logicians have proved:

(Snag) *There are very many complex computations that are not universal.*

The "almost all" in the PCE gives us some wiggle room, but at this point we'd do well to back off even more. Suppose we weaken the range of application of the PCE. Rather than saying it applies to "almost all" complex computations, suppose we say it applies to "most naturally occurring" complex computations. And this gives us an alternate formulation of the PCE.

> • *Alternate Form of Wolfram's Principle of Computational Equivalence (PCE).* Most naturally occurring complex computations are universal.

This statement is probably still too strong.[132] Rather than insisting upon it, we might consider what we really plan to use the PCE *for.* My feeling is that the main use of the PCE is to draw the conclusion that many naturally occurring computations embody unsolvable problems.

So I think what we really need is the following *Natural Unsolvability Hypothesis.*[133]

> • *Natural Unsolvability Hypothesis (NUH).* Most naturally occurring complex computations have unsolvable halting problems relative to some target detector.

Think of a computation as an ongoing process, for example your life, or society, or a plant growing, or the weather. Relative to a given computation, we can formulate the notion of a *target state* as being some special status or behavior that the computation might eventually reach. The *halting problem* in this context is the problem of deciding whether a given input will eventually send your computation into one of the target states. And a halting problem is *unsolvable* if there's no computation, algorithm, or rule of thumb to detect which inputs won't ever produce a target state.

The NUH says that if you have some naturally occurring computation that isn't class one or class two, then there will probably be some simply computable notion of a target state that leads to an unsolvable halting problem.

Getting more symbolic, the NUH says that for most naturally occurring complex computations $P$, there will be a target detector algorithm Is$P$Done such that there is no $P$FailsToHalt with the property that, for every input In,

> $P$FailsToHalt(In) is True $\leftrightarrow$
> $P$(In) never produces a state Out such that Is$P$Done(Out).

Note that the PCE implies the NUH. For if most naturally occurring complex computations are universal, it follows from Turing's Theorem that they also have unsolvable halting problems. Going in the other direction, the NUH does *not* imply the PCE. The NUH claims only that certain computations have unsolvable halting problems, and does *not* claim that these computations are universal. The good thing about the NUH is that, unlike the PCE, the NUH has no difficulties with the many nonuniversal computations that have unsolvable halting problems. The NUH has a better chance of being true and is easier to defend against those who doubt the validity of Wolfram's analysis of computation.

The downside of the NUH is that it's a little hard to understand. Too mathematical. Like, the *regular* Godfather makes you an offer you can't refuse; but the *mathematician* Godfather makes you an offer you can't understand.

Even though I myself did my doctoral thesis work in mathematical logic, I *still* find it a bit hard to think about unsolvable halting problems. It's like there's one too many negations in the definition. So I expect that the notion is especially difficult for the layperson.

A possible concern about the NUH is that perhaps it's so weak a statement that it's trivially true. Recall that our current definition of a computation's being complex is that it be nonterminating, nonrepeating, and nonnested—where "nested" means "having a regularly branching iterative form." But it isn't immediately *obvious* (at least not to me) that any computation that's complex in this sense must have an associated unsolvable halting problem. So the NUH *does* seem to be making an interesting assertion.

What I'd like to do now is to try to make the import of the NUH a bit clearer by giving some examples.

To begin with, I'll give some informal examples where the NUH might apply; then I'll discuss some more rigorous examples. Table 21 lists a variety of real-world computations. In each row, I suggest a computation, a notion of "target state," and a relevant question that has the form of wanting to detect initial states that fail to produce a target state.

Assuming that the NUH applies to these computations with these particular definitions of target state, we're faced with unsolvability, which means that none of the questions in the third column can be answered by finding a simple way to detect which inputs will set off a process that never leads to one of the target states.

Now let's look at three formal examples of complex computations that are likely to have unsolvable halting problems relative to a certain target state detector. The unsolvable problems would be the following:

- It's provably impossible to detect which programs will make your *computer* hang or enter an endless loop.
- Assuming the NUH, it may be impossible to detect which inputs to a *cellular automaton* will generate certain kinds of desired target states, such as having an especially large glider cross the world's central cell.
- Assuming the NUH, it may be impossible to detect which starting configurations will make a *flocking simulation* generate certain kinds of desired target states, such as having all the simulated critters bunched in the center of the virtual world.

| Computation | Target States | Unsolvable halting problem |
|---|---|---|
| The motions of the our solar system | Something rams into Earth | Which possible adjustments to Earth's orbit can make us safe forever? |
| The evolution of our species as we spread from world to world | Extinction | Which possible tweaks to our genetics might allow our race survive indefinitely? |
| The growth and aging of your body | Developing cancer | Which people will never get cancer? |
| Economics and finance | Becoming wealthy | Which people will never get rich? |
| Economics and finance | Going broke | Which people will never go broke? |
| Crime and punishment | Going to jail | Which kinds of careers allow a person to avoid incarceration forever? |
| Writing a book | It's obviously finished | Which projects are doomed from the outset never to be finished? |
| Working to improve one's mental outlook | Serenity, tranquility, peace | When is a person definitely on the wrong path? |
| Finding a mate | Knowing that *this* is the one | Who is doomed never to find true love? |
| Inventing something | *Eureka!* | Which research programs are utterly hopeless? |

**Table 21 Unsolvable Halting Problems in Everyday Life**

*Each row lists a generalized kind of computation, a relevant notion of a target state, and the probably unsolvable question of detecting which inputs lead to a computation that never reaches a targeted state. We can think of the first column as being computations P, the second as representing target state detectors IsPDone, and the third as representing questions that could be solved by computations of the form PFailsToHalt. The import of the NUH is that these kinds of PFailsToHalt computations don't exist.*

Regarding the *computer* example, think of the executable programs that I run on my PC. Certain programs with certain data fall into endless searches that perpetually hog most of the computer's processing power and thereby make the machine unusable. But, with other data, these programs reach a satisfactory target state in which their usage of the machine drops to some very minimal level. It would be nice to detect the bad program-and-data combinations in advance.

In other words, I'm thinking of my PC as a computation MyPC that I initialize with an In state consisting of a program and some data. In symbols I'll call this computation MyPC(In). At any given time $t$, there will be a unique state Out of my PC such that MyPC(In, $t$) = Out. The IsMyPCDone(Out) target detector will, produce, let us say, a True when the test program's current usage of the computer processing power has dropped to less than one percent.

Given the protean nature of a PC, we know that the MyPC computation is universal. Therefore, by Turing's Theorem, it has an unsolvable halting problem, which means that there's no endless search detector MyPCFailsTo-Halt such that MyPCFailsToHalt(In) returns True precisely whenever the program-and-input combination In is a bad apple that'll send my machine into endless thrashing.

In other words, there can never be an automated method for detecting bad programs.

For the *cellular automaton* example, think of the rule known as Brian's Brain (see figure 130). We can speak of a computation Brain such that if In and Out are cell patterns and $t$ is a time span, Brain(In, $t$) = Out means that running $t$ steps of the Brain rule on In produces Out. For the sake of the purity of the argument, we suppose that, as time goes by, we keep adding computational resources so that the CA never has to hit a barrier or wrap around on itself.[134]

**Figure 130: The Brain Halting Problem**

Now let's suppose that our IsBrainDone(Out) target detector is looking for a connected glider of size over one hundred cells that touches one particular cell called the center cell. IsBrainDone(Out) computes the value True if the pattern Out contains such a glider, otherwise IsBrainDone(Out) computes the value False.

Does Brain with this particular IsBrainDone have a solvable halting problem?

In this case, we almost don't need the PCE. With a little effort, I think someone could prove that Brian's Brain is in fact a universal computation and then extend the proof to show that Brain with the indicated IsBrainDone does indeed have an unsolvable halting problem. Lacking such a proof, however, I can fall back on NUH and draw the same conclusion.

So I'm saying there's no endless search detector computation BrainFails ToHalt for Brain with IsBrainDone. That is, there is no BrainFailsToHalt such that if BrainFailsToHalt(In) is True, then Brain(In) will never produce an Out pattern that contains a hundred-cell glider touching the center cell.

Lacking such a BrainFailsToHalt shortcut, all I can do is run the rule step-by-step and watch what happens. If I'm fated never to see that hundred-cell glider, I have no way of knowing when to stop waiting.

Finally, let's look at the *flocking* simulation example (figure 131). Consider a computation Flock such that if In is an input pattern, $t$ is some period of time, and Out is some other pattern, then Flock(In, $t$) = Out means that Flock acting on the pattern In produces the pattern Out at time $t$.

**Figure 131: The Flock Halting Problem**

Suppose that I want to decide which starting patterns will produce an output state where all the boids are bunched up in a small area at the center of the simulation world. In this situation, my IsFlockDone(Out) computation will work by, let us say, summing up the distances of the boids from the center, then entering the state True or False according to whether or not the sum is less than 0.1.

If this particular pair of Flock and IsFlockDone computations have a solvable halting problem, then there is some FlockFailsToHalt computation that will return True if the boids never bunch up.

Certainly Flock isn't a simple computation; the boids fly along very gnarly paths, and the computation is quite evidently class four. If we accept the full PCE, we might boldly speculate that Flock is universal and that you can emulate any computation at all by setting up the boids in a certain way.

If we're a bit more cautious, we might apply the NUH and conclude only that the halting problem in question is unsolvable, meaning that we have no endless search detector FlockFailsToHalt for Flock with IsFlockDone. FlockFailsToHalt would tell me in a finite amount of time if the boids that begin in a starting pattern In will fail to bunch up with the requisite degree of precision.

Lacking an endless search detector, all I can do is run the boid simulation and watch to see if the boids ever do form that tight bunch in the center. And I have no way of knowing how long I should wait. Even if, after a hundred thousand updates, I still haven't seen the boids cluster at the center, I must still wonder if, when I wait a bit longer, maybe they'll fall into formation.

Note that, so far as we know, the NUH could be wrong. There could be some complex computations that *do* have solvable halting problems for every possible target detector. But as one delves into these questions, it begins to seem as if, for just about any class three or class four process we examine, there will indeed be a way to view it as a computation for which there are endless searches, and for which at least one target detector poses an unsolvable halting problem.

As one last illustration of the NUH, consider Wolfram's wonderfully elementary example of a complex computation from arithmetic: powers of three. That is, we look at the sequence that arises if we keep multiplying by three: 1, 3, 27, 81, 243, . . . As you can see from figure 132, what seems to be a class three or class four pattern results.

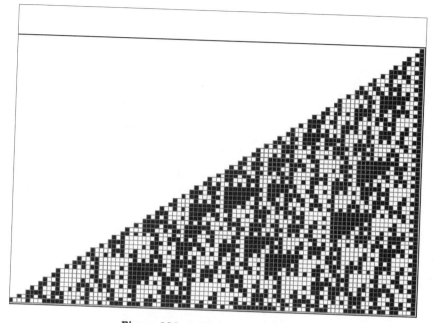

**Figure 132: Arithmetic Is Gnarly**

*Each row of this image represents a successive power of three. The numbers are "written out" in binary, with the black-and-white cells representing, respectively, ones and zeros. Thus the top row is binary 1, the second row is binary 11, which is what we normally call three, the third row is binary 1001, which is what we normally call nine, and so on.*

To me it seems likely that the question of whether an arbitrary bit pattern In will ever be found as part of any row of this complex pattern is unsolvable. Some patterns turn up early and often, and some patterns can be ruled out for number-theoretic reasons. But there could well be a residue of patterns that you can search for only by computing more and more rows—with no way of knowing if you might be computing new rows forever. With a little finesse, this potentially unsolvable problem can be viewed as a halting problem for a powers-of-three computation with a particular target detector.[135] My sense is that there is no computation that can detect every In that will fail to appear in any row of the powers of three.

Once again, the NUH says that every naturally occurring complex computation $P$ will harbor an unsolvable halting problem relative to some everywhere-defined target state detector Is$P$Done. Figure 133 illustrates the NUH.

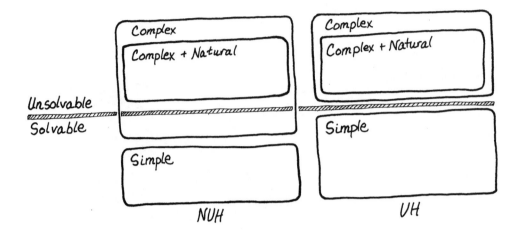

**Figure 133: The NUH and the Unsolvability Hypothesis (UH)**

*In these two diagrams, I use the horizontal gray line to separate the solvable from the unsolvable computations. The diagram on the left is the most general kind of situation one might have in which the NUH is true. The diagram on the left shows the situation if a stronger form of the NUH is true. The NUH says that for any naturally occurring complex computation there will be at least one notion of target state such that there's no way to decide which inputs will cause the computation to produce one of those target states. In the stronger UH form, we assert the unsolvability of all complex computations.*

I'm inclined to think that we may be able to drop the qualifier "naturally occurring" from the NUH and get a stronger Unsovability Hypothesis (UH) as illustrated. I think it's in fact possible that *all* complex computations have associated with them some unsolvable halting problem.

- *Unsolvability Hypothesis(UH).* All complex computations have unsolvable halting problems relative to some target detector.

My reasoning is as follows. We're using complex to mean class three or class four, and simple to mean class one or class two. If $P$ is a simple computation, then for every input In, $P(\text{In})$ reaches a fixed state, enters a periodically repeating loop, or generates a series of nested repetitions. These behaviors are essentially finite, and any questions about them you can pose will have simple answers. Thus, we don't expect simple computations to have unsolvable halting problems. But if $P$ is complex, then it's in some sense essentially infinite. And whenever infinity enters the picture, we expect to find something that escapes finite description.[136]

## 6.3: *Faster and Smarter*

In this section I want to discuss the meaning and the plausibility of the *Principle of Computational Unpredictability (PCU)*. Figure 134 illustrates the content of this principle.

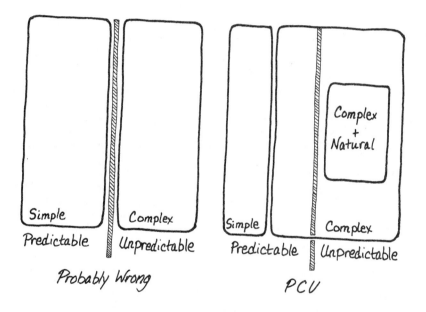

**Figure 134: The PCU**

*In these two diagrams, I use the vertical gray lines to separate the predictable from the unpredictable computations. The diagram on the left shows an incorrect estimate of the relationship between complexity and predictability: We know that some complex computations are in fact predictable (because they run much slower than necessary). The diagram on the right shows the situation that I believe to be true. The PCU says that any naturally occurring complex computation will be unpredictable. Although complex predictable computations exist, the PCU claims that such computations are not found in natural situations.*

- *Principle of Computational Unpredictability (PCU).* Most naturally occurring complex computations are unpredictable.

In order to give a more detailed discussion of the PCU, I need to formulate a more precise definition of unpredictability than I've given before. I'm going to say that *P* is *unpredictable* if there isn't any computation *Q* that emulates *P* and runs *exponentially* faster. When I first discussed this notion in section *1.2: A New Kind of Science,* I finessed the question of speed and simply spoke of a *Q* that runs "drastically faster" than *P.*

So now I'm going to need to explain what I mean by "runs exponentially faster." The study of computational speed makes up a large branch of theoretical computer science. And not without reason—the issue is also of great practical significance.

Thanks to the eternal search for improved computational speed, the job of being a software engineer never gets any easier. Even though the hardware keeps getting faster, people's expectations grow even more rapidly. One year, users are excited about playing a two-dimensional Pac-Man game on their cell phones—but a year later, they expect to see a three-dimensional racing game on the cell phone display, and for the game to be networked so as to allow for multiple players. Further down the line, users may be looking for holograms, for brain-to-brain interfaces, for games that include artificially intelligent simulations of all the personages currently in the day's news—there's no end in sight. Programmers continually search for ways to make their computations run faster.

Let me play the Devil's advocate for a minute. Why *should* programs run faster? What's the big rush? What's the point of making a boring process a hundred times faster than before? It'll just be a hundred times as boring. Do you gain anything by receiving and deleting a thousand spam ads in the same time that it used to take to process ten of them?

And when we turn to naturally occurring computations, speeding them up also seems worse than useless. Suppose I view my life as a computation called MyLife such that MyLife(Birth, 84 years) = Death. Do I really want to double the speed of MyLife to get an "improved" FastMyLife such that FastMyLife(Birth, 42 years) = Death? Physical time flows at its own rate and it's best to accept this. When I start wishing things would happen faster, it means I'm in a state of poor mental health.

But of course I recognize that there are practical situations where it really is useful to find faster computational methods. In this section we'll mainly be talking about situations where you are running a computation Fast that emulates some other computation Slow. If your superduper Fast is swifter than the run-of-the-mill Slow, you may have an opportunity to gain something. I list a few examples of these wished-for scenarios in table 20.

| The world's slow computation | Your *fast* mental shortcut computation | Your gain |
|---|---|---|
| A partner's mood swings | You see what's coming | You mollify your partner before things turn ugly |
| Having a child with someone | A (largely unconscious) assessment of your mutual compatibility | You form a satisfactory family |
| A rabbit's escape path | Foxy instincts about the rabbits' moves | You catch the rabbit |
| Tacklers' rush paths | An experienced running back's expectations | You score a touchdown |
| Ponderous bureaucratic deliberations | Nimble lone-gun decision-making | You outwit the establishment |
| Crowd motions in the checkout lanes | Mentally simulating human behavior | You check out quick |
| Stock market behavior. | Rules of thumb and technical number-crunching | You get rich |
| Carrying out an exhaustive search for the proof of a theorem | Using your deep insight, subconscious illumination, and nonlinear speculations | You're the first to prove the theorem |

**Table 20: Uses of Prediction (Dept. of "You Wish")**

*These are examples of situations where you might hope to use a fast mental computation to emulate some naturally occurring slow computation, thereby gaining something. As we'll be discussing in this section, in most cases the notion of the faster emulation is just a dream and is not actually achievable. The appropriate answer to those who think they can reliably make any of these predictions is: "You wish."*

Now think of a particular computation and suppose that you have a target detector that signals if and when the task has reached a state where you consider it to be done. Examples of how to reach a target state might be: Simulate a certain amount of virtual time in an artificial world, find the solution to an equation, or bring the performance of a system up to some specified standard.

With this in mind, we define the *runtime* of a task as the amount of time it takes until the computation reaches a targeted state. The runtime depends both upon the computation $P$ and upon the particular input In that you feed into it.

In comparing computational speeds, we find it useful to view runtime as a function that maps *input sizes* into times. For a given input size $N$, runtime($N$) is the time that elapses until a targeted state will be found for a typical input of size $N$.

How exactly do we measure the size of an input? In principle, an input might have several sizes associated with it—such as the width and height of a rectangle. But to keep things simple, we try to use a single number to specify an input's size. Examples of input sizes would be the following: the number of symbols in an input string, the cell diameter of an input pattern in a CA grid, the highest exponent used in a set of input equations, the number of creatures placed into a simulation world, or the amount of virtual time to be simulated in such a world. In the last example, the virtual targeted *simulation* time need not match the *computation* time; it might take, for instance, a year of computer time to calculate a second's worth of virtual time in a simulation of a chemical reaction involving millions of particles. It's the *computation* time that we associate with the runtime.

Note that we sometimes have a choice of which input size we view as the variable $N$. If I'm simulating, let us say, cars in traffic, I could view the input size as being either the number of cars that I'm simulating or the amount of virtual time that I want to simulate. In the car example it's actually more useful to think of the number of cars as being the input size $N$. So I might say that when I talk about the speed of a traffic simulation, I'm asking how much computational runtime it takes to simulate, say, one virtual hour of traffic involving $N$ cars.

The speed of a computation is often measured in terms of how rapidly its runtime grows as the input sizes go up, as suggested in figure 135 and table 21.[137]

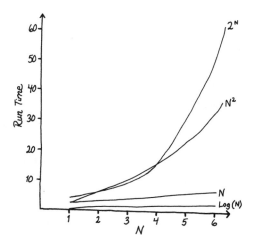

**Figure 135: Growth Rates for Runtime as a Function of Input Size**

*Once N gets large enough, the various runtime functions are ordered as you'd expect.*

| Rough bound on the runtime for inputs of size N | Computational speed | Speed class |
|---|---|---|
| $k \cdot \log(N)$ | Log $N$ time | LOG |
| $k \cdot N$ | Linear time | LIN |
| $k \cdot N^2$ | Quadratic time | $N^2$ |
| $k \cdot N^3$ | Cubic time | $N^3$ |
| Any polynomial p(N) | Polynomial time | P |
| $2^{(p(N))}$ for some polynomial $p$ | Exponential time | EXP |
| $2^{(2^{\wedge}(p(N)))}$ for some polynomial $p$ | Double-exponential time | EEXP |
| No describable bounding function | Runtime unbounded | Unsolvable |

**Table 21: Some Computational Speed Classes**

*These are "rough" bounds in the sense that we don't bother to mention the less important terms of the bounding function. For instance, having an $N^2$ bound really means that there are constants k, b, and c such that for sufficiently large N, the runtime on any input of size N will be less than $k \cdot N^2 + b \cdot N + c$. Also recall that a "polynomial" in N is any algebraic expression you can write as a sum of powers of N multiplied by real-number coefficients.*

Generally, if the runtime is any polynomial function of the input sizes, the computation is viewed as *feasible;* otherwise the computation is *unfeasible.* Thinking again of a traffic simulation, if the simulation requires quadratic time, you can fairly comfortably handle a thousand cars, as it's reasonable to imagine performing a million computational steps for an update. But if the simulation uses exponential time, you can forget about simulating a thousand cars, because $2^{1,000}$ is an insanely big number.

To clarify the ideas, let's discuss the runtime speeds of six specific kinds of computation, arranged in increasing order of difficulty.

- Pencil-and-paper calculation
- Cellular automata
- Simulated flocking
- Tuning a neural network
- Playing a board game like Go
- Performing universal computation

We begin by analyzing the runtime involved in *pencil-and-paper calculation.* As I mentioned in section *1.3: Reckoning a Sum,* it takes about a dozen steps to reckon the sum:

$$275$$
$$+\ 484$$

How we characterize the speed of this computation depends on how we choose to describe the size $N$ of the inputs.

If, on the one hand, I characterize the input size of the problem $(275 + 484)$ as being the maximum number of digits in the numbers, then the input size would be $N = 3$. And in this case, addition with arithmetic is a linear time computation, whereas counting by one takes exponential time relative to $N$.

If, on the other hand, I view the input size of the problem $(275 + 484)$ as being the size of the largest number involved, then the size would be $N = 484$. In this case, performing the addition by using arithmetic is what's called a logarithmic time computation, whereas counting by ones uses linear time relative to $N$.[138]

This distinction points out the importance of what we might call the "pre-processing" or "translation" stage in which an input is put into a format acceptable for a computation you're testing. When we compare the run speeds of totally different kinds of computations, we need to take into account the runtime of any input translation computation that you use in preparing an input to Slow for use by an emulating computation Fast.

Now let's look at the runtime involved in producing the rows of a one-dimensional *cellular automaton.* In particular, suppose I seed a one-dimensional CA like Rule 45 with a pattern that is $R$ cells across, and that I want to know what the $N$th row will look like. Let's make two assumptions here. First, we reduce our work by assuming that updating a line of identical cells is a trivial operation, so that I only need to compute the new values of cells that have an actively changing cell in their neighborhood. Second, we increase our work by assuming that there's no limit to the width of our CA world. As illustrated in figure 136, the update zone spreads out to either side of the seed zone. Computing row $N$ of a start pattern that's $R$ cells wide takes a time on the order of $R{\cdot}N + N^2$. Given that R is fixed for any particular computation, as we let $N$ get larger, the size of $N^2$ eventually swamps the size of $R{\cdot}N$, so we simply call this a quadratic time computation. That is, computing the future of a finite pattern in a one-dimensional CA is quadratic in the number of rows to be computed. A similar analysis shows that computing the future of a finite seed pattern in a two-dimensional CA world is *cubic* in the number of updates requested.[139]

As the next example of runtime, consider simulating the *flocking behavior* of $N$ boids for some fixed number of updates. At each update, we need for each boid to consider its distance from every other boid. Each of the $N$ boids needs to know its distance from all of the other $N$ boids, which makes for $N{\cdot}N$ or $N^2$ distance pairs to consider. So we say that running a boid simulation has quadratic time relative to the number of boids.[140]

If we generalize a boid simulation to simulating the interactions of the members of a society of $N$ members, it's easy to imagine models in which we need to look at people's interactions with other pairs of people—as when a person might, let us say, tell person $A$ something about person $B$ depending on the relationship between $A$ and $B$. In this case, the simulation would

**Figure 136:**
**A One-Dimensional CA's Runtime Varies with Number of Rows Squared**

*This picture shows one-dimensional CA Rule 45, seeded with a ten-cell pattern in the first row and updated through the fortieth row. Rule 45 is one of my favorites because its white cells make cute animal cracker shapes like elephants and giraffes. The rule has the slightly nasty property that a 000 neighborhood updates to 111 and vice versa, leading to alternating stripes in the blank zones. But those stripes can be filled in with essentially no computational overhead. I've drawn lines to mark out the zones of real computation; two triangles and a central rectangle. (I'll ignore the fact that the rule grows more slowly on the left so that, strictly speaking, I wouldn't have needed to do a full update computation for all the cells in the left triangle.) If we write R for the width of the seed pattern and N for the number of rows, the rectangle holds N·R cells and each triangle holds (N·N)/2 cells.*

become cubic time. And modeling still more complicated social interactions could push the time up to higher and higher powers of $N$.

Now consider the runtime involved in trying to *tune a neural network*. We want to adjust the connection weight values for a neural network with $N$ links between the neurons. The input is the untuned network, and the target state condition is that the network should, let us say, recognize a hundred different faces with an accuracy of some predetermined amount.

If I were to randomly test out weight values, I'd be embarking on an exponential time computation. But if I instead use the back-propagation method described earlier, it seems likely that the computation will usually converge to good weight values in polynomial time.

Note, however, that the back-propagation method only works for certain types of neural networks and for certain types of target state detectors. If a system is chaotically sensitive to small changes in the connection weights, tuning the network may turn out to be an exponential time problem after all.[141]

As our next example of computational runtime, consider *the board game Go* (see figure 137). As you may know, Go is a game played on a square grid that we can view as a matrix of $N \times N$ cells. Players alternate turns of marking a grid cell with a white or a black stone. The goal is to surround regions of open cells and to surround groups of your opponent's stones—if you successfully cut some stones off from access to open cells you capture them. The standard Go boards use $N = 19$, but the game is essentially the same—although more complex—for any $N$. Now suppose that In is a given position of black and white stones on an $N$ by $N$ Go board. The computation of deciding whether black or white wins is likely to require exponential time in $N$. The reason is that Go is sufficiently complex that in order to figure out how a game might evolve, you have to look at essentially all of the possible board positions, given that any cell can be in any of three states (blank, white, or black) and that there are $N \cdot N$ cells; this makes for $3^{(N \cdot N)}$ possibilities—which can also be written as $2^{(k \cdot N \cdot N)}$ for a proper choice of $k$.

As it turns out, we don't have to go to the mysterious East to find board games that are likely to be exponentially hard. If you generalize our familiar game of checkers to an $N$ by $N$ board, you also get a game such that, in all likelihood, it takes exponential time to decide if a given position is a win for red or for black.[142]

As our final example of runtime, consider a *universal computer U,* and suppose that $U$ has a special target state called Halt. If I feed $U$ an input In, the computation $U$(In) results. Rather than defining runtime as a function of input size $N$ as in the other examples, it's going to be useful here to think of runtime as a function of input states In.

We'll define $U$'s runtime function runtime(In) as follows. If the computation $U$(In) ever enters the Halt state, then we let runtime(In) be the computation time that it took to reach the Halt state. And in the cases where the computation $U$(In) never produces the Halt state, we view runtime(In) as undefined.

**Figure 137: My Son Beating Me at Go**

*Rudy Jr. has been able to beat me at every known board game since he was five. Computing if I will win from a given board position is easy: the answer's always No. But computing whether someone else in my position could possibly win is probably exponential in the size of the board.*

Can we bound runtime(In) by some function expressed in terms of the size *N* of the input? Suppose *L* is a simple, everywhere-defined computation mapping integers into integers.

- *Definition.* The function L *bounds* U *'s runtime function* means that whenever In is an input of size *N* and runtime(In) is defined, then runtime(In) < *L(N)*.
- If there is an everywhere defined *L* that bounds *U*'s runtime function, we say that *U is runtime bounded.*
- Otherwise, we say *U is runtime unbounded.*

As it turns out, logicians have proved a lemma to the effect that *any* computation with an unsolvable halting problem is runtime unbounded. (Mathematicians call a small, useful result a "lemma" because in Greek the word means "I help." The proof of the Unboundedness Lemma can be found in the *Technical Appendix.*)

- *Unboundedness Lemma.* Any computation with an unsolvable halting problem is runtime unbounded.

Recall from Turing's Theorem that every universal computation has an unsolvable halting problem. So the Unboundedness Lemma also tells us that *every universal computation is runtime unbounded.*

The Unboundedness Lemma is a powerful result. Suppose $L(N)$ is any mathematical function that's defined on all the integers—examples might be $N^2$, $N^{100}$, $10^N$, $10^{(10^\wedge N)}$, and so on. If $P$ is a computation with an unsolvable halting problem, then the Unboundedness Lemma tells us that $L$ must fail to bound $P$'s runtime. This means that there are going to be infinitely many inputs In with for which $P(\text{In})$ does in fact reach a targeted halting state, but not before more than $L(N)$ steps have elapsed—with $N$ as usual being the size of In. The point is that when you start up $P(\text{In})$, you have absolutely no way of knowing how long you may need to wait for the computation to halt.

Since the lemma holds for *any* computation with an unsolvable halting problem relative to some target detector—and not just for universal computations—we can combine it with the NUH to get the following:

- *Corollary to the NUH.* Most naturally occurring complex computations are runtime unbounded relative to some target detector algorithms.

This corollary tells us that there is no way to estimate how long you'll need to wait when you're waiting for a naturally occurring system to do something special—in the sense of producing a targeted output state. "Am I doing the right things to write a best seller?" "Wait and see."

So now we've learned a few things about computational runtime. Recall that I got onto this topic because I wanted to delve into the notion of unpredictability that we used in the Principle of Computational Unpredictability: *Most naturally occurring complex computations are unpredictable.*

- *Definition.* A computation is *predictable* if there is another computation that emulates it and is exponentially faster. Otherwise it's *unpredictable.*

In order to make the definition clear, I need to say a bit about what I mean by *emulation* and by *exponentially faster.* For purposes of this discussion, let's use the names Slow and Fast for the two computations. And to simplify things, let's assume that Fast and Slow use the same kinds of inputs and that they both share the same notion of a target state. In this simplified situation,

- *Fast emulates Slow* means that for any input state In and any target state Out, Slow(In) produces Out if and only if Fast(In) produces Out as well.

Suppose that we indeed have a situation where Fast emulates Slow. And suppose that Slow(In) and Fast(In) both produce the target state Out. In this case we let *slowtime* be the time that Slow(In) takes to reach Out; and we let *fasttime* be the time that Fast(In) takes to reach Out.

- *Fast is faster than Slow* means that fasttime < slowtime whenever fasttime and slowtime are as just described. And if we can always assert that $10^{fasttime}$ < slowtime, we say that *Fast is exponentionally faster than Slow.*[143]

I illustrate the notion of faster computation in figure 138.

In searching for a definition of unpredictability, my first instinct was to look at those computations $P$ that run at *maximal speed* in the sense that no $Q$ that emulates $P$ is faster than $P$. That is, $P$ operates at maximal speed if no other computation can do the same things as $P$, faster than $P$. But it turns out that this notion seems not to apply to many of the computations we are studying—in particular, *no computations performed by PCs are of maximal speed.*

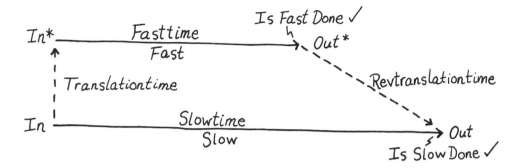

**Figure 138: Faster Computation**

*The Fast computation can do in fasttime what the Slow computation does in slowtime. In this figure I've depicted the more general case in which the two computations might possibly use different sets of states. For this reason, I've included two translation functions, indicating that In is translated into In\*, and Out\* is reverse translated into Out. To fairly compare the relative speed of two functions, we take the translation overhead into account. So what we'd really want for our "Fast is faster than Slow" condition is translationtime + fasttime + revtranslationtime < slowtime. In honest comparisons where you aren't trying to sneak a lot of computation into the translation steps, the translation times are linear functions of the sizes of the states being translated.*

Why not?

The problem is that any PC computation can be sped up by a linear factor. This can be done by improving your hardware in two different ways.

- Using a *faster processor.*
- Adding memory so as to be able to use larger *lookup tables.*

Regarding *faster processors*—that's what Moore's Law is all about. Any PC computation can be made faster by running it on a newer, faster machine.

The notion of *lookup tables* is subtler. Let's return once again to the example of using arithmetic to do an addition. How is it that you write 5 + 4 = 9 in a single computational step? Why don't you need to count on your fingers? It's because you learned the simple sums by heart in elementary school. You learned a lookup table.

Any digital computation can be sped up with lookup tables. Imagine a case where you want a computation that can return the value of some gnarly mathematical function $f$ for all the values of $i$ between one and one million. One way to do it would be to code up an algorithm for $f$ and turn it into a computation Slow such that given input $i$, the computation Slow($i$) applies the algorithm to $i$ and halts when it's crunched out an answer. But what I could do instead would be to precompute all of the values $f(1)$, $f(2)$, . . ., $f(1,000,000)$ and store all these numbers in a multimegabyte lookup table called, let us say, TableMillion. And now I can create a computation FastMillion which has TableMillion built right into its code. FastMillion calculates $f(i)$ in just a few steps: look up the value of $f(i)$ in TableMillion and halt! FastMillion will be faster than Slow, at least for inputs up to one million.

As a sidelight, note that, thinking in terms of how much space the source code might occupy on your hard drive, FastMillion is going to be a *larger* program than Slow, for the data in that big TableMillion lookup table is going to be part of FastMillion's code.

Is FastMillion maximally fast? Well, no, for FastMillion only has that lookup table for the first million possible inputs. If I plan to evaluate $f(i)$ for $i$ ranging up to a billion, then I could make a still faster computation FastBillion that uses a billion-row TableBillion.

At first it might seem that once I go out to $i$ values above a billion, the computations Slow, FastMillion, and FastBillion would all be on an equal footing. But, with their characteristic cunning, programmers can find ways to create lookup tables that will be useful all the way down the line—akin to the way that your times table for the numbers zero to nine helps you in multiplying arbitrarily large numbers. If the lookup tables are cleverly designed, FastMillion can be faster than Slow for *all* inputs $i$.[144]

As an elementary example of using a lookup table to make a program run faster for every input, let's consider a one-dimensional CA like the Rule 45 that I illustrated in the last section.

Suppose that, rather than updating the cells one at a time, I choose to update blocks of, say, six cells at once. Because each cell needs to see its left and right neighbors, in order to update a given block of six cells, I actually need to look at eight cells: my stretch of six cells plus one more cell on the left and one more on the right. So, in order to be able to update six cells at once, I construct a lookup table with two columns: the 256 possible eight-cell blocks are listed in the left column, and the properly updated version of the corresponding central six cells is listed in the right column.

And now I can update a row of, say, twenty-four cells by grabbing off four overlapping eight-cell neighborhoods as shown in figure 139. Twenty-four single-cell update steps are replaced by four six-cell update steps. The net effect is a linear speedup.

Although the notion of using a lookup table sounds like a software issue, it's really a matter of hardware. Whether or not a PC can use a large lookup table comes down to how much rapidly accessible memory the machine has. As John Walker used to say, "If you've got the memory, baby, I've got the time."[145]

Summing up, any known PC computation can be run faster by using two kinds of hardware improvements: faster processors and more memory. Note, however, that although the souped-up machine will be faster than the old machine, it won't be *exponentially* faster. We'll have fasttime < slowtime, but fasttime isn't going to be so tiny that $10^{\text{fasttime}}$ < slowtime. [Or, putting it in terms a mathematician would be more likely to use, we won't have fasttime < log(slowtime).]

Given that so many computations will in fact allow for a linear speedup but not for an exponential speedup, I choose to define *unpredictable* as being a weak-enough concept to apply to these kinds of computations.

- *Definition. P is unpredictable* if and only if there is no *Q* that emulates *P* and is exponentially faster than *P*. Otherwise *P* is *predictable*.

And I use *strongly unpredictable* to characterize those computations that don't allow for any kind of speedup at all.

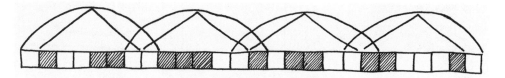

**Figure 139: Updating a One-Dimensional CA in Chunks**

*Assume the cells at the extreme ends stay fixed in the blank state. The picture shows how to update the inner cells in four chunks. You look at the cells under a curved arch to update the cells under the corresponding pointed arch.*

- *Definition. P is strongly unpredictable if and only if there is no Q
that emulates P and is faster than P.*

Note that none of the computations performed by your desktop computer is *strongly unpredictable,* for, as we just discussed, they all allow for linear speedups. But it may be that in the natural world some strongly unpredictable computations can be found. figure 140 illustrates the fact that being unpredictable is a weaker notion than being strongly unpredictable.

As I discuss in the Technical Appendix, we're not really interested in trying to make the predictable-unpredictable distinction for simple computations—for these computations all exhibit unsurprising behavior that can easily be described in advance. The predictable-unpredictable distinction is primarily of interest only for complex computations.

Here are two quick examples where a version of a slow computation is predictable by an exponentially faster version.

- *Computing the Nth power of 3, that is,* $P(N) = 3^N$. The slow way
is to start with a single tally mark on a piece of scratch paper

**Figure 140: Predictability, Unpredictability, and Strong Unpredictability**

*The predictable computations allow for exponential speedups and the unpredictable ones don't. Within the unpredictable computations, the strongly unpredictable ones don't allow for any speedup at all.*

and manually triple the number of marks on the paper $N$ times. It's exponentially faster to compute $P(N)$ by using arithmetic and positional digit notation. So the slow computation is predictable. Knowing how to do the fast computation involves knowing about arithmetic.

- *Computing the location P( N) of an idealized frictionless moving body after N seconds.* The slow way is to carry out a simulation consisting of a long chain of tiny time steps. It's exponentially faster to compute $P(N)$ by using an algebraic formula. So the slow computation is predictable. Knowing how to do the fast computation involves knowing calculus and Newton's laws to get the formula, and knowing algebra and arithmetic to apply the formula.

Note that in both of these examples, a computation is predicted by another computation that's based on more advanced modes of thought. As I mentioned above, our ability to achieve linear speedups with improved hardware implies that PC programs aren't *strongly* unpredictable. But, setting aside any doubts about the PCU, we expect that the complex computer programs in daily use are unpredictable in the weaker sense of not allowing for an exponential speedup.[146] After all, programs are improved to have a good level of speed before being marketed.

And I'm inclined to agree with the PCU's claim that most naturally occurring computations are unpredictable—in the sense that they can't be collapsed by an exponentially faster emulation. But there is a slight, nagging possibility that some future conceptual advance might render many of our computations predictable after all. I'll return to this point later.

I have a sense that my new terms *predictable, unpredictable,* and *strongly unpredictable* may still feel a bit slippery for some readers, so let me review their definitions one more time.

- *Predictable.* A computation is predictable if there's a way to speed it up exponentially.
- *Unpredictable.* A computation is unpredictable if there's no way to speed it up exponentially.

• *Strongly unpredictable.* A computation is strongly unpredictable if there's no way to speed it up at all, not even by a linear factor.

And now let's look at how these concepts apply to computations drawn from the four higher levels of reality: physics, biology, the mind, and society.

*Physics.* Physics is famous for laying down concise laws describing the behavior of nature. So we might expect most physical processes to be predictable. In point of fact, this isn't true.

A classic example of a physics prediction is the orbital motions of objects under the influence of one another's gravitational fields. Predictable? Well, no. As I mentioned in section *2.3: Chaos in a Bouncing Ball,* if more than two bodies are involved, we are faced with an essentially chaotic three-body problem. Yes, we can make exponentially fast algebraic predictions for quite a long period of time, but eventually the multiple interactions of the bodies throw off any formulaic laws—and we're thrown back upon step-by-step emulation as the possible means of prediction; and this breaks the exponential speedup. The emulation of a large number of orbital years will require a computation time that's some linear function of the number of years, and that's as good as you can do. Therefore many-body orbital computation is unpredictable. Is the computation *strongly* unpredictable as well? At first glance, it seems like we ought to be able to run a step-by-step emulation very fast and thus get a linear speedup, destroying strong unpredictability. But I don't think this is actually the case. The problem? No emulation is perfect.

My sense is that most complex physical processes *are* strongly unpredictable in the sense that they represent computations that can't be run any faster at all. Think of surf hitting a rock and shooting a plume into the air. Those incredibly intricate little bumps and wiggles in the foam—no way will anyone ever be able to produce a detailed, accurate, long-term emulation of a wave by any means short of making a physical copy of the wave.

When Gaia gets gnarly, there's no improving on her speed. Pour milk in your coffee, build a fire, watch a cloud, notice the air's motions when made visible by smoke or fog—these are strongly unpredictable computations one and all.

At the level of basic physics we have no power to speed up the hardware.

If a leaf trembles in the breeze, there's no way to make the fluttering go faster than its natural rate. If you increase the velocity of the wind, you'll be looking at an essentially different computation, for at different wind speeds, the leaf's behavior inhabits differently shaped chaotic attractors.

Yes, if I had a *movie* of the fluttering leaf, I could play the movie at double speed—but that doesn't seem to be something we can do with events that aren't yet in the past. Speaking science fictionally, it's fun to imagine a speedup ray that makes processes run faster. And maybe a slowdown ray to do the opposite. But in reality, I don't see this happening. The fluttering leaf is strongly unpredictable; if you want to find out what it'll do next, all you can do is watch and wait.

But—couldn't an exceedingly powerful PC simulate the leaf motions faster than they happen? Well, here we run into the problem of sensitive dependence upon initial conditions—such as the leaf's geometry and the air current's precise velocity. Given the rate at which chaotic computations diverge, and given the expected computational richness of chaotic motion, it's highly unlikely that we could simulate a fluttering leaf with enough accuracy to match the real leaf for more than a fraction of a second.

The problem is partly that physical systems seem analog rather than digital. The impossibility of getting a precise digitized measurement of a physical state not only frustrates our ability to emulate physics on a souped-up PC; it also blocks our ability to "hash" physical states into code numbers to be used as indices into lookup tables.

But what if physics *were* fundamentally a digital computation, perhaps like a giant CA, or perhaps something a bit more like a theorem-proving machine. A digital physics is logically possible—indeed, there's some movement in this direction not only among hard-core universal automatists but also on the part of physicists.

A digital physics admits the logical possibility of getting a precise digital copy of the wave or the windblown leaf, and of using a faster processor and a big lookup table to make a physical computation run faster than it does in the real world.

The problem here is: What kind of hardware runs my high-speed reality emulation? An alternate universe? Or perhaps there's a Cosmic Fry's Electronics that sells upgraded versions of our standard-issue reality engine?

Well, never mind about how the reality upgrade is to be accomplished. Let's just suppose that it's possible. Then what? Well, then physics is no longer strongly unpredictable. But—and this is a key point—it would still be unpredictable.

Why? Because, insofar as we believe in the Principle of Computational Unpredictability, there are no *exponentially* fast shortcuts for predicting the outcome of a naturally occurring complex computation.[147]

*Biology.* Let's focus on the issue of morphogenesis, that is, let's think about how an egg or a seed grows into an animal or a plant. To be quite definite, let's think about a fertilized human ovum that grows through the fetal stages to become a baby. Would it be possible to predict the baby's appearance?

Certainly we have some limited types of prediction tests regarding, for instance, the baby's sex and lack of birth defects. But what about predicting the pattern of pores on the baby's nose, the locations and curls of the baby's individual hairs, or the detailed network connections of the baby's brain? Even identical twins are different, if you take a magnifying glass to them.

As I discussed in section *3.2: The Morphogenesis of a Brindle Cow,* the processes that grow a baby are complex parallel computations unlikely to allow for an exponential speedup. So fetal growth is in this sense unpredictable.

Is the growth of an organism *strongly* unpredictable? In my *Ware* novels, I play with the science-fictional notions of rapidly tank-growing a clone of a person's adult body, and of somehow copying the same person's "software" onto the fresh tank-grown clone. The result: a new person who looks, thinks, and acts just like the original person.[148]

But just because I can imagine a linear speedup of fetal growth, that doesn't mean it's really possible. The problem is that the growth of an organism is a physical process and most complex physical processes are likely to be strongly unpredictable.

If cell differentiation is driven by a CA-like reaction-diffusion rule, for instance, the rule is going to be highly sensitive to how rapidly the relevant morphogen molecules diffuse past the cells' membranes and through the amniotic fluid. And when we're talking about something like molecular diffusion rates, we're talking about basic physical processes that tend to be definitely pegged to their own particular rates of change.

In other words, if you tried to speed-grow a fetus, you'd be likely to end up with something that looked more like a stork or a cabbage leaf than like a baby.

So my guess is that biological processes are not only unpredictable but strongly unpredictable. The only way they could allow for linear speedups would be if, once again, we could find some kind of reality upgrade to make the underlying physics go faster.

One cautionary note. Everything dies, so there's a sense in which all biological processes are simple class one computations. For most inputs In and most times $t$, an organism's output state $P(\text{In}, t)$ is "Sorry, I'm dead now." Bummer.

I guess we need to say that we're only comparing the computational run speeds of events that occur before an organism's demise. Putting it differently, I'm analyzing the computational power of idealized biological systems that could in principle live for an indefinitely long time.

*The mind.* Due to the computational complexity of our brains' neural networks, it seems clear that our mental processes are unpredictable. Indeed, given that your thoughts emerge from physically based biological processes, your stream of consciousness is in all likelihood *strongly* unpredictable.

We sometimes have the illusion of speeding up our mental computations for short periods of time by chemical means. This is the appeal of the stimulants, ranging from caffeine to crack cocaine to conotoxins (the hallucinogenic venom of the CA-decorated cone shell snail). As mankind's biotechnological skills advance, various other kinds of brain speedups may emerge, perhaps electrical as well as chemical. But it's not clear if any of these speedups can produce an accelerated emulation of what the brain would actually have been doing had it been left alone. So in that sense, the brain's normal behavior isn't being successfully predicted. As a practical matter, artificially induced brain speedup is often accompanied by a decreased ability to focus on a specific task. Our painstakingly evolved neurons aren't meant to be supercharged.

Much more to the point is the manner in which education and life experience teach us to draw conclusions faster. To some extent this is a matter of learning to group similar situations, to map an ensemble of situations to a single compact abstraction, and to use the abstraction as a bookmark that selects a response from a neural lookup table. As we grow older, our lookup tables grow and our responses become linearly faster and more stereotyped. The speed increase is the good news; the bad news is the loss of flexibility. "Eh?"

Even more dramatic than the accumulation of experience are the quite rare occasions when we attain an insight that sheds light upon large areas of our mental experience. These dramatic cases represent exponential rather than linear speedups.

If I say that exponential mental speedups occur, does this mean that the flow of thought is predictable after all? No. I have two reasons for saying that the occasional exponential speedup doesn't render the stream of thought predictable.

The *first* has to do with self-reference. Your mind is in fact the only "hardware" with enough information to try to run a computation that predicts the actions of your mind. And your thoughts are what we might call self-modifying code. You reach some partial kind of enlightenment, your mental landscape changes, you begin thinking faster. But this new, faster thought mode is once again unpredictable by you. It's like you can never manage to stand upon your own shoulders.

The *second* reason why I don't think the possibility of enlightenment makes my mind predictable is that my mental life is so multifarious. Speeding up one level doesn't mean speeding up all levels. Even if I become able to understand certain special kinds of situations in an exponentially faster way, this doesn't imply that I will ever be able to emulate, say, my emotional states and my fleeting fancies any faster than they arise.

Sometimes, when bored and unhappy, I begin to feel that my brain states are in fact predictable. "Same old, same old." I see the same faces and think the same dull thoughts. But, if I can muster enough alertness, I see that the details of my thoughts are a bit different each day.

The clouds in the sky are never precisely the same, and my thoughts don't precisely repeat either. Even when—at a coarse scale—I feel my homeostatic processes to be locked into a class two repetition, the details are truly class four.

Becoming aware of this is, I would say, a source of liberation. See the gnarl!

As in the biological case, I could say that because I'm going to die, my whole lifetime's stream of consciousness could be collapsed into a single very large lookup table containing my state of mind for each moment of my life—assuming that mental states could somehow be finitely recorded. Does this mean that my thoughts were predictable after all?

Certainly that's not my *intended* meaning of predictability. After all, that giant lookup table did require a big computational investment. My simple formalized definition of predictability doesn't fully capture this subtlety. Possibly future writers on these topics will find a better and more intricate formulation of predictability. I am, after all, only an *early* geek philosopher.

An alternate way to avoid the trap of finitude is to say that an analysis of my mind's predictability should be carried out as if I were to live forever. This isn't as unrealistic as it sounds. Suppose that my mind Ru could in fact be represented by an neural-net-equipped digital lifebox model RuLifebox. Being pure software, RuLifebox is then immortal, in that there's no upper bound to how long a time it can be run. So then it's not a simple or predictable computation.

*Society.* Most of the things I said about an individual mind hold for a society's hive mind. And the mortality issue that plagues biological and mental computations is perhaps not so applicable to a society because, at least in principle, it seems a society need never die. Societies evolve into other societies rather than dying. Barring a huge extinction catastrophe, our history could go on forever—with humanity leaving Earth for the stars, and perhaps even making it past whatever cosmic cataclysms our universe as a whole may be in for.

In the discussion of the mind, I mentioned that certain kinds of insight can in fact make a mind run exponentially faster. Relative to the hive mind, I'd say that exponential speedups have arisen at several of the stages in the human history of technology.

The development of a common language, for instance, allows all the members of a society to think faster. The speedup seems more than merely linear, as entirely new kinds of cooperation become possible. And the introduction of writing, of the printing press, of telephones, and of the Web—each of these has brought about a large and possibly exponential speedup in the computation rate of the hive mind as well. My sense is that the introduction of language and the successive communication enhancements have sped up the hive mind's activities to the same degree that using numbers speeds up the process of arithmetic.

How about the predictability of some specific social computations? The classic example would be the daily Dow stock market index. Think of "Dow" as an ongoing computation that spits out a specific number every day. Given the intense effort and utter lack of success on the part of technical market analysts, it seems that Dow is strongly unpredictable and cannot be sped up by even a few minutes.

As a side issue, the Dow computation is also *unsolvable* in the sense that there will be no way to compute correct answers to target-detecting questions of the type "Will such and such a pattern of ups and downs ever occur?" We might also wonder if Dow is *universal,* although it's far from obvious how one might actually use it to emulate other kinds of computations.

In the preceding discussion—and, for that matter, throughout this book— I've repeatedly insisted that naturally occurring complex processes are unpredictable. This is, once again, not a provable fact, but an hypothesis.

- *Principle of Computational Unpredictability (PCU).* Most naturally occurring complex computations are unpredictable.

Note that the PCU asserts that only *naturally occurring* computations won't be predictable. The only support for the PCU is empirical, that is, the PCU seems to be true for all the naturally occurring complex computations that Wolfram and others have looked at. But, once again, the PCU remains only a conjecture.

The restriction to naturally occurring computations is important for, as I'll now explain, there *are* artificially slowed-down complex computations that allow for exponential speedups.

Given any PC computation $P$, we can think of a slow, predictable computation Dumb$P$ that does the same thing as $P$. The idea is to have Dumb$P$ waste a lot of time. One way to do this is to have Dumb$P$ have a region of "scratch paper" memory that starts out with one mark in it. Dumb$P$ acts just like $P$, except that, after each step of $P$ that it emulates, Dumb$P$ goes off to the side and wastes time by doubling the number of marks in the scratch paper memory. If $P$ takes n steps to do something, then Dumb$P$ will take on the order of $2^n$ steps—thanks to all that doubling. This means that $P$ runs exponentially faster than Dumb$P$. So Dumb$P$ is predictable.

Note that Dumb$P$ has some bogus time-wasting code in its program. So we might suppose that if a program $P$ has minimal length, then $P$ is likely to be unpredictable. Certainly there are many programs of minimal length. But as we saw in our discussion of lookup tables, it's often the case that longer programs will run faster than smaller programs.

Human intellectual history teaches us that there can be speedup methods much subtler than eliminating waste or using lookup tables. Think once again of the invention of language and writing, of positional notation and arithmetic, of calculus and Newton's laws. Truly epochal advances bring exponential speedups in their wake.

The PCU is very much a case-by-case empirical hypothesis, and, given any complex computation, we're haunted by the faint possibility that there might be a subtler or more intricate computation that is in fact exponentially faster.[149]

Now I'll sum up sections *6.2: The Computational Zoo* and the present section 6.3 *Faster and Smarter* with a map that shows what I believe to be the layout of the computational zoo (see figure 141). Keep in mind that the Natural Unsolvability Hypothesis says that naturally occurring complex computations are *unsolvable,* whereas the Principle of Computational Equivalence says that naturally occurring complex computations are *unpredictable.* These principles are logically independent, so in my map the principles make distinctions along perpendicular axes.

The diagram reflects my opinion that the NUH and the PCU are true for naturally occurring complex computations—such as complex personal computer applications, the dynamics of physical systems, the growth of organisms, the processes of the human mind, and the workings of human society.

The most interesting part of my map is the "downtown" region that I labeled "Naturally Occurring." In figure 142, I zoom in to map the downtown region of the computational zoo, indicating some of the landmark computations we've discussed.

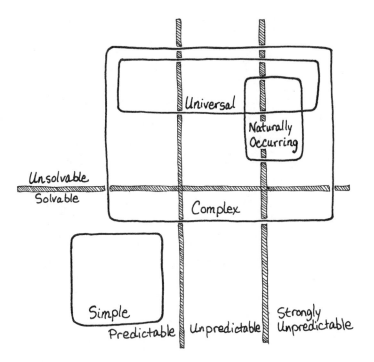

**Figure 141: My Map of the Computational Zoo**

*The horizontal line separates the solvable from the unsolvable computations, as suggested by the Natural Unsolvability Hypothesis (NUH). The first vertical line separates the predictable from the unpredictable computations, as suggested by the Principle of Computational Unpredictability (PCU). The second vertical line separates the unpredictable from the strongly unpredictable computations.*

In figure 142, I have the PC computations (which really include the digital CAs) on the left, as these all allow for linear speedups. CA Rule 110 is known to be universal; and it's my conjecture that Rule 30 will prove to have some unsolvable halting problems but fail to be fully universal. I regard most of the more naturalistic computations as being both universal and strongly unpredictable, which means, once again, that they can emulate any possible computation and that they don't allow for any kind of speedup at all. These include, from top to bottom, the flow of a society's *culture,* an individual person's stream of thought, the development of a plant or animal from a seed or *fetus,* the turbulent flow of any fluid such as the water in *surf* or the air we breathe, the historical sequences generated by a society's *politics,* and our friend the *fluttering leaf.* It may be that I'm overoptimistic and that some of these computations aren't actually universal, but I would still expect all of them to embody some kind of unsolvable halting problem. One example of a nonuniversal naturally occurring computation might be the Dow index of the *stock market*—simply because it may be too lacking in fine structure to be universal.

One final, rebellious thought. It would be very interesting if the PCU were totally wrong. I'm thinking of a situation where some beings vastly more intelligent than us come up with higher-order concepts to produce gargantuan computations that can run exponentially faster than all the computations around us. These godlike yet finite minds would be capable of scanning

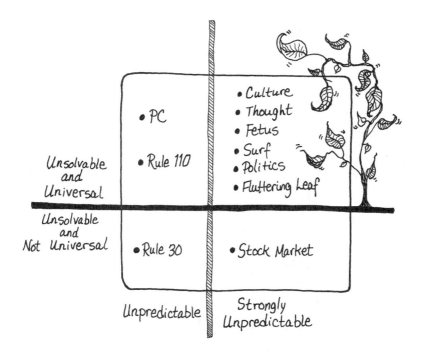

**Figure 142: Naturally Occurring Computations**

*The vertical line separates unpredictability from strong unpredictability, and the horizontal line separates universality from mere unsolvability. The computations on the left can be sped up by a linear factor, and those on the right can't be sped up at all. The computations on the top are universal (and thus unsolvable as well), whereas the computations on the bottom are unsolvable but not universal.*

today's Earth and in a matter of seconds correctly predicting every single detail of the twenty-four hours to come: your dreams tonight, the finest vortices in the water flowing down your shower drain tomorrow morning, the entire contents of tomorrow's evening news.

In the tome you hold, I've laboriously assembled arguments why such beings can't exist. But, hey, maybe I'm wrong.

If you look at the intellectual history of the human race, you'll notice that there aren't really all *that* many new ideas we've come up with. A lot of what scientists and artists occupy themselves with is putting old wine in new bottles. Maybe there's a whole level of thought that simply hasn't occurred to us yet—a breakthrough as radical as calculus, as radical as positional arithmetic notation, as radical as language.

But we do know this: Any deterministic processes capable of speeding up our complex naturally occurring computations would be unlike anything we've ever seen.[150]

## 6.4: *Random Truth*

The philosopher Gottfried Wilhelm Leibniz is perhaps best known for the fierce controversy that arose between him and Sir Isaac Newton over the invention of calculus. The *S*-like integral sign that we use to this day in expressions like $\int f(x)\ dx$ is in fact a notation invented by Leibniz.

When Leibniz was a youth of nineteen, he wrote a paper called "De Arte Combinatorica," in which he tried to formulate a universal algebra for reasoning, in the hope that human thought might some day be reducible to mathematical calculations, with symbols or characters standing for thoughts.

> But to return to the expression of thoughts by means of characters, I thus think that controversies can never be resolved, nor sectarian disputes be silenced, unless we renounce complicated chains of reasoning in favor of simple calculations, and vague terms of uncertain meaning in favor of determinate characters.
>
> In other words, it must be brought about that every fallacy becomes nothing other than a calculating error, and every sophism

expressed in this new type of notation becomes in fact nothing other than a grammatical or linguistic error, easily proved to be such by the very laws of this philosophical grammar.

Once this has been achieved, when controversies arise, there will be no more need for a disputation between two philosophers than there would be between two accountants. It would be enough for them to pick up their pens and sit at their abacuses, and say to each other (perhaps having summoned a mutual friend): "Let us calculate."[151]

Let's refer to this notion as Leibniz's dream—the dream of finding a logical system to decide all of the things that people might ever disagree about. Could the dream ever work?

Even if the dream were theoretically possible (which it isn't), as a practical matter it wouldn't work anyway. If a universal algebra for reasoning had come into existence, would, for instance, Leibniz have been able to avoid his big arguments with Newton? Fat chance. People don't actually care all that much about logic, not even Leibniz. We just pretend to like logic when it happens to be on our side—otherwise we're, like, *to hell with logic.*

This said, there's a powerful attraction to Leibniz's dream. People like the idea of finding an ultimate set of rules to decide everything. Physicists, for instance, dream of a TOE—short for Theory of Everything. At a less exalted level, newspapers and TV are filled with miracle diets—simple rules for regulating your weight as easily as turning a knob on a radio. On the ethical front, each religion has its own compact set of central teachings: Buddha's Eight Noble Truths, Moses's Ten Commandments, the Hindu Rules of Dharma, Christ's Two Commandments, the Five Pillars of Islam, and so on. And books meant to help their readers lead happier lives usually offer a simple list of rules to follow. (Sneak preview: my list, which appears in section *6.5: The Answers,* contains six suggestions: *turn off the machine, see the gnarl, feel your body, release your mind, open your heart, be amazed.*)

But, as I hinted above, achieving Leibniz's dream is in fact logically impossible. And I'm going to spend the rest of this section explaining why.

In order to truly refute Leibniz's dream, we need to find a precise way to formulate it. As it happens, formal versions of Leibniz's dream were first developed in the twentieth century.

An early milestone occurred in 1910, when the philosophers Bertrand Russell and Alfred North Whitehead published their monumental *Principia Mathematica,* intended to provide a formal logical system that could account for all of mathematics. And, as we'll be discussing, hand in hand with the notion of a formal system came an exact description of what is meant by a logical proof.

There were some problems with the Russell-Whitehead system, but by 1920 the mathematician David Hilbert was confident enough to propose what came to be known as *Hilbert's program:*

- We will discover a complete formal system, capable of deciding all the questions of mathematics.
- We will prove that this system is free of any possible contradiction.

As Hilbert put it, "The conviction of the solvability of every mathematical problem is a powerful incentive to the worker. We hear within us the perpetual call: There is the problem. Seek its solution. You can find it by pure reason, for in mathematics there is no *ignorabimus.*" You've got to love a guy who's so scholarly that he can't help but lapse into Latin. That last word means, as you probably realize, "we will not know."

For a decade, scientists could dream that Hilbert's program might come true. And meanwhile mathematics and much of physics were being recast as formal systems. Scientific theories could now be viewed as deterministic processes for determining the truth of theorems. Leibniz's dream was nearly at hand!

But then, in 1930, the logician Kurt Gödel proved there can *never* be a formal system of the kind sought by Hilbert's program. Every possible formal system must always have some kind of hole in it. And then Turing came along and made the situation even worse.

And now, thanks to my analysis of computation, I've found that, given any formal system about science, that is, any candidate for Leibniz's dream, there are going to be lots of sentences about the natural world that are undecidable for that formal system—in the sense that the system can't prove the given sentence to be true and can't prove it to be false.

- *Principle of Natural Undecidability.* For most naturally occurring complex processes and for any correct formal system for science, there will be sentences about the process that are undecidable by the given formal system.

It'll take the rest of this section for me to explain how I arrived at this claim. Let's begin by defining what I mean by a formal system. A *formal system* F can be characterized as having four components:

- A set of symbols
- A rule for recognizing which finite strings of symbols are grammatical sentences
- A rule for deciding which sentences are to be regarded as the axioms of the system
- Some inference rules for deducing sentences from other sentences

We also put a finiteness condition on the rules F uses—the grammar rule, the axiom rule, and the inference rules. These rules must be finitely describable in the same sense that a computation is finitely describable. Indeed, we can think of these rules as simple computations that halt on every input by returning a True of a False.

Although a formal system can be thought of as a meaningless game with symbols, in reality we create formal theories to encapsulate our knowledge of the world. One gain in creating a formal system is that the rigorous process of codifying the system can give us fresh insights into the domain we're trying to describe. In this context it's often felt that the shorter and more compact we can make a formal system, the better is the job that we've done.

Compactness can, however, be overdone—it's perhaps even more important that the formal system should have a pleasing aesthetic form. And even more essential than compactness or beauty is that the formal system should be able to prove a lot of things, and the shorter the proofs, the better.

Given that the main purpose of a formal system is to prove things, I should now explain what I mean by a formal proof.

A *proof* of a sentence S from the formal system F is a sequence of sentences, with the last sentence of the sequence being the targeted sentence *S*. Each preceding sentence must either be an axiom or be a sentence that is arrived at by combining still earlier sentences according to the inference rules. If a sentence is provable from F, we call it a *theorem* of F.

Combined with the notion of proof, a formal system becomes the source of a potentially endless number of theorems. Aided by a formal system, we mentally reach out into the unknown and produce facts about entirely new situations.

Now let's think of a formal system as a computation. There are several ways one might do this, but what's going to be most useful here is to work with a computation *F*Provable that captures the key aspect of a formal system: It finds theorems. Our *F*Provable will try to detect—so far as possible—which strings of symbols are theorems of F. That is, for any proposed provable sentence *S*, the computation *F*Provable*(S)* will carry out the following computation.

- If *S* fails to be a grammatical sentence *F*Provable*(S)* returns False.
- Otherwise *F*Provable starts mechanically generating proofs from the formal system F in order of proof size, and if *S* appears at the end of a proof, *F*Provable*(S)* returns True.
- If *S* is a grammatical sentence but no proof of *S* is ever found, then *F*Provable*(S)* fails to halt.

As it turns out, if F is a powerful enough formal system to prove the basic facts of arithmetic, then *F*Provable will be a universal computation. And then, by Turing's Theorem, *F*Provable has an unsolvable halting problem.[152]

As I mentioned in section *6.4: Faster and Smarter*, if a computation has an unsolvable halting problem, then there's no way to put a bound on how long a computation may actually take before it halts. In terms of the *F*Provable computation, this means that even very short theorems can have unbelievably long proofs.

Fermat's Last Theorem is a famous example of a short theorem with a long proof. Sometime around 1630, the French mathematician Pierre de Fermat wrote the following conjecture in the margin of a book: "There are no whole nonzero numbers $x, y, z$, and $n$ such that $n$ is greater than 2 and $x^n + y^n = z^n$."

Some 360 years later, in 1994, the Princeton mathematician Andrew Wiles succeeded in proving the theorem. His paper on the subject spans 108 pages in an advanced mathematical journal—and in order to flesh out the details, one would have to add tens of thousands of pages of introductory, intermediate, and advanced material.[153] Yes, FProvable(Fermat's Last Theorem) halts, but it has a very long runtime.

Let's come back to Leibniz's dream. Suppose we could formulate some wonderfully rich and inclusive formal system F that includes mathematics, physics, biology, human psychology, and even the laws of human society. And then, just as Leibniz said, whenever we're asked if some statement $S$ about the world were true, we'd set the computation FProvable($S$) in motion, and the computation would eventually return True—provided that $S$ is provable as well as true.

One cloud on the horizon is that, as I just mentioned, the fact that FProvable has an unsolvable halting problem means we might have to wait a really long time for True to pop out. And if $S$ isn't provable, then FProvable($S$) is going to run forever. And, again due to the unsolvability of the halting problem, there's no endless search detector FProvableNeverHalts that we might use to filter out the unprovable sentences $S$.

Hmm. Let's delve deeper.

To begin with, we're going to need another definition.

There's this nice feature about logic, which is that our formal systems have a negation operator ~. If $S$ is a sentence, ~$S$ means "not $S$." That is, $S$ is false if and only if ~$S$ is true.

Using this notion of negation, we can formulate the notion of consistency.

- *Definition.* F is consistent if and only if there is no sentence $S$ such that F proves $S$ and F proves ~$S$.

According to the usual rules of logic, if a theory proves even one contradiction, then it will go ahead and prove everything possible. So an inconsistent theory is useless for distinguishing between true and false statements about the world. We can reasonably suppose that our proposed Leibniz's-dream-type theory F is consistent.

Now on with the delving. Let's see what happens if we try to beat the unsolvability of the halting problem by setting up a computation for answering the question "Is $S$ provable?" (figure 143).

Since F is consistent, we won't ever have the embarrassing situation of turning on both lights. But there's another unpleasant possibility that might arise. What if *neither $S$ nor ~S* is provable from F In? this case, neither of the little lights ever gets turned on.

Well, as it turns out, the neither-nor case *does* happen. A lot! The reason has to do with—the unsovability of the halting problem for *F*Provable.

In order to dig still further, we need yet another definition.

- *Definition.* If F is a formal system and $S$ is a particular statement such that F proves neither $S$ nor ~S, we say *S is undecidable for* F.

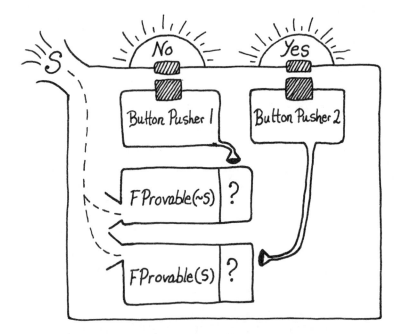

**Figure 143: Is $S$ provable? Let Us Calculate!**

*This device is designed to return a Yes or No answer to the question "Is S provable?" To simplify the diagram, we assume that we already know that S is a grammatical sentence in the language of F. Given such an input S, my device starts working on two computations, FProvable(~S) and FProvable(S). The two button-pushers watch for one of the computations to halt in the state True.*

A priori, we can see that there are four possible situations regarding the behavior of the "Is $S$ provable?" computation in figure 143 (see table 22).

| | FProvable(~S) returns True | FProvable(~S) doesn't halt. |
|---|---|---|
| **F Provable(S) returns True** | F proves both $S$ and $\sim S$, meaning F is inconsistent | F proves $S$ |
| **F Provable(S) doesn't halt** | F proves $\sim S$ | F proves neither $S$ nor $\sim S$, meaning that $S$ is undecidable for F |

**Table 22: Four Kinds of Provability and Unprovability**

*Given a formal system F and a sentence S, we can distinguish four cases: F is inconsistent, S is provable, ~S is provable, or S is undecidable.*

In their optimism, the early mathematical logicians such as David Hilbert hoped to find a formal system F such that the undecidable and inconsistent cases would never arise. As I mentioned earlier, Hilbert's program proposed finding a provably consistent formal system F that could decide all mathematical questions. But Hilbert's hopes were in vain. For according to the following theorem, (which I'll prove in the Technical Appendix) any formal system designed along the lines of Leibniz's dream or Hilbert's program will leave infinitely many sentences undecidable.

- *Undecidability Corollary to Turing's Theorem.* If F is a consistent formal system as powerful as arithmetic, then there are infinitely many sentences that are undecidable for F.

Actually, as I mentioned earlier, it was Kurt Gödel who first proved the existence of undecidable sentences. He found a sentence $G$ that in some sense says, "I am not provable by F." And then Turing improved on the result.[154]

What are Turing's undecidable sentences like? Well, there are all kinds of them, more than you can imagine. Indeed, there's an enhanced version of the Undecidability Corollary saying that the range of undecidable sentences extends beyond any simple characterization that you might come up with.

But, just to have something concrete to think about, it's worth noting that the very simplest undecidable sentences express a fact whose confirmation would require an endless search. Search is the bugaboo of computation.

To be more specific, let's use the variable $G$ to stand for one of the simplest kinds of undecidable sentences. We don't necessarily need to get into having $G$ say something metamathematical about provability—as Gödel did for the very first such result. Instead, a simple undecidable $G$ sentence might be characterized in terms of some algebraic property $g[n]$ that a number $n$ might have. In the simplest cases, we can say that $G$ is equivalent to a sentence of the following form.

- For all $n$, $g[n]$ isn't true.

The expression $g[n]$ can be thought of as being a simple algebraic formula. A more compact way to express $G$ is: "For all $n$, $\sim g[n]$". And it might be that we have more than one variable involved, so that we have a sentence of the form "For all $m$ and $n$, $\sim g[m, n]$."

I don't know of any conveniently short one-variable formulas $g[n]$ that produce an undecidable sentence $G$; all the ones I know of would involve rather large numerical parameters. But it's possible that the two-variable sentence "For all $m$ and $n$, $m^2 \neq n^5 + 6n + 3$" may actually be undecidable.[155]

It's interesting, though a bit dizzying, to compare and contrast two related ways of talking about a sentence $S$. On the one hand, we can ask if $S$ is true or false in the real world of numbers, and we can ask if $S$ or $\sim S$ happens to be provable from F. In the case where the sentence is one of our $G$ sentences of the form "There is no $n$ such that $g[n]$," only three of these possibilities can occur, as indicated in figure 144.

Let's say a bit about the three possibilities.

*G is false, and ~G is provable.* If a sentence $G$ of the form "For all $g$, $\sim g[n]$" is false, then there actually will be a specific $n$ such that $g[n]$ holds in the world of numbers, and F will be able to prove the instance $g[n]$ simply by checking the equation. Therefore, F will be able to prove $\sim G$.

*G is true, and G is provable.* If a sentence $G$ of the form "For all $g$, $\sim g[n]$" is true in the world of numbers, there really won't be any $n$ such that $g[n]$. Now in some of these cases, there may be a clever proof of this general fact from F. I call such a proof "clever" because it somehow has to prove in a finite

**Figure 144: Proof and Truth for a Simple G**

*The points in the big rectangle represent sentences of the form "There is no n such that g[n]", where g is some simple formula. And provability is relative to a consistent formal system F. The unshaded zone contains sentences undecidable by F.*

number of symbols that $g[n]$ is impossible for *every n*. Andrew Wiles's proof of Fermat's Last Theorem is this type of proof. A simpler example would be the proof of the irrationality of 2, which involves arguing that for no whole numbers $n$ and $m$ do we have $n^2 = 2m^2$, because if $n^2 = 2m^2$ were true, you could never finish canceling common factors of 2 from the two sides of the equation. A general proof doesn't get bogged down at looking at every possible value of $n$ and $m$. It has to use some kind of tricky reasoning to cover infinitely many cases at once.

*G is true, and G is not provable.* In these cases, there is no clever proof. The only way F could prove *G* would be to look at every possible number $n$ and show that $g[n]$ isn't true—but this would take forever. In a case like this it's almost as if *G* only *happens* to be true. At least as far as F can see, there's no overarching reason *why* $g[n]$ is impossible for every $n$. It's just that, as chance would have it, in the real world there *aren't* any such $n$. And thus *G* is undecidable by F.

The computer scientist Gregory Chaitin suggests that in a case like the third, we think of *G* as a *random truth.* It's not true for any deep, theoretical reason. It's just something that turns out to be so.[156]

So far I've been looking at undecidable sentences *G* of the form "There is no *n* such that *g*[*n*]," but these aren't really the best kinds of undecidable sentences to think about. Because these *G* have the property that when they're undecidable, they're also true! This is weird, and it tends to bother some people a lot.

But there's no paradox here, no contradiction. All we're seeing is the crumbling of Leibniz's dream, the crash of Hilbert's program. For any consistent formal system F that's as strong as arithmetic, there are going to be sentences *S* that F will neither prove nor disprove. And some may well be true.

There's an endless supply of undecidable sentences *S* beyond the simple kinds of sentences *G* that I've been discussing. These more complex sentences *S* don't have the unsettling property of being in some sense so obviously true that one feels puzzled about why F can't prove them. It's really these kinds of sentences that Chaitin has in mind when he speaks of "random truths."

Some initial examples of the next level of complexity might be "For each *m* there is an *n* such that *g*[*m, n*]" or "There is an *m* such that for all *n, g*[*m, n*]." And with sentences like this we can see the full range of possibilities regarding truth and provability (see figure 145).

In the real world, either *S* or ~*S* will be true, regardless of F's inability to prove either one of them. And if they're unprovable, then they're random truths, brute facts that hold for no particular reason.

So far, my examples of random truths have been sentences about natural numbers. But maybe you don't care about numbers that much. That's fine, but I can still zap you. Because, if we accept the NUH, and we assume that any natural process can be regarded as a computation, then we can apply our undecidability corollary to *any* complex natural process!

I arrive at this conclusion as follows. First of all, we have the following lemma:

- *Unsolvability and Undecidability Lemma.* If *P* is a computation with an unsolvable halting problem, and F is a correct formal theory, then there will be infinitely many sentences about *P* that are undecidable for F.

In this lemma, by the way, I'm using the phrase "correct formal theory" to mean a formal theory that doesn't prove things that are false. The idea behind the proof of the lemma is that there have to be lots of sentences

**Figure 145: Proof and Truth for Arbitrary Sentences**

*The points in the big rectangle represent arbitrary sentences for a formal theory* F. *The unshaded zone contains sentences undecidable by* F. *These are what we might call random truths.*

about $P$ undecidable for F, for otherwise F could solve $P$'s unsolvable halting problem. I'll say a bit more about this in the Technical Appendix.

And now we get to the payoff. If we assume either Wolfram's PCE or our weaker NUH, then most naturally occurring complex processes will have an unsolvable halting problem. If we combine this with the Unsolvability and Undecidability Lemma, we get the following:

- *Principle of Natural Undecidability.* For most naturally occurring complex processes, and any consistent correct formal system for science, there will be sentences about the process that are undecidable by the given formal system.

What makes the *Principle of Natural Undecidability* especially attractive is that the undecidable sentences are not just about arithmetic. They're about the behavior of actual real world processes.

No matter how thoroughly you try and figure the world out, there are infinitely many things you can't prove. Table 23 lists some examples of potentially undecidable sentences.

Nobody will ever manage to bounce a golf ball a thousand times in a row off a putter head.

There are an endless number of planets in our universe.

There are an endless number of planets with people indistinguishable from you.

No human will ever be born with six functioning arms.

No cow's spots will ever spell out your first name in big puffy letters.

Every year with a big birth-rate increase is followed by a big war.

The left wing will dominate American politics more often than the right wing does.

Mankind will evolve into higher forms of life.

The majority of times that you move to a different line in a supermarket, the new line goes slower than one of the lines you didn't pick.

New races of intelligent beings will emerge over and over for the rest of time.

The time of our cosmos extends forever.

**Table 23: Undecidability Is Everywhere**

It often happens in the history of science that some oddball new category is discovered—such as undecidable sentences about the natural world. At first nobody's sure if any phenomena of this kind exist, but then there's some kind of logical argument why these oddball things have to occur. And then, as time goes on, more and more of the curious entities are discovered until finally they're perceived to be quite run-of-the-mill.[157]

Undecidability is everywhere, and random truth abounds.

## 6.5: The Answers

In closing, I'll offer some answers to three of the big questions that I've been circling around.

- What is reality?
- What is the meaning of life?
- How can I be happy?

*What is reality?* An answer to this question often has the following format: "Everything is_____."

This specific style of answer is what philosophers call a *monism,* that is, an assertion that there is one single kind of substance that underlies all of the world's diverse phenomena. You might alternatively believe in, say, *two* different kinds of substances and be advocating a form of *dualism,* perhaps opting for matter and mind. For that matter, you can be a *pluralist* and say that reality is made up of all sorts of fundamentally different kinds of processes and entities.

I've always had a predilection for monisms, and over the years I've tried out lots of different ways to fill in the blank. I present some of my proposed answers in the motley table 24. In each row I have the key word for the answer, some aspects of what I take this answer to mean, some remarks about my experiences with this answer, and my approximate age when this answer first became of interest to me. I never actually abandon any of my answers, by the way, it's as if they're layered on top of each other, or as if they're a race of artificially alive "meme" creatures nested in my brain. I do recognize that one or another of my suggested "answers" may appear too paltry or specialized to be a basis for an entire ontology of the universe. But, hey, I get enthusiastic about things.

| Answer | Aspects of this answer | Experiences with this answer in my life, and my approximate age when it first took hold in me | |
|---|---|---|---|
| Family | Childhood before differentiation. Memories, talk, sharing, learning how to behave, learning language. | In some ways my parents are still with me; my father in my heartbeat, my mother in the rhythm of my breath. | 0 |
| Society | Rules, strangers. The pecking order. | School. I'm a heavily pecked low-ranking chicken in the fourth through ninth grades. It's as if, for those years, "The Ugly Duckling" was the story of my life. | 8 |
| Self | Thoughts, reflections, desires, fears, plans, simulations, fantasies. | Autumn, dusk, waiting for my mom to pick me up at school, playing with the other boys. It's like suddenly I wake up. A chaotic bifurcation. I have a moment of feeling my future self looking back at this moment. | 9 |

| Answer | Aspects of this answer | Experiences with this answer in my life, and my approximate age when it first took hold in me | |
|---|---|---|---|
| God | The God of religion, the pantheist God as Cosmos, God as philosophical Absolute, God as mystical One, the spiritual God as all-pervasive universal force. "The light is everywhere." | My father becomes an Episcopal priest. I try to take church seriously, but the specific dogmas seem too odd. "You've got to be kidding." Over the years, I have a couple of visions of the One, and eventually, in an effort to change my habits, I become willing to ask *something* for guidance and help. It seems to work. | 12 |
| Science fiction | Sense of wonder, goofs and eyeball kicks, transformation of mundane reality. | Random stories in anthologies in the Louisville Free Public Library. Then Heinlein, Sheckley, Dick, Lovecraft. I begin writing my own science fiction when I'm thirty. Writers I enjoy later on include Gibson, Sterling, Shirley, Laidlaw, Di Filippo, Doctorow, and Stross. | 13 |
| Nature | The web of life. And even the inanimate things are as interesting as if they were alive. Wind, water, fire. | I go to boarding school in the Black Forest for a year when I'm twelve; it makes a deep impression. And I love walking in the pastures near my home in Louisville. I'm fascinated by a particular stream, and when I see it iced over one winter, I imagine the moving bubbles beneath the ice are a model for fragments of the One that split off for a time to act as individual souls. | 13 |
| Literature | Tales. Sketching characters. Capturing perceptions and internal monologue. Personae as masks the author dons. Hoaxes. Presenting a sensibility. | Joyce. Kerouac. Burroughs. Pynchon. Borges. Poe. I get to be part of the cyberpunk school of science-fiction writers, then hone my own transreal style of literature. I become interested in the patterns of literature, which leads me to Joseph Campbell's *The Hero with a Thousand Faces*, which serves as a blueprint for my epic novel, *Frek and the Elixir.* | 18 |
| Science | Explanations via laws about unseen primitive entities: atoms, heat, magnetism, genes. | In high school I begin reading *Scientific American* and popular science books. I don't learn much in college; I can't integrate it into my then-paramount focus on trying out the Beat lifestyle. But I always love the texture of science, the odd deductions, the curious phraseology. | 18 |

| Answer | Aspects of this answer | Experiences with this answer in my life, and my approximate age when it first took hold in me | |
|---|---|---|---|
| Sex | Pure pleasure. Sensuality. Skin as sense organ. A way to turn off rational thought. | At some level, everything really *is* about sex. As Jorge Luis Borges wrote in an essay, "The Sect of the Phoenix," that appears in his book *Labyrinths*: "The Secret is sacred but is always somewhat ridiculous; its performance is furtive and even clandestine and the adept do not speak of it. There are no decent words to name it, but it is understood that all words name it or, rather, inevitably allude to it." | 20 |
| Marriage | Companionship, love, sharing, communication at a near telepathic level. | My wife is my oldest continuous friend, and my best connection to my youth. She was there. | 21 |
| Music | Beats, chords, embodied logic, emotional color. | Bo Diddley, Flatt and Scruggs, the Beatles, Zappa, the Stones, the Ramones, Rancid, NOFX, Muddy Waters and the endless boogie of the blues. | 21 |
| Politics | Power. War. Fear, greed, hatred. | I permanently lose faith in our government when they try to send me to die in Vietnam. And it hasn't gotten any better. Politics is a steady drain on psychic energy and mental equilibrium. I perpetually struggle not to get sucked in. | 22 |
| Math | The bare forms of thought. A universal language of science. Gnarly, weird shapes and counterexamples. | Grad school: my breakthrough comes when I teach calculus and finally understand it. My survey of math, *Mind Tools,* and my anthology of others' math stories, *The Mathenauts.* | 22 |
| Children | Passing on information. DNA + nurture + teach + love. | It's a blessing to have children. Their faces and voices, their cuddliness, the fascination of seeing them grow. | 23 |
| Logic | Rules of deduction applied to axioms. | Studying mathematical logic. I meet a few times with Kurt Gödel in Princeton, the ultimate guru of my life. "The *a priori* is very powerful." | 24 |
| Mysticism | Three central teachings of mysticism: "All is | Most of my friends are uneasy about mysticism, but I find it to be uncluttered and in some sense | 24 |

| Answer | Aspects of this answer | Experiences with this answer in my life, and my approximate age when it first took hold in me | |
|---|---|---|---|
| Mysticism *(continued)* | One, the One is unknowable, the One is right here." | obviously true. Some favorite works: Aldous Huxley, *The Perennial Philosophy*; Baba Ram Dass, *Be Here Now*; D. T. Suzuki, *The Field of Zen*; Rudolf Otto, *Mysticism East and West*; and the exhilarating section 6 of Ludwig Wittgenstein, *Tractatus logico-philosophicus*: "There are, indeed, things that cannot be put into words. They *make themselves manifest*. They are what is mystical." | 24 |
| Teaching | Passing on memes. Watered-down parenting. | Altruistic social good. You get to learn on the job and there are good work hours. A lecture is an evanescent form of performance art. The downside is academic politics. I don't manage to get tenure until I'm fifty. | 26 |
| Space | Higher dimensions. Matter as curved space. Time as a kind of space, leading to the spacetime of Einstein and Minkowski. Parallel worlds as sheets of spacetime. | I fall in love with Edwin Abbott's *Flatland*. His character A Square becomes a lifelong imaginary friend. I began lecturing on higher dimensions in my first teaching job, under the aegis of a Foundations of Geometry course. My first published book is about the fourth dimension, a few years later I write another: *The Fourth Dimension*. My novel *Spaceland* is a gnarly Y2K homage to *Flatland*. | 28 |
| Infinity | Infinite sets make up the forms of reality. The endless malleability of infinite sets can model objects, thoughts, and even the divine. | My Ph.D. thesis is on set theory. I like finding infinity in mathematics as it seems like the start of an exact mysticism and theology. I publish *Infinity and the Mind*. | 30 |
| The body | Jogging, cross-country skiing, cycling, backpacking, yoga. The different forms of exercise turn attention from thought loops to the muscles, the breath, and the body's motions. | I dig the runner's high. The rhythm of the skier. The rushing flow of the downhill bicyclist. I love how empty the woods are when I backpack; nature is always out there, doing her thing. Yoga wrings out the pains that dwell in my back from my years of hunching over the computer; yoga makes breathing into a sensual pleasure. | 32 |

| Answer | Aspects of this answer | Experiences with this answer in my life, and my approximate age when it first took hold in me | |
|---|---|---|---|
| Publishing | Teaching without personal contact; information transmission freed of space and time. | Writing is congenial for me. I'm better on paper than face-to-face. *The Lifebox, The Seashell, and The Soul* is my twenty-sixth published book. It's a constant unrelenting struggle to get in print. | 34 |
| Fractals | Infinitely detailed self-similar patterns. Fractals synthesize infinity and space. And they're deeply gnarly. | I can hardly contain my delight when I encounter the Mandelbrot set at the Austin pad of my cyberpunk pal Bruce Sterling, who's using an Amiga and a program written by Charles Platt, another science-fiction writer. It's a new paradise. Until fractals and CAs, I'd never wanted to touch a computer. But then I wanted one—an interactive "microscope" for exploring this new land. | 38 |
| Cellular Automata | Simple locally-based rules that act in parallel, the same rule everywhere. Gnarly patterns and behaviors emerging. Colliding streams of gliders as the paradigm for class four computation. | I visit Toffoli and Wolfram at their institutions to write a magazine article about CAs. I'm converted on the spot. I get a job teaching computer science in San Jose. I get hold of Toffoli's CAM-6 accelerator board and begin writing CAs. John Walker hires me to work with him at Autodesk, programming *Rudy Rucker's CA Lab* package. I switch to continuous-valued CAs and create the CAPOW package with my students at San Jose State University. | 39 |
| Artificial life | Autonomous agents that don't need synchronization. Interacting simulations. Improve DNA-like genomes by fitness-proportional reproduction. The fitter a-life critters tend to be the gnarlier ones. | Starting in 1980, I imagine simulated robotic evolution in my *Ware* novels. Eventually the information evolves away from the robot hardware to soft plastic moldie limpware and then to the "freeware" of intergalactic wave signals. I'm thrilled to be part of the early Artificial Life conferences in Los Alamos and Santa Fe. I publish an *Artificial Life Lab* software package with the Waite Group, at which time I'm into Turing-machine ants, which leads to my novel *The Hacker and the Ants*. | 42 |

| Answer | Aspects of this answer | Experiences with this answer in my life, and my approximate age when it first took hold in me | |
|--------|------------------------|------------------------------------------------------------------------------------------------|---|
| Chaos | Deterministic yet unpredictable processes wander around upon a characteristic attractor. Gnarly processes have fractal strange attractors. A process can bifurcate, that is, hop to a new attractor. | Chaos is a key part of the 1980s California computer scene. A remark in James Gleick's best-selling *Chaos* teaches me to see chaos in the motions of objects in nature, e.g., swaying branches and fluttering leaves. I help program *James Gleick's Chaos the Software*, a retail product for Autodesk. Auto desk's stock drops and I'm back to teaching. | 42 |
| Love | Opening my heart. | The universe loves itself. I have a vision of this, hiking in Yosemite with my son. Love is practical in any situation: Nothing else really works. Lines to this effect in the classic of hippie philosophy: Thaddeus Golas, *The Lazy Man's Guide to Enlightenment.* "Go beyond reason to love: it is safe. It is the only safety." | 46 |
| Virtual reality | A computer graphical simulation of reality. | The short-lived cyberspace craze. My new friends at *Mondo 2000* view cyberspace as a drug. I help them edit an anthology called *Mondo 2000: A User's Guide to the New Edge.* We make the cover of *Time* magazine. | 47 |
| Compassion | Be kind, if only for selfish reasons: It helps you stay serene. | I always wanted to find enlightenment and it had never once crossed my mind that the quest might have something to do with trying to be a kinder person. I formulate an addition to my three central teachings of mysticism: "The One will help you if you ask." | 50 50 |
| The Web | Emergent global mind. The Library of Babel. The universal encyclopedia. | The Web isn't like television because you can do it yourself. You're a chef instead of a force-fed goose. I love the way that blogging lets everyone publish their memoirs. I dream of creating a huge online lifebox compendium of all my books and journals. | 52 |
| Painting | Blending colors and forms to please the eye. Ideas made visible. | I learn to paint so I can write *As Above, So Below: A Novel of Peter Bruegel.* The medium is wonderfully nondeterministic and analog. | 53 |

| Answer | Aspects of this answer | Experiences with this answer in my life, and my approximate age when it first took hold in me | |
|--------|------------------------|-----------------------------------------------------------------------------------------------|---|
| Software engineering | Learning to see software patterns, designing classes to hold data and methods, object-oriented programming, debugging and refining code. | Designing software is like doing mathematical logic, but it's a logic that lives and does things on its own. I'd always wanted to be an experimental scientist. Software engineering is exceedingly difficult to teach. I tell my students, "The only way to learn programming is to make every possible mistake. All I can do is show you how to make mistakes faster." My officemate Jon Pearce teaches me about software patterns, comparing them to literary archetypes. | 54 |
| Mind | Merging with reality. To be quantum-mechanically coherent is to not have specific opinions. To adopt one position or another is to be decoherent. Wave with it. | I lecture on the philosophy of computer science in Leuven, focusing on the mind for days at a time. I have satori in Paris. Any mental process we can explicitly describe can be simulated by a computer. But we know we are more than a computer program. The missing ingredient is of necessity not logically describable. Nick Herbert's "Quantum Tantra" paper suggests using quantum coherence for the nonlogical element. | 55 |
| Computer Games | Games bring all the interesting aspects of computers together: software engineering, graphics, artificial intelligence, artificial life, chaos, story, art, sound. A great new art form is on the point of being born. | I follow the evolution from *Pac-Man* to the virtual reality games of the present. I teach a course on game design for at San Jose State University for about ten years and write a book, *Software Engineering and Computer Games*. I don't actually *play* many games once my son graduates from high school. Programming them is the part I like. The metagame. | 56 |
| Computation | CAs, fractals, chaos, software engineering, virtual reality, artificial life, computer games, simulations, biotechnology, Social dynamics—all rolled into one. | The meanings of Wolfram's *A New Kind of Science* continue to reverberate. I come to see the study of computation as the ultimate and most fundamental form of science, even more fundamental than mathematics. I write *The Lifebox, the Seashell, and the Soul.* | 58 |

| Answer | Aspects of this answer | Experiences with this answer in my life, and my approximate age when it first took hold in me | |
|---|---|---|---|
| Pluralism | All the answers at once. Farewell to monism. Why *should* the world be simple? To fully engage with reality you need to involve your physical body, your emotions, and the whole of your mind. | As a young man, I read William James's book *A Pluralistic Universe,* in which he brings out the point that monism could well be wrong. And, now, after spending a couple of years writing about everything being a computation, I've had enough with monistic reductionism. I'm longing to write a novel again. | 59 |

**Table 24: Rudy's Answers**

As you might suspect at this point, I don't always think universal automatism is the whole answer. I don't always believe that everything is a computation.

I had a moment of disbelief while finishing the first draft of this chapter in September 2004. I went camping in Big Sur with my wife, Sylvia; it was a hot day, and I had the chance to stand in the cool clear flow of the Big Sur River, up to my neck in a big pool that accumulates right before the river flows across a sand bar into the Pacific (see figure 146). Standing there, I closed my eyes to savor the sensation of water and air. My arms were weightless at my sides, my knees were slightly bent, I was at perfect equilibrium. Each time I exhaled, my breath would ripple the water, and reflections of the noon sun would flicker on my eyelids. Exquisite—and, no, I wasn't high; I haven't been high since I was fifty.

I was all there, fully conscious, immersed in the river. And I became powerfully aware of a commonsense fact that most readers will have known all along.

"This isn't a computation. This is *water.*"

Mind you, I don't think it's a waste of time expending energy in trying to believe universal automatism. It's not that universal automatism is really *wrong.* It's more that sometimes it becomes too cumbersome a way to try to think of things. Like any scientific monism.

Why pretend that reality is any less rich than you know it to be? I'm drawn to pluralism.

If I had to pick only a handful of my answers, I'd still include computation—

**Figure 146:**
**Pool at the Mouth of the Big Sur River**

for I really do think Wolfram is onto something. But I'd want to include mysticism, love, and the body. And water. And the reflections in my brass desk lamp. And crows. And . . .

Once you move past monism, the next logical stopping point is the most comprehensive possible pluralism.

- *Reality is endlessly diverse.*

But wait. Did I just say that I don't believe everything's a computation? I'm abandoning one the main points that I seem to have been arguing for throughout this lengthy tome? Come *on,* Rudy!

Well, when I first drafted this section in September 2004, I was a little fed up with thinking about computation. But I don't want to pull back too far from universal automatism. Even though it's wearisome to continually view the world as being made of computations, this particular monism could really be true. By now it's March 2005, and, having celebrated my retirement with a pleasant dive vacation in Micronesia, I'm more inclined to give universal automatism more credence. There was in fact one specific moment when I came back into the fold; I described it in my journal notes for the trip to Micronesia (see the photos in figure 147.)

**Figure 147: Snapshots from Micronesia**

*Left to right and top to bottom: a rock island near Palau, kayaking along the edge of a rock island, a soft coral whose shape is a disk with a fractally folded edge, Zhabotinsky-scroll hard coral.*

• • •

Yesterday I went on a kayak tour in the rock islands of Palau. It was one of the best days of my life.

Our guides were three Palauans: Jake, Ding, and Rayna. They were great: wild lively locals, talking rapid-fire Palauan to each other all day. Jake was the very image of the old-style Micronesian chief, although later I found out he'd gone to college, started a career as an accountant, and had thrown that over to be a tour guide.

There were five of us tourists. The guides loaded five single-seat hard kayaks on a boat and motored out to our starting point. For the rest of the day, we kayaked in stages: we'd get to a location and the motor boat would be waiting there, we'd tie our kayaks to the boat, go snorkeling, climb up the ladder to the motor boat, replenish our supplies, and then remount our kayaks. Jake had six waypoints for us: a hidden underwater tunnel leading to a tree-lined lagoon filled with giant clams, a sunken ship from the 1930s, a little point where he speared a fish, a large lagoon with a beach where we had lunch, an underwater tunnel leading to a cave filled with blue light coming up from the water, and an arch connecting two bays with soft corals growing on the sandy bottom of the arch.

Coming into the lagoon for lunch I felt quite weightless; the water was so clear and unrippled, and the sand below it so white. It was as if my kayak were gliding through empty space. And quiet, quiet, quiet all around. Not a whisper of wind in the trees, only the gentle lapping of the waves, the occasional calls of birds and, of course, the sporadic whooping of the Palauans. I had such a wave of joy, wading around that lagoon, and a profound sense of gratefulness, both to the world for being so beautiful and to God for letting me reach this spot. I had another wave of these feelings a bit later when we were kayaking through a maze of small islands in shallow water, bays that no motor boat could reach. Peaceful, peaceful. Eden. The world as it truly is meant to be. I'm glad I lived long enough to get here.

High in the air above one of these sunny backwaters, I see a large dark—bird? It's the size of an eagle, and, no, it's a fruit bat, the sun shining through the membranes of its wings. The islands look like green clouds come to earth; mirroring their fluffy white brethren above.

In the last snorkel spot there are lovely pale blue and pink soft corals, branching alveolar broccolis on the sandy bottom of the archway connecting two bays. Fractals, in short. Swimming through the arch, I encounter a shoal of maybe ten thousand tiny tropical fish, like the fish you'd see in someone's home aquarium, little zebras or tetras. With my snorkel on, I marvel at their schooling motions, their bodies moving in a unison like iron filings in a field, their ropes and scarves of density emerging from the parallel computation of their individual anxieties. The turbulent water currents compute, as do the clouds in the sky, the cellular automaton reaction-diffusion patterns on the mantles of the giant clams, the Zhabotinsky scrolls of the shelf corals, the gnarly roots of plants on the land.

And I'm thinking that maybe, yes, maybe after all everything *is* a computation. Universal automatism gives me a point of view from which I can make sense of all these diverse forms I'm seeing here. Maybe I was wrong to want to "take it all back" in September. But what about my thoughts, can I see those as computations, too? Well, why *can't* they just be fractal broccoli, flocking algorithms, class four turbulence, cellular automaton scrolls. I ascribe higher significance to them, but why make so much of them. Are my thoughts really so vastly different from the life forms all around me in these lagoons? Why not relax and merge. All is One.

And if I find it useful to understand the One's workings in terms of computation, don't think that this reduces the lagoon to a buzzing beige box. The lagoon is not reduced, the lagoon is computing just as it is. "Computing" is simply a way to speak of the dance of natural law.

Speaking of dance, when we got back to the dive shop, Jake and Rayna were kidding around with this cute young California woman who's just moved to Palau and is supporting herself by working at the shop. Jake and Rayna start dancing and chanting, crouched, facing each other, their hands shaking in their air, slapping their thighs, vital and joyous, mythic archetypes, gnarly computations like me.

So, okay, I'll go for the universal-automatist answer to "What is reality?"

- *Reality is made of gnarly computations.*

Now to the next question. *What is the meaning of life?*

One appeal of monistic philosophies is that if we can reduce reality to one substance, there's some hope of finding a rule of behavior for that substance, and that rule may suggest a meaning for the world.

Let's see how this works if we believe in universal automatism. If I say that everything is a computation, I'm saying that everything is a deterministic process. And that means that reality is a weave of logical if-then statements, with each phenomenon linked to a cause. As an extreme example of universal automatism, Wolfram suggests that if we trace the world's computations all the way back, there may be some underlying supercomputation that generates not only the entire cosmos but also the underlying fabric of space and time. But then, of course, we'd have to ask why that particular supercomputation exists.

This leads to the so-called superultimate why question: "Why is there anything?" The question is inherently unanswerable, for no proposed solution can be enough. Given that the superultimate why question is impossible to answer, it's in some sense meaningless—but such a criticism doesn't remove the question's sting.

The great science writer Martin Gardner makes the point very clearly.

Even if quantum mechanics becomes "explained" as part of a deeper theory—call it *X*—then we can ask "Why *X*?" There is no escape from the superultimate questions: "Why is there something rather than nothing, and why is the something structured the way it is?" As Stephen Hawking recently put it, "Why does the universe go to all the bother of existing?" The question obviously can never be answered, yet it is not emotionally meaningless. Meditating on it can induce what William James called an "ontological wonder-sickness." Jean-Paul Sartre called it "nausea." [158]

The point here is that even if Wolfram were right, it doesn't seem as if knowing the world to be the result of some supercomputation would be of much use to us. We still wouldn't know where the supercomputation came from. And—perhaps even more important, we still wouldn't know *what it's for.*

And that, after all, is really what we're after when we ask about the meaning of life. It's not so much the *cause* that's puzzles us as the *purpose.* Does a person's life have a purpose?

Well, our studies of universal automatism do suggest one line of thought. Computationally rich class four behaviors are in an objective sense more interesting than those that die out, repeat, or have no discernible structure. So a universal automatist might say that the meaning and purpose of a human life is to produce gnarly class four computation.

Note that the notion of gnarly computation as the meaning of life fits in with the more humanistic worldviews.

The human artifacts we admire are computationally rich. An empty canvas is class one. Hack artwork is class two copying of existing artifacts. Ugly scuzz is class three. Great art is class four: gnarly.

The nobler emotions are computationally rich as well. Murderous rage forces some victim's computation into class one termination. Hatred throws the hater into a class two loop. Too needy a desire to please puts a person at the mercy of capricious class three inputs. Compassion is an ever-evolving class four process.

Get the picture?

- *The meaning of life is beauty and love.*

One last question. *How can I be happy?*

I'll offer a bouquet of six answers—one for each of the six levels of reality we discussed. After long and complex mental computation, I've compressed the answers to a couple of words apiece. A to-do list.

- *Turn off the machine.* Universal automatism teaches us that there's a common ground upon which to compare nature to PCs. But this doesn't mean that that PCs are as good as reality. Far from it. On the common ground, we can readily see that the natural world is incalculably more powerful and interesting than the odd flickering boxes we're wedded to in the Y2K era. I try not to let them run my life.

- *See the gnarl.* The air is a gnarly ocean; the leaves dance on the trees. I've always enjoyed watching clouds and water; and now I realize that the computations they're carrying out are fully as complex as anything in any book I might read. Each flickering shadow is a reminder of the world's unsolvable and unpredictable richness.

- *Feel your body.* There's always something interesting to feel in this wonderful meat computation that I'm privileged to inhabit. It's fun sometimes to think of my body as being very large—like an immense starship that I'm inside. I can focus on the inputs from all the different parts. Meanwhile my breath and heartbeat are gently chaotic. As a heavy computer user, I need to remember not spend more time upgrading my machine than I do in exercising my bod.

- *Release your thoughts.* Underneath the wanting and worrying is the great river of thought. I don't control much of the world, and things rarely turn out as I predict, so why waste my time in focusing on fears, desires, and expectations? And why invest all my energy in logic which, as we now know, only goes so far? Released from the class two channels of attachment, I can watch my mind like fireworks above a wavy sea.

- *Open your heart.* People are the most interesting and beautiful entities I'll ever see. Society isn't about the news and the leaders. It's about the people I run into every day. Recently I saw a show of photographs by Diane Arbus. Diane must have been such a character. She had a way of getting to the essential humanity of her subjects—ordinary people lovingly depicted and made fully human in all individuality. They always seem to be as interested in Diane as she is in them. People sense when you look at them with utter interest and compassion; they look back and smile.

• *Be amazed.* Our studies of computation teach us that none of our theories will ever get very far. Not everything can be explained, nor even expressed in words. We're fully immersed in the incomprehensible. Life is a mystery; it's good to savor this.

Lest this list seem preachy, let's say the advice is actually aimed at me. I need it. I forget the simplest things.

And I'm glad to see these slogans emerge from my book's long and gnarly chain of reasoning. They're a nice place to end up.

One last thought: perhaps our universe is perfect.

# *Technical Appendix*

In the first part of this appendix, I bring together the various definitions given in the main text and, where necessary, make them a bit more precise. In the second part, I prove a couple of results relating to Turing's Theorem.

Most of the mathematical material here can be found in books on *recursion theory,* that branch of mathematical logic that studies ways to formalize the notion of computation. Two very good books covering this material in terms of computation are Martin Davis's *Computability and Unsolvability* (New York: Dover Books, 1982) and Marvin Minsky's *Computation: Finite and Infinite Machines* (New York: Prentice Hall, 1967). Two more advanced books on recursion theory are Hartley Rogers's *Theory of Recursive Functions and Effective Computability* (Cambridge, Mass: MIT Press, 1987) and Piergiorgio Odifreddi's *Classical Recursion Theory* (Amsterdam: North-Holland, 1989).

I've chosen to present this material in a somewhat nonstandard style of my own devising, both to make it more self-contained and to make it fit in better with my book.

## A.1: Rudiments of Recursion Theory

Let's start by repeating my basic definition of a computation.

- *Definition.* A *computation* is a process that obeys finitely describable rules.

The computation is thought of as embedded in linear time. The states of the computation can be treated as either inputs or outputs, with earlier states being inputs relative to the later states, and the later states being outputs relative to the earlier states.

Since we think of the computation's input states and output states as being drawn from the same set of states, this means that when we want to input something like a number into a computation, we're really setting the computation into an initial state that both represents the number in some simple fashion and sets the computation into a start-up condition.

Now I'll make some more refined definitions. Following standard logical practice I'll write "iff" as shorthand for "if and only if." In practice, if a definition has the form "A iff B," where A is some newly defined phrase and B is some kind of condition, then the intent of the definition is this: "from now on, when I say 'A,' that's an abbreviation for condition B." Another context in which logicians use "iff" is when A and B are conditions whose meaning is independently clear. In such a situation, "A iff B" means "A and B are equivalent conditions" or "A implies B and B implies A."

In the following, we'll suppose that P is a computation (that is, a deterministic system) and that In and Out are two of the system's possible states. We'll use t to stand for the time variable. To be quite general we'll view t as a real number.

- *Definition.* P(In, t) = Out iff the following is true. If you initialize the computation P to be in state In and then let it run for a time interval of length t, you will find the computation to be in state Out.

Note that the output state Out is completely determined by the rules for P, the input In, and the amount of elapsed time t.

In order to formulate a definition of "feasibility," it will be useful to have a specific time value T, which is the length of time that we consider it feasible to wait for an output. For an individual human, T would certainly be less than a hundred years and, in practice, our T standard tends to be measured in days or hours. For interactive robotic-style applications, T may in fact be measured in seconds. In casual conversation, we often speak of feasibility when we really mean *T*-feasibility, with *T* being some implicitly agreed upon maximum time.

- *Definition.* The computation *P*(In ,*t*) = Out is *T-feasible* if *t* is less than *T*.

We're sometimes interested in expressing the fact that a computation starting with a given state eventually reaches some other state, whether or not the computation continues changing after reaching the targeted state.

- *Definition.* *P*(In) *produces state* Out iff there is some *t* such that *P*(In, *t*) = Out.

Sometimes we're more interested in reaching some certain targeted kind of output than we are interested in a computation's ongoing passage through various states. One notion is simply that *P* stops changing. Since *P* is deterministic, it must in fact begin repeating itself if it enters the same state two times in row. We define a helper computation Is*P*Frozen(Out), which detects outputs after which *P* ceases to change.

- *Definition.* If *P* is a computation, the *default target detector* Is*P*Frozen is a computation defined as having two outputs, True and False, and is computed as follows:
    Is*P*Frozen(Out) enters and remains in the state True iff *P*(Out, 1) = Out.
    Otherwise Is*P*Frozen(Out) enters and remains in the state False.

I'm using *P*(Out,1) to express the notion of the "next state after Out." If time is continuous rather than discrete, *P*(Out,1) isn't really the *next* state after Out, but really any state after Out is good enough for the definition. I avoid speaking about the *P*(Out, *t*) computation remaining in the same state for "all *t* > 0," as this would open up the unnecessary possibility of an endless search.

We're often interested in trying to find a way to determine which inputs will produce a unique output.

- *Definition.* Consider a computation *P.* We say *P halts on input* In iff there is an output Out such that

    *P*(In) produces Out, and

    Is*P*Frozen(Out) produces True.

    We can express this important case in any of the following ways:

    *P*(In) *halts at* Out, or *P*(In) = Out, or *P*(In) *returns* Out.

Note that I am introducing a bit of ambiguity in my notation here. On the one hand, I think of *P*(In) as being a process, but, on the other hand, if *P*(In) halts at Out, I'm allowed to write *P*(In) = Out. Perhaps in this latter case I should really write *P*(In) = $_{IsPFrozen}$Out.

Note the distinction between the weaker *P*(In) *produces* Out and the stronger *P*(In) *returns* Out. If *P*(In) returns Out, it's also true that *P*(In) produces Out, but not vice versa, for a *P* can easily start from In, pass through Out, and continue changing its state, possibly without ever reaching a state Out such that Is*P*Frozen(Out). There are many computations *P* and inputs In that *P*(In) will fail to halt; imagine, for example, a computation that simply keeps adding on ones forever.

- *Definition.* The computation *P is everywhere defined* iff

    *P* halts on each input.

I think being *everywhere defined* is really what we have in mind when we speak of a computation as being in *class one.* These are the computations that always run down and stop.

In talking about naturally arising computations, we'll be interested in more general conceptions of halting, which leads us to introduce the notion of a target detector.

- *Definition.* If *P* is a computation, then the auxiliary computation Is*P*Done with special states False and True is a *target detector* for *P* iff Is*P*Done(Out) returns a False or a True for any possible state Out of *P.* Is*P*Done, in other words, is everywhere defined. We call a target detector nontrivial if it's not constant, that is, it doesn't always return True or always return False.

If we don't specify an Is*P*Done target detector, we will assume we're using the default Is*P*Frozen target detector, which returns True if any further updates would leave the system in the same state.

We can relativize the notions of halting and being everywhere defined for specific Is*P*Done target detectors.

- *Definition.* Consider a computation *P* with the target detector Is*P*Done. We say *P with* Is*P*Done *halts on input* In iff there is an output Out such that
    *P*(In) produces Out, and
        Is*P*Done(Out) produces True.
  In this case we can also say that *P*(In) *halts at* Out *relative to* Is*P*Done, and if Out is the first such output, we can write *P*(In) = $_{\text{Is}P\text{Done}}$Out.

- *Definition.* The computation *P* with the target detector Is*P*Done *is everywhere defined relative to* Is*P*Done iff *P* with Is*P*Done halts on each of its inputs.

For the next definitions, let *P* and *Q* be computations, with their own sets of states, and define a translation between the two sets of states as follows.

- *Definition.* The computation *ptoq* is a *translation* from *P* to *Q* iff
    - (i) *ptoq* is everywhere defined, and
    - (ii) *ptoq* takes *P*'s states as inputs, and it always halts at states of *Q*, and
    - (iii) if $a_1$ and $a_2$ are different states of *P*, then *ptoq*($a_1$) is different from *ptoq*($a_2$).

In other words, the computation *ptoq* translates from *P* to *Q* iff the computation *ptoq* embodies a one-to-one everywhere defined function from states of *P* into states of *Q*.

In the case where the possible states of *P* and *Q* make up the set of all integers, what I'm calling a translation is exactly the same thing as what recursion theorists call a one-to-one total recursive function. In this case, the translation is reversible, in the sense that you can use the computation *ptoq* to define a translation *qtop* from $Q$ to $P$.

Now we can define the important notion of emulation. This definition has vexed me more than any other in this book. The reason is that I use emulation to define two rather disparate notions: universality and unpredictability. A universal computation emulates every other computation, and a (strongly) unpredictable complex computation reaches its target states faster than any computation that emulates it.

Which notion of emulation I use isn't that problematic for formulating the notion of universality. Generally a computation that's universal relative to one notion of emulation will be universal relative to another. But the details of the definition of emulation become crucial when we want to formulate a notion of Big being faster than Small in the sense that Big produces the same answers as Small, but faster.

In the main text, I gave this definition of emulation.

- *Definition of emulation.* Big *emulates* Small if there is an emulation code emulatesmall such that for any states In and Out,
    Small(In) returns Out if and only if
    Big(emulatesmall, In) returns Out.

We can state this definition in a more general way by allowing for the possibility that Big and Small use different languages by providing a helper translation computation smalltobig.

As defined above, a translation computation is quite simple and unproblematic; if $S$ is any possible state, smalltobig($S$) will return an answer after a finite amount of time, and if two states are different, their translations are different as well.

If I use a translation, I don't need to mention the emulation code because I might as well suppose that smalltobig(In) translation works by firstly translating the In string into appropriate symbols for Big, and by secondly prefixing the translated string with the emulatesmall code.

- *Definition of emulation (second version).* Big *emulates* Small if there is a translation smalltobig such that for any states In and Out,

Small(In) returns Out if and only if
Big(smalltobig(In)) returns smalltobig(Out).

In other words, Big emulates Small means that the compound computation Big(smalltobig(In)) returns the same outputs as smalltobig(Small(In)).

Actually, I think it would be better to explicitly introduce two translation functions, one for each direction, and to explicitly require that Big have a target state detector that in some sense emulates the behavior of Small's target state detector. Let's assume that this third version is my "real" definition of emulation. I don't state it this way in the main text, as I thought it might look too complicated for the casual reader.

- *Definition of emulation (third version).* Big with the translation smalltobig, the reverse translation bigtosmall, and the target state detector IsBigDone *emulates* Small with target state detector IsSmallDone iff
    for any In and Out, Small(In) = $_{\text{IsSmallDone}}$ Out iff
        there is BigOut such that
            Big(smalltobig(In)) = $_{\text{IsBigDone}}$ BigOut
            and bigtosmall(BigOut) = Out.

Figure 148 illustrates this third notion of emulation.
If we like, we can define a shorthand symbol for emulation.

- *Definition.* If Big emulates Small, we write Small $\leq_e$ Big

I want to make five comments about my much-pondered definition of emulation.

(1) In Turing machine and stored program examples of emulation, it's often the case that the emulation involves a specific emulation code. This leads to the version I mentioned in the main text—which assumes that you're simply using the identity translation.

**Figure 148: Big Emulates Small, Using Different Languages**

(2) We might define a notion of *simulation* that is stronger than emulation.

- *Definition.* Big *simulates* Small iff Big with smalltobig emulates
  Small and for any states In and Out,
     Small(In) produces Out iff
        Big(smalltobig(In)) produces smalltobig(Out).

Simulation is not what we are looking for when we want to find a computation Big that returns the same outputs of Small, but much faster. If Small wastes a lot of time, we'd prefer that the faster Big skip over some of Small's behavior. We only require that Big produce translations of those desirable outputs of Small that satisfy the target state detector IsSmallDone.

(3) As well as using emulation to compare the speed of computations, we use it to define the notion of universality. Here we almost feel that a universal computation should not only emulate, but also simulate any other computation.

But it turns out that if $U$ can emulate any computation, it can in some sense simulate any computation as well.

For suppose *P* is a computation and *U* is universal. Suppose that I define a computation *P*Timed that takes state and time pairs as inputs. And the behavior of *P*Timed(<In, *t*>) is to compute the state *P*(In, *t*) and halt. Now since *U* emulates *P*Timed, *U* is able to tell you all of the states that *P*(In) goes through, and this would seem to be as useful as having *U* explicitly simulate *P*.

(4) Suppose we are working with digital computations Small and Big whose states are integers, and which use integral time steps. In this case the what-produces-what information about computation Small can be encoded as the set of pairs <In, Out> such that for some *t*, Small(In) returns Out. And, using a standard encoding, the pair <In, Out> can be thought of as a single integer InOut. So we can use the set Small* of all such integers to answer any question of the form, "Does Small(In) return Out?" Suppose we form a similar set Big* for the computation Big. My definition of emulation can now be recast as follows.

- *Definition of emulation (version for integer states). Big emulates Small* iff there is a translation $f$ such that $n$ lies in Small* iff $f(n)$ lies in Big*.

In recursion theory, this notion of emulation is called one-one reducibility; in symbols this is written Small $\leq_1$ Big. There's a related notion called many-one reducibility, or Small $\leq_m$ Big, in which we allow the translation function to be many-to-one instead of one-to-one.

We might possibly use a many-to-one translation to formulate a concept of weak emulation. Weak emulation would be relevant to a situation where, for instance, I'm modeling a detailed analog physical process with lower-resolution floating point computer numbers. Here, several physically distinct states would map into a single computer state. But, as we know from chaos theory, this kind of emulation tends not to faithfully reproduce outputs, so the notion of weak emulation would seem to be of limited use.

(5) The notion of "emulation" most commonly used in recursion theory is called Turing reducibility. To formulate this notion we need to first define an oracle *O*Big for a computation Big. The *oracle O*Big is the function such that *O*Big(In) = Out if Big halts at Out, and *O*Big(In) = False if In happens to be a value for which Big never halts. And then we say that Small is Turing reducible

to Big iff Big can be defined as a computation that's allowed to use $O$Big as a helper computation, and we express this in symbols as Small $\leq_T$ Big.

For a universal automatist, Turing reducibility is a fantastical study of things that don't really exist. For, given that we don't expect an oracle $O$Big to be a computation in the first place, a universal automatist doesn't expect $O$Big to exist *at all,* so why would they care about what you *could* do if you had it? The issue is that if, like most interesting computations, Big doesn't have a solvable halting problem, then $O$Big can't be a computation because it solves Big's halting problem. So, for a universal automatist, Small $\leq_T$ Big becomes in most cases an "if wishes were horses, then beggars would ride," kind of statement in which we spin conclusions from a counterfactual antecedent. Of course if we take off the perhaps overly strict blinders of universal automatism, Turing reducibility becomes a beautiful theory of great interest, not unlike the Cantorian theory of infinite sets.

So that's it for my discussion of emulation. Onward.

I'll often be interested in how long a computation takes. For any computation $P$, we can define a related computation Runtime_$P$ (In, Out) that searches for the lowest value (if any) of $t$ for which the computation $P$(In, $t$) = Out.

- *Definition.* For each computation $P$, define a function Runtime_$P$ that takes pairs of states as inputs and returns time values. Runtime_$P$(In, Out) is the least value of t such that $P$(In, $t$) = Out, if there is such a $t$, and otherwise Runtime_$P$(In, Out) is undefined.

If one computation emulates another, we can compare their speed. Recall that Big emulates Small means that Big(smalltobig(In)) returns the same outputs as smalltobig(Small(In)).

We can define a special kind of special runtime for the emulation computation.

- *Definition.* Suppose Big emulates Small using the translation smalltobig. Also suppose that Small(In) produces Out. Define the emulation runtime *Runtime_BigSmallEmulation(In, Out)* to be Runtime_Big(smalltobig(In), smalltobig(Out)).

- *Definition.* If Big emulates Small, Big is faster than Small iff for all but a finite number of pairs In and Out,
  Runtime_BigSmallEmulation(In, Out) < Runtime_Small(In, Out).

We're primarily interested in situations where a computation Big is radically faster than $P$. For a computer scientist, if $s$ and t are runtimes, "$s$ is radically smaller than $t$" often means that s is so much smaller than $t$ that even $10^s$ is smaller than $t$ as well. A different way to express this is to say that $s < \log(t)$, where $\log(t)$ is defined as the power $p$ such that $10^p = t$. For a typical integer $N$, $\log(N)$ is approximately the number of digits that it takes to write $N$ out in decimal notation.

- *Definition.* If Big emulates Small, *Big is exponentially faster than Small* iff for all but a finite number of pairs In and Out,
  Runtime_BigSmallEmulation(In, Out) < log(Runtime_Small(In, Out)).

My initial idea was to say that $P$ is predictable iff there is a $Q$ that's exponentially faster than $Q$. But if I only define *unpredictable* to mean "not susceptible to being sped up," I have a problem. When a constant or repetitive computation is described as concisely as possible, we have a rule that no longer allows for *any* speedup, exponential or otherwise. Consider, for instance, the computation ZeroHalt that immediately halts in the state 0 no matter what input you give it. ZeroHalt is a class one computation that's certainly "predictable" in the colloquial sense of the word, but it's not the case that any other computation can emulate ZeroHalt any faster. ZeroHalt is already minimal.

This why I'll rule out the class one and class two computations in my formal definition of an "unpredictable" computation.

- *Definition. P is predictable* iff either of these conditions holds:
  (a) There is a $Q$ that is exponentially faster than $P$, or
  (b) P *is* simple (in the sense of being class one or class two).

- *Definition. P is unpredictable,* iff $P$ is not predictable.

- *Definition. P is strongly unpredictable* iff $P$ is not predictable and there is no $Q$ that is faster than $P$.

In *A New Kind of Science* and in his earlier papers, Stephen Wolfram describes notions of being "computationally reducible," and "computationally irreducible" which are meant, I believe, to have the same intended meaning as my "predictable" and "unpredictable." Wolfram doesn't quite make clear in *A New Kind of Science* that it is indeed *exponential* speed increases that he has in mind. But in conversation with me in 2003, he agreed that this was his intention, as it's easy to get *linear* speedups of PC computations simply by using more states.

The reason I prefer not to employ Wolfram's usage is that, for someone familiar with recursion theory, the phrase "computationally irreducible" looks odd. This is because in recursion theory we commonly say "*P* is reducible to *Q*" to mean something like "*Q* emulates *P*," for some notion of emulation. And given that universal computations can emulate any computation at all, any *P* is reducible to any of the many universal computations *U*, so in the recursion-theoretic sense there aren't any irreducible computations. I also like using "unpredictable" as this sounds more intuitively understandable than "irreducible." This said, I have to admit that perhaps Wolfram's use of "irreducible" does a better job of capturing the essence of the notion, that is, of being a computation that can't be crushed down and made exponentially more efficient.

## A.2: Turing's Theorem

- *Definition. U is a universal computation* iff for every computation *P*, *U* emulates *P*.
- *Turing's construction.* There is a universal computation *U*.

For many *P* and IsPDone pairs, it's hard to decide for an arbitrary input In if *P*(In) will halt. Suppose, for instance, that the inputs code up mathematical theorems, and that *P*(In) systematically looks for a proof Out of In, with *P*(In) halting at Out meaning that Out is indeed a proof of In. If In is some obscure or difficult question about mathematics, it may be impossible to decide if the computation *P*(In) is ever going to halt.

- *Definition.* The computation *P has a solvable halting problem* iff there is a computation *P*FailsToHalt that takes the same inputs as

*P* and has a special output state True such that for every input In, *P*FailsToHalt(In) = True iff *P*(In) doesn't halt. If P does not have a solvable halting problem, we say *P's halting problem is unsolvable.*

So if *P* has a solvable halting problem, this means there is a computation *P*FailsToHalt that detects the inputs for which *P* won't halt. We speak of *P*FailsToHalt as an *endless search detector for* P.

Turing showed how to construct a universal computation in his 1936 paper, "On Computable Numbers, with an Application to the *Entscheidungsproblem,*" which also contains his main result:

- *Turing's Theorem.* If *U* is a universal computation, then *U*'s halting problem is unsolvable.

Once again think of a *Turing machine M* as a computing head coupled to an endless one-dimensional tape divided into cells with symbols on it chosen from some finite alphabet. The head can be in any of some finite number of internal states. We assume there is one distinguished state that we call the "halted" state. At each update, the head reads the symbol in the tape cell corresponding to its current location, and then, on the basis of this symbol and the head's current state, the head writes a symbol into the cell, moves one cell to the left or right, and changes its internal state. If the head enters the halted state, no further updates take place.

In the section A.1 of this Appendix, we spoke of inputs and outputs as states of the machine, but when it comes to a Turing machine, we do better to think of the inputs and outputs as states of the machine's *tape.*

If *M* is a Turing machine and In is a string, we speak of *M*(In) as the computation that results from starting *M* out on a tape containing the string In. It may be that the computation halts, leaving a string Out on the tape that we call the output. In this case we can write *M*(In) = Out. It may also be that the computation *M*(In) never halts. A Turing machine may, for instance, fail to halt on a given input In because it embarks upon an endless, and unsuccessful, search for an integer satisfying some desired condition relative to the input In. For typical Turing machines there will in fact be infinitely many input values for which *M* fails to halt.

A Turing machine is specified by a program $E$ consisting of quintuples specifying how the machine maps possible pairs of <Internal State, Read Symbol> into triples of <Write Symbol, Move Direction, New Internal State>. We can think of $E$ as being coded up as an integer $e$, and we can speak of our machine $M$ as being the machine $M_e$ with code $e$.

I mentioned before that Turing constructs a universal Turing machine. Here's a bit more about how it's made. In this discussion, assume that we have a standard method of "parsing" a string into a pair of strings; the parsing process might involve, for instance, a one-to-one function that maps the set of all integers into the set of all pairs of integers.

- *Turing's construction.* Turing describes a *Universal Turing Machine*, called UTM for short. UTM codes up the behavior of all the $M_e$. For an input string $k$, we think of UTM($k$) as beginning its computation by parsing the string $k$ into a pair of strings $(e, a)$, where $e$ is a program code followed by an input code $a$. If the input string isn't properly formed, then the parsing fails and the machine simply halts. We will often write "UTM($e$, $a$)" instead of "UTM($k$) for the $k$ that encodes the program-input pair $(e, a)$." In saying UTM is universal, we mean that for each program code $e$ and each input $a$, UTM($e$, $a$) will emulate the computation $M_e(a)$. That is, if $M_e(a)$ halts and leaves string $b$ on the tape, then UTM($e$, $a$) also halts and leaves string $b$ on the tape. And if $M_e(a)$ doesn't halt, then UTM($e$, $a$) doesn't halt either.

Note that, depending upon how we set up our coding process and how we implement the details of the simulation, there are any number of different universal Turing machines. We'll assume that UTM is a specific example of a universal Turing machine, and to make our proofs a bit simpler, we'll think of the $k$, $e$, and $a$ inputs as actually being integers.

It's interesting to note that we get into an infinite regress if we let $u$ be the program code for UTM and try to compute UTM($u$, $u$). Sometimes regresses are pernicious, but here it simply means the computation UTM($u$, $u$) never halts, as in this case the UTM is beginning to simulate itself beginning to simulate itself beginning to simulate itself beginning . . . and never gets anything done.

Now let's sketch a proof of Turing's Theorem.

We'll use what mathematicians call a proof by contradiction. According to classical logic, if $D$ is a statement, then either $D$ or the negation $\sim D$ has to be true. If $\sim D$ is impossible, then I can conclude that $D$ must be true.

So now let UTM be a universal Turing machine. I want to prove that UTM does not have a solvable halting problem. To do this, I'll assume that UTM does have a solvable halting problem, and deduce a contradiction, thus showing that "UTM has a solvable halting problem" is impossible.

Suppose we have a computation UTMFailsToHalt solving UTM's halting problem, that is, UTMFailsToHalt($k$) returns True iff UTM($k$) fails to halt. We can safely assume that UTMFailsToHalt is modeled as a Turing machine. So now we can construct an impossible "antidiagonal" machine $A$ such that

(1) $A(a)$ = UTM($a$, $a$) + 1 at the inputs where UTM($a$, $a$) halts, and

(2) $A(a)$ = 0 for the (nonhalting) inputs where UTMFailsToHalt($a$, $a$) returns True.

Since we can constructively define $A$ from UTM and UTMFailsToHalt, $A$ is itself a Turing machine with a program code $a$ such that $A = M_a$. What makes $A$ an "antidiagonal" machine is that $A$'s behavior differs from that of each Turing machine $M_e$ on the input $e$. But this quickly leads to a contradiction, since now $A$ must differ from itself on input $a$. That is, $A(a) = M_a(a) =$ UTM($a$, $a$), by the definition of the UTM. But, by the definition of $A$, if UTM($a$, $a$) is defined, then $A(a)$ = UTM($a$, $a$) + 1, and if UTM($a$, $a$) fails to halt, then $A(a) = 0$. So in either case $A$ differs from itself at input $a$, which is a contradiction. Therefore the UTM didn't have a solvable halting problem after all.

Note that this proof suggests a possible construction that we *can* in fact carry out for UTM. We can always define a $K(a)$ = UTM($a$, $a$) + 1, and let $K(a)$ fail to halt when UTM($a$, $a$) fails to halt. If $K$ has program code $k$, the computation $K(k)$ simply fails to halt, and there's no contradiction. You can only get a contradiction in the counterfactual case where you have UTMFailsToHalt to tell you that UTM($a$, $a$) fails to halt.

Now I'll state and prove a stronger version of Turing's Theorem.

- *Turing's Theorem (variation 2).* If $U$ is a universal computation and IsUDone is a nontrivial target detector, then $U$ has an unsolvable halting problem relative to IsUDone.

The proof of this is much the same as the proof of the normal Turing's Theorem.

The only difference is in how I define the antidiagonal computation $A$. If IsUDone is a *nontrivial* target detector, this means that there are states good and bad such that IsUDone(good) returns True and IsUDone(bad) returns False. I define $A$ so that it halts at either good or bad according to the following rules.

(1) $A(a)$ = bad if UTM($a$, $a$) produces some string $b$ such that IsUDone($b$) returns True.

(2) $A(a)$ = good if UTMFailsToHalt($a$, $a$) returns True.

As in the previous proof, we find the string a such that $M_a$ = A. So then $A(a) = M_a(a) = $ UTM($a$, $a$), by the definition of the UTM. But, by the definition of $A$, if UTM($a$, $a$) halts relative to IsUDone, then $A(a)$ is the nonhalted state bad, and if UTM($a$, $a$) fails to halt, then $A(a)$ halts at good. So in either case $A$ differs from itself at input $a$, which is a contradiction.

There are other variations on Turing's Theorem. For example, if $U$ is universal, the following halting problem is unsolvable: Decide for a given pair <In, Out> whether $U$(In) produces Out. Indeed, just about any general problem you might pose involving endless searches will be unsolvable for the universal computation $U$; this remark is made precise in a statement called Rice's Theorem, which I won't go into here.

Now suppose that $P$ is a computation with an unsolvable halting problem. It turns out that in this case we can also say something about the runtimes of the computations that $P$ does perform: They're unpredictably large.

- *Definition.* If $P$ is a computation and $L$ is an everywhere-defined computation, we say that $L$ *runtime bounds* $P$ if and only if

for all but some finite number of inputs In
    if Runtime_$P$(In) is defined, then Runtime_$P$(In) < $L$(In).

In reading this definition, recall that Runtime_$P$(In) is only defined for those inputs for which $P$(In) halts.

- *Definition.* A computation $P$ is *runtime bounded* if there is an every-where defined $L$ which runtime bounds $P$. Otherwise, *P is runtime unbounded.*

As I discussed in section *6.3: Faster and Smarter,* when you have a run-time-unbounded computation $P$, you really have no way of knowing how long you may need to wait for a given computation $P$(In) to halt—there is no bound you can precompute on the basis of the size of the input In.

So are there any of these troublesome runtime-unbounded computations? Yes; this follows from the Unboundedness Lemma, which I'll now prove.

- *Unboundedness Lemma.* If $P$ has an unsolvable halting problem, then $P$ is runtime unbounded.

We prove the Unboundedness Lemma by what mathematicians call the method of contraposition. That is, if you want to prove that some statement of the form "if $D$, then $E$," it suffices to prove "if ~$E$, then ~$D$." So we'll prove that if $P$ is runtime bounded, then $P$ has a solvable halting problem.

The proof of the lemma hinges on the fact that if the everywhere-defined computation $L$ runtime bounds $P$, then we can use $L$ to solve the halting problem for $P$. Define a computation $P$FailsToHalt to solve the halting problem for $P$ as follows. For any In, compute $P$FailsToHalt(In) by computing $P$(In) for time $L$($t$). If the computation hasn't halted by then, you known it will run forever, so you can return True. So now $P$FailsToHalt(In) = True iff $P$(In) fails to halt.

Combining Turing's Theorem and the Unboundedness Lemma, we can reason that if $U$ is universal, then $U$ has an unsolvable halting problem, and therefore $U$ is runtime unbounded. We can also combine the Unboundedness Lemma with the NUH to conclude what I might call the *Corollary to the NUH,* that is, most naturally occurring complex computations are runtime unbounded relative to some target detector algorithms.

To end this section, let me discuss some of the results in section *6.4: Random Truth*. As this section was already fairly formal, I won't bother restating the definitions of formal theory, provability, consistency, and undecidability. We say that a formal system is *correct* if it doesn't prove false statements. One key result we need is the following:

> • *Unsolvability and Undecidability Lemma.* If *P* is a computation with an unsolvable halting problem, and F is a correct formal theory, then there will be infinitely many sentences about *P* which are undecidable for F.

Proof sketch: Since *P* has an unsolvable halting problem, we have an infinite set NonHalt of all In such that *P*(In) doesn't halt. Since F is correct, if In is in NonHalt, F won't prove "P(In) halts." But there also have to be an infinite number of In in NonHalt such that F won't prove "P(In) does not halt." For otherwise FProvable could be used to solve the halting problem for *P.* End of proof sketch.

As I mentioned in footnote 152, Turing was able to show that if F is a consistent formal system as powerful as arithmetic, then we can embed the construction of Turing machines within the theory of F, so that FProvable becomes a universal computation. By Turing's Theorem, this tells us that FProvable has an unsolvable halting problem. Combining this fact with the Unsolvability and Undecidability Lemma gives us the following result, mentioned in section 6.4, with the proof already sketched in footnote 154.

> • *Undecidability Corollary to Turing's Theorem.* If F is a consistent formal system as powerful as arithmetic, then there are infinitely many sentences which are undecidable for F.

Finally, note that if we combine the NUH with the Unsolvability and Undecidability Lemma, we get the following.

> • *Principle of Natural Undecidability.* For most naturally occurring complex processes, and any correct formal system for science, there will be sentences about the process that are undecidable by the given formal system.

# *Glossary*

**analog, digital.** Traditionally, digital computers use bits and numbers, whereas analog computers represent data as continuously varying quantities such as lengths (as in the slide rule) or voltages. The distinction is actually a bit hard to maintain, so now we just say that a computational system is said to be *digital* if its states range over a small set of discrete possibilities, and is said to be *analog* if it has a very large number of possible states.

**attractor.** The characteristic space and time patterns of processes. Four kinds of attractors typically occur: points, curves, gnarly patterns, and random-looking patterns. The interesting gnarly attractors are also known as strange attractors.

**bifurcation.** A bifurcation occurs when a system begins ranging over a completely different zone of possibilities within the space of all possible phenomena. The term bifurcation is a bit misleading, as a bifurcation doesn't necessarily have anything to do with something splitting into *two*. Bifurcation means nothing more than changing something about a system in such a way as to make its behavior move to a different attractor.

**Brian's Brain.** A cellular automaton rule using three different states: ready, firing, and resting. This rule is known for its very lively and gnarly activity, and can be regarded as a toy model of neuron stimulations in the human brain. Named after Brian Silverman.

**CA, cellular automaton.** A parallel computation that's carried out in a space of cells. The cell space can be one-, two-, three- or higher-dimensional. CAs are characterized by updating all their cells at once, by having the same update rule for each cell, and by having each cell only accept input from immediately neighboring cells.

**chaos.** A system is said to be chaotic if it a very slight change in the system's initial conditions very quickly produces easily visible changes in its behavior. The behaviors of chaotic systems often generate spacetime patterns that have fractal shapes, and which can be said to lie upon strange attractors.

**class one, two, three, and four.** These classifications are applied to computations or to patterns or behaviors that might be produced by computations. A computation is classified according to which of the following behaviors it shows. *Class one*: Enters a constant state. *Class two*: Outputs a repetitive or nested pattern. *Class three*: Produces messy, random-looking crud. *Class four*: Produces gnarly, nonrepeating, purposeful-looking patterns.

**complex.** A complex computation is in class three or class four, that is, it produces a messy, random-looking output or a gnarly, intricate output. Note that some authors use complex to mean class four exclusively, but we are not following this usage.

**complexity.** Complexity is used in various senses. In this book, we usually speak of complexity as a measure of computational sophistication, with the complexity scale increasing through the computation classes in the order class one, class two, class three, and class four. Even though the class four computations appear visually orderly in that we can distinguish moving glider patterns in them, they may be computationally more complex. A quite different meaning of complexity has to do with emulation.

A computation *P* is said to be as complex as *Q* if *P* is able to emulate the behavior of *Q*. The computations that are the most complex in this sense are the universal ones, which are also usually in class four and are thus maximally complex in the first sense of the word.

**computation.** A computation is any process that obeys finitely describable rules.

**Copenhagen interpretation.** Quantum mechanics consists of a set of rules that work very well at predicting the results of certain kinds of experiments. There is disagreement about the best way to interpret these rules in terms of some underlying reality. The popular Copenhagen interpretation says that systems evolve into overlapping superpositions of many different states, but that when you observe a system it somehow collapses down into being in a pure and precise state.

**critical state.** Parallel-computing systems in physics and society often get into critical states if they're subjected to lots of inputs over a long period of time. A system in a critical state is tuned to a point where an additional input can cause any one of a very wide range of reactions. The sizes of these reactions will be distributed according to a *power law.*

**digital.** See *analog.*

**emulation.** A computation Big is said to emulate another computation Small, if Big is able to mimic the input-to-output behavior of Small. Generally speaking, any personal computer can emulate any other personal computer.

**endless search detector.** If I have a computation *P* and an input In, I set in motion a computation *P*(In) that may or may not eventually reach a target state. An endless search detector is a computation of the form *P*FailsTo-Halt such that *P*FailsToHalt(In) is True if *P*(In) runs forever.

**feasible.** A computation with a given input is said to be feasible if it produces a useful answer in a reasonable amount of time.

**finite-element model.** A finite element model simulates a physical processes by dividing space into small cells and measuring time in small ticks. These models are closely related to *cellular automata.*

**gnarly.** A process or pattern is gnarly if it can be regarded as coming from a class four computation. To be gnarly is to be non repeating, purposeful-looking, and intricate. Examples in nature would be twisting tree roots, large ocean waves, or weathered human faces.

**intrinsically random.** A computation is said to be intrinsically random if it generates random-looking outputs, even in the absence of any additional inputs. Wolframs CA Rule 30 is an example of such a computation.

**irreducible.** See *unpredictable.*

**Life.** The cellular automaton known as the Game of Life uses two cell states, live and dead. Life is characterized by having a lot of activity that usually dies out. With the proper initial conditions, however, a Life CA can simulate any given computation. Invented by John Conway.

**many universes theory, multiverse.** One can interpret quantum mechanics to mean that there are many parallel universes—known as a multiverse—and that until we perform a measurement on a system, we don't know which universe we and the system are actually in. Even though it may not be strictly true, the notion of a multiverse is useful for understanding quantum computation.

**neuron, neural net.** A biological neuron is a cell in a brain. Computer scientists work with toy neurons that share some of the features of the brain cell: they sum up their inputs to get a stimulation level, and if the level is high enough, the neuron sends out a signal. Many artificially intelligent programs work by constructing computer models from these toy neurons.

**PCE, Principle of Computational Equivalence.** Wolfram formulates this principle as follows: Almost all processes that are not obviously simple can be viewed as computations of equivalent sophistication.

**PCU, Principle of Computational Unpredictability.** Although Wolfram doesn't explicitly formulate this principle, he argues for it. I express it as follows: Most naturally occurring complex computations are unpredictable.

**Planck length.** This is the length $1.6 \times 10^{-35}$ meters, a scale below which it's not clear if we can actually speak of continuous space. The existence of this minimal size level suggests that ultimate reality may in fact have a granular structure to it, akin to a CA.

**power law.** Suppose that I am looking at a variety of similar entities and measuring a quality $L$ of each entity. And now suppose that I count the number $N$ of entities that occur at each given quality level $L$. The distribution is said to obey a *histogram-style* power law provided that $N$ is proportional to the reciprocal of $L$ raised to some power. In *rank-style* power laws, $L$ is porportional to the reciprocal of $R$ raised to some power where $R$ is the popularity of an entity. The two kinds of power law are equivalent. Power laws occur very commonly in physical and social situations.

**pseudorandom.** A computation which generates reasonably random-looking outputs is said to be pseudorandom. It's not clear if any truly and absolutely random processes exist. For if the world were to be an immense deterministic computation of some kind, everything would have a cause of some kind, and thus be only pseudorandom.

**Rule 30, Rule 110.** Wolfram uses a particular system for numbering the 256 simplest kinds of CA rules. Two of the most famous rules have the numbers 30 and 110. Rule 30 generates completely random-looking output when started out with a single marked cell. Rule 110 produces wandering gliders that bounce off each other. Rule 110 is known to be a universal computation. These two rules are standard examples of, respectively, class three and class four computations.

**simple.** A simple computation is in class one or class two, that is, it reaches a fixed state and halts, it enters a periodic loop, or it produces an orderly nested pattern.

**speedup.** Any hardware or software improvement that is used to achieve a computational task in a faster way. A linear speedup reduces the runtime by some constant factor, whereas an exponential speedup reduces a runtime to the logarithm of its value—that is, an exponential speedup reduces a slowtime to a fasttime such that fasttime < log(slowtime), or, if you don't like logarithms, such that $10^{\text{fasttime}}$ < slowtime. The classic example of an exponential speedup is using positional arithmetic to do addition instead of counting on your fingers.

**target state detector.** If $P$ is a computation and In is an input, we say that the process $P$(In) halts if it reaches some constant state Out. More generally, we can define a target state detector Is$P$Done, and instead of requiring that $P$(In) reach a fixed state, we check to see if $P$(In) reaches a state Out such that Is$P$Done(Out) is True.

**transactional interpretation of quantum mechanics.** In the transactional interpretation of quantum mechanics we suppose that systems do have definite nonsuperposed internal states even before we measure them. In order to consistently maintain this view, it's necessary to accept that "effects" can send influences backward in time to affect their "causes." In this view the universe is something of a synchronistic whole.

**Turing's Theorem.** Alan Turing proved that if $U$ is a universal computation, then $U$ has an unsolvable halting problem.

**unpredictable, strongly unpredictable.** A computation as unpredictable if there is no way to exponentially speed it up by using a more efficient computation. Wolfram uses the word "irreducible" for the same concept. A computation is strongly unpredictable if it's impossible to even achieve a linear speedup of the computation.

**undecidable.** A sentence $S$ is undecidable for a given formal system if the system is unable to prove or to disprove $S$.

**universal computation.** A computation is universal if it able to emulate every other computation. Our familiar personal computers embody universal computations, and many natural phenomena may be universal computations as well.

**unsolvable halting problem.** A computation $P$ is said to have an unsolvable halting problem if there is no way to decide which inputs In will send $P$ in to an endless nonhalting process. We can speak of unsolvability relative to a special target detector Is$P$Done, and unsolvability in this sense means that there is no endless search detector $P$FailsToHalt such that $P$FailsToHalt(In) returns True precisely when $P$(In) will never produce a state Out such that Is$P$Done(Out) holds.

**NUH, Natural Unsolvability Hypothesis.** This hypothesis says: Most naturally occurring complex computations have unsolvable halting problems relative to some target detector. This hypothesis is weaker than Wolfram's PCE. The NUH also implies the Principle of Natural Undecidability: For most naturally occurring complex processes, and any correct formal system for science, there will be sentences about the process that are undecidable by the given formal system.

**Zhabotinsky scroll.** Many cellular automata produce moving lima-bean-shaped scrolls. These are called Zhabotinsky scrolls after the Soviet physicist who, with his colleague Belousov, produced these scrolls in chemical solutions. Zhabotinsky scrolls occur in many natural and social contexts.

# *Notes*

The book's Web site, www.rudyrucker.com/lifebox, has all the links mentioned here in clickable form.

CHAPTER 1: COMPUTATION EVERYWHERE

1. Be warned that I'm introducing a new usage here. In legal parlance, *automatism* is used to mean something done by the muscles without any conscious control— a spasm, a reflex twitch, a convulsion, or perhaps even sleep-walking would be examples of legal automatism. The surrealist artists used *automatism* to refer to works created with as little conscious control as possible, with a view to unveiling the workings of the subconscious by the mind—so-called automatic writing is an example of surrealist automatism. Spiritualists use *automatism* to describe a medium speaking under the control of a spirit. Philosophers have used *automatism* to refer to any kind of dull, plodding behavior—in the early 1900s, Henri Bergson often spoke of *transcending automatism* when discussing how the human spirit should rise above the low mechanistic workings of matter.

But I want to use *universal automatism* to refer to the idea that everything in the world is a kind of computation.

There actually *is* an existing philosophical word for a notion fairly closely related to what I'm calling automatism. This would be *computationalism,* which is the belief that the human mind can be modeled as a computation. Universal automatism can be thought of as a generalization of computationalism. Universal automatism says that not only is the human mind a kind of computation; everything else is a computation as well. A pleasant thing about speaking of universal automatism instead of about computationalism is that it frees me from some of the baggage associated with the years-long and by now somewhat stale philosophical debates about artificial intelligence.

Another reason I like using the phrase "universal automatism" is because of its linguistic association with "cellular automata," which are a kind of parallel algorithm often used to illustrate the belief.

2. A philosophical quagmire beckons from the side of the road. Underlying the notion of inputs and outputs is the assumption that our computing system is embedded in linear time, with clear notions of earlier and later states. This might not always be a safe assumption. If, for instance, one wants to argue that the spacetime fabric of the universe is the result of a cosmic computation, it's better not to sneak the notion of time into the cosmic computation that's supposed to explain space and time. Stephen Wolfram, for instance, takes this into account when he tries to describe a computational basis for the cosmos in chapter 9 of his *A New Kind of Science* (Champaign, Ill.: Wolfram Media, 2002), pp. 433–546. Another point is that if we seek to exorcise the demons of quantum mechanics by viewing reality as a multiverse of branching time, then we need to remember that if two states lie on different branches it may not make sense to say that one is earlier or later than the other. But for now, yes, we will think of our computational systems as having a clear flow of time.

3. Given that $P(\text{In})$ is really thought of as a *process* rather than a *function* that always returns a definite value, one might perhaps do better to write $P[\text{In}]$ instead of $P(\text{In})$, but my feeling was that using two kinds of brackets might make things look more confusing.

4. Actually, there's a way to achieve what's called a polynomial speedup of Gosper's original calculation by using the 1995 discovery of the Bailey-Borwein-Plouffe formula for extracting an arbitrary digit of pi (see http://mathworld.wolfram.com/BBPFormula.html). But this formula hasn't been *proved* to work; its predictions are only "highly probable." In any case, given that I define an unpredictable computation to be one that doesn't allow for an *exponential* speedup, we're still safe in calling Gosper's computation of pi unpredictable, at least for now.

5. This formulation of the PCE is quoted from *Wolfram, A New Kind of Science*, pp. 716–17.

6. The following quote is from Wolfram, *A New Kind of Science*, p. 741. In my Technical Appendix, I give a formal definition of what we might call either computational irreducibility or unpredictability: a computation $P$ is *unpredictable* if there is no computation Fast$P$ that emulates $P$ and that runs *exponentially* faster than $P$.

Although Wolfram gives the impression of believing the PCU to be provable, I feel that he's mistaken on this point—as I'll discuss in chapter 6 and footnote 149. The PCU is a *conjecture* about the types of naturally occurring computations that one might expect to find.

7. The Vichniac vote rule is discussed in Tommaso Toffoli and Norman Margolus, *Cellular Automaton Machines* (Cambridge, Mass.: MIT Press, 1987). The original reference is Gérard Vichniac, "Simulating Physics with Cellular Automata," *Physica 10D* (1984): 96–115.

8. Let's try to make precise the exact sense in which using digits is exponentially faster than counting by one. If we stick to our estimate that adding a column of two numbers takes ten steps, then adding two $N$-digit numbers with arithmetic takes $\text{Short}T = 10 \cdot N$ steps. Suppose $A$ is the smaller of the two numbers added. If $A$ has a $N$ digits, this actually means that $A = a \cdot 10^N$ for some real number a between 0.1 and 1. So adding the numbers by counting off the smaller number by ones takes $\text{Long}T = a \cdot 10^N$ steps. $\text{Long}T$ is exponentially larger than $\text{Short}T$ in the sense that $\text{Long}T$ is greater than $0.1 \cdot 10^{(0.1 \cdot \text{Short}T)}$. The two fixed factors of 0.1 are not considered to be a problem in this kind of size comparison; we're allowed to neglect linear factors as long as we say that $\text{Long}T$ is "on the order of" $10^{\text{Short}T}$.

9. Ada Augusta, Countess of Lovelace, "Notes on Menabrea's Sketch of the Analytical Engine," reprinted in Philip and Emily Morrison, eds., *Charles Babbage and His Calculating Engines: Selected Writings by Charles Babbage and Others* (New York: Dover, 1961), p. 252.

10. William Gibson and Bruce Sterling, *The Difference Engine* (New York: Bantam Books, 1991), pp. 136–137.

11. Arthur Burks, Herman Goldstine, and John von Neumann, "Preliminary Discussion of the Logical Design of an Electronic Computing Instrument," reprinted in John von Neumann, *Collected Works,* vol. V (New York: Macmillan, 1963), p. 35.

12. The paper is "On Computable Numbers, with an Application to the *Entscheidungsproblem,*" *Proceedings of the London Mathematical Society,* 42(2)(1936–37): 230–65. A link to this truly epochal paper can be found online at www.turing.org.uk/sources/biblio.html, and the paper is also reprinted with annotations in Martin Davis, ed., *The Undecidable,* (New York: Raven, 1965). It's said that Turing's definition of his machines was inspired by thinking about the kinds of computations that bank clerks do.

13. As I discuss in chapter 6 and in the Technical Appendix, computations that

have predictable halting behaviors are essentially simpler than those computations for that there's no way to tell in advance if a given input will initiate a computation that halts. Certainly it's possible to conceive of very complicated kinds of computations that always halt, but from a mathematician's standpoint, any rule that uniformly dies down to a constant state is class one. Gnarly computations need to be unpredictably immortal.

14. Rudy Rucker, *The Hacker and the Ants,* (New York: Avon Books, 1994), p. 8. The book originally came out in 1994, but a "Release 2.0" version has since appeared (New York: Four Walls Eight Windows, 2003).

15. From "Random Processes and Transformations," Proceedings of the International Congress of Mathematics (1950), vol. 2, pp. 264–275, 1952. 1950 reprinted in Stanislaw Ulam, *Sets, Numbers and Universes* (Cambridge, Mass.: MIT Press, 1974), p. 336.

16. Martin Gardner, "Mathematical Games: The fantastic combinations of John Conway's new solitaire game Life," *Scientific American* (October 1970), 120–23.

17. Steven Levy, *Hackers: Heroes of the Computer Revolution* (New York: Doubleday, 1984), p. 147.

18. There are some very good special-purpose Life simulators available on the Web, along with many bizarre pattern files. One of the best ones for Windows is called Life32, and can be found at *http://www.mindspring.com/~alanh/Life32/index.html.*

19. See E. R. Berlekamp, J. H. Conway, and R. K. Guy, *Winning Ways for Your Mathematical Plays,* Vol. 2 (New York: Academic Press, 1982). A second edition has appeared from AK Peters of Wellesley, Mass.

20. More about Fredkin's vision of the world as a CA can be on his Web site, http://www.digitalphilosophy.org/. See also the sketch of Fredkin in Robert Wright, *Three Scientists and Their Gods,* (New York: Random House, 1988).

21. Stephen Wolfram, "Computer Software in Science and Mathematics," *Scientific American* (September 1984): 188–203.

22. Rudy, Rucker, *Wetware,* (New York: Avon Books, 1988), p. 32.

23. The program was originally marketed as *Rudy Rucker's CA Lab: Rudy Rucker's Cellular Automata Laboratory* (Sausalito, Calif.: Autodesk, 1989). When Walker rewrote it as a Windows program, he renamed it *CelLab* to avoid a lawsuit from a sober-sided company called Computer Associates, who seemed to feel they "owned" the letters "CA." *CelLab* is available for free download from the book's Web site, www.rudyrucker.com/lifebox/.

24. The executable and source code for CAPOW are available for free download from the book's Web site. As I discuss at some length in the first section of chapter two, although a program like CAPOW is only *approximating* continuous numbers by means of digital approximations, the patterns that occur resemble those one might see if the numbers were in fact infinitely precise and fully continuous.

25. The Hodgepodge rule is described in M. Gerhardt, H. Schuster, and J. J. Tyson, "A Cellular Automaton Model of Excitable Media Including Curvature and Dispersion," *Science* 247 (1990): 1563–66. The RainZha rule first appears in Rudy Rucker, *CA Lab Manual* (Sausalito: Autodesk, 1989). The Hodgepodge and RainZha rules are based upon about thirty discrete states. These rules are both implemented in CelLab. The RainZha rule is a variation of a three-state earliest scroll-producing CA rule discovered by James Greenberg and Stuart Hastings in 1997; a good survey of Greenberg-Hastings rules can be found online at David Griffeath's "Primordial Soup Kitchen" Web site on CAs, http://psoup.math.wisc.edu/java/jgh.html.

The Winfree rule stems from Arthur T. Winfree, "Rotating Chemical Reactions," *Scientific American* (June 1974): 82–95; in this rule, each cell holds two continuous-valued real numbers, which we think of as the activator and the inhibitor. The Meinhardt rule is also a continuous-valued activator-inhibitor rule, found in Hans Meinhardt, *The Algorithmic Beauty of Sea Shells* (New York: Springer-Verlag, 1995). These rules are implemented in my CAPOW package. Further explanations of the rules in my figures can be found on my book's Web site, www.rudyrucker.com/lifebox/.

CHAPTER 2: OUR RICH WORLD

26. If desired, we can, however, implement a data type for "arbitrary precision reals," in which real numbers with any finite number of decimal places are allowed. Mathematical software such as Maple and Mathematica support these types. But the simple CA models I'll discuss are in fact based on the *float* type.

27. In other words, yes, if you try to model a continuous-valued real number by using a range of only ten or a hundred distinct values between zero and one, your simulation will be chunky and inaccurate and unable to support smooth-looking waves. But once you drop the granularity low enough to be using ten thousand or a hundred thousand or a million discrete values between zero and one, the behavior stabilizes and displays smooth wave–like behavior for hundreds of thousands of generations. In the size ranges and runtimes I've played with, my continuous-valued CAs already look the same as they would if we were really

using an infinity of values. I have more on this point in my paper, "Continuous-Valued Cellular Automata in Two Dimensions," in David Griffeath and Chris Moore, eds., *New Constructions in Cellular Automata* (New York: Oxford University Press, 2003), pp. 295–316.

28. Another point to make vis-à-vis relativity and computational models of the universe: If the universe really were to be the result of a digital computation, as Wolfram supposes it to be, this might put stricter constraints on cosmology than those required simply by general relativity, and perhaps there could, after all, be a consistent global notion of time.

29. The continuous-valued CA images in this book were all made with the CAPOW software. As I mentioned in chapter one, CAPOW is a Windows program that I developed with my computer science students at San Jose State University in the late 1990s. I've been tweaking and expanding the program ever since. The research was funded by a grant from the Electric Power Research Institute (EPRI) of Palo Alto, California.

30. Stanislaw Ulam, in *Collected Papers of Enrico Fermi,* Vol. 2, (Chicago: University of Chicago Press, 1965).

31. You might wonder why the spots in the cubic wave patterns are symmetric, whereas the quadratic wave spots are not. This has to do with the fact that cubing preserves the distinction between negative and positive numbers but squaring does not. For more information, see Dan Ostrov and Rudy Rucker, "Continuous-Valued Cellular Automata for Nonlinear Wave Equations," *Complex Systems* 10 (Fall 1997): 91–119. A project I'd like to see would be a surfing game based on a CA simulating nonlinear waves.

32. James Gleick, *Chaos: Making a New Science* (New York: Viking, 1987), p. 262.

33. See Gerald Jay Sussman and Jack Wisdom, "Chaotic Evolution of the Solar System," *Science* 257 (July 3, 1992). Or see Jack Wisdom's online pages about this, http://geosys.mit.edu/~solar/text/short.html.

Despite the inevitable long-term onset of chaos, at this time our digital orrery programs are quite highly developed, taking into account the mutual gravitational effects of the planets and the asteroids. John Walker recently became obsessed with finding out if and when there would ever be a time when, viewed from Earth, both Venus and Mercury would ever appear to cross or "transit" our Sun's disk at the same time. After running a computation for about three months he found that, yes, a double transit will occur on July 26 in the year 69163! See http://www.fourmilab.ch/documents/canon_transits/.

34. The computer scientist Gregory Chaitin has used a very similar counting argument to show that most integers $n$ must be Chaitin-Kolmogorov incompressible in the sense of $n$ not being equal to $T_e(0)$ for any Turing program code $e < n$; see, for instance, G. J. Chaitin, *The Unknowable* (New York: Springer-Verlag, 1999). For more on Chaitin's work, see footnote 156.

35. Later in the book I'll define quite precisely what I mean by unpredictable. I do need to acknowledge that although I'll be using "pseudorandom" as a synonym of "unpredictable," cryptographers and theoretical computer scientists have developed some rather more refined technical definitions for the concept of pseudorandomness.

36. The name arose because, historically, chaoticians first investigated the attractors of the logistic map, whose strange attractors *do* in fact change by having each point of the attractor split into two. There's a well-known picture of the logistic map's family of attractors, arranged to form a sideways-branching tree, with each attractor bifurcating to make the next one. Three good chaos references are: the best-selling book by James Gleick, *Chaos*; the cartoon-illustrated volume by Ralph Abraham and Chris Shaw, *Dynamics: The Geometry of Behavior,* 3rd ed. (Santa Cruz: Aerial Press, 2004); and the clear and profound paperback by Edward Lorenz, *The Essence of Chaos* (Seattle: University of Washington Press, 1993).

37. Richard Feynman, Robert Leighton, and Matthew Sands, *The Feynman Lectures on Physics* (Addison-Wesley 1963), p. 37–11.

38. The computer scientist Scott Aaronson, who enjoys quantum mechanics a lot more than I do, remarks that it would be better to say that quantum mechanics is like the rising tide that submerges a sand castle, and that wanting to deny quantum mechanics is as feckless as telling the tide not to rise. Maybe so. But, hey, as long as we're playing with images, how about this: When I try to explain quantum mechanics, I feel like a frightened former landowner singing the praises of a revolutionary regime that's taken away his home, or like a one-legged man trying to tap dance.

39. See Brian Greene, *The Elegant Universe* (New York: W. W. Norton, 1999) or Lee Smolin, *Three Roads to Quantum Gravity* (New York: Basic Books, 2001).

40. See Fredkin's Web site, http://www.digitalphilosophy.org/, and especially see chapter nine of Stephen Wolfram's *A New Kind of Science*. My impression is that Wolfram's approach is several orders of magnitude more sophisticated than Fredkin's.

41. John Cramer, "The Transactional Interpretation of Quantum Mechanics," *Reviews of Modern Physics* 58 (July 1986): 647–88. The paper is online at http://mist.npl.washington.edu/ti/.

42. Quoted in Rudy Rucker, *The Fourth Dimension* (Boston: Houghton Mifflin, Boston 1984), p. 136.

43. See also Stephen Wolfram's eye-opening discussion of CAs and reversibility in *A New Kind of Science,* pp. 435–57.

44. My writing notes for *As Above, So Below: A Novel of Peter Bruegel* (New York: Tor Books, 2003) can be found online at www.rudyrucker.com/bruegel.

45. Now, as I mentioned earlier, in some universes there can be synchronization problems with breaking spacetime into tidy spacelike sheets—but maybe our universe doesn't happen to be a troublesome one. Or maybe (just maybe!) the real picture is somewhat more complicated than what I've here proposed.

46. Let me say a bit more about how quantum mechanics treats wave functions as the fundamental realities. Suppose, for instance, that you have a particle (such as an electron) that can be located anywhere along the $x$-axis. A wave function for this type of "one-dimensional single-particle system" has the form $\psi(x)$, that is, for each location $x$, $\psi$ assigns a value. It's traditional to use the Greek letter psi, or $\psi$, for this purpose.

What makes $\psi$ interesting is that the value of $\psi(x)$ isn't a simple real number. No, it's a *pair* of real numbers, which we dras as arrows pointing away from the $x$-axis.

The wave functions for a single particle system tend to wind around the axis like vines around a beanpole. This is because the angle of the $\psi(x)$ arrow varies as well as the length of the arrow. In figure 149, the $x$-axis runs from left to right. We've drawn the graph of our wave function as a ribbon, to make it easier to see. Each point $x$ has a unique corresponding "arrow-tip" point $\psi(x)$ on the ribbon.

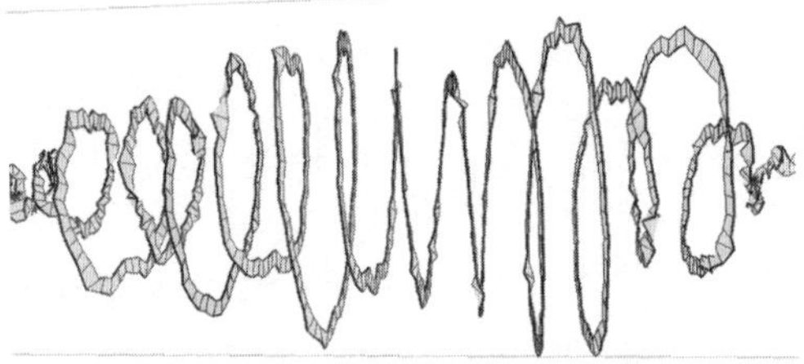

**Figure 149: A Random Wave Function**

Roughly speaking, for any specific location $x$, the distance of the $\psi(x)$ point from the axis measures the likelihood of finding the particle to actually be at $x$. Thus a particle that hasn't yet decided between two possible positions might have a wave function resembling figure 150.

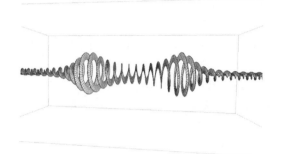

**Figure 150: Wave Function for a Particle with Two Likely Positions**

Having the $\psi(x)$ graph twist around the axis serves two purposes. It allows wave functions to cancel each other out, by having them be out of phase with each other. In addition, it allows wave functions to encode a particle's velocity. As it happens, if the velocity of a particle is known to be some specific value, this means that the wave function will resemble a smoothly coiling spring, as shown in figure 151.

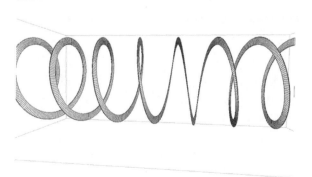

**Figure 151: Wave Function with Precise Velocity**

The uniform helix is a pure state for the velocity measurement. Since it's the same at every $x$ location, it holds no position information at all. What's a pure state for a position measurement? It's a somewhat unnatural kind of function; a line that, rather than coiling around the $x$-axis, runs right along the axis and then, at one particular position point, shoots up to a vastly tall vertical spike and then drops immediately back to the axis. Since it doesn't wrap around the $x$-axis, it holds no velocity information at all. In practice, the wave functions for actually existing particles combine these two features; they coil around the axis and they have higher amplitudes at some points than at others.

The deterministic aspect of pure quantum mechanics hinges on the fact that we have a simple rule for describing how a system's wave function $\psi(x)$ changes with time. First of all, to think of the wave function as being dependent on time, we write it as $\psi(x, t)$. The evolution of the wave function over time is summarized by a magically concise formula called Schrödinger's wave equation.

$$ih\frac{\partial}{\partial t}\psi(\vec{x}, t) = H\ \psi(\vec{x}, t)$$

I'm *not* going to try and explain Schrödinger's wave equation. Suffice it to say that it provides a fully deterministic rule for the behavior of a quantum system—up until such time as someone measures one of the system's attributes.

By the way, one possible problem with this highly mathematical worldview is that, after all, we don't really have much reason to believe that the world does support the existence of infinitely accurate real numbers such as are to be used in the wave functions. Schrödinger's intricate construction may turn out to be simply an approximation or averaging-out of some discrete and digital underlying reality such as, say, a couple of multidimensional CAs, such as the paired Physics and Metaphysics rules that I illustrated in section *2.5: What Is Reality?*

47. The jabberwocky oddity of this gate name reminds me of the title of Walter Tevis's story, "The Ifth of Oofth" (*Galaxy,* April 1957). As I recall, Tevis's story is about a guy who gets so bollixed up from time travel and hyperspace jumps that "the Ifth of Oofth" actually sounds like a reasonable date to him.

48. This algorithm was discovered by Peter Shor in 1994. A detailed popular account of it can be found in Julian Brown, *The Quest for the Quantum Computer*

(New York: Touchstone, 2000). In its hardback edition the book had the title *Minds, Machines, and the Multiverse.*

49. David Deutsch, *The Fabric of Reality: The Science of Parallel Universes—and Its Implications* (New York: Penguin, 1997). Deutsch has thought long and hard about quantum computers; among other things, he proved the existence of a universal quantum computer, and he devised a thought experiment intended to show that an artificially intelligent quantum computer could refute the idea that consciousness necessarily involves collapsing the wave function. Deutsch's thought experiment is nicely presented in Appendix C of Julian Brown's *The Quest for the Quantum Computer.* See also my section *4.8: Quantum Soul,* where I discuss physicist Nick Herbert's attempts to imagine our natural state of consciousness as being that of an uncollapsed wave function.

50. Rudy Rucker, *Wetware* (New York: Avon Books, 1988), pp. 83–86. I wrote *Wetware* in six weeks in Lynchburg, Virginia, of all places, in the spring of 1986, right before moving to Silicon Valley. Oozer's speech patterns are modeled on those of Neal Cassady, as twinked in Jack Kerouac, *Visions of Cody* (New York: McGraw-Hill, 1974).

CHAPTER 3: LIFE'S LOVELY GNARL

51. The quote is taken from a supposed interview with one Max Yukawa in Rudy Rucker, R. U. Sirius, and Queen Mu, eds., *Mondo 2000: A User's Guide to the New Edge* (New York: HarperCollins, 1992). Actually Max Yukawa was a character in my 1984 novel *Wetware* and the interview was a hoax. Although, to my eternal pride, the august and geekly *Jargon File* (http://www.catb.org/~esr/jargon/) of computer culture slang suggests that I coined the word *wetware,* I myself first saw the word in Bruce Sterling's novel *Schizmatrix* (New York: Arbor House, 1985), and Bruce says he got it from somewhere else that he can't remember.

52. Stuart Kauffman, *At Home in the Universe* (New York: Oxford University Press, 1995), p. 50. In the late 1960s Kauffman carried out some famous computer experiments on what he came to call random Boolean networks. You can play with these by using a Java applet by Torstein Reil found at http://users.ox.ac.uk/~quee0818/complexity/complexity.html.

53. Georg Hegel, *The Phenomenology of Mind* (New York: Harper & Row, 1967), pp. 75–76.

54. The complete reference for Turing's paper is Alan Turing, "The Chemical Basis

of Morphogenesis," *Philosophical Transactions of the Royal Society of London* 641 (1952) B237, 37–72. A good modern account of activator-inhibitor systems can be found in Philip Ball, *The Self-Made Tapestry: Pattern Formation in Nature* (New York: Oxford University Press, 1999).

55. The activator-inhibitor CA rules illustrated in this section are derived from work by Hans Meinhardt, *The Algorithmic Beauty of Sea Shells* (New York: Springer Verlag, 1995). Details about the rules I used for my images can be found on the book's Web page or in my paper, "Continuous-Valued Cellular Automata in Two Dimensions," in *New Constructions in Cellular Automata.*

56. This picture can be found in the online Turing archives at http://www. turingarchive.org/viewer/?id=476&title=25. More links and information about Turing's work on morphogenesis can be found on a page at Jonathan Swinton's Web site, http://www.swintons.net/jonathan/Turing/turbox.htm.

57. Brian Goodwin, *How the Leopard Changed Its Spots: The Evolution of Complexity* (Princeton, N.J.: Princeton University Press, 1994), pp. 168, 114.

58. Image made with Chaos program: Josh Gordon, Rudy Rucker, and John Walker, *James Gleick's Chaos: The Software* (Sausalito, Calif: Autodesk, 1990). At the time we wrote this program, computers were so slow that we had to use all kinds of odd tricks to make the program run fast enough.

59. Fuller's phrase in context: "I live on Earth at present, and I don't know what I am. I know that I am not a category. I am not a thing—a noun. I seem to be a verb, an evolutionary process—an integral function of the universe." See R. Buckminster Fuller, Jerome Agel, and Quentin Fiore, *I Seem to Be a Verb* (New York: Bantam, 1970).

I take the fluttering leaf analogy fairly seriously. My sense is that a fluttering leaf is not only as complex as the play of my emotions, but also as complex as the combined mental processes of my mind. My friend John Walker disputes this, arguing that real computational intelligence results not just from having a class four process, but from also having a lot of rapidly accessible and stable memory in which to store intermediate results; see his essay at http://www.fourmilab.ch/documents/comp_mem_nat_life/. A fluttering leaf only stores data within the subtleties of its motions, which doesn't seem like so accessible a form as being stored on a disk or in neurons. Walker feels that, thanks to its neural storage, a human mind really *is* doing more than most naturally occurring class four computations.

Reasonable as this view seems, I don't agree with it. I'm comfortable with viewing the mind as simply one among many universal computations found in the natural world. Yes, it's not *feasible* to model my brain as a fluttering leaf, but *in principle* the two computations are of the same power and sophistication. To me, this kind of deflating view of oneself comes as a relief and a stress-reducer. If I'm nothing more than a piece of dust dancing in the wind, what do I have to worry about?

60. See Robert May's popular essay, "The Best Possible Time to Be Alive," in Graham Farmelo, ed., *It Must Be Beautiful: Great Equations of Modern Science* (London, UK: Granta Books, 2002).

61. Kunihiko Kaneko, "Pattern Dynamics in Spatiotemporal Chaos," *Physica* 34D (1989): 1–41 investigates CAs based on a single species with a population value. See also Ralph Abraham, John Corliss, and John Dorband, "Order and Chaos in the Toral Logistic Lattice," *International Journal of Bifurcations and Chaos* 1(1) (March, 1991): 227–34. I have more details on their rule on my book's Web page, www.rudyrucker.com/lifebox.

62. From "The General and Logical Theory of Automata," 1948, reprinted in John von Neumann, *Collected Works,* Vol. 5 (New York: Macmillan, 1963), p. 315. The weird scenario described in this quote is reminiscent of a scene in Kurt Vonnegut Jr.'s *Sirens of Titan* (New York: Dell, 1971) where an unhappy robot tears himself apart and floats the pieces in a lake.

63. Christopher Langton, "Self-Reproduction in Cellular Automata," *Physica D* 10 (1984): 135–44.

64. *Wetware,* pp. 32–33.

65. The canonical source for information about L-systems is the lovely illustrated book, Przemyslaw Prusinkiewicz and Aristid Lindenmayer, *The Algorithmic Beauty of Plants* (New York: Springer Verlag, 1990). The L-system flower sequence can be found online at http://www.cpsc.ucalgary.ca/Research/bmv/vmm-deluxe/Plates.html.

66. Rodney Brooks, *Flesh and Machines: How Robots Will Change Us* (New York: Vintage Books, 2003), pp. 39–40.

67. Brooks, *Flesh and Machines,* pp. 184, 188.

68. Thomas Mann, *Doctor Faustus* (New York: Knopf, 1948), pp. 19–20.

69. The first book on genetic algorithms was John Holland, *Adaptation in Natural and Artificial Systems* (Lansing, Mich: University of Michigan Press, 1975). I have

drawn most of my information about the field from David Goldberg, *Genetic Algorithms in Search, Optimization and Machine Learning* (New York: Addison-Wesley, 1989).

70. Povilaitis worked with me on my book *Artificial Life Lab* (Corte Madera, Calif.: Waite Group Press, 1993). He also illustrated Rudy Rucker, *The Fourth Dimension: Toward a Geometry of Higher Reality* (Boston: Houghton Mifflin, 1984). See http://www.oxxide.com/index_dp.htm for more art by David Povilaitis.

71. The theme of whether the fittest a-life creatures are likely to be complex and gnarly is discussed in Chris Langton's classic paper "Life at the Edge of Chaos" in Christopher G. Langton, Charles Taylor, J. Doyne Farmer, and Steen Rasmussen, eds., *Artificial Life II* (New York: Perseus Books, 1991).

72. I'm supposing that I'll represent my real numbers by 32 bits each, as is customary. In this case, twelve real numbers require 384 bits, which we'll round up to an even 400. $2^{400} = (2^{10})^{40} \sim (10^3)^{40} = 10^{120}$. If you prefer, you could simply imagine an a-life creature based on a purely digital genome of 400 bits. Seth Lloyd's estimate appears in his paper, "Computational Capacity of the Universe," *Physical Review Letters* 88 (2002): online at http://arxiv.org/abs/quant-ph/0110141. See also Seth Lloyd and Y. Jack Ng, "Black Hole Computers," *Scientific American* (November 2004), 53–61.

73. Actually, it's not known if we really *do* achieve equally good search results if we use a deterministic pseudorandomizer instead of some cosmically unpredictable randomizer. The question is an open problem of theoretical computer science called the *P* versus BPP problem, where *P* is Polynomial Time and BPP is Bounded-Error Probabilistic Polynomial-Time. It's suspected that P = BPP, in which case replacing random numbers by pseudorandom numbers in an efficient algorithm is, in fact, okay.

In the context of search algorithms, I should mention the so-called No Free Lunch Theorems (NFL) proved by David Woldpert and William Macready. These results show that if we average across all possible search problems, no search algorithm is, on the whole, better than any other. The relevant papers can be found online at http://www.cs.uwyo.edu/~wspears/yin-yang.html. Religiously motivated creationists have begun arguing that the NFL theorems undermine the plausibility of Darwinian evolution. But the NFL results do not contradict the observable fact that Nature's genetic algorithms are in fact well-tuned for searching the idiosyncratically structured space of DNA strings. And the NFL theorems don't really come into play if, as I mentioned, we are searching not for the best possible solution, but simply for a reasonably good solution.

74. A classic a-life example of co-evolution is described in Danny Hillis, "Co-evolving Parasites Improve Simulated Evolution as an Optimization Procedure" in Langton, Taylor, Farmer, and Rasmussen, eds., *Artificial Life II*. This paper describes an experiment in which a genetic algorithm was used to discover an optimally fast algorithm for sorting lists of numbers. Hillis avoids getting stuck at the tops of small hills by simultaneously evolving the test cases that are best at demonstrating the nonfitness of proposed algorithms.

75. Rudy Rucker, *The Hacker and the Ants,* Release 2.0 (New York: Four Walls Eight Windows, 2002), pp. 185–88.

76. The idea of using "genomes" that are programs in the LISP computer language rather than strings of parameters was pioneered by John Koza, author of *Genetic Programming* (Cambridge, Mass.: MIT Press, 1992). Koza argues that it is better to be able to evolve actual computer *programs* instead of evolving *bit-strings* that still must be interpreted by computer programs. The reason LISP is so suitable for program evolution is that you can do crossover on LISP expressions by writing them as "parse trees" and swapping a branch of one tree with a branch of another tree. Nobody seems to be able to think of a way to do this for programs in ordinary C—simply cutting two C programs in half and sewing the different halves together won't produce working programs.

Note that Karl Sims uses a Koza-style evolution of LISP programs in the Gala-pagos demonstration shown in figure 75.

CHAPTER 4: ENJOYING YOUR MIND

77. See chapter eight of Rodolfo Llinás, *I of the Vortex: From Neurons to Self* (Cambridge Mass.: MIT Press, 2001).

78. Valentino Braitenberg, *Vehicles: Experiments in Synthetic Psychology* (Cambridge, Mass.: MIT Press, 1984). Braitenberg was at one time the director of the Max Planck Institute for Biological Cybernetics in Tübingen, Germany.

79. See my book, *Software Engineering and Computer Games* (Harlow, UK: Addison-Wesley, 2003), and the associated Web site, www.rudyrucker.com/computergames.

80. As a simple illustration of why continuous-valued computing units are richer than bit-valued units, consider trying to represent a round disk by a coarse grid

of tiles. If the tiles have to be black or white, you'll see jagged edges. But if the tiles can take on shades of gray, the jagged edges can be visually smoothed away. As in the physics simulations, the real numbers used by a PC aren't truly continuous; they're digital models of continuous numbers. If, again, we represent a real number by thirty-two bits, then we're "only" allowing for four billion different real numbers.

81. The face-recognition example that I discuss is taken from Tom M. Mitchell, *Machine Learning* (Boston: WCB McGraw-Hill, 1997). See my Web page www.cs.sjsu.edu/faculty/rucker/cs156.htm for links, source code, and details.

82. This slogan's first appearance may be in John Hertz, Anders Krogh, and Richard G. Palmer, *Introduction to the Theory of Neural Computation* (Redwood City, Calif.: Addison-Wesley, 1991).

83. The Brian's Brain illustration was made using a terrific Java Web applet called MJCell. This rapid and powerful applet was written by the Polish programmer Mirek Wojtowicz and can be viewed at Mirek's site, http://www.mirekw.com/ca/mjcell/mjcell.html.

84. I describe my original position in *Infinity and the Mind* (Princeton, N.J.: Princeton University Press, 1982), p. 184. The scripture passage is Exodus 3:14. The Hebrew word translated as "I AM" is " 'hyh," which might better be rendered as "I will be."

85. Antonio Damasio, *The Feeling of What Happens* (New York: Harcourt, New York 1999), pp. 170–71.

86. Legend has it that the Japanese programmer Itso Yamaguchi got his inspiration for Pac-Man's wonderfully simple circle-missing-a-sector icon from—a pizza. This classic origin tale is mentioned as an aside in the wonderful novel by D. B. Weiss, *Lucky Wander Boy* (New York: Plume Books, 2003). The book is about a ne'er-do-well Angelino media worker who's obsessed with an obscure arcade game bearing the same name as the novel. Steven Poole, *Trigger Happy* (New York: Arcade, 2000) is a good nonfiction history of computer games. For a technical treatment of game programming, see my book, *Software Engineering and Computer Games,* or Andre La Mothe, *Tricks of the Windows Game Programming Gurus* (New York: Sams, 2002.)

87. R. D. Laing, *Knots* (New York: Pantheon Books, 1970), p. 84.

88. Rudy Rucker, *Software* (New York: Ace Books, 1982), p. 36. In quantum information theory there's quite a different kind of discussion concerning whether it

would be possible to precisely copy any physical system such as a brain. The so-called no-cloning theorem indicates that you can't precisely replicate a system's quantum state without destroying the system. If you had a quantum-state replicator, you'd need to destroy a brain in order to get a quantum-precise copy of it. This said, it's quite possible that you could create a behaviorally identical copy of a brain without having to actually copy *all* of the quantum states involved.

89. I first used the word in a short story, "Soft Death," *The Magazine of Fantasy and Science Fiction* (September 1986), 42–54. The main character's last name Leckesh is a near-anagram of the last name of my writer-idol Robert Sheckley.

90. *Saucer Wisdom* (New York: Tor Books, 1999), pp. 57–59.

91. Thomas Pynchon, *Gravity's Rainbow* (New York: Viking Press, 1973), p. 516.

92. The American big-number-naming convention that I present here is sometimes called the "short scale" and the less common European convention the "long scale." For full details, see the Wikipedia entry http://en.wikipedia.org/wiki/Long_scale.

93. See Hans Moravec, *Robot: Mere Machine to Transcendent Mind* (Oxford, Eng.: Oxford University Press, 1999), p. 54, and Ray Kurzweil, *The Age of Spiritual Machines* (New York: Penguin Books, 1999), p. 103.

94. See the classic works, Marvin Minsky, *The Society of Mind* (New York: Simon and Schuster, 1985) and Douglas Hofstadter, *Gödel, Escher, Bach: An Eternal Golden Braid* (New York: Basic Books, 1979).

95. A side remark on this third point. Suppose I write MR for the mind recipe algorithm which I'm describing here. If the working of MR is completely deterministic, then for any number of years $n$, there is a unique agent MR($n$) that represents the fittest agent produced by running MR for $n$ years. Suppose that MR(1,000,000) is an agent whose behavior is indistinguishable from that of a human mind. And suppose as well that the complete and detailed specification of the MR is humanly comprehensible. So then MR(1,00,000) is a concise and comprehensible description of a human mind. Q.E.D.

To me this is an interesting result precisely because I used to think it was false! That is, I used to believe that there could be no humanly comprehensible description of a system equivalent to the human mind. But now I see that I was wrong. For more on this point, see the "Preface to the 2005 Edition" in Rudy Rucker, *Infinity and the Mind* (Princeton, N.J.: Princeton University Press, 2005). I'm always happy when logic gets me to change my mind—if that never happened, there wouldn't be much point in using logic! The a priori is very powerful.

96. Suppose that a person's thought system can be formalized as a system *H*. As I discuss at greater length in footnote 102, Kurt Gödel's Second Incompleteness Theorem tells us that either (a) *H* is inconsistent or (b) *H* is consistent and *H* cannot prove the sentence Con(*H*) expressing the consistency of *H*. So if a robot *R* is in fact equivalent to *H*, then either (a) *R* is inconsistent or (b) *R* is consistent and neither *R* nor *H* can prove Con(*R*). In either case, the person *H* has no way of knowing in advance whether or not *R* may suddenly go berserk.

97. See Seth Lloyd and Y. Jack Ng, "Black Hole Computers," *Scientific American* (November 2004) 53–61.

98. Vinge's talk "The Coming Technological Singularity: How to Survive in the Post-Human Era" appeared in the Winter 1993 issue of the *Whole Earth Review* and is also available online at http://www-rohan.sdsu.edu/faculty/vinge/misc/singularity.html—or just Google for "Vinge Singularity." Regarding the Singularity-Rapture comparison I quote below, I first heard this phrase from Bruce Sterling, who ascribes it to Cory Doctorow, who says he got it from Charlie Stross, who in turn says he nicked it from Ken McLeod—cynical science-fiction writers one and all.

99. See Stephen Wolfram, *A New Kind of Science,* p. 750. In my Technical Appendix I explain why I prefer the word *unpredictable* to Wolfram's *irreducible*. By the way, some philosophers would remark that Wolfram isn't the first person to have proposed the "unpredictable determinism" solution to the problem of free will. But certainly he's done much to crystallize and clarify the argument.

100. Nick Herbert, "Holistic Physics, or, An Introduction to Quantum Tantra" from *Southern Cross Review,* available online at www.southerncrossreview.org/16/herbert.essay.htm. Also see his book, *Elemental Mind: Human Consciousness and the New Physics* (New York: E. P. Dutton, 1993).

101. Rudy Rucker, *Frek and the Elixir* (New York: Tor Books, 2004), pp. 371–373. See www.rudyrucker.com/frek for my writing notes on the book, including further discussions of interrogations and decoherence.

102. Mentioning the physicist-author Roger Penrose brings up the issue of J. Anthony Lucas's classic argument that Gödel's Second Incompleteness Theorem rules out man-machine equivalence, an argument that Penrose revived and popularized in the 1990s. This *fallacious* argument is such a thoroughly dead horse that I didn't want to mention it in the main text. But I'll give it another beating here, lest one of my readers thinks I have no clear opinion on the subject. Do

note that the Lucas-Penrose argument is a completely distinct issue from Penrose-Hameroff speculation that the brain can act as a coherent quantum computer. It's to Penrose's credit that he's associated with multiple controversial ideas!

Before continuing, I should explain the Gödel's Second Incompleteness Theorem is the result that if $F$ is a consistent formal system as strong as arithmetic, then $F$ cannot prove the sentence $Con\,(F)$. $Con\,(F)$ is the sentence that expresses the consistency of $F$ by asserting that $F$ will never prove, say, $0 = 1$. If we think of $h$ as being the index of the Turing machine $M_h$, we can write $Con\,(h)$ as shorthand for $Con(M_h)$.

The remainder of this note is directly quoted from "Preface to the 2005 Edition" in Rudy Rucker, *Infinity and the Mind.*

Suppose $h$ is an integer that codes the program for a device $M_h$ whose output is very much like a person's. Lucas and Penrose want to say that, (1) after hanging around with $M_h$ for a while, any reasonable person will feel like asserting $Tr(h)$, a sentence which says something like, "If I base a machine $M_h$ on the algorithm coded by $h$ I'll get a machine which only ouputs true sentences about mathematics." And (2) having perceived the truth of $Tr(h)$, any reasonable person will also feel like asserting $Con(h)$, a sentence which says something like, "If I base a machine $M_h$ on the algorithm coded by $h$ I'll get a machine which never generates any mathematical contradictions." But Gödel's Second Incompleteness Theorem shows that $M_h$ can't prove $Con(h)$, so now it looks as if any reasonable person who hangs around with a human-like $M_h$ will soon know something that the machine itself can't prove.

The philosopher Hilary Putnam formulated what remains the best counterargument in his 1960 essay, "Minds and Machines," which has been reprinted in A. R. Anderson, *Minds and Machines,* Prentice-Hall, 1964, pp. 43–59. (For Lucas's ripostes to such objections, see his genial if unconvincing essay, "A Paper Read to the Turing Conference at Brighton on April 6th, 1990," available online at http://users.ox.ac.uk/~jrlucas/Godel/ brighton.html.)

Putnam's point is simple. Even if you have seen $M_h$ behaving sensibly for a period of time, you still don't have any firm basis for asserting either that $M_h$ will always say only true things about mathematics or that $M_h$ will never fall into an inconsistency. Now if you were to have a full understanding of how $M_h$ operates, then perhaps you could prove that $M_h$ is consistent. But, in the case where $h$ is the mind recipe, the operation of the eventual $M_h$ is incomprehensibly intricate, and we will never be in a position to legitimately claim to know the truth of the sentence $Con(h)$ which asserts that $M_h$ is consistent. This is, indeed, the content of Gödel's Second Incompleteness Theorem. Rather than ruling out man-machine equivalence, the theorem places limits on what we can know about machines equivalent to ourselves.

And, really, this shouldn't come as a surprise. You can share an office or a house with a person $P$ for fifteen years, growing confident in the belief that $P$ is consistent, and then one day, $P$ begins saying and doing things that are completely insane. You imagined that you knew $Con(P)$ to be true, but this was never the case at all. The only solid reason for asserting $Con(P)$ would have been a systematic proof, but, given that you and $P$ were of equivalent sophistication, this kind of proof remained always beyond your powers. All along, the very fact that $Con(P)$ wasn't provable contained the possibility that it wasn't true. Like it or not, that's the zone we operate in when relating to other intelligent beings.

### CHAPTER 5: THE HUMAN HIVE

103. Craig Reynolds, "Flocks, herds, and schools: A distributed behavioral model," *ACM SIGGRAPH Computer Graphics* 21, no.4 (July 1987): 25–34. Available online at www.red3d.com/cwr/papers/1987/boids.html.

104. John Updike, *Verse* (New York: Crest Books, 1965), p. 174. "The Great Scarf of Birds" first appeared in Updike's poetry collection, *Telephone Poles* (New York: Knopf, 1963).

105. These pictures were made with my Boppers software, available from the book's Web site, www.rudyrucker.com/lifebox. Individual images can't fully capture the dynamic flocking effect; to see flocking in action, you might download Boppers, or just go online to one of Craig Reynolds's two terrific Web sites. Flocking applets and a Java-driven tutorial on flocking and other kinds of steering behaviors can be found at http://www.red3d.com/cwr/steer/. A second site has some C++ code for steering behaviors and includes, for instance, a great simulation of pedestrians in motion, this is http://opensteer.sourceforge.net/.

106. R. D. Laing, *Knots* (New York: Pantheon Books, 1970). The personal interaction knots I quote here appear on, respectively, pages 21, 5, and 26. And the Zen-like knot I quote from at the end of this section is from page 84.

107. The quote is from G. K. Chesterton's admiring biography of a Victorian painter,

*G. F. Watts* (London: Duckworth, 1904), p. 88. I originally found the quote in Jorge Luis Borges, "The Analytical Language of John Wilkins," in E. Monegal and A. Reid, eds., *Borges: A Reader* (New York: Dutton, 1981), p. 143.

108. In the summer of 2004, I returned to Naropa to teach a writing workshop. While there, I wrote a transreal science-fiction story about encountering a reborn clone of William Burroughs; slated to appear as Rudy Rucker, "MS Found in a Minidrive," in Chris Conlon, ed., *Poe's Lighthouse* (Forest Hill, Md.: Cemetery Dance Publications, 2005). *Transrealism* is, by the way, my term for somewhat autobiographical science fiction; see www.rudyrucker.com/writing for more information.

109. The view of language generation as an innate human skill is generally associated with Noam Chomsky, who simply called the brain's language generator "the black box." A good recent popularization of ideas about innate language skills is Steven Pinker, *The Language Instinct* (New York: HarperCollins, 1994).

110. I had hoped that this might be a difficult question to answer, but Scott Aaronson e-mailed me a short proof that the answer is no. "Proof: Let's make the identification Be=1, Bop=2, Lu=3. Then the question is whether we can derive 312 starting from 123 and 31, by concatenation and deletion of 11's, 22's, and 33's. Observe that in any valid string, the sum of the numbers following any '2' must be odd. For clearly 123 and 31 satisfy that property, and the property is preserved under concatenation and deletion. But 312 fails the property, which completes the proof." Oh well. I'm sure that, with a bit more effort than I'm willing to invest, one could find a simply stated and truly difficult tag problem. Let's say that finding such a system is left as an exercise for the reader. I'll post the best answers I get on the book's Web site, www.rudyrucker.com/lifebox/.

111. Most people just say "power law," but I find it useful to say *"inverse power law"* most of the time as a reminder that I'm looking for laws like $N = 1/L^2$ rather than laws like $N = L^2$. The denominator exponent $D$ might simply be 1, but often it's 2 or 3 or even a fractional quantity like 2.4. Don't let the notion of fractional powers freak you out. They represent a kind of interpolation. That is, if $3^2$ is 9 and $3^3$ is 27, we expect $3^{2.4}$ to lie somewhere in between, and indeed, it's about 14. If you like, you can think of raising something to 2.4 power as first raising it to the twenty-fourth power, and then taking the tenth root, since 2.4 is 24/10. But it's easier just to think of the operation as being something reasonable between squaring and cubing.

112. To make the formula a little cleaner, we might normalize both $N$ and $L$ to range between zero and one by dividing each of them by 130,600. This yields $N_f = N/136,000$ as the relative frequency of a type of word, and $L_f = L/136,000$ as the relative linkiness of a word. Substituting into our empirical result $N = 1,000,000/L^{2.4}$, if we replace $N$ by 136,000 $N_f$ and replace $L$ by 130,600 $L_f$, do some arithmetic and round off, we get $n_f = 0.069/L_f^{2.4}$

113. Albert-László Barabási, *Linked* (New York: Plume, 2003). Barabási has made a name for himself by his researches into the scale-free structures of the Internet. One of his key papers on the topic is Albert-László Barabási and Réka Albert, "Emergence of Scaling in Random Networks," *Science* 286 (1999): 509–12. Links to this and many more of Barabási's papers can be found on his Web site at http://www.nd.edu/~alb/public.html.

114. Zipf's book reference is: George Kingsley Zipf, *Human Behavior and the Principle of Least Effort* (Boston: Addison-Wesley, 1949). Mandelbrot's comment appears in his own extravagant work of genius: Benoit Mandelbrot, *Fractals: Form, Chance and Dimension* (San Francisco: W. H. Freeman, 1977), pp. 272–73. By the way, the Mandelbrotian word *gangue,* more commonly used in French, refers to otherwise worthless material in which valuable ores or gems may be found. It's pronounced like "gang" in English.

I went to Mandelbrot's house early in 2001, when I was involved in an abortive project to try to make a large screen (IMAX) science movie featuring some huge, prolonged zooms into the Mandelbrot set.

The movie, which was to be about fractals, had the working title *Search for Infinity,* a title that was dictated by the producer, Jeff Kirsch, director of the San Diego Space Center Museum. Jeff was (perhaps unwisely) committed to presenting the film as being about infinity instead of being about fractals, as he felt many more people would be interested in the former than the latter. And in a mathematical sense, fractals are indeed infinite, in that you can zoom into them, forever finding more levels of detail. It's an infinity in the small, rather than an infinity in the large.

The very talented filmmaker Ron Fricke (*Koyaanisqatsi* and *Baraka*) was committed to shooting the film, and I was going to write the script. Ron and Jeff were also bent on including Arthur Clarke in the movie as a character. And Ron wanted the movie to star a computer-brained space probe who was afraid to fly off into the endless void of interstellar space. Jeff had scored a development grant for the project from the National Science Foundation (NSF) and we worked on preparing a final proposal over a couple of years.

Taking all the story constraints into account, I put together ten or eleven successively more refined treatments for a film script; for the final version, see www.rudyrucker.com/writing/.

But, like so many films, the project was never realized. The sticking point was that we failed to get a needed $1 million grant from the NSF. One reason I visited Mandelbrot was, in fact, to try to win his support in case the NSF were to ask his opinion about the project, but Mandelbrot was unenthused about it, I don't know exactly why. One of his issues was that it was wrong to bill the film as being about infinity, when in truth it was about fractals—I actually agreed with him on this point, but this wasn't something that I could get Jeff and Ron to go along with.

By way of making my own book an extravagant gangue, I'm going to paste in excerpts of my journal entry of January 14, 2001, regarding my meeting with Benoit. I don't think I'm going to find another place to publish this, and it's interesting and somewhat relevant, so what the heck.

Mandelbrot is waiting for me at the end of his driveway; he's worried I might not find the house as the address on the curb is covered by snow. A white-haired balding man, stocky, somewhat diffident, he sees me, I wave, he doesn't wave back, not sure yet I'm the one he's waiting for, when I'm closer he says, "Are you Rudy Rucker?" We introduce ourselves, shake hands, I tell him I'm thrilled to meet him. In the house his wife Adèle greets us, Mandelbrot disappears to take a pee, I suppose, then we sit in a cold room with some armchairs. They don't seem to really heat their house. He sits on an odd modern chair with parts of it missing, a collection of black corduroy hot dogs. He wears a jacket, a vest, a shirt, trousers with a paper clip attached to the fly to make it easier to pull up and down. I guess he's 75. Rather rotund and, yes, a bit like the Mandelbrot set in his roundness and with the fuzz of hairs on his pate.

He starts talking almost right away, an incredibly dense and rich flow of information, a torrent. Fractal of course, as human conversation usually is, but of a higher than usual dimension. It's like talking to a superbeing, just as I'd hoped, like being with a Martian, his conversation a wall-of-sound paisley info structure, the twittering of the Great Scarab.

His wife listens attentively as we talk and from time to time she reminds him to tie up some loose thread.

He doesn't seem overly vain—as I'd heard him described by some rivals. Certainly he has good self-esteem, but I think it's well earned and justified.

I repeatedly feel a great urge to go out and have a cigarette. The firehose-stream of information in his strong French accent—I have to cock my ear and listen my hardest to process it. I'm conscious of his wife watching me listen to him. I imagine she's judging how well I seem to listen, and when once I smirk as he says something a bit self-aggrandizing, she catches my expression and I imagine her giving me a black mark.

He isn't clear exactly what Jeff is trying to do with the movie, how Jeff plans to fund it, what his (Mandelbrot's) role is supposed to be, etc. I explain it as best I can; we don't really expect Benoit to do much more than to say that he doesn't find our project totally absurd. He seems to want to exact some kind of concession; at the end I have the feeling that he considers Jeff's emphasis on "infinity" to be a deal-breaker, to the extent that there might have been a deal.

I mention how much he's affected my view of the world. Mention also that I'm as excited to meet him as I was to meet Gödel. Mandelbrot says, "Oh, Gödel didn't talk much, I saw him at the Institute, I was von Neumann's last student." I rejoinder, "Well, Gödel talked a lot when I saw him, I was working on something he was interested in," and Benoit is impressed.

In the event, it's not really like meeting Gödel because I'm not so young and starry-eyed that I see Mandelbrot as a mythopoetic guru. Yet it is like meeting Gödel in the sense that for these two special oasis hours midway in the long caravan of my life I'm talking to someone whom I feel to be smarter than me. An ascended master.

Since the meeting, I've been thinking some more about ways in which Mandelbrot resembled the Mandelbrot set; it's a conceit I'm bent on playing with. As I mentioned, he was rather round about the middle, even bulbous, and his clothes and his head were indeed adorned with any number of fine hairs. He appeared and disappeared from my view several times; he'd get up and leave the room and then return. Perhaps each time it was a different bud of him that came back in!

A key point in perceiving his multibudded nature is that his wife in many ways resembles him: accent, age, attire, knowledge about his work. She was in fact a mini-Mandelbrot set hovering near the flank of the larger bud I was talking to. The two of them were connected, of course, by a tendril of love and attention, rather hard to physically see.

At times I felt a bit of menace from Mandelbrot, as when he was repeatedly asking that we not bill the movie as being about infinity. I felt some anxiety that he might somehow do something against us if we didn't accede. He has, one imagines, a wide range of influences. What was going on here was that I was sensing the presence of the *stinger* at the tip of the Mandelbrot set. A stinger so fine as to be all but invisible, a stinger that, as he grew somewhat agitated, was twitching with rapid movements that made it yet harder to see. But, nevertheless, I could feel its whizzing passages through the air near me. Palpable menace.

115. A nice numerical example of Zipf's Law can be found on a Web page by computer scientist Jamie Callan of the University of Massachusetts, it's URL, http://web.archive.org/web/20001005120011/hobart.cs.umass.edu/~allan/cs6 46–f97/char_of_text.html. For the mother of all Zipf's Law Web pages, see Wentian Li's site, http://linkage.rockefeller.edu/wli/zipf/.

In reading about inverse power laws, you may notice that there are different types of power laws that people discuss. Our Zipf's Law graph shows a *rank style* power law that gives the quality level $L$ of an object of rank $R$ by a law of the form $L = c/R^D$. But our linkiness power law graph was a *histogram style* power law giving the number of objects $N$ of some quality level $L$ by a law of the form $N = c/L^D$. And to make things worse there are so-called *cumulative* power laws as well.

Although it's not quite obvious, the different types of laws are closely related, and we can, for example, convert our histogram-style word linkiness power law from earlier in this section into a rank-style power law of the form $L^* = 0.12/R^{0.7}$. Here $L^*$ is the *normalized linkiness* level of the $R$th word, that is, the linkiness number $L$ divided by the total number of words available in the dictionary file.

Let me say a bit more about the confusing fact that different researchers describe power laws in alternative ways. I'll couch the discussion in terms of our word linkiness study.

A *histogram* power law of has the form $N \sim 1/L^D$, meaning in this case that the number of words $N$ that have a given linkiness $L$ is proportional to an inverse power of $L$.

A *cumulative* power law in this case would say that for any linkiness $L$, the number of words $M$ having linkiness greater than or equal to $L$ is $M \sim 1/L^E$ for some exponent $E$.

A *rank* power law would say here that if we rank words from the most linked to the least, and if $R$ is a word's rank order, then the linkiness $L \sim 1/R^E$ for some exponent $F$.

These forms are in some way equivalent, although the numbers interrelate in an odd way. The report by Lada A. Adamic, *Zipf, Power-laws, and Pareto—A Ranking Tutorial* at http://www.hpl.hp.com/research/idl/papers/ranking/ranking.html, describes how we can get from histogram to cumulative to rank forms of the same law—and vice versa. (The names in Adamic's title refer, respectively, to the rank, histogram, and cumulative forms of power laws.)

Let's go over how to get from a histogram law to a cumulative law to a rank law in the case of the word linkiness example.

*Histogram.* I have $N = c/L^D$. $L$ is a linkiness level and $N$ is the number of words at that level. In my particular example, $c$ is 1,000,000 and $D$ is 2.4.

*Cumulative.* To get the number of words with linkiness greater than or equal to some value $L_0$, integrate $c \cdot L^{-D}$ from $L_0$ to infinity, integrating with respect to $L$. At this point, we have to assume $D > 1$, as otherwise the integral will be infinite. Integrating by taking the antiderivative, I get $(c/(1 - D)) \cdot L^{(1-D)}$ evaluated from $L_0$ to $\infty$, which cooks down to $(c/(D-1))/L_0^{(D-1)}$. So I can say that if $M$ is the number of words with linkiness greater than or equal to $L$, then

$$M = (c/(D-1))/L^{(D-1)}.$$

In our particular example, this becomes $M = 714{,}286/L^{1.4}$.

*Rank.* Suppose I rank words in order of linkiness as one, two, three, and so on, with the most-linked word at one. Suppose a word $w$ has rank $R$ and linkiness $L$. Note that the words with lower rank numbers have linkiness better than the word $w$, so in fact $R$ is the same as the quantity $M$ defined in the cumulative form of the power law, $M$ being the number of words with linkiness greater than or equal to the linkiness $L$ of word $w$. So I can write the cumulative form of the power law as $R = (c/(D-1))/L^{(D-1)}$. And now if I solve for $L$ in terms of $R$, I get

$$L = (c/(D-1))^{(1/(D-1))}/R^{(1/(D-1))}.$$

For our particular example, this becomes $L = 15{,}182/R^{0.7}$.

If we had started with the normalized form of the power law histogram for our linkiness experiment we would have gotten this rank law:

$$N_f = 0.12/R^{0.7}.$$

This last form is not too wildly different from the normalized Zipf's Law relating word frequency $W_f$ to word popularity rank $R$, that is, $W_f = 0.1/R$.

Might the linkiness rank result really be the same as Zipf's Law? It could be that when we measured the linkiness in terms of how many definitions a word is likely to appear in, we were really just measuring the frequency of the word's appearance.

In closing, let me just mention a few more examples of the rank laws that histogram laws produce:

The histogram law $N = c/L^{1.5}$ goes with the rank law $L = 4c^2/R^2$.

The histogram law $N = c/L^2$, has a nice simple rank law $L = c/R$.

The histogram law $N = c/L^3$ matches a rank law $L = (0.5 \; c)^{0.5}/R^{0.5}$.

Do note that this analysis won't work if you start with a histogram law of the form $N = c/L$, in which the denominator exponent $D$ is one. For then resulting rank-law denominator exponent $1/(D - 1)$ isn't well defined.

116. Around 1900, the Italian economist Vilfredo Pareto offered an explanation of why salaries in an organization might obey an inverse power law. A company is arranged like a pyramid, with more people at each successively lower level, and with the salaries at each level being smaller than the salaries at the level above.

If we take a simplified case where higher-level employees have two subordinates, each earning half as much as them, we end up with a histogram-style inverse power law, for if you look at the rows and number them with $i$ starting at zero, you see that the $i$th row has $2^i$ people getting $1/2^i$ as much as the boss. This means that if $N$ is the number of people with a given salary $L$, then $N = 1/L$.

In this binary employee tree case the rank law would be of the form $L = 1/R$. We can't use the logic of the previous note to derive this, but intuitively this rank law is reasonable here because, taken together, the rows previous to the $i$th row have a total of $2^i - 1$ people in them. So the salary $1/2^i$ for the $i$th row members is at least approximately equal to the reciprocal of their rank.

I'm kind of into the math thing right now, so I'll show how to get histogram and rank laws for the salaries in more general cases of organizational trees. Fun with algebra! Give sub subordinates to each employee above the bottom and suppose that each subordinate earns 1/Cut as much as his or her immediate boss. If we generate the organizational chart down to $i$ levels, again viewing level zero as being the single supreme boss at the top, then the people at the $i$th level will be getting a salary $L$ of $(1/\text{Cut})^i = (1/\text{Cut}^i)$ times the supreme boss's salary. And the *number* of people $N$ at the $i$th level will be $\text{Sub}^i$. So if we make a histogram chart of the number of people at each salary level, we'll be matching salaries $L = (1/\text{Cut}^i)$ to the numbers $N = \text{Sub}^i$. What I want to do now is to show that this means we can find a number $D$ such that $N = 1/L^D$. It turns out that letting $D$ be (log Sub)/(log Cut) will do.

To understand this, note that in formal mathematical contexts like this, we take log with respect to a certain number $e$, which is about 2.72, and the meaning of the log is that $y = \log x$ iff $e^y = x$. So, again, if we define $D$ to be (log Sub)/(log Cut), then $\text{Cut}^D = e^{(\log \text{Cut})(\log \text{Sub})/(\log \text{Cut})} = \text{Sub}$. We can see that $D$ will work as the exponent for our power law via the following chain of identities.

$$N = \text{Sub}^i = 1/(1/\text{Sub}^i) = 1/(1/(\text{Cut}^D)^i) =$$
$$1/(1/(\text{Cut}^i)^D) = 1/((1/\text{Cut}^i)^D) = 1/L^D.$$

In the simple case we began with, Sub and Cut are both 2, so we end up with $D = 1$. But if, for instance, each employee has ten underlings, each earning 70 percent as much as their boss, then Sub is 10 and 1/Cut is 7/10, so Cut is 10/7, and $D$ is about 6.5.

In his discussion of Zipf in *Fractals,* Mandelbrot argues that the Pareto style of argument can also be used to give a rough justification for an $N = 0.1/L^2$ histogram version of Zipf's' Law if we think of language as being made up of randomly generated strings of letters. Using the logic of the previous note, this histogram can be converted into the usual Zipf's Law $L = 0.1/R$.

117. A nonwriter might wonder why I'm talking about *advances* instead of about *royalties.* Strictly speaking, a book advance is supposed to be an approximation to the expected royalties that a book might earn in the first couple of years. But the actual amounts of royalties tend to be obscured in a fog of megacorporation accounting legerdemain, and practicing writers think in terms of the advance as being what they actually *get* for a book. Yes, once in a while a low-advance book becomes a runaway a best seller and, more commonly, a high-advance book may bomb, but the discrepancies are ironed out in the next round of advances. Few

writers stop at one book. The advances serve as a kind of rolling average of past royalties.

118. As some calculus students may recall, the area from one to infinity under the curve $1/x$ is infinite, but the area under $1/x^D$ for any $D > 1$ will be finite. If, for instance, we take $D$ to be 1.1, then the book advance formula becomes Advance = $1,000,000/Rank$^{(1.1)}$, and the total outlay for no matter how many writers will never exceed something on the order of $10 million.

119. This rule is credited to a 1987 paper by the Russian physicist Yakov Zeldovich. A generalization of the rule appears in Damián Zanette and Susanna Manrubia, "Role of Intermittency in Urban Development: A Model of Large-Scale City Formation," *Physical Review Letters* 79 (July 21, 1997): 523–26, available online at http://linkage.rockefeller.edu/wli/zipf/zanette97.pdf.

The paper has a formal proof that, if we let $L$ be population, $N$ be the number of cities of a given population size, and $R$ be the size rank of a city, then the Zeldovich rule generates a distribution with a histogram power law of the form $N = c/L^2$, which corresponds to a perfect Zipf-style rank law of the form $L = c/R$.

120. B. Malamud, G. Morein, and D. Turcotte, "Forest Fires: An Example of Self-Organized Critical Behavior," *Science* 291 (1998): 1840–42. This doesn't seem to be available for free online, but there is a PowerPoint presentation at http://eclectic.ss.uci.edu/~drwhite/Anthro179a/J-Doyle.ppt and a discussion of the paper at http://www.ent-consulting.com/articles/automata.pdf. Also, to see the Java applet showing the rule go to http://schuelaw.whitman.edu/JavaApplets/ForestFireApplet/.

In the description of the rule, I mention two transition probabilities. Typical values for the probability of lightning setting a tree on fire is 0.000006, and 0.03 for the probability of a dead tree coming to life. These particular values lie within a fairly large range that produces a critical state with inverse power law behavior.

121. The original paper was by Per Bak, Chao Tang, and Kurt Wiesenfeld. Per Bak wrote a popular and boldly titled book, *How Nature Works: The Science of Self-Organized Criticality* (New York: Springer-Verlag, 1996). A very good recent popularization of the same ideas is Mark Buchanan, *Ubiquity: The Science of History . . . Or Why the World Is Simpler Than You Think* (New York: Crown, 2000). If you search the Web, you can find some online Java applets of the sandpile model; see my book's Web site, www.rudyrucker.com/lifebox/, for a sample link.

To make the text definition of the rule a bit more precise:

In the sandpile CA, the cell states are integers ranging from zero to seven and the update rule is as follows:

(i) If a cell's value is greater than or equal to four, we subtract four from cell's value, so as to model a tumbling tower of sand.

(ii) For each of the cell's four neighbors Nabe, if Nabe has a value greater than four, we add one to the cell's value, so as to model sand tumbling in from a neighbor.

(iii) If the cell is on the edge of the rectangular simulation world, we set its value to zero, so as to represent the drop at the edge of the table.

122. In recent decades, scientists of every stripe have begun using the CA paradigm for parallel computation, although they don't always mention the phrase "cellular automata." For a survey of examples, see B. Chopard and M. Droz, *Cellular Automata Modeling of Physical Systems* (Cambridge, UK: Cambridge University Press, 1998).

A number of papers on power laws have a certain canonical form involving CAs.

(i) Observe that some quality level $L$ can be measured for instances of some commonly occurring phenomenon. Do a data analysis to find that the percentage $N$ of phenomena having level $L$ obeys a histogram-style inverse power law of the form $N = c/L^D$.

(ii) Create a (possibly continuous-valued) CA that simulates some aspect of the physical social phenomenon. Find a quality $L$ of the CA that seems to represent the quality $L$, and perform a data analysis of some runs of your CA to produce a histogram-style power law of the form $N = b/L^E$.

(iii) If possible, carry out an analytic proof of why your CA has the precise constants $b$ and $E$ in its power law. Suggest tweaks to your CA to bring $b$ and $E$ into closer accordance with society's observed $c$ and $D$.

Not all the papers of this kind explicitly *say* that they're using CAs. This may be because, perhaps due to the psychedelic beauty of CAs, their popularity with hackers, or the playfulness of many writings about the Game of Life, CAs have a somewhat unrespectable aura. Or it could be because Wolfram's somewhat controversial and radical work is deeply intertwined with CAs. Or it could be because it's not so well known that CAs can in fact use real numbers as their state values. Speaking as a fanatical cellular automatist, I think it's high time that our pet paradigm started getting its due!

The writing-related remarks in the rest of this section appeared in my essay, "Seek the Gnarl" in *Journal of the Fantastic in the Arts* 16.1 (Spring 2005).

123. In connection with tit-for-tat strategies, I should mention that there *are* certain kinds of very simple situations where they work. A classic experiment by Robert Axelrod explored a simulated world in which the agents carry out repeated sequences of deals with each other. At each round, an agent has the option of playing fair or of trying to cheat its partner. Axelrod ran a genetic algorithm to evolve the fittest dealing strategy, and found that the most successful strategy is for an agent to play fair or cheat in a given round according to whether its partner played fair or cheated on the previous round. Although in this particular world, such a tit-for-tat strategy works, this doesn't mean that the result generalizes to a political situation in which there are, after all, many more than two possibilities. The philosopher Patrick Grim has done some very interesting work running Axelrod-style rules on two-dimensional CA grids; see Patrick Grim, Gary Mar, and Paul St. Denis, *The Philosophical Computer: Exploratory Essays in Philsophical Computer Modeling* (Cambridge, Mass.: MIT Press, 1998).

124. Indeed, thinking up a simple and unpredictable model of the stock market is so hard that Wolfram's model doesn't quite fill the bill. The problem with Wolfram's rule is that it's equivalent to the elementary CA rule known as Rule 90, which we illustrated in chapter 1. And Rule 90 is a *predictable* class two rule, for each black cell in the initial row of a Rule 90 simulation sets off a recursive tree pattern, and the pattern of the whole simulation can be obtained by layering the individual tree patterns on top of one another. This means that if you know the starting row of this rule with full accuracy, you can in fact predict the contents of row $N$ in a brief amount of time on the order of $\log(N)$. The messy class three appearance of the rule is a kind of illusion; the pattern is really an overlay of a bunch of very predictable patterns. My thanks to Wolfram's assistant, Kovas Boguta, for pointing this out. I'd be interested to hear from readers who think of better models.

125. Stephen Wolfram remarks, in *A New Kind of Science,* pp. 367–368, that over the years he's often proposed very simple models for use in various fields. The initial reaction is surprise and disbelief that so rudimentary a model could yield anything interesting. Experts in the relevant field step in and make the model more complicated. And then at some point it's noticed that the bells and whistles can be removed after all, and that the original lean model produced results as good as the gussied-up version.

126. Buchanan, *Ubiquity,* pp. 231–33.

127. I found the quote in Paul Benedetti and Nancy DeHart, eds., *On McLuhan: Forward Through the Rearview Mirror* (Toronto: Prentice-Hall Canada, 1997), p. 70. This book is a collection of quotes from McLuhan and comments on him by his peers. The quote in question was taken from a 1966 Canadian Broadcasting Company TV interview called *This Hour Has Seven Days*.

The standard references are: Marshall McLuhan, *Understanding Media: The Extensions of Man* (New York: McGraw-Hill, 1964) and Marshall McLuhan and Quentin Fiore, *The Medium Is the Massage* (New York: Penguin Books, 1967). It's also illuminating to read the excellent biography, Philip Marchand, *Marshall McLuhan: The Medium and the Messenger* (New York: Ticknor & Fields, 1989). McLuhan didn't even drive a car—he said he didn't want to be a servomechanism for a machine!

128. For my drawings of many of the inventions described here, see the *Saucer Wisdom* Web site, www.saucerwisdom.com.

CHAPTER 6: REALITY UPGRADE

129. As a computer scientist, I would have preferred to number the eight options from zero to seven, so that their numbers would match the binary patterns of the 1s and 0s in the three columns of figures 123 and 124.

Another point is that perhaps some things will be Other, that is, not inside $T$, $P$, or $C$. If we wanted to take this possibility into account, we could have added a fourth dark dot to Figure 122, the dot standing outside all the circles and representing the region $\sim(T \cup P)$, where $\cup$ is the set-theoretic union symbol. If we want to take into account the possibility of there being things in this Other category, our eight ontologies would split into sixteen.

A final remark is that I'd be interested in hearing from readers who have more ideas about representative names to attach to the ontologies.

130. Now and then I get careless and express "$P(\text{In})$ returns Out" by writing $P(\text{In}) = \text{Out}$, but really I shouldn't do that, since I want to think of $P(\text{In})$ as being a process rather than its final value. As I suggest in the Technical Appendix, it would be better to write $P(\text{In}) = {}_{\text{Is}P\,\text{Done}}\text{Out}$.

In my pictures plotting a computation's state as changing in time, the curves are drawn as smoothly varying, but the more abrupt changes of state characteristic of digital computations could be represented by lines with right-angled stair-step jumps in them.

131. See the books on recursion theory referenced at the beginning of the Technical Appendix, and see Richard Shore, "Conjectures and Questions from Gerald Sacks's *Degrees of Unsolvability*," *Archive for Mathematical Logic* 36 (1997): 233–53. The paper is available online at http://www.math.cornell.edu/~shore/papers/pdf/sackstp3.pdf.

In point of fact, the Friedberg, Muchnik, and Sacks results regarding degrees of unsolvability were proved for an ordering $\leq_T$ known as Turing reducibility rather than the emulation degree comparison $\leq_e$ that I'm using here. As I discussed in the Technical Appendix, my $\leq_e$ is in fact equivalent to what recursion theorists call one-one reducibility $\leq_1$. But for $\leq$ it's also the case that pairs of incomparable degrees exist, that the degrees are dense, and that there are infinitely many degrees. This follows as a corollary to the Friedberg, Muchnik, and Sacks results for $\leq_T$ because $\leq$ is a weaker notion than $\leq_T$. And independent proofs of some of the same facts about $\leq$ result from work by J. C. E. Dekker, also in the 1950s. Dekker, my professor in a class on recursion theory at Rutgers, was a very formal man, pleasant and a good teacher.

132. When Wolfram formulated his PCE, he was well aware of the problem that there are infinitely many degrees of unsolvability. Therefore he phrased his PCE so that it has two loopholes. (See Stephen Wolfram, *A New Kind of Science*, pp. 734, 1130–31 for Wolfram's discussion.)

The loopholes are to be found in, respectively, the very first and very last phrases of the PCE, which I italicize here: *Almost all* processes that are not obviously simple can be viewed as computations *of equivalent sophistication*.

Regarding the first loophole, Wolfram is saying that complex nonuniversal Turing machines "almost never" occur in natural contexts. This is an interesting aspect of the PCE, in that it seems to say something about the kinds of processes that actually occur in the real world.

Keep in mind that Wolfram's work is *empirical*. Unlike physical experiments, computer science experiments are exactly reproducible, and thus have a touch of the mathematical or theoretical. But really his inspiration came from looking at lots and lots of computations in action. And to reduce experimenter bias, he made a point of conducting *exhaustive* surveys of various classes of rudimentary computations such as Turing machines and CAs. Wolfram describes his research as a process of exploring the computational universe.

To exploit the second loophole we might interpret "computations of equivalent sophistication" more broadly than "computations that can emulate each other." Wolfram feels that the processes by which logicians construct their intermediate-degree computations always depend so essentially on the use of an underlying universal computation that the constructed intermediate computations are in some as-yet-to-be-defined sense "as sophisticated as" the universal computations.

Now, so far as I know, all the existing constructions of intermediate-degree computations *do* use a universal computation somewhere in their proof. But it seems capricious to conclude that therefore *every* intermediate-degree machine in some way relies upon a construction involving a universal Turing machine.

Let me offer a historical analogy to make plausible the ubiquity of intermediate degrees.

An algebraic number can be expressed as the solution to some polynomial algebraic equation formulated in terms of whole numbers. The nonalgebraic numbers are dubbed the transcendental numbers. For many years, the only known transcendental numbers were of an artificial nature. But eventually mathematicians proved that certain familiar numbers such as pi are transcendental. By the same token, we may eventually recognize that some very familiar kinds of computations have unsolvable halting problems, but are not universal.

I think it's plausible that there may in fact be naturally occurring processes of intermediate degree. It's tempting to speculate that the one-dimensional CA Rule 30 itself is such a computation.

133. I considered calling this hypothesis the "Weak PCE" to emphasize its origin as a weakening of Wolfram's PCE. But since the conjecture's actual content has little connection with notions of equivalence, it seems more appropriate to call it the Natural Unsolvability Hypothesis. But in any case, it's definitely inspired by the PCE.

Regarding the target state detector Is*P*Done, note that I require this to be a computation that returns a True or a False for every input. That is, Is*P*Done is what I term *everywhere defined*. This condition is necessary so as to rule out the following target detector Is*P*DoneUniversal, which would serve to make any *P* with an infinite number of distinct possible outputs unsolvable. Let *U* be some universal Turing machine. Let Is*P*DoneUniversal(Out) return True if *U*(Out) halts, and return False if *U*(Out) doesn't halt. If *P* with Is*P*DoneUniversal were solvable, *U*'s halting problem would be solvable, which would be a contradiction.

Note that I formulate the NUH in a fairly weak form, requiring only that each naturally occurring complex $P$ have at least *one* everywhere defined target detector computation Is$P$Done that yields an unsolvable halting problem. But for many computations, unsolvability will hold for *all* nontrivial target detectors, as I mention in the Technical Appendix.

134. Note that if I'm limited to a CA world of some finite size, say a thousand by a thousand pixels, the patterns in a finite CA world must eventually run out of possibilities and begin repeating themselves. And this means that any halting problem would in fact be solvable. The issue here is that a finite CA is really a class-two computation, albeit one with a very long period.

In particular, in a thousand-by-thousand Brian's Brain rule with its three distinguishable states per cell, there are only $3^{\text{million}}$ patterns the board can display. And if I just run the rule till it repeats itself, then I will know by then whether or not a particular target state—such as the hundred-cell glider—is ever going to appear.

But waiting until the computational system runs out of possibilities isn't the kind of "prediction" that we have in mind. After all, $3^{\text{million}}$ is an exceedingly large and unfeasible number, whose decimal expression would be something like a one with half a million zeros after it. When I say that I can't find an oracle for Brian's Brain, I mean that there's no quick and dirty computation that might tell me within, let us say, a million or so steps whether or not a given pattern will or will not ever appear when Brian's Brain is started up on such and such a pattern in a thousand-by-thousand world.

My point is that we do still think of Brian's Brain as a class four computation, even though it must repeat itself when run upon a finite grid. A class two computation is meant to be one that *quickly* repeats itself, and which is unable to take advantage of having more room to compute in. A class four computation, on the other hand, only repeats itself after it has pretty much exhausted all the available options of the computational environment where it's being run.

It might be that in a future analysis, someone will find a nice way to work the feasibility issue into the formulations of the computation classes and of related conjectures such as the NUH.

135. Let $K$ be the following computation: $K(\text{In})$ saves a copy of In and computes powers $3^t$. I can think of the output of $K(\text{In}, t)$ as a pair <Row, In> consisting of the binary expression Row for $3^t$ set down to the left of the binary expression for In. And Is$K$Done(Out), that is, Is$K$Done(<Row, In>) checks if the pattern In appears inside Row.

I admit it seems just a little slippery of me not to be using just the plain powers-of-three computation. I could avoid this slight awkwardness by formulating the notion of target detector so that it takes two arguments, as in Is*P*Done(In, Out).

136. Some might object to my bringing infinity into the discussion. The thing is, I'm trying to introduce some mathematical rigor. And the distinction between finite and infinite is absolute and clear, while distinctions between feasible and unfeasible are necessarily relativistic and vague. So rather than saying that a computation is complex if it's unfeasible to find a repeating pattern in it, I prefer to say that a computation is complex if it has no finite repeating blueprint at all. And rather than talking about complex computations whose halting problems have no *feasible* solution, I think it's more useful to talk about complex computations whose halting problems have no finite solution at all.

But, as I already mentioned in footnote 134, there may be some interesting way to replace "infinite" by "unfeasible" in the definitions of the computation classes and the formulation of the NUH.

Another point to make is that, if the UH really holds, then having an unsolvable halting problem could in fact serve as the definition of a complex computation.

137. Theoretical computer scientists use the runtime measure as a criterion of what they call computational complexity. In this context, they are using "complexity" *not* in the Wolfram sense of "gnarliness" but rather in the sense of "difficulty."

Computations can be compared not only according to how much runtime they use, but also according to how much memory or scratch paper they require. Still other distinctions can be introduced by allowing a computation to make guesses, to consult oracles about other computations, to carry out statistical experiments, and perhaps even to carry out quantum-mechanical measurements. Some four or five hundred of these theoretical complexity classes have been named, and you can find many of them listed on Scott Aaronson's Web site, "The Complexity Zoo," http://www.complexityzoo.com.

Perhaps the most widely discussed complexity class is the one known as *NP*. Let me quickly describe it here.

Suppose Test is a computation and that you have an input In of size $N$, a target state Out, and a minimal time $t$ such that Test(In, $t$) = Out. Now if $t$ is a polynomial function of $N$, then we say that Test is a polynomial time computation, a member of the computational class called $P$. But suppose that $t$ is instead comparable to $2^N$ in size. In this case, we can say that Test is an exponential time computation, a member of the computational class called EXP.

What about the computational class *NP*, whose the initials stand for nondeterministic polynomial time? A computation Test is said to be *NP* if there is a polynomial time computation IsTestDone(In, Out) that can check in polynomial time if Out is indeed a target output for the computation Test(In). The idea is that in an *NP* computation we can limit the (probably) exponential *search* aspect of the program to making guesses about the desired outputs, but *checking* if the outputs are *good* is to be a polynomial time process.

The name "nondeterministic" for this class is an unfortunate choice of nomenclature. After all, in any useful sense of the word *computation,* a truly *nondeterministic* computation wouldn't be a computation at all. The so-called nondeterministic computations are best thought of as deterministic computations that alternate between two stages: (search) generate a batch of possible outputs, (check) check if any of these outputs is the correct one, (search) generate some more possible outputs, (check) check if any of these is the correct one, and so on. *Exhaustive search computations* would be a far better name than *nondeterministic computations.*

Although it's widely believed that there are *NP* computations that aren't in *P,* nobody has been able to prove this. Many *NP* problems *U* are known to be *NP*-complete in the sense that an oracle for *U* could be used to solve all the other *NP* problems in polynomial time. A classic survey can be found in Michael Garey and David Johnson, *Computers and Intractability: A Guide to the Theory of NP-Completeness* (San Francisco: W. H. Freeman, 1979).

138. The logarithm base ten of a number $N$ is the power $p$ such that $10^p = N$. A simpler way to think of it is that log($N$) is approximately the number of digits that it takes to write $N$ in our familiar decimal notation. As I discussed in footnote 8, given that reckoning a sum with arithmetic involves only a few manipulations of the digits, its evident that summing a pair of numbers of roughly the same size $N$ is going to be something like $k \cdot$log($N$) steps—where $k$ is some constant factor. Therefore we can call this a logarithmic time computation.

139. For sparsely spreading CAs like Conway's Game of Life, one can drastically improve on $N$-cubed performance. The trick here is to keep track of which cells are active, and only to update cells that are adjacent to active cells. Given a Life pattern of size $M$ that doesn't get much bigger over time, computing $N$ updates of

the pattern becomes linear in $N$; although if the pattern grows by shooting out gliders, the rate becomes quadratic in $N$. Further speed enhancements are achieved by building a lookup table of recurring blocks of cells, so that, after a bit, the program becomes able to do a single-step update of a recurring pattern of, say, sixteen by sixteen cells—I discuss the lookup-table approach a bit further on in the main text. To find state-of-the-art Game of Life simulators, Google for *xlife* or Life32. For example, Life32 for Windows by Johan Bontes, can be found at http://psoup.math.wisc.edu/Life32.html.

For practical purposes, we very often do limit the size of a CA world to some maximum size $R$, either by clamping the border cells to zero, or by allowing the CA patterns to "wrap around" from one edge to the other. In these cases, we do well to think of there as being two input sizes: the world size $R$ and the requested number of updates $N$. It's fairly evident that the runtime of computing $N$ rows of a one-dimensional CA of fixed size $R$ will be on the order of $R{\cdot}N$ —you're filling in a space-time rectangle of $R$ by $N$ cells. Computing $N$ updates of a two-dimensional CA with fixed width $N$ is on the order of $R^2{\cdot}N$. And computing $N$ updates of a three-dimensional CA with fixed width $R$ is on the order of $R^3{\cdot}N$—which is why we don't see many large, fast three-dimensional CA simulations! A cubical grid with a mere hundred cells per edge has a million cells inside it.

140. We can actually shave the number of distance computations down to $N{\cdot}(N-1)/2$, for a boid doesn't need to compute the distance to itself, and once you compute the distance for one member of the pair of boids, the other member can use the same distance number. But, in the rough-and-ready language of runtime estimation, this is still said to be quadratic in $N$, or on the order of $N^2$.

141. Let me explain why a random search would take exponential time. Suppose we were to use coarse real numbers represented by sixteen bits each. So then there would be $2^{16}$ possible ways to choose one number. And choosing $N$ real numbers at random would be a matter of choosing $N{\cdot}16$ bits, which can be done $2^{(16{\cdot}N)}$ ways.

Although I think it should be possible to prove the polynomial time convergence of back propagation for the synapse weights to solve a given local set of problems, I don't recall having actually seen such a proof. Note also that converging to good weights for the test cases isn't the same as finding good weights for all the other unsupervised examples that one might run across.

I *have* seen a paper showing that the exact convergence time is chaotically sensitive to the initial random weights that you start it in: John Kolen and Jordan Pollack, "Back Propagation Is Sensitive to Initial Conditions," *Complex Systems* 4, no. 3 (1990) 269–80. Available online at Pollack's site, http://demo.cs. brandeis.edu/papers/bpsic.pdf.

142. See computer scientist David Eppstein's Web site http://www.ics.uci.edu/ ~eppstein/cgt/hard.html. The site summarizes some the known facts about the difficulty of various commonly played games, were they to be generalized to arbitrarily large boards. The reason I hedge my statements about these games is because we only know that these board-game problems are exponentially hard *if* there are computations that can be done using a polynomial amount of memory but which require an exponential amount of time. This assumption is called $P! = PSPACE$.

143. We could also express the second definition in terms of logarithms, where we let $\log(a)=b$ mean that $10^b = a$. With this notation, the definition becomes, "And if we can always assert that fasttime < log(slowtime), we say that Fast is exponentionally faster than Slow." I have a more detailed treatment of this chapter's definitions in the Technical Appendix.

144. A more sophisticated technique is for a long-running program to construct and store an ever-growing lookup table as it goes along. For this to work, the program needs a so-called hashing method for indexing states by simple numerical codes. And then, whenever the program has to laboriously update a state, it adds an entry to the lookup table, with the new entry matching the hash code to the updated state. The hacker demigod Bill Gosper at one time pushed this technique aggressively enough to create a "hash Life" scheme capable of computing $N$ updates of Life in $\log(N)$ runtime—at least for certain kinds of sparse and slowly growing start patterns.

145. In today's terminology, rapidly accessible memory takes the form of so-called RAM chips.

Lookup tables lay at the heart of the CAM-6 hardware accelerator that Toffoli and Margolus designed in the 1980s for speeding the Game of Life and other two-dimensional CAs. I still remember the joyous faces of my new hacker friends when I let them take the board out of my computer and fondle it. "It's nothing but memory chips!"

The CAM-6 functioned by representing a cell and its eight neighbors by sixteen bits of information. Rather than doing some if-then-else kinds of analysis to figure out the next state of the cell, the CAM-6 simply looked up the next state value in a $2^{16}$ member lookup table. In other words, 64K of RAM. (In 1986 that was a lot.) Once John Walker understood what was going on, he realized that we could emulate the CAM-6 board on any PC by simply having the PC use its own RAM for that 64K lookup table. And that led to our joint program, CA Lab, or celLab.

146. For purposes of philosophical discussion, I'm being rather strict here. That is, I'm sounding as if linear speedups are so puny as not to be worth noticing. But, in point of fact, linear speedups of our computer hardware repeatedly have been responsible for what amount to phase transitions in what computers mean to us.

Four quick examples: (a) Simply being able to lay out text on your computer screen as fast you can type is a luxury that only became available in the 1970s; before that, word processors didn't really exist. (b) The arrival of the IBM PC made it possible to have desktop drafting software, something that totally changed architecture and engineering. (c) In recent years, desktop computers have become able to emulate virtual realities as fast as humans expect the world to change, which has brought a whole new era of computer gaming that we've only begun to explore. (d) In coming decades we can expect to see reliable real-time speech recognition and convincing emulation of human facial features, leading to another phase transition in how we interact with our machines.

147. Before leaving physics, I should mention one other type of computation in this field. Physicists often predict various numerical constants, such as the mass of a fixed volume of carbon, the wavelength of light from an excited hydrogen atom, the viscosity of water, the resistance of a copper wire of a certain size, and so on. In each case, they aren't really predicting the outcome of one single experiment. They are, rather, talking about a computation Average($N$) that runs $N$ copies of an experiment and averages a certain measurement. And the claim is then that, for large enough $N$, Average($N$) becomes fixed. In other words, the prediction is that a certain computation Average is class one. Being class one, Average is in fact simple, so the whole issue of the predictability or unpredictability of complex processes doesn't come into play in an interesting way.

148. This notion was developed in my novels *Software* (New York: Ace Books, 1982) and *Wetware* (New York: Avon Books, 1988), and has since become something of a staple in commercial science fiction. *Software* was under option from 1990 to 2000 at Phoenix Pictures. Although a considerable amount of preproduction work was done—including eleven unsuccessful scripts—the option died. Right after Phoenix dropped my option, they released

the Arnold Schwarzenegger movie *The Sixth Day,* which I believe to have drawn inspiration from my work.

One of the central science-fiction conceits in *The Sixth Day* is the notion of taping someone's brain software and then loading that personality onto a tank-grown clone of the person—exactly as I described in *Wetware.* And, for that matter, in *The Sixth Day,* the software is copied to the new body by means of a flash of light, as in *Software.*

Imitators are prone to saying that the ideas they appropriate are "in the air." But the notion of tank-growing a clone and loading it up with one's brain software was a totally original notion when I first wrote about it in the early 1980s. It took me quite a long time to imagine this as a coherent scenario. The ideas were not in the air at all. The very notion of software was rather unfamiliar, let alone the notion of copying the software contents of a human brain.

The fact that the villain in *The Sixth Day* is called Drucker almost makes me think that the script writers were driven by a Raskolnikov-like obsession to confess their pilfering of my intellectual property. "Yes, I killed the old woman with an axe! Yes, I stole Dr. Rucker's ideas!" Drucker even wears small horn-rimmed glasses like me—my physical appearance was well known at Phoenix due to the occasional meetings I took there, on one occasion encountering the Terminator himself.

Oh well. At least I did get a fair amount of money from Phoenix over those ten years of option renewals. And, in the end, it was Governor Schwarzenegger who came through with the golden handshake that made it reasonable for me to retire from teaching in 2004. And now my book *Freeware* (New York: Avon Books, 1997) is under option to a different group, as is *Master of Space and Time* (New York: Thunder's Mouth Press, 2005). My life-computation may attain the movie target-state yet.

149. In *A New Kind of Science,* Wolfram seems to suggest that the PCE implies the PCU. He offers the following brief proof sketch of why a universal computation should be *unpredictable* (what he calls *irreducible*) in the sense that there won't be a computation that is exponentially more efficient than the universal computation.

"Consider trying to outrun the evolution of a universal system. Since such a system can emulate any system, it can in particular emulate any system that is trying to outrun it. And from this it follows that nothing can systematically outrun the universal system. For any system that could would in effect also have to be able to outrun itself" (*A New Kind of Science*, p. 742).

Wolfram's idea seems to be that if we (*thesis*) have a predictor computation that emulates our universal computation with faster runtime than that of actually running the universal computation, then (*antithesis*) having the universal computation emulate the predictor should also be faster than the universal computation, and then (*synthesis*) having the predictor emulate the universal computation's emulation of the predictor should be faster yet, and now we can use the synthesis as a new thesis, and get a yet-faster computation, and so on forever. But it would be impossible to have an endless sequence of smaller and smaller runtimes. Therefore a universal computation can't be predicted.

But if you think through some specific cases, we can see that this particular argument doesn't work. The descending chain will stop as soon as one crosses a cost-benefit condition whereby the overhead of simulation cost swamps the gain of the successive levels of simulation. Put differently, the antithetic step won't work very often.

To see why, think of the $P$ and Dumb$P$ example mentioned in the main text, and assume that both $P$ and Dumb$P$ are universal. If, then, we let Wolfram's universal computation $U$ be the Dumb$P$ computation, it's evident that $U$ is both universal and subject to an exponential speedup.

Suppose we try to apply Wolfram's argument to refute this. Our $U$ (that is, Dumb$P$) can emulate the faster computation $P$. But since $U$ (that is, Dumb$P$) is wired to carry out the wasteful tally doubling operation between each step, the computation of $U$-emulating-$P$ will *still* run slower than $U$, so the very first antithetic step fails and we get no further in Wolfram's proposed infinite regress.

150. Some might dream that quantum computation can break the bank of the PCU. Why not split into exponentially many universes, run a simple computation in each one, combine the answers, and achieve an exponential speedup? As a *practical* matter, it's not clear how good quantum computation can get, but suppose we're generous on this point and suppose that arbitrarily large ensembles can remain coherent over long periods of time. The *theoretical* problem is that some results suggest that the speedups we can gain from quantum computation may turn out to be at best polynomial.

A more radical objection to the dream of quantum computation would be that quantum mechanics may be fundamentally wrong.

151. The quote is from Gottfried Leibniz in, C. I. Gerhardt, ed., *Die philosophischen Schriften von Gottfried Wilhelm Leibniz,* (Vol. VII reprinted, Hildesheim: Georg Olms Verlag, 1978), p. 200. The quote is translated by the British philosopher George MacDonald Ross and can be found at http://www.philosophy.leeds.ac.uk/GMR/hmp/texts/modern/leibniz/analysis/analysis.html.

152. Turing's work showed that arithmetic is strong enough to emulate the running of Turing machines. More specifically, he showed that for any F as strong as arithmetic, we'll have a systematic computational method for converting any machine-input-output triple <*M*, In, Out> into a sentence *m_in_out* such that the following three statements are equivalent: (a) *M* (In) produces Out; (b) F proves *m_in_out*; and (c) *F*Provable(*m_in_out*) returns True.

This means that *F*Provable emulates *M*. Since we can do this for any machine *M,* this means that *F*Provable is a universal computation, so Turing's Theorem applies, and *F*Provable has an unsolvable halting problem.

153. Andrew Wiles, "Modular Elliptic Curves and Fermat's Last Theorem," *Annals of Mathematics* 141(3) (May 1995): 443–551; and Richard Taylor and Andrew Wiles, "Ring Theoretic Properties of Certain Hecke Algebras," in the same issue of *Annals of Mathematics.* The second paper patches a hole in the first paper! A lovely interview with Wiles appeared on the TV show *Nova*; the transcript can be found at http://www.simonsingh.net/Andrew_Wiles_Interview.html.

154. Here's a nutshell proof of the Undecidability Corollary to Turing's Theorem: Since F can model arithmetic, F is universal. Since F is universal, *F*Provable has an unsolvable halting problem. Since *F*Provable has an unsolvable halting problem, there is no endless search detector *F*ProvableFailsToHalt such that *F*ProvableFailsToHalt(*S*) returns True precisely for those cases in which *F*Provable(*S*) doesn't halt. But if every *S* were decidable by F, then *F*Provable(~*S*) could be used as an endless search detector for *F*Provable(*S*). End of proof.

I have more details in the Technical Appendix.

Actually, it was the supreme logician Kurt Gödel who first proved, in 1930, that undecidable sentences arise. We call a formal system F *complete* if for every sentence *S*, F proves *S* or F proves ~*S*. Otherwise we say F is *incomplete*.

*Gödel's First Incompleteness Theorem.* If F is a consistent finitely given formal system as powerful as arithmetic, then there is a specific sentence $G_f$ which is undecidable for F.

The proof of Gödel's First Incompleteness Theorem hinges on showing how to construct a long and complex integer $f$ that in some sense codes up the system F. And using this code interger he then constructs an algebraic formula involving a certain whole number parameter $p$, expressing the notion "P codes up a proof from the system F." These maneuvers are called *metamathematics.*

By using a clever diagonalization trick (which was in fact reused by Turing for his proof of Turing's Theorem), Gödel arranged it so that the meaning of $G_f$ can be viewed as having any of the three following forms: (a) There is no integer $p$ having the property of coding up a proof from F of sentence $G_f$; (b) $G_f$ is not a theorem of F; (c) $G_f$ does not appear among the sentences enumerated by the Turing machine $M_f$.

And then he deduces that $G_f$ is not a theorem of F and that $\sim G_f$ is not a theorem of F.

Mathematically, $G_f$ says there is no integer solution to a certain large and gnarly equation involving a polynomial, some exponentiation, and the humongous constant interger that in some sense encodes a full description of the formal system F.

For further details of Gödel's proof, see chapter four and excursion two in my book *Infinity and the Mind.*

155. The simplest kinds of properties $g$ that can be used for undecidability results of the "There are no whole numbers $n$ such that $g[n]$" are the so-called Diophantine equations, which are polynomial equations with integer coefficients. Actually we can generalize a bit, and look at sentences of the form "There are no whole numbers $n_1, n_2, \ldots n_k$ such that $g[n_1, n_2, \ldots n_k]$."

In 1970, the mathematicians Julia Robinson, Martin Davis, and Yuri Matiyasevich showed that among the sentences undecidable for any formal theory we'll find an infinite number of Diophantine equations that don't have any whole-number solutions, but for which we can't prove this fact.

The mathematician David Hilbert was involved in the background of this problem as well, for at the International Congress of Mathematicians in 1900 he proposed a list of what he considered to be really juicy problems. Hilbert's Tenth Problem was: Find an algorithm that determines if a given Diophantine equation has a solution in whole numbers. Robinson, Davis, and Matiyasevich showed that Hilbert's Tenth Problem leads to an unsolvable halting problem—and because of this we know that there have to be a lot of undecidable sentences stating that a given Diophantine equation has no solutions.

Wolfram feels that, in fact, there should be some exceedingly simple Diophantine equations of this kind (see *A New Kind of Science* p. 790). Perhaps his simplest example of a possibly undecidable formula based on a Diophantine equation is the following, which I mention in the main text: "For all $m$ and $n$, $m^2 \neq n^5 + 6n + 3$."

It may turn out that this statement is indeed true, so we will never have a proof by example that any such $m$ and $n$ *exist*. But it may also be that the *nonexistence* of such $x$ and $y$ will also be unprovable from existing mathematics, so a search for a proof would last forever.

156. Suppose that two computations can emulate each other, and that we are thinking of using one of them as a way to characterize some naturally occurring process. Which of the two computations will we prefer?

My thrust in this book has been to focus on computations that have shorter runtime. So if one computation is *exponentially* faster than the other, that's the one I prefer.

But what if one computation is only *linearly* faster than the other? In this case, the choice isn't so clear-cut. Why? Because if we keep looking for linearly faster computations, we may be letting ourselves in for an endless regress.

This is because for many processes, there is no *maximally* fast computation that emulates the process. As I discussed, any computation that can be emulated as a digital PC program is subject to a linear speedup produced by using faster processors and more RAM. These linear speedups stretch on until at some point one encounters basic limitations due to physical laws.

Now, many commonly occurring complex physical processes are already operating at this limiting speed. But if we want to talk about the relative speed of somewhat idealized PC programs, there's no need to push on to the physical limit. Two linearly comparable computations will end up at the same limit in any case.

Given two computations whose run speed differs only by a linear factor, might there be some criterion other than speed for selecting one or the other? Yes. Given two computations of linearly comparable speed, we might want to select the computation whose description size is smaller. A program with a smaller description is more concise and perhaps easier to talk about.

Before we can take this discussion any further, we have to assume that we have some simple, everywhere defined procedure for computing the *size* of a computation. In the domain of Turing machines or PC programs, a computation $P$ can be thought of as a digital program, so it's easy to define a function size($P$) to be simply the number of symbols in the program representing P.

When, for instance, you install a new executable program on your PC, the installer program checks if you have enough memory on your hard disk to hold all the bytes of the program. And once the new program is installed, you can use one of your desktop exploring tools to find the exact number of bytes that it uses. This number is what I mean by size($P$).

But when we look at physical, biological, mental, and social computations $P$, we're often dealing with computations that aren't expressed in any specific formal symbolism. These computations exist, and we may know more or less how they work, but, since they don't have to be run in the fiddling environment of a PC, these natural computations aren't fully expressed by a formal program.

One possibility (which admittedly has problems) might be to define the *size of a computation* to be the number of words it takes one person to tell another person how the computation works. What about the fact that physical computations can intimately involve physical quantities such as masses, field strengths, membrane permeabilities, reactivity, temperature, dendrite thickness, and the weather? Well, we can treat all of those things as additional inputs. The computation itself is just some rules describing how a system with all of those inputs will evolve over time. And its description is the number of words it takes to explain it.

The computer scientist Gregory Chaitin has studied the notion of computation size for many years. He uses the word elegant to describe computations of minimal size.

• *Definition.* A computation is *elegant* if there is no computation of smaller size that emulates it.

Chaitin argues that in science we are looking for elegant theories. We prefer a crisp, concise theory to a long, rambling one. The shorter theories are less likely to include extraneous junk. A computation that, for instance, generates a big lookup table from a few simple rules seems like a better explanation than a computation that just has the big lookup table hard-coded right in.

But, as a practical matter, extreme compression can make a description incomprehensible. And it can often be the case that there is no short helper program for generating a particular lookup table. And don't forget that there will be cases where a large program runs exponentially faster than the shorter one.

In 1965 Chaitin proved a curious theorem about elegance. Although informal counting arguments indicate there will be infinitely many elegant computations, any given theory is limited in its ability to prove that specific computations are elegant.

- *Chaitin's Theorem.* If F is a consistent finitely given formal system as powerful as arithmetic, then there will be a number $c_F$ such that F is unable to prove that any specific program of size greater than $c_F$ is elegant.

Quite briefly, the idea behind the proof of Chaitin's Theorem is that we find a certain $c_F$ related to the size of F and assume the theorem to be false. Then we define a program BerryF as: "The smallest program of size greater than $c_F$ which F can prove to be elegant." The phrase in quotes can be used to describe within F a program smaller than BerryF that emulates BerryF —contradicting the assumption that F proves BerryF to be elegant. Therefore Chaitin's Theorem must be true. You can find more details in my book *Mind Tools: The Five Levels of Mathematical Reality* (Boston: Houghton Mifflin, 1988), in G. J. Chaitin, *The Unknowable* (New York: Springer-Verlag, 1999), or in one of the numerous papers on Chaitin's home page, http://www.cs.auckland.ac.nz/CDMTCS/chaitin/.

Chaitin's Theorem tells that, unless we keep adopting stronger and stronger theories of mathematics, beyond some size level it becomes impossible to prove that computations are elegant. But this doesn't render the notion of elegance useless. It's still a reasonable criterion for selecting which of two computations to view as "better."

We can use simple counting arguments to show that in fact there must *be* elegant programs of every size. But Chaitin's Theorem shows that we can't *prove* the existence of these programs. Combining these two facts produces an endless supply of undecidable sentences of the form "There is an elegant program larger than $N$," and Chaitin's "random truths" are related to these sentences.

157. To illustrate how oddity spreads, I'll present a sustained analogy between the spread of undecidability and the rise of transcendental numbers in mathematics. It was Brian Silverman who suggested the analogy to me.

*History.* 300 BC. The Greeks worked primarily with real numbers that can be expressed either as the fraction of two whole numbers, or that can be obtained by the process of taking square roots. By the time of the Renaissance, mathematicians had learned to work with roots of all kinds, that is, with the full class of algebraic numbers—where an algebraic number can be expressed as the solution to some polynomial algebraic equation formulated in terms of whole numbers. The non-algebraic numbers were dubbed the *transcendental* numbers. And, for a time, nobody was sure if any transcendental numbers existed.

*Analogy.* 1920. In David Hilbert's time, it seemed possible that, at least in mathematics, every problem could be decided on the basis of a reasonable formal system. This was the inspiration for Hilbert's program.

*History.* 1884. The first constructions of transcendental real numbers were carried out by Joseph Liouville. Liouville's numbers were, however, quite artificial, such as the so-called Liouvillian number 0.110001000000000000000010000 . . . , which has a one in the decimal positions $n!$ and zero in all the other places. Someone might readily say that a number like this is unlikely to occur in any real context. (The term $n!$ stands for "$n$ factorial," which is the product $1 \cdot 2 \cdot \ldots \cdot n$ of all the integers from one to $n$.)

*Analogy.* 1930. Kurt Gödel proved the existence of some particular undecidable algebraic sentences. These sentences were somewhat unnatural. Relative to a given formal system F, they had the form "This sentence is not provable from F," or the alternate form, "The contradiction $0 = 1$ is not provable from the formal system F."

*History.* 1874. Georg Cantor developed his set theory and showed there are an infinite number of transcendental numbers. Someone could say that Cantor's transcendental numbers aren't numbers that would naturally occur, that they are artificial, and that they depend in an essential way upon higher-order concepts such as treating an infinite enumeration of reals as a completed object.

*Analogy.* 1936. Building on Gödel's work, Alan Turing proved his theorem on the unsolvability of the halting problem. He immediately derived the corollary that there are infinitely many undecidable sentences of mathematics and that these sentences came in quite arbitrary forms. Even so, the specific examples of such sentences that he could give were still odd and somewhat self-referential, like Gödel's undecidable sentences.

*History.* 1873. Charles Hermite proved that the relatively nonartificial number $e$ is transcendental.

*Analogy.* 1965. On an entirely different front, Paul J. Cohen proved that an important question about infinite sets called the continuum hypothesis is undecidable from the known axioms of mathematics. (Cohen's proof built on an earlier result proved by Kurt Gödel in 1946.) 1970. Back in the realm of unsolvable halting problems, Julia Robinson, Martin Davis, and Yuri Matiyasevich showed that, among the sentences undecidable for any formal theory, we'll find an infinite number of polynomial Diophantine equations that don't have any whole-number solutions, but for which we can't prove this fact. This means that there is a very large range of ordinary mathematical sentences that are undecidable.

*History.* 1882. Ferdinand von Lindemann proved that the garden-variety number pi is transcendental.

*Analogy.* 2002. Wolfram pointed out that his PCE implies that undecidability is all around us in the natural world. And, as I've discussed here, the NUH is enough to draw the same conclusion!

158. Martin Gardner, "Science and the Unknowable," *Skeptical Inquirer* (November–December, 1998), available online at http://www.findarticles.com/p/articles/mi_m2843/is_n6_v22/ai_21275519. See also the great essay, Paul Edwards, "Why," in *The Encyclopedia of Philosophy* (New York: Macmillan, 1967), Vol 8, pp. 296–302.

When I was in high school, I read a translation of Jean-Paul Sartre's 1938 novel *Nausea* (New York: New Directions, 1959), and it had a tremendous effect on me. Indeed, I loved *Nausea* so much that I inserted four quotes from it into my transreal autobiographical science-fiction novel *The Secret of Life* (New York: Bluejay Books, 1995).

Sartre's novel concerns a young man named Roquentin who becomes overwhelmed by the meaninglessness of existence. At the book's high point (p. 181), Roquentin is in a public garden and he's staring at the gnarly trunk and roots of a tree and he feels a kind of nausea at (as I would now put it) the complexity, unpredictability, and unsolvability of the biocomputation. But then Roquentin reaches a kind of enlightenment: "I got up and went out. Once at the gate, I turned back. Then the garden smiled at me. I leaned against the gate and watched it for a long time. The smile of the trees, of the laurel, *meant* something; that was the real secret of existence."

# *Image Credits*

Most of the photos are by Rudy Rucker (RR). The drawings are by Isabel Rucker (IR), mostly based on original drawings by Rudy Rucker. Most of the computer graphics images were made by RR. All other images are used with the permission of the credited owners.

The programs used by RR include the following:

*Boppers,* a public domain program, originally distributed with *Rudy Rucker's Artificial Life Lab* (Waite Group Press, Corte Madera 1993).

*CelLab,* a public domain program, originally distributed with CA Lab: Rudy Rucker's Cellular Automata Laboratory (Autodesk Inc., Sausalito 1989).

*CAPOW,* a public domain program, distributed online by Rudy Rucker, originally developed under a grant from the Electric Power Research Institute (EPRI) of Palo Alto, California.

*NKS Explorer,* a program sold by Wolfram Inc. The NKS Explorer images are used with the permission of Wolfram Inc.

*Mathematica,* a program sold by Wolfram Inc.

*CA3D,* a program written by Harry Fu as part of his doctoral work at San Jose State University. The CA3D images are used with the permission of Harry Fu, www.ctechnet.com/ca3d/ca3dapplet.htm.

Boppers, CelLab, and CAPOW can be downloaded for free from the book's Web site, www.rudyrucker.com/lifebox.

For each figure we list the number, caption, and credit below.

1. *A Dialectic Triad, The Lifebox, the Seashell, and the Soul.* IR.

2. *Six Cone Shells.* Scott and Jeanette Johnson, http://www.geocities.com/uwkwaj/.

3. *An Intellectual Stairway to Heaven.* IR.

4. *Time Line with Inputs and Outputs.* IR.

5. *Layers of Computation.* IR.

6. *William Gosper, Programmer King.* Stephen Jones, smj@sdf.lonestar.org.

7. *The Spectrum of Complexity.* RR.

8. *Simulated Bird Flocking.* RR, using Boppers.

9. *Mandelbrot sets.* RR, using Chaos.

10. *The Vichniac Vote Rule.* RR, using CelLab.

11. *Excerpt from the U.S. Income Tax Form 1040.* Internal Revenue Service.

12. *Woven Portrait of Joseph Marie Jacquard.* IR, based on original at CNAM, Musée des arts et métiers.

13. *A Detail of Scheutz's Difference Engine.* Smithsonian Institution, Photo number 74-11269.

14. *A Turing Machine History.* RR, using NKS Explorer.

15. *Processor and Memory Ribbon.* IR.

16. *Architectures of Turing Machine vs. Personal Computer.* IR.

17. *Networked Personal Computers.* IR.

18. *Network Architecture.* IR.

19. *Architecture of 1D and 2D CAs.* IR.

20. *Stanislaw Ulam Demonstrating the MANIAC Computer.* Los Alamos National Laboratory, 1955.

21. *A Cell Neighborhood in Conway's Life.* IR.

22. *A Life CA Soup, and the Glider Gun.* RR, using CelLab.

23. *Five Kinds of CA Behavior* RR, using NKS Explorer.

24. *Maxine Headroom.* RR, using the RC component of CelLab.

25. *Cellular Automata Scrolls.* RR, using CelLab and CAPOW.

26. *A 3D CA with Scrolls* RR, using CA3D.

27. *Class four Scrolls.* RR, using CelLab.

28. *Ed Hardebeck and Brian Silverman Building Tinkertoy Computer.* Brian Silverman.

29. *Local and Global Memory Access for Parallelism.* IR.

30. *1D Heat CAs with Varying Rates of Diffusion.* RR, using CAPOW.

31. *2D Wave CA, Two Views.* RR, using CAPOW.

32. *Fermi-Pasta-Ulam Quadratic and Cubic Nonlinear Waves.* RR, using CAPOW.

33. *A Ball Computes Bin to be Left or Right.* IR.

34. *Bounce Magnification.* IR.

35. *The Secret Machinery of the Universe.* RR.

36. *Von Karman Vortex Streets.* (a) Maarten Rutgers, (b) NASA.

37. *Water in a Stream.* RR.

38. *A Deterministic One-Dimensional CA Creating Gnarly-Looking Flow.* RR, using CAPOW.

39. *Rule 30, Started from a Single Black Cell.* RR, using NKS Explorer.

40. *"As Above, So Below" Gnarly Clouds and Water.* RR.

41. *Tree, Cloud, Mind, Mountain.* RR.

42. *The Beamsplitter.* IR.

43. *Interferometer.* IR.

44. *Reversed Time Signals Explain Synchronicity.* IR.

45. *Evolving A Spacetime Across Paratime.* IR.

46. *Peter Bruegel's Hunters in the Snow.* Kunsthistorisches Museum (KHM, Wien).

47. *Bruegel's Belgian Wagon. Detail of Hunters in the Snow.* Kunsthistorisches Museum (KHM, Wien).

48. *Spacetime Diagram of a Reversible One-Dimensional CA.* RR, using CelLab.

49. *A Physics and a Metaphysics to Explain All of Spacetime.* IR.

50. *An Interferometer as a NOT Gate.* IR.

51. *Beamsplitters as Square-Root-of-NOT Gates.* IR.

52. *A Two-For-One Quantum Computation.* IR.

53. *A Computational Architecture for Quantum Mechanics.* IR.

54. *Junk DNA Cover.* Painting by John Allemande for *Isaac Asimov's Science Fiction Magazine,* January, 2003. Image is copyright © 2002 Dell Magazines. Used with permission.

55. *A Spot on a Dog.* RR.

56. *Spots Generated by a Rule Using an Activator and an Inhibitor.* RR, using CAPOW.

57. *Turing's Cow Spots.* University of SouthHampton and King's College Cambridge 2003.

58. *Activator-Inhibitor Systems.* RR, using CAPOW.

59. *Scrolls Generated by Activator-Inhibitor Rules.* RR, using CAPOW.

60. *A Cone Shell Sitting on a CA Simulation of its Pattern.* Hans Meinhardt.

61. *Gnarl in Water and Wood.* RR.

62. *The Morphogenesis Architecture.* IR.

63. *The Computational Architecture of Homeostasis.* IR.

64. *A Pendulum and Two Magnets Simulating Three Conflicting Drives.* RR, using Chaos.

65. *From Generation to Generation.* IR.

66. *Time Sequences from the Logistic Map.* IR.

67. *Discrete Ecology Simulations May Produce Scrolls.* RR, using CelLab.

68. *Kaneko-Abraham-style Logistic Diffusion.* RR, using CAPOW.

69. *Continuous Ecological Simulations Can Produce Scrolls.* RR, using CAPOW.

70. *Langton's Self-Reproducing Cellular Automaton Pattern.* RR, using CelLab.

71. *Aristid Lindenmayer Holding a Weed at the First Artificial Life Conference.* Kevin Kelly.

72. *L System.* IR.

73. *Plant Forms based on L-systems.* Przemyslaw Prusinkiewicz and James Hanan.

74. *Crossover.* IR.

75. *Karl Sim's Galapagos Program Evolves Biomorphic Forms.* Karl Sims.

76. *A Smooth Fitness Landscape.* IR.

77. *Parallel Hill-Climbing.* IR.

78. *A Rugged Fitness Landscape.* IR.

79. *A Mind Connects Sensors to Effectors.* IR.

80. *A Toy Car That Straddles a Stripe.* IR.

81. *A Flagellate's Swimming Reflexes.* IR.

82. *Gnarly Braitenberg Vehicles.* Casey Reas.

83. *Logic Gates for a Walker.* IR.

84. *A Brain Neuron.* IR. Adapted from F. Crick and C. Asanuma, "Certain Aspects of the anatomy and Physiology of the Cerebral Cortex," in J. McClelland and David Rumelhart, eds., *Parallel Distributed Processing,* Vol. 2. (Cambridge, Mass: MIT Press, 1986), p. 337.

85. *Brain Neurons Connnected to Sensors and Effectors.* IR.

86. *The Neocortex, Divided into Upper, Middle and Deep Layers.* IR.

87. *A Simplified Diagram of the Neocortical Layers' Throughput.* IR.

88. *Computer Neuron Models.* IR.

89. *A Neural Net to Recognize Smiles and Frowns.* IR.

90. *Generalized Face Recognizer.* IR.

91. *A CA Made of Neurons.* IR.

92. *A Glider in the Brian's Brain Rule.* IR.

93. *The Brian's Brain Cellular Automaton.* RR, using MJCell by Mirek Wojtowicz.

94. *More Cellular Automata Scroll Patterns.* RR, using CAPOW.

95. *Cellular Automaton Patterns Like a Mind with Thoughts and Obsessions.* RR, using CAPOW.

96. *Another 3D CA with Scrolls.* RR, using CA3D by Harry Fu.

97. *The Self, the World and the Self Experiencing at the World.* IR.

98. *Towards a Neurology of Consciousness.* IR.

99. *Consiousness and Empathy for Computer Game Creatures.* IR.

100. *Is This Dog Conscious?* RR.

101. *Wheelie Willie Thinks of Infinity and of Nothing.* RR. From Rudy Rucker, *Infinity and the Mind.*

102. *Grandchildren with a Lifebox.* RR. From Rudy Rucker, *Saucer Wisdom.*

103. *Moore's Law Forever?* RR.

104. *Hans Moravec's Plot of Brain Speed and Brain Size.* Hans Moravec, *Robot: Mere Machine to Transcendent Mind* (Oxford: University Press, 1999).

105. *The Unpredictable China CA.* RR, using CAPOW.

106. *The Author with Nick Herbert at an April Fool's Day Parade.* RR.

107. *Sparkling Dew.* RR.

108. *Two Flocks.* RR, using Boppers.

109. *The Queensboro Bridge.* RR.

110. *This is a Pear.* RR.

111. *Word Associations.* IR.

112. *A Bell Curve and a Scale Free Distribution.* IR.

113. *Inverse Power Law Distribution for Word Linkiness.* RR, using Mathematica.

114. *Zipf's Law for The Lifebox, The Seashell, and the Soul.* John Walker.

115. *Different Distributions of Book Advances.* IR.

116. *The Zeldovich CA Model of the Formation of Cities.* RR, using CAPOW.

117. *The Forest Fire CA.* RR, using CAPOW.

118. *Sandpile Cellular Automata.* RR, using CAPOW.

119. *Self-Generating Cascades in a Nonlinear Wave CA.* RR, using CAPOW.

120. *John Walker.* RR.

121. *Wolfram's Stock Market Model.* RR, using NKS Explorer.

122. *Computations are Thoughts and Physical Processes.* RR.

123. *The "Natural" First Four Ontologies.* RR.

124. *The "Supernatural" Second Four Ontologies.* RR.

125. *Producing or Returning an Output.* IR.

126. *Target Detector.* IR.

127. *An Unsuccessful Solution to A Halting Problem.* IR.

128. *A Solvable Halting Problem.* IR.

129. *Degrees of Unsolvability.* IR.

130. *The Brain Halting Problem.* IR.

148. *Big Emulates Small, Using Different Languages.* IR.

149. *A Random Wave Function.* RR, using Mathematica.

150. *Wave Function for a Particle with Two Likely Positions.* RR, using Mathematica.

151. *Wave Function with Precise Momentum.* RR, using Mathematica.

The page-border images at the chapter heads were made by RR using CAPOW. More details about the images are on the book's Web site www.rudyrucker.com/lifebox.

# Index

reproduction
  by artificial life, 185–190
  by biological systems, 153–159
  reward distribution, 346–352
  Reynolds, Craig, 29, 317–320
  robots. *See* artificial life
  Rule 30, 111–113
  runtime speeds, 416–423, 478–479
  Russell, Bertrand, 442

**S**

sandpile models, 354–359
satire, 364–365
scale-free distribution, 341–342, 351, 352
Scheutz, Georg, 38
scientific speculations, 364
scrolls, 73–76, 164–165, 183, 185,
  244–245, 248–249
search engines, 58
search methods, 199–207
selection, 197
self-awareness, 253–267
sensations, 218–220
sensibility, innate, 252
sensors, 218–219
set theory, 265, 267
simulated annealing, 201, 203–204
simulations, 86, 104–105, 475–476
  of evolution, 283, 288–292
  limitations of, 209–210
  unpredictable, 115
Singularity, 292–294
skills, 14
smoke tendrils, 93
social commentary, 364–365
social systems, 365–373
social upheavals, 371–373
society, 315
  distribution of rewards in, 346–352
  response of, to cultural artifacts,
    351–359
  unpredictability of, 435–436
  *See also* group behaviors
software, 14, 36
  brain emulation, 281–292
solar system, 107
soul, 8
spacetime, 128–133

species distribution, 182–184
speed, computational, 414–430, 478–479
stairway to heaven, 9–10
steering behaviors, 319–322
stock market, 368–371, 436
stored program architecture, 36–37,
  40, 41
strange attractors, 101, 116
subject matter, 361–362
sums, reckoning, 31–36
superhuman machines, 292–294
supernaturalism, 393
supplemental inputs, 104
symbiosis, 176–177
synapses, 227, 228–229, 238
synchronization, 92

**T**

tables, 15
tag systems, 337–338
target detectors, 15, 17, 395–397,
  471–473
target states, 47, 395, 405–407, 471
technological innovations, 374–380
  future, 381–382
telepathy, 334–335
thought, 20, 239–249
  abstract, 287
  as computation, 264–267
  consciousness and, 253–267
  definition, 389
  distraction from, 251–252
  mind-body connection and, 220
  moods and, 249–252
  patterns, 245–249, 336–339
  recurrent, 244–245
  reprogramming, 250–252
  trains of, 240, 242–244, 247
  unpredictability of, 433–435
thought experiments, 364
  Aint Paint, 145–149
  Hello Infinity, 383–386
  Kind Rain, 311–313
  Lucky Number, 1–3
  Million Chakras, 77–79
  Terry's Talker, 213–216
thought loops, 240–242
  escaping, 250–252